RISC Systems
and Applications

C³ INDUSTRIAL CONTROL, COMPUTERS AND COMMUNICATIONS SERIES

Series Editor: **Professor Derek R. Wilson**
University of Westminster, England

RISC Systems and Applications

Daniel Tabak

Department of Electrical and Computer Engineering
George Mason University
Fairfax, Virginia 22030, USA

RESEARCH STUDIES PRESS LTD.
Taunton, Somerset, England

JOHN WILEY & SONS INC.
New York · Chichester · Toronto · Brisbane · Singapore

RESEARCH STUDIES PRESS LTD.
24 Belvedere Road, Taunton, Somerset, England TA1 1HD

Marketing and Distribution:

Australia and New Zealand:
Jacaranda Wiley Ltd.
GPO Box 859, Brisbane, Queensland 4001, Australia
Canada:
JOHN WILEY & SONS CANADA LIMITED
22 Worcester Road, Rexdale, Ontario, Canada

Europe, Africa, Middle East and Japan:
JOHN WILEY & SONS LIMITED
Baffins Lane, Chichester, West Sussex, UK, PO19 1UD

North and South America:
JOHN WILEY & SONS INC.
605 Third Avenue, New York, NY 10158, USA

South East Asia:
JOHN WILEY & SONS (SEA) PTE LTD.
37 Jalan Pemimpin 05-04
Block B Union Industrial Building, Singapore 2057

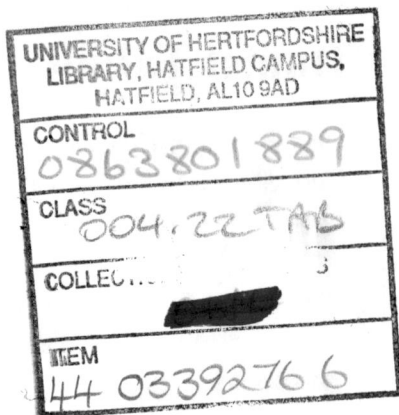

Library of Congress Cataloging-in-Publication Data   1 3 MAR 1996
Tabak, Daniel, 1934-
     RISC systems and applications / Daniel Tabak.
         p. cm. -- (Industrial control, computers, and communications
series ; 12)
     Includes bibliographical references and index.
     ISBN 0-86380-188-9 (hardback : alk. paper : Research Studies
Press). -- ISBN 0-471-96027-6 (hardback : alk. paper : John Wiley)
     1. RISC microprocessors. 2. Reduced instruction set computers.
     I. Title. II. Series.
     QA76.5.T295 1995
     004'.3--dc20   95-16403
                                               CIP

British Library Cataloguing in Publication Data
A catalogue record for this book is available from the British Library.

ISBN 0 86380 188 9 (Research Studies Press Ltd.) *[Identifies the book for orders except in America.]*
ISBN 0 471 96027 6 (John Wiley & Sons Inc.) *[Identifies the book for orders in USA.]*

Typeset by Abracadabra!, Tingewick, Buckingham, England
Printed in Great Britain by SRP Ltd., Exeter

To my grandchildren
Elior and Maayan

Trademarks

i286, i386, i387, i486, Pentium, i860, ICE, Paragon are trademarks of Intel Corporation.

M68000, MC68000, MC68010, MC68020, MC68030, MC68040, MC68060, M88000, MC88100, MC88200, MC88110 are trademarks of Motorola, Inc.

Alpha AXP, AXP, DEC, PALcode, PDP-11, VAX, VMS, Digital are trademarks of Digital Equipment Corporation.

CRAY, CRAY T3D, and CRAY C90 are trademarks of Cray Research, Inc.

IBM, PowerPC, IBM PC, XT, AT, PS/2, RS/6000 are trademarks of International Business Machines Corporation.

MIPS R2000, R3000, R6000, R4000, R4400, R8000, R10000 are trademarks of MIPS Technologies, Inc.

Silicon Graphics, Challenge, Indy, Irix are trademarks of Silicon Graphics, Inc.

Sun, SPARC, UltraSPARC are trademarks of Sun Microsystems, Inc.

SuperSPARC is a trademark of Texas Instruments.

PA-RISC, PA-7100, PA-7200, PA-8000 are trademarks of Hewlett-Packard Company.

Am29000 is a trademark of Advanced Micro Devices, Inc.

Connection Machine is a registered trademark of Thinking Machines Corporation.

Cm, CM-5, Cmost are trademarks of Thinking Machines Corporation.

Acknowledgement

Parts of chapters 1, 2, 6 to 12 have appeared in the author's "Advanced Microprocessors", second edition, 1995, chapters 5, 6, 14 to 20, and are reproduced here courtesy of McGraw-Hill, Inc. Front cover: CRAY T3D (Alpha-based) network, courtesy of Cray Research, Inc. Back cover: Silicon Graphics CHALLENGE server, photo courtesy of Silicon Graphics Computer Systems.

Series Editor's Foreword

The current Vice President of the United States Albert Gore Jnr, speaking to the US Congress in 1989 as Senator Gore, said:

> "High performance computing is a fulcrum. Government action applied here can powerfully influence the outcome of the overall struggle. I look forward to your consideration of the legislation. Mr President, I ask unanimous consent that a copy of my Bill be printed in the record."

That Bill was the National High Performance Computer Technology Act, and it was printed in the Congressional Record Vol 135, No 54, May 18th, 1989.

The Bill had its origins in a Presidential report, published during President Reagan's period of office, in which it was proposed that 'grand computer challenges' would require 'teraflop' computers and hence stretch computer performance by three orders of magnitude, i.e. gigaflops to teraflops. The insatiable demand for more computer power is satisfied in part by RISC technology, and Daniel Tabak has now rewritten his *RISC Systems* to include all the recent innovations in microprocessor architecture and multiprocessor workstation configurations that are striving to reach this teraflop target.

Silicon process technology continues to be developed. Today, four-layer metallisation and 0.5 micron features, yielding 10 million transistors, clocked at 100MHz 'plus' are standard volume products. Within sight are 0.2 micron features with 100 million transistors, and clocked at 500MHz. In my original foreword to Daniel Tabak's first RISC Architecture Book (1987) I wrote:

> "The most important challenge facing electronic systems engineers is the development of methods and techniques that utilise the reliability and manufacturing capacity that is available with modern methods of electronic circuit fabrication."

That is still true today in that we now have multiple execution units on chip, providing concurrent execution of instructions: pipelines — once the province of high-performance vector machines — are now routinely incorporated at the chip level; and, of course, significant amounts of cache memory to provide fast memory access to match processing speed with instruction and data retrieval. Utilising 100 million transistors efficiently on a single chip represents a major intellectual challenge in the next five years.

The social dimension of this ubiquitous technology is just beginning to emerge — the first 'Video on Demand' trials are currently taking place in Cambridge, UK, using ICL's 'Goldrush' Mega Server that is based on SPARC RISC technology. The massive public awareness and increase in E-mail and the use of World Wide Web (WWW) are relatively recent phenomena, as are multi-media workstations. Indeed, as I write this foreword, the launch of what is predicted to be the world's largest ever volume product, Windows 95, is reputedly going to provide a universal Graphical User Interface for the millennium.

In this book, Daniel Tabak has presented state-of-the-art RISC technology and its applications. It is the applications that are now driving the technology, because the technology now belongs to the users and not the technologists. It is the search for volume sales that now dominates computer products. Computers are now a mass-market product; and in that context there is major 'need to know', by engineers and students alike, about the latest and most important design methodologies and applications that the RISC approach has made possible.

This book is another extremely important contribution from Daniel Tabak and one that is a great pleasure to welcome to this series. To Daniel Tabak, I would say on behalf of the readers: thank you for your energy and tenacity in bringing forward this third book, *RISC Systems and Applications*. We all appreciate your initiative and clarity of expression.

Derek Wilson
London, 1995

Preface

The development and appearance of new advanced RISC-type microprocessors continues at a tremendous pace. Five years after the appearance of "RISC Systems" in 1990, there is a whole generation of new, far more advanced and higher-performing systems. The older systems have new generations of more powerful microprocessors. There are also some new systems, coming from manufacturers that can be considered as 'old timers' in the computer industry. New features rarely practiced before, such as a dual cache and instruction level parallelism, are now pervasively implemented in this generation's processors. A new book, a follow-up to "RISC Systems", describing the new systems, is certainly called for.

Like "RISC Systems", the book is intended for advanced undergraduate and graduate students of electrical and computer engineering, computer science, and other fields having an interest in computing systems. It can also serve practicing engineers and computer professionals. The text assumes a basic knowledge, by the reader, of computer organization and architecture. The goal of the book is to present the basic principles of RISC along with the description of a number of leading experimental and commercial RISC systems. The above presentation is concluded with a comparative evaluation of RISC systems and a detailed discussion of some of their most notable applications.

The current text was completely reorganized, and over three-quarters of it contains new material which did not appear in "RISC Systems". The book is subdivided into three Parts containing a total of eighteen chapters. The first Part (chapters 1 to 5) constitutes an introduction to RISC, featuring basic relevant principles and some examples of RISC experimental prototypes. The introductory first chapter is dedicated to a very important feature in RISC systems practice: pipelining and instruction level parallelism (ILP). The second chapter introduces the reader to the basic concepts of RISC, its properties, practices, advantages, and shortcomings. The next two chapters describe two pioneering experimental RISC prototypes: the Berkeley RISC in chapter 3, and the Stanford MIPS in chapter 4. Chapter 5 includes the description of a number of other notable experimental RISC systems, including some original research projects managed by the author, performed with his associates and students.

Part two constitutes a reference source for a number of notable high-performance, commercial RISC-type systems. It does not purport to be a substitute for a user manual for each of the systems described in this part. However, the description includes the most important features of the system's architecture, organization, and implementation. The systems covered in Part two include the DEC Alpha AXP (chapter 6), the IBM/Motorola/Apple PowerPC family (chapter 7), the Sun SPARC family (chapter 8), the MIPS Rx000 family (chapter 9), the Intel i860 (chapter 10), the Motorola M88000 family (chapter 11), the Hewlett-Packard Precision Architecture family (chapter 12), and the INMOS Transputer (chapter 13).

Part three is dedicated to the evaluation and applications of the RISC systems described in the first two parts. The systems described earlier are compared and some of their benchmark performance results are described in chapter 14. The next three chapters are dedicated to a detailed description of some of the most notable applications of RISC systems: multiprocessors (chapter 15), workstations (chapter 16), and real-time systems (chapter 17). Concluding comments are given in chapter 18. The text concludes with a glossary of abbreviations for the convenience of the reader. "RISC Systems" was used by the author as one of the texts in a senior (last-year undergraduate) course on computer design. The current text will be used in the same way. RISC has become a predominant approach in modern computer design. For this reason, the topics of RISC principles, practices, and applications should be integrated within any program of computer engineering and related areas.

The author and his associates have been working on RISC-related research and development since the late seventies. The author would like to express his appreciation to a number of colleagues and students for their valuable contributions, cooperation and comments. These include Dr. Donna J. Quammen (George Mason University), the originating architect of MULTRIS, Dr. Helnye Azaria, a former Ph.D. advisee (Ben Gurion University), the designer of the CMOVE and MODHEL systems, former students at GMU, contributors to the MULTRIS and MIRIS projects, D. Richard Miller, David K. DuBose, Robert Senko, Gordon Leeuwrik, Dimitrios K. Fotakis, Jean M. Davila, Andrew Phillips, and Scott Goldstein.

The author obtained valuable comments from outstanding professionals directly involved with the development of the advanced microprocessors discussed in the text. The author would like to express his thanks for valuable comments and information to Dr. Richard Sites (DEC), Don Adams (Cray Research), Charles Moore (IBM), Steve Krueger (TI), Dr. Mark Tremblay (Sun Microsystems), Chris Rowen (MIPS), Charlie Price (MIPS), Steve Proffitt (MIPS), Shabbir Latif (MIPS), Roger Golliver (Intel), Keith Diefendorff (Motorola), Philip Brownfield (Motorola), Dennis Brzezinski (Hewlett-Packard), Martin Whittacker (Hewlett-Packard), Doug Hunt (Hewlett-Packard).

The author would like to thank Professor Derek Wilson, the series editor, and Mrs. Veronica A. Wallace, Managing Director of Research Studies Press Ltd., for valuable comments and continued support. Last, but not least, the author would like to thank his wife Pnina for her everlasting patience, understanding, and moral support.

Contents

PART 1

INTRODUCTION TO RISC

CHAPTER 1

Introduction: High-Performance Pipelined Systems

1.1 The Instruction Pipeline: A First Step to High Performance

An obvious way to increase computer performance is to improve the realization technology and increase the frequency of operation of the system. This is certainly pursued by all computer manufacturers. Systems operating at a frequency exceeding 200MHz are already available commercially (such as the DEC Alpha AXP, see Part 2), and systems whose frequency exceeds 300MHz are reported by some company laboratories (again, future Alpha AXP implementations). During the past years, computer developers have been pursuing another way of increasing computer performance, in parallel with improving technology: namely, different ways of parallel processing [Hwan 93, Tabk 90].

Pipelining is one of the most commonly used features of parallel processing [Hays 88, HePa 90, Hwan 93, Stal 93]. An operation is subdivided into a number of elementary sub-operations, say k. We then form a k-stage system and execute the above sub-operations in each stage, one after the other. Thus, a k-stage pipeline is formed. If we continue to send data into the pipeline, then at any time the k-stage pipeline will handle k sets of data simultaneously, performing an elementary sub-operation on each of the k sets of data at each of the k stages. The pipeline is analogous to a manufacturing production line, consisting of a number of stages. At each stage some operation is performed on a product, until the final product is obtained at the last stage.

We differentiate between two basic types of pipeline:

1. *Instruction pipeline* — where different stages of instruction fetch and execution are handled in a pipeline.
2. *Arithmetic pipeline* — where different stages of an arithmetic operation are handled along the stages of a pipeline.

The discussion will concentrate on the details of the operation of the instruction pipeline. This topic is crucial in the design considerations of modern microprocessors. The arithmetic pipeline is also very important. However, it involves the details of design of the arithmetic logic unit (ALU), a topic completely outside of the scope of this text. A good coverage of arithmetic pipelines can be found in [Hays 88, Hwan 93].

The discussion of the instruction pipeline will start with a simple example of a four-stage pipeline ($k = 4$). The four stages are:

(1) **F — fetch.** The instruction is fetched into the CPU.
(2) **D — decode.** The instruction is decoded. The register file is accessed for operands.
(3) **E — execute.** The instruction is executed.
(4) **W — write-back.** The result of the execution is written back, that is, stored.

A time diagram of the above pipeline is illustrated in Fig. 1.1. A similar pipeline is actually practiced in the integer unit of Intel 860 and other systems (see Part 2). The diagram shows four stages of execution of four subsequent instructions: i, $i+1$, $i+2$, and $i+3$. It similarly continues in both directions prior to instruction i, and after instruction $i+3$. One can observe that at any time the pipeline is busy on some aspect of four consecutive instructions simultaneously.

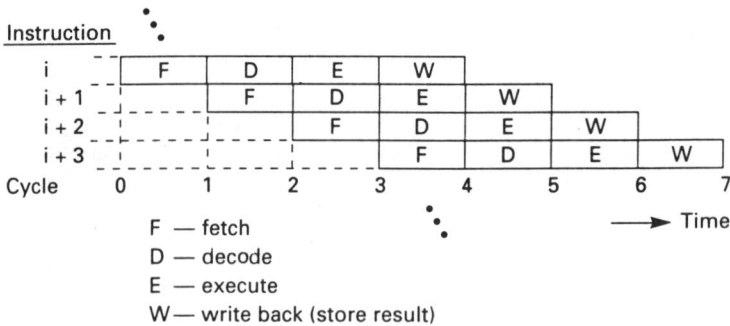

Fig. 1.1   An example of a four-stage pipeline

The diagram in Fig. 1.1 is drawn under idealized conditions, assuming that the pipeline execution proceeds in a smooth manner. This is not always the case. It is assumed in the diagram that every one of the four stages can be completed in a single cycle. While it may be assumed that the decoding will not take more than one cycle, it may not be assumed about the other operations. If an instruction consists of more than one word, and the data bus is only one word wide, the fetch may take more than one cycle. Only in systems where all instructions are no longer than the width of the data bus may we assume a single-cycle fetch at all times. The most difficult thing is to achieve single-cycle execution. This is certainly not always possible, particularly for instructions such as multiply, divide, and floating-point operations. As will be argued later in chapter 2, only in RISC systems can we achieve single-cycle execution for most instructions (Intel 860 is RISC-type). Completing the storage of the result in a single cycle W is not a problem if the result is stored in one of the CPU registers. However if the result is to be stored in an off-chip memory, it may take more than one cycle. As will be seen in chapter 2, all operations in RISC systems are register-to-register. This means that the result is always stored in a CPU register, and therefore there is no problem to complete stage W in a single cycle.

There are other potential problems that may disrupt the smooth execution of a pipeline. If we have to access memory to fetch an instruction (stage F) for one instruction, and access memory to store the result of the other (stage W) at the same time, we have a conflict. If an instruction depends on the result of the preceding one, that is, it uses as an operand the destination of the previous instruction, we have another problem. If one instruction happens to be a branch or a jump instruction, we have to interrupt the flow of instructions in the pipeline, and switch to another flow of instructions. All these phenomena which tend to disrupt the smooth execution of a pipeline, as shown in Fig. 1.1, are generally called *pipeline hazards* [HePa 90]. Pipeline hazards, and ways to minimize their effect, will be discussed in detail in the next section.

1.2 Pipeline Hazards

We can define three types of pipeline hazard [HePa 90]:

1. *Structural hazards*, which arise from resource conflicts when the hardware cannot support all possible combinations of instructions in simultaneous overlapped execution in different pipeline stages.
2. *Data hazards*, which arise when an instruction depends on the results of a previous instruction in a way that is exposed by the overlapping of instructions in different stages of the pipeline.
3. *Control hazards*, which arise from the appearance of branch, jump, and other control flow change instructions in the pipeline.

We shall discuss each pipeline hazard type separately.

Structural hazards

Let us check which system resources are used in each stage of the pipeline in Fig. 1.1:

Pipeline Stage	Resources Needed
F	PC, MAR, Address and Data bus
D	Decoder, internal bus
E	ALU, MAR, Address and Data bus
W	Internal bus

where PC = program counter, MAR = memory address register, ALU = arithmetic logic unit.

Looking at the fourth cycle in Fig. 1.1, we can see that the MAR and the address and data buses are needed in the E stage of instruction $i+1$ (to possibly fetch an operand from memory during the execution stage), and at the same time they are needed in stage F of instruction $i+3$ (to fetch the instruction). The internal bus is needed during the D stage of instruction $i+2$ (to transfer data from the register file) and, at the same time, during the W stage of instruction i (to store the final result in the register file). We definitely have a conflict of resources in this case, that is a structural hazard.

The effects of structural hazards can be alleviated by replication of resources. For instance, if we have a dual cache, one for code, and one for data, with separate access buses and MARs, the CPU can access the code cache at stage F of one instruction, and simultaneously the data cache in stage E of another instruction. Using multiple internal buses with a multiport register file will alleviate the problem of the simultaneous use of internal buses and register file access by different instructions, at different pipeline stages. Such features are indeed practiced by modern microprocessors. Another problem that may arise is due to the necessity of incrementing the PC after the instruction was fetched. If we attempt to use the ALU, there will be a conflict with another instruction at its E stage. This problem can be solved by featuring a special incrementing logic circuit dedicated to the PC, as practiced in most systems.

Data hazards

Dealing with data hazards can be best explained by example. Consider a sequence of two arithmetic instructions:

add r3, r2, r1; $(r3)+(r2) \rightarrow r1$, register r1 is the destination.

sub r4, r1, r5; $(r4)-(r1) \rightarrow r5$, register r1 is a source.

Let us look more closely at the pipelined execution of the two instructions:

Cycle:	1	2	3	4	5
add	F	D	E new (r1) calculated here	W (r1) stored here	
sub		F	D (r1) read here	E	W

Looking at the above sequence we can easily see that, while the new value in r1 will be stored during cycle 4, an attempt to read it will be made in cycle 3 during stage D of the sub instruction. If nothing is done about it, the sub instruction will use the old, stale value in r1, and a wrong result will be obtained. This is the essence of a data hazard.

The simplest way to deal with it is to stall the pipeline for two cycles:

Cycle:	1	2	3	4	5	6	7
add	F	D	E	W			
sub		F	ST	ST	D	E	W

where ST = stall in the pipeline.

Doing it this way, and this is a very simple solution, we lose two cycles, but make sure that the new value in r1 is used for the sub instruction.

There is of course a more sophisticated solution, requiring a hardware investment. The new value of r1 is actually calculated at cycle 3 in the E stage of add. It is then needed in cycle 4, which is the E (execution) cycle of the sub. What can be done in this case is to capture the new value to be stored in r1 in a special register at the output of the ALU, and *forward* it back to the ALU input as an operand for the subsequent sub instruction. The storage of the new value in the r1 register can then proceed in the W stage of add (cycle 4) as usual. Meantime, the sub instruction receives the new value at the beginning of its E stage and a correct result is now obtained. This method is called *forwarding*. A block diagram illustrating the forwarding method is shown in Fig. 1.2 [HePa 90].

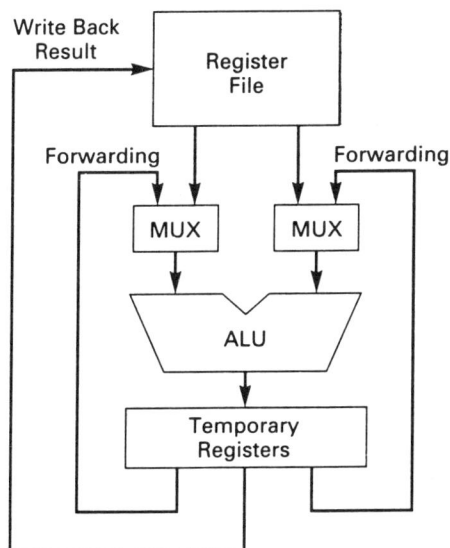

Fig. 1.2   Forwarding scheme

Not all types of data hazard can be resolved by forwarding. It was possible to do so in the previous case because the actual calculation in the first instruction was completed during the E cycle. The reason for that was that it was a register-to-register operation, executable within a single cycle. This will not be the case in a memory access instruction, such as a load. Even if the data item is loaded from an on-chip data cache, one needs a cycle to calculate the effective address and complete the virtual to physical address translation, and then a cycle to access the data cache, bring in the data item, and store it in the destination register. The result of a load instruction is not available at the end of the E stage, and no forwarding can be accomplished.

Example: Given the instruction sequence:

load memr, r1; (memr) → r1, r1 is the load destination.

add r1, r2, r3; (r1) + (r2) → r3, r1 is the add source.

The add instruction will have to be stalled until the end of the W stage of the load, when the new value will be stored in r1. The total delay in the pipeline will be two cycles.

When the detection of a pipeline hazard and the subsequent pipeline stall are performed by the hardware, the mechanism is called a *pipeline interlock*. Of course, this may also be accomplished by software, as it was done in the early members of the MIPS family of microprocessors [HePa 90, Tabk 90b, Part 2 of this text]. One method of hardware-based keeping track of data hazards is by *scoreboarding*. There is a special scoreboard register whose bits represent CPU registers. If register ri is a destination in a certain instruction, bit i of the scoreboard register is set. It is cleared when the instruction is completed. As long as bit i is set, no other instruction may use register ri. Scoreboarding was recently used mainly in RISC-type systems. More on scoreboarding will be said in chapter 2 on RISC.

In general, data hazards may be classified as follows [HePa 90]:

Assume instruction i occurs before instruction j.
1.   **RAW — read after write.** Instruction j attempts to read a source before instruction i writes into it.
2.   **WAR — write after read.** Instruction j attempts to write into a destination before instruction i reads it.
3.   **WAW — write after write.** Instruction j attempts to write into an operand before it is written into by instruction i (an out of order write). This can happen in pipelines where a write is performed in more than one stage. It cannot happen if a write is performed in the W stage only.

Control hazards
When an instruction within a pipeline turns out to be a jump or branch instruction, the instructions subsequent to it in the pipeline must be flushed, and a new target instruction fetched. This is the essence of a control hazard in a pipeline. In order to minimize the effect of a control hazard (that is, minimize the number of instructions flushed from the pipeline) the following steps must be taken:

1. Detect the branch as early as possible in the pipeline. If it is an unconditional branch, this can easily be done in stage D. For a conditional branch it is more difficult, since a condition must be tested after the instruction is decoded, taking up more time.

2. Attain the target address and load it into the PC as early as possible. If the target address must be computed following some addressing mode, an extra cycle may be required.

Branch target cache

One of the ways of reducing the delay caused by a control hazard is to have a *branch target cache* (BTC) in the CPU. A branch target cache contains a set of some first instructions or addresses of possible branch targets. If a branch target happens to be present in the branch target cache, it takes must less time to fetch it into the pipeline than if one had to access memory for it.

The most simple way of handling a control hazard is to stall the pipeline until the arrival of the target instruction, while flushing the prefetched instructions following the branch instruction. If the branch was detected in the D stage, the PC loaded fast, and the target instruction was readily available in the branch target cache, only a single cycle may be lost. Otherwise, the pipeline may be stalled for more cycles.

Branch prediction

Another way of dealing with control hazards is by *branch prediction*. One can design the hardware assuming (predicting) that the branches will be *not-taken*. In this case, instructions following the branch will continue to be executed. When and if it turns out that the branch is actually taken, the pipeline is stopped, results of the instructions following the branch are flushed, and the correct target instruction is fetched. Similarly, one can design the system with a branch *taken* prediction performing in a similar manner. The outcome of a branch-prediction policy is strongly program dependent. On the average, it may work either way, and nothing may be gained by branch prediction. There are systems, such as Intel i960 microcontrollers [HiTa 92], which offer the user an option of taking up the policy of branch taken or not-taken prediction. This is helpful if the user has specific and reliable information about the branching behaviour of the program.

Delayed branch

A method of reducing the penalty of control hazards, practiced in many RISC-type systems, is the method of the *delayed branch*. In this case, the instruction following the branch is always executed, while the branching is delayed for a whole cycle. Thus, no cycles are usually lost, and at least, the number of lost cycles is minimized. More on delayed branch in chapter 2 on RISC. Although the delayed-branch method was widely utilized in the first generations of RISC-type systems (the Motorola M88000 family features the delayed branch as a user option), its use becomes too complicated in the new superscalar systems where two or more instructions are fetched and processed simultaneously. Superscalar systems and *instruction level parallelism* (ILP) are discussed in the next section.

1.3 Instruction Level Parallelism (ILP)

Instruction level parallelism can be defined as a technique of simultaneous issue and processing of multiple instructions within a single processor (CPU). In an n-issue ILP system, n instructions are issued per CPU cycle, and n results per cycle may be attained.

A more formal definition of ILP is given by Rau and Fisher [RauF 93]:

ILP is a family of processor and compiler design techniques that speed up execution by causing individual machine operations, such as memory loads and stores, integer and floating-point operations, to execute in parallel.

We distinguish the following main types of ILP:

Superscalar, where a number of instructions are issued simultaneously each cycle. A two-issue superscalar execution, in a four-stage pipeline, is illustrated in Fig. 1.3(a).

Superpipelined, where a number of instructions are issued within a cycle, but not simultaneously. In an n-issue superpipelined system, a new instruction is issued every 1/n of a cycle. A two-issue superpipelined system is illustrated in Fig. 1.3(b). It is in analogy with running the pipeline at a double frequency. Similarly, an n-issue superpipelined system is in analogy with running the system at a frequency n times as fast [Joup 89, JoWa 89].

Some authors [HePa 94] characterize superpipelined execution as '*superpipelined* processors, an informal term suggesting a deeper pipeline than the five-stage model'. It is felt that defining the superpipelined concept by the depth of the pipeline is a rather vague way of doing it. The definition in [Joup 89] is more precise and clear.

VLIW — *very long instruction word*, where an instruction contains multiple operation codes with their operand specifications. The design of a notable VLIW system is described in [Colw 88]. The details of VLIW operation are outside the scope of this text.

Most modern microprocessors implement superscalar operation, two-issue, three-issue, or four-issue. The multichip IBM POWER2 is a six-issue superscalar. Some computer manufacturers are currently working on even higher-issue superscalar systems (such as eight-issue). The only superpipelined system produced to date is the MIPS R4000 and R4400 (see Part 2).

In an n-issue superscalar system, n instructions are fetched and decoded simultaneously. Subsequently, they must also be executed simultaneously in order to keep the advantage of a superscalar operation and attain n results per cycle. In

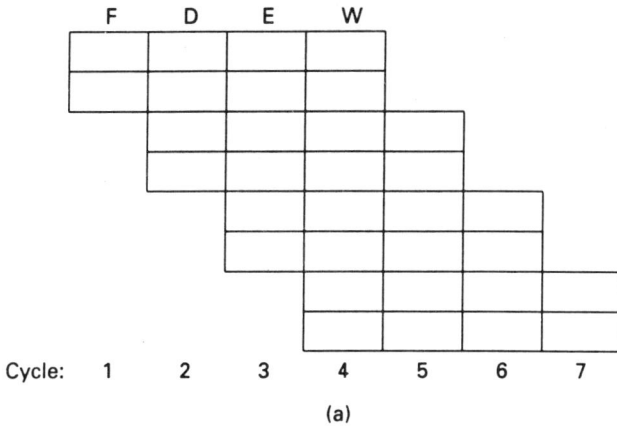

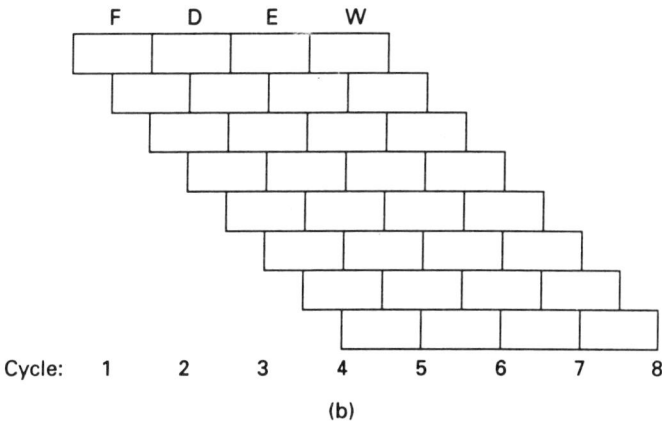

Fig. 1.3 Superscalar and superpipelined execution. (a) Two-issue superscalar; (b) two-issue superpipelined

order to execute n instructions simultaneously, we need to have n operation resources, some of which may be replicated. For instance, if we fetch two integer arithmetic instructions at the same time, we need two integer units to process them simultaneously.

Suppose we have an adequate number of resources. This alone will not solve all possible problems arising in superscalar operation. There is also a problem of data dependence. As argued earlier in this chapter, data dependence poses a serious hazard even in regular pipelines. It is much more serious in superscalar systems. If two or more dependent instructions are fetched simultaneously, forwarding will not be applicable, and stalling one of more of the pipelines might be unavoidable.

In a two-issue superscalar it is not difficult to group most programs into pairs or independent instructions. This can be done by either the user or the compiler. In three- or four-issue systems such grouping is more difficult, but still possible. However, more stalling should be expected. If we keep increasing the issue, the class of programs where instructions can be grouped into larger independent groups will get smaller and smaller. In a large-issue system (eight-issue and up), dependence among instructions issued together should be expected, multiple pipeline stalling may occur, and the resources may be underutilized most of the time. For this reason, most of the existing superscalar systems are two-issue, three-issue, or four-issue. There may be some manufacturers, however, who are working on higher-issue systems. Their success remains to be seen in the future. Some methods of dealing with hazards in superscalar systems are briefly surveyed in the following paragraphs.

Register renaming
A feature alleviating some of the data hazard problems in superscalar operation is *register renaming*. Register renaming prevents stalling of the completion of load operations by allowing the load operation to complete even though some previous operation using the same destination register as an operand has not yet moved into the decode stage and accessed that register. Even though it appears that the original contents of the register are destroyed by allowing the load operation to complete before the previous instruction has accessed the register, the load operation is actually loading temporarily another register. To be more specific, let us say that the load destination register is rd. Then, there would exist temporarily two rd registers: the original and the new. All *previous* instructions to the load, specifying rd, that are waiting in a queue to execute, access the register containing the *original* rd content, and all instructions *subsequent* to the load instruction, specifying rd, access the register containing the *new* content of rd. Register renaming is accomplished by implementing more physical registers than appear to be available to the programmer. For instance, the user model may contain officially 32 registers, while in reality there are 40 registers: eight extra registers for register-renaming implementation. The above description of the register-renaming implementation corresponds to such a feature in the FPU of the IBM RS/6000 [BaWh 90] and in the PowerPC implementations (see also chapter 7). There actually exist a number of ways of realizing the same concept which serves to solve the problem of possible out-of-order execution in superscalar systems [BuPa 93, HwPa 87, MPVa 93, SmPl 85].

Speculative execution
There exist many hazards in multiple-issue superscalar execution, such as data and control hazards, discussed earlier. If the execution of some instructions in the program is delayed until the resolution of uncertainties (such as whether a branch is or is not taken), valuable computing time may be lost. In order to save time, some modern designs have adopted a policy of executing instructions, tentatively

assuming a certain condition (such as a taken branch), correcting the results in case the assumption turns out to be incorrect. Such an approach is called *speculative execution*. Speculative execution is implemented in PowerPC 620 for instance (see chapter 7). The 620 speculatively executes instructions up to four unresolved branches. When implementing speculative execution, one must keep track of all possible outcomes in order to attain eventually correct results. An orderly approach to keeping track of possible outcomes is called: *state maintenance mechanism* [BuPa 93]. It is defined as follows:

State maintenance mechanism
Implementation of techniques involving the modification of the architectural machine state before it is known if such a modification is dictated by the correct sequential execution of the program. The implementation of this mechanism requires management of the machine state such that correct execution can be asserted [BuPa 93]:

1. Reorder buffer [SmPl 85].
2. History buffer [SmPl 85].
3. Checkpointing [HwPa 87].

These mechanisms will be described in the next paragraphs.

Reorder buffer
Implementation of the *reorder buffer* (ROB) [SmPl 85] involves updating the architecturally visible register file strictly in-order, while allowing instruction execution to proceed our-of-order [BuPa 93]. Instructions are put into a FIFO queue in the order in which they were issued. When an instruction completes execution, possibly out-of-order, its result is placed in the appropriate slot in the FIFO queue, rather than in the register file. The queue, in turn, updates the register file in-order, at a time when a possible error, resulting from an out-of-order execution, can be avoided. For instance, in the Power PC 604 implementation (chapter 7), within the dispatch unit logic, a reorder buffer (ROB) entry is allocated for each instruction, and dependency checking is done between the instructions in the dispatch queue [P604 94]. The rename buffers are searched for the operands as the operands are fetched from the register file. Operands that are written by other instructions ahead of the one in the dispatch queue are given the tag of that instruction's rename buffer. Otherwise, the rename buffer or the register file supplies either the operand or a tag. As instructions are dispatched, the fetch unit is notified that the dispatch queue can be updated with more instructions. An instruction is retired from the ROB when it has finished execution and all instructions ahead of it have been completed. The instruction's result is written into the appropriate register file and is removed from the rename buffers at or after completion.

History buffer

In the implementation of the *history buffer* [SmPl 85] the register file is updated as instructions complete execution, however the previous register values are maintained in a LIFO queue. The LIFO queue is arranged with a slot for each instruction in order of issue. The LIFO contains the history of the register file values. The head of the queue (bottom of the stack) contains the oldest instruction in the queue, and when it completes execution it is discarded from the queue. When an instruction causing an exception reaches the head of the queue, the register file is reconstructed by copying the history buffer back into the register file beginning with the tail of the queue (top of stack). For a mispredicted branch we 'undo' only those instructions issued since that branch [BuPa 93].

Checkpointing

A *checkpoint* is defined as a point in a dynamic instruction stream at which the machine state is preserved in some way to allow efficient restoration of the architecturally visible machine state [BuPa 93, HwPa 87]. It involves tagging checkpointed entities (such as physical registers) with a bit field which indicates the checkpoints at which the entry exists. There is a single bit for each checkpoint that the machine is capable of supporting. If the bit corresponding to the current checkpoint is set, then this physical register is the most recent reference to the associated architected register. By manipulating the content of this bit field, the register instance can be propagated to subsequent checkpoints or can be overwritten (by clearing the current bit). Backing up the machine requires returning to a previous set of physical to architected mappings. This is accomplished by treating a previous checkpoint as the current one. Similarly, retiring a checkpoint that is no longer needed simply requires clearing the corresponding bit in these bit fields [BuPa 93, HwPa 87].

Other methods of improving superscalar performance are described in the following paragraphs.

Branch history table

In recent superscalar implementations, such as the PowerPC 604 and 620 (see chapter 7), a *branch history table* (BHT) is implemented. A multiple-entry (512 on the 604, 2048 on the 620) provides two bits per entry, indicating four levels of dynamic prediction: **strongly not-taken, not-taken, taken,** and **strongly taken**. The history of a branch's direction is maintained in these two bits. Each time a branch is taken the value is incremented (with a maximum value of three meaning strongly taken). When a branch is not taken, the bit value is decremented (with a minimum value of zero meaning strongly not-taken). If the current value predicts taken and the next branch is taken again, the BHT entry then predicts strongly taken. If the next branch is not taken, the BHT then predicts taken.

Reservation station

A number of superscalar systems (such as PowerPC 604 and 620; see chapter 7) implement a *reservation station* (RS) to process branches within a *branch processing unit* (BPU). All branches, conditional and unconditional, are placed in a reservation station (RS) until conditions are resolved and they can be executed. At that point, branch instructions are executed in order. A special completion unit is notified whether the prediction was correct.

Register mapping

Another method recently proposed to deal with out-of-order execution is the method of *register mapping* [MPVa 93]. Only one set of physical registers is maintained. The registers defined by the system architecture are mapped into a subset of the available physical registers. This mapping changes as the instructions are issued. The association of the *architected registers* with *physical registers* is maintained in a *mapping table*. Correct results are maintained by repeated references to the mapping table [MPVa 93].

1.4 Concluding Comments

Pipelining and ILP can improve significantly system performance. These features are therefore implemented in a vast majority of new systems created in past years. The implementation of these features is not limited to RISC (see chapter 2). For many years pipelining has been implemented in numerous CISC systems, such as the DEC VAX and the Motorola M68000 families. As will be discussed in more detail in chapter 2 on RISC, efficient handling of even a regular pipeline depends strongly on the ability to fetch an instruction in a single cycle, and then execute it in a single cycle. Such a requirement is even more important in superscalar systems, when a number of pipelines are run in parallel. In CISC systems we have multiword instructions which must be fetched in more than one cycle. Many CISC instructions execute in more than one cycle because of their complexity and memory access for operands during execution. On the other hand, with the uniform single-word instruction size in RISC systems, all of the instructions can be fetched in a single cycle. Because of RISC simplicity and restricted memory access, most of RISC instructions execute in a single cycle. Therefore, RISC systems will handle pipelining and ILP more efficiently than CISC systems. The details of RISC principles and its properties will be discussed next in chapter 2.

16

CHAPTER 2

The Concept of RISC

2.1 Introductory Comments: RISC vs. CISC

The microprocessor families Intel x86 and Motorola M68000 [Tabk 94] are known for their abundant instruction sets, multiple addressing modes, and multiple instruction formats and sizes. Their control is microprogrammed, and different instructions execute within a different number of cycles. The control units of such microprocessors are naturally complex, since they have to distinguish between a large number of opcodes, addressing modes, and formats. This type of system belongs to the category called *complex instruction set computer* (CISC). Although many CISC microprocessors are pipelined, there exists an inherent difficulty in managing a pipeline (see chapter 1) in a system with a variety of instruction sizes and different instruction execution lengths.

As opposed to the traditional CISC design, in the early eighties there emerged a new trend of computer design called RISC — *reduced instruction set computer* [HePa 90, PaDi 80, PaSe 82, Patt 85, Tabk 87, Tabk 94]. What is 'reduced' in a RISC? Practically everything: the number of instructions, addressing modes, and formats. In an ideal RISC all instructions have the same size (usually 32 bits) and execute within a single CPU cycle. In practice, only the majority of the instructions (over 80 percent in most RISC systems) execute in a single cycle. The relative properties of CISC versus RISC systems will now be elaborated in more detail.

A CISC system with a large menu of features implies a larger and more complicated decoding subsystem, preceding the complex control logic. Logic signals will usually have to propagate through a considerable number of gates, increasing the duration of delays and slowing down the system. In a microprogrammed environment (and most CISCs are microprogrammed), increased complexity will directly result in longer microroutines and therefore their longer execution to produce all necessary microoperations and their corresponding control signals to execute an instruction.

One of the ways to increase the speed of execution on any computer is to implement pipelining (see chapter 1). For a pipeline with n stages, we can get the system to deal with n subsequent instructions simultaneously. Consider a simple two-stage instruction pipeline:

Stage One: Fetch, F
Stage Two: Execute, E

Assume a simple model where each of the above stages takes just a single CPU cycle to complete. We get the following instruction-time (in CPU cycles) layout for three subsequent instructions:

Cycle:	1	2	3	4
instr.　i :	F	E		
i + 1:		F	E	
i + 2:			F	E

All three instructions are fully taken care of in four cycles. It should also be mentioned that instruction $i-1$ is executed during cycle 1, while instruction $i+3$ is fetched during cycle 4. At any cycle, two instructions are being worked on in this simple two-stage pipeline.

The above streamlined pipeline model does not occur in CISC systems. The instructions are of different length; while some can be fetched in a single cycle, others need more. Different instructions are executed in a different number of cycles. A more realistic example on a CISC can be the following:

Cycle:	1	2	3	4	5	6	7
instr.　i :	F	E	E	E			
i + 1:		F			E		
i + 2:			F	F		E	E

It takes now seven cycles to execute three instructions (in the previous model it would take six cycles to handle all three instructions without a pipeline). Because of the disparity in instruction lengths and execution times, some instructions have to be suspended and wait for a few cycles within the pipeline. Instruction $i+3$ can be fetched starting with cycle 5, and its execution can begin no earlier than cycle 8.

The above example illustrates that there is a difficulty in implementing an instruction pipeline efficiently in a CISC-type system. In actual systems, instruction pipelines have more than two stages (usually three to six for integer operations and more for floating-point). If there are considerable differences between lengths and execution cycles of different instructions, which can appear in the CPU in any order, the pipeline design and utilization will be much more complicated. This complication will be even more severe for superscalar or superpipelined systems (see chapter 1).

The complexity of a CISC system would imply a long design time with a significant probability of design errors. In a complex system the errors will take a long time to locate and correct. By the time a CISC system is designed, built, and tested, it may become obsolete from the standpoint of the state of the art of the current computer technology, in which significant advances occur on a quarterly basis (sometimes even more frequently).

A large instruction set presents too large a choice for the compiler of any high-level language (HLL). This in turn makes it more difficult to design the optimizing stage of a CISC compiler. This stage would have to be longer and more complicated in a CISC system. Furthermore, the results of this 'optimization' may not always yield the most efficient and the fastest machine-language code.

Some CISC instruction sets contain a number of instructions particularly specialized to fit certain HLL instructions. However, a machine-language instruction that fits one HLL may be redundant for another and would constitute an excessive effort for the designer. Such a machine may have a relatively low cost-benefit factor.

Considering the pipeline operation example discussed above, one can see that an efficient system operation can be attained if all instructions take the same number of cycles for the fetch and execution stages. If the above take a single clock cycle, the operation will naturally be the speediest for a given technology. The designer should therefore strive to achieve uniform, single-cycle fetch and execute operations for each instruction implemented on the computing system being developed.

A single-cycle fetch can be achieved by keeping all instructions at a standard size. The standard instruction size should be equal to the basic word length of the computing system, which is usually equal to the number of data lines in the system bus, connecting the memory (where the program and data are stored) to the CPU. At any fetch cycle, a complete single instruction will be transferred to the CPU. For instance, if the basic word size is 32 bits and the data part of the system bus (the data bus) has 32 lines, then the standard instruction length should be 32 bits, as it is today in most systems. Some systems have a double bus, in and out of chip (64 bits), thus being able to fetch two instructions at a time.

Achieving uniform (same time duration) execution of all instructions (desirably in a single cycle) is much more difficult than achieving a uniform fetch. Some instruction executions may involve simple logical operations on a CPU register (such as clearing the register) and can be executed in a single CPU clock cycle without any problem. Other instructions may involve memory access (load from or store to memory, fetch data) or multicycle operations (multiply, divide, floating-point) and may be impossible to be executed in a single cycle. In order to attain better performance the designer should strive to achieve a situation where most of the featured instructions are executable in a single cycle.

Ideally, we would like to see a *streamlined* and *uniform* handling of all instructions, where the fetch and the execute stages take up the same time for any instruction (in the two-stage pipeline model) — preferably a single cycle. This is one of the first and most important principles inherent in the RISC design approach. All instructions go from the memory to the CPU, where they are executed, in a constant stream. Each instruction is executed at the same pace, and no instruction is kept waiting. The CPU is kept busy all the time. Having thus introduced the basis of the RISC idea, we will discuss the RISC properties in detail in the next section.

2.2 RISC Properties

As argued in the preceding section, some of the necessary conditions to achieve a streamlined operation in a RISC-type system are:

1. Standard, fixed size of the instruction, equal to the computer word length and to the width of the data bus (with the stipulation that in some new systems the word length and/or the data bus may be an integer multiple of the instruction size, as it is in the new 64-bit systems and in some 32-bit systems with a 64-bit data bus).
2. Standard execution time of all instructions, preferably within a single CPU cycle (with the stipulation that a minority of instructions, such as divide, will have to be executed in more than a single cycle).

One might raise the following argument: why not pack two instructions into a single word, transferred into the CPU on the data bus? Considering a 32-bit system, why not have some simple instructions of 16-bit length? In a 32-bit system, two 16-bit instructions can be packed into a single 32-bit word and fetched together. This would seem to enhance the speed of operation. On the other hand, having instructions of both 16 and 32 bits is contrary to the principle of uniformity in size of all instructions and does not permit a continuous streamlined handling at all times. Having more than one size of instructions also tends to complicate the decoding and other logic. Then why not have a standard 16-bit instruction? A 16-bit standard instruction is not practical in modern computers. Of course, a considerable number of simple single-operand instructions could be 16 bits in length. The trend in modern computer design is to have three-operand instructions. This permits efficient encoding of operations with different source operands and a different destination in a single instruction (with a two-operand format, two instructions would be required). A 32-bit format is needed for three-operand instructions. This will also permit a larger range for immediate values and address displacements. Therefore, since it is impracticable to have all instructions of halfword (16-bit) length, they all should be a full word (32-bit) long, as they are in most modern systems.

   Requiring all of the instructions to be of the same length is not in itself sufficient to ensure streamlined handling for all cases. It is also essential to have relatively simple decoding and control subsystems. A complex control unit will introduce extra delays in producing control signals, which in turn will tend to interfere with the expected streamlined and uniform handling of all instructions. An obvious way of significantly reducing the complexity of the control unit is to provide a reduced number of choices (a reduced 'menu') of instructions, data and instruction formats, and addressing modes. A reduction in the number of operation possibilities will first of all simplify the design and speed up the operation of the decoding subsystem, since it will have many fewer items to distinguish. Since there are fewer instructions and addressing modes, the control unit needs less logic circuitry to implement them. For a reduced menu, the control unit will be simpler and less costly to design, manufacture, and test. The reduction of the operations menu has been one of the primary points made by the original proposers of the RISC idea [PaDi 80].

How much is reduced? There is no definite answer to this question. One can only inspect the menu of the existing RISC-type systems (see Part 2), comparing them to the CISCs (such as VAX with 304 instructions, 16 addressing modes, and over 10 different instruction lengths). Based on a number of existing systems one can tentatively adopt the following constraints for a RISC menu:

Number of instructions: less than or equal to 128
Number of addressing modes: less than or equal to four
Number of instruction formats: less than or equal to four

Realizing that it might not be practical to hope that all instructions will execute in a single cycle, one can request that at least 80 percent should.

Which instructions should be selected to be on the reduced instruction list? The obvious answer is, the ones used most often. A number of earlier studies [Fair 82, Kate 85, PaDi 80] established that a relatively small percentage of instructions (10 to 20 percent) takes up about 80 to 90 percent of execution time in an extended selection of benchmark programs. Among the most often executed instructions were data moves and arithmetic and logical operations. Another criterion for selection is the *general* support of HLL. This is an important consideration, supporting the reduction of the semantic gap [Myrs 82] between the basic machine design and the HLLs, particularly since over 90 percent of all programming is done in HLL. The term *general support* is stressed, as opposed to the support of a particular HLL. In other words, one should strive to provide features that tend to support HLLs in general (such as support for procedure handling, parameter passing, and process management), as opposed to a particular HLL (such as Pascal or FORTRAN).

It was mentioned earlier that one of the reasons preventing an instruction from being able to execute in a single cycle is the possible need to access memory to fetch operands and/or store results. The conclusion is therefore obvious: we should minimize as much as possible the number of instructions that have to access memory during the execution stage. This consideration brought forward the following RISC principles, adopted on all of the existing systems of this category:

1. Memory access, during the execution stage, is done by *load* and *store* instructions only.
2. All operations, except load and store, are *register-to-register*, within the CPU. Systems featuring the above two rules are said to be adhering to a *load/store memory access architecture*.

Most of the CISC systems are microprogrammed, because of the flexibility that microprogramming offers the designer [Hays 88]. Different instructions usually have microroutines of different length. This means that each instruction will take a different number of cycles to execute. This contradicts the principle of a uniform streamlined handling of all instructions. Uniform handling of instructions can be achieved by using hardwired control, which is also faster. In hardwired control, a set of input signals is passed through a logic network to produce a set of control signals [Hays 88]. In such a system, uniformity of instruction handling is easily achieved. Therefore, RISC-type systems should have *hardwired control*.

In order to facilitate the implementation of most instructions as register-to-register operations, a sufficient number of CPU general-purpose registers has to be provided. A sufficiently large register set will permit the temporary storage of the intermediate results needed as operands in subsequent CPU operations. This, in turn, will reduce the number of memory accesses by reducing the number of load and store operations in the program, speeding up its run time. A minimal number of 32 general-purpose CPU registers has been adopted by most industrial RISC systems designers. Design considerations for establishing the size of the CPU register file are discussed in section 2.4.

A summary of the basic points of RISC definition is given in Table 2.1. It is not a rigorous, acceptable by all, definition. In fact, some systems, advertised as RISC-type, violate some of the points in Table 2.1. The above points should be viewed as guidelines, explaining the nature of RISC. Loosely speaking, a system satisfying the majority of these points could be accepted as a RISC. Naturally, the more of these points are satisfied, the closer is the system to being recognized as a 'full-fledged RISC'.

Table 2.1 RISC Definition

A RISC system satisfies the following properties:

1. Single-cycle execution of all (or at least most, over 80 percent) instructions.
2. Single-word standard length of all instructions.
3. Small number of instructions, not to exceed about 128.
4. Small number of instruction formats, not to exceed about four.
5. Small number of addressing modes, not to exceed about four.
6. Memory access by load and store instructions only.
7. All operations, except load and store, are register-to-register, within the CPU.
8. Hardwired control unit.
9. A relatively large (at least 32) general-purpose CPU register file.

In addition to the basic properties, forming the essence of RISC systems, summarized in Table 2.1, a number of features are practiced in many actual RISC systems. These features are not necessarily unique to RISC-type systems, and do not constitute a part of its definition. In fact, they might well be adopted by any CISC-type system, and indeed some of them have been.

One of the most important practices in modern computer design to be discussed here is the machine support of HLL. Although most of the programming is done in HLLs, the basic computer design of earlier generations did not provide any hardware-based support for HLL features, such as array management, handling of procedure parameter passing, typing and classifying information, process and memory management. Usually, a wide *semantic gap* existed between the HLL and the machine design [Myrs 82]. In the early generations of computers this gap had to be narrowed and bridged by software. A wide semantic gap would in general cause more complicated and hence more costly and less reliable system software. Lately, many systems (such as the VAX [Leon 87, LeEc 84]) have started to incorporate features supporting HLLs in their basic design, thus narrowing the semantic gap.

The support of HLL features is mandatory in the design of any computing system, be it RISC or CISC. It is a rather complicated matter and has to be approached very carefully. Loading the design with a great number of HLL features and instructions (some of which may happen to be used rather rarely) may result in a very complex and low-throughput system. A better approach is to investigate statistically the frequency of usage of various HLL features and to run a substantial number of benchmark programs written in HLL. Such experimental work has indeed been performed by the Berkeley team during the design of their RISC I and RISC II [Kate 85, PaSe 82, Patt 85]. This investigation suggested that the procedure call-return is the most time-consuming operation in typical HLL programs. The percentage of time spent on handling local variables and constants turned out to be the highest, compared to other variables. Based on that, the Berkeley team decided to support HLLs in their RISC design by supporting efficiently the handling of local variables, constants, and procedure calls, while leaving less frequent HLL operations to instruction sequences and subroutines. In other words, the Berkeley team decided to support HLLs by enhancing the performance of the most time-consuming HLL features and operations. Many other subsequent RISC designs followed this policy, obtaining reasonable HLL support and narrowing the semantic gap, while maintaining the simplicity and low complexity of the designed system.

One of the mechanisms supporting the handling of procedures, and their parameter passing in particular, is the feature of the *register window*. It was adopted by the Berkeley RISC designers and later featured on the Pyramid [Tabk 87] and the Sun SPARC (Part 2).

The register file is subdivided into groups of registers, called windows. A certain group of i registers, say r0 to r(i − 1), are designated as *global registers*. The global registers are accessible to all procedures running on the system at all times. On the other hand, each procedure is assigned a separate window within the register file. The window base (first register within the window) is pointed to by a field called *current window pointer* (CWP), usually located in the CPU's *status register* (SR), as illustrated in Fig. 2.1. If the currently running procedure is assigned the register window J, taking up registers K, K + 1, ..., K + W − 1 (where W is the number of registers per window), the CWP contains the value J, thereby pointing to the base of window J. If the next procedure to execute takes up window J + 1, the value in the CWP field will be incremented accordingly to J + 1.

REGISTER FILE

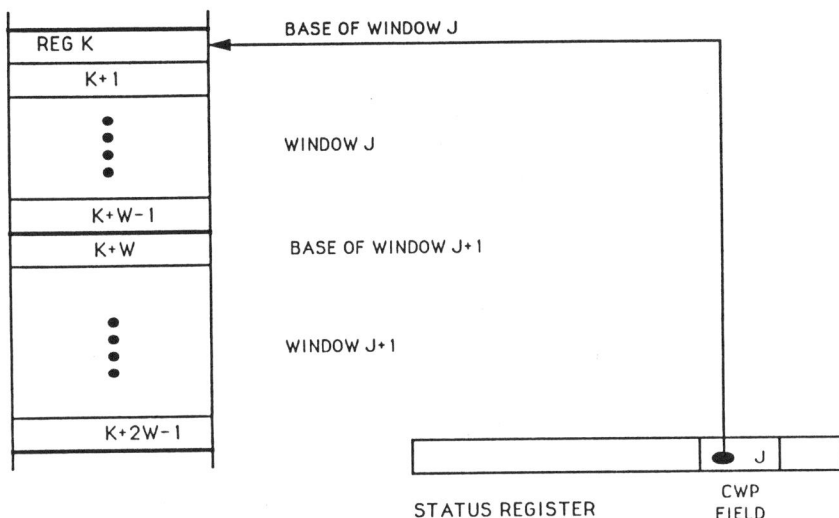

Fig. 2.1   Register windows

Register windowing can be particularly adapted to efficient parameter passing between calling and called procedures by partial overlapping of the windows, as illustrated in Fig. 2.2. The last N registers of window J are the first N registers of window J + 1. If the procedure taking up window J calls a procedure, which in this design will necessarily be assigned the next window J + 1, it can pass N parameters to the called procedure by placing their values into registers (K + W − N) to (K + W − 1). The *same* registers will be automatically available to the called procedure without any further movement of data. Naturally, the procedure call will cause the CWP field to be incremented by one. In a computer with a small register file, parameters are passed by placing them on stack or any other data structure in memory. Extra traffic on the CPU to memory bus is necessarily involved, taking up additional time.

Although register windowing has been implemented primarily on RISC-type systems, the concept is not directly connected with RISC principles, listed earlier. Theoretically, register windowing could be implemented on any system. However, an important point has to be noted. Modern implementations involve the use of VLSI chips. A CISC control unit takes up a large percentage of the chip area,

REGISTER FILE

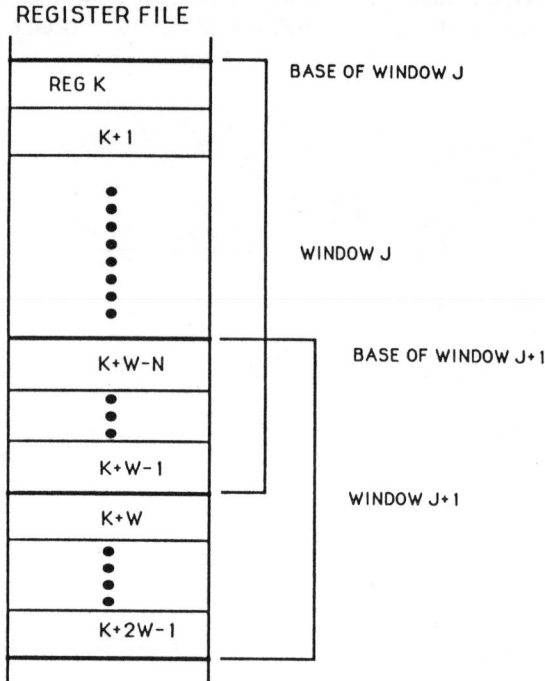

Fig. 2.2   Partially overlapping windows

leaving very little space for other subsystems and basically not permitting a large register file, needed for an efficient implementation of windowing. A RISC control unit takes up a much smaller percentage of the chip area, yielding the necessary space for a large register file. The overall size of a CPU register file is a debatable matter, to be discussed in more detail in section 2.4.

Most modern computers use a number of parallel processing approaches to speed up operations [Hwan 93]. In particular, the *pipelining* technique is widely used (see chapter 1). Pipelining was already featured in the third-generation computers such as the CDC 6600, and it became widely implemented later on (VAX 8600, MC68040, and many others). Pipelining was widely used on various CISC systems even before the RISC approach became popular, and the concept is not really a part of RISC definition. However, as argued earlier in this section, a streamlined RISC can handle pipelines more efficiently. Pipelining is indeed implemented in practically all modern high-performance RISC systems. Moreover, the most recent systems implement more than one pipeline by using the *superscalar* approach (see chapter 1).

Another design feature, associated with pipelining, which became very popular on some RISC systems, is that of the *delayed branch*. The problem occurs in systems where instructions are prefetched (they are always prefetched in an instruction pipeline), right after a branch. If the branch is conditional, and the condition is not satisfied (an unsuccessful, not taken branch), then the next instruction, which was prefetched, is executed, and since no branch is to be performed, no time is lost. If on the other hand the branch condition is satisfied (a successful, taken branch), or the branch is unconditional, the next prefetched instruction is to be flushed and another instruction pointed to by the branch address is to be fetched in its place. The time dedicated to the prefetching of the flushed instruction is lost. Such loss of time is remedied by using the delayed-branch approach.

Consider the following example:

CLR r2; clear register r2

CMP r1, 10; check the difference (r1) − 10

BZ adr1; if (r1) − 10 = 0, branch to adr1

Next instruction; otherwise, execute next instruction

where (r1) is the content of register r1. The nature of the 'next instruction' is immaterial (can be any) and ';' represents the beginning of a comment. The next instruction was prefetched and will be flushed if (r1) − 10. The first instruction can be placed between the branch and the next instruction, as follows:

CMP r1, 10

BZ adr1

CLR r2

Next instruction

The reshuffling of the instructions does not change the result. The instruction 'CLR r2' is now prefetched following the branch. Applying the *delayed branch* principle and assuming a successful branch, the execution of the branch [placing the value of the branch address 'adr1' into the program counter (PC)] is delayed until the following prefetched instruction (CLR r2) is executed. No time is lost, and there is no change in the intended program operation since r2 had to be cleared anyway before the branch, and it did not influence the branch condition (check whether the value stored in another register r1, is equal to 10).

The delayed-branch technique may be implemented on any system, be it RISC or CISC. It so happens that it was implemented on some RISC systems. The reason why it was not implemented on CISCs is that CISCs have more serious problems associated with handling the pipeline (see section 2.1), and the extra complexity associated with the introduction of a delayed branch is not going to be of significant help and is not worth while. Implementing the delayed branch in superscalar systems, with multiple parallel pipelines, is too complicated, and for this reason not practiced in such systems.

There is another problem associated with the handling of instruction pipelines. It is the problem of data dependency, discussed in chapter 1. Consider the following sequence of instructions:

LOAD memr, r1; load CPU register r1 from memory location memr

ADD r1, r2, r3; (r1) + (r2) → r3

The register r1, loaded from memory by the first instruction, is needed as an operand in the execution of the next instruction. It is important that the add instruction should use the new value in r1, attained after the completion of the load. Assuming both instructions can be fetched in a single fetch cycle (F), the load from memory would usually require an extra execute cycle (E). We have the following pipeline scheme:

load	F	E	E
add		F	E

The add is ready to execute before the new value in r1 is available. Unless appropriate steps are taken, the old value in r1 may be used, yielding a possibly incorrect result.

A method currently used to deal with such a case is called *scoreboarding*. A special CPU control register, called the *scoreboard register*, is set aside for this purpose. Assume that there are 32 CPU registers, as is the case in most RISCs. The scoreboard register will then be 32 bits long. Each of its bits represents one of the 32 CPU registers. For instance, bit 0 represents r0, bit 1 represents r1, and so on. In general, if register ri (i = 0, 1, ..., 31) is involved as a destination in the execution of any instruction, bit i in the scoreboard register will be set. As long as bit i is set, any subsequent instruction in the pipeline will be prevented from using ri in any way until bit i is cleared. This will happen as soon as the execution of the instruction, which caused bit i to be set, is completed.

In the previous example, bit 1 of the scoreboard register will be set until the load is complete. The execution of the add instruction will be held (H cycle) until bit 1 is reset:

load	F	E	E	
add		F	H	E

A cycle may be lost, but the final result is correct. Scoreboarding is used in a number of RISC-type systems, but it is not a property characterizing RISC.

Another feature, implemented in a number of RISC-type systems, is separate data and code caches, or the dual cache [HaVZ 90, Hays 88, HePa 90]. Some manufacturers refer to this feature as 'Harvard architecture'. It should be borne in mind, however, that in the original Harvard design the separation of data and code referred to the *main memory*. In most RISC-type systems of today, and even in some CISCs, only the primary cache is usually separated into data and code parts; the secondary cache (if implemented [HePa 90, Przy 90]) and the main memory store both code and data. Dual cache is practiced today both on RISC and CISC systems; it is not a part of the RISC definition.

Practically all most recent RISC systems and some CISCs practice *instruction level parallelism* (ILP), superscalar design in most cases and superpipelined in a few (see chapter 1). This practice, although implemented in most recent RISCs, is not a part of the RISC definition.

To summarize, the features implemented in RISC systems, but not necessarily constituting the basic principles of RISC, are:

1. HLL support.
2. Implementation of register windows.
3. Pipelining.
4. Delayed branch.
5. Scoreboarding.
6. Dual cache.
7. Instruction level parallelism.

The basic principles and properties of RISC having been discussed, an evaluation of RISC, presenting its advantages and disadvantages, will be taken up in the next section.

2.3 RISC Evaluation
Advantages of RISC
The advantages of RISC will be discussed from a number of points of view:

VLSI realization
Computing speed
Design cost and reliability
HLL support

RISC shortcomings will be presented subsequently.

RISC and VLSI realization. The VLSI-viewpoint argumentation was one of the principal points presented by the original RISC proponents at Berkeley in 1980 [PaDi 80]. As argued earlier, a RISC has relatively few instructions, few addressing modes, and few instruction formats. As a result, a relatively small and simple (compared to CISC) decoding and executing hardware subsystem of the CPU is required. This yields the following results when we contemplate the realization of a computing system by VLSI chips:

1. The chip area, dedicated to the realization of the control unit (the so-called control area) is considerably reduced. For example, the control area on RISC I took up six percent of the chip area [PaSe 82]; on RISC II, 10 percent; and on the CISC Motorola MC68020, 68 percent. In general, the control area for CISCs might take up over 50 percent of the chip area. Therefore, on a RISC VLSI chip, there is more area available for other features. There is a higher chance of fitting a whole CPU and some additional features on a chip (cache, floating-point unit, part of the main memory, memory management unit, I/O ports).
2. As a result of the considerable reduction of the control area, the RISC designer can fit a large number of CPU registers (138 on RISC II) on the chip. This in turn enhances the throughput for a large class of programs.
3. By reducing the control area on a VLSI chip and filling the area by 138 identical registers, we actually increase the *regularization factor* of the chip. The regularization factor is defined [Latt 81] as the total number of devices on the chip, excluding ROMs, divided by the number of drawn devices (such as registers, ALUs, counters, and other subsystems). It is the effective number of devices on the chip that we get for each device that we draw. Basically, the higher the regularization factor, the lower the VLSI design cost. While the regularization factor for MC68000 was 12, it was 25 for RISC I [Patt 82].
4. The GaAs VLSI chip realization technology is currently limited to a relatively low density compared to CMOS. Therefore, since a RISC reduces the control area, it represents an attractive approach for GaAs, single-chip, CPU realization [Milu 86].

The computing speed aspect. As explained earlier, the essence of a RISC is its uniform, streamlined handling of all (at least most) of the instructions. The RISC design approach is particularly suitable for a more efficient handling of pipelines (compared to CISC). As a result of the uniformity of instruction size and duration of execution, wait or hold periods in the pipeline are reduced to a minimum. These factors contribute significantly to the increase in computing speed.

A simpler and smaller control unit in a RISC has fewer gates. This results in shorter propagation paths (fewer gates to propagate through) for the control unit signals, yielding a faster operation.

A significantly reduced number of instructions, formats, and modes results in a simpler and smaller decoding system. As in the case of the simpler control unit, the decoding operation is faster on a RISC.

A hardwire-controlled system with a reduced control unit will in general be faster than a microprogram-controlled one — particularly if the latter has instructions corresponding to microroutines of different lengths, some of which may be considerably long.

A relatively large (32 or more) CPU register file tends to reduce CPU-memory traffic to fetch and store data operands. Data items that are needed often can be kept in CPU registers. This tends to save computing time, particularly for programs handling large amounts of data.

A large register set can also be used to store parameters to be passed from a calling to a called procedure, to store the information of a process that was preempted by another, and to store the information of an interrupted program. Without an adequate CPU register file, all of the above information would have to be stored in memory. This would cause extra CPU-memory traffic for the storage, and later, for the eventual restoration of the above information. All in all, a considerable amount of computer time can be saved by a large register set in a number of different events.

The delayed-branch technique also contributes to the enhancement of speed by preventing the flushing (and thus a waste) of prefetched instructions in case of a successful branch.

From the quantitative point of view, we can say that the RISC design contributes to the reduction of the program run or to the increase of speed by reducing the number of clock cycles per instruction. This follows from the basic characterization of RISC, which minimizes the number of cycles (ideally, to one) needed to execute each instruction.

Design cost and reliability considerations. A relatively small and simple control unit in a CPU will usually yield the following design cost and design reliability benefits:

1. It will take a shorter time to complete the design of a RISC control unit, thus contributing to the reduction in the overall design cost.
2. A shorter design time would reduce the probability that the end product will be obsolete by the time the design is completed.
3. A simpler and smaller control unit will have a reduced number of design errors and, therefore, a higher reliability.
4. Because of the simplicity and low number of instruction formats (usually not above four) and the fact that all instructions have the same standard length, instruction will not cross word boundaries and an instruction cannot wind up on two separate pages in a virtual memory. This eliminates a potential difficulty in the design of a virtual memory management subsystem.

High-level language (HLL) support. Several of the modern CISC systems, such as the VAX [Leon 87], have many features in their machine design that support directly functions which are common in HLLs (procedure management, array operations, array index testing, information typing and protection, memory management, and others). Several CISC systems have machine-language instructions that are either identical or very similar to some HLL instructions. As it turns out, the RISC design also offers some features that directly support common HLL operations and simplify the design of certain HLL compilers:

1. Since the total number of instructions in a RISC system is small, a compiler (for any HLL), while attempting to realize a certain operation in assembly language, will usually have only a single choice, as opposed to a possibility of several choices in a CISC. This will make that part of the compiler shorter and simpler in a RISC.

2. The availability of a relatively large number of CPU registers in a RISC permits a more efficient code optimization stage in a compiler by maximizing the number of faster register-to-register operations and minimizing the number of slower memory accesses.

3. The 'register windows' arrangement in a RISC CPU permits fast parameter passing between procedures and constitutes a direct support of HLL handling of subroutines and procedures.

4. All in all, a RISC instruction set presents a reduced burden on the compiler writer. This in turn tends to reduce the time of preparation of RISC compilers and their cost [PaDi 80, PaSe 82].

5. A simplified instruction set in a RISC provides an opportunity to eliminate a level of translation at run time in favor of translating at compile time (since the RISC compiler is simpler).

RISC shortcomings

RISC shortcomings are directly related to some of its points of advantage. The principal RISC disadvantage is its reduced number of instructions. Since a RISC has a small number of instructions, a number of functions, performed on CISCs by a single instruction, will need two, three, or more instructions on a RISC. This in turn will cause the RISC code to be longer. More memory will have to be allocated for RISC programs, and the instruction traffic between the memory and the CPU will be increased [FIMM 87]. Recent studies have shown [PaSe 82] that, on the average, a RISC program will be about 30 percent longer than a CISC program performing the same function. This is because only a minority of the instructions are used most of the time [Fair 82], and this minority is usually featured on RISC systems. This consideration has been taken seriously by most commercial RISC systems manufacturers. In fact, a number of commercial RISCs feature more than 100 instructions (see Part 2), compared to fewer than 40 on the Berkeley RISC.

The CPU register file played an important role in the discussion of RISC advantages in this section. Modern microprocessors also feature a sizeable on-chip cache. The relative merits of these features will be discussed in the next section.

2.4 On-chip Register File vs. Cache Evaluation

A controversial feature of a number of RISC systems is the large (sometimes over 100) CPU register file. Some of its potential advantages are quite obvious, and have already been mentioned in the preceding section. By keeping data values to be used as operands in the program in the CPU register file, the overall data traffic between the memory and the CPU is reduced. If the register set is small, many intermediate results, even if needed later in the program, have to stored in memory, only to be fetched again at a later time. With a large register set, intermediate results and any other data can be kept in CPU registers for as long as they are needed. A large register set also permits efficient parameter passing between procedures. With a small register set, all of the parameters have to be stored in memory and fetched from it whenever needed, increasing the CPU-memory traffic.

In a multitasking environment, the processor is often switched between different tasks. Each task has a certain set of data associated with it called the *task context* or the *task state*. The context of the interrupted task has to be saved. It is usually saved in memory and later retrieved when the interrupted task is reinstated. If the CPU has a large register file and the task context is limited to a finite subset of the CPU registers, the context can be saved in *another subset* of the CPU register file, saving on CPU-memory traffic. The same can be said about saving the basic information of an interrupted program. A large enough CPU register file can be configured by the designer to serve, optionally, as a stack or a data queue, if needed (see chapter 5). Without a large CPU register file, the above data structures have to be configured in the memory, and any communication with them constitutes extra CPU-memory data traffic. Having a large number of identical registers on the CPU chip increases its regularization factor and thus reduces the VLSI design and manufacturing cost.

On the other hand, having a large, on-chip CPU register file is plagued with disadvantages. The register address decoding system will be more complicated for a larger register file, increasing the access time to any of its registers. The use of window pointers in some systems also tends to increase the register address decoding time. Elaborate window management policies may also complicate the CPU logic, raising the cost and slowing down the operation. A large register file takes up more space on a chip. Some designers may decide that it is more important to put other resources on the chip (cache, special function units), and have only a modest (32) CPU register file.

In all systems where all of the CPU registers are saved in memory during a context switch, a large register file will take more time to store and later to retrieve. In addition, some compiler techniques make more efficient use of relatively small register files (16 to 32 registers). The advantages and disadvantages of a large (over 32) CPU register file, discussed above, are summarized in Table 2.2. Most RISC-type commercial processors have 32 registers for the *integer unit* (IU) and separate 32 registers for the *floating-point unit* (FPU).

As can be seen, the question of the optimal size of the CPU register file is a controversial one, requiring additional research. Despite some obvious advantages, certain studies have cast doubt on the benefit of a large register set [FIMM 87, Wall 88]. The simulation experiments in these studies were conducted with somewhat contrived rather than actual models of widely used computers. For this reason, the recommendations resulting from the above are indicative rather than conclusive. More extensive experimental results are needed.

Table 2.2 Large CPU Register File

Advantages

1. Speed-up of operations by reducing CPU-memory traffic.
2. Procedure parameter passing support within the CPU.
3. Multitasking context switching and interrupt handling support within the CPU.
4. On-chip stack and/or queue of data.
5. Increase in the chip regularization factor.

Disadvantages

1. Longer access time.
2. If window pointers are used, longer to decode register address.
3. Register file takes up more chip space.
4. Elaborate window policies complicate CPU logic.
5. Advanced compiler technology makes efficient use of relatively small register files.
6. If all CPU registers are saved on a context switch, a large register file will take more time to store or retrieve.

An alternative to a large register file is the use of a cache. The cache is now implemented in practically all modern computing systems. In order to compare the relative merits of a cache and a register file, let us look at some of their properties, listed in Table 2.3.

Since cache addresses are actually memory addresses (usually 32 bits), they would take longer to decode than register file addresses (seven bits for 128 registers, for instance). Moreover, three direct register addresses can easily be packed into a 32-bit instruction format. With memory addressing, single-word instruction length (32 bits), a three-operand addressing would necessarily be indirect. This would imply a longer access time compared to the direct mode. If the cache is on the same chip with the CPU, the access time will be comparable to that of a register file, but still at least a cycle longer because a complete 32-bit address must be calculated for the cache access, according to the specified addressing mode.

Table 2.3 On-chip Cache vs. Register File

Cache	CPU Register File
1. Addressed as locations in memory — long addresses.	Separate register addressing — short addresses.
2. Has to be tens of kbytes to be effective.	About 128 registers (512 bytes) will have significant effect on performance.
3. Information loaded in units of lines (blocks).	Information can be loaded individually to each register.
4. Slower access (EA calculation, virtual to physical address translation).	Faster access.
5. Information loaded based on prefetch and replacement policies.	Any information can be loaded at any time by the user.
6. Usually inaccessible by the user.	Fully accessible by the user.
7. Possibility of a miss.	No miss.

In many systems the user has no direct control over the manipulation of the cache. The cache is usually managed either by the hardware or by OS. On the other hand, the CPU register file is usually general purpose (or most of it), fully accessible by the user.

A simulation study, using VHDL, on the relative merits of on-chip cache vs. register file, was recently reported [MaTA 91]. The simulation was conducted for a model of the RISC-type Intel i860XR (see Part 2) which has an 8 Kbyte data cache, and 32 CPU registers (32 for IU and 32 for FPU). The simulation was conducted using the Linpack benchmark for the floating-point register file. The results are illustrated in Fig. 2.3. The horizontal axis represents the on-chip data cache, and the vertical axis represents computing time. There are four curves for different sizes of the register file: 32 (the existing one), 64, 128, and 256. One can see from Fig. 2.3 that doubling the register file from 32 to 64 registers improves considerably the performance. After that, only a modest improvement is achieved. This is in line with the previous discussion about the size of the register file: it is advantageous to increase it only up to a point. It can also be seen from Fig. 2.3 that one needs hundreds of thousands of bytes of cache to achieve the performance attainable by several hundreds of bytes of register file. The conclusion is that although cache can improve performance considerably, we should not give up the register file. The register file should be kept at a size of 32 to 64 registers. Most modern RISC systems have 32 IU and 32 FPU registers, for a total of 64 CPU registers.

2.5 Overview of RISC Development and Current Systems
As can be seen from the preceding discussion in this chapter, the RISC concept is not quite clear cut; it has both advantages and shortcomings. It has encountered

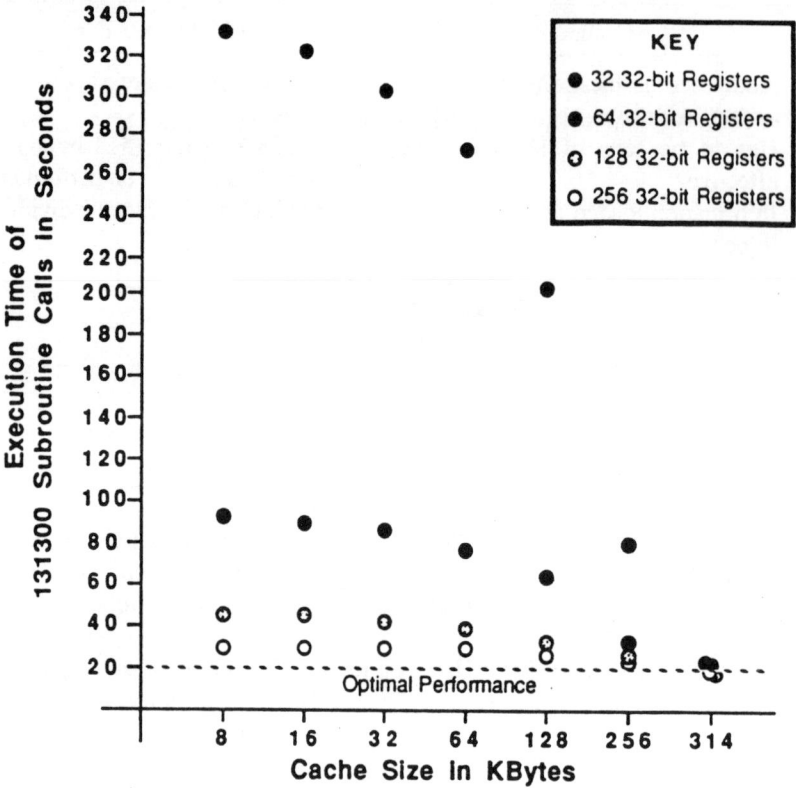

Fig. 2.3   Register/cache ratio vs. performance

opposition right from its inception [ClSt 80], in the same issue where it was first publicly announced [PaDi 80]. The RISC controversy continued over a number of years [Colw 85]. Notwithstanding the controversy, an important fact is notable: there is a considerable number of commercial computer products (see Part 2) announced as RISC-type by their manufacturers. To be sure, some of them do not adhere to all of the RISC properties specified in Table 2.1. One particular RISC 'violation' is in the number of instructions. In some systems such as IBM RS/6000 it is close to 200. Some of the announced RISC-type systems are more 'RISCy' than others; however, all of them strive to achieve a uniform and streamlined handling of all (or at least most) instructions.

The reason for the success of the RISC idea, despite its criticism, is the proven performance of RISC-type systems, attained over the years. Some examples of experimental results, demonstrating RISC system benchmark performance, compared to some CISCs, will be presented in Part 3.

⟍Among the RISC manufacturers there are companies which started with a RISC product, such as MIPS Computer Systems (now a part of Silicon Graphics) with its Rx000 series, and Sun Microsystems with its SPARC (see Part 2). There are other manufacturers, known for their CISC microprocessor families, who also started their own RISC system families, such as:

Intel, with its x86 family [Tabk 94], starting the RISC i860 family,
Motorola, with its M68000 family [Tabk 94], starting the RISC M88000 family and joining IBM and Apple in the PowerPC endeavor.

Of particular note is IBM which actually was the first to start with the development of an experimental RISC system, the 801 (see also chapter 5), and now features the RISC System 6000 and POWER2 (see Part 2). This effort is continued jointly by the cooperation of IBM, Motorola, and Apple in creating a new RISC-type family of microprocessors, called PowerPC, with the 6xx series (see Part 2).

Digital Equipment Corporation (DEC), some of whose professionals opposed the RISC idea in the beginning [ClSt 80], now features its own RISC product, the Alpha AXP (see Part 2), considered to be the fastest microprocessor of the early and mid nineties.

Practically all new RISC-type products, as well as some CISCs, are superscalar. The MIPS R4000 and R4400 are two-issue superpipelined (see chapter 1).

The application of RISC processors is widening. Generally speaking, most RISC processors are universal and their field of application is not limited. However, some of the most notable recent RISC applications are in workstations, multiprocessors, and real-time systems, primarily because of their superior performance, at a relatively low cost. The application area of RISCs is expected to widen in the future (see Part 3).

CHAPTER 3

The Berkeley RISC

3.1 Introductory Comments

After discussing some general issues regarding RISC-type systems, the Berkeley RISC will be presented in this chapter. The Berkeley RISC I and RISC II are the first systems bearing this name and the first to be realized on a VLSI chip. In this chapter, unless stated otherwise, the term 'RISC' will imply the specific Berkeley RISC system (I or II, as specified).

The aspects of architecture, organization and realization of RISC I and II will be described. By 'architecture' we mean the image that the computing system presents to the machine-language programmer and the compiler writer [Myrs 82]. This usually includes the complete list of all CPU registers, flip-flops and other parts accessible to the user by any instruction, data and instruction formats, the complete instruction set and any other details that the programmer has a need to know.

By 'organization' one should understand the complete details of the configuration, interconnections and other pertinent data of all the subsystems included in the computer, such as ALU, control subunits, I/O ports, buses, pins and others. By 'realization' one should understand the details of the hardware structures and circuit components chosen to construct the system. Details about the VLSI technology, materials and other pertinent data are to be mentioned. Although all aspects will be presented, a particular stress will be given to the architectural properties of RISC.

3.2 RISC Architecture
3.2.1 General Description

The RISC is a 32-bit machine, with each byte in memory individually addressed. It recognizes the following integer, signed (two's complement) and unsigned data formats:

Word	32 bits
Halfword	16 bits
Byte	8 bits

The RISC does not have a floating-point facility. In a word or a halfword, the least significant byte has the lowest address. All data items in memory are aligned in such a way that they do not cross word boundaries. If we start storing in the memory byte items, their addresses will be 0, 1, 2, 3, 4, 5, ... and so on. For halfwords we will have only even addresses 0, 2, 4, 6, ... and for words: 0, 4, 8, 12 (addresses 0 and those divisible by four). The data bus between the CPU and the memory is 32 bits wide and every memory-read operation fetches 4 bytes at a time into the CPU.

An example of a memory packing could be the following:

bits	31	24 23	16 15	8 7	0	*word*
	byte 3	byte 2	byte 1	byte 0		0
	halfword 6		halfword 4			4
	halfword 10		halfword 8			8
	halfword 14		halfword 12			12
	word 16					16

The bits in a word are numbered so that bit 0 is the least significant, and bit 31 the most significant.

The CPU has a total of 138 32-bit working registers, R0, R1, ..., R137 available to the user. However, each program or procedure, running on the RISC, 'sees' only 32 CPU registers. The multiple registers are used for parameter passing between calling and called procedures and for the storage of local variables by each procedure. This point will be elaborated in more detail later on. The first ten registers R0, R1, ..., R9, called the *global registers*, are seen by all of the procedures running on the RISC and they contain the global variables of the program. Register R0 contains always zero (R0 = 0) and it is used to synthesize addressing modes and operations which are not directly available on the RISC. It can be written into but its contents will remain zero nevertheless.

When a signed eight- or 16-bit data value is stored in a 32-bit register it is automatically sign-extended, while being placed in the register's least significant part. The remaining, most significant part of the register is filled with the sign of the data value (1 for negative, 0 for positive). In the case of eight- or 16-bit unsigned data values, it works similarly; only the most significant part of the register is filled with zeros.

A whole word (32 bits) is used to specify addresses in RISC. Thus, the RISC logical address space is 2^{32} bytes or 4 Gbytes.

3.2.2 The Instruction Formats
The RISC is a three-address (operand) machine with two sources and a destination specified in the instruction. There are also some two- and single-address (operand) instructions. The RISC architecture distinguishes two basic instruction formats:

(a) The Short-Immediate Format

This format is used for all register-to-register instructions and for register-indexed load, store and control-transfer instructions.

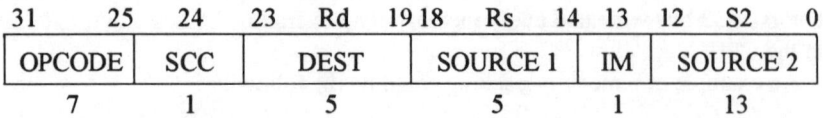

31	25	24	23	Rd	19 18	Rs	14 13	12	S2	0
OPCODE		SCC	DEST			SOURCE 1		IM	SOURCE 2	
7		1	5			5		1	13	

The individual fields of the instruction format have the following interpretation:

OPCODE   Seven bits, contains the operation code of the instruction. Although there is space for 128 opcodes, the RISC I has 31 and the RISC II only 39 instructions.

SCC   One bit, when set this bit determines whether the condition codes (flags) of the CPU will be affected by the instruction.

DEST   Five bits, determines one out of 32 possible destination registers, Rd.

SOURCE 1   Five bits, one of the source registers, Rs (out of 32).

IM = 0   the low-order five bits of the SOURCE 2 field (13 bits) specify the second source register; eight bits of SOURCE 2 are unused.

IM = 1   SOURCE 2 is interpreted as a 13-bit, sign-extended constant.

SOURCE 2   13 bits, represents the second source operand S2, as explained above.

(b) The Long-Immediate Format

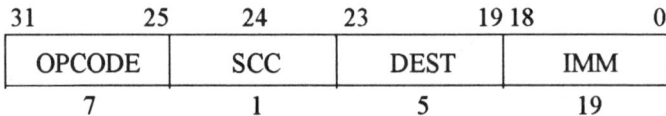

31	25	24	23	19 18	0
OPCODE		SCC	DEST		IMM
7		1	5		19

This format is used for all PC-relative instructions and for all branches. The OPCODE and the SCC field are interpreted as in the Short-Immediate Format.

DEST   Five bits, interpreted in two ways:
(a) As a five-bit destination register, Rd,
(b) For branch instructions, its four least significant bits constitute the *condition code*, while the leftmost bit is unused.

IMM   19 bits, interpreted as a sign-extended constant.

3.2.3 The Addressing Modes

Formally, there are two basic addressing modes:

(1) Indexed mode, (Rx) S2
    Effective Address = Rx + S2

(2) PC-Relative, Y
   Effective Address (EA) = PC + Y

Mode (1) can be used to synthetize the following modes:

(a) Base-Absolute (Direct), Rx = Rb, S2 = imm
    EA = Rb + imm
(b) Register Indirect, Rx = Rp, S2 = R0 = 0
    EA = Rp
(c) Indexed for a linear byte array a[i], assuming Ra points to the base of a[.],
    Rx = Ri, S2 = Ra
    EA = Ra + Ri

3.2.4 The Instruction Set

The RISC I has 31 instructions and the RISC II has 39. RISC II has all of the 31 RISC I instructions plus an extra eight LOAD/STORE (five LOAD, three STORE) instructions. All of the eight extra RISC II instructions use the PC-Relative addressing mode, while the original LOAD/STORE instructions of RISC I (but also available on RISC II) use the Indexed mode.

The complete list of the RISC II 39 instructions is given in Table 3.1. The additional eight instructions of RISC II are indicated. The RISC instructions are subdivided into four categories:

1. Arithmetic-Logic Instructions (12).
2. Memory Access: LOAD/STORE Instructions (16).
3. Branch and CALL Instructions (7).
4. Miscellaneous Instructions (4).

The instructions are listed in Table 3.1 in the above order.

In the Operation column of Table 3.1, when we write Rs + S2, we mean — the contents of Register Rs plus either the contents of the register, specified by S2, or the immediate constant, specified by S2. The above sum can serve as an effective address in memory, and the contents of the memory location, starting at that address, are denoted by M[Rs + S2]. Of course, different ['addends'] can be substituted in this expression:

M[Rx + S2]

M[PC + Y]

but the meaning remains the same.

The jump conditions, expressed by COND, are the following [Kate 85]:

Table 3.1 RISC II Instruction Set

Instruction Name	Assembly Notation	Operation
Arithmetic-Logic Instructions		
1. Integer Add	ADD Rs, S2, Rd	Rd <-- Rs + S2
2. Add with Carry	ADDC Rs, S2, Rd	Rd <-- Rs + S2 + C
3. Integer Subtract	SUB Rs, S2, Rd	Rd <-- Rs - S2
4. Subtract with Carry	SUBC Rs, S2, Rd	Rd <-- Rs - S2 - C
5. Integer Subtract Reverse	SUBI Rs, S2, Rd	Rd <-- S2 - Rs
6. Subtract Reverse with Carry	SUBCI Rs, S2, Rd	Rd <-- S2 - Rs - C
7. Logical AND	AND Rs, S2, Rd	Rd <-- Rs and S2
8. Logical OR	OR Rs, S2, Rd	Rd <-- Rs or S2
9. Logical Exclusive OR	XOR Rs, S2, Rd	Rd <-- Rs XOR S2
10. Shift Left	SLL Rs, S2, Rd	Rd <-- Rs shifted by S2
11. Shift Right Logical	SRL Rs, S2, Rd	Rd <-- Rs shifted by S2
12. Shift Right Arithmetic	SRA Rs, S2, Rd	Rd <-- Rs shifted by S2
LOAD/STORE Instructions		
13. Load Long	LDXW (Rx) S2, Rd	Rd <-- M[Rx + S2]
14. Load Short Unsigned	LDXHU " "	" = "
15. Load Short Signed	LDXHS " "	" = "
16. Load Byte Unsigned	LDXBU " "	" = "
17. Load Byte Signed	LDXBS " "	" = "
18. Load Relative Long II	LDRW Y, Rd	Rd <-- M[PC + Y]
19. Load Relative Short Unsigned II	LDRHU " "	" = "
20. Load Relative Short Signed II	LDRHS " "	" = "
21. Load Relative Byte Unsigned II	LDRBU " "	" = "
22. Load Relative Byte Signed II	LDRBS " "	" = "
23. Store Long	STXW Rm, (Rx) S2	M[Rx + S2] <-- Rm
24. Store Short	STXH " "	" = "
25. Store Byte	STXB " "	" = "
26. Store Relative Long II	STRW Rm, Y	M[PC + Y] <-- Rm
27. Store Relative Short II	STRH " "	" = "
28. Store Relative Byte II	STRB " "	" = "

	Instruction	Assembly Notation	Operation
Branch and CALL Instructions			
29.	Conditional Jump	JMPX	COND, (Rx) S2	PC <-- Rx + S2
30.	Conditional Relative Jump	JMPR	COND, Y	PC <-- PC + Y
31.	Call and Change Window	CALLX	Rd, (Rx) S2	Rd <-- PC, next PC <-- Rx + S2 CWP <-- CWP - 1
32.	Call Relative and Change Window	CALLR	Rd, Y	Rd <-- PC, next PC <-- PC + Y CWP <-- CWP - 1
33.	Return and Change Window	RET	COND, (Rx) S2	PC <-- Rx + S2 CWP <-- CWP +1
34.	Call an Interrupt Pr	CALLI	Rd	Rd <-- last PC, next CWP <-- CWP - 1
35.	Return from Interrupt Pr	RETI	COND, (Rx) S2	NXTPC <-- Rx + S2, next CWP <-- CWP + 1
Miscellaneous Instructions			
36.	Load Immediate High to Restart Delayed Jump	LDHI	Rd, Y	Rd <31:13> <-- Y, Rd <12:0> <-- 0
37.	Load Last PC (Save Value for Restarting Pipeline) Pr	GETLPC	Rd	Rd <-- last PC
38.	Load Status Word	GETPSW	Rd	Rd <-- PSW
39.	Set Status Word Pr	PUTPSW	Rm	PSW <-- Rm

Comments

II - Instruction available on RISC II only (not on RISC I).
Pr - Privileged (System) Instructions.
S2 - Either a CPU register or a 13-bit immediate constant.
M[Rx + S2] - Memory location contents, whose effective address starts at Rx + S2.
Y - immediate 19-bit constant.
Rd, Rx, Rm - CPU registers. When in an equation - their contents.
Long - 32-bit word
Short - 16-bit word
COND - Branch condition (specified in the text). When COND=0, it represents an unconditional branch.
CWP - Current Window Pointer, points to the window of the currently active procedure.

Hexadecimal Code	Assembly Notation	Name of Condition
0	—	Unconditional Jump
1	GT	Greater Than
2	LE	Less or Equal
3	GE	Greater or Equal
4	LT	Less Than
5	HI	Higher Than
6	LOS	Lower or Same
7	LO or NC	Lower Than or No Carry
8	HIS or C	Higher or Same or Carry
9	PL	Plus
A	MI	Minus
B	NE	Not Equal
C	EQ	Equal
D	NV	No Overflow
E	V	Overflow
F	ALW	Always

Some of the instructions in RISC I have different mnemonics [PaSe 82] than those in RISC II [Kate 85]:

RISC I	RISC II
SUBR	SUBI
SUBCR	SUBCI
LDL	LDXW
LDSU	LDXHU
LDSS	LDXHS
LDBU	LDXBU
LDBS	LDXBS
STL	STXW
STS	STXH
STB	STXB
JMP	JMPX
CALL	CALLX
CALLINT	CALLI
RETINT	RETI

However, their operation is essentially the same.

The opcodes of the RISC II instructions are the following [Kate 85]:

	000XXXX	001XXXX	010XXXX	011XXXX
XXX 0001	CALLI	SLL		
XXX 0010	GETPSW	SRA		
XXX 0011	GETLPC	SRL		
XXX 0100	PUTPSW	LDHI		
XXX 0101		AND		
XXX 0110		OR	LDXW	STXW
XXX 0111		XOR	LDRW	STRW
XXX 1000	CALLX	ADD	LDXHU	
XXX 1001	CALLR	ADDC	LDRHU	
XXX 1010			LDXHS	STXH
XXX 1011			LDRHS	STRH
XXX 1100	JMPX	SUB	LDXBU	
XXX 1101	JMPR	SUBC	LDRBU	
XXX 1110	RET	SUBI	LDXBS	STXB
XXX 1111	RETI	SUBCI	LDRBS	STRB

For instance, to obtain the opcode of AND, we take the three bits of the column with the four bits of the row to form: 001 0101.

3.2.5 The CPU Registers

As mentioned before, the RISC has 138 32-bit working registers R0, R1, ..., R137, available to the user, 32 registers per program or procedure. The first 10 registers R0, R1, ..., R9 are called the *global registers*. They are visible to *all procedures* running in the system. In addition, each procedure sees 22 *window registers*, R10 to R31 (see Fig. 3.1), subdivided into three groups:

Name	Number of Registers	Registers
HIGH	6	R31 to R26
LOCAL	10	R25 to R16
LOW	6	R15 to R10

There can be a total of eight windows. Each window is pointed to by a three-bit field CWP (Current Window Pointer) of the Processor Status Word, PSW (bits 10–12). The PSW register (13 bits) is visible to the user and can be manipulated by the GETPSW and PUTPSW (privileged) instructions. Each window is identified by a *window number*, ranging from 0 to 7.

Registers R16 to R25 (LOCAL) of each procedure contain the local scalar variables of that procedure. Registers R10 to R15 (LOW) of the procedure contain the parameters passed by this procedure to the procedure that it is calling. Registers

Registers

			Parameters passed to this procedure by the calling procedure
R31 ⎰	6	HIGH	
⋮ R26			
R25		LOCAL	Local scalar variables of this procedure
⋮	10		
R16			
R15	6	LOW	Parameters passed by this procedure to the called procedure
⋮ R10			
R9	10	GLOBAL	Global variables seen by all procedures
⋮ R0			

WINDOW REGISTERS

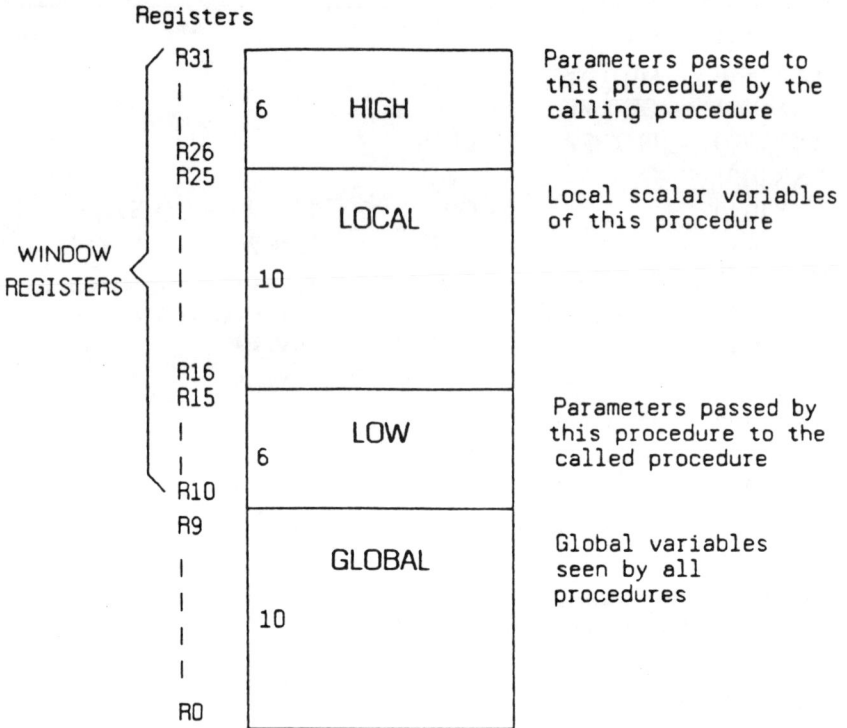

Fig. 3.1 CPU registers seen by each procedure

R26 to R31 (HIGH) contain the parameters passed to this procedure by the procedure which called it (see Fig. 3.2).

The Processor Status Word (PSW) is a 13-bit register, structured as follows:

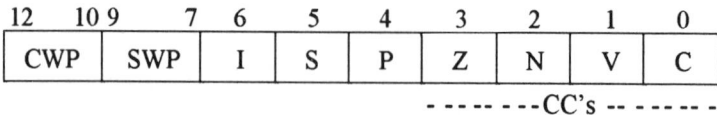

12 10	9 7	6	5	4	3	2	1	0
CWP	SWP	I	S	P	Z	N	V	C

- - - - - - - - CC's - - - - - - - -

where:

CWP Current Window Pointer, 0 to 7, specifies the window of the currently active procedure.

SWP Saved Window Pointer, identifies the youngest window that has been saved in memory. Not visible to the regular user.

I Interrupt enable bit.

S System mode bit.

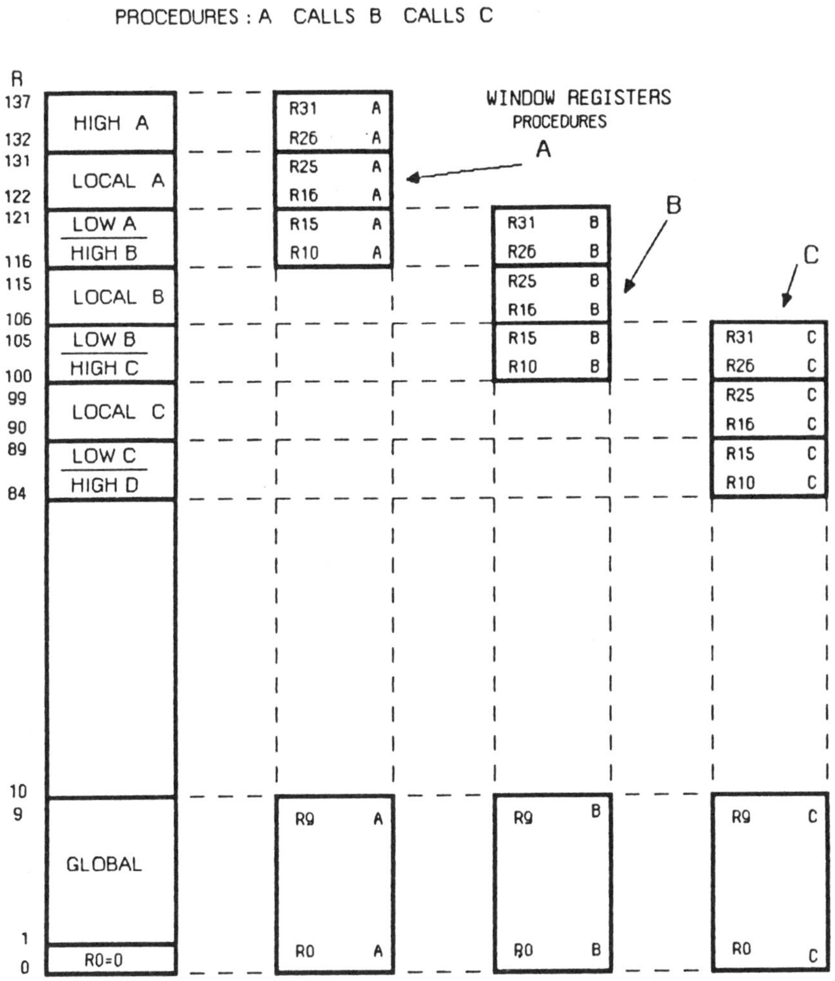

PROCEDURES : A CALLS B CALLS C

Fig. 3.2   RISC working registers

P   Previous system mode bit.
CC   Condition Codes (Flags):
               Z   Zero
               N   Negative
               V   oVerflow
               C   Carry

The CPU working registers can be identified by an addressing pair:

Window Number. Register Number

Register	Window Number.	Reg. assignment	
137		7.25	Window 7 locals
---		---	
---		---	
---		---	
128		7.16	
- - - -	- - - - - - - - - -		
127	6.31	7.15	Window 6 input arguments
---	---	---	Window 7 passed arguments
---	---	---	
---	---	---	
122	6.26	7.10	
- - - -	- - - - - - - - - -		
121	6.25		
---	---		
---	---		
---	---		
112	6.16		Window 6 locals
- - - -	- - - - - - - - -		
111	6.15	5.31	Window 6 passed arguments
---	---	---	Window 5 input arguments
---	---	---	
---	---	---	
---	---	---	
---	---	---	
---	---	---	
32	---	1.16	Window 1 locals
- - - -	- - - - - - - - -		
31	0.31	1.15	Window 0 input arguments
---	---	---	
---	---	---	
26	0.26	1.10	Window 1 passed arguments
- - - -	- - - - - - - - -		
25	0.25		Window 0 locals
---	---		
---	---		
---	---		
16	0.16		
- - - -	- - - - - - - - -		
15	0.15	7.31	Window 0 passed arguments
---	---	---	
---	---	---	
10	0.10	7.26	Window 7 input arguments
- - - -	- - - - - - - - -		
9			Global Registers

0			

The Window Number ranges from 0 to 7 and the current value is always stored in the CWP field of the PSW. The Register Number ranges from 10 to 31. Each procedure occupies a specific window and has a Window Number assigned to it. The window distribution in the register file has the form [Kate 85] shown on page 46.

As we can see, the registers dedicated to the windows (R10–R137) are arranged in a *circular organization*, with eight windows (labelled 0 to 7) occupying the register file at any one time. In fact, there is a virtually unbounded capability of the absolute procedure nesting depth. Whenever there is a procedure call and there is no more space in the register file, a *register file overflow* (trap) occurs, and the parameters are pushed on stack (in the main memory). The SWP points to the youngest window that has been saved in memory. Mechanically, the criterion for a register file *overflow* is the event when a *call* instruction attempts to modify CWP so that it becomes equal to SWP. Symmetrically, there is also an *underflow trap* when a *return* instruction attempts to modify CWP so that it becomes equal to SWP. Tamir and Sequin [TaSe 83] have investigated this aspect of RISC architecture and concluded that the best strategy, for most practical cases, is to save only one window per overflow trap. For eight windows there can be actually seven nested procedure activations.

Other CPU registers visible to the user (all 32 bits):

Instruction Register (IR) — contains the instruction to be executed next.
Program Counter (PC) — contains the address of the next-to-be-executed instruction (in IR). Used for PC-relative addressing mode.
Next PC (NXTPC) — contains the address of the instruction to be executed subsequently after the one contained in the IR.
Last PC (LSTPC) — contains the address of the instruction which just finished executing. Not visible to the regular user. Its purpose is to hold the value to the PC when an instruction is aborted due to an interrupt. The PC, in turn, holds the value of the NXTPC, while NXTPC is used for fetching the first instruction of the interrupt handler (interrupt service routine).

All three PCs always have a 0 least significant bit, since RISC instructions are always halfword aligned in the main memory. The three PCs are needed for the handling of delayed jumps and interrupts, to be discussed later in this chapter.

3.2.6 RISC Pipeline

Most of the RISC operational instructions are of the register-to-register type:

Rs1 op Rs2 → Rd

Here, the second source operand S2 is one of the CPU registers Rs2 (the alternative being a 13-bit immediate value). The above operation can be easily subdivided into three principal stages:

(1) Read Rs1 and Rs2 (or get PC or IMM).

(2) Perform the operation on Rs1 and Rs2.

(3) Write the result into the destination register Rd.

LOAD and STORE instructions, the only ones that access memory, require an additional cycle to complete their execution.

The RISC I has a basic two-stage pipeline. Each instruction cycle has the form:

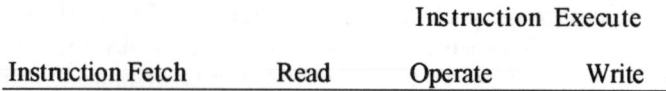

Instruction Execute

Instruction Fetch	Read	Operate	Write

And a sequence of instructions I1, I2, I3 ...:

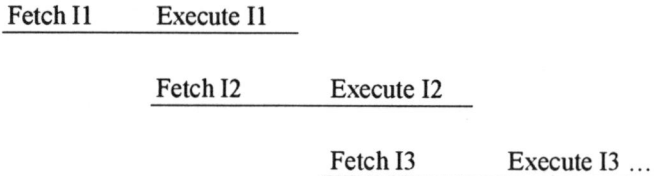

Fetch I1	Execute I1		
	Fetch I2	Execute I2	
		Fetch I3	Execute I3 ...

The RISC II separates the last stage of the execute subcycle, namely the writing into Rd, into another pipeline stage. Thus, the RISC II instruction pipeline has three stages:

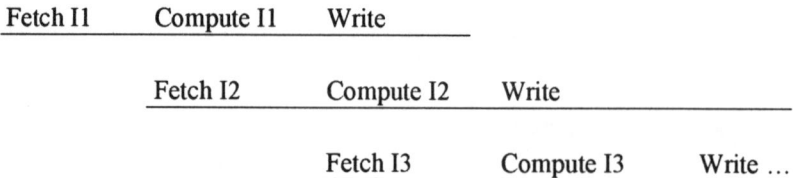

Fetch I1	Compute I1	Write		
	Fetch I2	Compute I2	Write	
		Fetch I3	Compute I3	Write ...

Usually, the pipelining issue belongs to the organization of the computing system, rather than to its architecture. It may be completely transparent to the user, who does not really have a need to know about it (such as with the VAX 8600 which is a pipelined machine with an architecture identical to the VAX 11/780). However, in RISC, due to the *delayed jump* facility (see chapter 2), at least the compiler writer has to be aware of the pipeline. Therefore, in RISC it is a part of the architecture. The burden of the delayed jump is taken up by the compiler writer. To facilitate the implementation of the delayed jump there are three PCs: NEXTPC, PC and LSTPC, as specified in the previous section.

Only one memory access at a time (fetch instruction, LOAD, STORE) is possible on the RISC. Therefore, during the execute stage of a LOAD or STORE instruction, there is no possibility of fetching the next instruction and the pipeline is *suspended* for a whole cycle.

3.2.7 RISC CPU-Memory Data Interface

The RISC architecture supports three basic data types:

Words	32 bits
Halfwords	16 bits
Bytes	8 bits

The CPU-memory data bus is 32 bits wide, and 4 bytes are always transmitted along it. All instructions are 32 bits long, and they are aligned along word boundaries (addresses divisible by four in the byte-addressable memory). Thus, there is no particular problem in the instruction-fetching operation.

In a memory-read (LOAD instruction) operation a whole word is always read into the CPU, even if the LOAD instruction involved only a byte or a halfword (16 bits). For instance, a word at address 20 is composed of 4 bytes at addresses 20, 21, 22, 23 (or two halfwords at addresses 20 and 22). If we LOAD byte 21, say into register R5, the whole 32-bit word at address 20 will be read into the CPU. However, only byte 21 will be loaded into the least significant byte of R5. If the LOAD was signed (LDXBS or LDRBS), the byte in R5 will be sign extended. If it was unsigned (LDXBU or LDRBU), the three most significant bytes of R5 will be filled with zeros. The LOAD operation works similarly with halfwords.

For memory-write (STORE instruction) operations the CPU always transmits a full 32-bit word, notwithstanding the exact data item specified by the instruction. If the STORE involves a byte or a halfword, only that part of a word in memory is to be overwritten. The two least significant bits of the 32-bit Effective Address (EA), supplied by the CPU, establish the byte within the word that is to be overwritten. In addition we use two special control outputs from the CPU:

WIDTH code W
WIDTH code H

The word-overwriting rules are as follows:

Instr.	WIDTH code W	WIDTH code H	EA 1:0	Word bits to be overwritten			
				31:24	23:16	15:8	7:0
STW	ON	OFF	00	W	W	W	W
STH	OFF	ON	00			W	W
			10	W	W		
STB	OFF	OFF	00				W
			01			W	
			10		W		
			11	W			

Example: Given EA = 00007A61 (hex), WIDTH code W = WIDTH code H = 0

Obviously EA $\langle 1:0 \rangle = 01$ and according to the above rules we overwrite bits $\langle 15:8 \rangle$ in the word at address 00007A60 (hex).

3.2.8 Interrupt
The exceptions of the RISC are subdivided into two categories:

Interrupts (external)
Traps (internal)

The main Interrupts and Traps and their corresponding Interrupt Vectors (addresses for the Interrupt Service Routine) are:

Interrupts	Vectors (hexadecimal)	
Reset pin pulsed high	8000	0000
Interrupt Request pin pulsed high	8000	0010

Traps	Vectors (hexadecimal)	
Illegal opcode	8000	0000
Privileged opcode in user mode (while S = 0)	8000	0000
Address misalignment	8000	0000
Register File Overflow	8000	0020
Register File Underflow	8000	0030

The priorities of the above are:
    8000 0000 highest priority
    8000 0030 medium priority (30,20 cannot occur simultaneously)
    8000 0020
    8000 0010 lowest priority

The Reset pin interrupt is non-maskable. All other interrupts can be disabled by setting bit I = 0 in the PSW.

Suppose I = 1 (interrupt enabled) and an interrupt request arrives in the middle of an instruction cycle of instruction i. The following, hardware-based, events will occur automatically:

(1) Instruction i is aborted; it will not complete its execution. A memory write (STORE) that may have started will be allowed to complete.
(2) Instruction i + 1 that may have been prefetched during cycle i is discarded. It is replaced by a hardwired instruction

    CALLI   R25   (with SCC = 0)

which places the value in LSTPC into the register R25. The LSTPC contains at this point the value in PC, when the interrupt request arrived.
(3) The PSW is modified as follows:
   I = 0   (disable interrupts)
   P = S   (S bit saved into the P bit)
   S = 1   (transfer into system mode)
(4) The Interrupt Vector value is loaded into NXTPC. This value constitutes the address of the next instruction to be fetched and executed by the CPU.

In addition, between points (2) and (4), the value in NXTPC must also be saved. We have:

$$NXTPC \rightarrow PC \rightarrow LSTPC$$

Subsequently the interrupt service routine (interrupt handler) must save the value in LSTPC by its first instruction, which is

GETLPC   R24   ;   R24 ← LSTPC

After the completion of the interrupt handling, the PC values are to be restored by [Kate 85]:

JMPX   ALW, (R25) 0
RETI   ALW, (R24) 0

where ALW is the 'always' condition (see section 3.2.4).

3.3 RISC Organization

The organization of RISC I is sketched in Fig. 3.3 and that of RISC II in Fig. 3.4. Only a part of the RISC subsystems and their interconnections is shown in these Figures. One of the main differences between the RISC I and II organizations is that RISC I has a three-bus Register File Cell (buses A, B, C), while RISC II Register File Cell has only two buses (A and B). In addition, the RISC I register file has fewer (78) registers. The redesign of the Register File Cell in RISC II permitted the achievement of a more compact cell — about 2.5 times smaller than the three-bus RISC I cell. The saving in the chip area gave the designers more flexibility in the allocation of the chip area to other on-chip resources. To make the two-bus pipeline operation more effective and to avoid idle time in the utilization of the register file, a third stage has been introduced into the instruction pipeline (see section 3.2.6). The writing of the result of instruction i, into the register file, occurs while the ALU is executing instruction $i + 1$ and at the same time instruction $i + 2$ is being fetched.

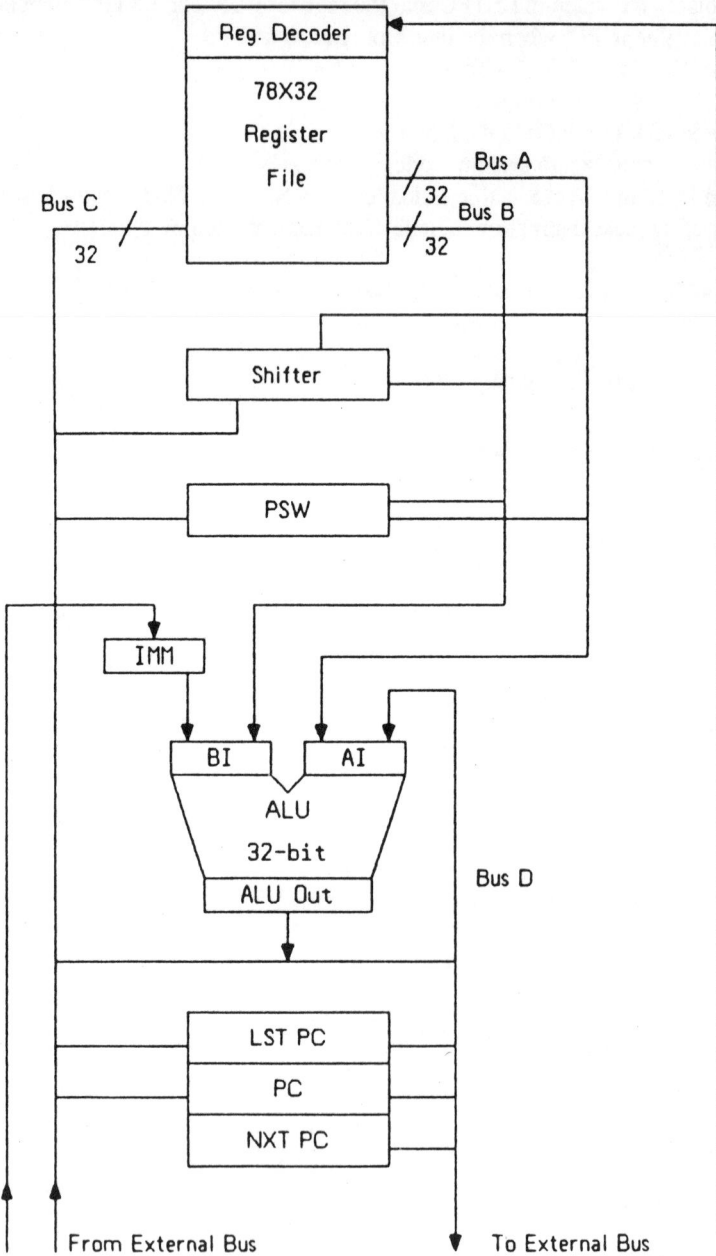

Fig. 3.3 RISC I organization

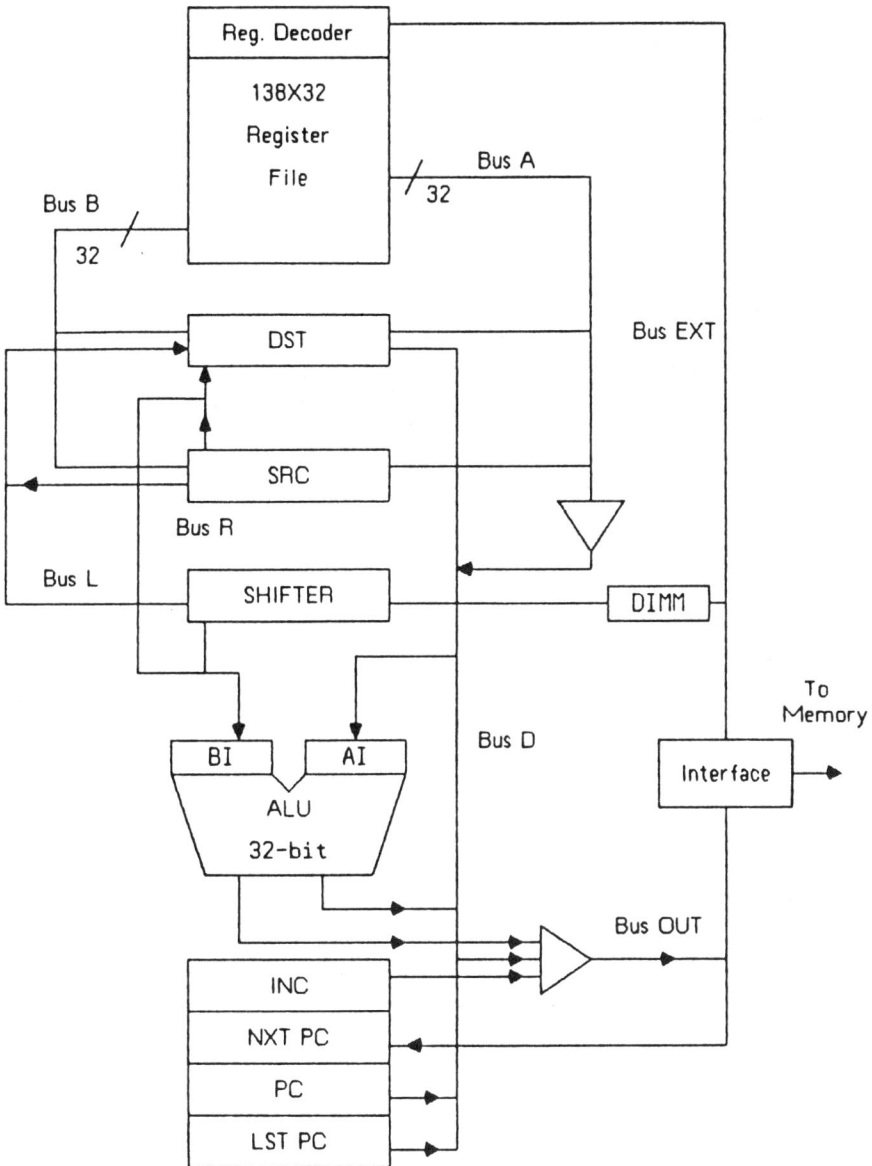

Fig. 3.4 RISC II organization

The abbreviations used in Figs. 3.3 and 3.4 are:

PSW   Processor Status Word register

IMM	Immediate latch
DIMM	Data In/Immediate latch
AI, BI	two input latches to the ALU
INC	Incrementer
DST	Destination latch, serving as a temporary pipeline latch
SRC	Source latch for the shifter

The communication between the RISC chip and the outside devices is established through a set of the following interconnection pins [Kate 85]:

Name	Bits
Address/Instruction/Data	32
Clock phases (in)	4
Reset (in)	1
Interrupt Request (in)	1
Interrupt Acknowledge (out)	1
WIDTH code W (out)	1
WIDTH code H (out)	1
Read/Write (out)	1
System Mode (out)	1
Instruction/Data (out)	1
Instruction Length (in)	1
Total	45

3.4 RISC Realization

The RISC I was realized on a single NMOS (lambda at 2 microns) chip in 1981 [PaSe 82]. Some of its design metrics, compared to the Z8000 and MC68000 commercial microprocessors, were:

Metric	Z8000	MC68000	RISC I	RISC II
Total devices	17500	68000	44000	41000
Total minus ROM	17500	37000	44000	41000
Drawn devices	3500	300	1800	
Regularization factor	5.0	12.1	25	20
Area, MIL^2	60000	69000	124000	
Size of Control, MIL^2	37000	35000	7000	
Percentage of control	53%	50%	6%	10%
Time to first silicon (months)	30	30	19	
Design effort (man * months)	60	100	15	18
Layout effort (man months)	70	70	12	12

From the above data we can see the considerably higher regularization factor, lower control area share, and lower design and layout effort of RISC, as argued in the discussion of the RISC advantages in chapter 2. It should also be noted that RISC is a 32-bit machine, while Z8000 and MC68000 are 16-bit machines (notwithstanding the 32-bit CPU registers of 68000).

The RISC II was realized in 1983, using the same NMOS technology as in the RISC I. It used smaller geometries, i.e. lambda = 1.5, was about half the size of RISC I and it runs with a 12MHz clock (330ns per instruction, compared to 500ns, 8MHz, of RISC I).

As the semiconductor technology becomes more advanced and more transistors can be incorporated on a chip, the next subsystem to be included on chip will be the instruction cache. This will be the key and primary ingredient that produces an improvement in the overall throughput. In the meantime, an extra instruction cache NMOS chip, which incorporates 44500 transistors for use in conjunction with RISC II, has been proposed [Kate 85].

CHAPTER 4

The Stanford MIPS

The Stanford MIPS [Henn 82,84, Przy 84] was the second RISC processor, developed in academia, and following the Berkeley RISC very closely on the time scale. However, as will be seen from the subsequent description, it is considerably different from the Berkeley system. The basic differences, to be elaborated in the next section, are a relatively small CPU register set and more extensive reliance on software on the Stanford MIPS, compared to the Berkeley RISC.

A commercial RISC processor, based on a significantly extended Stanford MIPS, was brought to industry through MIPS Computer Systems, Inc. (Sunnyvale, CA), and will be described in chapter 9.

The MIPS RISC-type machine was developed at the Stanford University between 1981 and 1983. The MIPS acronym stems from 'Microprocessor without Interlocked Pipeline Stages'. The exact meaning of this will be explained later in this section.

The MIPS is a 32-bit machine. Its standard Word is defined to be 32 bits long and it is *word addressable*. However, *byte addressing* in MIPS is supported using a set of instructions for manipulating *byte pointers*, which are single addresses, whose two low-order bits are used to specify a byte within a word.

The MIPS Instruction Set is defined at two levels:

1. *User Level* — or *Assembly Language Instruction Set*, defines instructions that are *unpacked*, that is all have a standard length of 32 bits, and have no pipeline dependencies or branch delays.
2. *Machine Level* — low level, run by the processor. Generated only by a single program, the *Reorganizer*. The Reorganizer does all implementation-dependent optimization and isolates the user-level instruction set from the implementation details.

Each macroinstruction is similar to a single microinstruction (the control is hardwired), requiring very simple and fast decoding. All instructions are executed within the same time interval, a *single data memory cycle*. The instructions have either two or three operands. There are four *addressing modes*:

1. Immediate;
2. Based with Offset;

3. Indexed;
4. Base Shifted.

The MIPS instructions are subdivided into four groups (types) of *instruction pieces*:

1. ALU;
2. Load/Store;
3. Control Flow;
4. Special Instructions.

Up to two simple (and possibly unrelated) instruction pieces are packed together, during *reorganization*, into an instruction word of 32 bits.

(1) *ALU pieces*: All register-to-register, two or three operand formats. Use less than half of an instruction word.

(2) *Load/Store pieces*: Use 16 to 32 bits. When they are less than 32 bits, they are packaged with an ALU piece which is executed during the execution stage of the pipeline.

(3) *Control Flow pieces*: Include straight jumps, compare instructions and relative jumps. All branch instructions have a delay in their effect of one instruction; the next sequential instruction is always executed.

(4) *Special Instructions*: Support procedure and interrupt linkage.

There is no direct floating-point operation support on MIPS; a coprocessor is needed for this type of operation. There is support for page faults, externally generated interrupts, and internally generated traps (arithmetic overflow and software generated exceptions). Support for an off-chip instruction cache implementation is provided.

Some examples of MIPS instruction pieces, classified by four groups, are provided as follows:

(1) *ALU*

   Add src1, src2, dst; src2 + src1 $\rightarrow$ dst

   Sub src1, src2, dst; src2 − src1 $\rightarrow$ dst (Subtract)

                              Total instructions in this group: 13

(2) *Load/Store*

   Ld [src1 + src2], dst ; M[src1 + src2] $\rightarrow$ dst (Load)

   Mov src, dst   ; src $\rightarrow$ dst (Move)

   St src1, A[src]   ; src1 $\rightarrow$ M[A + src] (Store)

                              Total: 10

58

(3) *Control Flow*

Bra dst ; PC + dst → PC (Branch)

Jmp dst ; dst → PC (Jump)

Total: 6

(4) *Special*

SavePC A; PC → M[A]

Total: 2

Total MIPS Instructions: 31

There are no condition codes for conditional jumps. Instead, there are *compare and branch* operations.

There is a 16 32-bit CPU register file (32 registers on a more recent model MIPS-X), organized as a two-port structure. The large register file with the register window, as in the Berkeley RISC, has not been adopted in the Stanford MIPS system. On the other hand, in addition to the PC, there are four registers to hold the four previous PC values. They are needed to backtrack and restart instructions in case of a fault. In addition, there is a register to hold the *future* PC value, a feature which supports the branch instructions. The branch address for a conditional branch is calculated for a given instruction and stored in the future PC register. Only if the specified condition is satisfied is the content of future PC transferred into the regular PC. The above four registers are not architecturally visible.

Although the *virtual address* is 32 bits long, packaging constraints permitted only 24 address pins. Thus, the *physical address space* is 2^{24} = 16 MWords (32 bits each), equal to 64 Mbytes. The MIPS has separate Instruction and Data Memories, and their accesses are interleaved.

The MIPS supports a large, uniform addressing space for each process and fast context switching between processes. A process is defined as the smallest unit of programming activity which can be scheduled to run on a processor. Each process address (virtual address) space is 4 GWords = 2^{32} Words (1 Word = 32 bits). Each process has its own process identification number incorporated into the virtual memory address. Not all of the virtual to physical address translation could be included on the same chip. The hardware design supports the inclusion of an off-chip Translation Lookaside Buffer (TLB) for the address translation.

The general tendency in the MIPS design was to shift complexity from hardware to software. Its instruction set easily maps into a microinstruction set involving very simple decoding. The compiler, however, is required to be more sophisticated than the Berkeley RISC, because it performs a compact and time-efficient mapping between higher-level instruction constructs and the simplified instruction set. The advantages of moving the complexity from hardware to software are:

(a) Complexity is paid for (in computing time) only once during compilation.

(b) Design effort is concentrated on the software, rather than on constructing a complex hardware engine, which is hard to design, debug and efficiently utilize. VLSI environment makes hardware simplicity important.

There exists presently Pascal, FORTRAN and C compilers for the MIPS. A MIPS compiler incorporates two basic parts:

(1) *Code Generator* — produces a stream of simple operations, independent of all resource interaction, branch delays and instruction combinations.

(2) *Code Reorganizer* — performs the following operations on the *generated code*:

    (a) Assembles and packs one or two independent operations (instruction pieces) into each 32-bit instruction word.

    (b) Moves appropriate instructions into the words following each delayed branch.

    (c) Reorders instructions within each basic block to eliminate resource conflicts.

The above code reorganization saves, on the average, about 30% of execution time.

The MIPS has a five-stage instruction pipeline, with three active instructions residing in the pipeline at any time. One instruction is initiated every two clock cycles. The stages of the pipeline and their individual tasks are as follows:

Stage Name	Task
1. IF — Instruction Fetch	Send PC value, fetch instruction, increment PC.
2. ID — Instruction Decode	Decode instruction.
3. OD — Operand Decode	Compute effective address of operand, fetch operand, use ALU.
4. OS/EX — Operand Store/(SX) Execution	Send operand to memory if store, use ALU if execution.
5. OF — Operand Fetch	Receive operand if load.

Naturally, not all of the pipeline stages are needed for each instruction. The timing of the pipeline stages for a sequence of instructions looks as follows:

Instr.	Cycle									
	1	2	3	4	5	6	7	8	9	10
i	IF	ID	OD	SX	OF					
i+1			IF	ID	OD	SX	OF			
i+2					IF	ID	OD	SX	OF	
									... and so on	

Taking, for instance, the sequence of CPU cycles 5 and 6, we see that during this two-cycle period the ALU is busy with stages OD and SX of instruction $(i+1)$, the Instruction Memory is busy with stages IF and ID of instruction $i+2$, while the Data Memory is busy with stage OF of instruction i and stage SX of instruction $(i+1)$. We can observe an efficient utilization of resources in this pipeline organization.

Considering the general operation and management of a pipeline, one can envisage an event when one component of an instruction in a pipeline may refer to a value that is computed in an earlier instruction. Because the earlier instruction may still be executing, the value may not be available, and a *pipeline timing hazard* is present. A hardware mechanism, called a *pipeline interlock*, prevents the latter instruction from continuing until the needed value is available. An interlock mechanism adds significantly to the hardware overhead. Its elimination from the hardware allows a simpler design. Interlocks can be eliminated by *reordering* the instructions and by inserting NOP operations, wherever necessary. In MIPS, the reordering to eliminate interlocks is done by the code *reorganizer* within the compiler. Since MIPS does not have hardware interlocks (the problem is handled by software), its name is *M*icroprocessor without *I*nterlocked *P*ipe *S*tages.

The *delayed-branch* principle is also practiced in the MIPS design. Each branch instruction always executes one succeeding instruction. If the branch instruction references memory, as in an indirect jump, two succeeding instructions are fetched and executed. If an exception occurs during a branch, three consecutive PC values are saved in CPU registers, especially predesigned for this purpose.

The MIPS CPU organization is shown in Fig. 4.1. It has a 32-bit full CLA (Carry Look Ahead) ALU. The total ALU delay is 80ns. The CPU has two 32-bit bidirectional buses, sixteen 32-bit general purpose registers and two memory interfaces, one for data and one for instructions. The masking unit allows a machine address to be converted to a process virtual address. It also detects attempts to access illegal addresses and it raises an exception in such a case.

The MIPS was realized with NMOS, two-micron technology. With a 4MHz, 250ns clock cycle, it achieves a performance of 2 VAX 780 MIPS (Millions Instructions Per Second). It has 84 pins, allocated as follows:

Address	24
Data	32
Status Out	8
Status In	7
Clock, Power	9
Control	4
Total	84

The chip contains an equivalent of over 24000 transistors and its regularity factor is 12. Its area is relatively subdivided as follows:

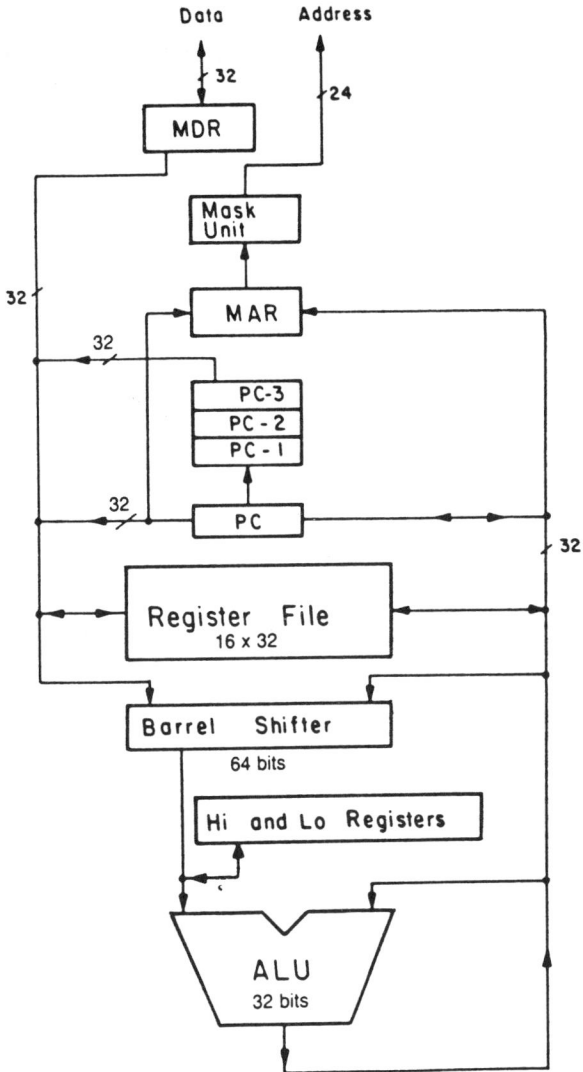

Fig. 4.1   MIPS organization

Datapath	39.2%
Control	18.2%
Periphery	42.6%
Total	100.0%

Compared to the Berkeley RISC, the MIPS control area is almost double: however, still considerably lower than the 50% of the CISCs. Another major difference is the regular CPU register file on MIPS: only 16 registers, compared to the 138 on RISC II. There are, however, 32 registers on the MIPS-X.

The MIPS-X is a two-micron CMOS, 150000 transistors chip. Its performance is about 20 millions of instructions per second (MIPS) at 20MHz.

CHAPTER 5

Experimental RISC Systems

5.1 The IBM 801

The IBM 801 system was the first RISC-type system to be developed as an experimental computer. As attested by the system developers [Radi 83], the following principles were examined during the design:

(1) System orientation towards the *pervasive use of HLL programming* and a sophisticated compiler.
(2) A *primitive instruction set* which can be *completely hardwired.*
(3) Storage hierarchy and I/O organization to enable the CPU to *execute an instruction* at almost *every cycle.*

Referring back to chapter 2, we can see that the above principles fit quite well to the points of definition of a RISC-type system. Since the development of the IBM 801 started in 1975, it can definitely be regarded as the first RISC-type machine, although it has never been called by that name.

The IBM 801 is a 32-bit machine. Both its addresses as well as arithmetic data are 32 bits long. Two's complement arithmetic is being used. Instructions are also fullword (32 bit) long, aligned on fullword boundaries in memory. In fact, all operands are aligned in memory on boundaries, consistent with their size. The instructions are executed in a single cycle of 66ns, achieving an overall speed of 10 MIPS. There is a total of 120 machine-language instructions. However, this instruction set is intended for the compiler writer only. The regular user is supposed to program in HLL only. A PL.8 (subset of PL/1) compiler has been developed along with the 801 system. The compiler also accepts Pascal programs, producing compatible object code so that PL.8 and Pascal procedures can call one another.

Memory is accessed by Load/Store instructions only. Only two addressing modes are used for memory access:

Base + Index
Base + Displacement

For Branch target specifications, the following three addressing modes can be used:

Absolute 26-bit address
Instruction Address Register (IAR) + Displacement
(signed 16 or 26 bit)
Register + Register

The last two addressing modes are not conceptually different from the two memory reference addressing modes. Thus, we really have only three different addressing modes on the 801. In general, instructions may have three register operands.

Multiplication is supported by the MULTIPLY STEP instruction. A 32 × 32-bit, 64-bit product, multiplication is accomplished in 16 cycles. Similarly, division is supported by the DIVIDE STEP instruction. A 64/32-bit, 32-bit quotient, 32-bit remainder division is accomplished in 32 cycles.

The 801 architecture supports a *Branch with Execute* feature. When the branch target is fetched, the CPU executes the instruction following the branch. This is practically the same as the delayed branch (chapter 2).

Example: The code sequence:

LOAD R1, A
BNZ L   ; Branch on Non Zero

is converted by the compiler into a Branch with Execute sequence:

BNZX L   ; Branch on Non Zero and Execute
LOAD R1, A; executed while the instruction
             ; at address L is being fetched.

There is A total of 32 CPU registers. That was a considerably large number for a system of 801's size in 1975, although it is substantially lower than the 138 of RISC II, completed in 1982. Of all the experimental RISC prototypes, the register window idea has been implemented on the Berkeley RISC and GMU MIRIS and MULTRIS only (in a way different from the Berkeley RISC though, as described in section 5.3).

The system's Cache memory is split into a

(1) Data Cache
(2) Instruction Cache

with asynchronous fetching of instructions and data from memory. A block diagram is shown in Fig. 5.1. The Block (Line) size for either cache is 32 bytes. The basic store unit is 4 bytes = 32 bits. Explicit instructions for cache management have been defined. Thus, in the 801 system, the cache is a part of the architecture, visible to the programmer (at least to the compiler writer).

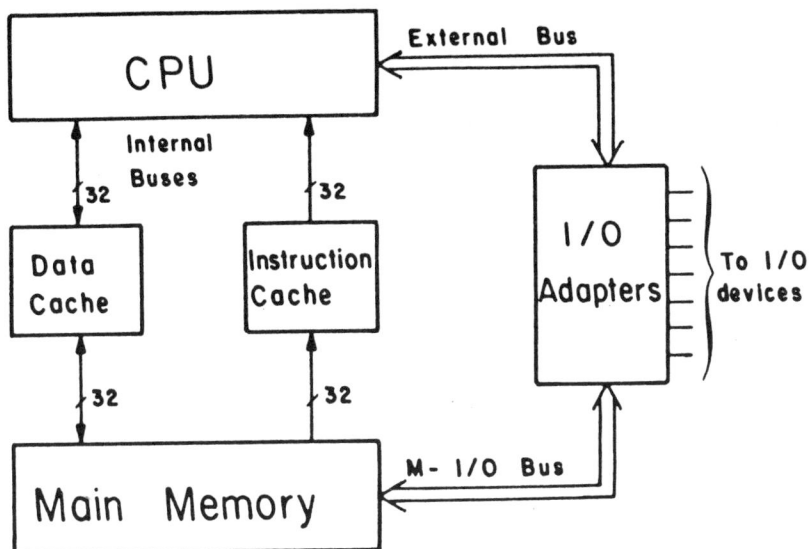

Fig. 5.1   IBM 801 interconnections

The hardware prototype of the IBM 801 has been realized with Motorola ECL (Emitter Current Logic) 10K DIP (Dual Inline Packages) MSI chips. It was completed in 1980.

5.2 The Berkeley SOAR and SPUR

After having completed the development of the RISC II in 1981, the Berkeley team continued with the design of two new, special purpose, RISC-type systems: the Smalltalk On A RISC (SOAR) [Ungr 87, UnPa 87] and the Symbolic Processing Using RISC (SPUR) [Adms 86, KaPa 86].

Smalltalk-80 is an object-oriented programming environment, developed by Xerox Corp. in Palo-Alto, CA, and implemented on their Dorado computing system [Deut 83, GoRo 83]. Before the creation of SOAR, Smalltalk-80 had to be run on relatively expensive computing systems. One of the main motivations of SOAR designers was to create a simple and inexpensive system, capable of running Smalltalk-80 in an efficient, high-performance manner. A number of architectural innovations were built into the SOAR to speed up Smalltalk-80 operations [Ungr 87, UnPa 87].

Smalltalk-80 does not have type of operands declarations. This causes a significant overhead since a type check has to be performed before the execution of an operation. SOAR designers improved the Smalltalk-80 performance by introducing hardware supported *data tagging*. There are two types of tagged data: integers and pointers (as required by the Smalltalk-80 environment), denoted by the most significant bit in a 32-bit SOAR word (bit 31), as illustrated in Fig. 5.2. For integers, bit 31= 0, and for pointers, bit 31 = 1. Bits 28–30 are used as a *tag* field for pointers. The tag is actually used as a *generation tag*, associated with the object pointed to by the pointer. It is particularly used during store operations while reclaiming storage space. The SOAR reclaim policy requires that a list be updated whenever a pointer to a new object is stored in an old object. While computing the memory address, the store instruction compares the generation tag of the data being stored with the generation tag of the memory address. If the latter is smaller, the store is completed; otherwise, a list update exception is generated.

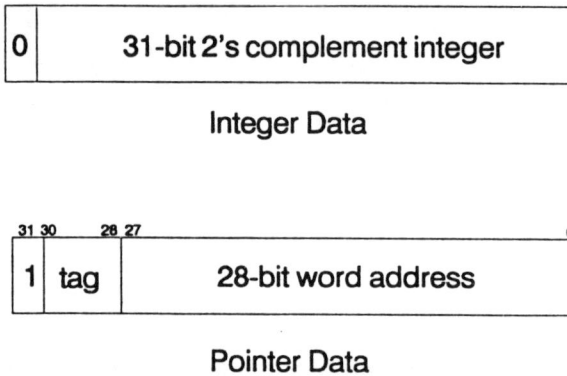

0	31-bit 2's complement integer

Integer Data

31 30	28 27	0
1	tag	28-bit word address

Pointer Data

Fig. 5.2   SOAR tagged data formats

For arithmetic and comparison operations, SOAR assumes that the operands are integers and begins the execution of the operation immediately, simultaneously checking the tags. Most often (in over 92% of all cases) both operands are integers and the correct result is available after one cycle. If not (the operands are pointers), SOAR aborts the operation and traps to routines that carry out the appropriate computation for the data types.

SOAR architecture uses *compare-and-skip* instructions for integer comparisons. It does not have conventional condition codes. Conditional jumps are implemented by a sequence of a conditional skip and an unconditional jump. SOAR jump instructions contain the absolute address of the target instruction. Because no address computation is required, SOAR eliminates the instruction prefetch penalty for jumps. If the condition in the conditional skip is met, the program skips the jump. Otherwise, the prefetched jump is executed.

SOAR has a standard 32-bit word instruction length. Most instructions take one cycle to execute. Loads, stores and returns are executed in two cycles. There are three basic instruction formats:

(1) Calls and jumps, with a 28-bit word address of target.
(2) Three-operand, with a six-bit opcode and five-bit fields of source 1, source 2

and destination registers. Source 2 can alternately serve as a 12-bit immediate constant.

(3) Store, with a six-bit opcode and two source fields.

Memory is word addressed. Separate instructions insert or extract bytes from words. There are 21 instruction types including arithmetic (add, sub), logical (and, or, xor), shift (sll, srl, sra), byte manipulation (insert, extract), load/store (including load/store multiple, loadm, storem), skip, trap, nop and program control (call, jump, ret).

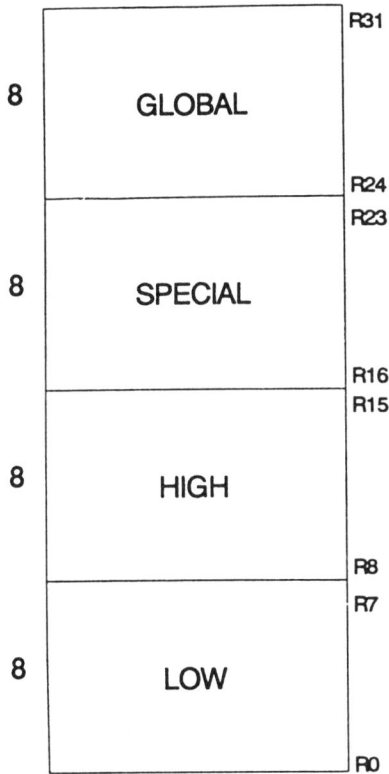

Fig. 5.3   Register file for each subroutine on the SOAR

SOAR, like RISC I and II, efficiently supports subroutine calls and returns by using the overlapping register window approach (chapter 3). Each subroutine running on the SOAR sees three-bit CPU registers, as illustrated in Fig. 5.3. The above 32 registers are subdivided into four groups of eight registers:

(1) LOW, R0–R7, contain parameters passed to the called subroutine.

(2) HIGH, R8–R15, contain parameters received from the calling subroutine.

(3) SPECIAL, R16–R23, include:

R16, rzero, always zero (as R0 on RISC I or II).

R17, Program Counter, PC.

R18, shb, Shadow B, input to ALU.

R19, sha, Shadow A, input to ALU.

R20, Saved Window Pointer, SWP (memory address of object leader of the most recently saved register window).

R21, tb, Trap Base, base address of the interrupt and trap vector area.

R22, Current Window Pointer, CWP (index of on-chip register set serving as a HIGH-window).

R23, Processor Status Word, PSW.

(4) GLOBAL, R24–R31, for system software such as trap handlers.

The register window arrangement for three consecutive nested routines A, B and C, is illustrated in Fig. 5.4. It is understandably similar to that of the Berkeley RISC (chapter 3), although somewhat different. In addition to the 16 global and special registers, there are 64 window registers, permitting a seven-deep routine nesting on chip. The total number of CPU registers is 80. When the number of routine activations exceeds the on-chip register capacity, SOAR traps to a software routine that saves the contents of a set of registers in memory. Load- and store-multiple instructions, to speed register saving and restoring, are available. These instructions can transfer eight registers in nine cycles (one instruction fetch and eight data accesses). These instructions have the ability to operate on non-contiguous data; the increment between memory references is given by the source 2 field.

Another way SOAR supports subroutine handling and reduces overhead is by decreasing the time taken to find the target of a call. Once computed, the target's address is cached in the instruction stream for subsequent use [Ungr 87]. This feature is called *in-line caching*. Subsequently, the SOAR call instruction contains the absolute address of its destination. A call or jump can be recognized by examining only one bit. This makes it possible to detect these instructions in time to send the incoming data back to the memory as an address. Thus, a call or jump executes in one cycle. The above call or jump handling mechanism is called the *fast shuffle*.

The SOAR return instruction performs one compulsory and three optional functions, specified by the low-order three opcode bits. The compulsory function is a transfer of control to the calling (or interrupted) routine. The optional functions are:

(1) Enable interrupts, yielding a return from interrupt instruction.

(2) Increment the CWP for returning from a normal call.

(3) Initialize local registers to zero, according to the Smalltalk-80 requirements.

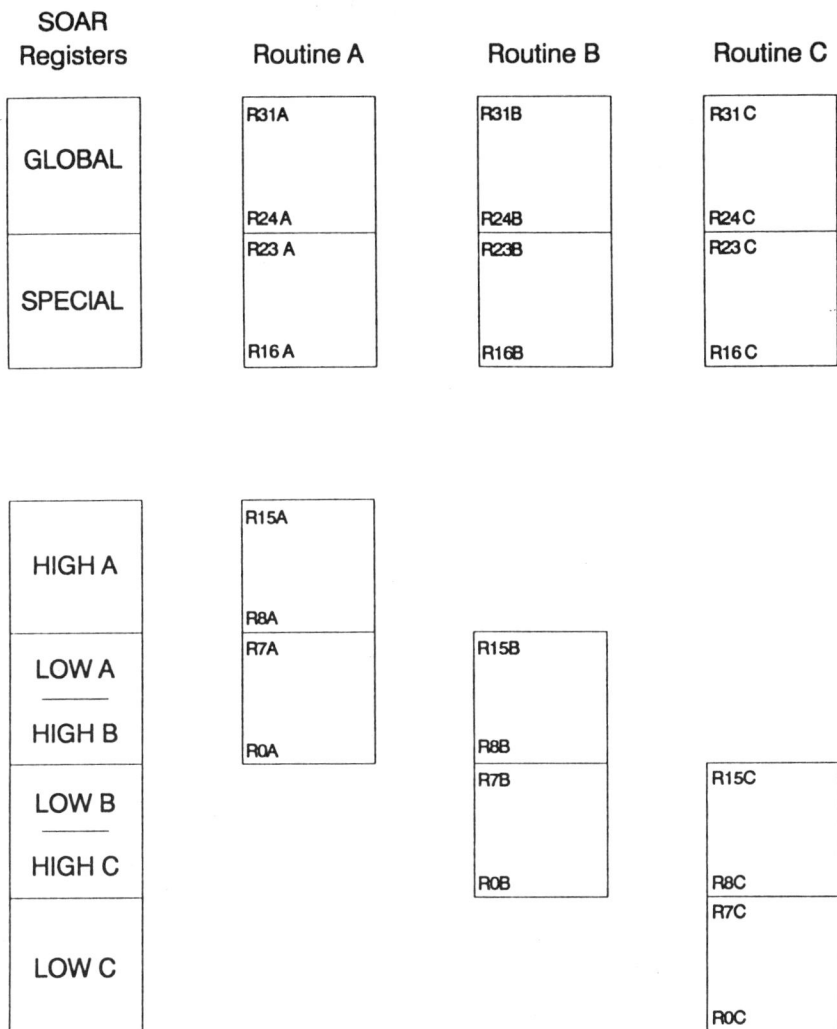

Fig. 5.4 SOAR register windows

Each call in Smalltalk-80 needs a new *activation record*, containing local variables and other data of the new object. SOAR caches activation records in the on-chip register file, achieving higher speed. If the number of activations exceeds the number of on-chip register windows, an overflow occurs. It is backed by an overflow stack in memory. Pointers to activation records are rare, so SOAR's hardware merely detects these and causes a trap at the appropriate time. The first trap occurs when a reference to an activation record is created. Pointers to activation records have all the tag bits (Fig. 5.2) set. When such a word is stored into memory, the tag check causes a trap. At the time of the trap, the high-order bit of the activation record's return address is set. Setting this bit indicates that the activation record may outlive its parent. Since these records are normally allocated and freed Last-In-First-Out (LIFO), we label such anomalously long-lived activation records as non-LIFO. The return instruction then traps if the return address has the high-order bit set — this lets software save this activation record.

To reduce the cost of trapping, SOAR implements *Shadow Registers* that catch the operands of the trapping instructions. SOAR does not support nested interrupts or traps in order to reduce complexity. There is an Interrupt Enable bit (bit 6) in the Program Status Word (PSW); it is reset upon an interrupt or trap. When an interrupt or trap occurs, the instruction that is executing is aborted before it can change any values in registers. The address of the aborted instruction is saved in R7. I/O interrupts are disabled by clearing the interrupt enable bit in the PSW. This freezes the Shadow Registers, which normally track the ALU inputs. A vector is constructed from the trap base register, the opcode of the aborted instruction, and the trap source. Finally, the control is transferred to the vectored location [Ungr 87].

The SOAR datapath is illustrated in Fig. 5.5. It contains a dual-port register file, ALU, PC, Memory Address Latch and a Destination Latch. The three-stage SOAR pipeline is illustrated in Fig. 5.6. Because of the *fast shuffle* feature, described above, jumps and calls execute in a single cycle and cause no delay in the pipeline. Conditional branches are synthetized with a skip and an unconditional jump. This takes two cycles. The datapath allows two simultaneous reads or one write to the register file. Each execute cycle is divided into three nonoverlapping phases (Fig. 5.6):

(1) Decode the instruction and precharge the bus.
(2) Read source registers onto the buses.
(3) Compute results in the ALU and, simultaneously, store back the result from the previous instruction into its destination register.

The result of instruction i is not actually stored into its destination register until the end of instruction $i+1$. Forwarding logic hides this delay; if instruction $i+1$ attempts to read the destination register of instruction i, the desired value is forwarded from the destination latch at the output of the ALU.

The SOAR is a four-micron NMOS, 35700 transistors, 3 W power dissipation chip. Its performance is 400 nsec/instruction, or 2.5 MIPS. Its primary disadvantage is that it needs an extra 700 Kbytes of memory to run Smalltalk-80, compared to the Dorado, which needs just one Mbytes. This is a common RISC-type system disadvantage (chapter 2). A SOAR-based board, that operates with a Sun workstation, was constructed at Berkeley.

Another Berkeley RISC-spinoff system is the Symbolic Processing Using RISC (SPUR) workstation [KaPa 86]. It was aimed at applying RISC concepts to

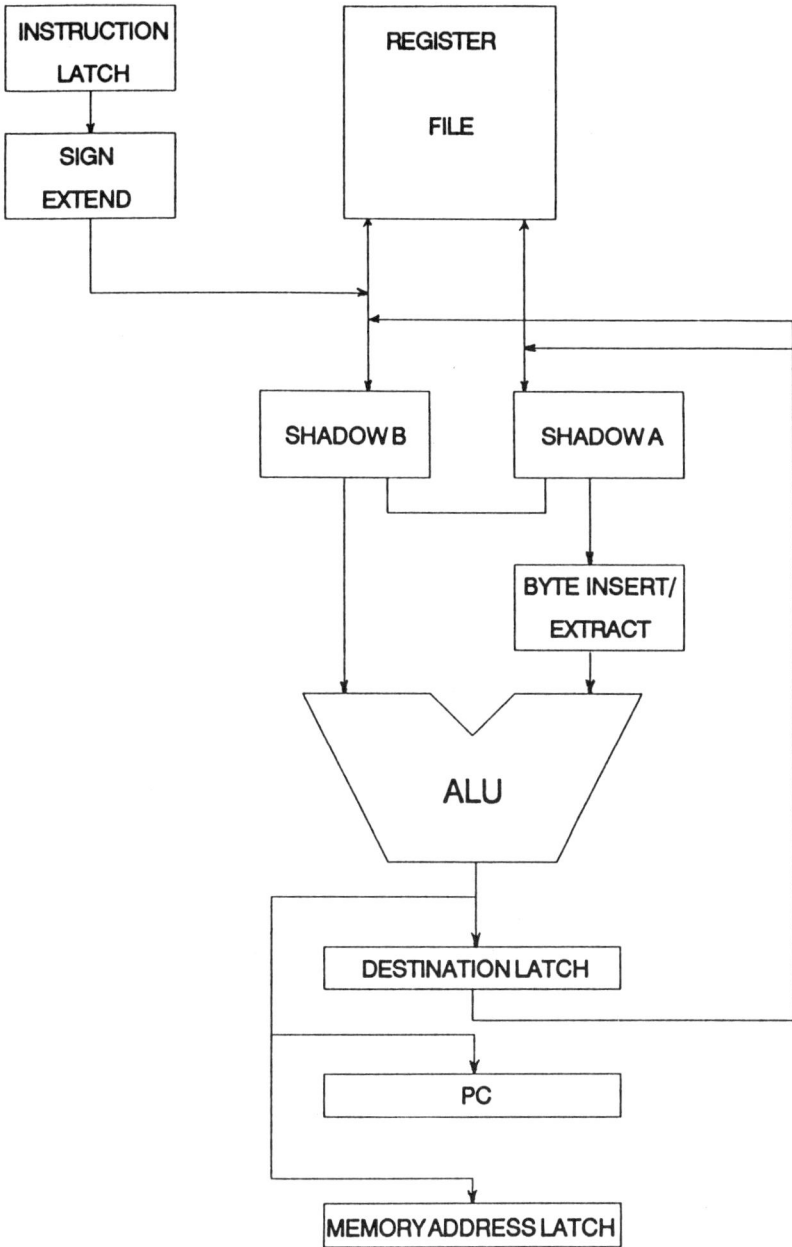

Fig. 5.5   The SOAR datapath

```
                    CYCLE:      k-1        k         k+1
INSTRUCTION


      i-1                     execute   write-back
      i                        fetch     execute    write-back
      i+1                                 fetch      execute
```

PHASE OF EXECUTE CYCLE: 1   2   3

```
                                    decode,     read       ALU,
                                    precharge  register  write-back
                                      bus
```

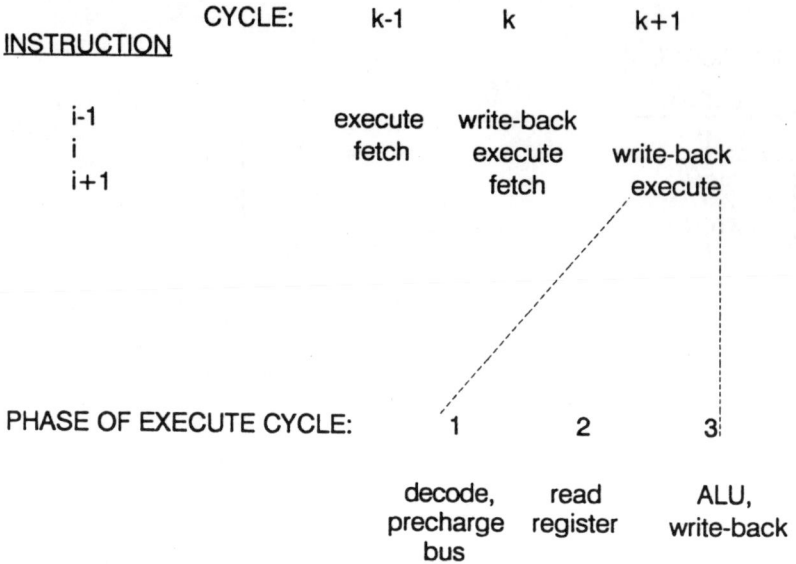

Fig. 5.6 The SOAR pipeline

the support of LISP programming environments [Gabr 85]. The SPUR incorporates custom-designed processor nodes and off-the-shelf memory and I/O boards. SPUR may include up to 12 processor nodes, interconnected by the SPUR bus into a multiprocessor system. The TI NuBus was chosen as the system bus.

The processor node board is composed of the following major parts:

(1) Custom-designed VLSI, 32-bit, RISC-type CPU. It features 40-bit tagged (32 bits data, eight bits tag) architecture and a load-store/register-register instruction set.
(2) A VLSI, custom-designed, memory/cache management chip, implementing a cache coherency protocol and virtual memory management.
(3) A custom-designed floating-point coprocessor, implementing the IEEE standard.
(4) A 128 Kbyte cache.

The board features a 64-bit data bus to accommodate double-precision floating-point values.

5.3 The GMU MIRIS and MULTRIS
A Microcoded RISC-type processor, MIRIS, was developed at the George Mason University (GMU) in Fairfax, Virginia [DuBo 88, DuFT 86, Tabk 87]. A bit-sliced (AMD2900) prototype was constructed.

Like most other RISC systems, it is a 32-bit processor with 32-bit data paths. All instructions are 32-bit long and each instruction is primitive enough to execute in a single cycle. The current, bipolar technology, used for the prototype, permits work at 10MHz, attaining a performance of 10 Millions of Instructions Per Second (MIPS).

The MIRIS is subdivided into two main parts (Fig. 5.7):

(1) The Program Control Section (PCS), along with the Program Memory (PM). Its functions are:

(a) Compute the address of the next instruction to be executed.

(b) Fetch the instruction from PM into the Instruction Register (IR).

(c) Decode the instruction, providing all of the necessary control signals on the control lines.

(d) Provide the appropriate hardware logic to recognize and handle interrupts.

(2) The Data Execution Section (DES), along with the Data Memory (DM), are physically separate from the PM. Its functions are:

(a) Execute all data processing tasks with the Arithmetic Logic Unit (ALU).

(b) Store current operands and results in the Register File (RF).

(c) Provide information about the status of the processor through an appropriate field of the Logical Status Word (LSW), allocated within the Program Status Control Unit (PSCU).

(d) Interface with the Data Memory (DM) to Load/Store operands.

The basic difference between the MIRIS and the other research prototypes of RISC (Berkeley and Stanford machines, IBM 801) is that the control of MIRIS is microcoded, while that of the others is hardwired. However, the MIRIS microcode does not have the standard structure with numerous microsubroutines, as in other microcoded machines. In MIRIS, each machine instruction always corresponds to just one 64-bit control word. All control words are stored in a maximum 256×64 Control Store PROM. Since, at the moment, there are only 64 instructions (no more than about 75 are expected at the end of the development), the Control Store is underutilized in the prototype. The most significant byte of each machine instruction is the opcode and at the same time a direct address to the 256×64 ($256 = 2^8$) Control Store. No decoding is needed. The short access Control Store produces practically immediately (within 30ns with the current realization) a 64-bit, horizontal Control Word (or Microinstruction), capable of activating up to 64 control lines simultaneously. Thus, a *streamlined*, microcode-based, instruction execution is achieved. At the same time, the design benefits from the usual microcode advantages of greater flexibility for modifications and error recovery, while maintaining a high speed of instruction handling (no decoding, control lines activated within 30ns).

The Control Store of MIRIS is very similar to the Nanomemory in the MC68000, and for this reason it has been so labelled. Of course, there is a big difference in the fact that MIRIS does not have the extra Micromemory level

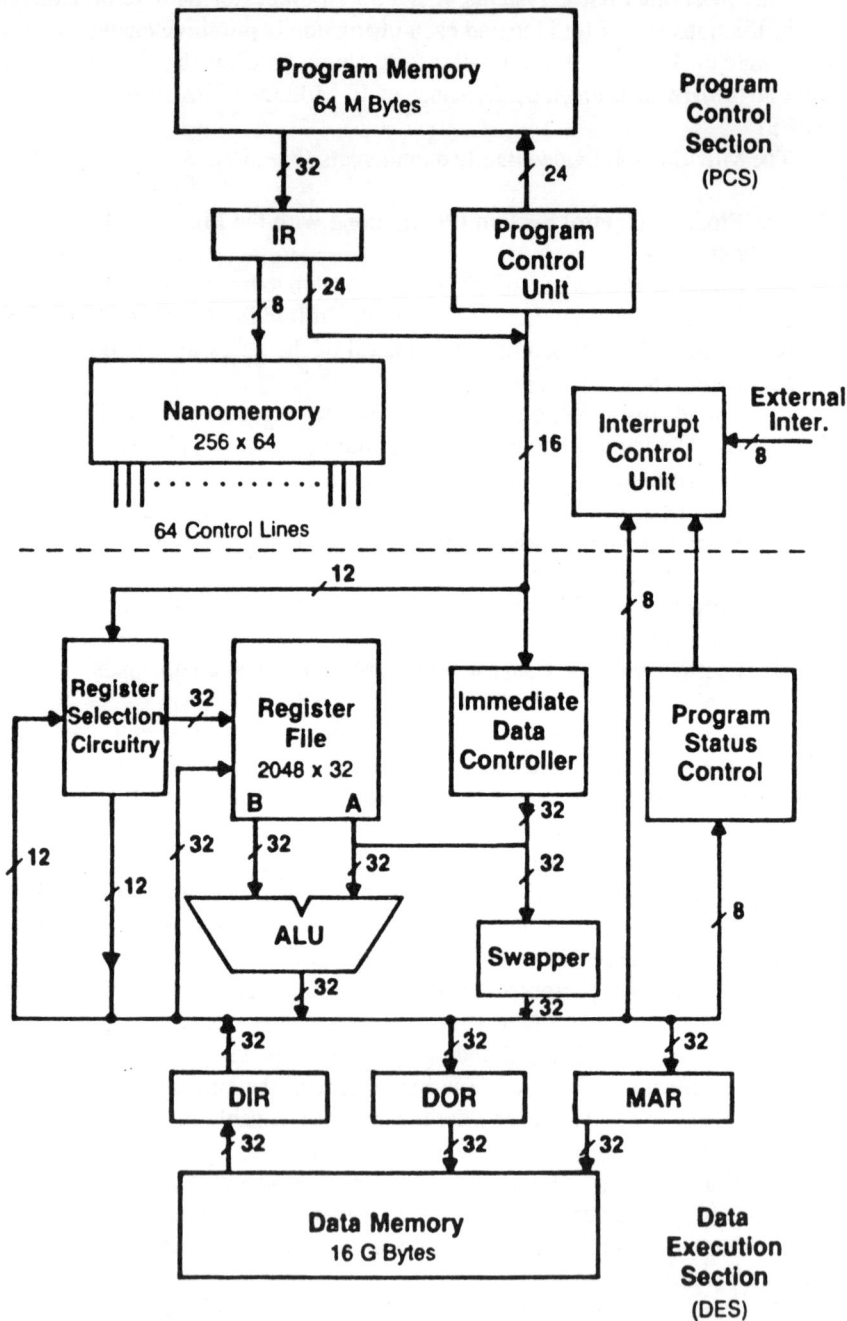

Fig. 5.7   Microcoded RISC (MIRIS)

available in the MC68000 [Hays 88, p. 361]. This is illustrated in Fig. 5.8.

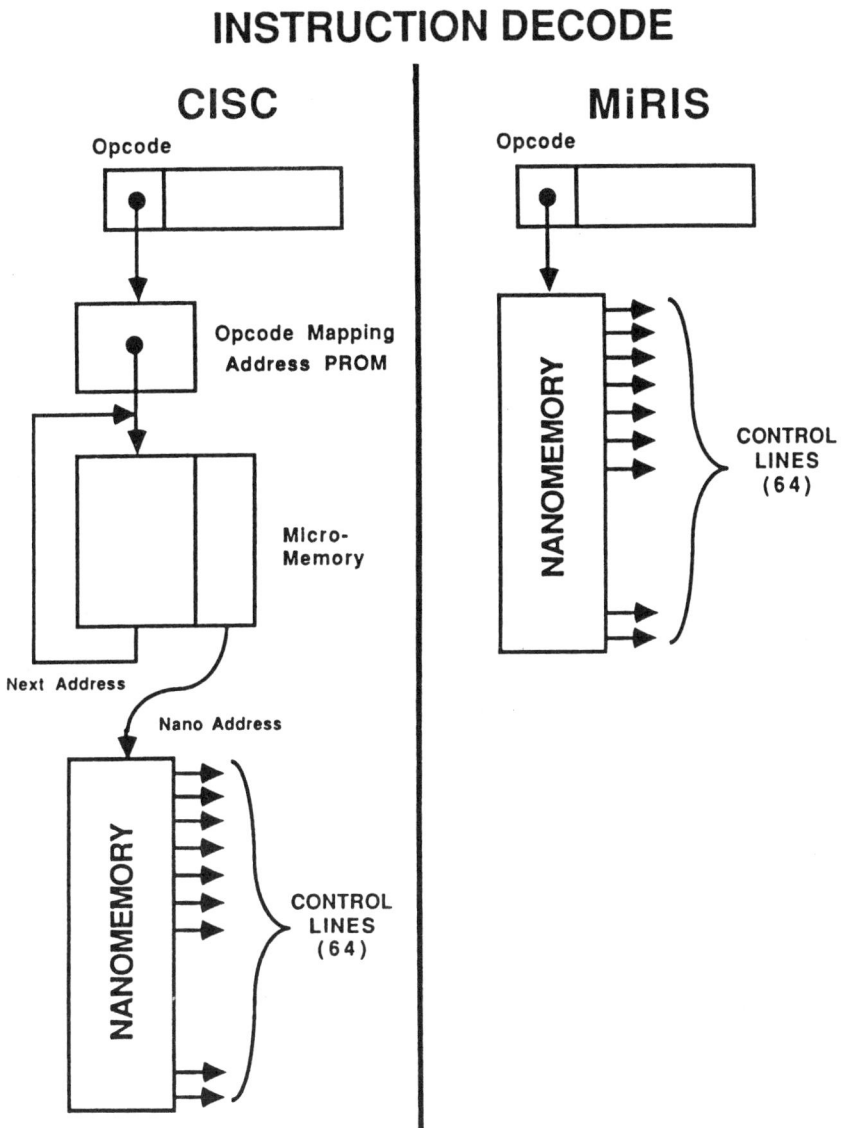

INSTRUCTION DECODE

CISC

Opcode

Opcode Mapping
Address PROM

Micro-
Memory

Next Address

Nano Address

NANOMEMORY

CONTROL
LINES
(64)

MiRIS

Opcode

NANOMEMORY

CONTROL
LINES
(64)

Fig. 5.8   A CISC and MIRIS microcode hierarchy

The Program and Data Memories can be accessed simultaneously. In fact, while the result of instruction (i − 2) may be executed by the ALU, while instruction i is being fetched and decoded (a practically immediate operation), thus forming a three-stage instruction pipeline.

The only data formats recognized by MIRIS architecture are:

8-bit Byte
16-bit Halfword
32-bit Word

Two's complement arithmetic is implemented.

The MIRIS has a set of 64 primitive instructions. Each instruction is executable within a single machine cycle and has a standard length of 32 bits. All instructions are subdivided into two major fields:

bits 31–24   : opcode
bits 23–0   : operand address

There is a one-to-one correspondence between each type of machine instruction, fetched from PM, and a single control word (nanoword, nanoinstruction) in the 256×64 Nanomemory. The eight-bit opcode is just a direct address into the Nanomemory ($256 = 2^8$) and no decoding is necessary. The machine has a capability of handling up to 256 primitive instructions. The design can be relatively easily expanded by adding new instructions if necessary, sometimes just by adding information to the Nanomemory PROM, while judiciously using the existing control lines interconnections.

The Program Memory (PM) is addressed only by a single 24-bit Direct Addressing Mode. It is Word (32 bit)-addressable. Thus, its size is 16 MWords or 64 Mbytes. All in all, the MIRIS architecture recognizes four formats for the Operand Address field, as illustrated in Fig. 5.9.

The value of the immediate operand is 16 bits wide within the address field. When transferred into a 32-bit register it can be placed in its high 31:16 or low 15:0 halfword and either 0 or 1 extended, according to the IS encoding:

IS	Placement	Extension Bit
00	low	0
01	high	0
10	low	1
11	high	1

The SRC and DST fields are each six bits wide. If the MSB of either is not set (0), then the lower five bits are used to address only the 32 global registers R0–R31. Otherwise, the lower five bits are combined with the six bits of either Port A and Port B fields in the LSW to form the 11-bit address of one of the 2048 CPU registers.

Each process in the MIRIS can 'see' a maximum of 96 registers out of the whole Register File (RF). The RF is implemented as a dual port memory in which the SRC and the DST registers can be accessed simultaneously and the result can

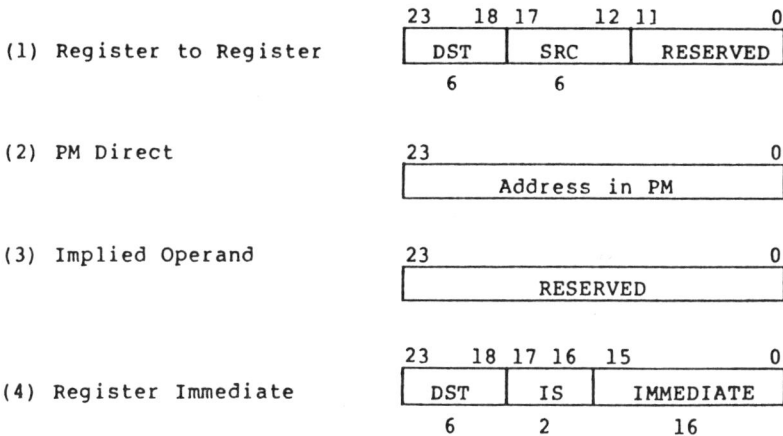

(1) Register to Register

23	18 17	12 11	0
DST	SRC	RESERVED	
6	6		

(2) PM Direct

23	0
Address in PM	

(3) Implied Operand

23	0
RESERVED	

(4) Register Immediate

23	18 17 16	15	0
DST	IS	IMMEDIATE	
6	2	16	

where:

SRC - Source
DST - Destination
IS - Immediate Selector

Fig. 5.9   MIRIS operand addressing formats

be stored back into the DST register — all within one CPU cycle (100ns). This is one of the reasons for the expected high throughput of MIRIS.

The Logical Status Word (LSW) format is illustrated in Fig. 5.10. It should be stressed that the LSW is not implemented in hardware as a single register. Its fields are realized in the Program Status Control Unit in different components. However, the contents of LSW in its entirety can be moved into any register using the available instruction:

SAVLSW DST ; DST ← (LSW)

The LSW can also be restored using:

RESLSW SRC ; LSW ← (SRC)

Generally, the saving of any information during a procedure call or an interrupt is done in the CPU register file instead of the Data Memory, thereby speeding up the operation.

As stated in the beginning of this section, the MIRIS system is organized as

31	24	23	22	16	15		12	11	6	5	0
MASK		I	RESERVED		C O N Z			PORT B		PORT A	

where:

MASK	–	8-bit interrupt mask field
I	–	Interrrupt Enable (I=1 : Enabled).
C	–	Carry Flag
O	–	Overflow Flag
N	–	Negative Flag
Z	–	Zero Flag
PORT B	–	upper six bit register file address, port B
PORT A	–	upper six bit register file address, port A

Fig. 5.10   The MIRIS Logical Status Word (LSW)

two basic parts (Fig. 5.7):

(1) The Program Control Section (PCS)
(2) The Data Execution Section (DES)

The PCS is composed of the following main units:

(a) *Program Control Unit* (PCU). Provides the address of the next instruction to be executed. It contains a 24-bit Program Counter (PC) register. The address is provided in a 24-bit direct format. The PCU is realized using six AMD2930 Program Control Unit chips. The chip contains a 17-register stack for nested subroutine return addresses.

(b) *Instruction Register* (IR). Stores the whole instruction (32 bits), fetched from the Program Memory (PM). It is loaded with a new instruction every clock cycle (100ns). The IR is realized by four TTL74S374 chips.

(c) *Nanomemory*. A 256 × 64 PROM Control Store. Each 64-bit Control Word constitutes a horizontal microcode entry, equivalent to a specific MIRIS instruction. The eight-bit opcode, stored in the eight most significant bits of IR, constitutes a direct address into the nanomemory. The nanomemory is realized by 16 AM27S21A (256 × 4 each) PROM chips, with an access time of 30ns.

(d) *Interrupt Control Unit* (ICU). Recognizes interrupts and passes control to interrupt service routines. Realized by an AMD2914 chip to handle eight interrupt sources.

(e) *Program Memory* (PM). Organized as a 16-MWord (64 Mbytes) memory. Accessed by the PCU. Access time: 100ns.

The DES includes the following:

(a) *32-bit Arithmetic Logic Unit* (ALU). Performs all of the data processing operations. Realized by eight AMD2903 chips along with AMD2902 chips for the Carry Look Ahead (CLA) logic circuitry.

(b) *Register File* (RF). The maximal configuration contains 2048 32-bit registers, realized by AMD29705 chips. The current, reduced prototype contains only 128 registers. It is easily expandable to its full size.

(c) *Data Memory* (DM). Technologically, approximately the same as the PM. Presently, it is of the same size, 64 Mbytes. It can be extended to $2^{32} = 4$ Gbytes.

(d) *DM Interface Registers.*

MAR — Memory Address Register

DOR — Data Output Register

DIR — Data Input Register

All three are 32-bit wide, realized by TTL74S374 chips. The MAR contains the address of the DM location accessed. The DOR serves as a buffer for data to be stored in DM, while DIR is a buffer for data fetched from DM.

(e) *Program Status Control Unit* (PSCU). An auxiliary logic unit, used to store the status information of the processor. Includes the LSW register data. Realized by an AMD2904 chip.

(f) *Immediate Data Controller.* Supplies immediately data values to the ALU. Realized by 16 74LS253 chips.

(g) *Swapper.* Swaps halfwords and bytes within 32-bit words. In addition it can perform a four-bit rotate left.

A Motorola 68000-based system serves as a front-end auxiliary coprocessor to handle the OS, I/O operations and diagnostics. The system memories are dual-port organized to permit simultaneous access by the service processor and by the MIRIS CPU. The overall MIRIS structure is shown in Fig. 5.11. An example of an activation of an instruction is shown in Fig. 5.12.

To summarize, the expected high throughput of MIRIS is due to the following factors:

(1) Streamlined handling of simple, primitive instructions.

(2) Avoidance of instruction decoding.

(3) Fast, horizontally microcoded Nanomemory.

(4) Large CPU dual-port register file (2048 × 32), which allows accessing two registers and storing a result — all in one cycle of 100ns. We have also an overall minimization of memory accesses.

(5) Register window (96 registers) mechanism for passing parameters. Only 48 registers are implemented in the prototype.

(6) Storage of data, due to an interrupt, in the register file, instead of in the main memory.

(7) Fast memory access; access time = 100ns.

(8) All instructions executed in a single cycle of 100ns.

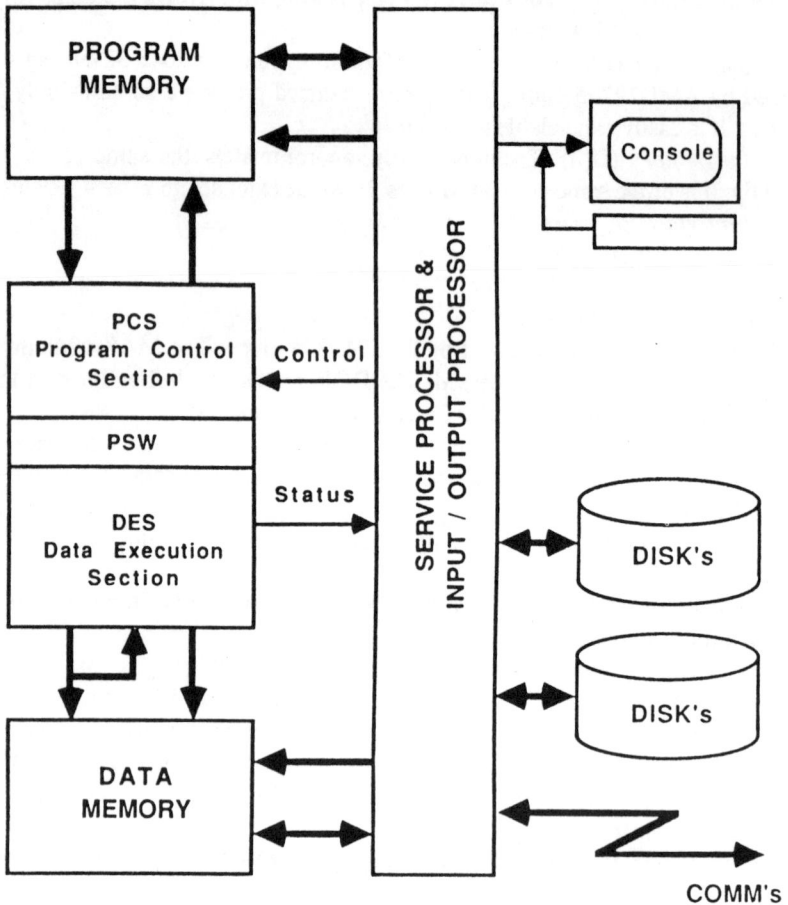

Fig. 5.11   MIRIS computer system overall structure

The above was achieved (1987) in a bit-sliced AMD2900 (10MHz) prototype. It stands to reason that an eventual, single-chip (excluding PM and DM) VLSI realization may yield even better results.

The MIRIS project was extended for multitasking operation, exemplified by an intermediate model called Parallel RISC (PARIS) [DuBo 88, QDuT 88]. The current-generation multitasking system i s called MULTRIS (MULTitasking RISC) [QuMT 89]. The MIRIS does not feature floating-point operations. A set of high-speed software floating-point procedures was developed for the MIRIS. Their performance was found to be competitive with that of other systems such as IBM 370/148, NS32081 (10MHz), MC68881 (8MHz), Intel 8087 (8MHz), VAX 11/750 and RISC II (12MHz) with a Weitek coprocessor. For double-precision

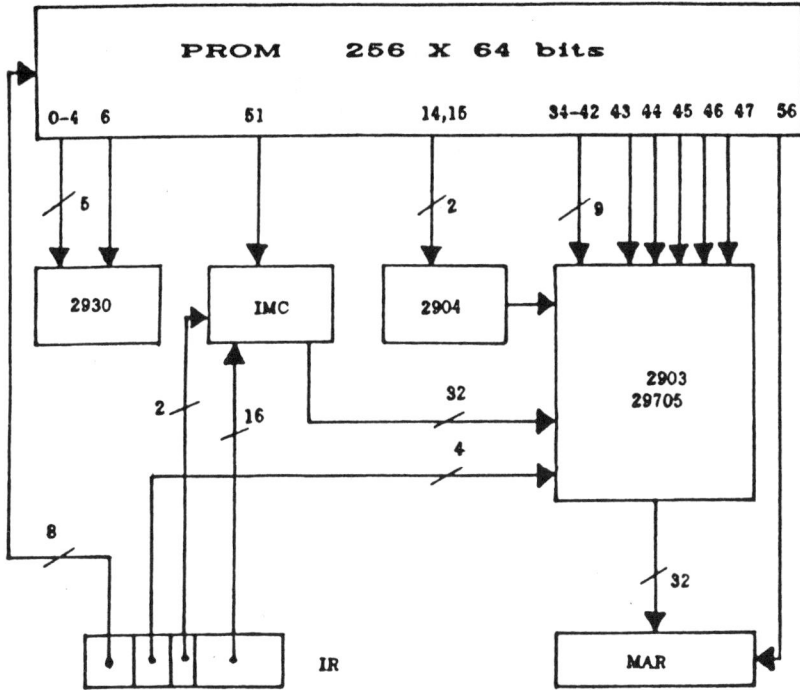

Fig. 5.12 Instruction interpretation
CAMAR SRC, IMM   MAR ← SRC + IMM

Whetstone it exceeded the Berkeley RISC II software performance (without a coprocessor) by an order of magnitude [DaPT 88].

The goal in the MULTRIS development was to design a system which offers the advantages of general registers, register stacks, and cache, but which minimizes some of the problems associated with them, discussed in chapter 2. The concept is called 'Threaded Register Windows'. Currently the basic unit of the thread is a register window, each of which contains 16 32-bit registers. The size of this window is experimental, and may be changed later. These windows do not overlap as do those of the Berkeley RISC II (chapter 3), but dual pointers supported by the architecture allow access to both a *calling* procedure's activation window and the *called* activation window — therefore any passed parameters need not be copies. The windows can be flexibly and dynamically configured to serve as:

(1) Activation Record Stacks: several windows may be dynamically linked together to form a stack to hold procedural activation records. Because no window overlap is required, the windows forming the stack need not be contiguous.
(2) General Purpose Traditional Data Stacks: the same linking approach can be used to form a traditional push/pop data stack. Implicit access to this stack is

supported by the architecture.

(3) General Purpose Queues: the architecture also supports implicit access to queues made up of linked register windows.

(4) Statically allocated windows to hold vital information for an interrupt handler or the operating system.

(5) Isolated packets of frequently used global or object oriented data.

The overhead involved in forming the links is low, and the architecture supports constructs which make it transparent to application programs.

There are many advantages to these structures. The activation record stack allows the run time system to have multiple stacks (or at least the tops of them) resident on-chip at one time. This allows tasks to save their most recently used and needed data in the fastest storage available, and not copy it at the time of a context switch. The result of this will be to make the performance gains achieved by other RISC machines available to multitasking systems.

The queue structure will allow task communications to occur within the domains of the fast on-chip storage, and will also facilitate scheduling. The additional availability of traditional stacks is advantageous since this structure is sharable by all procedures. That is, it is not tied directly to the procedure control structures. This structure would be useful to a compiler: to hold data from large procedural activation records (those which require more than 16 words); or to support recursive algorithms, such as those used to handle trees and graphs [AhHU 75].

The interior of the windows is accessed using a block relative address (register number). Therefore, the operand address is short, allowing for three operand instructions, and the compiler can assume that a dedicated set (one window) of registers is available for local and parameter storage. Dynamically allocated storage is initially allocated only in the windows. This is done by taking a 'free window' from a hardware supported (chip-resident) free-windows stack. Off-chip memory is allocated only if an overflow occurs. Which windows to overflow, or to underflow, can be computed in the background using information available from the operating system and guidance from the compiler. The additional processing time needed to choose which window to overflow can be regained by avoiding 'misses' and unnecessary memory allocations.

In the register window thread organization, register access is implicit through window pointers contained in the processor state. The processor state, saved in two process status words (PSW1 and PSW2), includes references to six windows at any one time. Additionally, there is always an implicit reference to the global window, giving an access to a total of 7×16 registers. Access is restricted to only these windows. This allows the scope of a procedure to be inherently protected. Because of the limited address field, it is impossible to accidentally access data outside the windows which have been allocated to a process.

Fig. 5.13 shows the organization of the processor state registers. Of the six windows, five are used to access user data. One, the 'Map Window' (MW in (PSW1)

31		26 25		18	17	16	15	14	13	12		7	6		3	2	0
OW		INT MASK		I	C	O	N	Z		MW			MWI				

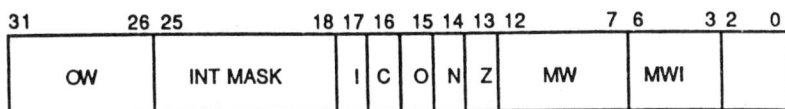

Program Status Word 1

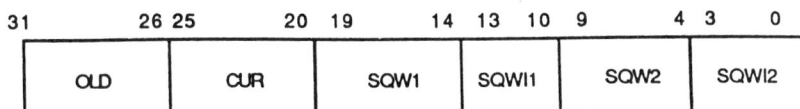

31		26 25		20	19		14	13		10	9		4	3		0
OLD		CUR			SQW1			SQWI1			SQW2				SQWI2	

Program Status Word 2

CUR	Current activation record window pointer
OLD	Previous (caller's) activation record window pointer
SQW1	Stack/Queue Window 1 pointer
SQWI1	Stack/Queue Window 1 index
SQW2	Stack/Queue Window 2 pointer
SQWI2	Stack/Queue Window 2 index
OW	'Object' Window pointer
MW	Map Window pointer
MWI	Map Window index
ICONZ	Interrupt enable, carry, overflow, negative, and zero flags

Fig. 5.13   Processor state registers

is used to manage activation record stacks. The five data window references are:

(1) The Current Window (accessible through CUR in PSW2) — containing the activation record of the currently active procedure.
(2) The Old Window (accessible through OLD in PSW2) — containing the activation record of the current procedure's dynamic parent. Any parameters which are passed are accessed directly using this pointer.

(3) Stack/Queue Window 1 (accessible through SQW1 in PSW2) — this window may be treated as a data stack, the head or tail of a queue, or a general data window.

(4) Stack/Queue Window 2 (accessible through SQW2 in PSW2) — this window may be treated as a data stack, the head or tail of a queue, or a general data window.

(5) An Object Window (accessible through OW in PSW1) — this window can be used to hold any additional program-controlled data pointer which, for example, can be used to access an object or frequently referred to globals.

The SQW pointers also have an intra-register displacement associated with them. A register address is expressed in the instruction using two fields. The first is a three-bit field indicating one of the windows; the second a four-bit field indicating one of the 16 registers in that window.

Register windows which are resident in the processor can be referenced by a six-bit window pointer (this provides for up to 64 windows). When a window is spilled to memory, it is still necessary to maintain a reference to the data it contains. In this architecture, windows are most easily spilled to specific locations in memory called 'window frames'. These frames are located in a specific region of data memory. The approach permits windows, whether spilled or not, to be referenced via a 16-bit pointer. If the upper 10 bits of the pointer are all zero, then the window is resident in the register bank in the window specified by the lower six bits. Otherwise, the full 16-bit value is used to form a memory (byte) address by shifting it left six bits. This indicates that window frames can only occur on 64-byte boundaries in memory.

The activation record stacks are represented by a list of windows, as shown in Fig. 5.14. Access to the top two windows is possible using the OLD and CUR pointers as described in the preceding section. To keep track of the 'thread' of windows allocated to the activation record stack, an additional window, the map window (MW), is needed. This serves as a map, or directory, of the stack. This map, which can be housed in any register window, contains a sequential list of six-bit window pointers identifying the register windows in the stack and defining their order. The return address value for each nested procedure call is stored here as well. There is also a flag field which indicates that the window has overflowed into memory. The MWI (Map Window Index) is used to index this window. If a procedure call depth greater than 15 exists in one task, the hardware will trap and create a link for an additional map window. One register (the link) is reserved to accommodate the doubly linked list (two 16-bit pointers to either memory resident window frames, or to another register window).

If it becomes necessary to overflow a window from a particular activation stack into memory, the MW plays an integral role. To start an overflow, a memory resident window image, a 'window frame', is allocated and a pointer to it is saved in the 'downward' link in the first location of the allocated window frame (referred to as the 'MW image'). Next, the activation record window to be spilled is copied

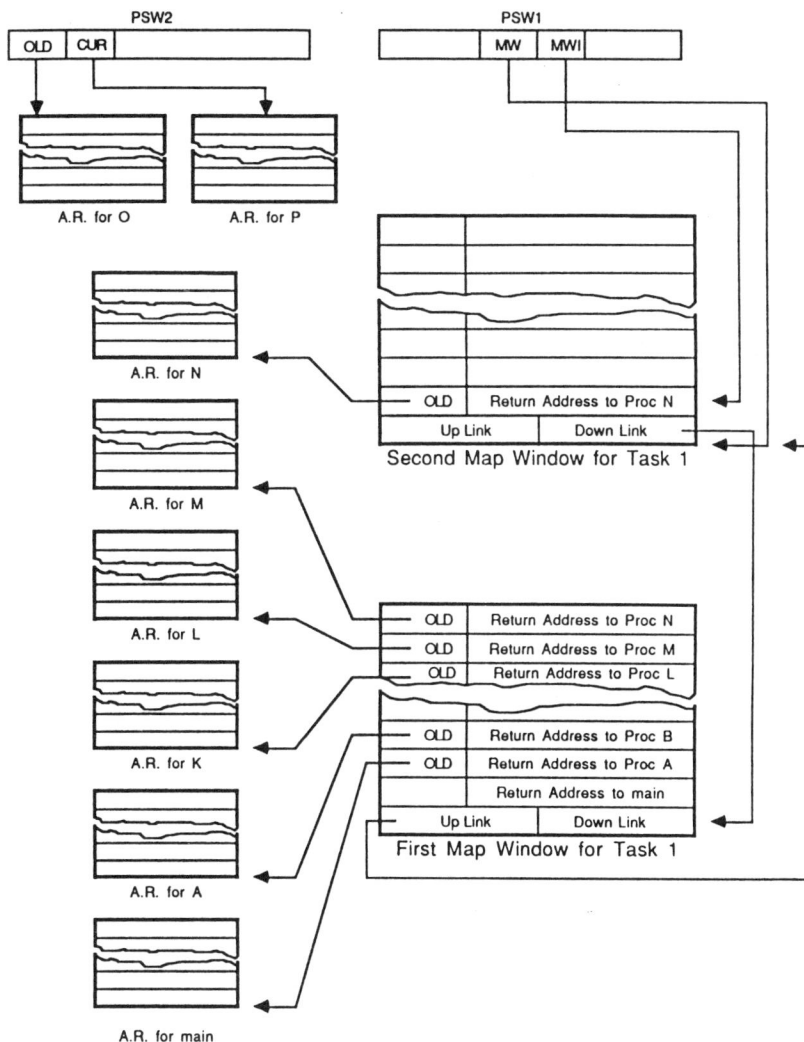

Fig. 5.14 Activation record stack thread maintenance

into a second memory window frame. The 16-bit pointer to this window frame is now saved in the MW image. When all 15 windows of this MW have been overflowed, the MW itself can be spilled. Since each MW contains a pair of 16-bit pointers (in R0), the MW linkage can be maintained whether or not the MWs are in memory or registers. When this procedure chain is reactivated, the windows must be copied back to register windows before control is transferred to them. Only those procedures that are about to be reactivated need be copied back.

If access is required to a variable down the procedure chain, this map (whether resident in memory or in register windows) can be used to traverse the chain.

To facilitate communication in multitasking systems, the threaded register windows can be reconfigured as queues or traditional push/pop stacks. The two SQW and SQW1 fields are used to support these structures. Four special instructions alter these pointers; POP, PUSH, ENQUEUE and DEQUEUE. All four instructions add or remove the single word elements from the stack/queue which is pointed to by the SQW plus SQW1. After each instruction the SQW1 is adjusted accordingly. When 15 elements have been pushed or queued, a software trap will link another window to the stack/queue.

The expandability of these structures, as illustrated in Fig. 5.15, is especially beneficial to queue management. In most conventional systems, queues are implemented in statically allocated storage and have a circular behavior. This requires that the memory allocated be sufficiently large to accommodate the entire queue, and that base and bound checks be done. Using the threaded register window concept the queue is register resident and occupies only the minimum number of windows needed to hold the current queue contents. As the queue grows and shrinks, register windows are automatically allocated and de-allocated. No checks for base/bounds need be performed.

The two SQWs allow access to both the head and the tail of a queue. However, frequently the entity which queues and the entity which dequeues are separate tasks. In Fig. 5.15, two tasks are accessing the same queue. The source task uses SQW2 to reference the queue's tail. The receiving task uses SQW1 to reference the queue's head. The choice of using SQW1 or SQW2 is arbitrary and can be left to programming convention.

The queue-empty condition or stack-empty condition is not automatically determined by the hardware but requires software support. However, there is a hardware aid provided. If during the execution of one of the four instructions SQW1 = SQW2 and SQWI1 = SQWI2 condition codes will be set.

Parts of the stack/queue can be overflowed to the memory window frames. In this case the links of its neighbor windows are changed to point to the memory frame address. Two such window frame pointers are accommodated in register 0 of each window.

As with other operations presented here, this set of queue/stack operations is designed to hide as much of the register window granularity from the applications programs as possible, without paying a large performance penalty.

Since the total task state is provided in the two PSWs, task context switches can be accomplished by simply saving two words. This saves the configuration of the activation stack and all other window-based data structures. If these two words were saved in registers, saving the current state would require two register-to-register moves, plus any additional logic needed to determine the storage location. In order to optimize a task context switch, any saved scheduler data, such as the location of task control blocks, scheduling queues, etc., should be made available as soon as the scheduler is passed control.

Sending Task's PSW2

OLD	CUR	SQW1	SQWI1	SQW2	SQWI2

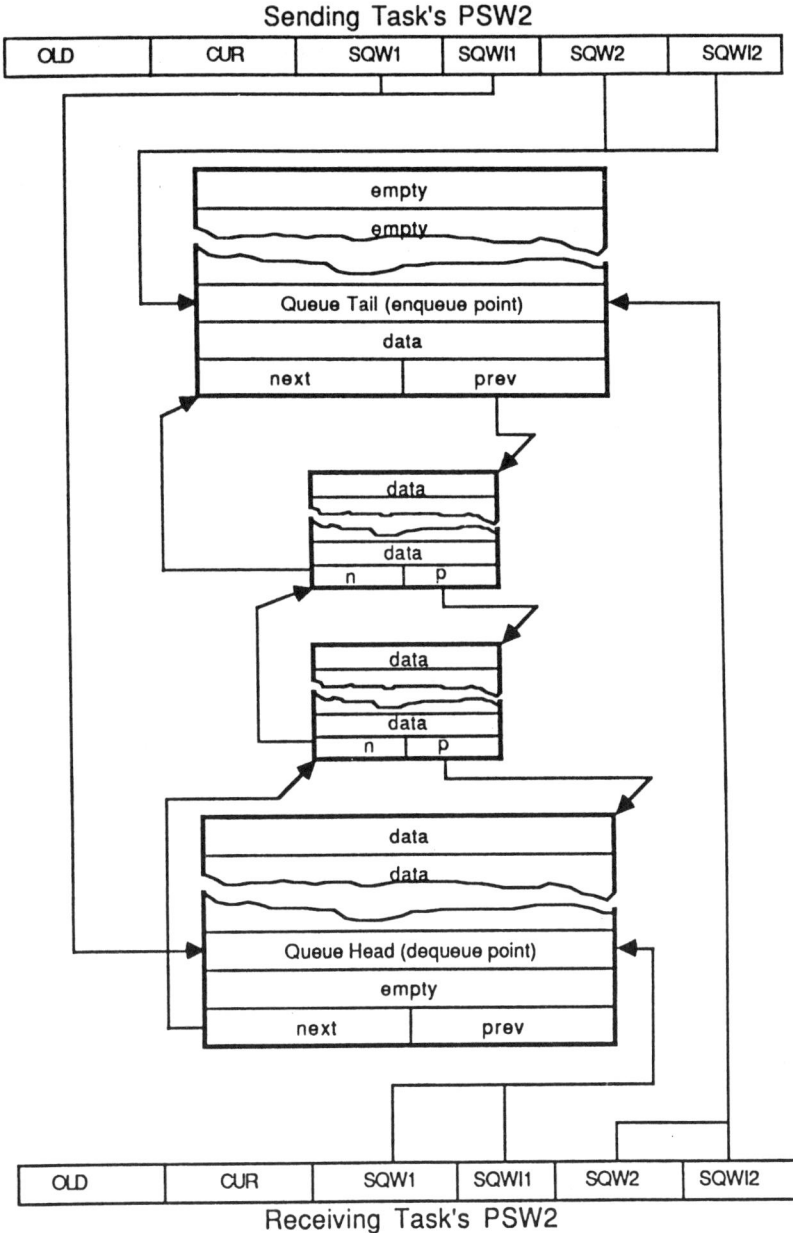

OLD	CUR	SQW1	SQWI1	SQW2	SQWI2

Receiving Task's PSW2

Fig. 5.15   Queue window management

To facilitate this, the architecture allows for a window to be pre-allocated for the scheduler's 'CUR' window. This window may be selected at system start-up, and a pointer to it saved in a special register called the Interrupt Control Register (ICR). There are 16 of these special registers, eight of which are reserved for hardware interrupt vectors. The other eight may be used for software traps. The ICR structure is shown in Fig. 5.16. The window pointer field permits the static allocation of a window for use by each interrupt handler. This window remains allocated even after the handler returns. There are many advantages to this static allocation. First, it reduces the chances of a window underflow exception occurring at the time of an interrupt. Second, the static nature of the window makes it nicely suited to serving as a buffer for interrupts involving data transfer.

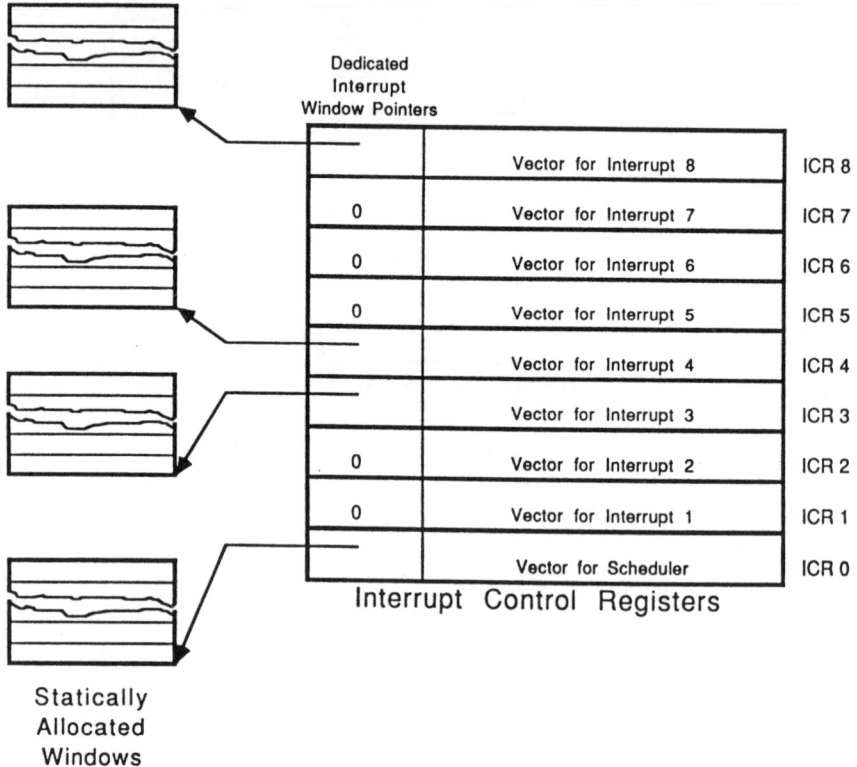

Fig. 5.16   Interrupt Control Registers (ICRs)

The 'CALLI' instruction is used for software traps. This instruction is similar to the CALL instruction except it need not select a window from the free list to be used as the new CUR window. Instead it checks the ICR window field. If it is non-zero, then the pre-allocated window is moved to CUR. This same process is used to service interrupts. It is not necessary to have a pre-allocated window — a value of zero in this field causes the interrupt to be allocated a new window, just as in a procedure call.

By using an instruction similar to a procedure call to transfer control to the scheduler, the PC and 'OLD' field of the currently active task is saved in that task's MW. Because of the symmetry of CALLI and CALL, once the selected task's PSWs have been loaded, the scheduler need only execute a return instruction (RET). The RETI instruction is provided for this. It is identical to RET except it does not return the window pointed to by CUR to the free list, unless the CUR entry in the interrupt's ICR is zero.*

A block diagram of MULTRIS is shown in Fig. 5.17 [Leeu 90]. It is to some extent similar to that of the MIRIS (Fig. 5.7). The handling of the instructions, fetched from the Program Memory, is basically the same. There is a dual bus system for simultaneous transfer of even- and odd-numbered word data. All buses are 32 bits wide. The burst mode control is used for fast transfer of 16-register windows to or from window frame locations in the Data Memory (dual-ported). MULTRIS contains a number of hardware units, in addition to the ALU, to speed up operations (multiplier, divider, shifter).

Notation used in Fig. 5.17:

DIRE — Data Input Register Even
DIRO — Data Input Register Odd
DORE — Data Output Register Even
DORO— Data Output Register Odd
MAG — Memory (Data) Address Generator
MAR — Memory Address Register
PC   — Program Counter
RE   — Result Even
RO   — Result Odd

A map of the Program Memory (PM) is shown in Fig. 5.18. Since all instructions are of single-word length (32 bits), it is word-addressable. The byte-addressable Data Memory (DM) is illustrated in Fig. 5.19. A map of the CPU registers file, consisting of 64 register windows (16 registers), along with the corresponding window frames in the DM, is shown in Fig. 5.20. A list of free window frames, implemented as a stack in DM, is maintained. It is shown in Fig. 5.21.

In addition to the PSW1 and PSW2 registers, shown in Fig. 5.13, there are three control registers:

SSW   — System Status Word,
OPR   — Overflow Pointer Register,
RB   — Implied Base Register,

---

* The paragraphs dealing with the Threaded Register Windows concept were written by Donna J. Quammen and D. Richard Miller.

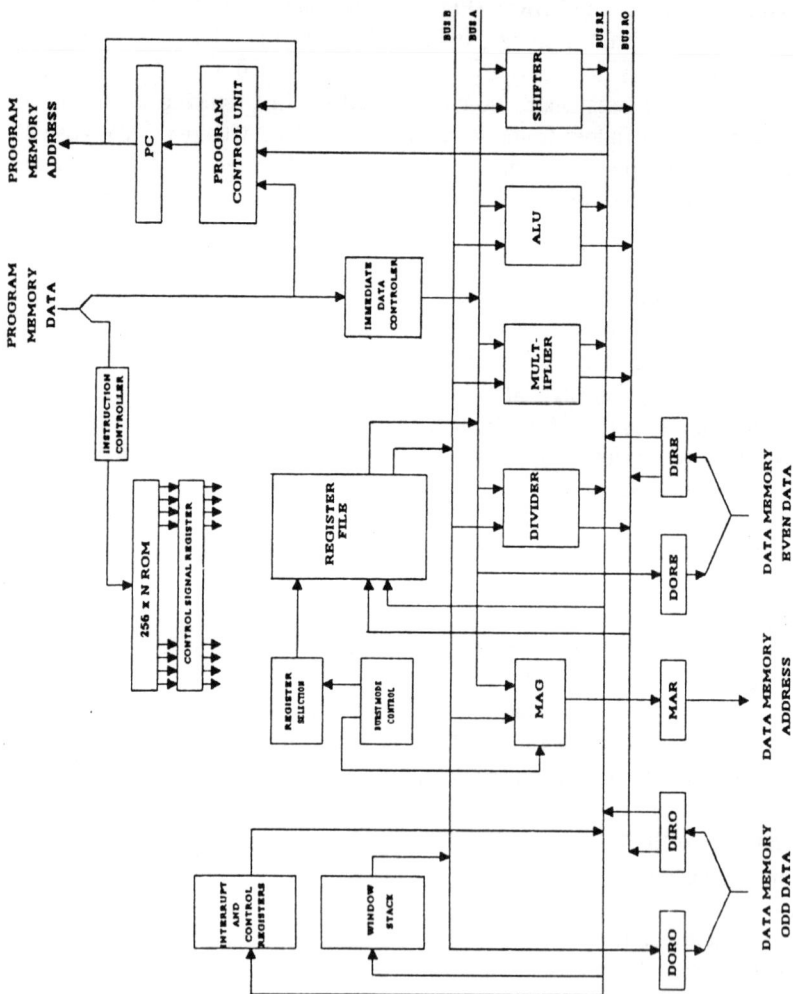

Fig. 5.17 MULTRIS block diagram

MULTRIS ARCHITECTURE
PROGRAM MEMORY
(PM)

word (32-bit) addressed
since all instructions are
32-bits long

16 MWords
(64 MBytes)
$2^{24} \times 32$

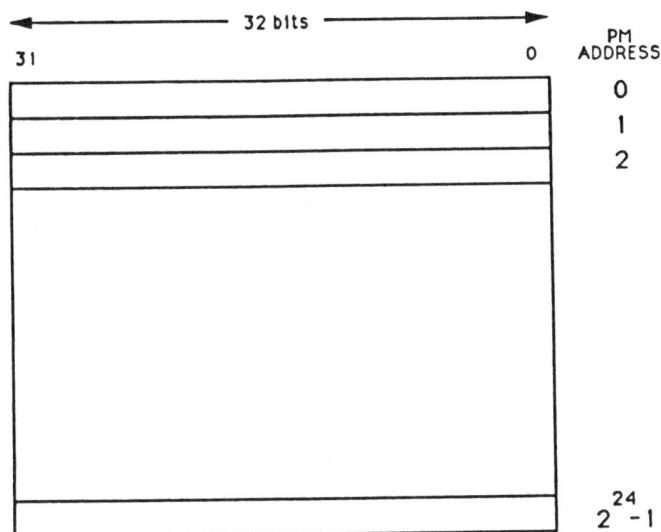

Fig. 5.18   Program memory

and 16 Interrupt Control Registers (ICRs, also shown in Fig. 5.16), illustrated in Fig. 5.22.

MULTRIS architecture features four instruction formats, shown in Fig. 5.23. There are three basic groups of instructions:

MULTRIS ARCHITECTURE
DATA MEMORY
(DM)

BYTE ADDRESSABLE AT ANY ADDRESS

HALFWORD ADDRESSABLE AT ANY EVEN ADDRESS

WORD ADDRESSABLE AT ANY ADDRESS DIVISIBLE BY 4

$$4 \text{ GBytes} \quad 2^{32}$$
$$2 \text{ GHWords} \quad 2^{31}$$
$$1 \text{ GWord} \quad 2^{30}$$

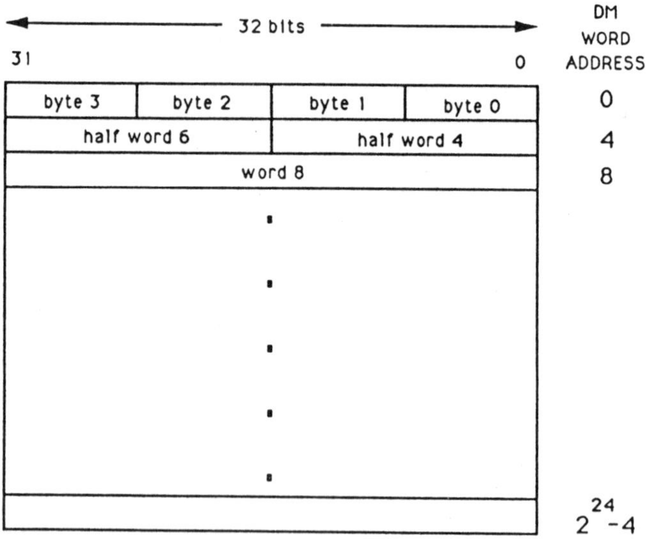

	32 bits			DM WORD ADDRESS
31			0	
byte 3	byte 2	byte 1	byte 0	0
half word 6		half word 4		4
word 8				8

$$2^{24} - 4$$

Fig. 5.19   Data memory

1. Data Movement (Tables 5.1 and 5.2),
2. Arithmetic-Logic (Table 5.3),
3. Program Control (Table 5.4).

MULTRIS ARCHITECTURE

REGISTER WINDOW ORGANIZATION

1024 32-bit Registers = 64x16x32
64 16-Register Windows

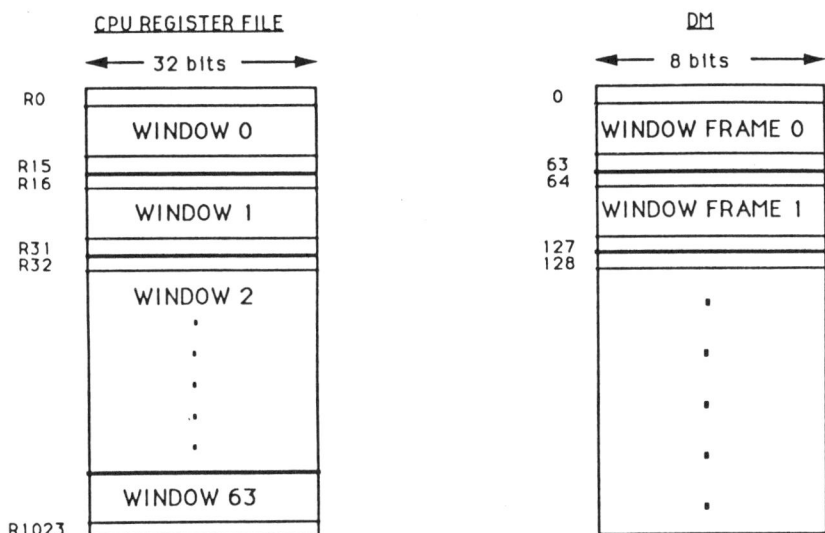

CPU REGISTER FILE   DM

◄─── 32 bits ───►   ◄─── 8 bits ───►

R0	0
WINDOW 0	WINDOW FRAME 0
R15 / R16	63 / 64
WINDOW 1	WINDOW FRAME 1
R31 / R32	127 / 128
WINDOW 2	.
. . . . .	. . . .
WINDOW 63	.
R1023	

DATA MEMORY (DM) IS BYTE ADDRESSED
EACH CPU REGISTER IS 32 BITS
THERE ARE 16 CPU REGISTERS PER WINDOW
WHICH MAPS TO DM AS FOLLOWS:

$$\frac{16 - 32\ \text{BIT WORDS}}{\text{REGISTER WINDOW}} \times \frac{4\ \text{BYTES}}{\text{WORD}} = \frac{64\ \text{BYTES OF DM}}{\text{PER WINDOW FRAME}}$$

Fig. 5.20   CPU register file and DM window frames

5.4 The BGU Single Instruction Computer

One of the principal characteristics of a RISC-type system (chapter 2) is a reduced number of machine-language instructions. By continuing to reduce the number of instructions, eventually the limiting case of a Single Instruction Computer (SIC) will be achieved. Such a case has indeed been considered in the past by several researchers [AzTa 80, 83a, Lipo 76, 78, TaLi 80]. The idea of constructing and

MULTRIS ARCHITECTURE

LIST OF FREE WINDOW FRAMES IN DM

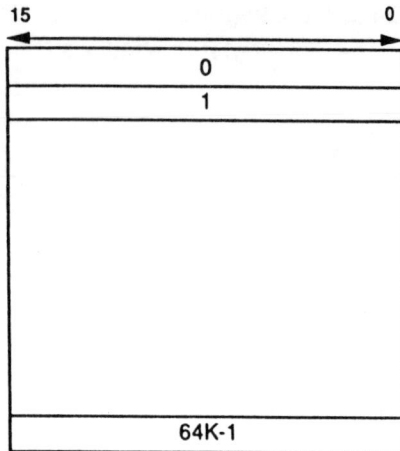

15		0
	0	
	1	
	64K-1	

Implemented as a stack in DM., with the top of the stack in one of the CPU windows.

Fig. 5.21   Free windows stack in DM

utilizing a SIC was originally proposed by Lipovski [Lipo 76]. Since the single instruction, implemented in the above system, was MOVE, the whole idea was designated as the 'MOVE Architecture'. Subsequently, a Conditional MOVE option was added to the system [Lipo 78] and it has been renamed as 'CMOVE Architecture'. The choice of MOVE as the single instruction has not been random. It is usually the most often used instruction in many programs. Indeed, a recent study [Fair 82] reports that data movement instructions are used with a frequency of 45% on the average. This is the highest frequency; the second most frequent instructions are the program modification instructions at 29%. Theoretically, one could build a SIC with a different instruction; however, based on practical considerations of frequency of usage, the MOVE implementation is fully justified.

A prototype of SIC (CMOVE Architecture) system of eight bits was constructed, for the first time, in the Digital Laboratory of the Department of Electrical and Computer Engineering at the Ben Gurion University (BGU) of the Negev in Beer Sheva, Israel [AzTa 83a] in 1982.

The principal basic properties of a CMOVE architecture system can be summarized follows:

System Status Word, (SSW):

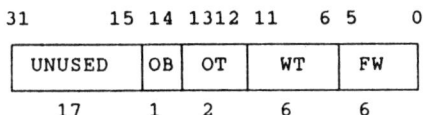

```
31          15 14 1312 11   6 5      0
```

UNUSED	OB	OT	WT	FW
17	1	2	6	6

FW : FREE WINDOWS, number of free windows left on the window stack

WT : WINDOWS TRANSFERRED, number of windows transferred to memory

OT : OVERFLOW TYPE, 00 Regular Task Activation
                    01 LIFO Stack

OB : OVERFLOW BIT, set on window overflow

Overflow Pointer Register, (OPR):

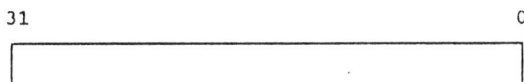

```
31                                    0
```

This register holds a data value that points to the beginning address in data memory where the _first_ overflowed window is stored.

Implied Base Register, (RB):

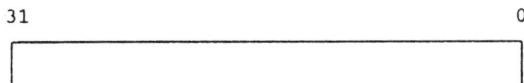

```
31                                    0
```

This register is used in any instruction that makes reference to RB.

Interrupt Control Registers, (ICRs):

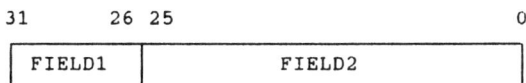

```
31      26 25                          0
```

FIELD1	FIELD2

FIELD1 : Dedicated Interrupt Window Pointer or 0

FIELD 2 : Interrupt Vector

Note: There are sixteen of the above Interrupt Control Registers.

Fig. 5.22   Control registers

MULTRIS ARCHITECTURE
INSTRUCTION FORMATS

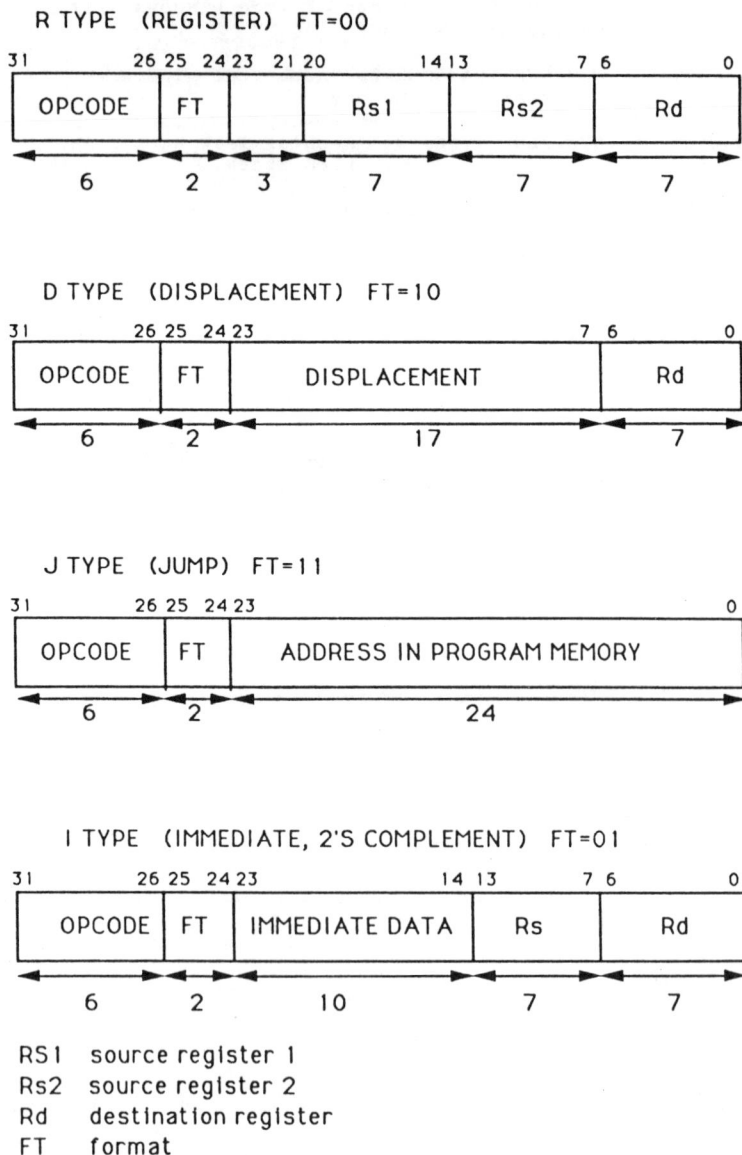

R TYPE (REGISTER) FT=00

OPCODE	FT		Rs1	Rs2	Rd
6	2	3	7	7	7

Bits: 31 · 26 25 · 24 23 · 21 20 · 14 13 · 7 6 · 0

D TYPE (DISPLACEMENT) FT=10

OPCODE	FT	DISPLACEMENT	Rd
6	2	17	7

Bits: 31 · 26 25 · 24 23 · 7 6 · 0

J TYPE (JUMP) FT=11

OPCODE	FT	ADDRESS IN PROGRAM MEMORY
6	2	24

Bits: 31 · 26 25 · 24 23 · 0

I TYPE (IMMEDIATE, 2'S COMPLEMENT) FT=01

OPCODE	FT	IMMEDIATE DATA	Rs	Rd
6	2	10	7	7

Bits: 31 · 26 25 · 24 23 · 14 13 · 7 6 · 0

RS1 source register 1
Rs2 source register 2
Rd destination register
FT format

Fig. 5.23 Instruction formats

Table 5.1 MULTRIS Architecture; Data Movement Instructions

			FORMAT
LOAD INSTRUCTIONS			
LDx (Rb,Ri),Rd	indirect based-indexed		
		DM address ((Rb)+(Ri)) ⟶ Rd	R
LDx disp(Rb),Rd	indirect base + displacement (10 bits)		
		DM address (disp + (Rb)) ⟶ Rd	I
LDx disp,Rd	indirect implied base + displacement (17 bits)		
		DM address (disp + (RB)) ⟶ Rd	D
LDC Imm,Rs,RC	load control register		
		Imm + (Rs) ⟶ RC	I
		RC = PSW1, PSW2, RB, SSW, OPR	
STORE INSTRUCTIONS			
STx Rs,(Rb,Ri)			R
STx Rs,disp(Rb)			I
STx Rs,disp			D
STC Imm,Rc,Rd	store control register		
		Imm + (RC) ⟶ Rd	I

where x is H for half word, B for byte, or blank for word (default)

PUSH Imm,Rs,SWP			I
	SWP -- stack window pointer = MW, SQW1, SQW2		
POP 0,SWP,Rd			I
ENQ Imm,Rs,SWP	Enqueue		I
DEQ 0,SWP,Rd	Dequeue		I

(a) The system has a single instruction (no opcode, no opcode decoding) with the following general structure:

MOVE FROM SOURCE, TO DESTINATION

SOURCE represents the address of the source location in memory, while DESTINATION represents the address of the destination location in memory.

(b) The instruction is executed in two machine cycles, FROM and TO.

(c) There are four addressing modes for each of the two timing cycles:

Table 5.2 MULTRIS Architecture; Window Load/Store Instructions

FORMAT

LDWL n, Rx, Rd; Load Window Low Pointer

   n = number of registers to move (default = 16)

   Rx (15-0) = pointer to base of window frame in DM to

      be moved to next free register window

   Rd = pointer to window which is loaded

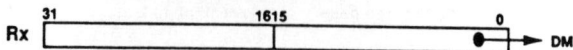

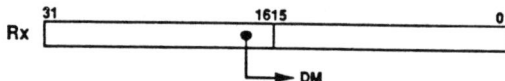

I

```
        31              1615                    0
    Rx [_____|_____●]─► DM
```

LDWH n, Rx, Rd; Load Window High Pointer

   n = number of registers to move (default = 16)

   Rx (31-16) = pointer to base of window frame in DM to

      be moved to next free register window

   Rd = pointer to window which is loaded

I

```
        31              1615                    0
    Rx [_____●|_____]
                        └─► DM
```

STWL n, Rx, Rd; Store Window Low Pointer

   n = number of register to move (default = 16)

   Rx (5-0) = pointer to register window to store

   Rd = pointer to base of destination window frame in DM

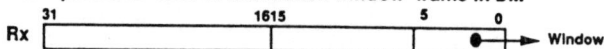

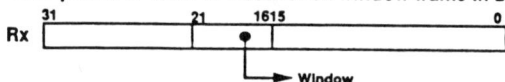

I

```
        31              1615          5      0
    Rx [_____|_____|_____●]─► Window
```

STWH n, Rx, Rd; Store Window High Pointer

   n = number of registers to move (default = 16)

   Rx (21-16) = pointer to register window to store

   Rd = pointer to base of destination window frame in DM

I

```
        31        21   1615               0
    Rx [_____|___●_|_____]
                      └─► Window
```

FROM Cycle	TO Cycle	Code
Direct	Direct	00
Immediate	Conditional	01
Indexed X	Indexed X	10
Indexed S	Indexed S	11
X and S are index registers		

(d) There are two memories:

   A Program Memory (PM) to store instructions

   A Main Memory (MM) to store data

(alternatively identified as a data memory).

Table 5.3 MULTRIS Architecture; Arithmetic-Logic Instructions

		FORMAT
ADD Rs1,Rs2,Rd	(Rs1) + (Rs2)⟶Rd	R
ADD Imm,Rs,Rd	(Rs) + Imm ⟶ Rd	I
ADD Imm,Rd	(Rd) + Imm ⟶ Rd	D
SUB Rs1,Rs2,Rd	(Rs2) - (Rs1)⟶Rd	R
SUB Imm,Rs,Rd	(Rs) - Imm ⟶ Rd	I
SUB Imm,Rd	(Rd) - Imm ⟶ Rd	D
OR Rs1,Rs2,Rd	(Rs1) OR (Rs2)⟶Rd	R
OR Imm,Rs,Rd	(Rs) OR Imm ⟶ Rd	I
OR Imm,Rd	(Rd) OR Imm ⟶ Rd	D
AND Rs1,Rs2,Rd	(Rs1) AND (Rs2)⟶Rd	R
AND Imm,Rs,Rd	(Rs) AND Imm ⟶ Rd	I
AND Imm,Rd	(Rd) AND Imm ⟶ Rd	D
COM Rs,Rd	Complement Rs⟶Rd (Imm=0 implied)	I
SLL Imm,Rs,Rd	Shift Logical Left Rs by Imm⟶Rd	I
SLR Imm,Rs,Rd	Shift Logical Right Rs by Imm ⟶Rd	I
SAL Imm,Rs,Rd	Shift Arithmetic Left Rs by Imm⟶Rd	I
SAR Imm,Rs,Rd	Shift Arithmetic Right Rs by Imm ⟶Rd	I
MUL Rs1,Rs2,Rd	Signed (Rs1)*(Rs2)⟶Rd, Rd+1 Rd=most sig, Rd+1=least sig	R
DIV Rs1,Rs2,Rd	Signed (Rs1)/(Rs2) ⟶Rd (Quotient)	R
MOD Rs1,Rs2,Rd	Remainder (Rs1)/(Rs2) ⟶ Rd	R

(e) The CPU consists mainly of a Central Controller and auxiliary logic circuitry. It includes eight registers, allocated in the first eight addresses of MM: 0 to 7. The registers are:

100

Table 5.4 Program Control Instructions

Instruction	Action	Format
JMP adr.pm	adr.pm -> PC	J
JMP disp,(Rb,Ri)	disp(Rb)(Ri)->PC	I
JCC adr.pm (see CC table)	If CC=TRUE then adr.pm -> PC	J
JCC disp,(Rb,Ri) (see CC table)	If CC=TRUE then disp(Rb)(Ri)->PC	I
CALL adr.pm	adr.pm -> PC	J
CALL disp,(Rb,Ri)	disp(Rb)(Ri)->PC	I
CALLI adr.pm	adr.pm -> PC	J
CALLI disp,(Rb,Ri)	disp(Rb)(Ri)->PC	I
RET	N/A	N/A
RETI	N/A	N/A

Condition Code Table:

Code (CC)	Indication	State
Z	zero result	Z set
NZ	non-zero	Z reset
N	negative	N set
P	pos. or zero	N reset
O	overflow	O set
NO	no overflow	O reset
C	carry	C set
NC	no carry	C reset

Address	Register	Comment
0	PC	Program Counter
1	JSR	Subroutine Register
2	X	Index Register
3	X – 1	Contains always (X) – 1
4	S	Index Register
5	S – 1	Contains always (S) – 1
6	C	Counter Register
7	C – 1	Contains always (C) – 1

(f) The CPU contains no ALU. Arithmetic and/or Logic operations are performed within I/O processors, denoted in this system as: Arithmetic Move Units (AMUs).

(g) For an m-bit word machine, the single instruction format for each of the two cycles (FROM, TO) consists of $m + 4$ bits, which is the word size of the Program Memory. It follows that:

m bits are used for the direct address either in MM or for the AMUs, and the four control bits are defined:

Two bits for four addressing modes, listed in (c)

One bit indicating MM or AMU space

One bit for an interrupt flag.

The instruction format of a CMOVE is shown in Fig. 5.24.

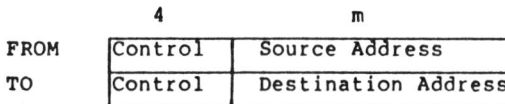

Fig. 5.24   CMOVE instruction format

The conditional mode of the TO cycle is implemented using an extra N flip flop (flag), which is loaded, automatically, with the sign bit of the word moved last. If $N = 1$, the condition is considered to be satisfied and the conditional move is performed. If $N = 0$, no move takes place and N is not affected.

Programming is done by the following symbolic notation:

$A \leftarrow B$

where B is the source and A, the destination symbolic address. If the move is conditional, we write

$A¢ \leftarrow B$.

To move immediate numbers we use the symbol #,

$A \leftarrow 20\#$

number 20 (decimal) is moved into location A. All address references refer to MM or AMU (depending on the space allocated). Only the Program Counter (PC, at MM location 0) refers to the Program Memory (PM). The PC is normally incremented in each memory cycle (by one for FROM and by one for TO). A branch operation is performed as follows:

$0 \leftarrow ADDR$

or

$JMP \leftarrow ADDR$

where ADDR is a symbolic branch address. Naturally, an immediate branch address can also be specified:

$JMP \leftarrow 100\#$.

It should be noted that addresses refer to the MM, while in the case of JMP or PC, the addresses refer to the PM.

The instruction: call a subroutine, say SUB1, is written:

$1 \leftarrow SUB1$

or

$JSR \leftarrow SUB1$.

The PC content, which is the address of the following instruction, is stored automatically in a special RTS register and restored to the PC after a return from the subroutine. The instruction: return from a subroutine, is written:

$JMP \leftarrow JSR$.

Each of the registers X, S and C has a companion register $X-1$, $S-1$ and $C-1$, respectively, which contains, automatically, its decremented value. Thus,

$X \leftarrow X-1$

decrements X, while

$X-1 \leftarrow X$

increments X.

In order to perform any arithmetic or logic operation, one has to use a special AMU, wired for the specific operation. For instance, in an AMU wired for addition, there would be an interconnection shown in Fig. 5.25. Moving the addends into registers A and B will automatically yield their sum in C.

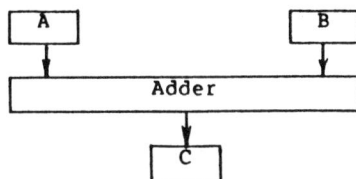

Fig. 5.25   AMU adder configuration

The SIC was intended from its inception to serve as a *special purpose controller* only. For this reasons it has not been mentioned in the previous chapters along with other RISC-type systems. Any comparison between the SIC and the other systems with respect, for instance, to the ability to handle complicated software, such as OS or HLL Compilers, would not be useful because the SIC has not been designed for such an implementation.

The implementation for which the SIC has been intended is for cases requiring very simple controllers with relatively brief and simple software. Particularly in large-scale systems, where a large number (hundreds, possibly thousands) of such controllers may be required, it may be more economical to use a very simple controller, instead of a full-scale off-the-shelf microprocessor CISC, with numerous but unnecessary instructions. An example of a potential use of a SIC-type controller could be the control of a signalized traffic intersection.

A complete design of a SIC prototype, using AMD2900 bit-sliced equipment, has been performed [AzTa 80, 83a]. Although only an eight-bit prototype has been constructed, the design can be readily implemented for any m-bit system. Since the realization equipment is known, precise performance evaluation can be made for any generated software. For a preliminary comparison with existing 16-bit microprocessors, a 16×16 multiplication subroutine was generated for a 16-bit CMOVE system operating at 8MHz. The CMOVE multiplication subroutine consists of a series of shifts and adds (performed by moves from one register to another), executed within an AMU (Arithmetic MOVE Unit). It was compared with the following microprocessors, which have a multiplication instruction in their assembly language:

Intel 8086 at 8MHz
Motorola 68000 at 8MHz
Zilog 8000 at 4MHz

The 16×16 multiplication in microseconds:

CMOVE	3.500
8086	18.125
68000	9.250
8000	17.500

Even if the CMOVE is run at 4MHz, it would perform the 16×16 multiplication in 7 microseconds. The regular 2900 operating frequency is actually 10MHz, and the CMOVE can perform the above operation in 2.8 microseconds. It should be pointed out that the above comparison studies were actually performed in 1981, taking into account the equipment available at that time. A distributed multiprocessing system, composed of hundreds of CMOVE processors, has also been designed [AzTa 81].

5.5 The BGU MODHEL System for RISCS Investigation

The objective of this section is to describe a special purpose computing system MODHEL, which has been developed to serve as a tool to investigate the properties of various RISC-type models.

There are quite a few models of RISC-type systems, each with a different combination of instructions in its instruction set. The question arises: which combination of instructions is a better choice? How do you choose an instruction set? Once an instruction set has been chosen, what will be the properties of the system? In order to attempt to answer the above questions, a special research tool, the MODHEL System [Azar 84, AzTa 83b, ShAz 85], has been proposed. It is a RISC-type system, which can be optionally activated as a different system with a different combination of instructions. The MODHEL is an experimental research system which is not intended to perform as a universal computer. The primary designation of MODHEL is to serve as an investigation tool in the study of the computing systems within the RISC Space (RISCS). Some results of studies of this type will be presented later in this section.

The particular and unique property of the MODHEL is that it consists of Modules of Instruction Subsets. Each module contains a group of two to six different instructions, and each module can be activated or deactivated during any specific operation of the system. In this way, a variety of RISC-type systems can be created and tested out on the same physical installation.

The current design contains eight instruction modules with the following instruction allocation:

Module	Notation	Instructions
0	M_0	Data Movement Instructions; MOVE, CMOVE
1	M_1	Program Control Instructions: JMP, JMPR, CALL, CALLR, RET
2	M_2	Arithmetic Instructions I; ADD, ADDC, SUB, SUBC
3	M_3	Shift and Rotate Instructions: SHIFT, ROTATE (Left, Right)
4	M_4	Logic Instructions; OR, AND, NOT, XOR
5	M_5	Arithmetic Instructions II; MULT, DIV
6	M_6	I/O Instructions; IN, OUT
7	M_7	Reserved; Option for Multiprocessing Support

Activating module M_0 only makes the MODHEL almost identical to the SIC or the CMOVE system, described in the previous section. Activating all of the eight modules makes MODHEL very close to the RISC I with its 31 instructions. As will be seen in the following description, the architectures of MODHEL and RISC I (or II) are very close (see also chapter 3). Activation of any other combination of modules will yield a different RISC-type system within the RISC computing space (RISCS). The following notation will be adopted: activation of module 0 only yields a system denoted by M_0,

activation of modules 0, 1: M_{01}
activation of modules 0, 1, 2: M_{012}
activation of modules 0, 2, 3: M_{023}

and so on.

No matter which combination of modules has been selected, the MODHEL has the following architectural properties:

(a) Word length: 32 bits.
(b) The MODHEL has a stack oriented architecture.
(c) There are two separate memories:
Program Memory (PM) to store programs;
Main Memory (MM) to store data.
All instructions, data items and addresses are each 32 bits long.
(d) MM is accessed by MOVE TO/FROM MM only (equivalent to STORE/ LOAD of RISC). Data is processed when it is in one of the CPU registers only.
(e) There is a single 32-bit Instruction Format, shown in Fig. 5.26.
(f) There are four Addressing Modes:

1. *Direct* to MM, 18 bits: SRC1, ADDR, SRC2.
2. *Indexed* to MM: SRC1, ADDR + (SRC2).
3. *Register Indirect* to MM: (SRC2)

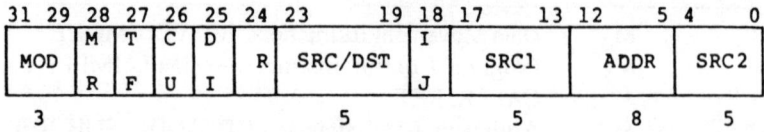

31	29	28	27	26	25	24	23	19	18	17	13	12	5	4	0
MOD		M R	T F	C U	D I		R	SRC/DST		I J		SRC1		ADDR	SRC2
3								5				5		8	5

where:

MOD	Module identifier (000 to 111).
MR	Access Memory or Register.
TF	TO MM cycle or FROM MM cycle.
CU	Conditional or Unconditional Move.
DI	Direct or Indirect Addressing Mode.
R	Relative address, when R=0, 18 least significant bits of the instruction form an address.
SRC/DST	Source or Destination Register.
IJ	Indirect Jump. Used by a Slave processor in a multiprocessing configuration to bring an address from the shared MM to its own PC.
SRC1	Source Register.
ADDR	8-bit address component.
SRC2	Index Register (when DI=1).

Fig. 5.26   MODHEL instruction format

SRC1 = ADDR = 0

4. *Immediate* in fields SRC1, ADDR, SRC2: 18 bits.

(g) There is a total of 138 CPU registers, with 32 (10 global, 22 window) seen by each procedure, as in RISC II (chapter 3).

The primary function of MODHEL is to serve as a research tool for RISCS investigations, and it has indeed been used in such capacity [Azar 84].

In order to be able to make a comparison with previous studies, the same benchmark programs as in [PaSe 82] have been used:

Puzzle A
Puzzle B
Ppuzzle
Qsort.

The following modules of the MODHEL have been used:

Module	Number of Instructions
0	6
1	5
2	4
3	4

A total of MODHEL configurations have been tested:

MODHEL Configuration	Total Number of Instructions
M_0	6
M_{01}	11
M_{02}	10
M_{012}	15
M_{0123}	19

For each benchmark program, the dynamic count (for a program run) of the occurrence of the instructions was taken. This was done for all MODHEL configurations, one after the other, listed above. The M_0 module, which has only MOVE-type instructions, is equivalent to the CMOVE system, described in section 5.4. The arithmetic operations are performed in the AMU in such a system. The dynamic count was then compared with the results of [PaSe 82] for the Berkeley RISC I and for the VAX 11/780. The results, specified in millions of occurrences of instructions, are as follows:

System	VAX	RISC I					
Program			M_0	M_{01}	M_{02}	M_{012}	M_{0123}
Puzzle A	10.01	10.11	20.55	20.55	15.05	15.05	10.11
Puzzle B	8.23	10.11	20.38	20.38	15.05	15.05	10.11
Ppuzzle	5.33	7.10	12.59	12.59	7.86	7.86	7.10
Qsort	1.05	1.63	2.26	2.08	1.70	1.70	1.70

The four benchmark programs activated from 17% to 36% of data movement instructions, 43% to 65% of arithmetic instructions and from 17% to 25% of program control instructions, including subroutine calls and returns. This is a reasonable mix for a test, and it fits, in a general way, the results in [Fair 82]. The above results indicate that, even if we use the 15-instruction configuration M_{012} and compare it to RISC I, we use 50% more instructions for Puzzle A and B, 10% more for Ppuzzle and only 4% more for Qsort. For the M_{0123} configuration the number of instructions, used dynamically, becomes practically identical to that of RISC I for all benchmarks. The M_{0123} contains 19 instructions, about 61% of RISC I. The above results are only indicative and, as yet, inconclusive. More experimentation work in RISCS is needed in order to be able to draw definite conclusions, which could provide an answer to the questions posed at the beginning of this section. The results obtained so far can only serve as an indication (but not as a proof) that RISC-type systems, with a very small number of instructions (even less than the 31 instructions of the Berkeley RISC I), can run the same benchmarks as the RISC I or the VAX 11/780 at a comparable speed. The MODHEL system can be used in a variety of experiments with a great number of benchmark programs in studies aimed to provide some answers to the above questions.

PART 2

COMMERCIAL RISC PROCESSORS

CHAPTER 6

The DEC Alpha AXP

6.1 Introductory Comments

Digital Equipment Corporation (DEC), or simply *Digital*, is well known for its pioneering minicomputer products, such as the PDP-11 family, and its superminicomputer VAX family. Both the PDP and the VAX families have been widely used in the whole world for many years. The VAX is an obvious example of a CISC architecture (see chapter 2), with its extensive instruction set, formats, and addressing modes. In parallel with extending the capabilities and the various models of the VAX, DEC researchers have been working on the development of their own RISC-type microprocessor. This development has culminated in the announcement of the Alpha AXP in 1991, the first Digital RISC. Prior to that, Digital had been using MIPS R2000 and R3000 RISC-type microprocessors (see chapter 9) in its DECstation family of workstations. The Alpha AXP has all of the attributes of its other RISC-type contemporaries. It practices instruction level parallelism (see chapter 1). Its first implementations have an on-chip FPU, MMU, and a dual primary cache (8 Kbyte code, 8 Kbyte data). Its more recent implementation (21164) has an on-chip unified secondary cache of 96KB (a unique feature so far). In some sense it can be said that it is ahead of its time: starting at 150MHz, and exceeding 200MHz, it surpasses all of its contemporaries in its frequency of operation (at least during the period of 1992 to 1995). It could be called indeed the fastest microprocessor of the early and mid nineties. The first product realizing the Alpha AXP architecture is labelled 21064. It starts a new Digital family of RISC-type microprocessors.

The architecture of Alpha AXP will be discussed in detail in the next section. Its physical realization and implementations will be presented in the subsequent one.

6.2 The Alpha AXP Architecture

The Alpha AXP is a 64-bit RISC-type architecture [Sits 92a,b, 93, McLe 93]. It essentially satisfies all of the RISC properties (see chapter 2). In particular, it features register-to-register operation and memory access by load and store instructions only. All of the Alpha instructions have a fixed length of 32 bits, as do practically all other RISC-type processors. Like most other RISC-type systems, Alpha features three-operand instructions. Since the Alpha is a 64-bit system, all of its CPU general-purpose registers are 64-bit. The bits in all registers are numbered so that the least significant bit (LSB) is 0, and the most significant bit (MSB) is 63. Alpha has two sets of 32 64-bit registers: one for the integer unit (IU): R0, R1, ..., R31, and one for the floating-point unit (FPU): F0, F1, ..., F31. Registers R31 and F31 are hardwired to contain a value zero at all times, similarly to most other RISCs (however, in other RISCs it is usually R0). Register R30 is designated as a stack pointer (SP). Otherwise, all other registers R0 to R29 and F0 to F30 do not have any prespecified tasks. The program counter (PC) is a separate 64-bit register (unlike the preceding VAX architecture where the PC is R15). All Alpha operations are done between the CPU 64-bit registers. The architecture also supports 32-bit integer operations. Alpha is byte-addressable; its basic addressable unit is the eight-bit byte. Memory is accessed using 64-bit virtual little-endian (the lowest byte has the lowest address) byte addresses. The minimum virtual address is 43 bits.

Data types

Alpha AXP architecture recognizes the following data types:

Integer data types

1. **Byte**, eight bits. Basic addressable unit.
2. **Word**, 16 bits. Two contiguous bytes starting on an arbitrary byte boundary. A word is addressed by the address of its least significant byte (the byte that contains bit zero).
3. **Longword**, 32 bits, Four contiguous bytes starting on an arbitrary byte boundary. A longword is addressed by the address of its least significant byte. In a longword integer, bit 31 (MSB) is the sign bit.
4. **Quadword**, 64 bits. Eight contiguous bytes starting on an arbitrary byte boundary. A quadword is addressed by the address of its least significant byte. In a 64-bit integer, bit 63 is the sign bit.

The Alpha integer data types are shown in Fig. 6.1

Although words, longwords, and quadwords may be stored at any byte address, better performance can be achieved if they are *naturally aligned*. That is, longwords are stored in addresses divisible by 4 (low-order two bits of the address are zero), and quadwords are stored in addresses divisible by 8 (low-order three bits are zero).

Floating point data types

Alpha AXP architecture features two groups of floating-point data types:

1. VAX floating-point formats, for backward compatibility with the VAX software.
2. IEEE Standard (ANSI/IEEE 754-1985) floating-point formats, as practiced in practically all other modern systems.

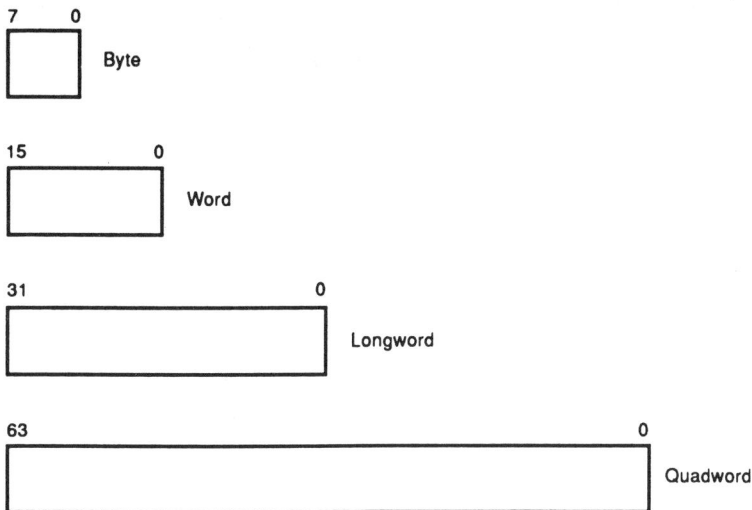

Fig. 6.1 Alpha integer data types

VAX floating-point formats
Alpha architecture features three VAX floating-point formats:

1. **F floating**, 32 bits
2. **G floating**, 64 bits
3. **D floating**, 64 bits.

The memory storage of the above formats is illustrated in Fig. 6.2, and their CPU floating register storage in Fig. 6.3. Although A may be any address in memory, better performance will be attained if A is naturally aligned (divisible by 4 for F, and by 8 for G and D formats). The main difference between the G and D formats is that G has an 11-bit exponent field, while D has an eight-bit one. Thus, the G format has a much higher range. The D format is not fully supported on the Alpha, and no D floating-point arithmetic operations are provided. For VAX compatibility, exact D floating-point arithmetic may be provided by software emulation.

In the F floating-point format, the eight-bit exponent encodes the values of 0 to 255. An exponent value of 0 together with a sign bit (S) of 0 is interpreted as an F datum of zero value. Exponent values of 1 to 255 represent true binary exponents of -127 to 127 respectively. Thus, the bias is 128. An exponent value of 0, together with a sign bit of 1, is interpreted as a *reserved operand*. An attempt to use a reserved operand in a floating-point instruction causes an arithmetic exception. The range of an F datum is approximately $0.29(10)^{-38}$ to $1.7(10)^{38}$ decimal. The

F_floating Datum

15 14   7 6   0

| S | Exp. | Frac. Hi | : A |
| Fraction Lo | | | : A + 2 |

G_floating Datum

15 14   4 3   0

S	Exp.	Frac. Hi	: A
Fraction Midh			: A + 2
Fraction Midi			: A + 4
Fraction Lo			: A + 6

D_floating Datum

15 14   7 6   0

S	Exp.	Frac. Hi	: A
Fraction Midh			: A + 2
Fraction Midi			: A + 4
Fraction Lo			: A + 6

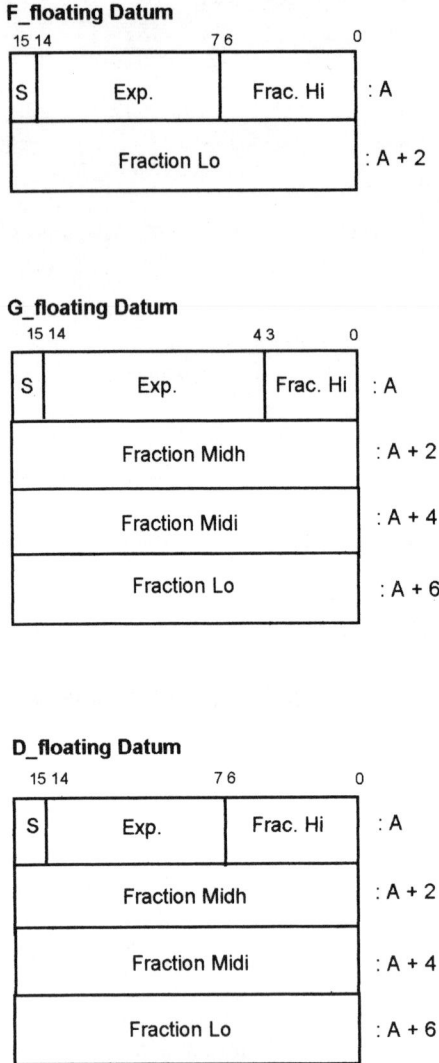

Fig. 6.2   Memory storage of VAX floating-point formats (*Courtesy of Digital Equipment Corp.*)

precision of an F datum is approximately 2^{-23}, typically 7 decimal digits.

In the G floating-point format, the 11-bit exponent encodes the values of 0 to 2047. An exponent value of 0, together with a sign 0, represent a zero value. Exponent values of 1 to 2047 represent true binary exponents of -1023 to 1023 respectively. An exponent value of 0, together with a sign bit of 1, represent a reserved operand. The G datum range is approximately $0.56(10)^{-308}$ to $0.9(10)^{308}$.

F_floating Register Format

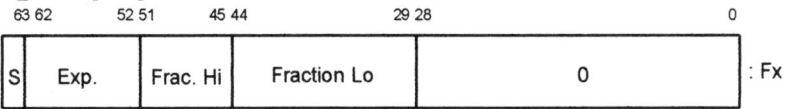

63 62	52 51	45 44	29 28	0	
S	Exp.	Frac. Hi	Fraction Lo	0	: Fx

G_floating Format

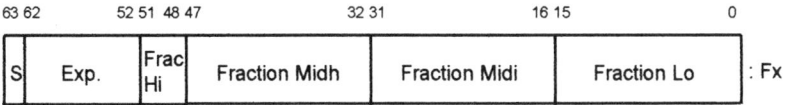

63 62	52 51 48 47	32 31	16 15	0	
S	Exp.	Frac Hi	Fraction Midh	Fraction Midi	Fraction Lo	: Fx

D_floating Register Format

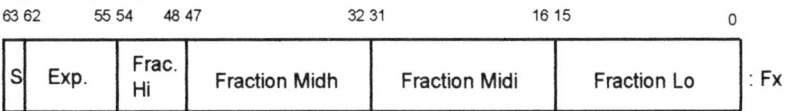

63 62	55 54 48 47	32 31	16 15	0	
S	Exp.	Frac. Hi	Fraction Midh	Fraction Midi	Fraction Lo	: Fx

Fig. 6.3 Register format of VAX floating-point formats *(Courtesy of Digital Equipment Corp.)*

The precision of a G datum is approximately 2^{-52}, typically 15 decimal digits. The precision of a D datum is approximately 2^{-55}, typically 16 decimal digits.

IEEE floating-point formats
The IEEE standard features the single-precision 32-bit (S floating), and the double-precision 64-bit (T floating) formats. Their memory and floating register storage are illustrated in Fig. 6.4. Location A may be anywhere in memory, but for better performance it should be naturally aligned, as in the case of the VAX formats.

Longword and quadword integers may be stored in FPU registers. Their storage in memory and in FPU registers is illustrated in Fig. 6.5.

Instruction formats
All Alpha AXP instructions are 32-bit (longword) long. The Alpha architecture features five basic instruction formats illustrated in Fig. 6.6. The notation used in Fig. 6.6 is the following:

Ra, Rb, Rc are integer register operands.
Fa, Fb, Fc are floating-point register operands.
disp is a displacement, added to the value in Rb to form a virtual address.
SBZ — should be zero.
LIT is an eight-bit literal value from 0 to 255.

All instruction formats have a six-bit (bits ⟨31:26⟩) major opcode field. Any unused

S_floating Datum

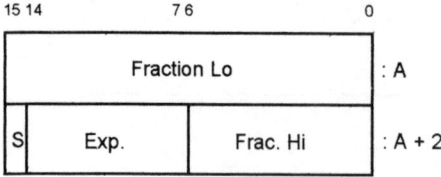

```
15 14          7 6              0
┌──────────────────────┬───┐
│      Fraction Lo     │ : A
├─┬──────────┬─────────┤
│S│   Exp.   │ Frac. Hi│ : A + 2
└─┴──────────┴─────────┘
```

S_floating Register Format

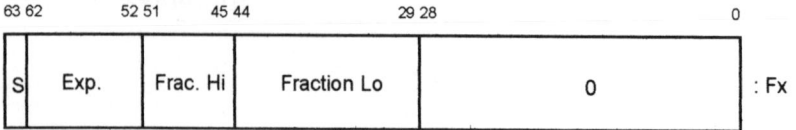

```
63 62      52 51    45 44        29 28            0
┌─┬────────┬────────┬──────────┬──────────────┐
│S│  Exp.  │Frac. Hi│Fraction Lo│      0       │ : Fx
└─┴────────┴────────┴──────────┴──────────────┘
```

T_floating Datum

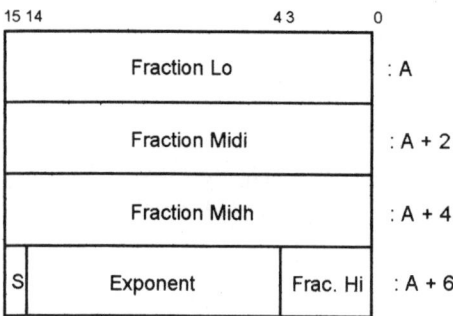

```
15 14                    4 3      0
┌──────────────────────────┐
│      Fraction Lo         │ : A
├──────────────────────────┤
│      Fraction Midi       │ : A + 2
├──────────────────────────┤
│      Fraction Midh       │ : A + 4
├─┬──────────────┬─────────┤
│S│   Exponent   │ Frac. Hi│ : A + 6
└─┴──────────────┴─────────┘
```

T_floating Register Format

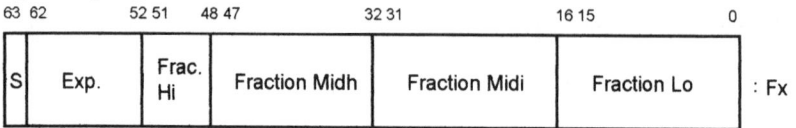

```
63 62      52 51  48 47        32 31          16 15         0
┌─┬────────┬─────┬────────────┬─────────────┬────────────┐
│S│  Exp.  │Frac.│Fraction Midh│Fraction Midi│Fraction Lo │ : Fx
│ │        │ Hi  │            │             │            │
└─┴────────┴─────┴────────────┴─────────────┴────────────┘
```

Fig. 6.4   Alpha IEEE floating-point formats *(Courtesy of Digital Equipment Corp.)*

register field (five bits) of an instruction (Ra, Rb, Fa, or Fb) must be set to a value of 31 (11111 binary). The five instruction formats will now be discussed separately.

(a) Memory instruction format
This format is used to transfer information between registers and memory, to load an effective address, and for subroutine jumps. The **Memory_disp** field is a byte offset. It is sign extended and added to the contents of register Rb to form a virtual

Longword Integer Datum

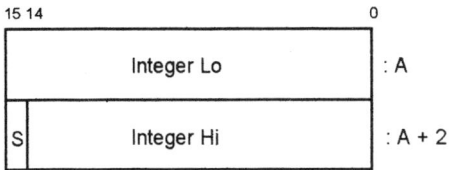

15 14   0

| Integer Lo | : A |
| Integer Hi | : A + 2 |

(S in left margin of Integer Hi row)

Longwood Integer Floating-Register Format

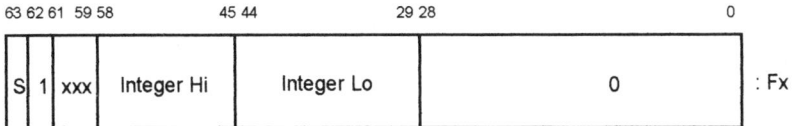

63 62 61 59 58   45 44   29 28   0

| S | 1 | xxx | Integer Hi | Integer Lo | 0 | : Fx |

Quadword Integer Datum

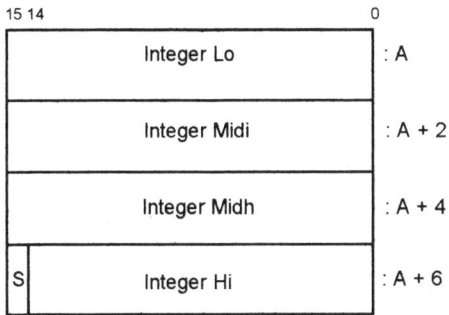

15 14   0

Integer Lo	: A
Integer Midi	: A + 2
Integer Midh	: A + 4
Integer Hi	: A + 6

(S in left margin of Integer Hi row)

Quadword Integer Floating-Register Format

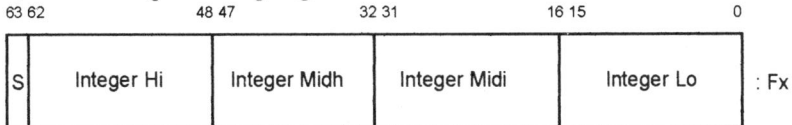

63 62   48 47   32 31   16 15   0

| S | Integer Hi | Integer Midh | Integer Midi | Integer Lo | : Fx |

Fig. 6.5   Integer data storage in memory and FPU registers *(Courtesy of Digital Equipment Corp.)*

address. The virtual address is used as a memory load/store address of a result value, depending on the specific instruction. For some instructions, the **Memory_disp** field is replaced by the **Function** field. It serves as an extension of the opcode that designates a set of miscellaneous instructions.

(b) Branch instruction format
The branch format is used for conditional branch instructions (in which case the Ra field contains the condition encoding) and for PC-relative subroutine jumps. As

118

Memory Instruction Format

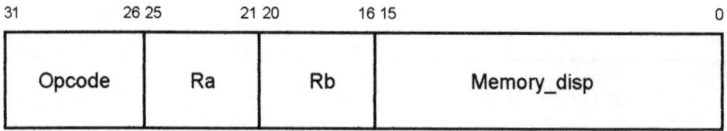

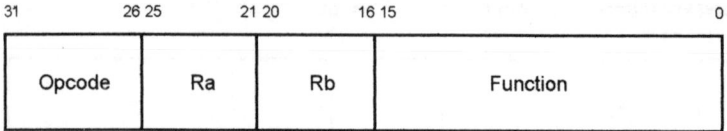

31	26 25	21 20	16 15	0
Opcode	Ra	Rb	Memory_disp	

31	26 25	21 20	16 15	0
Opcode	Ra	Rb	Function	

Branch Instruction Format

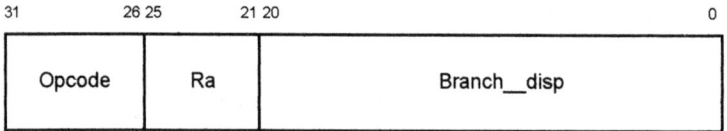

31	26 25	21 20	0
Opcode	Ra	Branch__disp	

Operate Instruction Format

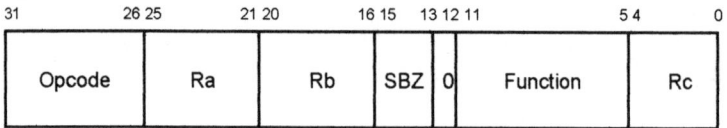

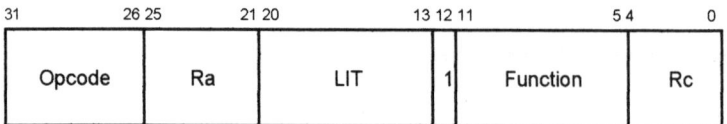

31	26 25	21 20	16 15	13 12 11	5 4	0
Opcode	Ra	Rb	SBZ	0 Function	Rc	

31	26 25	21 20	13 12 11	5 4	0
Opcode	Ra	LIT	1 Function	Rc	

Floating-Point Operate Instruction Format

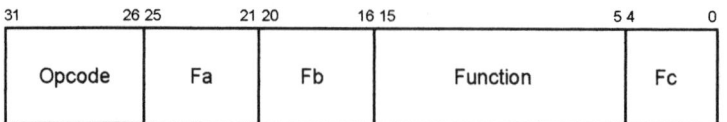

31	26 25	21 20	16 15	5 4	0
Opcode	Fa	Fb	Function	Fc	

PALcode Instruction Format

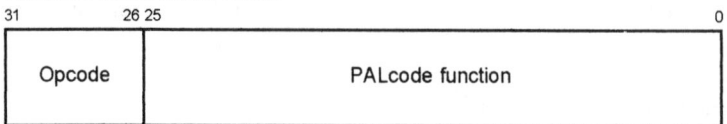

31	26 25	0
Opcode	PALcode function	

Fig. 6.6   Alpha instruction formats *(Courtesy of Digital Equipment Corp.)*

each instruction is decoded, the PC value is advanced to point to the next sequential instruction. The new PC value is referred to as the *updated PC*.

The **Branch_disp** field is treated as a longword offset. It is shifted left two bits (to address a longword boundary), sign-extended to 64 bits and added to the updated PC value to form the target virtual address.

(c) Operate instruction format

The operate instruction format is used for instructions that perform integer register-to-register operations. Fields Ra and Rb specify source operands. Field Rc specifies the destination. The **Function** field is an extension of the opcode. If bit 12 is 0, Rb specifies a source register operand. If bit 12 is 1, an eight-bit zero-extended literal constant is formed by bits $\langle 20:13 \rangle$ of the instruction. The literal is interpreted as a positive integer between 0 and 255 and is zero-extended to 64 bits.

(d) Floating-point operate instruction format

This format is used for instructions that perform floating-point register-to-register operations. The Fa and Fb fields specify floating-point register source operands. The Fc field specifies the destination. Floating-point convert instructions use a subset of the floating-point operate format and perform register-to-register conversion operations. The Fb operand specifies the source, the Fa field must be F31 (that is, zero), and Fc is naturally the destination.

(e) PALcode instruction format

The *privileged architecture library* (PAL) code format is used to specify extended processor functions (more on PALcode later in this section). The 26-bit **PALcode Function** field specifies the particular PALcode operation. The source and destination operands for PALcode instructions are supplied in fixed registers that are specified in the individual instruction descriptions. An opcode of zero and a PALcode function of zero specify the HALT instruction.

Addressing modes

The Alpha AXP architecture features four simple addressing modes, as practiced on RISC-type systems (see chapter 2):

1. Register.
2. Immediate.
3. Register indirect with displacement.
4. PC-relative.

Instruction set

The Alpha AXP architecture features the following types of instructions [Sits 92]:

1. Integer load and store.
2. Integer control.

3. Integer arithmetic.
4. Logical and shift.
5. Byte manipulation.
6. Floating-point load and store.
7. Floating-point control.
8. Floating-point operate.
9. Miscellaneous.

All of the instruction types will be discussed in this section group by group. Prior to that, some notation must be introduced. In most Alpha instructions, wherever applicable, the source operands are listed first, following the operation mnemonic, left to right, and the destination operand is listed last. The only exceptions are the load instructions (both integer and floating-point), where the destination register is listed first, following the instruction mnemonic.

An instruction operand is specified by the following attributes:

⟨name⟩. ⟨access type⟩ ⟨data type⟩

The ⟨name⟩ may be any of the registers: Ra, Rb, Rc, Fa, Fb, Fc, or:

disp — the displacement field of the instruction,
fnc — the PAL function field of the instruction,
#b — an integer literal operand in the Rb field of the instruction.

The ⟨access type⟩ is a letter denoting the operand access type. It may be one of the following:

Access Type	Meaning
a	Used in address calculation 'al' means scale by 4 (longwords) 'aq' means scale by 8 (quadwords) 'ab' means the operand is in byte units
i	The operand is an immediate literal
r	The operand is read only
m	The operand is both read and written
w	The operand is write only

The ⟨data type⟩ is a letter denoting the data type of the operand. It may be one of the following:

Data Type	Meaning
b	Byte
f	F_floating
g	G_floating
l	Longword
q	Quadword
s	S_floating
t	T_floating
w	Word
x	Specified by the instruction

Integer load and store instructions

The memory access integer load and store instructions (a total of 12) are summarized in Table 6.1.

Table 6.1 Integer Load and Store Instructions

Mnemonic	Operands	Operation
LDA	Ra.wq, disp.ab(Rb.ab)	Load address
LDAH	Ra.wq, disp.ab(Rb.ab)	Load address high
LDL	Ra.wq, disp.ab(Rb.ab)	Load SE longword
LDQ	Ra.wq, disp.ab(Rb.ab)	Load quadword
LDQ_U	Ra.wq, disp.ab(Rb.ab)	Load quadword unaligned
LDL_L	Ra.wq, disp.ab(Rb.ab)	Load SE longword locked
LDQ_L	Ra.wq, disp.ab(Rb.ab)	Load quadword locked
STL	Ra.rq, disp.ab(Rb.ab)	Store longword
STQ	Ra.rq, disp.ab(Rb.ab)	Store quadword
STL_C	Ra.mq, disp.ab(Rb.ab)	Store longword conditional
STQ_C	Ra.mq, disp.ab(Rb.ab)	Store quadword conditional
STQ_U	Ra.rq, disp.ab(Rb.ab)	Store quadword unaligned

where

SE - sign-extended

In all instructions in Table 6.1, except LDAH, the virtual memory address is computed by adding the content of register Rb to the sign-extended 16-bit displacement:

$$Ra \leftarrow Rbv + SE\,(disp)$$

where Rbv is the value in Rb and SE = sign extended.

For LDAH the displacement is multiplied by $65536 = 2^{16}$ and added sign-extended to Rbv:

$$Ra \leftarrow Rbv + SE\,(disp*65536)$$

The load locked and store conditional instructions are intended for multiprocessor implementation and will not be discussed in this section.

Integer control instructions

Integer control instructions include conditional and unconditional branch, branch to subroutine, and jump instructions. The integer control instructions (a total of 14) are summarized in Table 6.2.

The displacement field of the instruction is used to encode this information as follows:

disp⟨15:14⟩	Mnemonic	Predicted Target ⟨15:0⟩	Prediction Stack Action
00	JMP	PC+{4*disp⟨13:0⟩}	–
01	JSR	PC+{4*disp⟨13:0⟩}	Push PC
10	RET	Prediction stack	Pop
11	JSR_COROUTINE	Prediction stack	Pop, push PC

The four different opcodes set different bit patterns in disp⟨15:14⟩, and the hint operand sets disp⟨13:0⟩.

The updated PC value (updated after the instruction is fetched) is stored in register Ra, and then the PC is loaded with the target virtual address, supplied from register Rb. The low two bits of Rb are ignored. Fields Ra and Rb may specify the same register; the target address calculation using the old value of Rb is done before the new value is assigned.

The Alpha AXP architecture specifies three types of branching *hints* in instructions [Sits 93]:

(1) Architected static branch prediction rule: forward conditional branches are predicted not-taken, and backward ones taken. To the extent that compilers and hardware implementations follow this rule, programs can run more quickly with little hardware cost. This hint does not preclude doing dynamic branch prediction

Table 6.2 Integer Control Instructions

Mnemonic	Operands	Operation
BEQ	Ra.rq, disp.al	Branch if Rav = 0
BGE	Ra.rq, disp.al	Branch if Rav >= 0
BGT	Ra.rq, disp.al	Branch if Rav > 0
BLBC	Ra.rq, disp.al	Branch if Ra LSB = 0
BLBS	Ra.rq, disp.al	Branch if Ra LSB = 1
BLE	Ra.rq, disp.al	Branch if Rav <= 0
BLT	Ra.rq, disp.al	Branch if Rav < 0
BNE	Ra.rq, disp.al	Branch if Rav not = 0
BR	Ra.wq, disp.al	Unconditional branch
BSR	Ra.wq, disp.al	Branch to subroutine
JMP	Ra.wq,(Rb.ab),hint	Jump
JSR	Ra.wq,(Rb.ab),hint	Jump to subroutine
RET	Ra.wq,(Rb.ab),hint	Return from subroutine
JSR_COROUTINE	Ra.wq,(Rb.ab),hint	Jump to subr. return

where

>= is greater or equal

<= is less than or equal   '

not= is not equal

hint is an encoding to possible branch prediction logic.

in an implementation, but it may reduce the need to do so.

(2) Describes computed jump targets. Otherwise unused instruction bits are defined to give the low bits of the most likely target, using the same target calculation as unconditional branches. The 14 bits provided are enough to specify the instruction offset within a page, which is often enough to start a fastest-level instruction cache fetch many cycles before the actual target value is known.

(3) Describes subroutine and coroutine returns. By marking each branch and jump as 'call', 'return', or 'neither', the architecture provides in implementation enough information to maintain a small stack of likely subroutine return addresses. This implementation stack can be used to prefetch subroutine returns quickly.

The conditional move instructions and the branching hints eliminate some branches and speed up the remaining ones without compromising multiple instruction issue.

Example: Given a jump to subroutine instruction JSR R26, (R27), 0x4123;
The hint is the hexadecimal value 4123. The most significant two bits of the hint 01 specify that the computed jump is a call to a subroutine (JSR), and not a return or a regular jump. The remaining 14 bits of the hint (00 0001 0010 0011) are an offset of the most likely jump target (the most likely value to be in R27 at run time). The actual calculation using these bits is exactly as the PC-relative calculation: multiply by 4 (shift two bits left) and add to the updated PC.

Integer arithmetic instructions

The integer arithmetic instructions of Alpha (a total of 20) are listed in Table 6.3.
The operands for the integer arithmetic instructions may be of two forms:

Ra.rq, Rb.rq, Rc.wq

or

Ra.rq, #b.ib, Rc.wq

The ADD instructions work in general as follows:

$$Rc \leftarrow Rav + Rbv$$

For a longword (32-bit) addition ADDL, the high-order 32 bits of Ra and Rb are ignored, and the sum is sign-extended:

$$Rc \leftarrow SE[(Rav + Rbv)\langle 31:0\rangle]$$

In the scaled add instructions, register Ra is shifted left by two bits (for S4), or by three bits (for S8), and then added to Rb or a literal with the sum going to Rc. For a longword addition, the upper 32 bits of Ra and Rb are ignored.

In the compare instructions (CMPxx, CMPUxx), the value in register Ra is compared to the value in register Rb, or to a literal #b. If the specified relationship is true, the value one is stored into Rc. Otherwise, Rc is cleared.

Example: CMPLE R1, R2, R5; compare signed quadword less than or equal.

Rav = R1 = 50, Rbv = R2 = 100, Rav < Rbv; relationship LE (less or equal) is true, therefore Rc = R5 $\leftarrow$ 1

In the multiplication instruction MULQ, Rav is multiplied by Rbv and the 64-bit product is stored in Rc. In the longword multiply, the high 32 bits of Ra and Rb are ignored, and the sign-extended 32-bit product is stored in Rc.

Table 6.3 Integer Arithmetic Instructions

Mnemonic	Operation
ADDL	Add longword
ADDQ	Add quadword
S4ADDL	Scaled add longword by 4
S8ADDL	Scaled add longword by 8
S4ADDQ	Scaled add quadword by 4
S8ADDQ	Scaled add quadword by 8
CMPEQ	Compare signed quadword =
CMPLT	Compare signed quadword <
CMPLE	Compare signed quadword < or =
CMPULT	Compare unsigned quadword <
CMPULE	Compare unsigned quadword < or =
MULL	Multiply longword
MULQ	Multiply quadword
UMULH	Unsigned multiply quadword high
SUBL	Subtract longword
SUBQ	Subtract quadword
S4SUBL	Scaled subtract longword by 4
S8SUBL	Scaled subtract longword by 8
S4SUBQ	Scaled subtract quadword by 4
S8SUBQ	Scaled subtract quadword by 8

Thus, for MULQ: $Rc \leftarrow Rav * Rbv$

For MULL: $Rc \leftarrow SE[(Rav * Rbv)\langle 31:0 \rangle]$

If an overflow occurs in MULQ, the least significant 64 bits of the product are written into Rc. The upper 64 bits of the 128-bit product can be generated using the UMULH (unsigned multiply quadword high) instruction, in which only the upper 64 bits of the 128-bit unsigned product of Ra and Rb (or a literal) are stored into Rc.

For UMULH: $Rc \leftarrow$ Unsigned $(Rav * Rbv)\langle 127 : 64 \rangle$

In the subtract instructions, the value of Rb or a literal is subtracted from the value of Ra and the result is stored in Rc. As in ADD, the upper 32 bits of Ra and Rb are ignored in a longword subtraction, and the result is sign-extended.

For SUBQ: $Rc \leftarrow Rav - Rbv$

For SUBL: $Rc \leftarrow SE\,[(Rav - Rbc)\langle 31 : 0 \rangle]$

The scaled subtract instructions work in complete analogy with the scaled add instructions. For instance, in the S8SUBQ instruction, Ra is left-shifted by three bits before Rbv is subtracted from it, with the 64-bit difference going to Rc.

The Alpha AXP architecture does not feature an integer divide instruction; however, a floating-point divide is available.

Logical and shift instructions

The Alpha AXP logical instructions perform quadword Boolean operations. The conditional move instructions (not featured in most other systems) in this group perform conditional transfers from register to register without a branch. The shift instructions perform left and right logical shift and right arithmetic shift. These instructions (a total of 17) are summarized in Table 6.4.

The operand specification for the above instructions is:

Ra.rq, Rb.rq, Rc.wq

or

Ra.rq, #b.ib, Rc.wq

The logical operations are performed as follows:

Mnemonic	Operation
AND	$Rc \leftarrow Rav$ AND Rbv
BIC	$Rc \leftarrow Rav$ AND (NOT Rbv)
BIS	$Rc \leftarrow Rav$ OR Rbv
ORNOT	$Rc \leftarrow Rav$ OR (NOT Rbv)
XOR	$Rc \leftarrow Rav$ XOR Rbv
EQV	$Rc \leftarrow Rav$ XOR (NOT Rbv)

The pure complement function NOT can be performed by doing the ORNOT with Ra = R31 (always zero).

Table 6.4 Logical and Shift Instructions

Mnemonic	Operation
AND	Logical AND
BIC	Logical AND with complement
BIS	Logical OR
EQV	Logical equivalence (XORNOT)
ORNOT	Logical OR with complement
XOR	Exclusive OR
CMOVxx	Conditional move integer
SLL	Shift left logical
SRA	Shift right arithmetic
SRL	Shift right logical

Thus: ORNOT R31, Rb, Rb; 0 OR (NOT Rbv) = NOT Rbv → Rb.

The OR mnemonic may be used instead of BIS. It has the same meaning and it is accepted by the assembler.

The CMOVxx instruction (xx is the condition mnemonic) works by testing Rav for the specified condition. If the condition is true, the content of Rb is transferred to Rc. There are eight conditions featured on CMOVxx (thus there are eight CMOVxx instructions):

Condition (xx)	CMOVE if register Ra:
EQ	Equal to zero
GE	Greater than or equal to zero
GT	Greater than zero
LBC	Low bit clear
LBS	Low bit set
LE	Less than or equal to zero
LT	Less than zero
NE	Not equal to zero

In the shift instructions register, Ra is shifted left or right 0 to 63 bits. The bit count (by how many bits shifted) is either in register Rb (in $Rbv\langle 5:0\rangle$) or is given as a literal #b. The shifted result is stored in Rc. In the logical shift, zero bits are propagated into the vacated bit positions. In the arithmetic shift, the sign bit (Rav⟨63⟩) is propagated into the vacated bit positions.

Byte-manipulation instructions

The Alpha AXP architecture features five types of byte-manipulation instructions (a total of 24 instructions) within registers. This is an unusual feature compared to other systems. The byte-manipulation instructions can be used with the load and store unaligned instructions to manipulate short unaligned strings of bytes. The five types of byte-manipulation instruction will be discussed next one after the other, along with their particular options. All of the byte-manipulation instructions have the same operand specifications as the logical and shift instructions, described above.

1. Compare byte

This group contains a single instruction CMPBGE (Compare byte greater or equal). It does eight parallel unsigned byte comparisons between corresponding bytes of Rav and Rbv, storing the eight results in the low eight bits of Rc. The high 56 bits of Rc are set to zero. Bit 0 of Rc corresponds to byte 0 of Ra and Rb, bit 1 of Rc corresponds to byte 1, and so on. A result bit is set in Rc if the corresponding byte of Rav is greater than or equal to that of Rbv (unsigned). The compare byte instruction allows character-string search and compare to be done eight bytes at a time.

2. Extract byte

This group features seven options for the EXTxx instruction:

EXTxx Option	Extract:
BL	Byte low
WL	Word low
LL	Longword low
QL	Quadword low
WH	Word high
LH	Longword high
QH	Quadword high

The EXTxL shifts register Ra right by 0 to 7 bytes, inserts zeros into vacated bit positions, and then extracts 1, 2, 4, or 8 bytes into register Rc. Instruction EXTxH shifts register Ra left by 0 to 7 bytes, inserts zeros into vacated bit positions, and then extracts 2, 4, or 8 bytes into register Rc. The number of bytes to shift is specified by the three least significant bits of Rb (Rbv⟨2:0⟩) or by an immediate value of a literal #b. The number of bytes to extract is specified in the function code. Remaining bytes are filled with zeros. A single EXTxL instruction can perform byte or word loads (the load instructions work with longwords and quadwords only), pulling the datum out of a quadword and placing it in the low end of a register with high-order zeros. A pair of EXTxL/EXTxH instructions can perform unaligned loads, pulling the two parts of an unaligned datum out of two quadwords and placing the parts in result registers, where they are ready for combining into the full datum by a simple OR.

Example: Assume a quadword data item HGFE DCBA (a string of byte characters) is stored unaligned in two memory quadword locations: X(R11) and X+7(R11). The three least significant bits of X(R11) are 101(or 5). The value in X(R11) is CBAx xxxx, and the value in X+7(R11) is xxxH GFED (x is a 'don't care' byte). The following is a small program placing the complete quadword datum into register R1:

LDQ_U R1, X(R11); R1 ← CBAx xxxx

LDQ_U R2, X+7(R11); R2 ← xxxH GFED

LDA R3, X(R11); R3⟨2:0⟩ ← 101 (=5)

EXTQL R1, R3, R1; R1 ← 0000 0CBA

EXTQH R2, R3, R2; R2 ← HGFE D000

BIS R2, R1, R1; R1 ← HGFE DCBA

3. Byte insert
The byte insert instruction INSxx has seven options:

INSxx Option	Insert:
BL	Byte low
WL	Word low
LL	Longword low
QL	Quadword low
WH	Word high
LH	Longword high
QH	Quadword high

INSxL and INSxH shift bytes from register Ra and insert them into a field of zeros, storing the result in register Rc. Register Rbv⟨2:0⟩ or a literal #b selects the shift amount (0 to 7), and the function code selects the maximum field width: 1, 2, 4, or 8 bytes. The instructions can generate a byte, word, longword, or quadword datum that is spread across two registers at an arbitrary byte alignment.

4. Byte mask

The byte mask MSKxx instruction has seven options, the same as the byte insert and byte extract instructions (MSKBL, MSKWL, MSKLL, MSKQL, MSKWH, MSKLH, MSKQH). MSKxL and MSKxH set selected bytes of register Ra to zero, storing the result in register Rc. Register Rbv⟨2:0⟩ or a literal selects the starting position of the field of zero bytes, and the function code selects the maximum width: 1, 2, 4, or 8 bytes. The instructions generate a byte, word, longword, or quadword field of zeros that can spread across two registers at an arbitrary byte alignment. The INSxx and MSKxx instructions position new data and zero out old data in registers for storing bytes, words, and unaligned data.

5. Zero bytes

This group contains two instructions:

ZAP   Zero bytes
ZAPNOT   Zero bytes not

These instructions set selected bytes of register Ra to zero, and store the result in register Rc. Register Rbv⟨7:0⟩ or a literal selects the bytes to be zeroed; bit 0 of Rb corresponds to byte 0 of Ra, bit 1 of Rb corresponds to byte 1 of Ra, and so on. A result byte is set to zero if the corresponding bit of Rb is a one for ZAP and a zero for ZAPNOT. The ZAP instructions allow zeroing of arbitrary patterns of bytes in a register.

The CMPBGE and ZAP instructions allow very fast implementations of the C language string routines, among other uses.

Floating-point load and store instructions

The floating-point load and store instructions (a total of eight) move floating-point data between memory and floating-point registers. The instructions are summarized in Table 6.5.

In the load instructions, Fa is the destination register. The memory address is computed by adding a sign-extended displacement to Rbv for both load and store instructions. Register Fa serves as the source register in the store instructions.

Floating-point control instructions

There are six floating-point branch instructions. These instructions test the value of a floating-point register Fa, and conditionally change the value of the PC. The operand format for all six instructions is:

Fa.rq, disp.al

The instructions are summarized in Table 6.6.

These instructions use PC-relative addressing. If the specified condition for Fav with respect to zero is true, the displacement value, shifted left by two bits, is added to PC, to form a new branch target address.

Table 6.5 Floating-point Load and Store Instructions

Mnemonic	Operands	Operation
LDF	Fa.wf, disp.ab(Rb.ab)	Load F_floating
LDG	Fa.wg, disp.ab(Rb.ab)	Load G_floating
LDS	Fa.ws, disp.ab(Rb.ab)	Load S_floating
LDT	Fa.wt, disp.ab(Rb.ab)	Load T_floating
STF	Fa.rf, disp.ab(Rb.ab)	Store F_floating
STG	Fa.rg, disp.ab(Rb.ab)	Store G_floating
STS	Fa.rs, disp.ab(Rb.ab)	Store S_floating
STT	Fa.rt, disp.ab(Rb.ab)	Store T_floating

Table 6.6 Floating-point Branch Instructions

Mnemonic	Operation
FBEQ	Floating branch equal
FBGE	Floating branch > or equal
FBGT	Floating branch >
FBLE	Floating branch < or equal
FBLT	Floating branch <
FBNE	Floating branch not equal

Floating-point operate instructions
This is the largest group of instructions featured by the Alpha architecture for a total of 47. It can be subdivided into four categories:

1. Arithmetic   16
2. Convert   13
3. Compare   7
4. Miscellaneous   11

The floating-point arithmetic instructions are summarized in Table 6.7.

Table 6.7 Floating-point Arithmetic Instructions

Mnemonic	Operation
ADDF	Add F_floating
ADDG	Add G_floating
ADDS	Add S_floating
ADDT	Add T_floating
SUBF	Subtract F_floating
SUBG	Subtract G_floating
SUBS	Subtract S_floating
SUBT	Subtract T_floating
MULF	Multiply F_floating
MULG	Multiply G_floating
MULS	Multiply S_floating
MULT	Multiply T_floating
DIVF	Divide F_floating
DIVG	Divide G_floating
DIVS	Divide S_floating
DIVT	Divide T_floating

The operands for all floating-point arithmetic instructions are defined as follows:

Fa.rx, Fb.rx, Fc.wx

The four arithmetic operations are performed as follows:

Addition:	$Fc \leftarrow Fav + Fbv$
Subtraction:	$Fc \leftarrow Fav - Fbv$
Multiplication:	$Fc \leftarrow Fav * Fbv$
Division:	$Fc \leftarrow Fav / Fbv$

The floating-point convert operations are summarized in Table 6.8.

Table 6.8 Floating-point Convert Operations

Mnemonic	Operands	Operation
CVTLQ	Fb.rq, Fc.wx	Convert longword to quadword
CVTQL	Fb.rq, Fc.wx	Convert quadword to longword
CVTDG	Fb.rx, Fc.wx	Convert D_ to G_floating
CVTGD	Fb.rx, Fc.wx	Convert G_ to D_floating
CVTGF	Fb.rx, Fc.wx	Convert G_ to F_floating
CVTGQ	Fb.rx, Fc.wq	Convert G_floating to quadword
CVTQF	Fb.rq, Fc.wx	Convert quadword to F_floating
CVTQG	Fb.rq, Fc.wx	Convert quadword to G_floating
CVTQS	Fb.rq, Fc.wx	Convert quadword to S_floating
CVTQT	Fb.rq, Fc.wx	Convert quadword to T_floating
CVTTQ	Fb.rx, Fc.wq	Convert T-floating to quadword
CVTTS	Fb.rx, Fc.wq	Convert T_ to S_floating
CVTST	Fb.rx, Fc.wx	Convert S_ to T_floating

In all of the above operations, Fb contains the datum to be converted, and Fc is the destination where the converted datum is stored.

There are two types of floating-point compare instructions:

1. CMPGxx Compare G_floating, operands: **Fa.rg, Fb.rg, Fc.wq**
where xx may take the options:

EQ equal
LE less than or equal
LT less than

for a total of three instructions.

2. CMPTxx Compare T_floating, operands: **Fa.rx, Fb.rx, Fc.wq**
where xx may take the options EQ, LE, LT as for CMPGxx, and another option:

UN unordered

for a total of four instructions (total seven compare instructions).

In all of the floating-point compare instructions the operands in Fa and Fb are compared. If the specified relationship is true, a non-zero floating-point value (0.5 for CMPGxx, 2.0 for CMPTxx) is written into Fc. Otherwise, a true zero is written into Fc.

The floating-point miscellaneous operate instructions (a total of 11) are summarized in Table 6.9.

Table 6.9 Floating-point Miscellaneous Operate Instructions

Mnemonic	Operands	Operation
CPYS	Fa.rq, Fb.rq, Fc.wq	Copy sign
CPYSE	Fa.rq, Fb.rq, Fc.wq	Copy sign and exponent
CPYSN	Fa.rq, Fb.rq, Fc.wq	Copy sign negate
FCMOVxx	Fa.rq, Fb.rq, Fc.wq	Floating conditional move
MF_FPCR	Fa.rq, Fa.rq, Fa.wq	Move from FPCR
MT_FPCR	Fa.rq, Fa.rq, Fa.wq	Move to FPCR

The xx in FCMOVxx stands for six possible conditions:

EQ   equal to zero
GE   greater than or equal to zero
GT   greater than zero
LE   less than or equal to zero
LT   less than zero
NE   not equal to zero

featuring six floating-point conditional move instructions.

For the CPYS and CPYSN instructions, the sign bit of Fa is fetched (and complemented in the case of CPYSN) and concatenated with the exponent and fraction bits from Fb; the result is stored in Fc. For CPYSE, the sign and exponent bits from Fa are fetched and concatenated with the fraction bits from Fb; the result is stored in Fc. These instructions can be used to generate special operations not available in the regular instruction set, such as:

Register move: CPYS Fx, Fx, Fy
Floating-point absolute value: F31, Fx, Fy (F31 is always zero)
Floating-point negation: CPYSN Fx, Fx, Fy

In the FCMOVxx instructions, register Fa is tested and compared with zero. If the specified relationship xx is true, Fbv is moved to Fc. Otherwise, no operation is performed.

In the MF_FPCR and MT_FPCR instructions, the content of FPCR is moved to Fa, and Fav is moved to FPCR respectively. The same register Fa must be specified in all three fields.

Miscellaneous instructions

There are seven miscellaneous instructions, listed in Table 6.10.

Table 6.10 Miscellaneous Instructions

Mnemonic	Operands	Operation
CALL_PAL	fnc.ir	Call PAL routine
FETCH	0(Rb.ab)	Prefetch data
FETCH_M	0(Rb.ab)	Prefetch data, modify intent
MB	--	Memory barrier
WMB	--	Write memory barrier
RPCC	Ra.wq	Read process cycle counter
TRAPB	--	Trap barrier

The CALL_PAL instruction causes a trap to PALcode (discussed later in this section).

In the FETCH and FETCH_M instructions, an aligned 512-byte block of data is specified by Rbv. An implementation may optionally attempt to move all or part of this block (or a larger surrounding block) of data to a faster-access part of the memory hierarchy, in anticipation of subsequent load or store instructions that may access that data. The FETCH instruction is a hint to the implementation that may allow faster execution. The FETCH_M instruction gives the additional hint that modifications (store instructions) to some or all of the data block are expected.

The MB instruction is required only in multiprocessor systems. It facilitates synchronization between dependent iterations of loops, scheduled to run on different processors [Hwan93, Tabk 90]. The MB instruction guarantees that all subsequent load and store instructions will not access memory until after all previous load and store instructions have accessed memory, as observed by other processors. When strict ordering of operations is required, as in some multiprocessor synchronization operations, the MB instruction forces *serialization* of operations. Software then controls serialization, enforcing it only when necessary [McLe 93]. In Alpha implementations, the memory unit uses the MB instruction by retiring all previous load misses and write operations before sending the MB to the BIU. The instruction unit stalls new memory instructions until the MB has been completed [BaKe 95]. The memory unit implements the WMB instruction by ensuring that all write operations, that are pending in the write buffer at the time when the WMB is executed, are completed before any write operation added after the WMB is sent to the cache control unit. In the RPCC instruction the content of the process cycle counter (PCC) is written into Ra. The PCC is used for timing intervals in each processor in a multiprocessor system. The low-order 32 bits of PCC are incremented once per N CPU cycles. N is an implementation-specific integer with a possible value of 1 to 16.

The TRAPB instruction allows software to guarantee that, in a pipelined implementation, all previous arithmetic instructions will complete without incurring any arithmetic traps before any instructions after the TRAPB are issued.

Privileged architecture library (PAL) code
The PALcode [Sits 92b] provides a mechanism to implement the following functions without resorting to a microcoded machine:

1. Instructions that require complex sequencing as an atomic operation.
2. Instructions that require VAX-style interlocked memory accesses.
3. Privileged instructions.
4. Memory management control.
5. Context swapping.
6. Interrupt and exception dispatching.
7. Power-up initialization and booting.
8. Console functions.
9. Emulation of instructions with no hardware support.

PAL functions are implemented in Alpha architecture in standard machine code, resident in main memory. PALcode environment differs from the normal environment in the following ways:

1. There is complete control of the machine state, allowing all functions of the machine to be controlled.
2. Interrupts are disabled, allowing the system to provide multi-instruction sequences as atomic operations.
3. Implementation-specific hardware functions are enabled, allowing access to low-level system hardware.
4. Instruction stream memory management traps are prevented, allowing PALcode to implement memory management functions such as translation buffer (TB) fills.

PALcode uses the Alpha instruction set for most of its operations. There are five opcodes reserved to implement additional PALcode functions: PALRES 0, 1, 2, 3, 4. These instructions produce an illegal instruction trap if executed outside of the PALcode environment. PALcode is allocated space in the physical memory.

The Alpha AXP architecture is intended to be implemented on a series of high-performance microprocessor products. The first Alpha AXP implementations are described in the subsequent section.

6.3 Alpha AXP Implementations

The first implementation of the Alpha AXP architecture is the 21064 microprocessor chip [DECM 92, Dobb 92, McLe 93]. The 21064 is fabricated in a 0.75 micron CMOS technology utilizing three levels of metallization and optimized for 3.3 volt operation. The die size is 16.8 × 13.9 mm and it contains 1.68 million transistors. Its initial operating frequency is within the 150 to 200MHz interval. Power dissipation at 200MHz is 30 watts. The processor is a two-issue superscalar. The chip includes a dual cache, 8 Kbyte instruction and 8 Kbyte data. It also includes a four-entry, 32 byte-per-entry write buffer, a pipelined 64-bit integer execution unit with a 32 × 64 register file, and a pipelined FPU with a 32 × 64 register file of its own. The pin interface includes integral support for an external secondary cache of 128 Kbytes up to 8 Mbytes. The internal caches are direct-mapped. All caches have 32 bytes/line. The internal data cache is a write-through, read allocate, physical cache. The chip package is a 431-pin pin grid array (PGA) with 140 pins dedicated to power supply voltage and ground.

A block diagram of the 21064 is shown in Fig. 6.7. It features the following main subsystems:

IBOX — issues instructions (two at a time), maintains the integer pipeline, and performs PC calculations. It decodes two instructions in parallel and checks availability of resources. There is no out-of-order issue. There will be an issue if appropriate resources are available. If resources are not available for the first instruction, there will be no issue. The IBOX contains branch prediction logic, instruction translator buffers (ITBs), interrupt logic, and performance counters (issues, non-issues, total cycles, pipe dry, pipe freeze, cache misses). There are two ITBs:

1. Small-page ITB, eight-entry, fully associative, contains recently used instruction stream page table entries (PTEs) for 8 Kbyte pages.
2. Large-page ITB, four-entry, fully associative, for 512 × 8 Kbyte pages (4 Mbyte).

EBOX — integer execution unit. It contains a 64-bit adder, logic box, barrel shifter, bypassers, integer multiplier, 32 × 64 integer register file (IRF) with four read and two write ports.

ABOX — address generation unit. It contains address translation datapath, load silo, data cache interface, internal processor registers (IPRs), and the bus interface unit (BIU), and a 32-entry, fully associative data translation buffer (DTB). The load silo is a memory reference pipeline that can accept a new load or store instruction every cycle until a data cache fill is required. The BIU has an external 128-bit data bus.

FBOX — the FPU. It contains in addition to the operation units a 32×64 floating-point register file (FRF), and a user accessible floating-point control register (FPCR).

ICACHE — instruction cache. 8 Kbytes, direct-mapped, physical-addressed, 32 bytes/line.

DCACHE — data cache. 8 Kbytes, direct-mapped, physical-addressed, 32 bytes/line, write-through, read allocate.

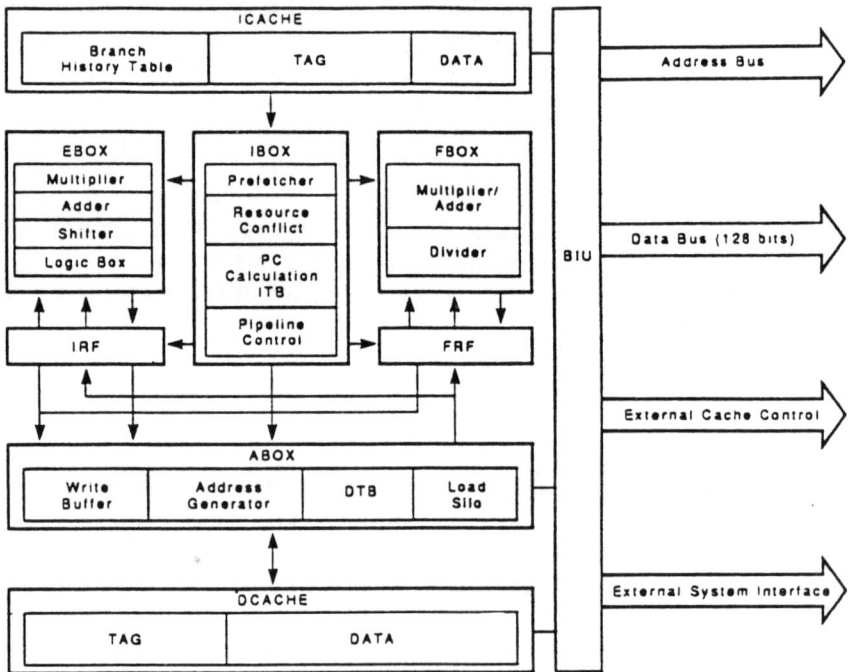

Fig. 6.7   Block diagram of the 21064 *(Courtesy of Digital Equipment Corp.)*

An example of an external interface interconnection of the 21064 is shown in Fig. 6.8 [Dobb 92]. It is designed to directly support an off-chip secondary cache (also called backup cache, or B-cache) that can range from 128 Kbytes to 8 Mbytes and can be constructed from ordinary SRAMs. The interface is designed to allow all cache policy decisions to be controlled by logic external to the CPU chip. There are three control bits associated with each B-cache line: valid (V), shared (S), and dirty (D). The chip completes a B-cache read as long as valid is true. A write is processed by the CPU only if valid is true and shared is false. When a write is performed, the dirty bit is set to true. In all other cases, the chip defers to an external state machine to complete the transaction. This state machine operates synchronously with the sysCLK output (see Fig. 6.8) of the chip, which is a mode-controlled submultiple of the CPU clock rate ranging from divide by 2 to divide by 8. It is also possible to operate without a B-cache. As shown in Fig. 6.8, the external cache is connected between the CPU chip and the memory system interface. The cache access begins with the address delivered on the adr_h lines and results in ctl, tag, data, and check bits appearing at the chip receivers within the prescribed access time. In 128-bit mode, B-cache accesses require two external data cycles to transfer the 32-byte ($256 = 2 \times 128$ bits) cache line across the 16-byte pin bus. In 64-bit mode, it is four cycles. This yields a maximum B-cache read bandwidth of 1.2 Gbytes/sec and a write bandwidth of 711 Mbytes/sec. Internal cache lines can be invalidated at the rate of one line per cycle using the dedicated invalidate address pins iAdr_h⟨12:5⟩.

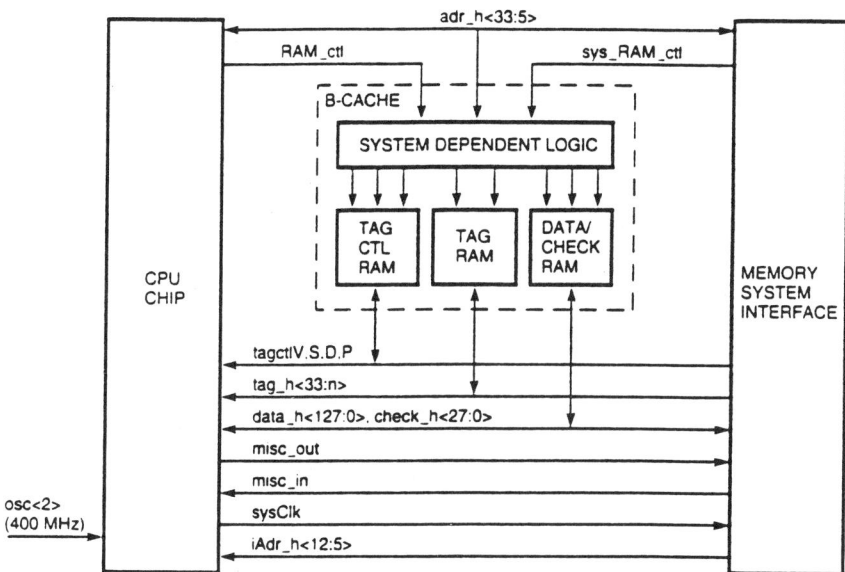

Fig. 6.8   CPU external interface *(Courtesy of Digital Equipment Corp.)*

The 21064 IU and FPU pipelines are illustrated in Fig. 6.9 [Dobb 92]. The pipeline stages are listed in Table 6.11. The integer pipeline is seven stages deep. The first four stages are associated with instruction fetching, decoding, and scoreboard checking of operands for possible data dependency (see chapters 1 and 2). Pipeline stages 0 through 3 can be stalled. Beyond stage 3, however, all pipeline stages advance every cycle. Most ALU operations complete in cycle 4

(A1). Primary cache accesses complete in cycle 6 (WR); so cache delay is three cycles. The instruction stream is based on autonomous prefetching in cycles 0 and 1 with the final resolution of ICACHE hit not occurring until cycle 5. The prefetcher includes a branch history table and a subroutine return stack. The architecture provides a convention for compilers to predict branch decisions and destination addresses, including those for register indirect jumps. The penalty for branch mispredict is four cycles.

The FPU pipeline is 10 stages deep. It is identical and mostly shared with the IU pipeline in stages 0 through 3. All operations, 32- and 64-bit have the same timing (except divide). Divide is handled by a nonpipelined, single bit per cycle, dedicated divide unit. In cycle 4 (F1), the register file data are formatted to fraction, exponent, and sign. In the first stage, adder exponent difference is calculated and a $3 \times$ (multiplicand) is generated for multiplies. In addition, a predictive leading 1 or 0 detector using the input operands is initiated for use in result normalization. In cycles 5 (F2) and 6 (F3), for add/subtract, alignment or normalization shift i s performed. For both single- and double-precision multiplication, the multiply i s done in a radix-8 pipelined array multiplier. I n cycles 7 (F4) and 8 (F5), the final addition and rounding are performed in parallel and the final result is selected and driven back to the register file in cycle 9 (FWR). With an allowed bypass of the register write data, floating-point delay is six cycles. The superscalar dual issue of instructions is restricted to the following pairs:

Any load/store in parallel with any operate
An integer operate in parallel with a floating-point operate
A floating-point operate and a floating-point branch
An integer operate and an integer branch.

The two instructions, issued together, can be swapped or serialized by hardware if required. The system supports pages of 8KB, 64KB, 512KB, and 4MB.

A number of subsequent Alpha AXP implementation microprocessors have been produced by DEC:

The **21064A** is a 0.5 micron, 3-metal layer, CMOS-5, 2.5 million transistors, 431-pin PGA microprocessor, running at frequencies ranging from 225 to 275MHz. It has double the on-chip cache of the 21064: 16KB instruction, 16KB data, for a total of 32KB.

The second major implementation of the Alpha AXP architecture is the 21164, announced in the fall of 1994 [BaKe 95]. It is a 9.3 million transistor, 0.5 micron CMOS microprocessor, operating at frequencies of 250 to 300MHz [EdRu 94]. The 21164 is a four-issue superscalar. It is the first microprocessor with an on-chip two-level cache. The primary on-chip cache, denoted as L1, is the same as the on-chip cache of the 21064: 8KB code and 8KB data. Both primary caches are direct-mapped with 32 bytes/line. The primary data cache implements a write-through

0 IF	1 SW	2 I0	3 I1	4 A1	5 A2	6 WR
CACHE ACCESS	SWAP PREDICT	DECODE	ISSUE RF READ	ALU1	ALU2	WRITE
				PC GEN	ITB	I-CACHE HIT/MISS
				VA GEN	DTB	D-CACHE HIT/MISS

ALU1 → → → }BYPASS

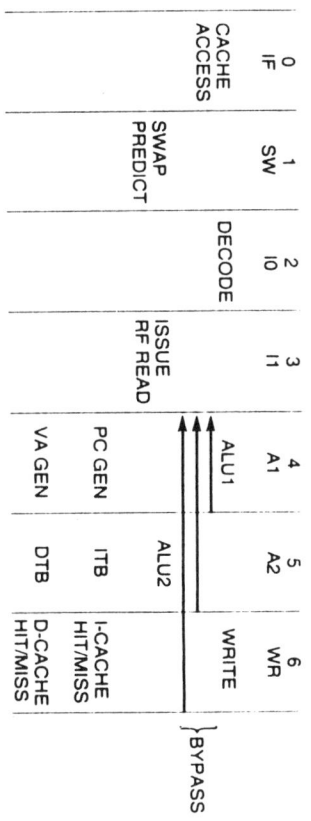

(a) Integer Unit Pipeline Timing

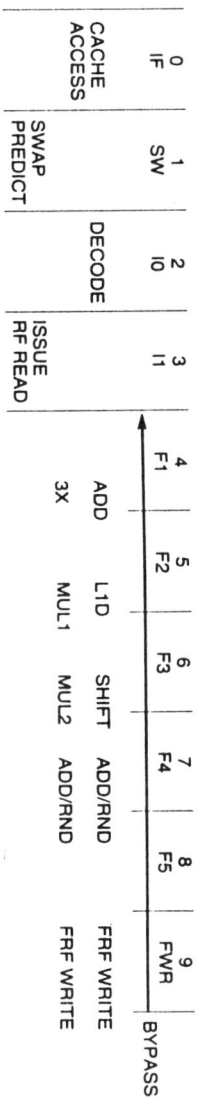

0 IF	1 SW	2 I0	3 I1	4 F1	5 F2	6 F3	7 F4	8 F5	9 FWR
CACHE ACCESS	SWAP PREDICT	DECODE	ISSUE RF READ	ADD	L1D	SHIFT	ADD/RND		FRF WRITE
				3X	MUL1	MUL2	ADD/RND		FRF WRITE

BYPASS

(b) Floating-point Unit Pipeline Timing

KEY:
PC GEN   GENERATE NEW PROGRAM COUNTER VALUE
VA GEN   GENERATE NEW VIRTUAL ADDRESS
ITB   INSTRUCTION TRANSLATION BUFFER
DTB   DATA TRANSLATION BUFFER

Fig. 6.9   21064 pipelines (Courtesy of Digital Equipment Corp.)

Table 6.11 Alpha AXP 21064 Pipeline Stages

COMMON STAGES:

0 IF *instruction fetch* - Fetch a pair of instructions from the Icache

1 SW *swap* - Inspect if any of the two fetched instructions go into the integer or FP pipeline. Swap their order if necessary. Perform branch prediction.

2 I0 *issue 0* - Check for interdependencies of the fetched instructions. Complete decoding and setup for next stage.

3 I1 *issue 1* - Read IU and FPU register files. Check and detect register conflicts. Issue instructions to the datapath function units.

INTEGER OPERATIONS STAGES:

4 A1 *computation cycle 1* - Single-cycle execution instructions completed and ready for forwarding. Ibox computes new PC value.

5 A2 *computation cycle 2* - ITB lookup. Continue longer-time IU computations.

6 WR *write* - Write result into IU register file.

MEMORY REFERENCE STAGES (LOAD/STORE):

4 AC Abox calculates effective address for data.

5 TB DTB lookup.

6 HM Dcache hit/miss detection and load into register file.

FLOATING-POINT STAGES:

4 - 8 F1 - F5 Floating-point calculations.

9 FWR Write result into FPU register file.

AC - address computation
DTB - data translation buffer
ITB - instruction translation buffer

policy. The on-chip secondary cache, denoted L2, is a unified (code and data on the same cache), 96KB, three-way set-associative with 64 bytes/line (there is a 32 byte/line option). It implements write-back and write-allocate policies. There is on-chip logic circuitry to interface to an external third-level cache, denoted L3. The external cache can be 1 to 64MB, direct-mapped, with 32 or 64 bytes/line, and with write-back and write-allocate policies. A block diagram of the 21164 is shown in Fig. 6.10.

Comparing Fig. 6.10 with the block diagram of the 21064 in Fig. 6.7, we can

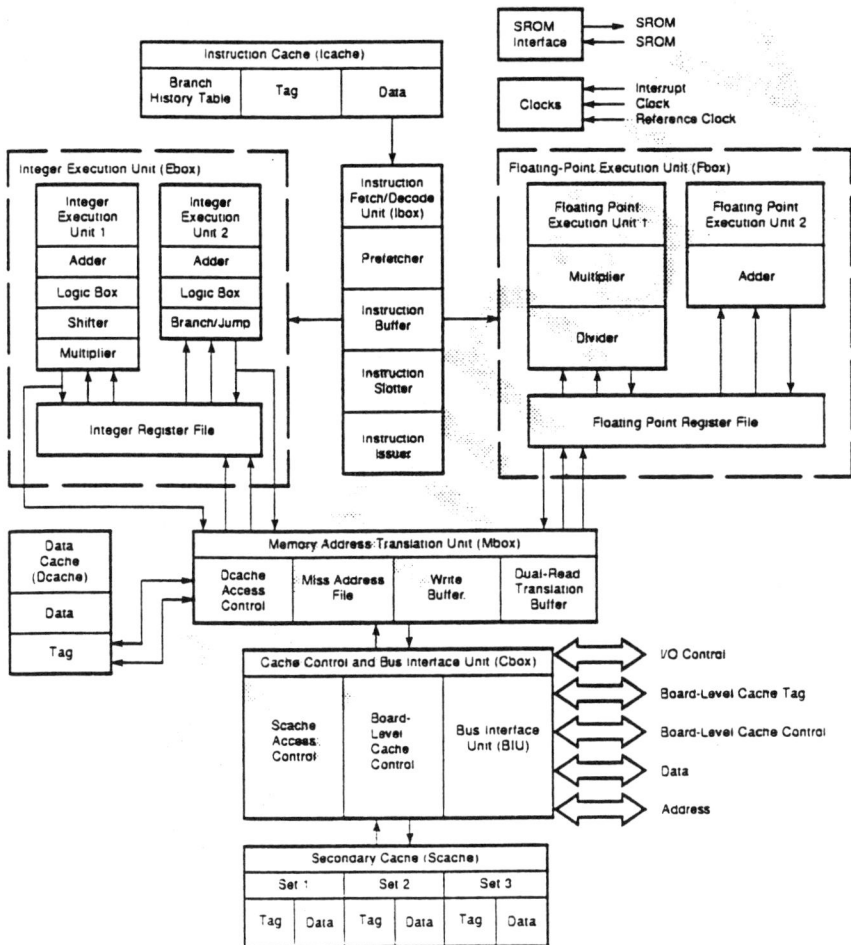

Fig. 6.10   DECchip 21164 block diagram *(Courtesy of Digital Equipment Corp.)*

see that the 21164 contains subsystems denoted in a similar manner, performing similar tasks: the Ibox, Ebox, and the Fbox. One major difference is that, while the Ebox of 21064 contained only one integer execution pipeline, the Ebox of the 21164 contains two such pipelines, capable of simultaneous execution. This certainly speeds up the performance of the 21164. Having more than one execution unit is very helpful in superscalar operation, where more than one integer instruction may be issued at the same time. The 21164 memory address translation unit, called Mbox, contains the address translation data path, a data translation buffer (DTB), load and store execution logic, the miss address file, and the write buffer address file. The 21164 implements a 43-bit virtual address and a 40-bit physical address. The DTB has 64 entries, it is fully associative, serving 8KB pages. The write buffer has six 32-byte entries. The cache control and bus interface unit, called Cbox, processes all accesses sent by the Mbox and implements all memory-related external interface functions, particularly the coherency protocol functions for write-back caching. It controls the L2 and L3 caches. The Cbox handles all instruction and data primary cache (L1) misses, performs the function of writing data from the write buffer into the shared coherent memory subsystem, and has a major role in executing the memory barrier instruction, used in multiprocessing. The Cbox also controls the 128-bit bidirectional data bus, address bus, and I/O control.

The 21164 pipeline structure, similar to that of the 21064 (Fig. 6.10, Table 6.11), is illustrated in Fig. 6.11. The first four stages of the pipeline are executed in the Ibox. The remaining stages of the pipeline are executed by other units (Ebox, Fbox, Mbox). The Ibox maintains state for all pipeline stages to track outstanding register write operations. The system sustains two independent loads per cycle, or an independent store per cycle.

In order to compare the performances of the 21164 and its predecessor 21064, some operations delays, expressed in CPU cycles, are listed in the following table. As we can see, the performance of the 21164 exceeds that of the 21064 by a factor of 1.5 to 2 for some operations, expressed in CPU cycles. Considering the fact that the 21164 can operate at a frequency of up to 300MHz, the factor is even higher.

Operation	21164	21064/21064A
Shift/byte	1	2
Integer multiply	8-16	19-23
Compare and branch	0	1
Floating-point	4	6
L1 data cache	2	3

The **21066** is a highly-integrated implementation of Alpha, whose on-chip functions include an I/O controller, IU, FPU, memory controller, graphics accelerator, instruction and data caches (8KB each, as on the 21064), and an external cache controller [McKi 94]. The 21066 is a 0.68 micron, three-metal layer, CMOS-4, 287-pin PGA microprocessor, running at 166MHz. The **21068** is a lower-frequency version of the 21066, running at 66MHz.

6.4 Concluding Comments
The first implementation of the Alpha AXP architecture, the 21064, running at a frequency of 150 to 200MHz, is listed in the October 1992 Guinness Book of Records as the world's fastest single-chip microprocessor [Sits 93]. The 21064A runs at 275MHz, and the 21164 runs at 300MHz. How long DEC will retain this status, considering the developing competition, remains to be seen.

Instruction Cache Read

Instruction Buffer, Branch Decode,
Determine Next PC

Slot by Function Unit

Register File Access Checks,
Integer Register File Access

Integer Operate Pipeline	IC	IB	SL	AC			
	0	1	2	3	4	5	6

First Integer Operate Stage

If Needed, Second Integer Operate Stage

Write Integer Register File

Arithmetic, logical, shift and compare instructions complete in pipeline stage 4 (1-cycle latency). C-MOV completes in stage 5 (2-cycle latency). IMULL has an 8 or 9-cycle latency. C-MOV or BR can issue in parallel (0-cycle latency) with a dependent CMP instruction.

Floating-Point Pipeline	IC	IB	SL	AC					
	0	1	2	3	4	5	6	7	8

Floating-Point Register File Access

First Floating-Point Operate Stage

Last Floating-Point Operate Stage

Write Floating-Point Register File

Memory Reference Pipeline	IC	IB	SL	AC								
	0	1	2	3	4	5	6	7	8	9	10	11

Dcache Read Begins

Dcache Read Ends

Use Dcache Data, Scache Tag Access

Scache Data Access Begins

Scache Data Access Ends

Use Scache Data, Fill Dcache

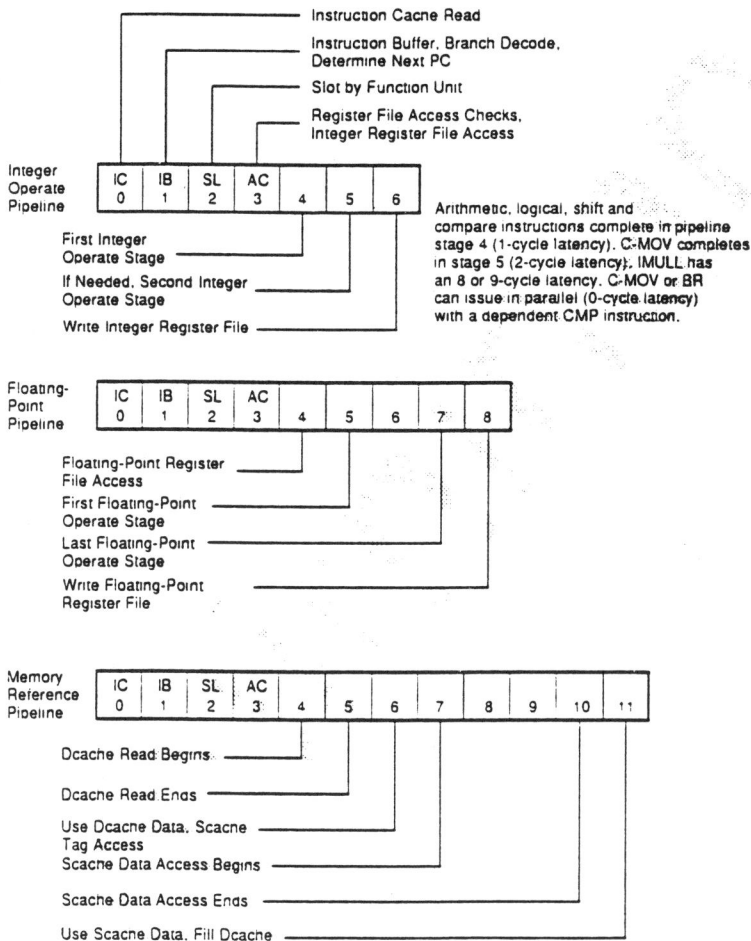

Fig. 6.11 Instruction pipeline stages *(Courtesy of Digital Equipment Corp.)*

The Alpha AXP architecture is certainly new for the most part. The Alpha AXP architecture was developed for a new 64-bit RISC-type processor family, while its predecessor at DEC, the VAX architecture, supported a CISC-type 32-bit family of superminicomputers. On the other hand, one cannot say that the Alpha AXP architecture starts a completely new page. The DEC VAX, and even the 16-bit PDP, are still alive within the Alpha AXP architecture through a number of features:

(a) Although the Alpha AXP is a 64-bit architecture, the terminology for data types has its roots in the 16-bit PDP family. A 'word' is still 16-bit, as it was in the PDP and the VAX. A 32-bit data item is a 'longword', as in the VAX. As can be seen from the subsequent chapters in this Part, most RISC-type systems use the term 'word' for 32-bit data, and 'halfword' for 16-bit data.

(b) The VAX floating-point format is kept on as an optional data type in the Alpha AXP architecture, featured in parallel with the IEEE Standard, which is adopted exclusively on all other modern systems, RISC and CISC.

(c) Some of the old PDP instruction mnemonics, such as BIS instead of OR, are still kept within the Alpha AXP architecture.

Nevertheless, the Alpha AXP architecture (along with the architecture of MIPS R4000, described in chapter 9) is a pioneer in 64-bit architectures. Most of its features are innovative and will probably appear in other future systems.

DEC designers are currently working on future extensions of the Alpha AXP architecture and future, more powerful implementations [McLe 93, Sits 93]. While initial implementations use only 43 bits of virtual address, they check the remaining 21 bits (of 64), so that software can run unmodified on later implementations that use all 64 bits. Similarly, while initial implementations use only 34 bits of physical address, the architected page table entry (PTE) formats and page size choices allow growth to 48 bits. By expanding into a 16-bit PTE field that is not currently used by mapping hardware, a further 16 bits of physical-address growth (for a total of 64 bits) can be achieved, if needed.

While initial implementations use only 8 Kbyte pages, the design accommodates limited growth to 64 Kbyte pages. Beyond that, page table granularity hints allow groups of 8, 64, or 512 pages to be treated as a single large page, thus effectively extending the page size range by a factor of over 1000 [Sits 93]. Each architected PTE format also has one bit reserved for future expansion.

There are a number of areas of instruction set flexibility designed into the architecture. Four of the six-bit opcodes are nominally reserved for adding integer and floating-point aligned octaword (128-bit) load/store instructions. Nine more six-bit opcodes remain for other expansions. In addition, the function field contains more room for further expansion.

One of the most notable intended applications of the Alpha AXP microprocessors is in the CRAY T3D *massively parallel processor* (MPP) system [Adms 94]. The CRAY T3D MPP will be described in detail in Part 3. We are going to see new, more powerful Alpha AXP architecture implementations and applications in the near future.

CHAPTER 7

The PowerPC Family

7.1 Introductory Comments

As mentioned in chapter 2, the development of the first RISC-type computer started in the mid-seventies at IBM with the experimental IBM 801 system [Radi 83; and see chapter 5], although the term 'RISC' was coined at Berkeley in 1980. The goal of the IBM 801 designers was to create a new system, oriented toward the pervasive use of high-level languages (HLL). The system was designed to execute an instruction at almost every clock cycle ('almost', because there are a few instructions, such as load or store, which access memory, multiply, divide, that cannot be executed in a single cycle). To achieve the above (see also chapter 2), a primitive instruction set, completely hardwired, was adopted. These are certainly RISC characteristics.

Subsequently, in the mid-eighties, a commercial RISC-type processor, the ROMP (Research Office products division Microprocessor), was announced by IBM [Tabk 87, chapter 4]. Compared to the 801, it had a smaller percentage of instructions executing in a single cycle and 65% of its instructions were 16 bits long, while the others were 32-bit. In contrast, all 801 instructions were uniformly 32 bits long. Thus, the ROMP appeared to be somewhat 'less of a RISC', compared to the original 801. The ROMP was used in the IBM RT 6150 and RT 6151 workstations.

The IBM next RISC-type system, announced in 1990, is the RISC System (RS)/6000 or RS/6000 [BaWh 90, GrOe 90]. Its architecture, which constitutes the basis of the RS/6000 design, is denoted by IBM as POWER (performance optimization with enhanced RISC). The RS/6000 will be described later in this chapter in section 7.4.

In 1991 IBM got together with Motorola and Apple to form a new alliance with a goal to seize the lead in the desktop computer industry by developing a new and powerful family of RISC-type microprocessors. This new family is called: the PowerPC family. This alliance puts together the vast experience of the three leading companies in hardware and software. It cuts significantly development costs and avoids useless duplication of effort [Burg 94, Dief 94, DiOH 94, McKi 94, MoSt 94, ShPh 94, WeSm 94].

The first PowerPC implementation is the PowerPC 601 microprocessor (also called MPC 601 by Motorola, and PPC 601 by IBM), to be described in section 7.3. It is followed by subsequent implementations such as MPC 603, 604, 620, and others in the near future. All these new systems are based on the PowerPC architecture [PoPC 93], derived from the IBM POWER architecture. The PowerPC architecture will be described in the next section 7.2 and its implementations in section 7.3.

7.2 The PowerPC Architecture

The PowerPC architecture can be viewed as consisting of the following three layers:

1. *User instruction set architecture* (UISA) — includes user-level registers, programming model, data types, addressing modes, and the base user-level instruction set (excluding a few user-level memory-control instructions).
2. *Virtual environment architecture* (VEA) — describes the semantics of the memory model that can be assumed by software processes and includes descriptions of the cache model, cache-control instructions, address aliasing, and other related issues.
3. *Operating environment architecture* (OEA) — includes the structure of the memory management model, supervisor-level registers, privileged instructions, and the exception model.

Systems based on the PowerPC architecture operate in two basic modes of operation: *user* and *supervisor* modes, similar to the M68000 family [Tabk 94]. It should be noted that the PowerPC architecture was designed from the beginning with future 64-bit implementations in mind. The PowerPC architecture was defined as a 64-bit architecture with a 32-bit subset [DiOH 94]. Its first three implementations, the 601, 603, and the 604, are 32-bit systems; however, the next implementation, the 620, is a 64-bit processor.

Register set and programming model

The PowerPC register set and programming model are shown in Fig. 7.1 [PoPC 93]. It is subdivided into two main parts, corresponding to the two modes of operation:

User programming model,
Supervisor programming model.

Programs executing in the supervisor mode can access all registers. Programs executing in the user mode can access registers in the user programming model only.

The *user programming model* includes the following registers:

General-purpose registers (GPR). The GPR file consists of 32 GPRs denoted as GPR0 to GPR31. The GPRs are 32-bit wide in 32-bit implementations, and 64-bit wide in 64-bit implementations (Fig. 7.1 shows a 32-bit implementation). The

USER PROGRAMMING MODEL

FPR0
FPR1
•
•
•
FPR31
0   63

GPR0
GPR1
•
•
•
GPR31
0   31

Condition Register

CR
0   31

Floating Point Status and Control Register

FPSCR
0   31

SUPERVISOR PROGRAMMING MODEL

Segment Registers

SR0
SR1
•
•
•
SR15
0   31

Machine State Register

MSR
0   31

User-Level SPRs

SPR1	XER—Integer Exception Register
SPR8	LR—Link Register
SPR9	CTR—Count Register

0   31

Supervisor-Level SPRs

SPR18	DSISR—DAE/ Source Instruction Service Register
SPR19	DAR—Data Address Register
SPR22	DEC—Decrementer Register
SPR25	SDR1—Table Search Description Register 1
SPR26	SRR0—Save and Restore Register 0
SPR27	SRR1—Save and Restore Register 1
SPR272	SPRG0—SPR General 0
SPR273	SPRG1—SPR General 1
SPR274	SPRG2—SPR General 2
SPR275	SPRG3—SPR General 3
SPR282	EAR—External Access Register
SPR284	TB—Time Base
SPR285	TBU—Time Base Upper
SPR287	PVR—Processor Version Register
SPR528	IBAT0U—IBAT 0 Upper
SPR529	IBAT0L—IBAT 0 Lower
SPR530	IBAT1U—IBAT 1 Upper
SPR531	IBAT1L—IBAT 1 Lower
SPR532	IBAT2U—IBAT 2 Upper
SPR533	IBAT2L—IBAT 2 Lower
SPR534	IBAT3U—IBAT 3 Upper
SPR535	IBAT3L—IBAT 3 Lower
SPR536	DBAT0U — DBAT 0 Upper
SPR537	DBAT0L — DBAT 0 Lower
SPR538	DBAT1U — DBAT 1 Upper
SPR539	DBAT1L — DBAT 1 Lower
SPR540	DBAT2U — DBAT 2 Upper
SPR541	DBAT2L — DBAT 2 Lower
SPR542	DBAT3U — DBAT 3 Upper
SPR543	DBAT3L — DBAT 3 Lower
SPR976	DMISS —Data TLB Miss Address Register[1]
SPR977	DCMP—Data TLB Miss Compare Register[1]
SPR978	HASH1—PTEG1 Address Register[1]
SPR979	HASH2—PTEG2 Address Register[1]
SPR980	IMISS—Instruction TLB Miss Address Register[1]
SPR981	ICMP—Instruction TLB Miss Compare Register[1]
SPR982	RPA—Real Page Address Register[1]
SPR1008	HID0—Hardware Implementation Register 0[1]
SPR1010	HID2 —Instruction Address Breakpoint (IABR) [1]

0   31

[1] MPC603-only registers. These registers are not necessarily supported by other PowerPC processors

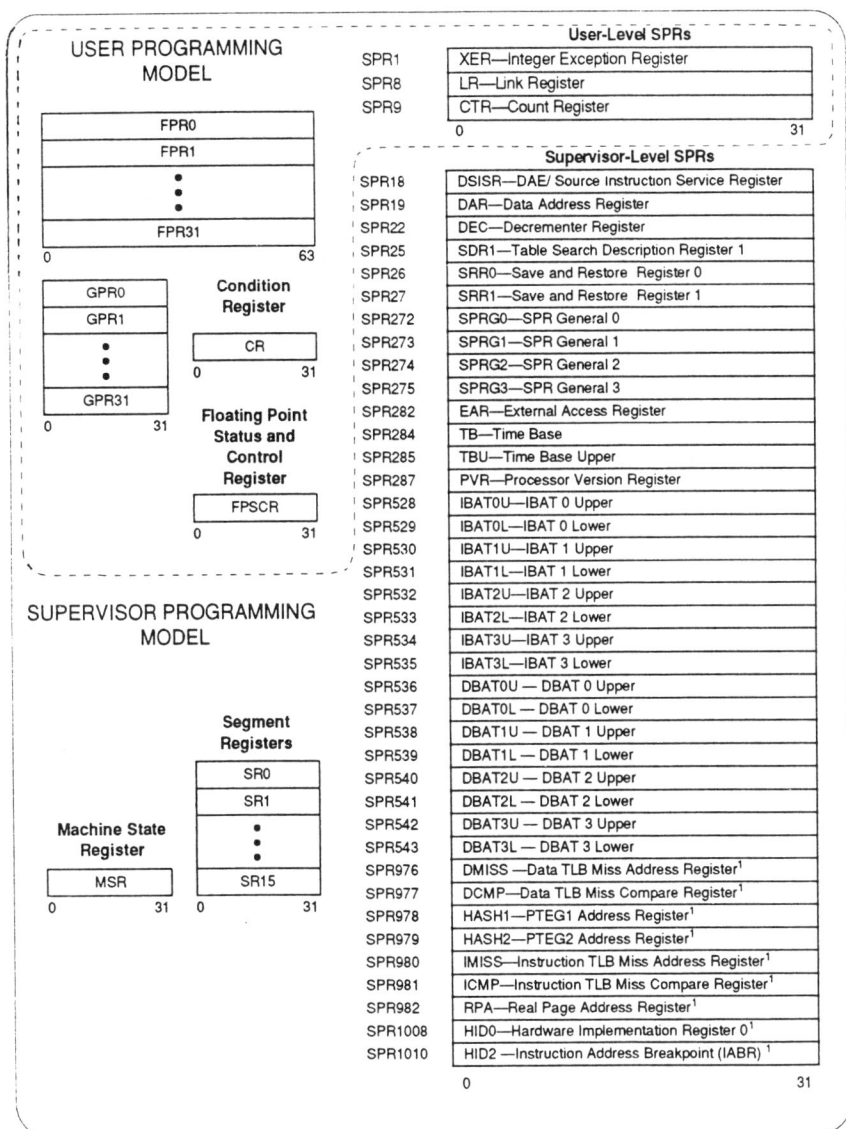

Fig. 7.1   PowerPC programming model — registers *(Courtesy of Motorola, Inc.)*

PowerPC architecture is extended to a full 64 bits, but has a 32-bit subset. Note that in the PowerPC architecture the most-significant bit (MSB) is bit 0, and the least-significant bit (LSB) is bit 31, contrary to the practice in most other microprocessors (a 'legacy' from the IBM 360/370 architecture). The GPRs serve as the data source and destination for all integer instructions and provide addresses (as base or index registers) for all memory access instructions.

Floating-point registers (FPR). The FPR file consists of 32 64-bit registers denoted as FPR0 to FPR31. The FPRs serve as data source or destination for floating-point instructions. They can contain single- or double-precision IEEE 754 Standard floating-point data [IEEE 85].

Floating-point status and control register (FPSCR). The 32-bit FPSCR contains all floating-point exception signal bits, exception summary bits, exception enable bits, and rounding control bits needed for compliance with the IEEE 754 Standard.

Condition register (CR). The 32-bit CR is divided into eight four-bit separate condition registers, CR0 to CR7, that reflect the result of certain arithmetic operations and provide a mechanism for testing and branching.

There are three *special-purpose registers* (SPR) in the user programming model (the other SPRs are in the supervisor programming model):

1. *Integer exception register* (XER). 32 bit. Contains the integer carry and overflow bits.
2. *Link register* (LR). 32 bit. The LR can be used to provide the branch target address and to hold the return address after branch and link instructions.
3. *Count register* (CTR). 32 bit. The CTR is decremented and tested automatically as a result of branch and count instructions.

The 32-bit *condition register* (CR) reflects the results of certain operations and provides a mechanism for testing and branching. The CR is subdivided into eight four-bit separate condition registers, CR0 to CR7, shown in Fig. 7.2.

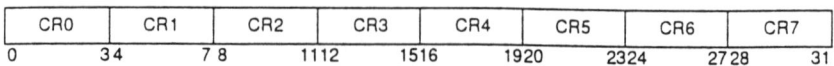

CR0	CR1	CR2	CR3	CR4	CR5	CR6	CR7
0 3 4	7 8	11 12	15 16	19 20	23 24	27 28	31

Fig. 7.2   Condition register (CR) *(Courtesy of Motorola, Inc.)*

The CR condition registers can be set in the following ways:

1. Specified fields in the CR can be set by a move instruction from a GPR (**mtcrf** or **mcrfs**).
2. Specified fields of the CR can be moved from one CRi field to another with the **mcrf** instruction.
3. A specified field of the CR can be set by a move (**mcrxr**) from the XER register.
4. CR logical instructions can be used to operate on specified bits in the CR.

5. CR0 can be the implicit result of an integer operation.
6. CR1 can be the implicit result of a floating-point operation.
7. A specified CR field can be the explicit result of either an integer or floating-point compare operation. This property can be used for comparing a number of values through a sequence of compare instructions.

Setting CR0 and CR1 is an optional implicit result, controlled by opcode.
   Instructions are provided to test individual CR bits. The CR is cleared by a hard reset. The CRi bit settings for compare operations are:

Bit 0, less than, LT for integer, FL for floating-point,
Bit 1, greater than, GT for integer, FG for floating-point,
Bit 2, equal, EQ for integer, FE for floating-point,
Bit 3, summary overflow, SO for integer, unordered, FU (or UO) for floating-point.

The CR0 field has special setting interpretations, if set from arithmetic, rather than compare, instructions:

Bit 0, negative (LT), set when the result is negative,
Bit 1, positive (GT), set when the result is positive,
Bit 2, zero (EQ), set when the result is zero,
Bit 3, summary overflow (SO), set on overflow.

   The XER register upper three bits (bits 0, 1, 2) are of particular importance in conjunction with the functions of the CR. These upper bits of XER are:

Bit 0, *summary overflow* (SO) is set whenever an instruction (except **mtspr**) sets the overflow bit (bit 1, OV) to indicate overflow and remains set until software clears it (with the **mtspr** or **mcrxr** instruction). It is not altered by compare instructions or other instructions that cannot cause an overflow.
Bit 1, *overflow* (OV) set to indicate that an overflow has occurred during execution of an instruction. The OV bit is not altered by compare instructions or other instructions that cannot cause an overflow. It is cleared by an arithmetic instruction that does not cause an overflow.
Bit 2, *carry* (CA) set to indicate that a carry out of bit 0 (MSB) occurred during execution of an instruction.

The XER register is cleared by hard reset.
   The *supervisor programming model* includes (see Fig. 7.1):

Machine state register (MSR). The MSR defines the state of the processor.
Segment registers (SR). The 32-bit 16 SRs are present only in 32-bit PowerPC implementations.

The remaining registers are SPRs, some of which are implementation dependent.

The bits of the *machine state register* (MSR), shown in Fig. 7.3, are used as follows:

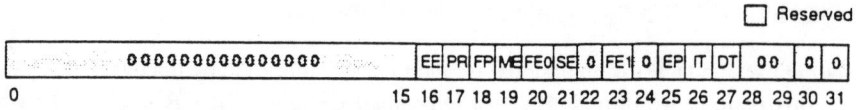

☐ Reserved

| 0000000000000000 | EE | PR | FP | ME | FE0 | SE | 0 | FE1 | 0 | EP | IT | DT | 0 0 | 0 | 0 |

0   15 16 17 18 19 20 21 22 23 24 25 26 27 28 29 30 31

Fig. 7.3   Machine state register (MSR) *(Courtesy of Motorola, Inc.)*

Bit 16, *external interrupt enable* (EE) — external interrupts enabled when EE = 1, disabled when EE = 0.

Bit 17, *privilege level* (PR) — the processor can only execute user-level instructions when PR = 1, and all instructions when PR = 0.

Bit 18, *floating-point available* (FP) — floating-point available for processor execution when FP = 1, and unavailable when FP = 0.

Bit 19, *machine check enable* (ME) — machine check exceptions enabled when ME = 1, disabled when ME = 0.

Bits 20 and 23, *floating-point exception modes 0 and 1* (FE0 and FE1) — two encoded bits:

FE0	FE1	Mode
0	0	Floating-point exceptions disabled
0	1	Floating-point imprecise nonrecoverable
1	0	Floating-point imprecise recoverable
1	1	Floating-point precise mode

Bit 21, *single-step trace enable* (SE) — single-step operation when SE = 1, normal execution when SE = 0.

Bit 25, *exception prefix* (EP) — specifies an exception vector offset,

     when EP = 0, exceptions are vectored to the physical address 000n nnnn (hex)

     when EP = 1, exceptions are vectored to the physical address FFFn nnnn (hex)

Bit 26, *instruction address translation* (IT) — instruction address translation enabled when IT = 1, disabled when IT = 0.

Bit 27, *data address translation* (DT) — data address translation enabled when DT = 1, disabled when DT = 0.

Other bits of the MSR are reserved.

The supervisor model registers can be subdivided into the following categories:

Configuration registers, including:

MSR, described above.
Hardware implementation dependent register 0 (HID0, also denoted SPR1008, see Fig. 7.1). This register is used to control various functions within the processor, such as locking, enabling, and invalidating the on-chip caches.
Processor version register (PVR, also denoted SPR287). It is a read only register that identifies the version (model) and revision level of the PowerPC implementation processor.

Memory management registers, including:

Instruction block address translation (BAT) registers (SPR528 to SPR535, see Fig. 7.1).
Data BAT registers (SPR536 to SPR543).
Segment registers (SR) (SR0 to SR15).
Search description register 1 (SDR1, also denoted SPR25). SDR1 specifies the page table format use in logical to physical address translation for pages.
The SR and BAT registers will be discussed in conjunction with memory management of specific PowerPC implementations in section 7.3.

Exception handling registers, including:

Data access and alignment exception (DAE)/Source instruction service register (DSISR, also denoted SPR18) defines the cause of data access and alignment exceptions.
Data address register (DAR, also denoted SPR19) holds the address of an access after an alignment or data access exception.
Save and restore registers 0 and 1 (SRR0 and SRR1, also denoted SPR26 and SPR27, respectively). The SRR0 is used for saving the address of an instruction that caused an exception, and the address to return to when a return from interrupt (**rfi**) instruction is executed. The SRR1 is used to save machine status on exceptions and to restore machine status when an **rfi** instruction is executed.

Miscellaneous registers, including:

Decrementer register (DEC, also denoted SPR22), a decrementing counter that provides a mechanism for causing a decrementer exception after a programmable delay.
External address register (EAR, also denoted SPR282). The EAR controls access to the external control facility through the external control in and out word indexed instructions.
Time base facility (for writing) (TBL, or TB, and TBU, also denoted as SPR284 and SPR285, respectively). The time base registers TBL and TBU together

provide a 64-bit time base register. The registers are implemented as a 64-bit counter, with the least-significant bit being the most frequently incremented. The PowerPC architecture defines that the time base frequency be provided as a subdivision of the processor clock frequency.

In addition to the above, there are two similar registers in the user VEA layer, for reading, called TBR268 and TBR269 (the supervisor model registers belong to the OEA layer of architecture).

Data types

The PowerPC architecture recognizes the following integer data types:

Operand	Size (bytes)	Size (bits)	Address Bits 28–31 if Aligned
Byte	1	8	xxxx
Halfword	2	16	xxx0
Word	4	32	xx00
Double word	8	64	x000

Best performance is always attained when data operands are aligned. The PowerPC architecture supports both big-endian and little-endian byte ordering [Tabk 94]. The default byte ordering is big-endian (true for the MPC 601 so far). Byte ordering can be changed to little-endian by setting a bit in the MSR register.

PowerPC architecture implements the IEEE 754-1985 Standard single- and double-precision floating-point formats [IEEE 85].

Addressing modes

As in all RISC-type systems, all operations are register-to-register, using the two modes:

1. *Register direct*; the operand is in a GPR or FPR.
2. *Immediate*; the operand is a part of the instruction.

An effective address (EA) to memory is needed in two classes of instructions:

Load and store.
Branch.

The appropriate addressing modes for the above are:

For **load and store** instructions:

1. *Register indirect*; a GPR register contains the address of the operand in memory.
2. *Register indirect with immediate index*; an immediate displacement d (called

in PowerPC architecture *d operand* or *immediate index*) is added to the value in a GPR to form an EA.
3. *Register indirect with index*; the content of two GPR registers, one serving as register indirect and the other as index, is added to form the EA. Any GPR can serve as a register indirect or index register.

For **branch** instructions:

1. *Immediate addressing*; the branch address is a part of the instruction. It is sign-extended to form a target EA. This mode is generally called *direct* or *absolute*.
2. *Link register indirect*; the target EA is in the link register.
3. *Count register indirect*; the target EA is in the count register.

Instruction formats
Some of the main instruction formats of the PowerPC architecture are shown in Fig. 7.4 [PoPC 93]. All PowerPC instructions are 32-bit long. The format in Fig. 7.4(a) is used for most operations. The upper six bits (0 to 5) contain the opcode. The opcode is extended into the subopcode field (bits 22 to 30). The two register source operands are in fields A (bits 11 to 15) and B (bits 16 to 20). The destination operand is in field D (bits 6 to 10). Control bit OE (bit 21) enables overflow detection when set (OE = 1). Control bit Rc (bit 31), called the *record bit*, updates CR if set (Rc = 1). In the PowerPC assembly notation of instructions, the order of the operands is usually the same as in the instruction format.

Example: add rD, rA, rB; rD ← (rA) + (rB)

Any GPR (integer operation) and any FPR (floating-point operation) can serve as rA, rB, or rD in this example.
   Operations with an immediate operand have the format shown in Fig. 7.4(b). The SIMM field (bits 16 to 31) provides for the storage of a 16-bit immediate operand.

Example: addi rD, rA, SIMM; add immediate, rD ← (rA) + EXTS(SIMM)

where EXTS(SIMM) is a sign-extended SIMM field.
   The format in Fig. 7.4(b) can also be used by load and store instructions using the register indirect with immediate (displacement) addressing mode. In this case, field A stores the register indirect encoding, while field D is used for the destination register for load, and for the source register for store instructions.
   The format in Fig. 7.4(c) is used for branch instructions. The LI field is the *immediate address field*. If the *absolute address bit* AA (bit 30) is clear (AA = 0), the LI is shifted two bits left, filling the two lower bits with zeros, and added (sign-extended) to the instruction address to form the branch target address. If AA = 1,

156

opcode	D	A	B	OE	subopcode	Rc

0　　　　5 6　　　　　10 11　　　　15 16　　　　20 21 22　　　　　　　30 31

OE = extended arithmetic bit
Rc = record bit

(a)

opcode	D	A	SIMM

0　　　　5 6　　　　10 11　　　15 16　　　　　　　　　　　31

(b)

opcode	LI	AA	LK

0　　　　5 6　　　　　　　　　　　　　　　　　29 30 31

AA = absolute address bit
LK = link bit
LI = immediate address field

(c)

opcode	BO	BI	BD	AA	LK

0　　　　5 6　　　　10 11　　　15 16　　　　　　29 30 31

(d)

opcode	D	A	B	C	subopcode	Rc

0　　　　5 6　　　　10 11　　　15 16　　　20 21　　　25 26　　30 31

(e)

opcode	D	A	B	subopcode	0

0　　　　5 6　　　　10 11　　　15 16　　　20 21　　　　　　30 31

(f)

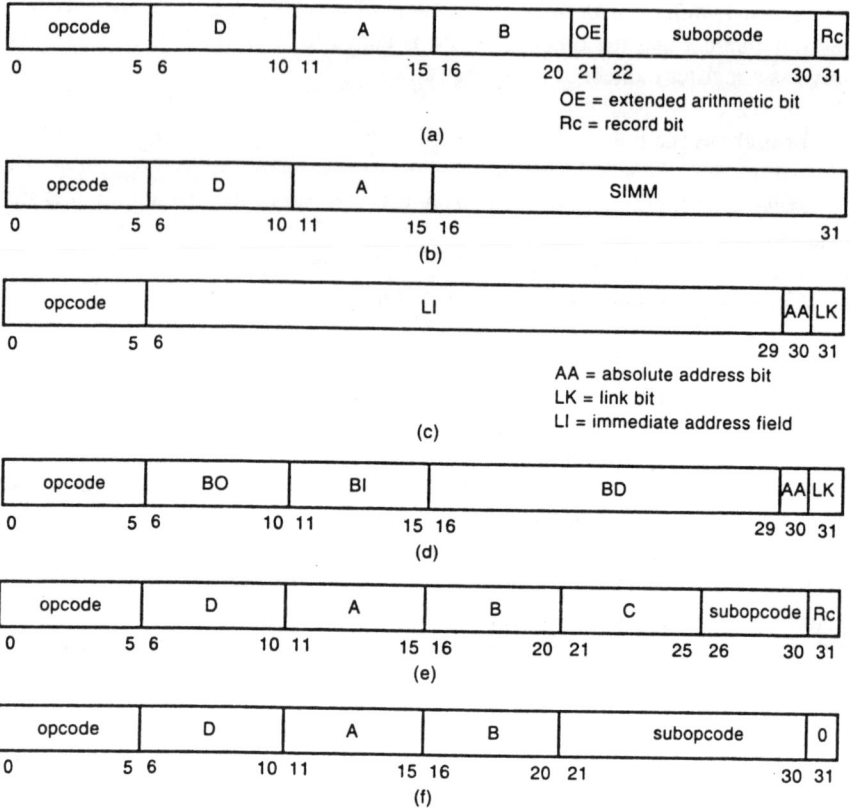

Fig. 7.4　　PowerPC main instruction formats. (a) Register-to-register operations; OE = extended arithmetic; Rc = record bit; (b) Immediate operations, load/store register indirect and immediate; (c) Branch. AA = absolute address bit, LI = immediate address field; LK = link bit; (d) Branch conditional; (e) Combined arithmetic (floating-point multiply and add); (f) Load/store register indirect and index

the shifted as above and sign-extended LI field constitutes the branch target address (direct, or PowerPC immediate addressing mode). If the *link bit* LK (bit 31) is set (LK = 1), then the EA of the instruction following the branch instruction is placed into the LR.

The *branch conditional* instruction format is illustrated in Fig. 7.4(d). The BO field specifies the conditions under which the branch is taken. The BI field specifies the bit in the CR to be used as the condition of the branch. The BD field is used to form the branch target address. The AA and LK bits are used in a manner similar to that of the unconditional branch, shown in Fig. 7.4(c). The

PowerPC architecture features composite instructions, involving floating-point multiply and add, for instance.

Example: fmadd frD, frA, frC, frB; frD ← (frA) * (frC) + (frB)

The format for such an instruction is shown in Fig. 7.4(e).
The format in Fig. 7.4(f), similar to the format in Fig. 7.4(a), is used for load and store instructions using the register indirect with index addressing mode. The A field is used for the register indirect, and the B field is used for the index register. As before, the D field serves as a destination for load and as a source for store instructions.

Instruction set
The PowerPC instruction set is listed in Table 7.1 in alphabetical order.
Some of the instructions, such as integer arithmetic, have four forms of operation.

Example: Take for instance the **add** instruction. Its three additional forms are:

add.	add with CR update
addo	add with overflow update (in XER)
addo.	add with overflow (in XER) and CR updated.

If we use just the 'add' instruction, neither CR nor XER bits will be affected by the outcome. The use of 'add.' will affect the CR condition code bits. The use of 'addo' will affect the OV bit of XER (set on overflow), but the SO bit of CR will not be affected. The use of 'addo.' will affect both the CR and XER registers.
Most floating-point instructions have just the additional 'mnemonic.' option.

Example: fadd   floating-point add,
       fadd.   floating-point add with CR update.

The branch **b** and branch conditional **bc** have four different options. The three additional options are (in addition to **b**):

ba *branch absolute*, AA = 1, LK = 0; the branch target address is the sum of the shifted LI field and the address of the branch instruction.
bl *branch then link*, AA = 0, LK = 1. The LI field is the target address, and the address of the next instruction is placed in LR.
bla *branch absolute then link*, AA = 1, LK = 1: a combined effect of **ba** and **bl**.

The same options are also in effect for the branch conditional (**bc**) instruction: **bca**, **bcl**, and **bcla**. Some instructions, such as **andi.** or **andis.**, come with the CR update option only.
PowerPC instructions are subdivided into the following categories [PoPC 93]:

Table 7.1 PowerPC Instruction Set

Mnemonic	Operation
1. add	add
2. addc	add carrying
3. adde	add extended
4. addi	add immediate
5. addic	add immediate carrying
6. addic.	add immediate carrying and record
7. addis	add immediate shifted
8. addme	add to minus one extended
9. addze	add to zero extended
10. and	and
11. andc	and with complement
12. andi.	and immediate
13. andis.	and immediate shifted
14. b	branch
15. bc	branch conditional
16. bcctr	branch conditional to CTR
17. bclr	branch conditional to LR
18. cmp	compare
19. cmpi	compare immediate
20. cmpl	compare logical
21. cmpli	compare logical immediate
22. cntlzw	count leading zeros word
23. crand	CR AND
24. crandc	CR AND with complement
25. creqv	CR equivalent
26. crnand	CR NAND
27. crnor	CR NOR
28. cror	CR OR
29. crorc	CR OR with complement
30. crxor	CR XOR
31. dcbf	data cache block flush
32. dcbi	data cache block invalidate
33. dcbst	data cache block store
34. dcbt	data cache block touch
35. dcbtst	data cache block touch for store
36. dcbz	data cache block set to zero
37. divs	divide short
38. divw	divide word
39. divwu	divide word unsigned
40. eciwx	external control input word indexed
41. ecowx	external control output word indexed
42. eieio	enforce in-order execution of I/O
43. eqv	equivalent
44. extsb	extend sign byte
45. extsh	extend sign halfword
46. fabs	floating-point absolute value

Table 7.1 (continued)

Mnemonic	Operation
47. fadd	floating-point add
48. fcmpo	floating-point compare ordered
49. fcmpu	floating-point compare unordered
50. fctiw	floating-point convert to integer word
51. fctiwz	fl-pt. convert to int. word with round to zero
52. fdiv	floating-point divide (single-precision)
53. fmadd	floating-point multiply-add (single-precision)
54. fmr	floating-point move register
55. fmsub	floating-point multiply-subtract (single-precision)
56. fmul	floating-point multiply (single-precision)
57. fnabs	floating-point negative absolute value
58. fneg	floating-point negate
59. fnmadd	fl-pt. negative multiply-add (single-precision)
60. fnmsub	fl-pt. neg. multiply-subtract (single-precision)
61. frsp	floating-point round to single-precision
62. fsub	floating-point subtract (single-precision)
63. icbi	instruction cache block invalidate
64. isync	instruction synchronize
65. lbz	load byte and zero
66. lbzu	load byte and zero with update
67. lbzux	load byte and zero with update indexed
68. lbzx	load byte and zero indexed
69. lfd	load floating-point double-precision
70. lfdu	load fl-pt. double-prec. with update
71. lfdux	load fl-pt. double-prec. with update indexed
72. lfdx	load fl-pt. double-prec. indexed
73. lfs	load floating-point single-precision
74. lfsu	load fl-pt. single-prec. with update
75. lfsux	load fl-pt. single-prec. with update indexed
76. lfsx	load fl-pt. single-prec. indexed
77. lha	load halfword algebraic
78. lhau	load halfword algebraic with update
79. lhaux	load halfword algebraic with update indexed
80. lhax	load halfword algebraic indexed
81. lhbrx	load halfword byte-reverse indexed
82. lhz	load halfword and zero
83. lhzu	load halfword and zero with update
84. lhzux	load halfword and zero with update indexed
85. lhzx	load halfword and zero indexed
86. lmw	load multiple word
87. lswi	load string word immediate
88. lswx	load string word indexed
89. lwarx	load word and reverse indexed
90. lwbrx	load word byte-reverse indexed
91. lwz	load word and zero
92. lwzu	load word and zero with update

Table 7.1 (continued)

Mnemonic	Operation
93. lwzux	load word and zero with update indexed
94. lwzx	load word and zero indexed
95. mcrf	move CR field
96. mcrfs	move to CR from FPSCR
97. mcrxr	move to CR from XER
98. mfcr	move from CR
99. mffs	move from FPSCR
100.mfmsr	move from MSR
101.mfspr	move from SPR
102.mfsr	move from SR
103.mfsrin	move from SR indirect
104.mtcrf	move to CR fields
105.mtfsb0	move to FPSCR bit 0
106.mtfsb1	move to FPSCR bit 1
107.mtfsf	move to FPSCR fields
108.mtfsfi	move to FPSCR field immediate
109.mtmsr	move to MSR
110.mtspr	move to SPR
111.mtsr	move to SR
112.mtsrin	move to SR indirect
113.mulhw	multiply high word
114.mulhwu	multiply high word unsigned
115.mullw	multiply low
116.mulli	multiply low immediate
117.nand	NAND
118.neg	negate
119.nor	NOR
120.or	OR
121.orc	OR with complement
122.ori	OR immediate
123.oris	OR immediate shifted
124.rfi	return from interrupt
125.rlwimi	rotate left word immediate then mask insert
126.rlwinm	rotate left word immediate then AND with mask
127.rlwnm	rotate left word then AND with mask
128.sc	sytem call
129.slw	shift left word
130.sraw	shift right algebraic word
131.srawi	shift right algebraic word immediate
132.srw	shift right word
133.stb	store byte
134.stbu	store byte with update
135.stbux	store byte with update indexed
136.stbx	store byte indexed
137.stfd	store floating-point double-precision
138.stfdu	store floating-point double-precision with update

Table 7.1 (continued)

Mnemonic	Operation
139.stfdux	store fl-pt. double-precision with update indexed
140.stfdx	store floating-point double-precision indexed
141.stfs	store floating-point single-precision
142.stfsu	store floating-point single-precision with update
143.stfsux	store floating-point single-prec. with update indexed
144.stfsx	store floating-point single-precision indexed
145.sth	store half word
146.sthbrx	store half word byte-reverse indexed
147.sthu	store half word with update
148.sthux	store half word with update indexed
149.sthx	store half word indexed
150.stmw	store multiple word
151.stswi	store string word immediate
152.stswx	store string word indexed
153.stw	store word
154.stwbrx	store word byte-reverse indexed
155.stwcx	store word conditional indexed (CR0 field affected)
156.stwu	store word with update
157.stwux	store word with update indexed
158.stwx	store word indexed
159.subf	subtract from
160.subfc	subtract from carrying
161.subfe	subtract from extended
162.subfic	subtract from immediate carrying
163.subfme	subtract from minus one extended
164.subfze	subtract from zero extended
165.sync	synchronize
166.tlbie	TLB invalidate entry
167.tw	trap word
168.twi	trap word immediate
169.xor	XOR
170.xori	XOR immediate
171.xoris	XOR immediate shifted

1. *Integer instructions.* There are four integer instruction types:

a. *Integer arithmetic*, including add, addi, addis, addic, subf, subfic, addc, subfc, adde, subfe, addme, subfme, addze, subfze, neg, mulli, mullw, mulhw, mulhwu, divw, divwu.

b. *Integer compare*, including cmp, cmpi, cmpl, cmpli.

c. *Integer logical*, including and, andi, andis., or, ori, oris, xor, xori, xoris, nand, nor, eqv, andc, orc, extsb, extsh, cntizw.

d. *Integer rotate and shift*, including rlwinm, rlwnm, rlwimi, slw, srw, srawi, sraw.

2. *Floating-point instructions.* There are five floating-point instruction types:

a. *Floating-point arithmetic,* including all arithmetic instructions starting with 'f' (Table 7.1).

b. *Floating-point Multiply-Add,* including all combined multiply-add and multiply-subtract instructions starting with 'f' (Table 7.1).

c. *Floating-point rounding and conversion,* including frsp, fctiw, fctiwz.

d. *Floating-point compare,* including fcmpu and fcmpo.

e. *Floating-point status and CR,* including mffs, mcrfs, mtfsfi, mtfsf, mtfsb0, mtfsb1.

f. *Floating-point move,* including fmr.

3. *Load and store instructions.* There are nine load and store instruction types:

a. *Integer load,* including lbz, lbzx, lbzu, lbzux, lhz, lhzx, lhzu, lhzux, lha, lhax, lhau, lhaux, lwz, lwzx, lwzu, lwzux.

b. *Integer store,* including stb, stbx, stbu, stbux, sth, sthx, sthu, sthux, stw, stwx, stwu, stwux.

c. *Integer load and store with byte reversal,* including lhbrx, lwbrx, sthbrx, stwbrx.

d. *Integer load and store multiple,* including lmw and stmw.

e. *Integer move string,* including lswi, lswx, lscbx, stswi, stswx.

f. *Memory synchronization,* including eieio, isync, lwarx, stwcx., sync.

g. *Floating-point load,* including lfs, lfsx, lfsu, lfsux, lfd, lfdx, lfdu, lfdux.

h. *Floating-point store,* including stfs, stfx, stfsu, stfsux, stfd, stfdx, stfdu, stfdux.

4. *Flow control instructions,* including b, bc, bclr, bcctr, crand, cror, crxor, crnand, crnor, creqv, crandc, crorc, mcrf, sc, rfi, twi, tw.

5. *Processor control instructions,* including mtspr, mfspr, mtcrf, mcrxr, mfcr, mtmsr, mfmsr.

6. *Memory control instructions,* including dcbi, dcbt, dcbtst, dcbz, dcbst, dcbf, mtsr, mtsrin, mfsr, mfsrin, tlbie.

7. *External control instructions,* including eciwx and ecowz.

Examples:

subf	rD, rA, rB; (rB) – (rA) $\rightarrow$ rD
mullw	rD, rA, rB; low-order 32 bits of (rA) * (rB) $\rightarrow$ rD
mulhw	rD, rA, rB; high-order 32 bits of (rA) * (rB) $\rightarrow$ rD
divw	rD, rA, rB; low-order 32 bits of (rA)/(rB) $\rightarrow$ rD

To compute the remainder, remainder = dividend – (quotient) * (divisor):

divw	rD, rA, rB; quotient $\rightarrow$ rD
mullw	rD, rD, rB; (quotient) * (divisor) $\rightarrow$ rD

subf	rD, rD, rA; (rA) – (rD) = remainder $\rightarrow$ rD
srw	rA, rS, rB; shift rS right by a number of bits specified by rB (bits 26–31), zeros on left, shifted result $\rightarrow$ rA
stwx	rS, rA, rB; (rS) $\rightarrow$ (EA), EA = (rA) + (rB)
fmr	frD, frB; frD $\leftarrow$ (frB)
cmpw	CRi, rA, rB; rA and rB are compared, affecting the flags in the CRi field
beq	CRi, target; if in the cmpw above (rA) = (rB), bit EQ in CRi is set, branch to target

Exceptions

The PowerPC architecture supports four types of exception:

1. *Synchronous, precise*. Caused by an instruction. All instruction-caused exceptions are handled precisely; that is, the machine state at the time the exception occurs is known and can be completely restored.
2. *Synchronous, imprecise*. Involves imprecise floating-point exceptions. May or may not be restartable.
3. *Asynchronous, precise*. Involves maskable external interrupt exceptions.
4. *Asynchronous, imprecise*. Involves non-maskable imprecise exceptions such as system reset and machine check.

When exceptions occur, information, such as the instruction that should be executed after control is returned to the original program and the content of the MSR, is saved in the save/restore registers SRR0 and SRR1 (SPR26 and SPR27), program control passes from user to supervisor level, and software begins execution of the exception handler.

7.3 PowerPC Implementations
PowerPC 601
The PowerPC 601, also called MPC 601, is the first microprocessor implementation of the PowerPC architecture. It is a 66MHz, 2.8 million transistors, 0.6 micron, four-layer metal CMOS, packaged in 304-pin ceramic quad flat pack microprocessor [AlBe 93, BAMo 93, Moor 93, PaSi 93, PoPC 93]. Its power dissipation is 9W at 3.6V, 66MHz operations. It is a three-issue superscalar system (see chapter 1). The MPC 601 block diagram is shown in Fig. 7.5.

The *instruction unit* (Fig. 7.5) prefetches instructions from the cache and places them in the *instruction queue*, illustrated in Fig. 7.6. The instruction queue has space for eight instructions in slots Q0 to Q7. The eight instructions can be

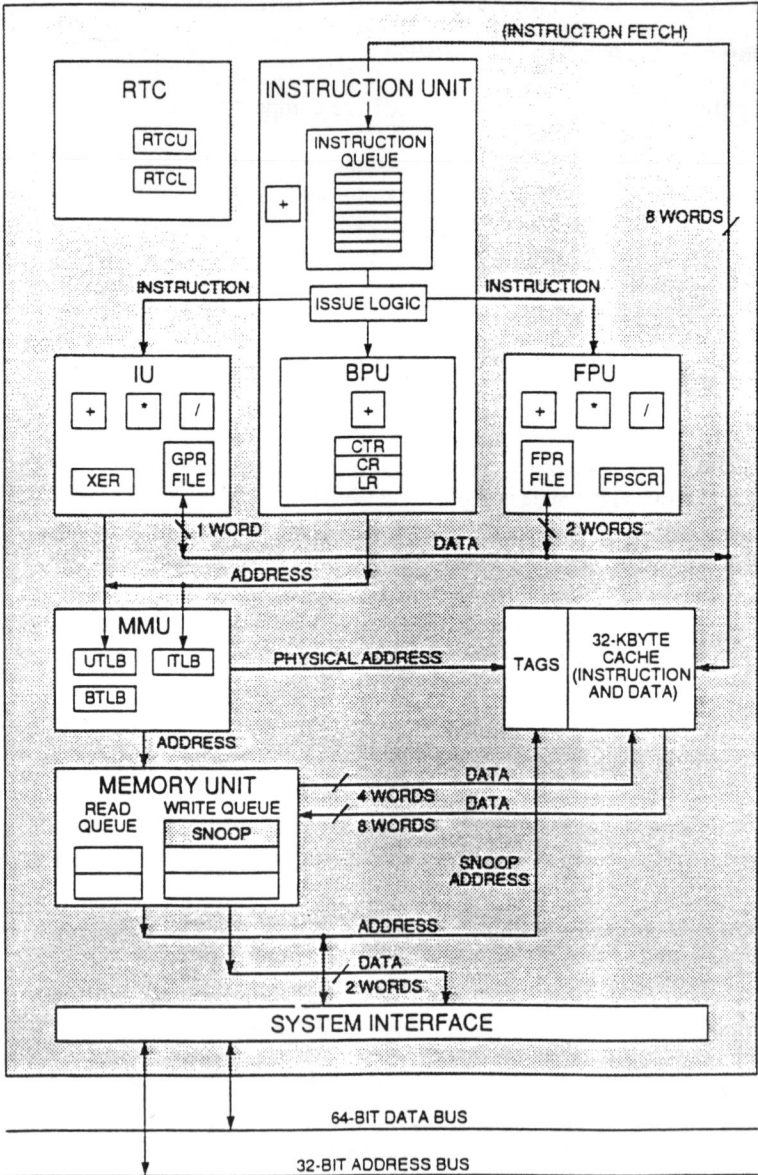

Fig. 7.5 MPC 601 block diagram *(Courtesy of Motorola, Inc.)*

loaded into the queue in one cycle (there are 32*8 = 256 bits leading from the cache to the instruction unit). Instructions move from the top of the queue (Q7) towards the bottom (Q0) and a full range of shift amounts through the queue is supported. The instruction queue (Q4 to Q7) provides buffering to reduce the need to access the cache. Some initial decoding is performed in the lower half (Q0 to Q3). Only three instructions at a time can be issued to the execution units. Some instructions can be issued out of order from any of the bottom four queue entries.

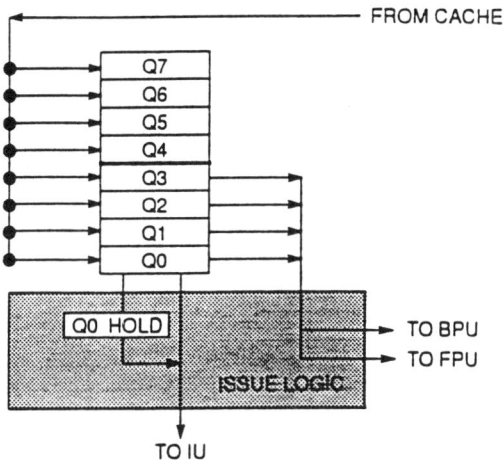

FROM CACHE

Q7
Q6
Q5
Q4
Q3
Q2
Q1
Q0

Q0 HOLD

TO BPU
TO FPU

ISSUE LOGIC

TO IU

Fig. 7.6   Instruction queue *(Courtesy of Motorola, Inc.)*

The MPC 601 has three independent execution units:

1. *Integer unit*, IU. It is a 32-bit unit executing all integer and memory access instructions (including those required for floating-point registers). The IU contains an ALU, a multiplier, a divider, the *integer exception register* (XER or SPR1, see Fig. 7.1), and the 32-register 32-bit GPR file (Fig. 7.1).
2. *Floating-point unit*, FPU. The FPU contains a single-precision multiply-add array, a divider, the 32-register 64-bit FPR file, and the FPSCR (Fig. 7.1). The FPU contains two additional instruction buffers which allow floating-point instructions to be issued from the general instruction buffer even if the FPU is busy, making instructions available for issue to the other execution units (by vacating space in the instruction buffer). The FPU adheres to the IEEE 754-1985 Standard.
3. *Branch processing unit*, BPU. The BPU looks through the bottom half of the instruction queue for a conditional branch instruction and attempts to resolve it early. It also performs CR look-ahead operations on conditional branches. The BPU uses a bit in the instruction encoding to predict the direction of unresolved conditional branches. When an unresolved conditional branch is predicted, the processor prefetches from the predicted target stream. Therefore, when an unresolved

conditional branch is encountered, the processor prefetches instructions from the predicted target stream until the conditional branch is resolved.

The BPU contains an adder to compute branch target addresses and three SPRs: the LR (SPR8), the CTR (SPR9), and the CR (see Fig. 7.1). The BPU calculates the return pointer (address of the instruction following the subroutine call) for subroutine calls and saves it in the LR. The LR may also contain the branch target address for the *branch conditional to LR* (**bclr**) instruction. The CTR contains the branch target address for the *branch conditional to CTR* (**bcctr**) instruction. Because the BPU uses dedicated registers rather than GPRs or FPRs, execution of branch instructions is independent of the execution of integer and floating-point instructions.

Three simultaneously issued instructions can execute simultaneously only if they are of the appropriate type to be issued to the three independent execution units, that is, if one instruction is integer, one floating-point, and one branch. If two back-to-back integer instructions are encountered, they will be executed in sequence through the IU, although branch and floating-point instructions may be dispatched from behind.

The MPC 601 features four types (physically three pipelines) of pipeline of different depth [Moor 93]:

1. *Branch pipeline*, two stages:
   Fetch
   Dispatch, decode, execute, predict; all in one cycle
2. *Integer instructions pipeline*, four stages:
   Fetch
   Dispatch, decode
   Execute
   Write-back
3. *Load/Store instructions pipeline*, five stages:
   Fetch
   Dispatch, decode
   Address generation
   Cache
   Write-back
   Stages fetch, dispatch, decode, address generation (or execute), and write-back, are physically the same on pipelines 2 and 3. The cache stage is used by pipeline 3 only.
4. *Floating-point pipeline*, six stages:
   Fetch
   Dispatch
   Decode
   Execute 1
   Execute 2
   Write-back

The load/store pipeline needs an extra cycle for cache access (more cycles will be needed in case of a cache miss). The floating-point pipeline also needs extra cycles for some operations, particularly those of double-precision.

The MPC 601 MMU, shown in Fig. 7.7, supports up to 4 Petabytes (2^{52} bytes) of *virtual memory* and 4 Gbytes (2^{32} bytes) of *physical memory*. The MMU also controls access privileges for these spaces on block and page granularities. The MPC has three types of TLB:

1. *Unified TLB* (UTLB), 256-entry, two-way set-associative, for 4 Kbyte pages.
2. *Block TLB* (BTLB), four-entry, fully associative, for blocks (optionally 128KB to 8MB).
3. *Instruction TLB* (ITLB), four-entry, fully associative, most recently used instruction address translations.

The BPU generates all instruction and data addresses. After a *logical address* (LA) is generated, its upper-order bits, LA0 to LA19 (Fig. 7.7), are translated by the MMU into physical address bits PA0 to PA19. Simultaneously, the lower address bits, A20 to A31, are directed to the on-chip cache (discussed later in this section) to point to the appropriate set and the data item accessed. After translating the address (or rather its upper 20 bits), the MMU passes the upper 20 bits to the cache for tag match lookup. The untranslated lower bits are concatenated with the translated upper bits to form a physical address accessing the external memory.

The 16 32-bit *segment registers* (SR), shown in Figs. 7.1 and 7.7, control both the page and I/O controller interface address translation mechanism. One of the SRs is selected by the four highest-order address bits LA0 to LA3. The contents of the selected SR are concatenated with the low-order 28 bits of the logical address to generate an interim 52-bit *virtual address*. Page address translation corresponds to the conversion of this virtual address into the 32-bit physical address. In most cases, the physical address for the page resides in the UTLB. If there is a miss in the UTLB, the processor automatically searches the page tables in memory.

Block address translation, done by the BTLB, occurs in parallel with page translation and is similar to it, except that there are fewer upper-order LA bits to be translated, since blocks are much larger than 4KB pages.

For instruction accesses, the MMU first performs a lookup in the four-entry ITLB. In case of a miss in ITLB, UTLB and BTLB are looked up.

The MPC 601 *memory unit* (Fig. 7.8) contains read and write queues that buffer operations between the external interface and the cache. These operations result from load and store instructions for which a cache miss occurred, and operations required to maintain cache coherency, such as dirty line copybacks. As shown in Fig. 7.8, the read queue contains two elements and the write queue contains three. Each element of the write queue can contain eight words (256 bits

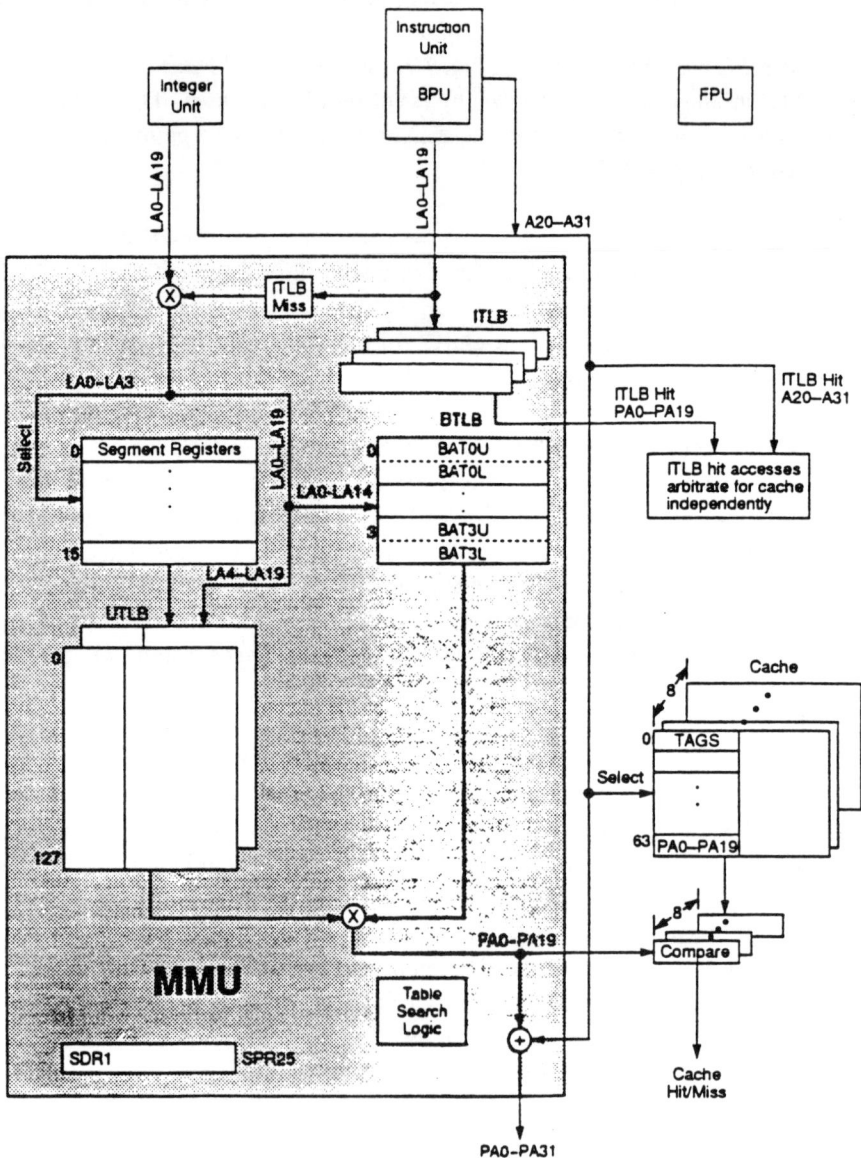

Fig. 7.7 MMU block diagram *(Courtesy of Motorola, Inc.)*

or 32 bytes). Each element of the read queue contains 32 address bits and control information bits.

The MPC 601 has a 32 Kbyte unified (code and data in the same cache), eight-

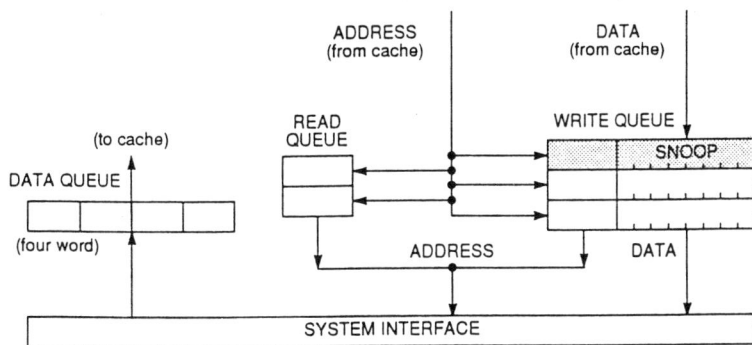

Fig. 7.8   Memory unit *(Courtesy of Motorola, Inc.)*

way set-associative, 64 bytes/line cache, illustrated in Fig. 7.9. Each line is divided into two eight-word sectors, each of which can be snooped, loaded, flushed, or invalidated independently.

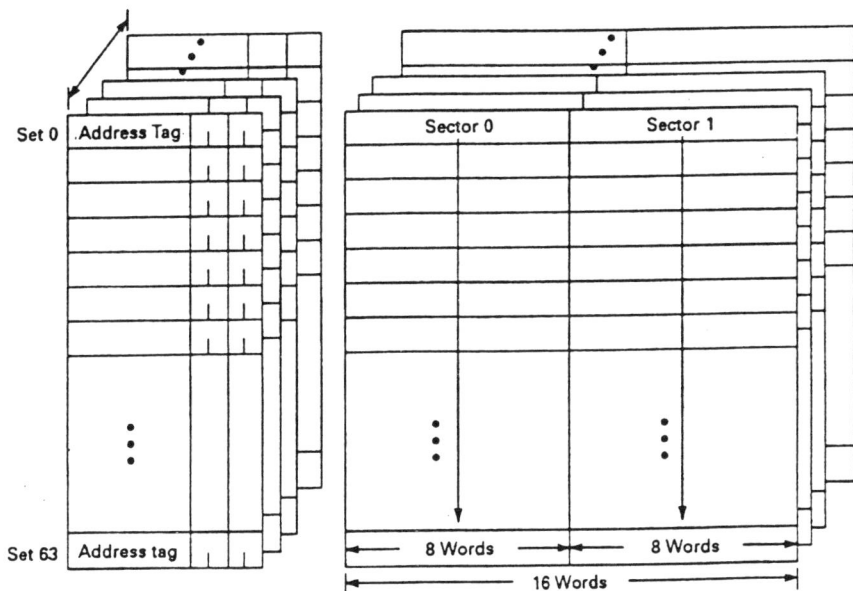

Fig. 7.9   Cache unit organization *(Courtesy of Motorola, Inc.)*

The size of the cache being 2^{15} bytes, line size 2^6 bytes, we have:

$2^{15} / 2^6 = 2^9$ lines in the cache, and
$2^9 / 2^3 = 2^6$ sets in the cache.

In forming the address accessing the cache, we need six bits to identify each byte in a line, and six bits to identify the set (total of 12 bits also constituting the internal page offset in a 4KB page), leaving 20 bits for the TAG.

PowerPC implementations can control access modes on a page or block basis, featuring:

Write-back/write-through options,
Cache-inhibited mode,
Memory coherency.

The cache coherency is handled by the *modified, exclusive, shared, invalid* (MESI) protocol [AlBe 93, PoPC 93], featuring the following four states:

1. *Modified*; the cache line was modified, and it holds the only valid data for this address.
2. *Exclusive*; the cache line holds data identical to the data at this address in memory. No other cache has these data.
3. *Shared*; the cache line holds data identical to the data at this address in memory and perhaps in one other cache.
4. *Invalid*; the data in the cache line are invalid.

Each sector has two bits that store the encoding for the above four states. An LRU algorithm is used for cache-line replacement. The cache organization is specific to the MPC 601 implementation.

The MPC 601 implements the following classes of exception:

1. Asynchronous imprecise for machine check and system reset.
2. Asynchronous precise for external interrupts.
3. Synchronous precise for instruction-caused exceptions.

The external signals of the MPC 601 are shown in Fig. 7.10. PowerPC has adopted a set of interface signals similar to that of the Motorola MC88110 (see chapter 11), but not identical. The 64-bit external data bus should be particularly noted.

PowerPC 602
The PowerPC 602 is a low-power realization of the PowerPC architecture, aimed at the embedded processor market. The 602 is a 0.5 micron CMOS; it has one million transistors and runs at 66MHz. Its power expenditure at that frequency is 1.2 watts, dropping to 2 milliwatts when on standby. The processor has four functional units: IU, branch, load/store, and a single-precision only FPU. Dual-precision floating-point computations (if needed) will have to be carried out in software. The 601 IU can multiply a byte of data by a word of data every cycle. This is helpful in graphics and compression applications, where data are frequently

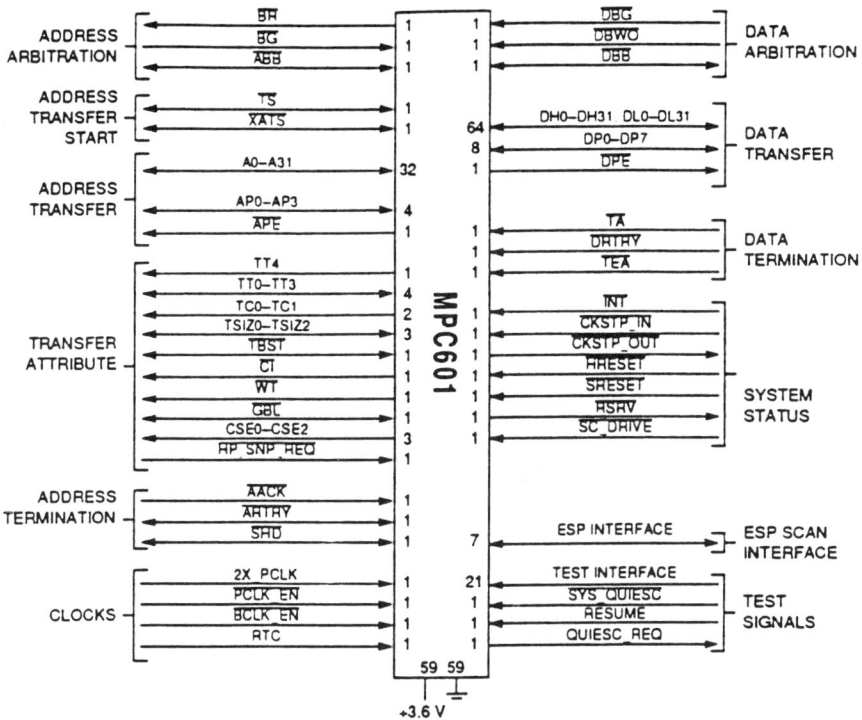

Fig. 7.10   MPC 601 signal groups *(Courtesy of Motorola, Inc.)*

presented as a byte stream. The IU can also add data items in logarithmic form, without a need to have them decoded first. This is helpful for digital signal processing (DSP) operations, such as handwriting and speech recognition. The PowerPC 602 has a dual cache, 4KB instruction and 4KB data. The caches are two-way set-associative. Its data and address pins are multiplexed.

PowerPC 603

The MPC 603 is the first low-power implementation of the PowerPC architecture [Burg 94, Dief 94, DiOH 94]. Like the 601, the 603 is a three-issue superscalar. As opposed to the 601, which carries some of the IBM POWER architecture, the 603 is the first purely PowerPC implementation. A block diagram of the MPC 603 is shown in Fig. 7.11.

The 603 instruction unit contains a sequential fetcher, an instruction queue, a BPU, and a dispatch unit. The fetcher can fetch two instructions at a time from the instruction cache over a 64-bit internal bus. The instruction queue (IQ) holds six instructions. Instructions are dispatched to their respective execution units from the dispatch unit at a maximum rate of two instructions per cycle. The dispatch unit

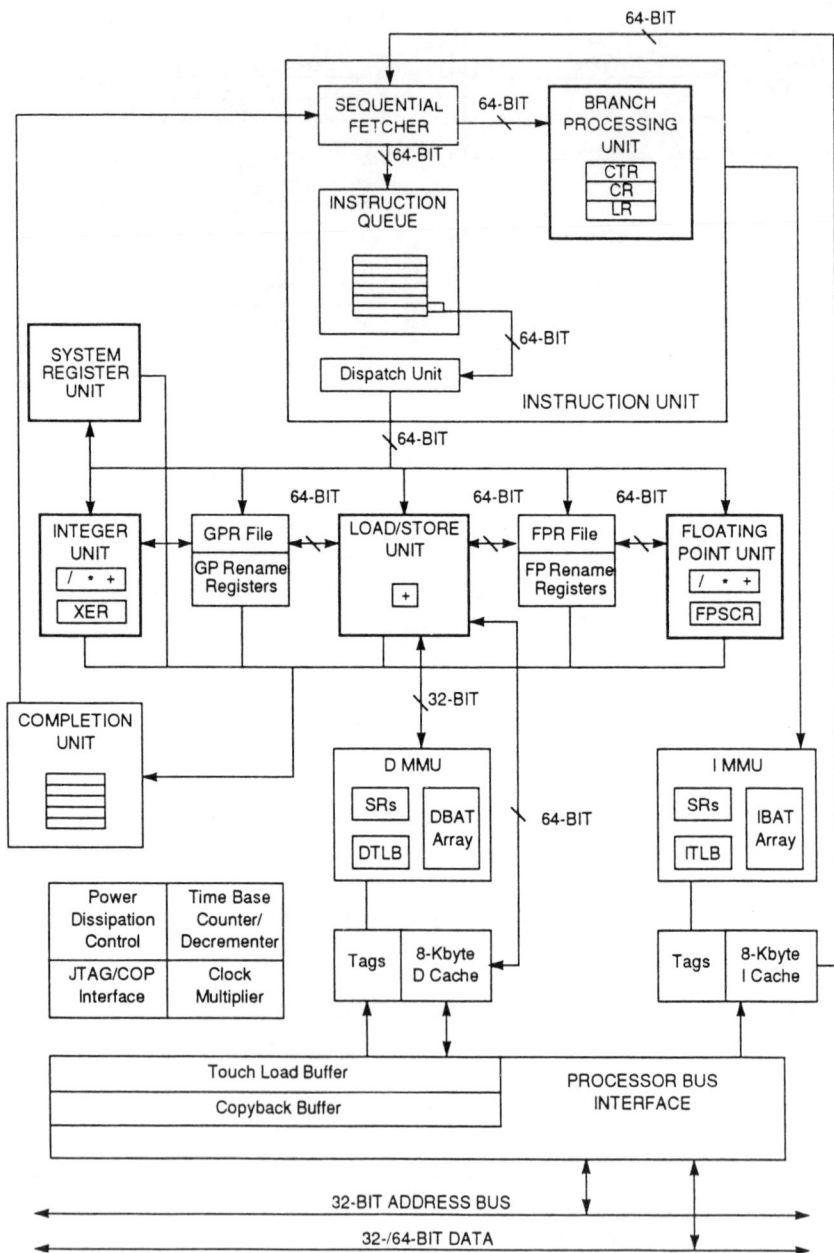

Fig. 7.11   MPC 603 block diagram *(Courtesy of Motorola, Inc.)*

performs source and destination register dependency checking, determines dispatch serializations, and inhibits subsequent instruction dispatching as required.

The BPU receives branch instructions from the fetcher and performs CR look-ahead operations on conditional branches to resolve them early. The BPU uses a bit in the instruction encoding to predict the direction of the conditional branch. Therefore, when an unresolved conditional branch instruction is encountered, the processor fetches instructions from the predicted target stream until the conditional branch is resolved. The BPU contains an adder to compute branch target addresses and three user control registers, LR, CTR, and CR (see section 7.3). The BPU calculates the return address for subroutine calls and saves it in the LR for certain types of branch instruction.

The MPC 603 features five execution units: IU, FPU, load/store unit (LSU), system register unit (SRU), and a completion unit. The SRU executes various system-level instructions, including condition register logical operations and move to/from special-purpose register instructions. The completion unit tracks instructions from dispatch through execution, and then retires, or completes them in program order. Instruction state and other information required for completion is kept in a FIFO queue of five completion buffers. A single completion buffer is allocated for each instruction once it enters the dispatch unit.

The MPC 603 features a dual MMU (one for instructions, I MMU, one for data, D MMU, see Fig. 7.11), and a dual cache, 8 Kbyte instruction, 8 Kbyte data (total 16 Kbytes). Each MMU has a 64-entry TLB. Each cache is two-way set-associative with 32 bytes/line. The LRU replacement policy is used. The data cache is write-back.

A more recent version of the 603 is the PowerPC 603E. The 603E is a 0.5 micron, 100MHz microprocessor with essentially the same structure as the 603. The cache on the 603E is double however: 16KB instruction, 16KB data (as opposed to 8KB each on the 603). The 603E caches are four-way set-associative, as opposed to two-way on the 603.

PowerPC 604

The PowerPC 604 or MPC 604 was announced in the Spring of 1994. It is a four-issue superscalar microprocessor implementing the PowerPC architecture. A block diagram of the MPC 604 (or simply 604) is shown in Fig. 7.12. A detailed scheme of its internal data paths, stressing the separate transmission of operands and results, is illustrated in Fig. 7.13 [P604 94].

Similarly to the 603, the 604 instruction unit is composed of an instruction fetcher, an eight-word instruction queue, the BPU, and a dispatch unit. The fetcher transfers two instructions per cycle to the instruction queue from the instruction cache (I-cache) over a 64-bit internal bus (see Fig. 7.12). The instruction queue consists of two four-entry queues: a decode queue (DEQ), where the four instructions are decoded, and a dispatch queue (DISQ), from which four instructions are transferred to the dispatch unit simultaneously. The dispatch unit provides the logic for checking the instructions and dispatching them to the

174

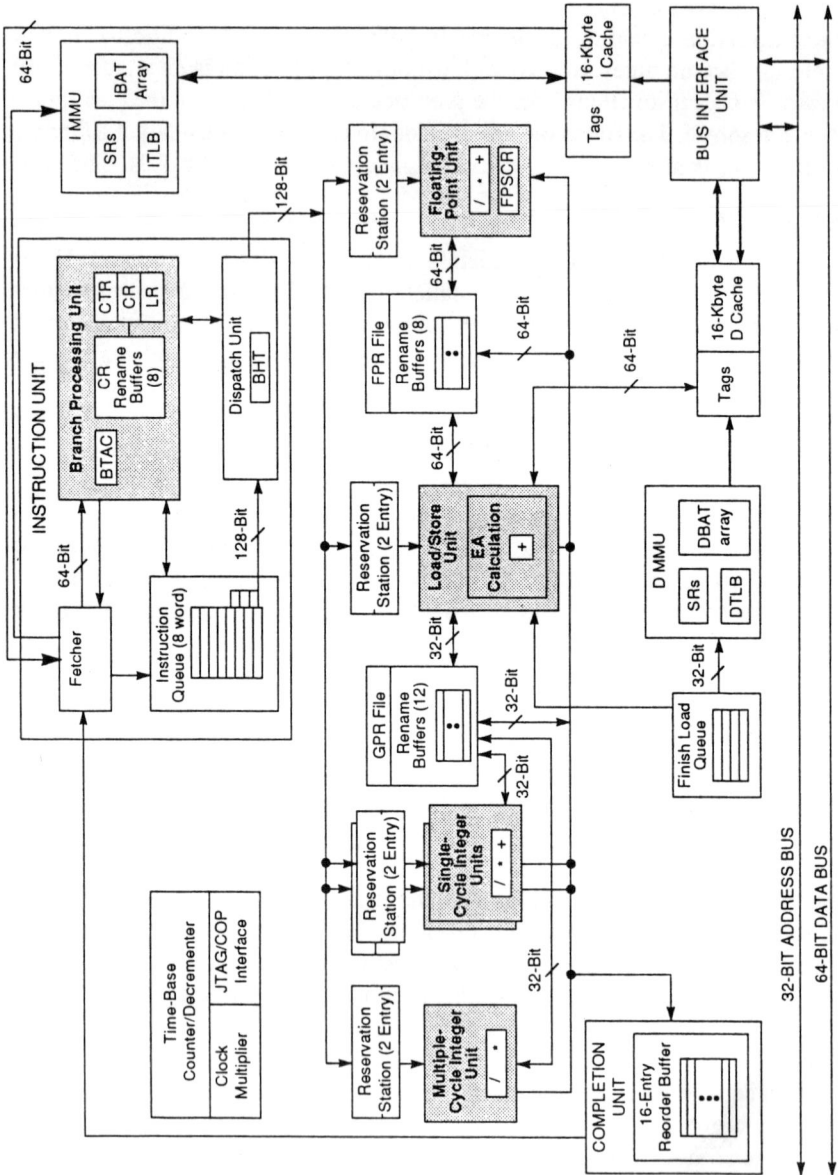

Fig. 7.12 Block diagram of PowerPC 604 *(Courtesy of Motorola, Inc.)*

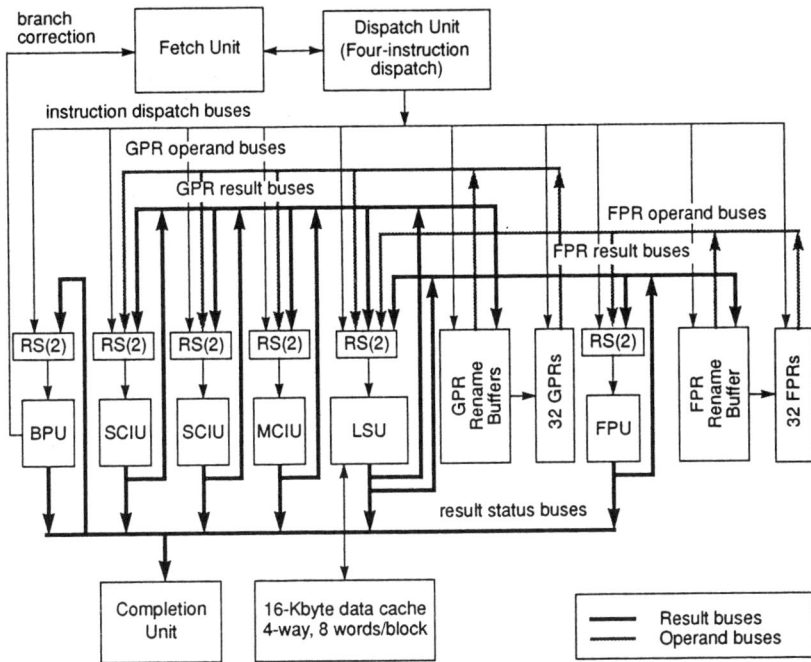

Fig. 7.13   MPC 604 block diagram — internal data paths *(Courtesy of Motorola, Inc.)*

appropriate execution units. The dispatch unit contains the branch history table (BHT) which helps in effective handling of branch instructions.

The 512-entry BHT provides two bits per entry, indicating four levels of dynamic prediction: **strongly not-taken, not-taken, taken,** and **strongly taken.** The history of a branch's direction is maintained in these two bits. Each time a branch is taken the value is incremented (with a maximum value of three meaning strongly taken). When a branch is not taken, the bit value is decremented (with a minimum value of zero meaning strongly not-taken). If the current value predicts taken and the next branch is taken again, the BHT entry then predicts strongly taken. If the next branch is not taken, the BHT then predicts taken.

Within the dispatch unit logic a reorder buffer (ROB) entry is allocated for each instruction, and dependency checking is done between the instructions in the dispatch queue [P604 94]. The rename buffers are searched for the operands as the operands are fetched from the register file. Operands that are written by other instructions ahead of the one in the dispatch queue are given the tag of that instruction's rename buffer. Otherwise, the rename buffer or the register file supplies either the operand or a tag. As instructions are dispatched, the fetch unit is notified that the dispatch queue can be updated with more instructions (the concept of register renaming is explained in chapter 1).

The BPU is used for branch instructions and CR logical operations. All branches, conditional and unconditional, are placed in a reservation station (RS) until conditions are resolved and they can be executed. At that point, branch instructions are executed in order; the completion unit is notified whether the prediction was correct. The BPU also executes CR logical instructions, which flow through the reservation station as the branch instructions (see Figs. 7.12 and 7.13).

The completion unit retires executed instructions from its ROB (see Fig. 7.12) and updates register files and control registers. The completion unit recognizes exception conditions and discards any operations being performed on subsequent instructions in program order. The completion unit can quickly remove instructions from a mispredicted branch, and the decode/dispatch unit begins dispatching from the correct instruction path. An instruction is retired from the ROB when it has finished execution and all instructions ahead of it have been completed. The instruction's result is written into the appropriate register file and is removed from the rename buffers at or after completion.

To avoid contention for a given register location, the 604 provides rename registers for storing instruction results before the completion unit commits them to the architected register (see also chapter 1). Twelve rename registers are provided for the GPRs, 12 for the FPRs, and eight for the CR. When the dispatch unit dispatches an instruction to its execution unit, it allocates a rename register for the results of that instruction. The dispatch unit also provides a tag to the execution unit identifying the result that should be used as the operand. When the proper result is returned to the rename buffer, it is latched into the RS. When all operands are available in the RS, the execution can begin. The completion unit does not transfer results from the rename registers to the destination registers until any speculative branch conditions preceding it in the completion queue are resolved and the instruction itself is retired from the completion queue without exceptions. If a speculatively executed branch is found to have been incorrectly predicted, the speculatively executed instructions following the branch are flushed from the completion queue and the results of those instructions are flushed from the rename registers.

The MPC 604 has six execution units: two single-cycle IUs (SCIU), a multiple-cycle IU (MCIU), an FPU, a BPU, and a load/store unit (LSU), as illustrated in Figs. 7.12 and 7.13. Each SCIU consists of three subunits: an adder/comparator, a subunit for logical operations, and a subunit for performing rotates, shifts, and count leading zero operations. These subunits handle all one-cycle arithmetic and logic instructions. Only one subunit can execute an instruction at a time. The MCIU consists of a 32-bit integer multiplier/divider.

The MPC 604 has a six-stage instruction pipeline, illustrated in Fig. 7.14. The pipeline stages are [P604 94]:

1. **Instruction fetch**, IF. The fetch unit loads the DEQ with instructions from the I-cache and determines from what address the next instruction should be fetched.

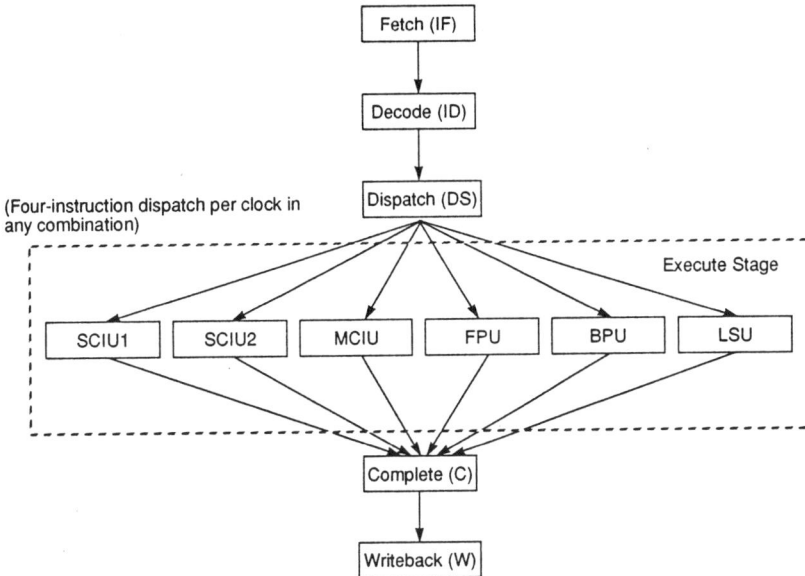

Fig. 7.14   MPC 604 pipeline diagram *(Courtesy of Motorola, Inc.)*

2. **Instruction decode**, ID. All time-critical decoding is performed on instructions in the DISQ. The remaining decode operations are performed during the next dispatch stage.

3. **Instruction dispatch**, DS. The not-time-critical decoding is completed. Dispatch logic determines when an instruction can be dispatched to the appropriate execution unit. At the end of the DS stage, instructions and their operands are latched into the execution input latches or into the unit's RS. Logic in this stage allocates resources such as the rename registers and ROB entries.

4. **Execute**, E. The instruction flow is split among the six execution units, some of which consist of multiple pipelines. An instruction may enter the execute stage from either the DS stage or the execution unit's RS. At the end of the E stage, the execution unit writes the results into the appropriate rename buffer entry and notifies the completion stage that the instruction has finished execution. The execution unit reports any internal exceptions to the completion stage and continues execution, regardless of the exception.

5. **Complete**, C. The C stage ensures that the correct machine state is maintained by monitoring instructions in the completion buffer and the status of instruction in the E stage. When instructions complete, they are removed from the ROB. Results may be written back from the rename buffers to the register as early as the C stage. If the completion logic detects an instruction containing exception status or if a branch has been mispredicted, all subsequent instructions are cancelled, any results in rename buffers are discarded, and instructions are fetched from the correct

instruction stream.

6. **Write-back**, W. Any information in the rename buffers that was not stored (written back) during the C stage, is written back in the W stage.

The 604 MMU structure is similar to that of the 603, supporting a 4 Petabytes (2^{52}) virtual address space, and a 4 Gigabytes (2^{32}) physical address space. The MMU is dual: one for instructions and one for data (see Fig. 7.12). Each TLB has 128 entries (double the size of 603's), and it is two-way set-associative. The 604 features a dual cache: 16 Kbytes I-cache, 16 Kbytes D-cache (a total of 32 Kbytes on-chip cache). Each cache is four-way set-associative with 32 bytes/line. The data cache is write-back supporting the MESI cache coherency protocol.

PowerPC 620

The PowerPC 620 implements the 64-bit version of the PowerPC architecture. It has a structure very similar to that of the 604: it has the same type of six execution units and it is a four-issue superscalar. The 620 is a 0.5 micron, four-metal layer chip. It is a seven-million-transistor microprocessor with an on-chip dual cache of a total of 64KB: 32KB I-cache, 32KB D-cache. It has on-chip logic to control an off-chip second-level cache of 1 to 128MB. The chip runs initially at 133MHz, and it recently attained a frequency of 200MHz.

A block diagram of the PowerPC 620 is shown in Fig. 7.15. Comparing it with the block diagram of the PowerPC 604 in Fig. 7.12, it can be observed that the two systems have a very similar structure, as stated above. The main structural differences between the 604 and the 620 can be summarized as follows:

Processor:	604	620
BHT entries	512	2048
CR rename buffers	8	16
I-cache to fetcher bus (bits)	64	156
GPR rename buffers	12	8
LSU reservation station entries	2	3
Caches (KB each)	16	32
D MMU queues	Finish Load	Load, Finish Store Completed Store

The 620 uses four mechanisms to support dynamic branch prediction in the fetch and dispatch stages of its pipeline: the *branch target address cache* (BTAC), the *count register renaming*, the *LR stack*, and the *branch history table* (BHT). The BTAC contains the target address of previously executed branch instructions. It is accessed by the fetch address in the fetch stage of the pipeline. The BTAC is organized as a 256-entry, two-way set-associative cache. It contains only the target address of those branches that are predicted to be taken. If the fetch address hits in the BTAC, the target address is used in the next cycle to fetch the next set of

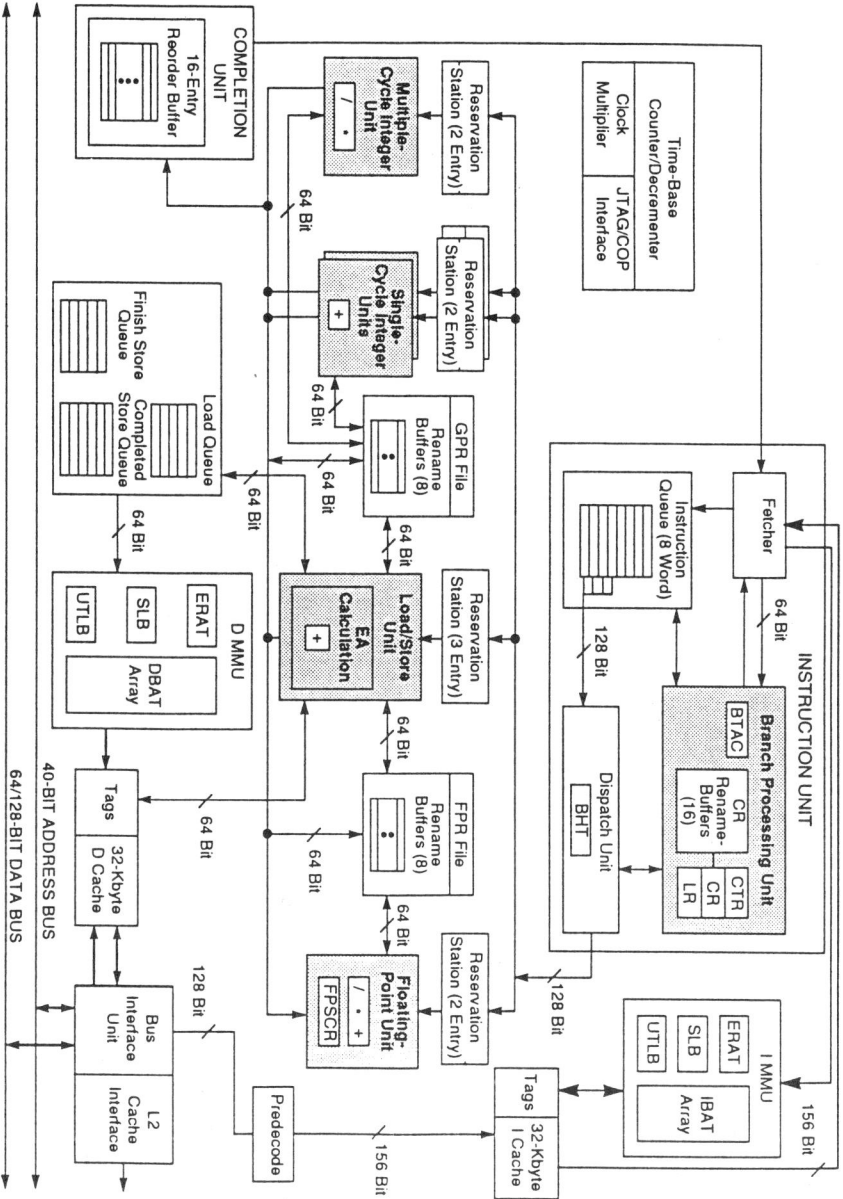

Fig. 7.15 PowerPC 620 block diagram *(Courtesy of Motorola, Inc.)*

instructions. If there is a miss to the BTAC, the fetcher assumes sequential program flow and generates the appropriate sequential address based on the number of instructions received from the I-cache. The fetch address, and not the first branch address, is sufficient to access the BTAC, since the BTAC always contains the first predicted taken branch instruction beyond the current fetch address. In the dispatch stage, unconditional branches are identified and conditional branches may be resolved as taken branches. The instruction prefetch will then be redirected to the correct target address if this branch was predicted not taken by the fetch stage.

For a conditional branch instruction whose condition depends on the value of the count register, the prediction is made based on the count register value. If the prediction is different from the current prefetch direction, the prefetch is redirected. To accelerate branch instructions that read or modify the count register, the count register is renamed with a shadow register. The shadow registers are updated when a branch instruction is dispatched, even if it is from a predicted (as opposed to resolved) execution path. The future values kept in these shadow registers are also used to form branch predictions. If a prediction is correct, there is no penalty. If not, the shadow registers are restored to the proper state so that the instructions fetched from the correct path can be dispatched and executed.

To accelerate subroutine call and return sequences, an eight-entry LR stack is implemented. In the PowerPC architecture (see section 7.2), a branch instruction that has the LINK bit set is used for a subroutine call, and that saves the return address in the LR. A branch to LR instruction is used for return from a subroutine. For nested subroutines, the LR must be saved before another subroutine call. When the 620 executes a branch with the LINK bit set, the return address is stored into a shadow LR as well as pushed into the LR stack. When a branch to LR is encountered, an entry from the stack is pulled off and used speculatively as the branch target address. This allows continuous instruction prefetching without waiting until the LR is restored. The LR stack provides accurate branch target prediction unless the stack overflows or the program does not save and restore the LR properly. The LR prediction is resolved at the completion time of the branch instruction, and the pipeline will be flushed if a misprediction is detected.

The BHT is used for predicting branch instructions whose condition depends only a bit in the CR. The BHT is a 2048-entry (512-entry on the 604), direct-mapped table. Each entry in the table stores four prediction stages (as in the 604): strong taken, weak taken, weak not-taken, and strong not-taken. The BHT is updated when the branch instruction is executed. The BHT prediction also controls the BTAC update. If the branch is predicted to be taken for the next encounter, it is added to the BTAC. If not, it is deleted from the BTAC. When dynamic branch prediction is disabled, static branch prediction is used for branch instructions whose condition depends on a bit in the CR. For static branch prediction, the Y bit in the instruction along with the direction of the branch determine which way the branch should be predicted. If static branch prediction determines the branch should be taken, then it is added to the BTAC.

The 620 features speculative execution of instructions taking advantage of the parallelism exposed by predicting branches. The 620 speculatively executes instructions for up to four unresolved branch instructions. The results of speculatively executed instructions are kept in temporary storages, such as rename registers, reorder buffers, and shadow registers. These temporary storages contain a part of the processor's future state that will be copied to its architectural state as the corresponding instructions are completed. Each temporary storage area is purged in the event of a branch misprediction or other exceptional event. This provides the basis for a precise exception mechanism since the processor's architectural state represents, at all times, the results of instructions completed in program order.

The 620 has a five-stage instruction pipeline (as opposed to six stages on the 604): fetch, dispatch, execute, complete, write-back. After the instructions are transferred from the outside, they pass through a predecoder (see Fig. 7.15) on their way to the internal code cache (I-cache). The predecoded instructions reside in the I-cache until the instruction unit fetches them. Because of this predecoding, the remainder decoder logic is merged into the dispatch stage of the processor instruction pipeline. This effectively shortens the 620 pipeline from six stages (as on the 604) to five stages [ThRy 94]. The 620 pipeline diagram is similar to that of the 604, shown in Fig. 7.14, except that there is no separate decode stage between the fetch and the dispatch stages.

The 620 has a separate load/store unit (LSU) like the 604. For a load operation, the cache is first accessed from the LSU, and the data are forwarded to the execution units as well as to the rename buffer in the case of a cache hit. All store operation data are added to the five-entry *finished store queue* (FSQ) after they are translated. As each store operation is completed, it is moved along with the store data received from the register file into the six-entry *completed store queue* (CSQ) without waiting for the store to actually take place in the cache or memory. The D-cache is capable of serving one completed store and one load every cycle if there are no address conflicts between the load and store addresses. If a store misses in the cache, it is moved to the store miss register. While the store miss is being served, all later stores are held off in the CSQ to ensure that stores are performed in program order. Load accesses that miss in the D-cache are captured in the load miss register and a bus request is generated to load the missing line.

The 620 implements a two-level MMU. The first-level MMU uses separate 64-entry, fully-associative *effective-to-real address translation* (ERAT) buffers for instruction and data address translation. These are backed up by the second-level MMU, which has a shared 20-entry, fully associative *segment lookaside buffer* (SLB) and a shored 128-entry, two-way set-associative TLB. The first 16 entries of the SLB are also used to implement the segment registers to support 32-bit operation systems. The management of these buffers and the loading of table entries from the segment table/page table in the memory to these buffers are done entirely in hardware in compliance with the PowerPC architecture's segmented paged virtual memory system. In addition, the 620 also implements the architected instruction/data block address translation (IBAT/DBAT) registers, which facilitate the address translation of large contiguous areas of memory, ranging from 128KB to 256MB.

The 620 cache organization is illustrated in Fig. 7.16. The data cache can store 32KB of data with an additional 4KB used for byte parity bits for error detection. It is organized as eight-way 'semi-associative' with 64 bytes per line. Conventional eight-way set-associative caches read out all eight potential cache lines' tags from the selected set and then select one line based on the tag comparison results. This is done on every cycle and introduces speed and power consumption problems. The 620 data and instruction caches, however, use part of the effective address bits to preselect a line from the selected set. This speeds up the line selection process. The 620 data cache can handle one load and one store every cycle, and when hit, both will finish in one cycle. While serving a load miss, the 620 data cache can continue performing other loads which hit the cache. If a second miss occurs, it will be queued in the LSU and serviced when the first miss is finished. The data cache can operate with a write-back or write-through policy programmable on a per page or per block basis. It implements an LRU replacement algorithm. Coherency is maintained by implementing the MESI protocol.

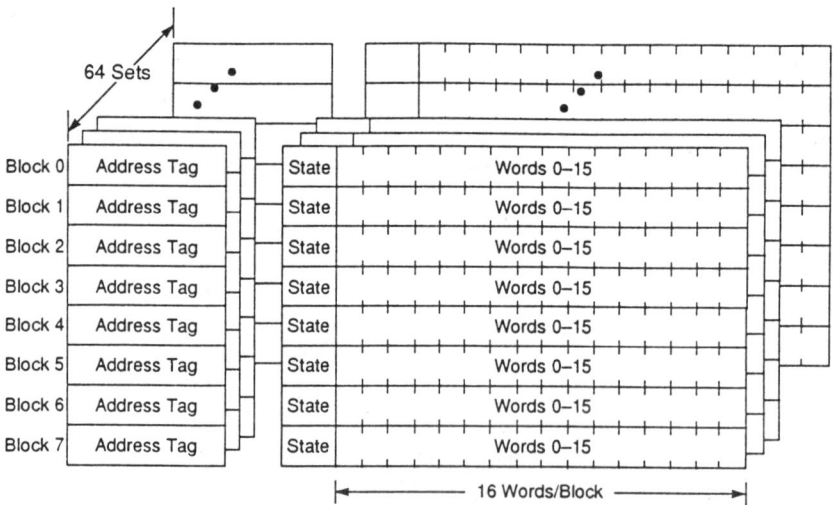

Fig. 7.16   Cache unit organization *(Courtesy of Motorola, Inc.)*

The 620 instruction cache is similarly organized except for the following differences. First, it contains an additional 7KB of predecode information and 1KB for parity, which makes the total size of I-cache 40KB. The predecode bits are generated when instructions are loaded from the secondary cache (L2) or memory. Second, it has a *cache reload buffer* (CRB) that holds the most recently loaded cache line until the next cache miss. The reload buffer is also accessed during normal instruction fetch; so it is essentially a one-line virtual cache.

The 620 has an on-chip secondary cache (L2) controller. The L2 is configurable from 1 to 128MB. It is unified, direct-mapped, physically indexed and tagged, with 64 bytes/line. The L2 data interface to the 620 chip is 128 bits wide. It implements the MESI cache coherency protocol.

The PowerPC 620 signal groups are shown in Fig. 7.17. Particular attention should be paid to the two separate 128-bit data interfaces (one for general data transfer and one for L2 interface) and a 40-bit separate address bus.

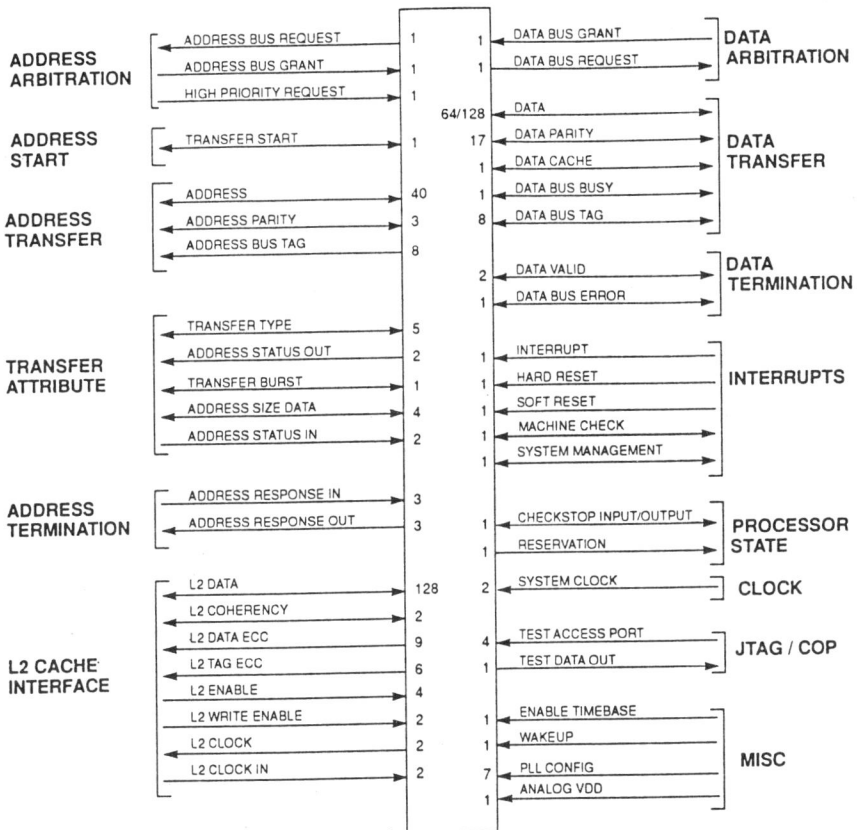

Fig. 7.17   PowerPC 620 microprocessor signal groups *(Courtesy of Motorola, Inc.)*

Some of the properties of the PowerPC processors are summarized in the following table [Dief 94, SmWe 94]:

Processor:	601	603	604	620
Transistors* 10^6	2.8	1.6	3.6	7.0
Peak frequency, MHz	100	80	100	150
Instruction cache, KB	32*	8	16	32
Data cache, KB	–	8	16	32
Cache associativity	Eight-way	Two-way	Four-way	Eight-way
Line size, bytes	64	32	32	64
Pins	304	240	304	625

* The 601 cache is unified, storing both instructions and data

7.4 The IBM RS/6000

The IBM RS/6000 is a predecessor of the PowerPC architecture. The PowerPC architecture is taken mostly from the IBM POWER (performance optimized with enhanced RISC) architecture, on which the RS/6000 is based. Most of the POWER instructions are actually implemented by the PowerPC architecture. About 34 POWER architecture instructions were not implemented by PowerPC [PoPC 93]. A block diagram of the RS/6000 system is shown in Fig. 7.18 [BaWh 90, GrOr 90].

The primary RS/6000 subsystems, shown in Fig. 7.18, are:

Instruction cache unit — ICU
Fixed-point unit — FXU
Floating-point unit — FPU
Data cache unit — DCU
Storage control unit — SCU
Initial program load — IPL
Read-only storage — ROS
I/O channel controller — IOCC
Serial link adapter — SLA
System I/O bus — SIO bus
Description language code — DSL code.

The bus size is expressed in Fig. 7.18 in units of W (word = 32 bits). Each block in Fig. 7.18 represents a separate chip (except blocks designated as memory cards, native I/O, and IPL ROS). If we count the FPU chip, we can say that the RS/6000 CPU is realized on three chips. The ICU contains an 8 Kbyte instruction cache and a *branch processor*. The branch processor processes the incoming instruction stream from the instruction cache and feeds a steady flow of instructions to the FXU and the FPU. The RS/6000 is a four-issue superscalar; however, only a specific combination of four instructions can be executed simultaneously (one branch, one integer, one floating-point, and one CR instruction, for instance). The branch processor provides all of the branching, interrupt, and condition code functions within the system.

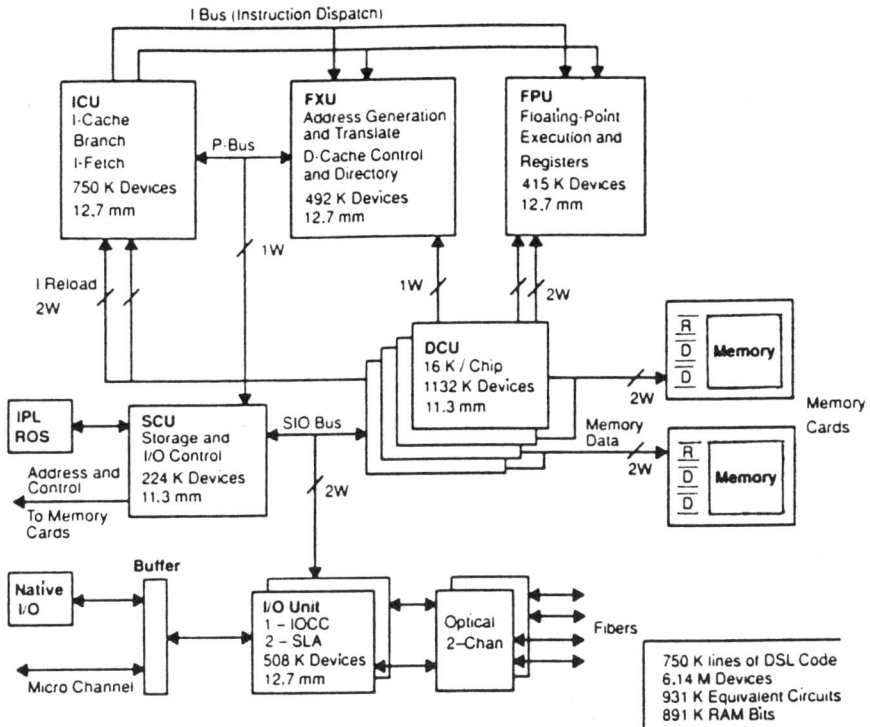

Fig. 7.18   RS/6000 block diagram *(Courtesy of IBM Corp.)*

There exists also a single-chip version of the RS/6000 called RSC. The RS/6000 instruction pipeline has five stages: fetch, dispatch, decode, execute, write-back; somewhat different, but close to the MPC 601 integer pipeline. IBM has followed up the POWER line of system development with a new system called POWER2 [WeSm 94]. The processor of POWER2 is a six-issue superscalar. Of the six issued instructions, two can be issued to the FXU, two to the FPU, and two to the ICU. Up to two branches per cycle may be issued, but only if the first conditional branch is not taken. The POWER2 is an eight-chip high-performance system, operating at frequencies of up to 72MHz. The basic architecture of the POWER2 is almost identical to that of POWER, with very minor differences. POWER2 has a 32 Kbyte instruction cache, located on the same chip with the branch unit. It is two-way set-associative with 128 bytes/line. The 256 Kbyte data cache is implemented on four chips. It is four-way set-associative with 256 bytes/line. A more advanced version of the eight-chip system is called POWER2+. Its block diagram is shown in Fig. 7.19. The names of the basic subsystems (ICU, FXU, FPU, DCU, SCU) are the same as in the initial RS/6000 and POWER2. The ICU on-chip I-cache is the same as in POWER2, 32KB. The primary D-cache, implemented on up to four DCU chips, is 128KB. The new POWER2+ subsystem is a secondary cache L2, configurable for 512KB, or lMB, or 2MB. The secondary cache is direct-mapped with 128 bytes/line.

7.5 Concluding Comments

The MPC 601 is only the starting implementation of the PowerPC family, endeavored by IBM, Motorola, and Apple. The 603, 604, and 620 are implementations of the pure PowerPC architecture, whereas 601 is a 'bridge' chip implementing a superset of the IBM POWER and PowerPC architectures. Many more MPC 6xx-family systems are undoubtedly under development. How they will compare with other top RISC performers, such as the DEC Alpha AXP (see chapter 6), only future experience will tell. As far as applications go, Apple has already announced new PowerPC-based 'Mac' PCs and workstations.

187

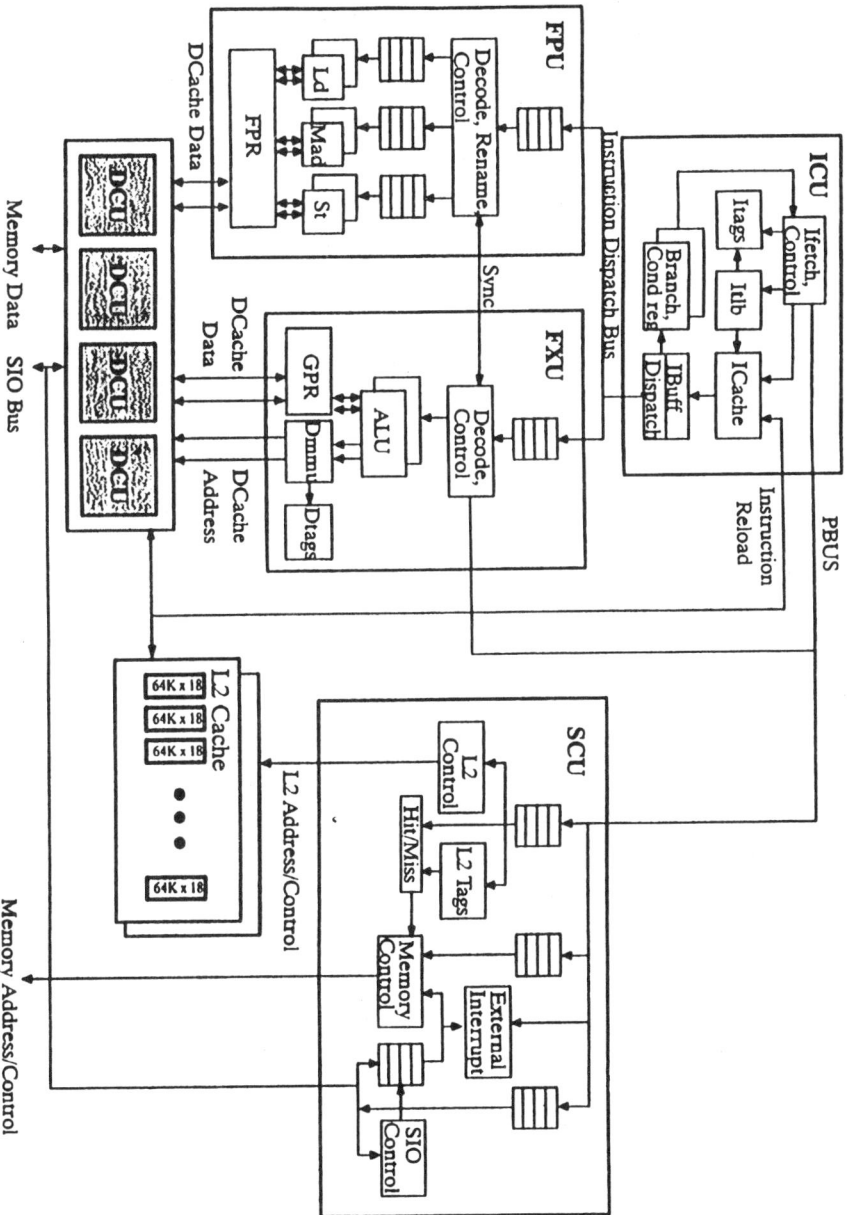

Fig. 7.19 POWER2+ block diagram (*Courtesy of IBM Corp.*)

CHAPTER 8

The Sun SPARC Family

8.1 Introductory Comments

The SPARC architecture was initiated by Sun Microsystems, Inc., in Mountain View, CA. Before announcing the SPARC, Sun Microsystems produced a very popular family of M68000-based Sun workstations. One of the things that differentiates SPARC from other RISC-type systems is that Sun does not have a history of preceding microprocessors, RISC or CISC; so it had no software compatibility constraints to worry about. SPARC designers could start from a clean slate. Another thing that differentiates Sun from other RISC microprocessor manufacturers is that it does not manufacture the chips it designs. Sun Microsystems designed the SPARC architecture, and then produced the workstations implementing the SPARC microprocessors (the famous and very popular SPARCstations). The actual manufacturing of microprocessors implementing the SPARC architecture is licensed out to a number of chip manufacturing companies in the USA, Europe, and Japan (the situation may somewhat change in the future with Sun starting to market the SPARC microprocessors as well). In fact, the very first marketed implementation of the SPARC was manufactured by the Japanese Fujitsu Microelectronics, Inc. The latest top-level SPARC implementations are the SuperSPARC and the UltraSPARC: a joint venture of Sun Microsystems and Texas Instruments (TI) in Houston, Texas.

The name SPARC stands for *scalable processor architecture* [Garn 88, KlWi 88, Paul 94, Sprc 90, Tabk 94]. The concept of *scalability*, as seen by the SPARC creators, is the wide spectrum of its possible price/performance implementations, ranging from the microcomputers to supercomputers [Garn 88]. The scalability of the SPARC can also be interpreted in the number of CPU registers than can be used in various versions of products, implementing the SPARC architecture. The SPARC architecture follows the Berkeley RISC design philosophy [Kate 85, PaSe 82, Patt 85, Tabk 94] by its stressing of the importance of the relatively large CPU register file and by implementing similar register window features (see also chapter 2). This will be further elaborated in the next section describing the SPARC architecture.

8.2 SPARC Architecture
Register file
SPARC architecture features a comparatively large CPU register file of over 100 registers. As in the Berkeley RISC, any procedure funning on the SPARC can access only 32 registers, denoted r0 to r31. Eight of the registers (r0 to r7) are *global*, accessible by all procedures. The other 24 registers are the *window registers*, assigned to each procedure, with an overlap of eight registers between procedures. The 24 window registers are subdivided into three groups of eight registers each, as illustrated in Fig. 8.1, for a sequence of three nested procedures.

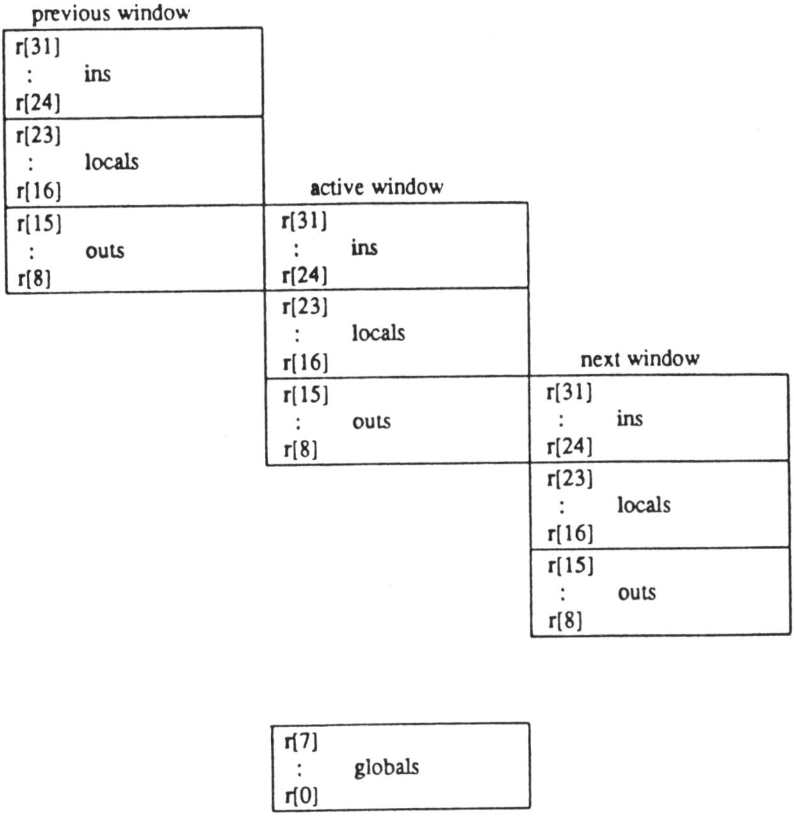

Fig. 8.1   Three overlapping windows and globals *(© Copyright Sun Microsystems, Inc. 1987)*

The group subdivision of the window registers is:

r31 – r24   *ins*, contain parameters passed to the procedure by the calling procedure.
r23 – r16   *locals*, contain local parameters of the procedure.

r15 – r8   *outs*, contain parameters passed to the called procedure.

As can be seen in Fig. 8.1, the outs registers of the calling procedure are physically the ins registers of the called procedure. The calling procedure passes parameters to the called procedure through its outs registers, which are the ins registers of the called procedure. The register window of the currently running procedure, called the *active window*, is pointed to by the *current window pointer* (CWP) in the *processor state register* (PSR).

The number of windows (NWINDOWS) that can be used in different versions of the SPARC ranges from 2 to 32, for a total number of general-purpose *integer unit* (IU) registers (including the eight globals) ranging from 48 to 548, respectively. Most current SPARC implementation microprocessors feature eight windows for a total of 136 registers. Implemented windows are contiguously numbered 0 to (NWINDOWS – 1). An example of an eight-window implementation, where the windows are circularly interconnected, is shown in Fig. 8.2.

The CPU contains a 32-bit control register called *window invalid mask* (WIM). Each bit of WIM, w_i (i = 0, 1, ..., 31), corresponds to one of the possible 32 windows (even if less than 32 are implemented). If $w_i = 1$, window i is considered to be invalid, and a trap condition exists. The CPU's *program counter* (PC) is a separate register, not included in the general-purpose register file. SPARC implementations may have several PCs containing addresses of subsequent instructions.

Some of the SPARC IU registers have specially designated tasks. The r0 is hardwired to a zero value, as it is in many other RISC-type systems. A CALL instruction writes its own address into the *outs* register r15. The CWP is *decremented* with a SAVE instruction on a procedure call and *incremented* by a RESTORE instruction on a procedure return. Procedures can also be called without changing the window.

Suppose that in the case of NWINDOWS = 8 (Fig. 8.2), window 0 is the currently running active window. In this case, CWP = 0. Since window 0 is the last free window, when the procedure using window 0 calls another procedure a *window overflow* occurs. A new register window wraps around to overwrite the previously used window 7, whose contents must be saved in the memory by software. After a return, and when the register file was out of windows, we have a *window underflow*. Software must restore previously used register windows in this case. A window overflow trap is caused by the overflow. The overflow trap handler uses the locals of window 7 for pointers into the memory where the overflowed window is stored. Window 7 is invalidated during the trap handling by setting bit w_7 of the WIM register.

Data types
SPARC architecture recognizes the following data types, shown in Fig. 8.3:

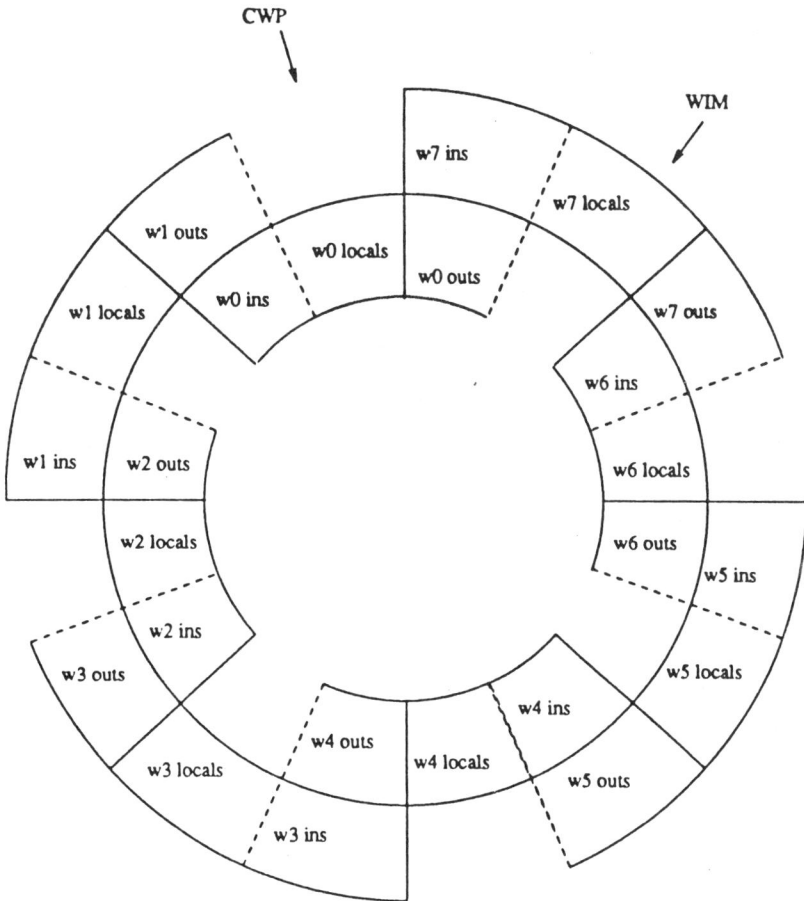

Fig. 8.2   Circular stack of window registers *(© Copyright Sun Microsystems, Inc. 1987)*

Integer
Signed, unsigned byte   8 bits
Signed, unsigned halfword   16 bits
Signed, unsigned word   32 bits
Doubleword   64 bits
Floating-point (IEEE 754-1985 Standard)
Single-precision   32 bits (exponent: 8 bits, fraction: 23 bits)
Double-precision   64 bits (exponent: 11 bits, fraction: 52 bits)
Quad-precision   128 bits (exponent: 15 bits, fraction: 112 bits)

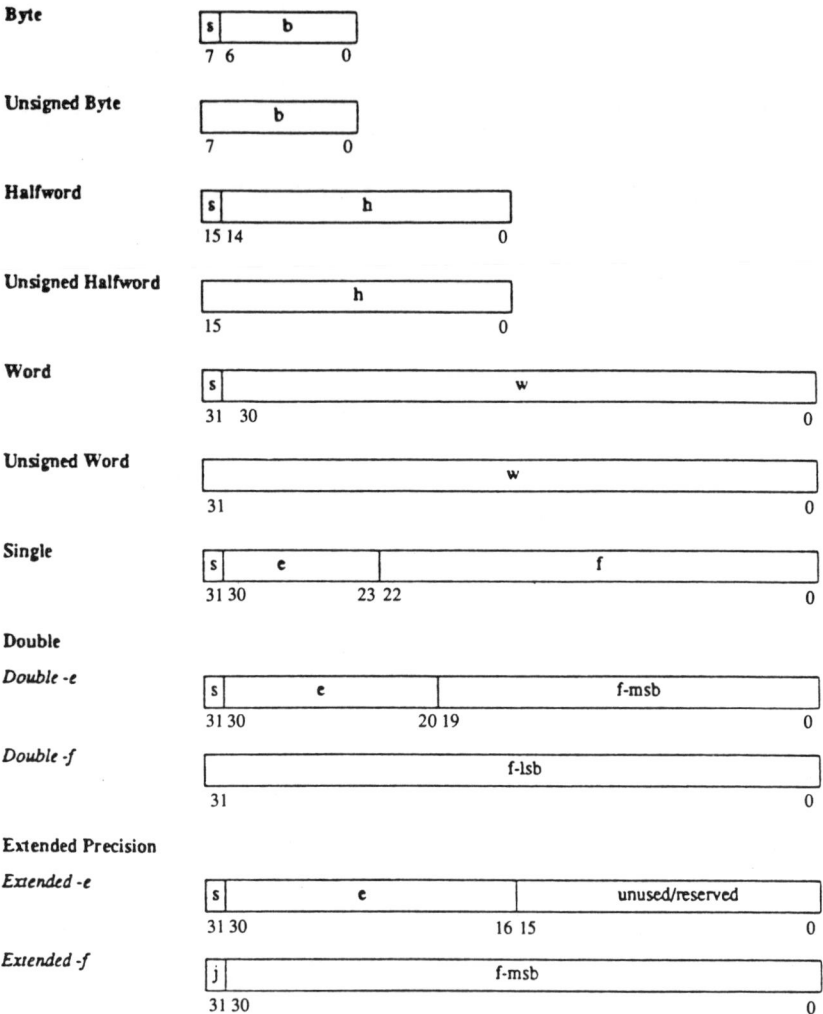

Fig. 8.3 Processor data types *(© Copyright Sun Microsystems, Inc. 1987)*

The halfwords are aligned on two-byte address boundaries (even addresses), words on four-byte boundaries (addresses divisible by four), and doublewords on eight-byte boundaries (addresses divisible by eight). The storage of the data types in memory is illustrated in Fig. 8.4. A big-endian byte ordering is used.

Instruction formats

The SPARC instruction formats are shown in Fig. 8.5. There are three basic instruction format types:

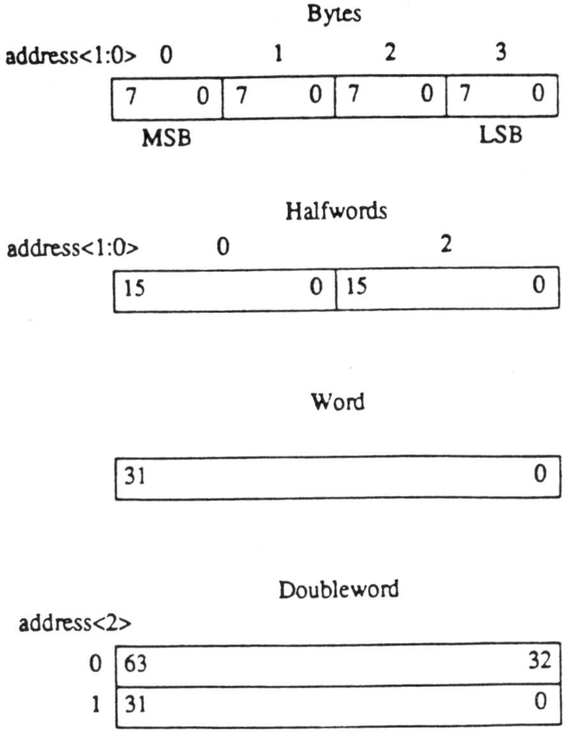

Fig. 8.4   Address conventions *(© Copyright Sun Microsystems, Inc. 1987)*

1. CALL
2. Branch instructions
3. Operate instructions (register-to-register).

As can be seen in Fig. 8.5, the operations instructions implement three-operand addressing, and all formats are of a single word length (32 bits). The fields in the instructions have the following designation:

op   bits 31, 30 in all formats. They are interpreted as follows:

Format 1: CALL

op	disp30

31 29   0

Format 2: SETHI and Branches (Bicc, FBfcc, CBcc)

op	rd	op2	imm22
op	a	cond	op2	disp22

31 29 28 24 21   0

Format 3: Remaining instructions

op	rd	op3	rs1	i	asi	rs2
op	rd	op3	rs1	i	simm13	
op	rd	op3	rs1	opf	rs2	

31 29 24 18 13 12 4 0

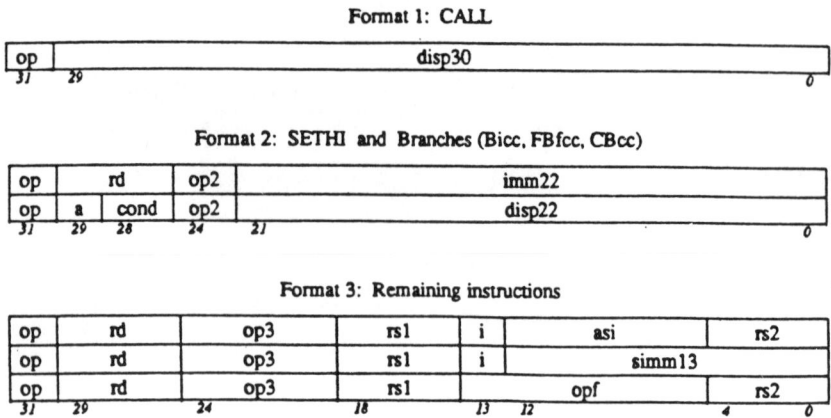

Fig. 8.5   SPARC instruction formats *(© Copyright Sun Microsystems, Inc. 1987)*

op	instruction
01	Call
00	Bicc, FBfcc, CBccc, SETHI
10 or 11	All other instructions

op2   bits 24 to 22 in format 2. Selects the instruction as follows:

op2	instruction
000	UNIMP
010	Bicc
100	SETHI
110	FBfcc
111	CBccc

rd   bits 29 to 25 in formats 2 and 3. Selects the source register for store instructions and the destination register for all other instructions.

a   bit 29 in format 2. Annul bit. Changes the behavior of the instruction encountered immediately after a control transfer.

cond   bits 28 to 25 in format 2. Selects the condition code for conditional branches.

imm22   bits 21 to 0 in format 2. A 22-bit constant value used by the SETHI instruction.

disp22   bits 21 to 0 in format 2. A 22-bit sign-extended word displacement for branch instructions.

disp30   bits 29 to 0 in format 1. A 30-bit sign-extended word displacement for PC-relative call instructions.

op3   bits 24 to 19 in format 3. Opcode extension.

i   bit 13 in format 3. Selects the type of the second ALU operand for non-floating-point operation instructions.
$i = 0$: the second operand is in a register rs2.
$i = 1$: the second operand is sign-extended simm13.

asi   bits 12 to 5 in format 3. An eight-bit address space identifier generated by load and store alternate instructions.

rs1   bits 18 to 14 in format 3. Selects the first source operand register.

rs2   bits 4 to 0 in format 3. Selects the second source operand register.

simm13   bits 12 to 0 in format 3. A sign-extended 13-bit immediate value.

opf   bits 13 to 5 in format 3. Identifies a floating-point operate instruction.

Addressing modes

Besides the standard *register direct* and *immediate* addressing modes, there are only three addressing modes for memory access:

1. *Register indirect with displacement*; register + signed 13-bit constant.
2. *Register indirect indexed*; register1 + register2.
3. *PC-relative*; used in CALL instructions with a 30-bit displacement.

Instruction set

The SPARC architecture features the following types of instructions:

1. Load/store
2. Arithmetic/logical/shift.
3. Control transfer.
4. Read/write control registers.
5. Floating-point operate.
6. Coprocessor operate (not needed on latest highly integrated implementations).

The SPARC instruction set is summarized in Table 8.1.

The load and store instructions (the only ones to access memory) generate a 32-bit byte address. In addition to the address, the processor always generates a nine-bit *address space identifier* (**asi**), interpreted as follows:

Table 8.1 SPARC Instruction Set

Opcode	Name
LDSB (LDSBA†)	Load Signed Byte (from Alternate space)
LDSH (LDSHA†)	Load Signed Halfword (from Alternate space)
LDUB (LDUBA†)	Load Unsigned Byte (from Alternate space)
LDUH (LDUHA†)	Load Unsigned Halfword (from Alternate space)
LD (LDA†)	Load Word (from Alternate space)
LDD (LDDA)†	Load Doubleword (from Alternate space)
LDF	Load Floating-point
LDDF	Load Double Floating-point
LDFSR	Load Floating-point State Register
LDC	Load Coprocessor
LDDC	Load Double Coprocessor
LDCSR	Load Coprocessor State Register
STB (STBA†)	Store Byte (into Alternate space)
STH (STHA†)	Store Halfword (into Alternate space)
ST (STA†)	Store Word (into Alternate space)
STD (STDA†)	Store Doubleword (into Alternate space)
STF	Store Floating-point
STDF	Store Double Floating-point
STFSR	Store Floating-point State Register
STDFQ†	Store Double Floating-point Queue
STC	Store Coprocessor
STDC	Store Double Coprocessor
STCSR	Store Coprocessor State Register
STDCQ†	Store Double Coprocessor Queue
LDSTUB (LDSTUBA†)	Atomic Load-Store Unsigned Byte (in Alternate space)
SWAP (SWAPA†)	Swap r Register with Memory (in Alternate space)
ADD (ADDcc)	Add (and modify icc)
ADDX (ADDXcc)	Add with Carry (and modify icc)
TADDcc (TADDccTV)	Tagged Add and modify icc (and Trap on overflow)
SUB (SUBcc)	Subtract (and modify icc)
SUBX (SUBXcc)	Subtract with Carry (and modify icc)
TSUBcc (TSUBccTV)	Tagged Subtract and modify icc (and Trap on overflow)
MULScc	Multiply Step and modify icc
AND (ANDcc)	And (and modify icc)
ANDN (ANDNcc)	And Not (and modify icc)
OR (ORcc)	Inclusive-Or (and modify icc)
ORN (ORNcc)	Inclusive-Or Not (and modify icc)
XOR (XORcc)	Exclusive-Or (and modify icc)
XNOR (XNORcc)	Exclusive-Nor (and modify icc)
SLL	Shift Left Logical
SRL	Shift Right Logical
SRA	Shift Right Arithmetic
SETHI	Set High 22 bits of r register
SAVE	Save caller's window
RESTORE	Restore caller's window
Bicc	Branch on integer condition codes
FBfcc	Branch on floating-point condition codes
CBccc	Branch on coprocessor condition codes
CALL	Call
JMPL	Jump and Link
RETT†	Return from Trap
Ticc	Trap on integer condition codes

Opcode	Name
RDY RDPSR† RDWIM† RDTBR†	Read Y register Read Processor State Register Read Window Invalid Mask register Read Trap Base Register
WRY WRPSR† WRWIM† WRTBR†	Write Y register Write Processor State Register Write Window Invalid Mask register Write Trap Base Register
UNIMP	Unimplemented instruction
IFLUSH	Instruction cache Flush
FPop	Floating-point Operate: FiTO(s.d.x), Fis.d.x)TOi FsTOd, FsTOx, FdTOs, FdTOx, FxTOs, FxTOd, FMOVs, FNEGs, FABSs, FSQRT(s.d.x), FADD(s.d.x), FSUB(s.d.x), FMUL(s.d.x), FDIV(s.d.x), FCMP(s.d.x), FCMPE(s.d.x)
CPop	Coprocessor operate

(© Copyright Sun Microsystems, Inc. 1987)   † privileged instruction

asi (decimal)	Assignment
0 – 7	Implementation-definable
8	User instruction space
9	Supervisor instruction space
10	User data space
11	Supervisor data space
12 – 255	Implementation-definable

Examples:

LDSB   addr, rd; bad signed byte from memory at address addr into register rd.

LD   addr, rd; load word from addr into rd.

Most of the arithmetic-logical instructions have dual versions (such as ADD and ADDcc) that modify the integer condition codes (icc) as a side effect.

Examples:

ADD   rs1, rs2, rd; (rs1) + (rs2) → rd, no icc modification.

ADDcc   rs1, rs2, rd; (rs1) + (rs2) → rd, icc modified.

In some SPARC assemblers, registers are denoted as follows:

%0 to %31   all general registers r0 to r31.
%g0 to %g7   global registers, same as %0 to %7.
%o0 to %o7   outs registers, same as %8 to %15.
%l0 to %l7   local registers, same as %16 to %23.
%i0 to %i7   ins registers, same as %24 to %31.

Examples:

SUB   %12, %11, %15; (r12) – (r11) → r15.

AND   %5, %3, %1; (r5) AND (r3) → r1.

The SETHI (set high 22 bits of rd) instruction writes a 22-bit constant from the instruction into the high-order bits of the destination register rd. It clears the low-order 10 bits of rd and does not change the condition codes. It can be used to construct a 32-bit constant using two instructions. It is used in the following form (format 2):

SETHI   const22, rd; const22 is a 22-bit constant number.

There are five types of control transfer instruction:

1. Conditional branch (Bicc, FBfcc, CBccc).
2. Jump and link.
3. Call (CALL).
4. Trap (Ticc).
5. Return from trap (RETT).

Each of the above can be further categorized according to whether it is

(1) PC-relative or register-indirect

or

(2) delayed or nondelayed.

A PC-relative control transfer computes its target address by adding the (sgifted) sign-extended immediate displacement to the PC value. A control transfer instruction is *delayed* if it transfers control to the target address after a one-instruction delay. This is essentially the *delayed-branch* feature, described in chapter 2. The a (annul) bit in format 2 influences the execution of the *delay instruction*, which follows the branch instruction. The annul operation is as follows:

a	Type of Branch	Delay Instruction Executed?
1	Unconditional	No
	Conditional, taken	Yes
	Conditional, not taken	No
0	Unconditional	Yes
	Conditional, taken	Yes
	Conditional, not taken	Yes

A procedure that requires a register window is invoked by executing both a CALL (or JMPL) and a SAVE instruction. A procedure that does not need a register window, a so-called *leaf routine*, is invoked by executing only a CALL (or a JMPL). Leaf routines can use only the *outs* registers. The CALL instruction stores PC, which points to the CALL itself, into register r15 (an outs register). The JMPL (jump and link) instruction stores PC into the specified register.

Example: JMPL   addr, rd; PC stored in rd.

The SAVE instruction is similar to an ADD instruction, except that it also decrements the CWP by one, causing the active window to become the previous window, thereby saving the caller's window.
Example: SAVE   rs1, rs2, rd; the operands rs1 and rs2 are from the previous (old) window and rd is in the new window, addressed by the new value in the CWP field.

A procedure that uses a register window returns by executing both a RESTORE and a JMPL instruction. A leaf procedure returns by executing a JMPL only. The RESTORE instruction (also similar to an ADD) increments the CWP by one, causing the previous window to become the active window, thereby restoring the caller's window. Also, the source registers for the addition are from the current window, while the result is written into the previous window. Both SAVE and RESTORE compare the new CWP against the WIM to check for window overflow or underflow.

The SPARC architecture features the following multiprocessor operation support instructions:

SWAP — exchanges the content of an IU register with a word from memory, while preventing other memory accesses from intervening. SWAP is an *atomic* instruction.
LDSTUB — *atomic load and store unsigned byte*, reads a byte from memory into an IU register and then rewrites the same byte in memory to all 1's, while precluding intervening accesses. Can be used to construct *semaphores*.

The floating-point instructions, featured by the SPARC architecture, which were mentioned in Table 8.1, are listed in more detail in Table 8.2.

SPARC architecture was developed during the past years through several versions. Version 8 (V8), implemented on the SuperSPARC (see section 8.3), included:

1. SPARC reference MMU, reducing the time involved in porting an OS to a newly designed hardware platform.
2. Suggested address space identifier (ASI) assignments, facilitating the manufacture of systems compatible with the SPARC architecture. ASI addressing

Table 8.2 Floating-Point SPARC Instructions

Mnemonic	Operation
FiTOs,d,q	Convert integer to floating-point s,d,q
F(s,d,q)TOi	Convert floating-point s,d,q to integer
FsTOd,q	Convert floating-point single to d,q
FdTOs,q	Convert floating-point double to s,q
FqTOs,d	Convert floating-point quad to s,d
FMOVs	Move floating-point single
FNEGs	Negate floating-point single
FSQRTs,d,q	Floating-point square root s,d,q
FADDs,d,q	Floating-point add s,d,q
FSUBs,d,q	Floating-point subtract s,d,q
FMULs,d,q	Floating-point multiply s,d,q
FDIVs,d,q	Floating-point divide s,d,q
FsMULd	Floating-point multiply single produce double
FdMULq	Floating-point multiply double produce quad
FCMPs,d,q	Floating-point compare s,d,q
FCMPEs,d,q	Floating-point compare no exceptions s,d,q

Where
s - single-precision
d - double-precision
q - quad or extended-precision
Note: instructions FsMULd and FdMULq are new on the SuperSPARC and have not been featured in earlier SPARC implementations.

allows the OS to take advantage of eight address bits in addition to a normal address. ASIs can be used for MMU interrogation, cache flushing, and other high-performance features.

3.   Integer multiply and divide instructions.

4.   Basic multiprocessor support.

5.   Standardized application binary interface (ABI) software information for software developers, ensuring that third-party software would be portable to systems implementing the SPARC architecture.

The SPARC version 9 (V9) architecture [WeGe 94] enhances V8 by providing explicit support for:

1.   64-bit addresses and 64-bit integer data; integer registers and virtual addresses extended to 64 bits.

2.   Advanced optimizing compilers.

3.   Superscalar implementations.

4.   Advanced OS.

5.   Fault tolerance.

6.   Faster trap handling and context switching.

7.   Big- and little-endian byte ordering.

8.   32 64-bit, double-precision floating-point registers (16 additional registers).

9.   Condition codes for both 32- and 64-bit data types.

10. Four sets of floating-point condition code registers (up from one), allowing more parallelism.

V9 main instruction set changes include [WeGe 94]:

1. Speculative loads.
2. Branch prediction in new branch instructions, avoiding pipeline delays.
3. The instruction **branch on register value** reduces instruction count and increases parallelism.
4. 64-bit integer multiply and divide.
5. Conditional move instructions.
6. A new barrier instruction.
7. Compare-and-swap instruction.
8. Prefetch instruction.

The SPARC V9 architecture defines a new memory model called *relaxed memory order* (RMO). The RMO allows the CPU hardware to schedule memory accesses (load/store) in nearly any order, as long as the program attains a correct result. Hence, the hardware can instantaneously adjust to resource contentions and schedule accesses in the most efficient order, leading to much faster memory operations and better overall performance [WeGe 94].

In addition to the instruction set, available under the SPARC V9 architecture, an additional *visual instruction set* (VIS) was developed for the UltraSPARC implementation [Kohn 95]. The purpose of the VIS is to provide a standard multimedia capability for SPARC-based systems. The VIS is well suited for parallel processing of graphics data. The VIS allows the support of:

1. Video conferencing.
2. Video decoding with broadcast quality (720×480 pixels, 30 frames/sec).
3. Three-dimensional visualization.
4. Stripped-down systems where the CPU does all the required graphics manipulation.

The VIS data types are *pixels* and *fixed data* Pixels consist of eight-bit unsigned integers contained in a 32-bit word. Fixed data consist of either four 16-bit fixed-point components, or two 32-bit fixed-point components, both contained in a 64-bit doubleword.

The VIS features the following types of instruction:

conversion
arithmetic/logical
address manipulation
memory access
motion estimation, use in video compression algorithms.

8.3 High-Performance SPARC Implementations
The SuperSPARC

The SuperSPARC is a 3.1 million transistors, 0.8 micron, three-layer metal BiCMOS, 293 ceramic pin grid array (PGA) microprocessor, manufactured by Texas Instruments (TI) in cooperation with Sun Microsystems [BlKr 92, SSPC 92]. The processor chip contains an IU, FPU, MMU, and a dual cache (20KB code, 16KB data, total: 36KB). A block diagram of the SuperSPARC is shown in Fig. 8.6.

The SuperSPARC is a three-issue superscalar system. The SuperSPARC can issue and execute three instructions every cycle subject to the following constraints:

1. Maximum of two integer results.
2. Maximum of one data memory reference.
3. Maximum of one floating-point arithmetic instruction.
4. Terminate group of instructions after each control transfer.

Data dependencies (see chapter 1) are solved on the SuperSPARC by:

1. *Cascading* dependent instructions in the same group.
2. *Forwarding* dependent instructions in consecutive groups.

The block diagram in Fig. 8.6 shows the details of the structure of the IU. There are four ALUs and a shifter. The lower leftmost ALU is used for address computations; its output is forwarded to the MMU and the data cache. The other three ALUs are used for data processing. If we have two integer instructions which are data-dependent, the first instruction can be executed in one of the upper ALUs, forwarding the result and another operand to the lower ALU, completing both computations within a single cycle. After that, both results are stored in the IU register file.

The SuperSPARC integer pipeline consists of four stages (cycles). Each cycle has two phases. The pipeline eight phases are:

1. **F0** Instruction cache (I-cache) access and TLB lookup.
2. **F1** I-cache match detect. Four instructions sent to the instruction queue (iqueue).
3. **D0** Issue one, two, or three instructions. Select register indices for load/store instructions.
4. **D1** Read register file for load/store instructions. Resource allocation for ALU instructions. Evaluate branch target address.
5. **D2** Read register file for ALU operands. Calculate EA for load/store instructions.
6. **E0** First stage of ALU. Data cache (D-cache) access and TLB lookup. Floating-point instruction dispatch.

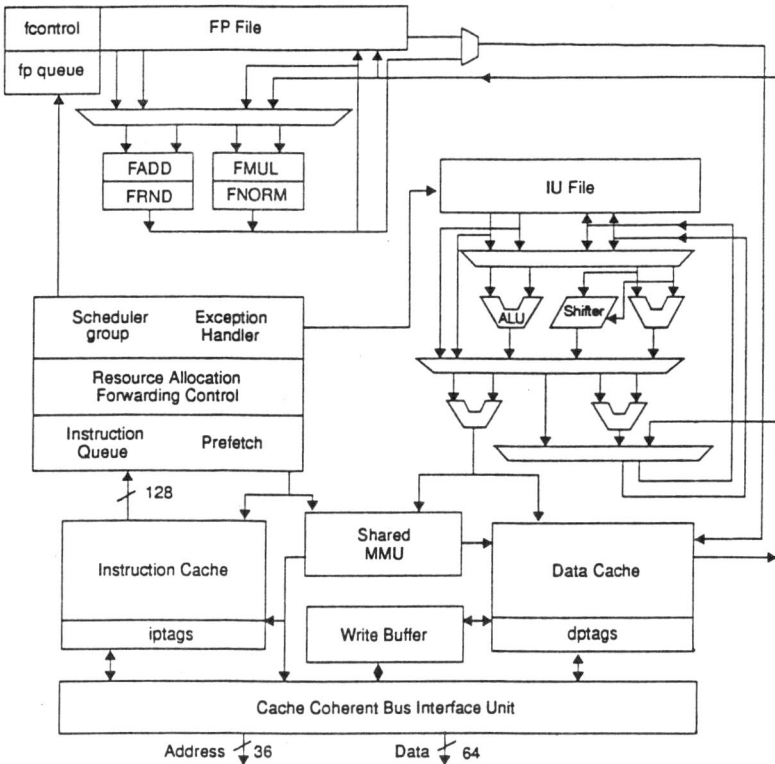

Fig. 8.6 SuperSPARC functional block diagram *(Courtesy of Sun Microsystems, Inc., and TI, Inc.)*

7. **E1** Second stage of ALU. D-cache match detect. Load data available. Resolve exceptions.

8. **WB** Write back result into the register file. Retire store into the store buffer.

The FPU pipeline is tightly coupled to the integer pipeline. An operation may be started every cycle; the delay of most floating-point operations is three cycles. In the E0 phase, one floating-point arithmetic instruction is selected for execution and its operands are read during E1. Two stages of execution delay are required for the double-precision FPU adder and FPU multiplier. The first cycle of the adder examines exponents, aligns mantissas, and produces a result. The first cycle of the multiplier computes and adds partial products. Independent second stages round and normalize the result of the respective units. Forwarding paths are provided to chain results of one FPU operation into the source of a subsequent operation.

Fig. 8.7 illustrates an example of pipelined execution of a set of ALU

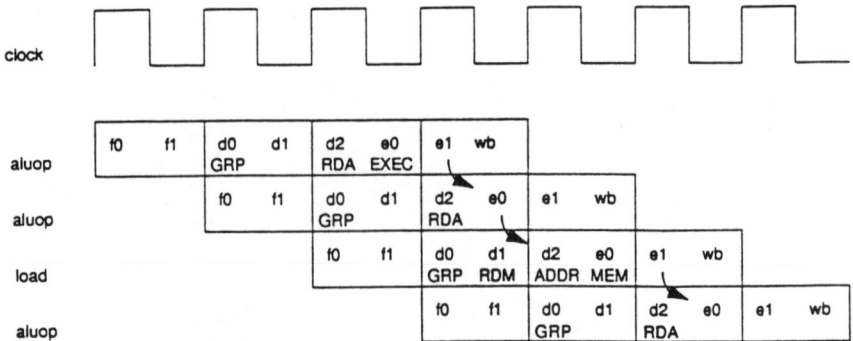

Fig. 8.7   Pipelined execution of load with forwarding.
GRP — issue group of instructions
RDA — read register file for ALU operands
EXEC — execute
RDM — read register file for memory access
ADDR — calculate EA
MEM — D-cache access
(Courtesy of Sun Microsystems, Inc., and TI, Inc.)

operations, with a load instruction in between. Up to four instructions can be fetched during the (F0,F1) cycle, but only up to three instructions can be issued as a group (**GRP**) during the D0 phase. Forwarding of results between subsequent groups of instructions is shown by arrows in Fig. 8.7.

Pipelined execution of a set of instructions, which includes a conditional branch, is shown in Fig. 8.8. A taken branch case is in Fig. 8.8(a), and a non-taken case in Fig. 8.8(b). The original sequential instructions are denoted as S1 and S2, an the target instructions as T1, T2, T3, and T4. The delay instruction, placed after the conditional branch instruction (BNE in this example), is denoted by DI, while C1 refers to the certainty instruction stream. The SuperSPARC processor can group the compare (CMP) and the conditional branch instruction (BNE), to speed execution. The processor statically predicts that all branches are taken. When a control transfer instruction relative to the PC is issued, its DI is fetched concurrently. During the D1 phase, the target address (TA) is computed. As the branch instruction enters phase D2, the target instruction stream is fetched (FT). The fetch completes as the DI advances to phase D1 and the compare and branch instructions enter phase E0. The compare instruction computes new integer condition codes in phase E0, and the branch direction is resolved. When a branch is taken, all sequential path instructions (S1 and on; grouped together with the DI) are invalidated (squash S1), as shown in Fig. 8.8(a). When branch is not taken (untaken), sequential path instructions (SA+) remain valid and the target instructions (T1 and on) fetched are discarded. This scheme does not introduce a

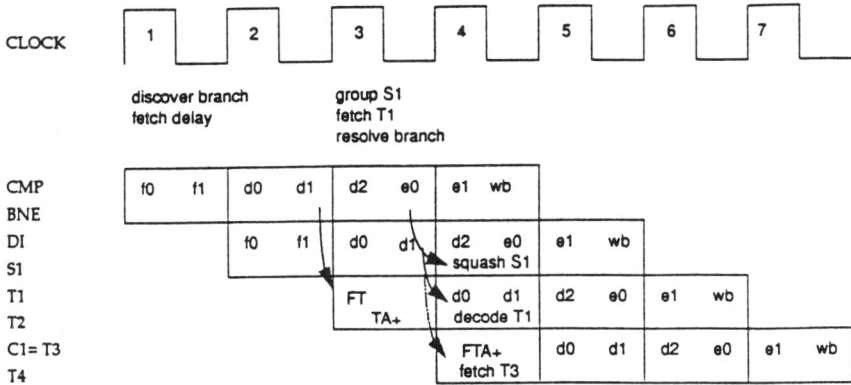

Fig. 8.8(a) Taken conditional branch *(Courtesy of Sun Microsystems, Inc., and TI, Inc.)*

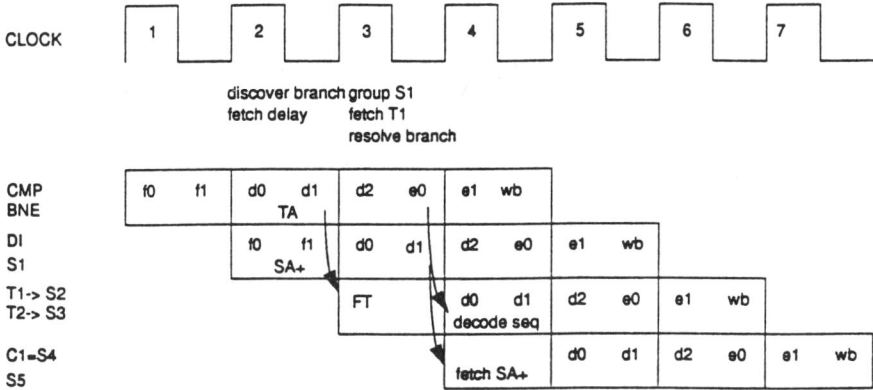

Fig. 8.8(b) Untaken conditional branch *(Courtesy of Sun Microsystems, Inc., and TI, Inc.)*

pipeline bubble (stall) for either branch path. The PC and prefetch PC values for *both* directions are precomputed. The SuperSPARC branch implementation can execute non-taken branches somewhat more efficiently than taken branches.

The SuperSPARC implements a *precise exception* model. At any given time there can be up to nine instructions in the IU pipeline and four more in the floating-point queue. Exceptions and the instructions that caused them propagate through the IU pipeline. They are resolved in the execute stage before their results can modify visible state in the register file, control registers, or memory.

The FPU consists of a *floating-point controller* (FPC), two independent pipelines FADD and FMUL, a floating-point queue, and a 32-bit 32-register floating-point file (FP file, Fig. 8.6). The FP file is organized as 16 64-bit doublewords to optimize double-precision performance. Each 32-bit word of the

FP file can be accessed separately, however. The FP file has three read and two write ports. The FPC is tightly coupled to the IU pipeline and is capable of executing a floating-point memory event and a floating-point operation in the same cycle. The FPC also handles floating-point exceptions.

There are two types of floating-point instructions:

1. **FPOPs** — floating-point operations, such as add, multiply, convert and so on.
2. **FPEVENTs** — floating-point events, such as load/store to/from floating-point registers, load/store to/from floating-point status register, store floating-point queue, integer multiply, and integer divide. FPEVENTs are executed by the FPU but do not enter the FPU queue. The FPU pipeline consists of four stages:

1. **FRD** — decode and read.
2. **FM/FA** — execute multiply or add.
3. **FN/FR** — normalization and rounding.
4. **FWB** — write back to FP file.

All floating-point instructions are issued by the IU in the E0 phase of the IU pipeline. Once issued, the floating-point instructions proceed through the FPU pipeline. The FPU pipeline stalls the IU pipeline in a few situations: the FPU queue will become full after several long-delay FPU arithmetic instructions are encountered in close proximity. Forwarding paths are provided to chain the result of one FPOP to source operands of a subsequent FPOP without stalling for an FP register write. Similarly, an FPEVENT load can forward data to FPOP source operands and an FPOP result can forward data to an FPEVENT store.

All FPU instructions start in order and complete in order. They are executed in one of the two independent units: FADD and FMUL. These instructions are held in a first-in-first-out (FIFO) queue that holds up to four entries. Each entry can hold a 32-bit FPOP instruction and a 32-bit FPOP address.

An FPU exception remains pending until another FPOP or FPEVENT is requested by the IU. It will be reported to the subsequent floating-point instruction at that time.

The SuperSPARC has a dual cache: 20 Kbyte instruction and 16 Kbyte data cache for a total of 36 Kbyte on-chip primary cache. There is support for an external, second-level 1 Mbyte cache. Fig. 8.9 shows the SuperSPARC MMU and cache organization. This organization uses the term 'set' in a different manner than in the computer literature [HaVZ 90, Hays 88]. In the SuperSPARC, a set is a block of data of 4 Kbyte, the page size in this system. The instruction cache contains five such sets for a total of five pages or 20 Kbytes. The data cache contains four such sets for a total of four pages or 16 Kbytes. Based on this, the instruction cache is said to be five-way set-associative, and the data cache is four-way set-associative. Both caches use a pseudo LRU replacement algorithm. The line size on the instruction cache is 64 bytes, and on the data cache it is 32 bytes. The instruction cache is accessed by a 128-bit fetch path, allowing the fetching of

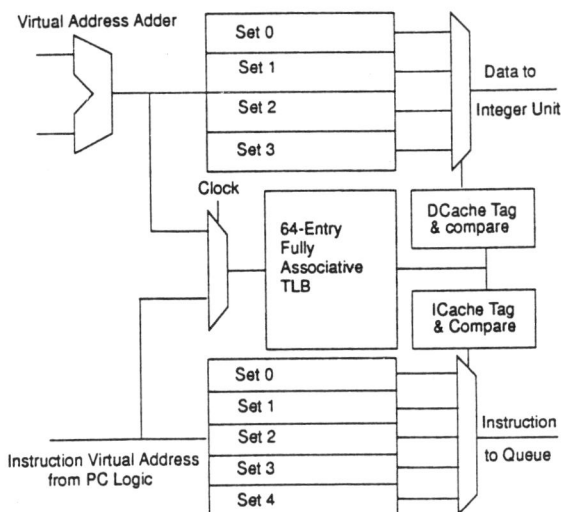

Fig. 8.9   Cache/MMU organization *(Courtesy of Sun Microsystems, Inc., and TI, Inc.)*

four instructions simultaneously. The data cache is accessed by a 64-bit path, allowing transmission of double-precision floating-point data in one bus cycle. The hit rate for SPEC 92 was reported by Sun to be 98% for the instruction cache and 90% for the data cache. The caches are physically addressed. The SuperSPARC TLB has 64 entries, and it is fully associative.

The following instructions, not available on the early SPARC implementations, are featured by the SuperSPARC:

UMUL (UMULcc): unsigned integer multiply (and modify icc).
SMUL (SMULcc): signed integer multiply (and modify icc).
UDIV (UDIVcc): unsigned integer divide (and modify icc).
SDIV (SDIVcc): signed integer divide (and modify icc).
STBAR: store barrier.
FsMULd: floating-point multiply single produce double.

There is a second-generation SuperSPARC implementation — the SuperSPARC II [SSII 95]. SuperSPARC II is a 0.72 BiCMOS, 90MHz, 3.1 million transistors, 313 pin ceramic PGA microprocessor. The main differences in SuperSPARC II design, compared to the first-generation SuperSPARC, are:

1. Higher frequency of operation (90MHz).
2. Redesign of the pipeline. The major change is the elimination of decode stage D2 and increasing the WB stage to a full cycle.

The SuperSPARC II four pipeline stages are:

F (Fetch) — fetch instruction from memory into the instruction prefetch queue.

D (Decode, Grouping, Read register file) — selects an in-order instruction group from the candidate instructions at the head of the instruction queue prefetch buffer. Checks scoreboard dependencies and inserts pipeline bubbles when dependencies cannot be met by forwarding. Assigns execution unit resources to specific instructions in the selected instruction group. Reads memory reference address registers. Generates branch target address. Manages next PC value. Reads operand registers.

E (Execute) — performs IU execution. Dispatches floating-point commands.

WB (Write-back) — stores results.

3. Redesign of IU register file. The register file is accessed only once per cycle in SuperSPARC II (as opposed to twice in SuperSPARC). The SuperSPARC II register file has 10 ports: eight read and two write (four ports on SuperSPARC). This eliminates the need for a double access per cycle. This also eliminates the need of multiplexing operands as on the SuperSPARC.

4. Five-stage FPU pipeline (four stages on SuperSPARC).

The five SuperSPARC II FPU stages are:

Fd (Dispatch) — decodes the new FPU instruction from the IU pipeline or the FPU queue. Reads the register file for new operands. Checks dependency between instructions and determines candidates for execution. Forwards load data into source operands.

Fp (Pre-process) — checks instruction operands for subnormal numbers. Prepares operands for the next stage (Fx). Starts a small portion of execution.

Fx (Execute) — execution in either the add, multiply or divide/square root execute stage. The Fx stalls for floating-point divide or square root until an unrounded result is computed.

Fr (Rounding) — results from the Fx stage are rounded.

Fw (Write-back) — store results, report traps when exceptions are detected.

5. Split TLB (as opposed to a unified 64-entry TLB on the SuperSPARC):

64-entry for the D-cache
16-entry for the I-cache.

The UltraSPARC

The UltraSPARC is a 64-bit, 0.5m CMOS, four-metal layer, 167MHz microprocessor, manufactured by TI (as is the SuperSPARC) [Gree 95, Kohn 95]. It is a four-issue superscalar with six execution units: two integer, two floating-point, one LSU, and one branch unit. Its block diagram is shown in Fig. 8.10. The

UltraSPARC has a nine-stage instruction pipeline, illustrated in Fig. 8.11. The first three stages and the last two stages are the same for integer and floating-point operations. The fourth to seventh stages are separate, allowing a single stage for integer and three stages for floating-point execution. The UltraSPARC maintains binary compatibility with all previous SPARC systems, including the SuperSPARC and the microSPARC.

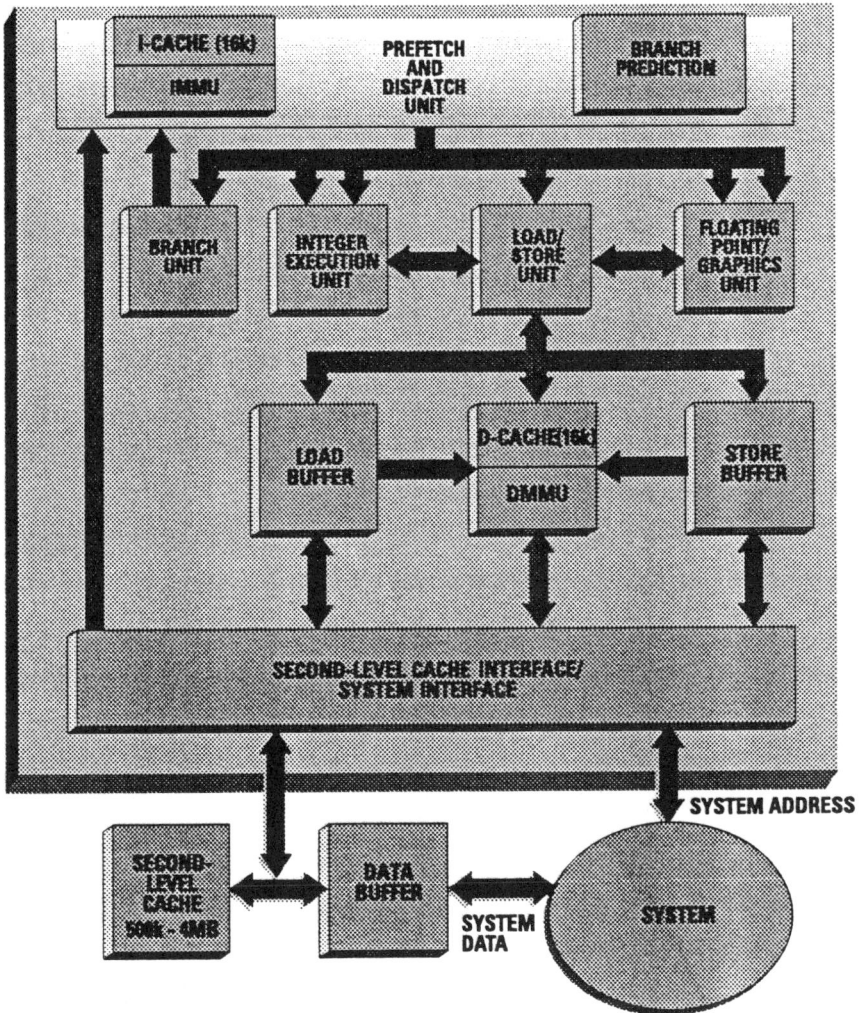

Fig. 8.10   UltraSPARC block diagram *(Courtesy of Sun Microsystems, Inc.)*

A 12-entry instruction buffer decouples the prefetching of instructions from their execution. The prefetching of instructions is based on the current flow of

F	D	G	E	C	N1	N2	N3	W
Fetch	Decode	Grouping	Execution	Cache Access				Writeback
Instructions are fetched from I-cache	Instructions are decoded and placed in the instruction buffer	Up to 4 instructions are grouped and dispatched. Register file accessed	Integer instructions are executed and virtual address calculated	D-cache access	Determines D-cache hit or miss, dTLB hit or miss	Load miss enters load buffer	Traps are resolved	All results are written to the register files. Instructions are considered committed

R	X1	X2	X3
Floating point and graphics instructions are further decoded and register file accessed	Start execution	Execution continued	Finish execution

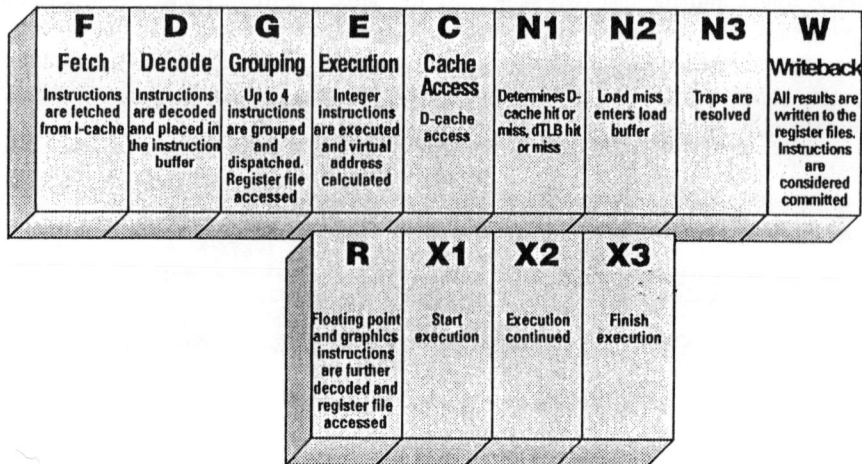

Fig. 8.11   UltraSPARC pipeline *(Courtesy of Sun Microsystems, Inc.)*

instructions and dynamic branch prediction. Up to four instructions are fetched per cycle and stored in the instruction buffer. The UltraSPARC prefetch and dispatch unit is illustrated in Fig. 8.12. The UltraSPARC uses dynamic branch prediction to predict the outcome of branches. This capability allows the processor to prefetch instructions and prepare them for the various execution units, shown in the lower part of Fig. 8.12. The branch prediction mechanism is based on a two-bit four-state machine that predicts branches based on the specific branch's most recent history. Since the history of a branch may change every time it is encountered, the prediction is dynamic in nature. Associated with each pair of instructions in the I-cache is a two-bit prediction field, indicating one of four possible branch prediction states: strongly taken (ST), lightly taken (LT), lightly not taken (LNT), and strongly not taken (SNT).

The two-bit branch prediction scheme is particularly efficient for looping branches — the most likely use for a branch. The processor only changes predictions for branches in steady state after two mispredictions, which is a suitable arrangement for loops. For instance, the prediction of the branch is set to strongly taken for a loop in a steady state. When the processor exits the loop, it changes the prediction bits to lightly taken. If the branch is not taken again, the prediction becomes strongly not taken.

The UltraSPARC integer execution unit (IEU) is shown in Fig. 8.13. It features two ALUs for integer arithmetic, logical and shift operations, integer multiply (two bits per clock), integer divide (one bit per clock), and an eight-window register file (as in other SPARC processors).

The UltraSPARC floating-point/graphics unit (FGU), shown in Fig. 8.14, features five separate functional units which support floating-point and graphics

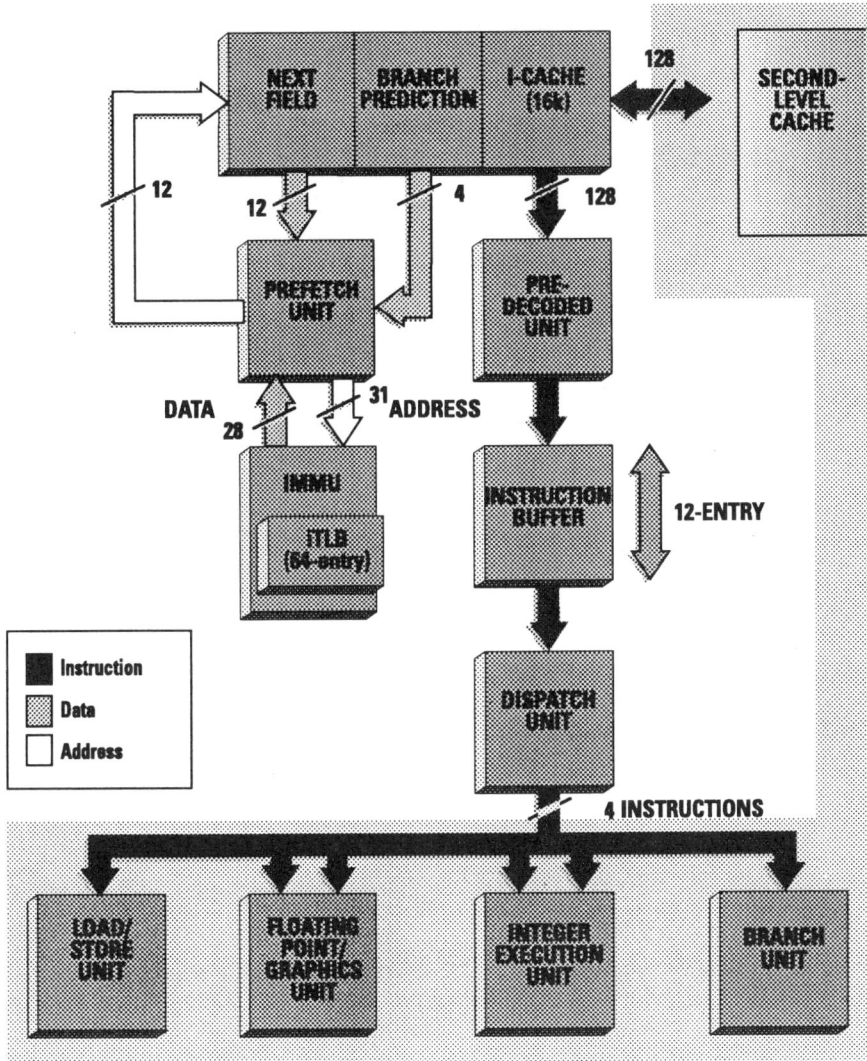

Fig. 8.12   Prefetch and dispatch unit *(Courtesy of Sun Microsystems, Inc.)*

operations. Its register file contains 32 double-precision 64-bit registers. The high floating-point bandwidth is two floating-point operations per cycle. The floating-point operations delay is one to three cycles, except for divide (12 cycles for single and 22 cycles for double precision) and square-root instructions.

The UltraSPARC load/store unit (LSU) is illustrated in Fig. 8.15. It includes the D-cache, a load buffer and a store buffer. The nine-deep load buffer eliminates stalls caused by a D-cache miss during a load operation. When a D-cache miss

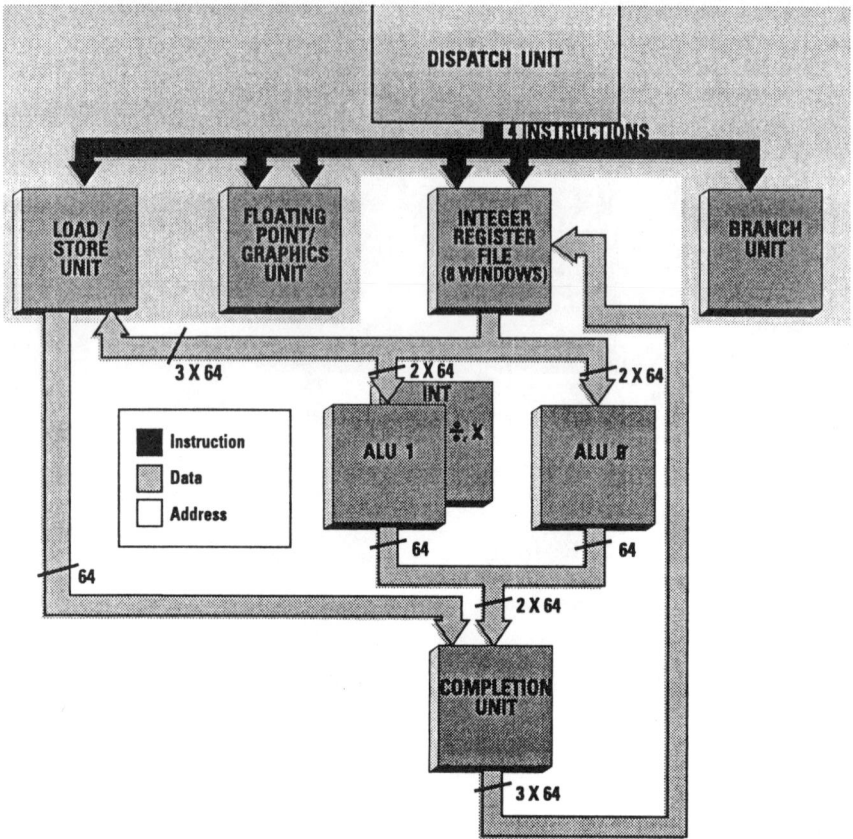

Fig. 8.13   Integer execution unit *(Courtesy of Sun Microsystems, Inc.)*

occurs, the unit gets the missed data from the second-level cache (L2) while the next several instructions are executed without a pause (assuming the subsequent instructions do not need the loaded value as an operand). This unit can accommodate up to nine outstanding loads without stalling, providing enough time for the processor to locate the data in L2 and load it (assuming no subsequent data dependencies; see chapter 1). To minimize pipeline stalls on a store miss, an eight-deep store buffer is featured. The decoupled tag and data portion in the store buffer both have separate address buses to L2. This enables the processor to determine a store bit or a miss ahead of, and independently from, the data transfer. Once the hit/miss information is obtained, a data transfer can occur simultaneously with the tag check of a later store. The decoupling of the tag and data in the store buffer supports a store throughput of up to one store per cycle. Store hits update L2, while store misses allocate a new line into L2 without updating main memory. Although

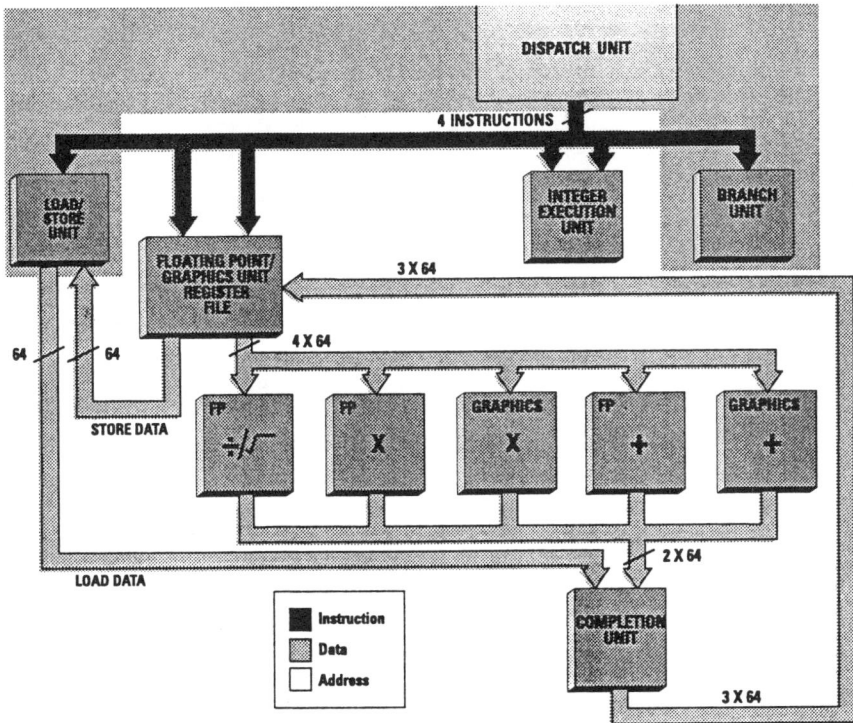

Fig. 8.14 Floating-point/graphics unit *(Courtesy of Sun Microsystems, Inc.)*

accesses to main memory take longer, the store buffer can successfully hide the delay from the processor.

The UltraSPARC memory system interface is illustrated in Fig. 8.16. Its 128-bit data bus supports a memory bandwidth of 600 MB/sec. It supports a 44-bit virtual address and a 41-bit physical address. The UltraSPARC MMU can accommodate different page sizes of any combination of 8KB, 64KB, 512KB, and 4MB. The UltraSPARC has a dual MMU: one for instructions and one for data. Each MMU has a fully associative, 64-entry TLB. Data buffers, which connect the processor to the system, serve to isolate the interaction between the CPU and L2 from the system bus. The data buffers also minimize the overhead of data transfers from the processor to the system during writebacks and non-cacheable store operations. These buffers include a read buffer that can hold a 64-bit line coming from main memory due to a miss in L2 or a non-cacheable read. There are several buffers receiving data from the processor. Two 64-byte buffers are included for writebacks, block stores and transmitted interrupt vectors. There are also eight 16-byte non-cacheable store buffers and a 64-byte snoop buffer for maintaining cache coherency. To shorten miss delays and enhance the bandwidth to and from the

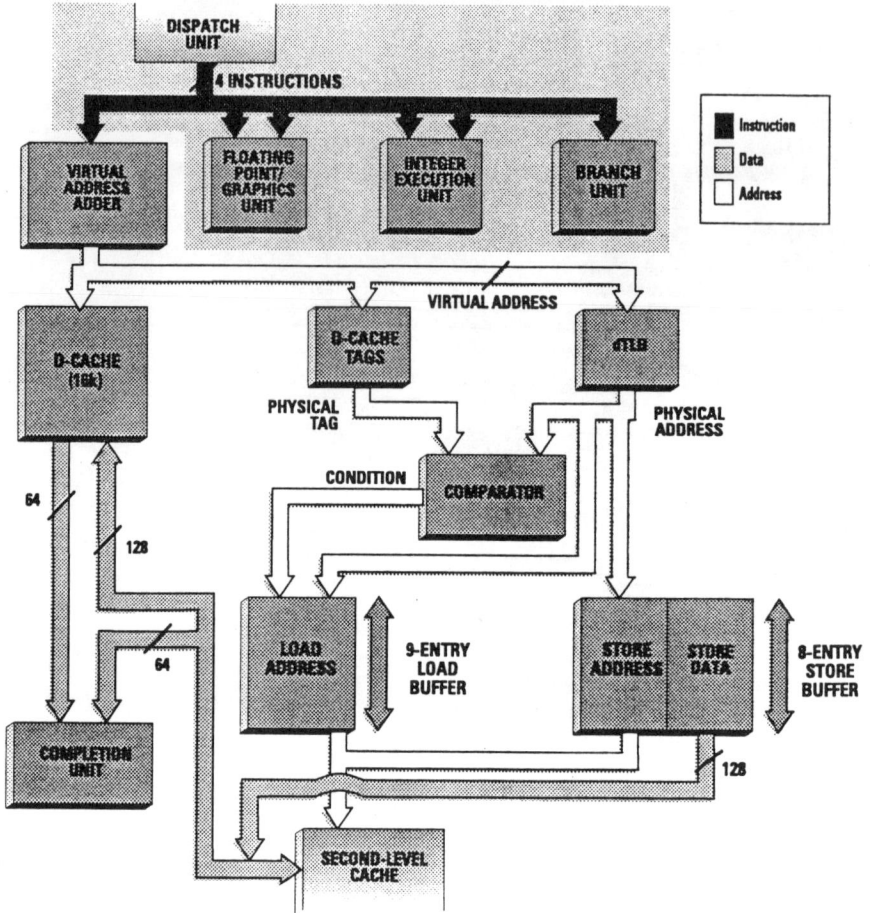

Fig. 8.15 Load/store unit *(Courtesy of Sun Microsystems, Inc.)*

system, the data buffers allow operations to overlap. A transaction between the buffers and the system can be handled while the processor simultaneously accesses the external second-level cache (L2).

Along with the data buffers, UltraSPARC also supports unique block load/store commands. These commands allow the processor to execute 64-byte load and store operations directly from/to main memory. The block load/store commands avoid 'cache pollution' by eliminating data allocation to the D-cache and the L2 and by going directly to the floating-point registers. This ability to load and store large amounts of information is especially valuable for graphics-intensive applications. Advanced graphics operations, such as real-time video, require the system to update the image 30 times per second. With the above capability the system can move images directly from main memory to the screen fast enough to

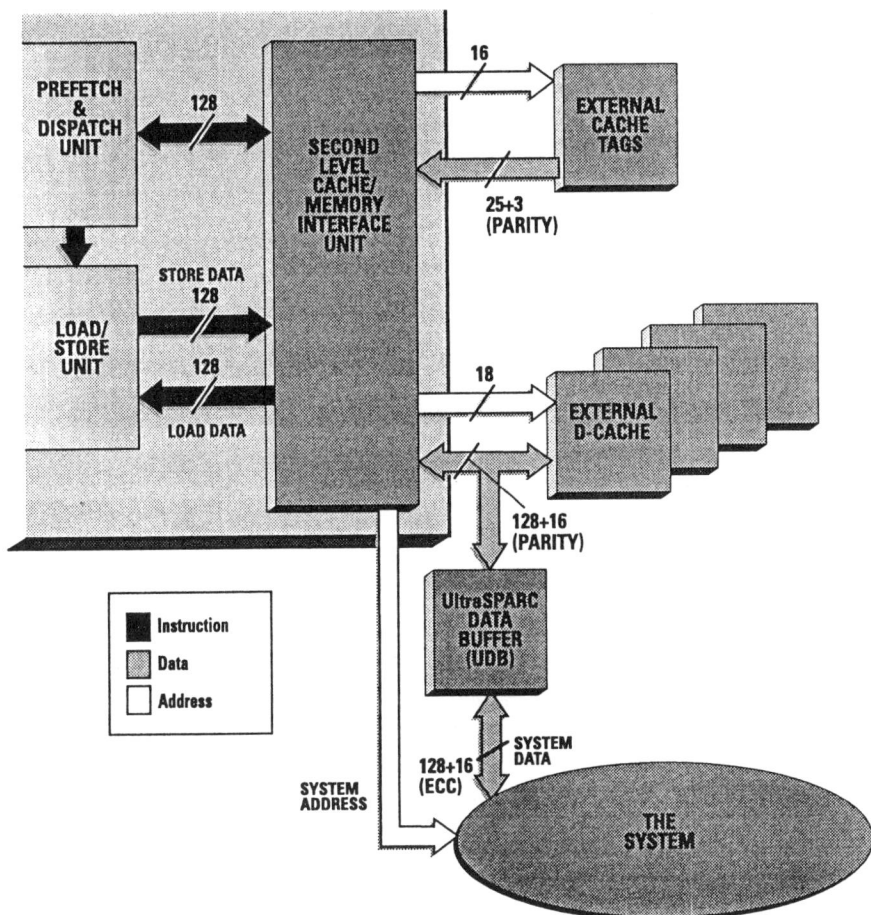

Fig. 8.16   Memory system *(Courtesy of Sun Microsystems, Inc.)*

eliminate screen flicker.

The UltraSPARC I-cache is 16KB, two-way set-associative with 32 bytes/line. It is physically indexed and contains physical tags. The D-cache is 16KB, direct-mapped, write-through with 32 bytes/line. Each line consists of two 16-byte sub-blocks. The UltraSPARC contains on-chip logic capable of controlling an off-chip second-level cache (L2) of 512KB to 4MB. The L2 is physically indexed and physically tagged. It is unified, direct-mapped, 64 bytes/line, and it implements a write-back policy. It includes the contents of the on-chip I-cache and D-cache. Adding the VIS feature [Kohn 95] to the UltraSPARC required only a 3% increase in die area, but resulted in significantly improved graphics capabilities over existing processors.

8.4 Earlier SPARC Implementations

The very first SPARC architecture implementations included a CPU chip with a single-ALU IU, a register file (usually 136 registers from the start), PCs, PSR, and a few other control and status registers. The FPU, MMU, and cache had to be realized on separate chips. Some of the first manufacturers to implement the SPARC architecture were Fujitsu Microelectronics, Inc. (Japan), Cypress Semiconductor (Ross Technology), Bipolar Integrated Technology, Inc. (BIT), LSI Logic Corporation, and Texas Instruments (TI), the manufacturer of the SuperSPARC.

The original Cypress SPARC CPU was labeled CY7C601. Cypress followed it up by a subsequent model called *HyperSPARC*, or CY7C620. The HyperSPARC is a two-issue superscalar, with over 1 million transistors, containing on-chip IU and FPU, operating at 55.5MHz (later versions are promised to run at up to 100MHz), with a 64-bit-wide data bus. The MMU and cache have to be configured outside of the CPU chip.

TI also features a lower-level, scalar, single-pipeline microprocessor, called *MicroSPARC*. The MicroSPARC is a 0.8 micron, 800 000 transistor, 5V, consuming 3.5W at 50MHz. It contains an IU, FPU, and a modest on-chip dual cache of 4KB code and 2KB data. A more recent version, MicroSPARC II, will operate within the frequency interval of 40 to 100MHz.

8.5 Concluding Comments

There exist numerous implementations of the SPARC architecture, manufactured by a number of companies all over the world. Many more are currently being developed, and undoubtedly new SPARC-architecture more powerful microprocessors will be announced in the near future. It is quite possible that some new versions of the SuperSPARC and UltraSPARC will be higher-issue superscalar systems, operating at higher frequencies.

CHAPTER 9

The MIPS Family

9.1 Introductory Comments

Similarly to Sun Microsystems, MIPS Computer Systems, Inc. (currently called MIPS Technologies, Inc.) is a creator of an original RISC-type architecture. Similarly to Sun, MIPS performs the architectural design and licences the actual chip manufacturing to other companies. MIPS, however, manufactured workstations and other computer systems based on these chips (again, similarly to Sun). MIPS RISC microprocessors have been adopted as CPUs by notable computer systems manufacturers, such as DEC in its DECstation systems, Silicon Graphics in its Indigo workstations and Challenge servers (see chapter 16), and many others. The commitment of Silicon Graphics to the MIPS architecture was so great, in fact, that the two companies merged in 1992. The MIPS architecture and business model, however, remain open.

The MIPS system originated at Stanford University in the early eighties [Hein 93, Henn 82, Henn 84, HePa 90, Przy 84, Tabk 94]. The MIPS acronym stands for *microprocessor without interlocked pipeline stages*. The reason for the above name is that, initially, MIPS pipeline hazards were handled by *software* (by the MIPS compiler), as opposed to hardware pipeline interlocks, practiced on other systems (see also chapters 1 and 4). However, more recent MIPS systems, starting with the R4000, have hardware interlocks. Thus, the MIPS acronym has more of an historical significance, and it does not quite fit the latest MIPS processors.

Some of the MIPS developers at Stanford, together with other professionals, founded the MIPS Computer Systems company, which continued the development of the MIPS into a successful commercial product. MIPS developers have designed the R2000, R3000, R6000, R4x00, R8000, and R10000 RISC processors, which can be denoted in general as Rx000 families, to be described in the following sections in this chapter. All of the above are implementations of the MIPS architecture, to be described in the next section. It should be noted, however, that there exist four levels of backward-compatible architectural levels MIPS I, II, III, and IV (level IV being the latest).

9.2 MIPS Architecture

Register file

The MIPS user-visible CPU integer registers are shown in Fig. 9.1. There are 32 general-purpose registers r0 to r31, a program counter (PC), and two registers that hold the results of integer multiply and divide operations:

HI — multiply and divide register higher result (remainder for divide),
LO — multiply and divide register lower result (quotient for divide).

All registers shown in Fig. 9.1 are 64-bit for 64-bit microprocessor implementations. The same registers are 32-bit for 32-bit implementations.
   Two of the general-purpose registers have a special function:

r0 is hardwired to a zero value, as in most RISC-type systems (see chapter 2).
r31 is the *link register* for *jump and link* instructions. It may be used for other purposes when it is not used in conjunction with the jump and link instruction.

All other registers, r1 through r30, are free to be used by the programmer in any way. However, a practical system must reserve some registers for use by the exception handler since there is no information pushed on a stack. Existing systems reserve registers r 26 and r27 for use by the OS kernel. In such a case, they may not be used by a user level program.

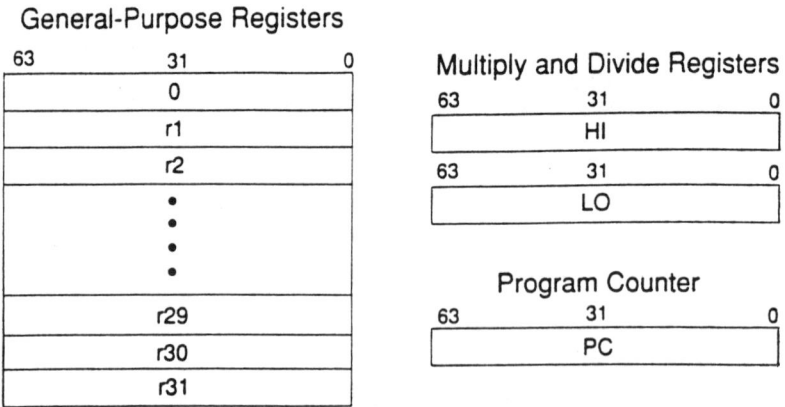

General-Purpose Registers

63	31	0
	0	
	r1	
	r2	
	•	
	•	
	•	
	•	
	r29	
	r30	
	r31	

Multiply and Divide Registers

63	31	0
	HI	

63	31	0
	LO	

Program Counter

63	31	0
	PC	

Register width depends on mode of operation: 32-bit or 64-bit

Fig. 9.1   CPU registers *(Courtesy of MIPS Computer Systems, Inc.)*

The floating-point register file in the FPU is shown in Fig. 9.2. It consists of:

1.   32 *floating-point general-purpose registers* FGR0 to FGR31. As shown in Fig. 9.2, the register configuration depends on the value of the *FR bit* in the *status register* (SR; contains the operating mode, interrupt enabling, and the diagnostic states of the processor). If FR = 1, the FGRs are 64-bit wide; and if FR = 0, the FGRs are 32-bit wide.
2.   *Control/status register* FCR31. The 32-bit FCR31 contains control and status

data. It controls the arithmetic rounding mode and the enabling of user-mode traps. It also identifies exceptions that occurred in the most recently executed instructions.
3. *Implementation/revision register* FCR0. The 32-bit FCR0 specifies the implementation and revision number of the FPU.

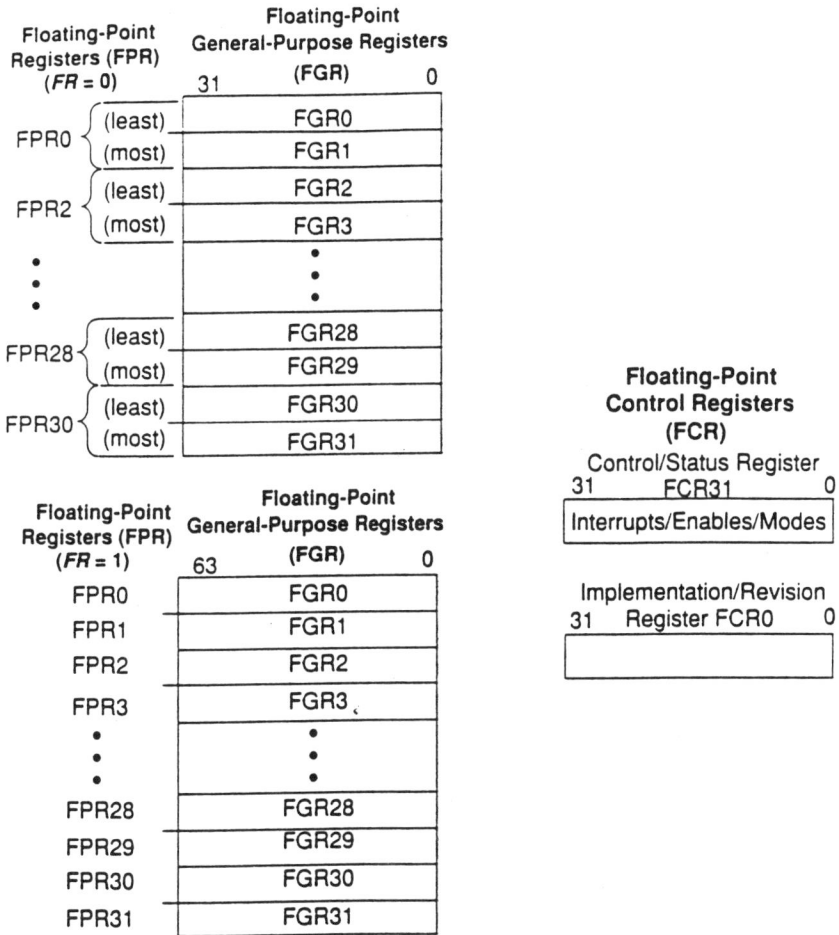

Floating-Point Registers (FPR) (FR = 0)	Floating-Point General-Purpose Registers (FGR)
FPR0 { (least) (most)	FGR0 / FGR1
FPR2 { (least) (most)	FGR2 / FGR3
FPR28 { (least) (most)	FGR28 / FGR29
FPR30 { (least) (most)	FGR30 / FGR31

Floating-Point Control Registers (FCR)

Control/Status Register 31 FCR31 0 Interrupts/Enables/Modes

Floating-Point Registers (FPR) (FR = 1)	Floating-Point General-Purpose Registers (FGR)
FPR0	FGR0
FPR1	FGR1
FPR2	FGR2
FPR3	FGR3
FPR28	FGR28
FPR29	FGR29
FPR30	FGR30
FPR31	FGR31

Implementation/Revision 31 Register FCR0 0

Fig. 9.2 FPU registers *(Courtesy of MIPS Computer Systems, Inc.)*

Data types
The MIPS architecture recognizes the following data types:

Byte — eight bits,
Halfword — 16 bits,

220

Word — 32 bits,
Doubleword — 64 bits.

Byte ordering within a word can be configured as either big-endian or little-endian. The MIPS floating-point formats conform to the IEEE 754-1985 Standard [IEEE 85], featuring the 32-bit single-precision and 64-bit double-precision.

Addressing modes
The MIPS architecture features the following addressing modes:

Register.
Immediate.
PC-relative.
Relative indirect (base register), with or without offset (displacement).

Instruction formats
The three MIPS architecture instruction formats are summarized in Fig. 9.3, along with the specification of the different fields. MIPS instructions must be aligned on word boundaries in the memory.

I-Type (Immediate)

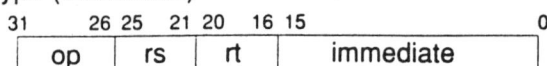

31	26 25	21 20	16 15	0
op	rs	rt	immediate	

J-Type (Jump)

31	26 25	0
op	target	

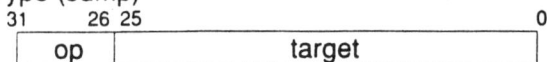

R-Type (Register)

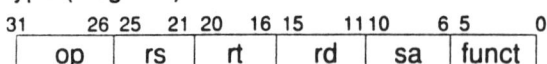

31	26 25	21 20	16 15	11 10	6 5	0
op	rs	rt	rd	sa	funct	

op	is a 6-bit operation code
rs	is a 5-bit source register specifier
rt	is a 5-bit target (source/destination) register or branch condition
immediate	is a 16-bit immediate value, branch displacement or address displacement
target	is a 26-bit jump target address
rd	is a 5-bit destination register specifier
sa	is a 5-bit shift amount
funct	is a 6-bit function field

Fig. 9.3   CPU instruction formats *(Courtesy of MIPS Computer Systems, Inc.)*

Instruction set

MIPS architecture defines four coprocessors, denoted CP0 through CP3. CP0, incorporated on the CPU chip, supports the virtual memory system and exception handling. CP1 is the FPU coprocessor, incorporated on the CPU chip in the latest implementations. CP2 is reserved for future definition by MIPS, and CP3 is used to provide certain extensions to the MIPS *instruction set architecture* (ISA). The basic instruction set (ISA), common to all MIPS Rx000 microprocessors, is listed in Table 9.1. Table 9.2 lists instructions that are extensions to the ISA in latest implementations.

The on-chip coprocessor CP0 special instructions are listed in Table 9.3. The FPU instructions are listed in Table 9.4.

Examples:

    Load word: LW rt, offset (rs);

The I-type format (Fig. 9.3) is used. The rt field represents the destination CPU register. The rs field points to the base register. The immediate field contains a 16-bit offset (displacement sign-extended to 32 bits), added to the content of rs to form the memory EA, whose content is loaded into rt.

    Subtract: SUB rd, rs, rt; rd ← (rs) − (rt), R-type format.

    Multiply: MULT rs, rt; R-type format (rd not used), (rs) ∗ (rt) → (HI, LO) 64-bit product.

    Divide: DIV rs, rt; R-type format (rd not used), $(rs)/(rt)$ quotient → LO, remainder → HI.

    Jump: J target; J-type format.

The 26-bit target field is shifted left two bits, combined (on the left) with the four most significant bits of the current PC value, to form the jump target address. The delayed branch feature (see chapter 2) is implemented on the scalar implementations of the MIPS.

Jump and link: JAL target;
Used as a subroutine call. Works exactly the same way as the jump, except that the address of the instruction after the delay slot, (PC) + 8, is placed in the *link register* r31.

Branch on equal: BEQ rs, rt, offset; I-type format.
The contents of registers rs and rt are compared. If equal, the program branches to a new target address. The new target address is computed from the sum of the address of the instruction in the delay slot (following BEQ) and the 16-bit offset, shifted left two bits and sign-extended to 32 bits.

Table 9.1 CPU Instruction Set (ISA)

OP	Description	OP	Description
	Load and Store Instructions		**Multiply and Divide Instructions**
LB	Load Byte	MULT	Multiply
LBU	Load Byte Unsigned	MULTU	Multiply Unsigned
LH	Load Halfword	DIV	Divide
LHU	Load Halfword Unsigned	DIVU	Divide Unsigned
LW	Load Word	MFHI	Move From HI
LWL	Load Word Left	MTHI	Move To HI
LWR	Load Word Right	MFLO	Move From LO
SB	Store Byte	MTLO	Move To LO
SH	Store Halfword		**Jump and Branch Instructions**
SW	Store Word		
SWL	Store Word Left	J	Jump
SWR	Store Word Right	JAL	Jump And Link
	Arithmetic Instructions	JR	Jump Register
	(ALU Immediate)	JALR	Jump And Link Register
ADDI	Add Immediate	BEQ	Branch on Equal
ADDIU	Add Immediate Unsigned	BNE	Branch on Not Equal
SLTI	Set on Less Than Immediate	BLEZ	Branch on Less than or Equal to Zero
SLTIU	Set on Less Than Immediate Unsigned	BGTZ	Branch on Greater Than Zero
		BLTZ	Branch on Less Than Zero
ANDI	AND Immediate	BGEZ	Branch on Greater than or Equal to Zero
ORI	OR Immediate		
XORI	Exclusive OR Immediate	BLTZAL	Branch on Less Than Zero And Link
LUI	Load Upper Immediate	BGEZAL	Branch on Greater than or Equal to Zero And Link
	Arithmetic Instructions		**Coprocessor Instructions**
	(3-operand, R-type)	LWCz	Load Word to Coprocessor z
ADD	Add	SWCz	Store Word from Coprocessor z
ADDU	Add Unsigned	MTCz	Move To Coprocessor z
SUB	Subtract	MFCz	Move From Coprocessor z
SUBU	Subtract Unsigned	CTCz	Move Control to Coprocessor z
SLT	Set on Less Than	CFCz	Move Control From Coprocessor z
SLTU	Set on Less Than Unsigned	COPz	Coprocessor Operation z
AND	AND	BCzT	Branch on Coprocessor z True
OR	OR	BCzF	Branch on Coprocessor z False
XOR	Exclusive OR		
NOR	NOR		**Special Instructions**
	Shift Instructions	SYSCALL	System Call
SLL	Shift Left Logical	BREAK	Break
SRL	Shift Right Logical		
SRA	Shift Right Arithmetic		
SLLV	Shift Left Logical Variable		
SRLV	Shift Right Logical Variable		
SRAV	Shift Right Arithmetic Variable		

(Courtesy of MIPS Computer Systems, Inc.)

Table 9.2 Extensions to the ISA

OP	Description	OP	Description
	Load and Store Instructions		**Multiply and Divide Instructions**
LD	Load Doubleword	DMULT	Doubleword Multiply
LDL	Load Doubleword Left	DMULTU	Doubleword Multiply Unsigned
LDR	Load Doubleword Right	DDIV	Doubleword Divide
LL	Load Linked	DDIVU	Doubleword Divide Unsigned
LLD	Load Linked Doubleword		**Jump and Branch Instructions**
LWU	Load Word Unsigned	BEQL	Branch on Equal Likely
SC	Store Conditional	BNEL	Branch on Not Equal Likely
SCD	Store Conditional Doubleword	BLEZL	Branch on Less than or Equal
SD	Store Doubleword		to Zero Likely
SDL	Store Doubleword Left	BGTZL	Branch on Greater Than Zero Likely
SDR	Store Doubleword Right	BLTZL	Branch on Less Than Zero Likely
SYNC	Sync	BGEZL	Branch on Greater than or
	Arithmetic Instructions		Equal to Zero Likely
	(ALU Immediate)	BLTZALL	Branch on Less Than Zero And
DADDI	Doubleword Add Immediate		Link Likely
DADDIU	Doubleword Add Immediate	BGEZALL	Branch on Greater than or Equal to
	Unsigned		Zero And Link Likely
		BCzTL	Branch on Coprocessor z True Likely
	Arithmetic Instructions	BCzFL	Branch on Coprocessor z False Likely
	(3-operand, R-type)		**Exception Instructions**
DADD	Doubleword Add	TGE	Trap if Greater Than or Equal
DADDU	Doubleword Add Unsigned	TGEU	Trap if Greater Than or Equal Unsigned
DSUB	Doubleword Subtract	TLT	Trap if Less Than
DSUBU	Doubleword Subtract Unsigned	TLTU	Trap if Less Than Unsigned
	Shift Instructions	TEQ	Trap if Equal
DSLL	Doubleword Shift Left Logical	TNE	Trap if Not Equal
DSRL	Doubleword Shift Right Logical	TGEI	Trap if Greater Than or Equal Immediate
DSRA	Doubleword Shift Right Arithmetic	TGEIU	Trap if Greater Than or Equal
DSLLV	Doubleword Shift Left		Immediate Unsigned
	Logical Variable	TLTI	Trap if Less Than Immediate
DSRLV	Doubleword Shift Right	TLTIU	Trap if Less Than Immediate Unsigned
	Logical Variable	TEQI	Trap if Equal Immediate
DSRAV	Doubleword Shift Right	TNEI	Trap if Not Equal Immediate
	Arithmetic Variable		
DSLL32	Doubleword Shift Left		**Coprocessor Instructions**
	Logical + 32	DMFCz	Doubleword Move From Coprocessor z
DSRL32	Doubleword Shift Right	DMTCz	Doubleword Move To Coprocessor z
	Logical + 32	LDCz	Load Double Coprocessor z
DSRA32	Doubleword Shift Right	SDCz	Store Double Coprocessor z
	Arithmetic + 32		

(Courtesy of MIPS Computer Systems, Inc.)

Table 9.3 CP0 Instructions

Op	Description
DMFC0	Doubleword Move From CP0
DMTC0	Doubleword Move To CP0
MTC0	Move to CP0
MFC0	Move from CP0
TLBR	Read Indexed TLB Entry
TLBWI	Write Indexed TLB Entry
TLBWR	Write Random TLB Entry
TLBP	Probe TLB for Matching Entry
ERET	Exception Return

(Courtesy of MIPS Computer Systems, Inc.)

9.3 High-Performance MIPS Implementations
MIPS R4000 family

The MIPS R4000 is a 64-bit, 1.3 million transistors, 1 micron CMOS, 447-pin microprocessor. It is a two-issue superpipelined system, with an external frequency of 50MHz, and the internal pipeline running at a double frequency 100MHz. It has an on-chip FPU and a dual cache of 8KB code and 8KB data, for a total of 16 Kbytes. Although the R4000 is a fully fledged 64-bit system, its instructions are uniformly 32-bit, as specified in section 9.2.

There is also a more advanced version of the R4000: the R4400. The R4400 is architecturally identical to the R4000. The R4400 is a 0.6 micron CMOS, containing 2.2 million transistors, with a double cache of 16KB code and 16KB data, for a total of 32 Kbytes. Its initial model external frequency is 75MHz, and the internal pipeline runs at 150MHz. A later R4400 model runs at 100MHz external and 200MHz pipeline frequency.

In addition to the above, there is another version, the R4200, produced by MIPS and NEC (Japan). The R4200 combines the integer and the floating-point processing in the same functional area on the chip. It has a dual non-symmetric cache: 16KB code, 8KB data, for a total of 24 Kbytes. Its external frequency is 40MHz (internal 80MHz) with a power dissipation of 1.5W. It has a simpler five-stage pipeline, as opposed to the R4000 or R4400 eight-stage pipeline (to be discussed in detail later in this section). The R4200 is manufactured by NEC, and it is strongly targeted for embedded designs.

Another implementation of the same architecture is the Integrated Device Technology (IDT; Santa Clara, CA) and Toshiba (Irvine, CA) R4600. It has essentially the same features as the R4400, except that it has a shorter pipeline (five stages, as opposed to eight on R4400) and its caches are two-way set-associative (other R4x00 systems are direct-mapped). The Toshiba R4600 is fully denoted as TC86R4600. It is a 208-pin microprocessor, available at frequencies of 100 and

Table 9.4 FPU Instruction Summary

OP	Description
	Load/Store/Move Instructions
LWC1	Load Word to FPU
SWC1	Store Word from FPU
LDC1	Load Doubleword to FPU
SDC1	Store Doubleword From FPU
MTC1	Move word To FPU
MFC1	Move word From FPU
CTC1	Move Control word To FPU
CFC1	Move Control word From FPU
DMTC1	Doubleword Move To FPU
DMFC1	Doubleword Move From FPU
	Conversion Instructions
CVT.S.fmt	Floating-point Convert to Single FP
CVT.D.fmt	Floating-point Convert to Double FP
CVT.W.fmt	Floating-point Convert to Single Fixed Point
ROUND.w.fmt	Floating-point Round
TRUNC.w.fmt	Floating-point Truncate
CEIL.w.fmt	Floating-point Ceiling
FLOOR.w.fmt	Floating-point Floor
	Computational Instructions
ADD.fmt	Floating-point Add
SUB.fmt	Floating-point Subtract
MUL.fmt	Floating-point Multiply
DIV.fmt	Floating-point Divide
ABS.fmt	Floating-point Absolute value
MOV.fmt	Floating-point Move
NEG.fmt	Floating-point Negate
SQRT.fmt	Floating-point Square Root
	Compare Instructions
C.cond.fmt	Floating-point Compare
	Branch on FP Condition
BC1T	Branch on FPU True
BC1F	Branch on FPU False
BC1TL	Branch on FPU True Likely
BC1FL	Branch on FPU False Likely
.fmt	format specifier
.cond	condition specifier

(Courtesy of MIPS Computer Systems, Inc.)

133MHz (internal frequency). The Toshiba R4600 operates with a 3.3V power supply with a power expenditure of 2.5W at 100MHz. The R4600 does not have multiprocessing features and external cache control. Its power dissipation is typically 4W.

A block diagram of the R4000 is shown in Fig. 9.4. One can clearly see in it the IU, FPU, CP0, and the dual cache.

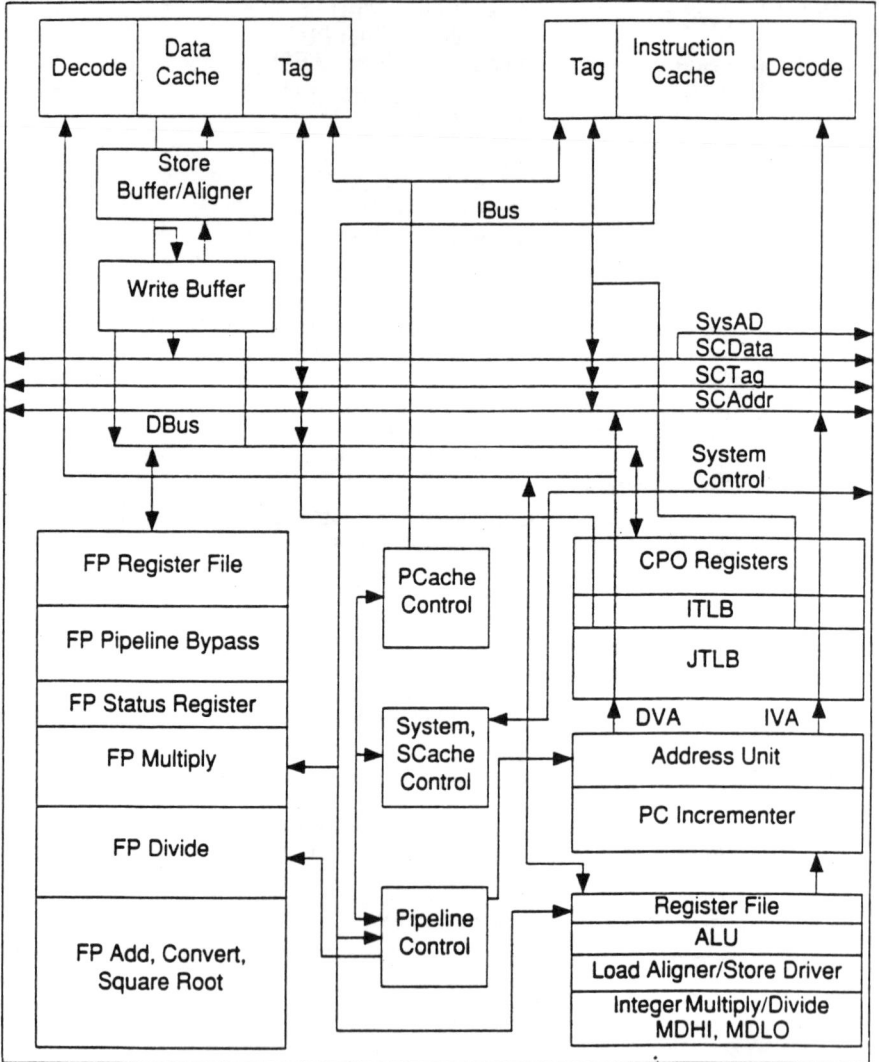

Fig. 9.4   R4000 internal block diagram *(Courtesy of MIPS Computer Systems, Inc.)*

The R4000 eight-stage instruction pipeline is shown in Figs. 9.5 and 9.6. Fig. 9.5 shows the eight pipeline stages for eight consecutive instructions, while

Fig. 9.6 illustrates the details of the pipeline operation. One can see in Fig. 9.5 the issue of two consecutive instructions, one every half master clock cycle, in a two-issue superpipelined operation (see chapter 1).

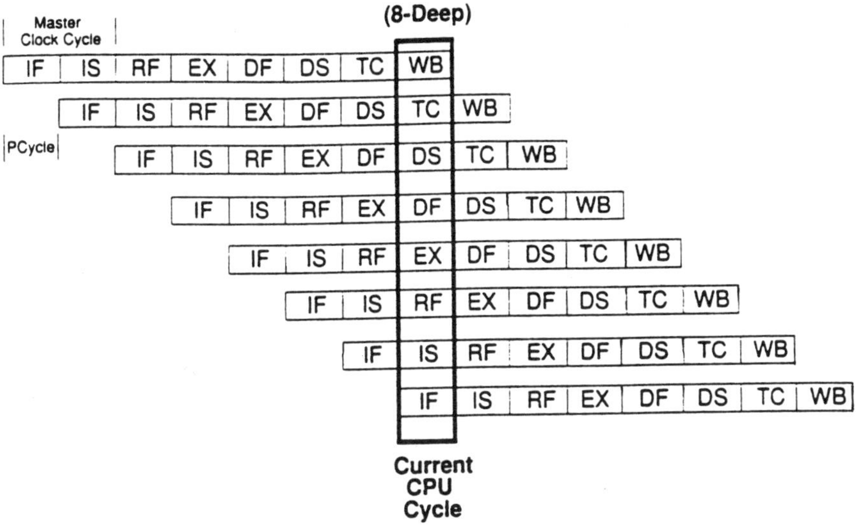

Fig. 9.5 R4000 pipeline and instruction overlapping *(Courtesy of MIPS Computer Systems, Inc.)*

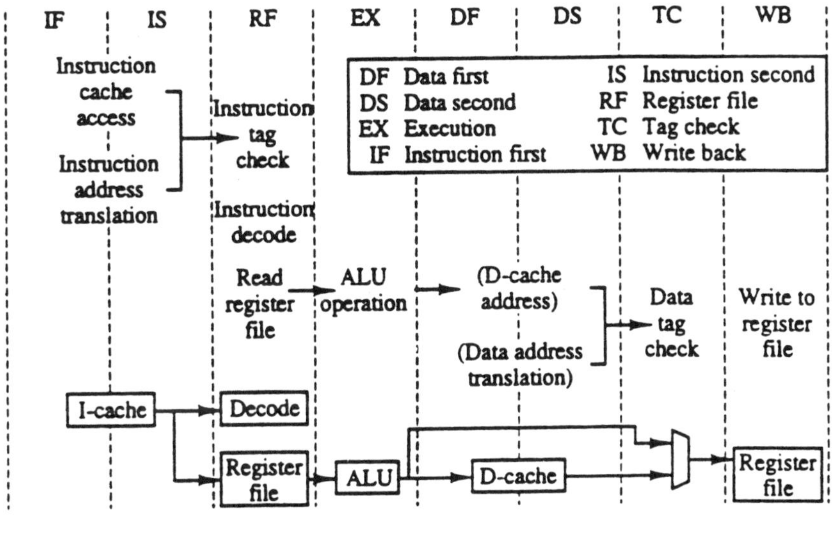

Fig. 9.6 R4000 hardware pipeline stages *(Courtesy of MIPS Computer Systems, Inc.)*

The R4000 pipeline stages are the following [MR40 91, Hein 93]:

1. **IF** — *instruction fetch, first half.* An instruction address is selected by the branch logic, and the instruction cache fetch begins. The *instruction TLB* (ITLB) begins the virtual to physical address translation.
2. **IS** — *instruction fetch, second half.* The instruction cache fetch and the ITLB translation are completed.
3. **RF** — *register fetch.* The instruction decoder decodes the instruction and checks for interlock conditions. The instruction cache tag is checked against the page frame number obtained from the ITLB. Any required operands are fetched from the register file.
4. **EX** — *execution.* For register-to-register instructions, the ALU performs the arithmetic or logical operation. For load and store instructions, the ALU calculates the data virtual address. For branch instructions, the ALU determines whether the branch condition is true and calculates the virtual branch target address.
5. **DF** — *data fetch, first half.* For load and store instructions, the data cache fetch and the data address translation begin. For branch instructions, the target address translation and TLB update begin. Register-to-register instructions perform no operations during the DF, DX, and TC stages.
6. **DS** — *data fetch, second half.* For load and store instructions, the data cache fetch and data address translation are completed. The shifter aligns the data to the word or doubleword boundary. For branch instructions, the target address translation and TLB update are completed.
7. **TC** — *tag check.* For load and store instructions, the cache performs the tag check. The physical address from the TLB is checked against the cache tag to determine if there is a hit or a miss.
8. **WB** — *write-back.* For register-to-register instructions, the result is written back to the register file. Load, store, and branch instructions perform no operation during this stage.

The above pipeline has a branch delay of three cycles and a load delay of two cycles. Any pipeline interrupts are handled by *hardware interlocks.* In that respect, the design of the R4000 deviates from the original Stanford MIPS.

The R4000 FPU is shown in Fig. 9.7 [MR40 91]. Like the IU, the FPU uses a load/store oriented instruction set, with single-cycle load and store operations. Floating-point operations are started in a single cycle, and their execution is overlapped with other fixed-point or floating-point operations. The FPU conforms to the IEEE 754-1985 Standard. The FPU has three operation units, adder, multiplier, and divider, subject to the following constraints:

Adder: allows one clock cycle overlap between each newly issued instruction and the instruction being completed. The adder can overlap operations, to some degree, with the multiplier.
Multiplier: allows up to two pipelined MUL.[S,D] instructions to be processed as

long as:
1. Two idle cycles are required after MUL.S,
2. Three idle cycles are required after MUL.D.
Divider: handles only one non-overlapped divide instruction in its pipeline at any one time.

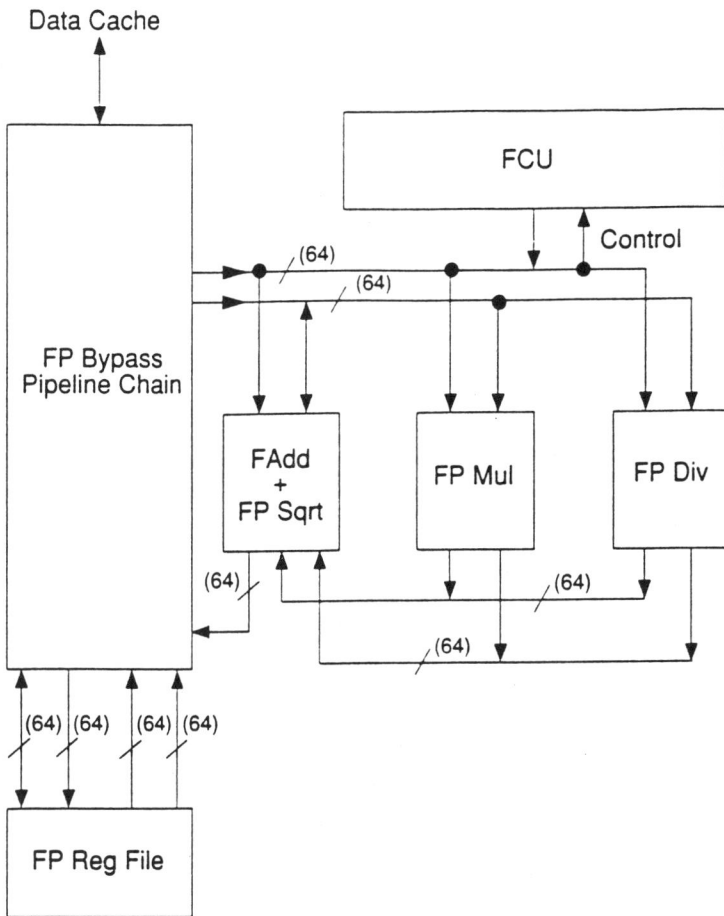

Fig. 9.7　FPU functional block diagram *(Courtesy of MIPS Computer Systems, Inc.)*

Both R4000 caches are *direct-mapped*, 8KB each, organized with either a four-word (16-byte) or eight-word (32-byte) line. The write policy for the data cache is *write-back*. Each line of the instruction cache has associated with it, in addition to a 24-bit address tag, a valid bit and a parity bit. Each line of the data cache has associated with it, in addition to a 24-bit address tag, a two-bit line state indicator and a write-back bit. The *write-back bit* indicates when the cache line contains modified data that must be written back to memory or to the secondary cache. There are four states defined for the primary on-chip data cache:

1. **Invalid** — The cache line does not contain valid information.
2. **Shared** — The line contains valid information and may be present in another cache. The line may or may not be consistent with memory, and may or may not be owned.
3. **Clean exclusive** — The line contains valid information and is not present in any other cache. The line is consistent with memory and is not owned.
4. **Dirty exclusive** — The line contains valid information and is not present in any other cache. The line is inconsistent with memory and is owned by the processor.

The above states are particularly used in protocols for maintaining cache coherency in multiprocessing systems [Hwan 93].

The R4000 contains on-chip logic to interface to an optional external *secondary cache*. It can be configured either as a unified or as a dual cache. The interface is designed to support the following secondary cache parameters: direct mapping, write-back policy for data, with optional line size of four-word (16-byte), eight-word (32-byte), 16-word (64-byte), or 32-word (128-byte). The secondary cache line has associated with it, in addition to a 19-bit address tag, a three-bit *primary cache index* and a three-bit line state indicator (five states).

The primary cache index provides a pointer to the virtual address of primary cache lines that may contain data from the secondary cache line. The five secondary cache states are:

1. **Invalid** — The line does not contain valid information.
2. **Shared** — The line contains valid information and may be present in another cache. The line may or may not be consistent with memory, and is not owned.
3. **Dirty shared** — The line contains valid information and may be present in another cache. The line is inconsistent with memory and is owned.
4. **Clean exclusive** — The line contains valid information and is not present in any other cache. The line is consistent with memory and is not owned.
5. **Dirty exclusive** — The line contains valid information and is not present in any other cache. The line is inconsistent with memory and is owned.

The primary cache **shared** state corresponds to the secondary cache states **shared** and **dirty shared**.

The secondary cache may be configured to have a total size of 128KB to 4MB. There are 128 data lines between the CPU chip and the secondary cache.

The R4000 *virtual address space* is defined for two modes:

1. The 32-bit mode: 32-bit address; maximal user process size is 2GB = 2^{31}

bytes.
2. The 64-bit mode: 64-bit address; maximal user process size is 1 TB = 2^{40} bytes.

The 36-bit *physical address space* is 64GB = 2^{36} bytes.
The R4000 functions in three operating modes:

1. *User*, regular operation for nonsupervisory programs.
2. *Supervisor*, intermediate mode which can be used to more easily build secure OS.
3. *Kernel*, most privileged mode, analogous to 'supervisor' mode in other systems.

The R4000 TLB has 48 entries. Each entry maps two consecutive pages, having the effect of a 96-entry TLB. Each TLB entry (page pair) can map a page pair of variable size.
There are three types of the R4000 processor:

1. R4000SC, a high-performance uniprocessor, 447-pin, secondary cache control.
2. R4000MC, large cache-coherent CPU for multiprocessors, 447-pin, secondary cache control.
3. R4000PC, for cost-sensitive systems, 179-pin, no support for secondary cache.

The pinout diagram of the R4000 is shown in Fig. 9.8. Of particular note are the 128 data lines for secondary cache interface on the right (SCData), and 64 address and data lines (multiplexed), interfacing to the system bus (SysAD).

MIPS R8000 system
The R8000 is a multichip implementation of the MIPS architecture. The system, illustrated in Fig. 9.9, consists of the following major parts [Rhod 94]:

1. R8000 processor (CPU).
2. R8010 FPU.
3. Tag RAM for L2 even addresses.
4. Tag RAM for L2 odd addresses.
5. Cache SRAM for L2 even data.
6. Cache SRAM for L2 odd data.
7. Cache controller.

The R8000 CPU is a 64-bit, Toshiba 0.7 micron VHMOSIII technology, 75MHz, 591-pin PGA microprocessor. It is a four-issue superscalar. Its block diagram is shown in Fig. 9.10. Owing to the existing on-chip hardware, it can execute in parallel two integer arithmetic or two load/store instructions (barring data dependencies; see chapter 1). The CPU implements the MIPS IV version of the

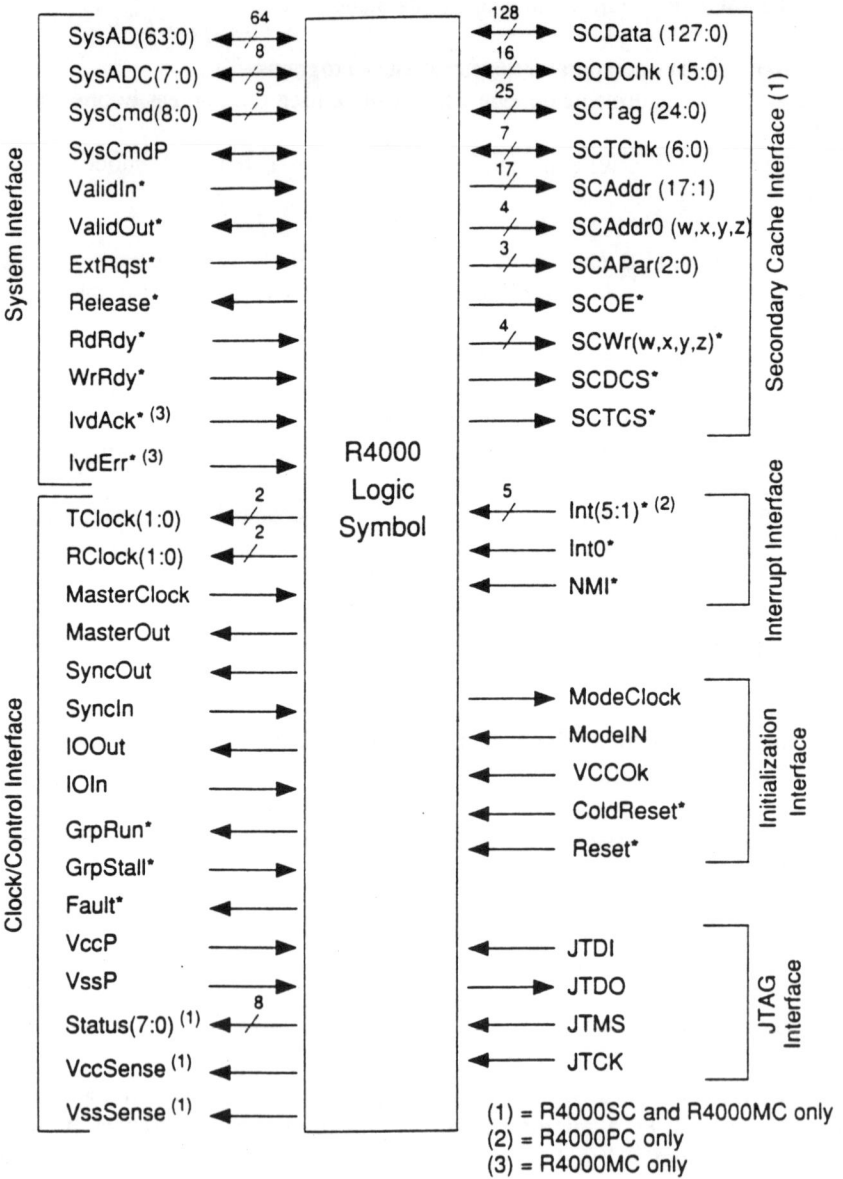

Fig. 9.8   R4000 logic symbol diagram *(Courtesy of MIPS Computer Systems, Inc.)*

To
Data
Buffers

Tag RAM Control

To
Data
Buffers

CACHE
CONTROLLER

Data Path Control

Cache
Controller ASIC

R8000 Microprocessor
Chip Set

Control

TBus

Tag

TAG
RAM
(even)

Index,
Sector,
Control

Status

R8000 CPU

Tag

Index,
Sector,
Control

Status

TAG
RAM
(odd)

Data
Set
Address

Address

Address

Data
Set
Address

STREAMING
CACHE
SRAM (even)

Load
Data

Control

Status

Load
Data

STREAMING
CACHE
SRAM (odd)

R8010 FPU

Store Data

Store Data

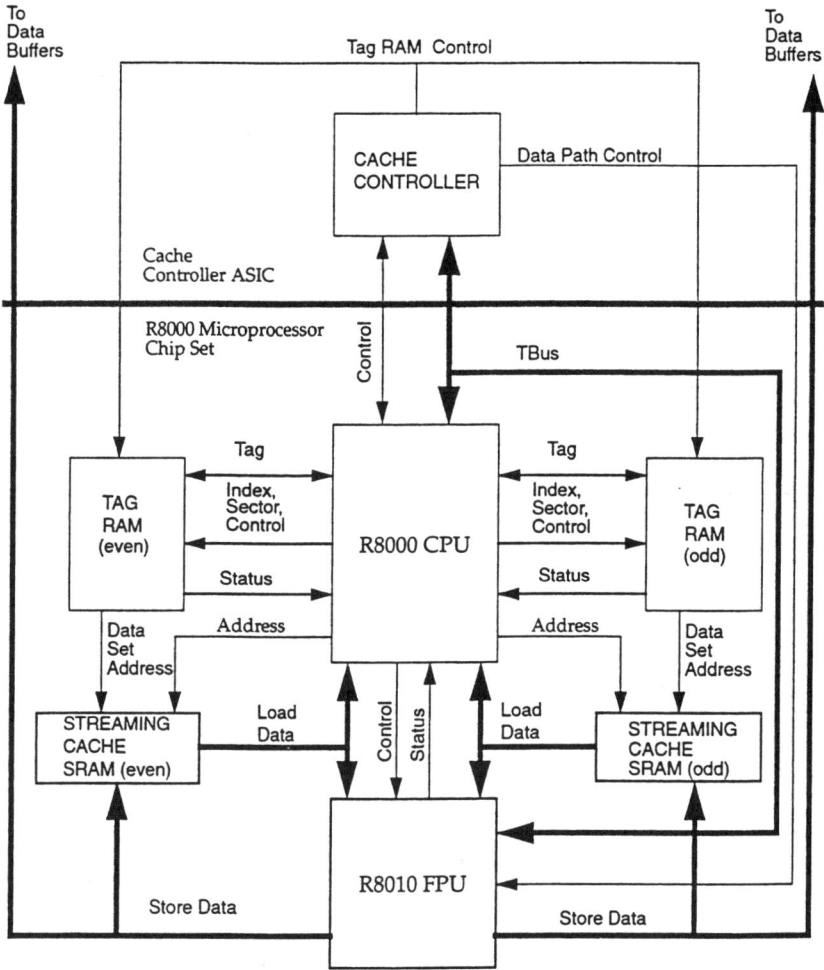

Fig. 9.9   R8000 microprocessor chip set block diagram *(Courtesy of MIPS Computer Systems, Inc.)*

MIPS instruction set. The additions and extensions of the MIPS IV to the MIPS instruction set (see section 9.2) are listed in Table 9.5.

The R8000 contains an on-chip dual cache: 16KB I-cache and 16KB D-cache. Both caches are virtually indexed and direct-mapped with 32 bytes/lines. The I-cache is single-ported and virtually tagged. The D-cache is dual-ported and physically tagged. The external secondary cache (L2) is 4MB, four-way set-associative. The on-chip TLB has 384 entries. It is dual-ported, three-way set-associative, supporting page sizes of 4, 8, 16, 64KB, 1, 4, and 16MB. There is also an on-chip 1024-entry (one entry per four instructions), direct-mapped branch

234

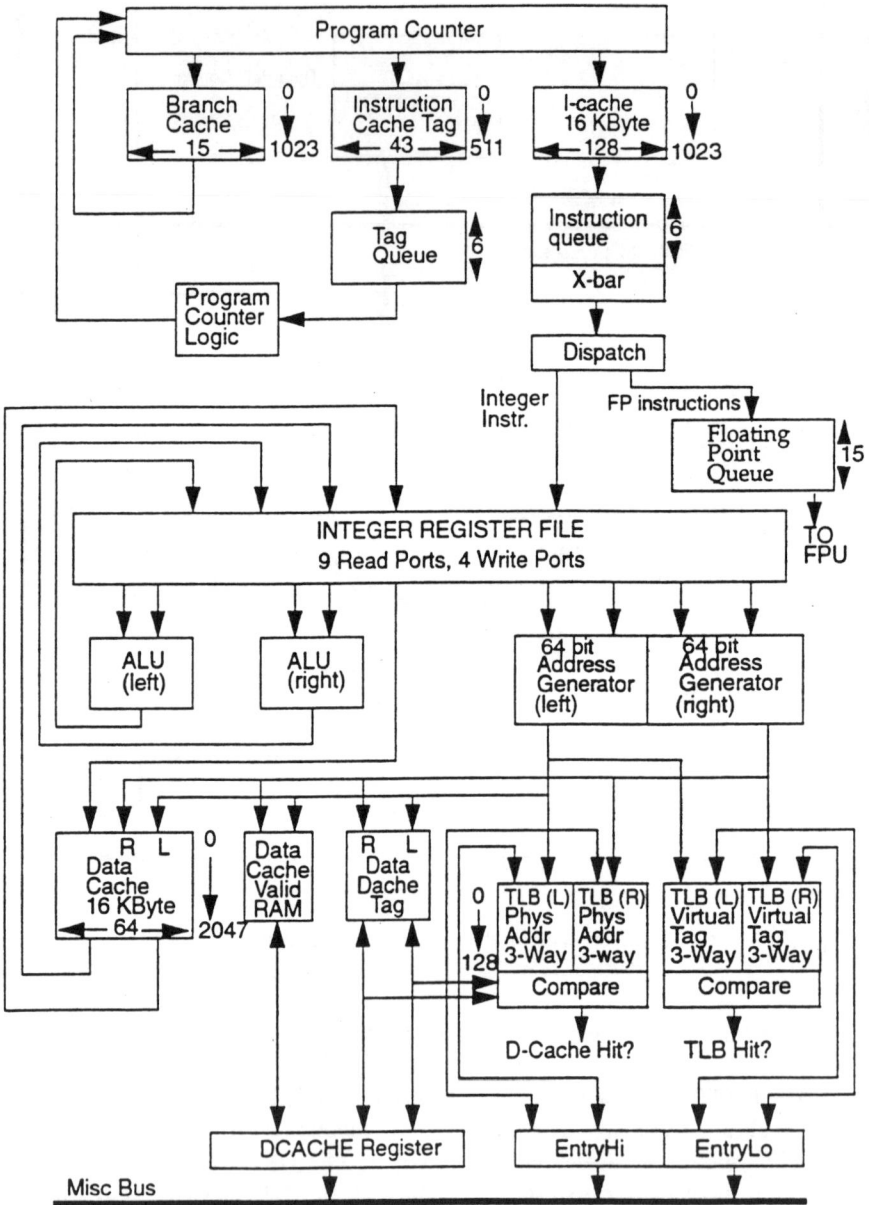

Fig. 9.10   R8000 microprocessor block diagram *(Courtesy of MIPS Computer Systems, Inc.)*

Table 9.5 MIPS IV Instruction Set Additions and Extensions

Instruction	Definition
BC1F	Branch on FP Condition Code False
BC1T	Branch on FP Condition Code True
BC1FL	Branch on FP Condition Code False Likely
BC1TL	Branch on FP Condition Code True Likely
C.cond.fmt (cc)	Floating Point Compare
LDXC1	Load Double Word indexed to COP1
LWXC1	Load Word indexed to COP1
MADD.sd	Floating PointMultiply-Add
MOVF	Move conditional on FP Condition Code False
MOVN	Move on Register Not Equal to Zero
MOVT	Move conditional on FP Condition Code True
MOVZ	Move on Register Equal to Zero
MOVF.fmt	FP Move conditional on Condition Code False
MOVN.fmt	FP Move on Register Not Equal to Zero
MOVT.fmt	FP Move conditional on Condition Code True
MOVZ.fmt	FP Move conditional on Register Equal to Zero
MSUB.sd	Floating Point Multiply-Subtract
NMADD.sd	Floating Point Negative Multipy-Add
NMSUB.sd	Floating Point Negative Multiply-Subtract
PFETCH	Prefetch Indexed --- Register + Register
PREF	Prefetch --- Register + Offset
RECIP.fmt	Reciprocal Approximation
RSQRT.fmt	Reciprocal Square Root Approximation
SDXC1	Store Double Word indexed to COP1
SWXC1	Store Word indexed to COP1

(Courtesy of MIPS Computer Systems, Inc.)

prediction cache. A MESI protocol is implemented for cache coherency.
The R8000 has a five-stage instruction pipeline:

1. F — fetch and partial decoding of the instruction. Branch prediction.
2. D — decode instruction, read register file, perform scoreboarding and dependency checks (see chapter 1).
3. A — generate the required memory access address (for load/store instructions).
4. E — ALU execution, D-cache access, TLB lookup, exception detection.
5. W — write the result into the register file.

The R8010 FPU is illustrated in Fig. 9.11. It has two floating-point execution units, capable of handling two floating-point instructions simultaneously (barring data dependencies).

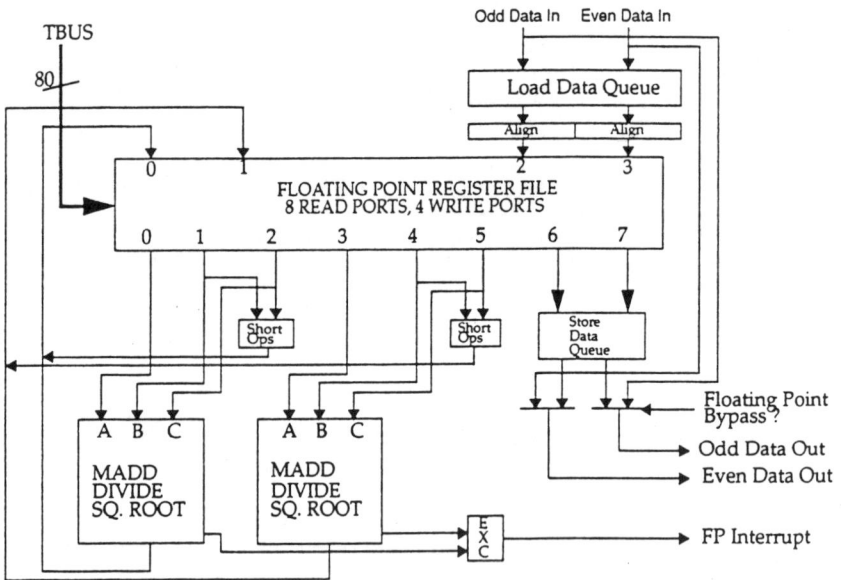

Fig. 9.11   R8010 floating-point unit block diagram *(Courtesy of MIPS Computer Systems, Inc.)*

MIPS R10000

The R10000 is a single-chip, 64-bit high-performance MIPS processor. It is a six-million-transistors, 0.5 micron CMOS, four-metal layer, 200MHz, 527-pin ceramic PGA (CPGA) microprocessor. It is a four-issue superscalar. One of its particular and unique features is the double size of its register files: both the integer and the floating-point register files have 64 64-bit physical registers each (32 architected registers and 32 rename registers, transparent to the programmer, in each file) [Hein

94]. The R10000 implements the MIPS IV instruction set architecture (ISA). The architecture implemented by the R10000 is also called ANDES (Architecture with Non-sequential Dynamic Execution Scheduling). A detailed block diagram of R10000 is shown in Fig. 9.12.

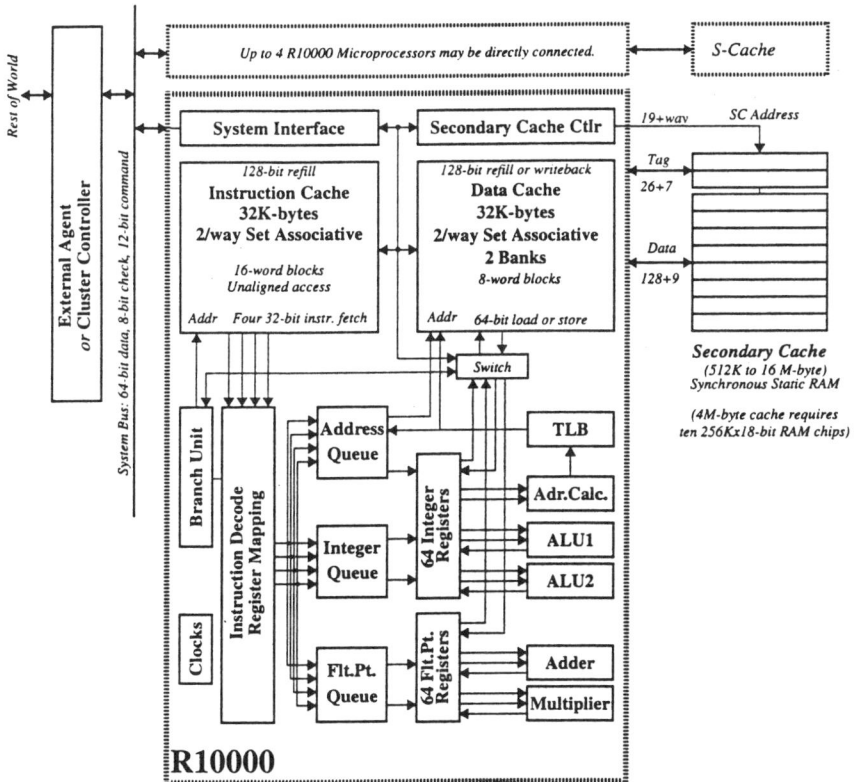

Fig. 9.12   Detailed block diagram of the R10000 processor *(Courtesy of MIPS Computer Systems, Inc.)*

The R10000 has an on-chip dual cache: 32KB I-cache, 32KB D-cache for a total of 64KB. The I-cache is two-way set-associative with 64 bytes/line. It uses an LRU replacement algorithm. Four instructions per cycle are fetched from the I-cache. The four fetched instructions are subsequently forwarded to the instruction decode and register rename (mapping) units. The instruction decode unit processes four instructions in parallel. In the register rename (mapping) unit, logical register numbers are replaced by physical register numbers. Integer registers are mapped using a 33-word-by-six-bit mapping table with four write and 12 read ports. Floating-point registers are mapped using a 32-word-by-six-bit mapping table with four write and 16 read ports. A 32-entry active list is kept of all instructions within the pipeline.

A branch unit handles branch instructions. One branch instruction per cycle is allowed. Conditional branches can be executed speculatively up to four-deep. The branch unit includes a 44-bit adder to compute branch addresses and a four-quadword branch resume buffer, used for reversing speculative branches. It also includes a branch link quadword which contains a link register for return from leaf subroutines.

At the exit from the register mapping (rename) unit there are three 16-entry queues: address, integer, and floating-point. The integer datapath includes a 64×64-integer physical register file with seven read and three write ports. There are two 64-bit ALUs:

1. ALU1 containing an ALU, shifter, and an integer branch comparator.
2. ALU2 containing an ALU, an integer multiplier and an integer divider.

The load/store pipeline starts with a 16-entry address queue. It implements a dynamic issue that uses the integer register file for base and index registers. The load/store pipeline includes:

1. A 16-entry stack for non-blocking load and store operations.
2. A 44-bit virtual address calculation unit.
3. A 64-entry fully-associative TLB, using a 40-bit physical address and a 44-bit virtual address.

Each TLB entry maps two pages, with variable page sizes ranging between 4KB and 16MB, in powers of four.

The floating-point pipeline starts with a 16-entry floating-point instruction queue. It contains the following subunits:

1. A 64×64-bit floating-point physical register file with five read and three write ports.
2. A 64-bit parallel multiply unit (three-cycle pipeline with two-cycle delay) which also performs move instructions.
3. A 64-bit add unit (three-cycle pipeline with two-cycle delay) which handles addition, subtraction, conversions, and other floating-point operations.
4. Separate 64-bit divide and square-root units which may operate concurrently.

The R10000 D-cache (32KB) is two-way set-associative with 32 bytes/line. It uses an LRU replacement algorithm. It features 64-bit load/store and 128-bit refill or write-back operations. The D-cache is arranged as two identical 16KB banks. It is two-way interleaved. The D-cache is virtually indexed and physically tagged. The R10000 system interface allows direct connection for small two- to four-way multiprocessor systems. There is a 128-bit data interface to a secondary off-chip cache (L2). The L2 may be configured from 512KB to 16MB using synchronous SRAMs. It is intended to be two-way set-associative with 64 or 128 bytes/line.

The R10000 features multiple pipelines, from five to seven stages, illustrated in Fig. 9.13. The integer arithmetic pipeline has five stages: fetch, decode, issue, execute (ALU), write result. The load/store pipeline has six stages: fetch, decode, issue, address calculation, access D-cache, write result. The floating-point pipeline has seven stages: fetch, decode, issue, execute 1, execute 2, execute 3, write result. To keep these pipelines busy (filled), instructions can be issued out of order, provided that all dependencies on previous instructions have been met. Register renaming (see chapter 1) is used to resolve dependencies between instructions, and to provide precise exception handling. The direction taken by each branch instruction is predicted, and instructions along the predicted path are speculatively executed. From a programmer's perspective, instructions are executed sequentially. When an instruction loads a new value into its destination register, the new value is immediately available for use by subsequent instructions [Hein 94].

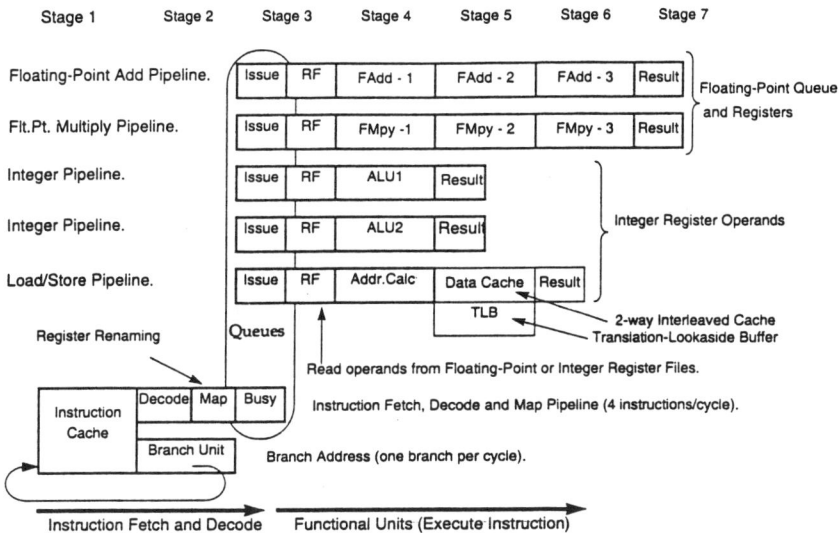

Fig. 9.13   Superscalar pipeline *(Courtesy of MIPS Computer Systems, Inc.)*

The R10000 implements out-of-order superscalar processing by using *dynamic issuing*. Fetched instructions are decoded and stored in queues. Each instruction is eligible to begin execution as soon as its operands become valid, independent of the original instruction sequence. In effect, the hardware rearranges instructions to keep its execution units busy. Although up to five instructions may begin execution during each cycle, some instructions (such as divide) take several or many cycles to complete. Thus, when a branch instruction is decoded, its branch condition (taken or not taken) may not yet be known. However, the R10000 processor can predict whether the branch is taken, and then continue decoding and executing subsequent instructions along the predicted path. When a branch prediction is wrong, the processor must back up to the original branch and take the other path. This technique is called *speculative execution*. Whenever the processor discovers that it mispredicted a branch, it aborts all speculatively executed instructions and restores the processor to the state it held before the branch [Hein 94]. This restoration takes one cycle in the R10000.

9.4 Earlier MIPS Implementations

Early MIPS implementation microprocessors (R2000, R3000, R6000) contained just an integer CPU and the CP0 on chip. The FPU was implemented on auxiliary chips (R2010, R3010, R6010). Some of the primary MIPS manufacturers are Integrated Device Technology (IDT), Inc. (Santa Clara, CA), LSI Logic Corporation (Milpitas, CA), Toshiba (Japan), NEC (Japan), and Performance Semiconductor Corporation (Sunnyvale, CA). The on-chip logic was designed to interface to a dual external cache from the beginning.

The R2000/R3000 pipeline (essentially the same as for R6000), illustrated in Fig. 9.14, has five stages:

1. *IF — instruction fetch*. Get instruction physical address from the TLB.
2. *ID — instruction decode*. Complete instruction fetch from external instruction cache. Read operands from the CPU register file while decoding the instruction.
3. *ALU — arithmetic logic unit*. Perform the required operation on the instruction operands.
4. *MEM — access memory*. Access external data cache for load or store instructions.
5. *WB — write-back*. Store ALU result or value loaded from the data cache into the register file.

9.5 Concluding Comments

Systems implementing the MIPS architecture microprocessors have been extensively implemented both by MIPS Computer Systems and by other companies in a wide range of workstations and other computing systems. Among some latest implementations one can mention the use of the R4400 in an up to 24 CPUs multiprocessor of the Nile series, produced by Pyramid Technology Corporation (San Jose, CA), which was one of the first manufacturers of commercial RISC-type systems in the early eighties [Tabk 87]. Tandem Computers built R4000-based high-reliability systems. Silicon Graphics (Mountain View, CA), which later merged with MIPS, produced a large variety of MIPS-architecture-microprocessor-based graphics workstations of the *Indigo* series. The Challenge line of multiprocessor servers from Silicon Graphics (see chapter 16), which began shipping in 1992, holds several records for general-purpose and scientific multiprocessing. Systems based on the R10000 will be announced in 1995 and 1996.

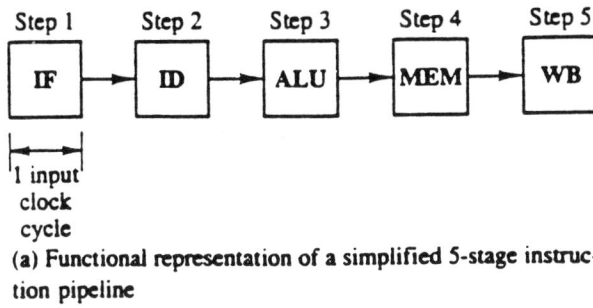

(a) Functional representation of a simplified 5-stage instruction pipeline

Clock cycle

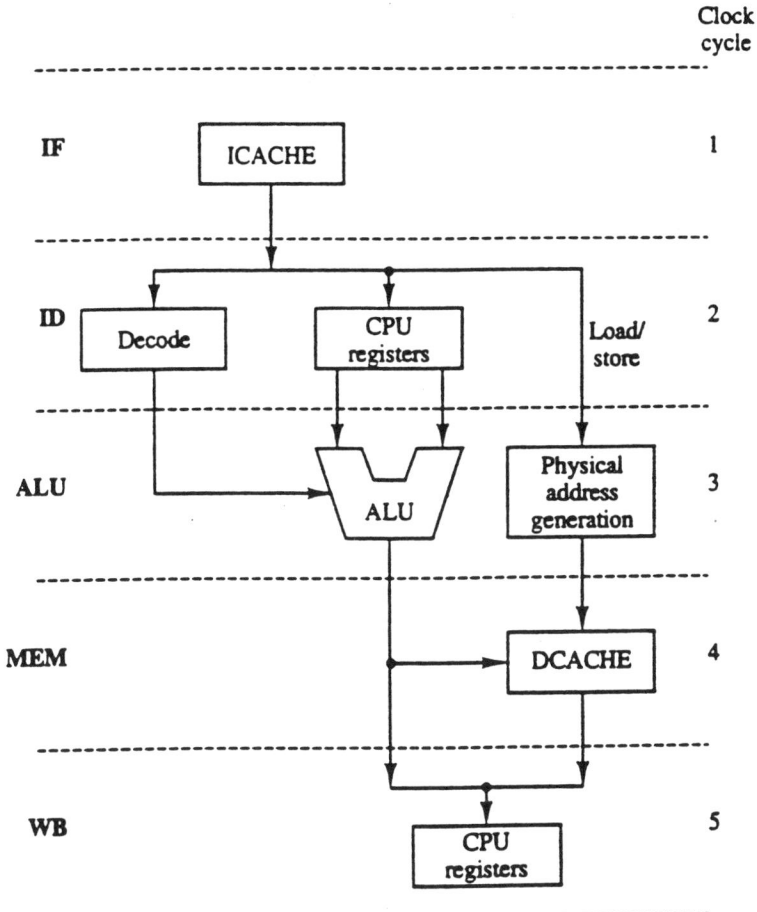

Note: stages IF and ALU may involve TLB look-up

(b) Simplified physical representation of a 5-stage instruction pipeline. (Here we assume the existence of an I-cache and a D-cache on chip.)

Fig. 9.14   MIPS R2000/R3000 pipeline *(Courtesy of MIPS Computer Systems, Inc.)*

CHAPTER 10

The Intel i860 Family

10.1 Introductory Comments

The Intel i860-family microprocessors (also known as 80860) are the first RISC-type products of Intel. For many years Intel was and still is a leader in the microprocessor industry, primarily known for its x86 CISC-type family [Tabk 94]. The i860 RISC was first announced in 1989 [Atki 91, KoMa 89]. It featured on-chip FPU, dual cache, and a graphics unit (first microprocessor with such a feature). The latest model, i860 XP, has an on-chip dual cache of a total of 32KB: 16KB instruction, 16KB data. Since its inception, the i860 has been implemented in a number of notable computing systems, such as Intel's latest massively parallel processing system, the Paragon.

The i860 architecture will be presented in the next section, following by details of its implementation. As is the case with other Intel microprocessors, the i860 is manufactured by Intel.

10.2 i860 Architecture

The i860 CPU registers are illustrated in Fig. 10.1. There are two separate sets of general-purpose registers:

1. *Integer register file*: thirty-two 32-bit registers, r0 to r31. Register r0 is permanently hardwired to a value of zero, as it is practiced in most RISC-type systems.

2. *Floating-point register file*: thirty-two 32-bit registers, f0 to f31. Registers f0 and f1 are permanently hardwired to a zero value. When accessing 64-bit floating-point values, an even-odd pair of registers can be used such as (f2,f3). When accessing 128-bit values, an aligned set of four registers (f0,f1,f2,f3), (f4,f5,f6,f8), ..., or (f28,f29,f30,f31), can be used. The instruction must designate the lowest register number of the set of registers containing 64- or 128-bit values. The register with the lowest number contains the least significant value.

The 32-bit *processor status register* (**psr**), shown in Fig. 10.2, contains the state information for the current process. The psr bits and fields are the following:

Bit 0, BR — break read, and *bit 1, BW — break write*, enable a data access trap when the operand address matches the address in the *data breakpoint register* (**db**), and a read or write, respectively, occurs.

INTEGER   FLOATING-POINT

32   0   64   0

	r0
	r1
	r2
	r3
	r4
	r5
	r6
	r7
	r8
	r9
	r10
	r11
	r12
	r13
	r14
	r15

f0
f2
f4
f6
f8
f10
f12
f14
f16
f18
f20
f22
f24
f26
f28
f30

epsr   psr

db

dirbase

fir

fsr

KR
KI
T
MERGE

r16
r17
r18
r19
r20
r21
r22
r23
r24
r25
r26
r27
r28
r29
r30
r31

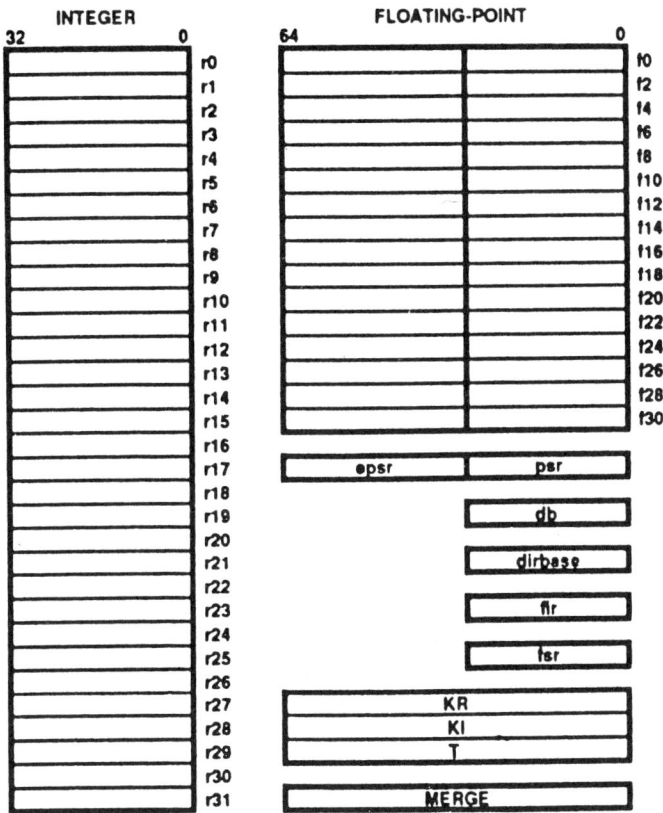

Fig. 10.1   80860 register set *(Courtesy of Intel Corporation)*

Bit 2, CC — condition code, set by various instructions according to tests they perform. The *branch on condition code* (**bc**) instructions test its value.

Bit 3, LCC — loop condition code, set and tested by the *branch on LCC and add* (**bla**) instruction.

Bit 4, IM — interrupt mode, enables external interrupts if set (IM = 1); disables interrupts if clear (IM = 0).

Bit 5, PIM — previous interrupt mode, and *bit 7, PU — previous user mode*, save the corresponding status bits (IM and U) on a trap, because those status bits are changed when a trap occurs. They are restored into their corresponding status bits when returning from a trap handler with a branch indirect instruction when a trap flag is set in the psr.

Bit 6, U — user mode, set when the processor is executing in the user mode; cleared when executing in the supervisor mode.

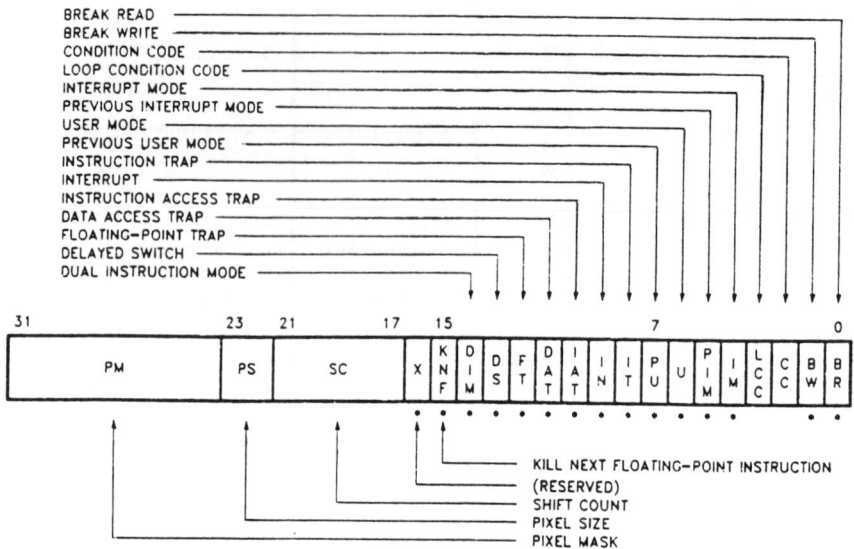

Fig. 10.2   Processor status register *(Courtesy of Intel Corporation)*

Bit 8, IT — instruction trap, bit 9, IN — interrupt, bit 10, IAT — instruction access trap, bit 11, DAT — data access trap, and bit 12, FT — floating-point trap are trap flags. They are set when the corresponding trap occurs. The trap handler routine examines these bits to determine which conditions have caused the trap.

Bit 13, DS — delayed switch, set if a trap occurs during the instruction cycle before the dual instruction mode is entered or exited.

Bit 14, DIM — dual instruction mode, set when a trap occurs if the processor is executing in dual-instruction mode (when the processor fetches two instructions on each clock cycle); cleared if it is executing in single-instruction mode.

Bit 15, KNF — kill next floating-point instruction, when set, the next floating-point instruction is suppressed.

Bits 17 to 21, SC — shift count, store the five-bit shift count (by how many bits shifted) used by the last right shift instruction.

Bits 22, 23, PS — pixel size, control pixel size according to the encoding:

PS	Pixel Size, bits	Pixel Size, bytes
00	8	1
01	16	2
10	32	4
11	Undefined	Undefined

Bits 24 to 31, PM — pixel mask, corresponds to pixels to be updated by the pixel store instruction (**pst.d**). If a bit of PM is set, then **pst.d** stores the corresponding pixel.

The KR, KI, and T registers are special-purpose registers used by the dual-operation floating-point instructions that initiate both an adder and a multiplier unit operation. These registers can store values from one dual-operation instruction and supply them as inputs to subsequent dual-operation instructions.

The MERGE register is used only by the vector-integer instructions. It accumulates (or merges) the results of multiple addition operations that use as operands the color intensity values from pixels or distance values from a buffer. The accumulated results can then be stored in one 64-bit operation.

Data types

The i860 architecture supports integer and floating-point data types. Load and store operations can reference 8-, 16-, 32-, 64-, and 128-bit operands. Integer operations are performed on 32-bit operands. Add and subtract instructions can also operate on 64-bit integers. Arithmetic operations on 8- and 16-bit integers can be performed by sign-extending the values to 32 bits and then using the 32-bit operations. Two's complement is used for signed values. When an 8- or 16-bit integer is stored in a 32-bit register, it is sign-extended to 32 bits.

The i860 supports the IEEE 754-1985 floating-point Standard formats of 32 and 64 bits [IEEE 85]. Graphics unit pixels of 8, 16, or 32 bits are supported. Regardless of the pixel size, the i860 always operates on 64 bits worth of pixels at a time.

Addressing modes

The i860 architecture features a few very simple addressing modes:

Register — the operand is in a CPU register.
Immediate — the operand is a part of the instruction.
Offset — absolute address into the first or last 32KB of the logical address space.
Register indirect with offset — EA = (reg) + offset : assembly notation: #const(reg).
Register indirect with index — EA = (reg1) + (reg2); assembly notation: reg1(reg2).

In addition, the floating-point load and store instructions may select *autoincrement* addressing. In this mode (reg2) is replaced by (reg1 + reg2) after performing the load or store. This mode makes stepping through arrays more efficient, because it eliminates one address calculation instruction.

Instruction formats

The i860-architecture instruction formats are illustrated in Fig. 10.3, along with the appropriate notation interpretation.

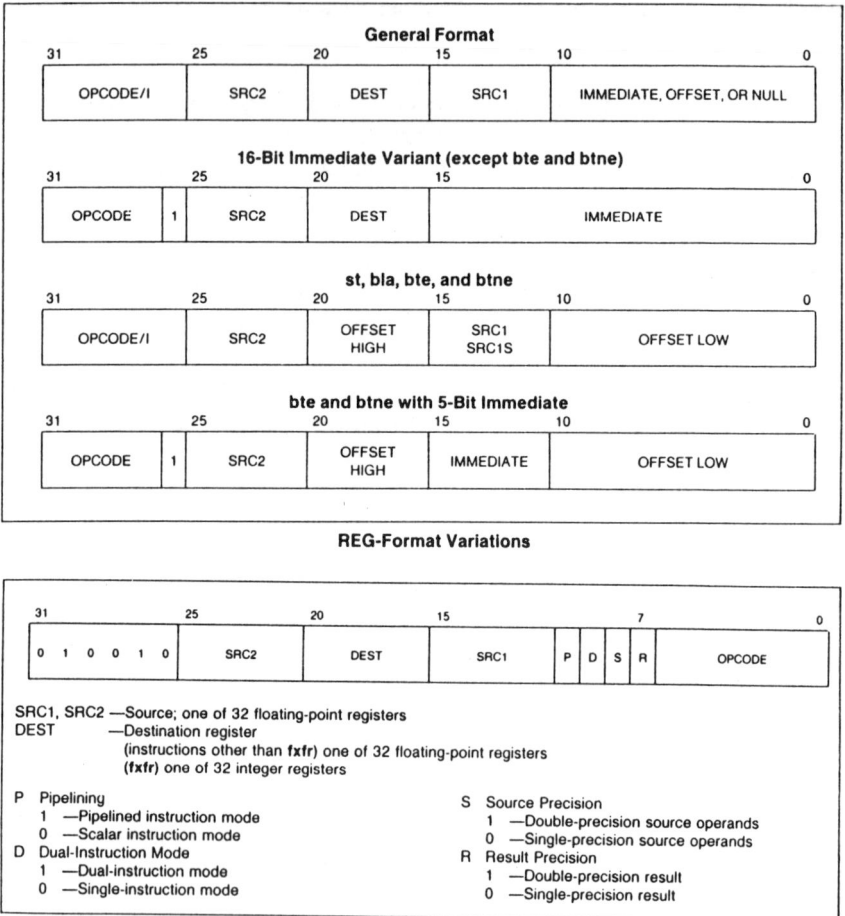

General Format

31	25	20	15	10	0
OPCODE/I	SRC2	DEST	SRC1	IMMEDIATE, OFFSET, OR NULL	

16-Bit Immediate Variant (except bte and btne)

31	25	20	15	0
OPCODE	1	SRC2	DEST	IMMEDIATE

st, bla, bte, and btne

31	25	20	15	10	0
OPCODE/I	SRC2	OFFSET HIGH	SRC1 SRC1S	OFFSET LOW	

bte and btne with 5-Bit Immediate

31	25	20	15	10	0
OPCODE	1	SRC2	OFFSET HIGH	IMMEDIATE	OFFSET LOW

REG-Format Variations

31	25	20	15	7	0
0 1 0 0 1 0	SRC2	DEST	SRC1	P D S R	OPCODE

SRC1, SRC2 —Source; one of 32 floating-point registers
DEST   —Destination register
           (instructions other than fxfr) one of 32 floating-point registers
           (fxfr) one of 32 integer registers

P Pipelining
   1 —Pipelined instruction mode
   0 —Scalar instruction mode
D Dual-Instruction Mode
   1 —Dual-instruction mode
   0 —Single-instruction mode

S Source Precision
   1 —Double-precision source operands
   0 —Single-precision source operands
R Result Precision
   1 —Double-precision result
   0 —Single-precision result

Floating-Point Instruction Encoding

Fig. 10.3   80860 instruction formats *(Courtesy of Intel Corporation)*

Instruction set

The i860 instruction set is listed in Table 10.1. It should be noted that the i860 does not feature integer multiply and divide instructions; in fact, it does not have a divide instruction at all. The multiplication operation is performed by the floating-point multiplier. In order to multiply two integers, the **fmlow.p** instruction (see Table 10.1) can be used. There is a floating-point *reciprocal value* instruction (**frcp.p**) which can be used to perform division via a Newton-Raphson approximation. There is also a *reciprocal floating-point square-root* (**frsqr.p**) instruction.

Examples:

adds src1, src2, rdest; add signed, $(src1) + (src2) \rightarrow rdest$.

subs src1, src2, rdest; subtract signed, $(src1) - (src2) \rightarrow rdest$.

ld.x src1(src2), rdest; load integer from memory $EA = (src1) + (src2)$ into rdest register.

.x denotes the size of the loaded operand:

.x = **.b**, 8-bit,
.x = **.s**, 16-bit,
.x = **.l**, 32-bit.

st.x src1, #const(src2); store integer from register src1 into memory $EA = (src2) + const$.

shl src1, src2, rdest; shift left logical src2 by (src1) bits $\rightarrow$ rdest.

mov src2, rdest; register-to-register move $(src2) \rightarrow rdest$.

The above move instruction is equivalent to:

shl r0, src2, rdest (r0 is permanently zero).

In most systems, the pipelines are transparent to the programmer and would thus not be a part of the architecture but of the organization. The i860 has several specific pipeline instructions, giving the user direct control over the pipeline operation. The pipelines are 'pushed' by the user and not by the clock. Therefore, in the i860 the pipelines are part of the architecture. Another interesting point to be noted is that pipelined loads of the i860 help 'hide' memory delays. The i860 pipeline instructions start with a 'p' (see Table 10.1), such as **pfmul.p**, **pfadd.p**, **pfsub.p**, and others.

Another form of parallelism featured by the i860 architecture is that it can execute both a floating-point and an integer instruction simultaneously. In such a case, the i860 operates as a *two-issue superscalar* (see chapter 1). Such parallel execution is called on the i860 *dual-instruction mode*. When executing in dual-instruction mode, the instruction sequence consists of 64-bit aligned instructions

248

Table 10.1 Instruction Set (1 of 2)

Core Unit		Floating-Point Unit	
Mnemonic	**Description**	**Mnemonic**	**Description**
Load and Store Instructions		**Register to Register Move**	
id.x	Load integer	fxfr	Transfer F-P to integer register
st.x	Store integer	**F-P Multiplier Instructions**	
fld.y	F-P load	fmul.p	F-P multiply
fst.y	F-P store	pfmul.p	Pipelined F-P multiply
pfld.y	Pipelined F-P load	pfmul3.dd	3-Stage pipelined F-P multiply
pst.d	Pixel store	fmlow.p	F-P multiply low
Register to Register Move		frcp.p	F-P reciprocal
ixfr	Transfer integer to F-P register	fsqr.p	F-P reciprocal square root
Integer Arithmetic Instructions		**F-P Adder Instructions**	
addu	Add unsigned	fadd.p	F-P add
adds	Add signed	pfadd.p	Pipelined F-P add
subu	Subtract unsigned	famov.r	F-P adder move
subs	Subtract signed	pfamov.r	Pipelined F-P adder move
Shift Instructions		fsub.p	F-P subtract
shl	Shift left	pfsub.p	Pipelined F-P subtract
shr	Shift right	pfgt.p	Pipelined greater-than compare
shra	Shift right arithmetic	pfeq.p	Pipelined equal compare
shrd	Shift right double	fix.v	F-P to integer conversion
Logical Instructions		pfix.v	Pipelined F-P to integer conversion
and	Logical AND	ftrunc.v	F-P to integer truncation
andh	Logical AND high	**Dual-Operation Instructions**	
andnot	Logical AND NOT	pfam.p	Pipelined F-P add and multiply
andnoth	Logical AND NOT high	pfsm.p	Pipelined F-P subtract and multiply
or	Logical OR	pfmam.p	Pipelined F-P multiply with add
orh	Logical OR high	pfmsm.p	Pipelined F-P multiply with subtract
xor	Logical exclusive OR	**Long Integer Instructions**	
xorh	Logical exclusive OR high	fisub.z	Long-integer subtract
Control-Transfer Instructions		pfisub.z	Pipelined long-integer subtract
br	Branch direct	fiadd.z	Long-integer add
bri	Branch indirect	pfiadd.z	Pipelined long-integer add
bc	Branch on CC	**Graphics Instructions**	
bc.t	Branch on CC taken	fzchks	16-bit Z-buffer check
bnc	Branch on not CC	pfzchds	Pipelined 16-bit Z-buffer check
bnc.t	Branch on not CC taken	fzchkl	32-bit Z-buffer check
bte	Branch if equal	pfzchkl	Pipelined 32-bit Z-buffer check
btne	Branch if not equal	faddp	Add with pixel merge
bla	Branch on LCC and add	pfaddp	Pipelined add with pixel merge
call	Subroutine call	faddz	Add with Z merge
calli	Indirect subroutine call	pfaddz	Pipelined add with Z merge
intovr	Software trap on integer overflow	form	OR with MERGE register
trap	Software trap	pform	Pipelined OR with MERGE register

(Courtesy of Intel Corporation)

with a floating-point instruction in the lower 32 bits and an integer instruction in the upper 32 bits (the i860 data bus is 64-bit in and out of the chip in all its implementations). Table 10.1 identifies which instructions are executed by the

Table 10.1 Instruction Set (2 of 2)

Core Unit	
Mnemonic	**Description**
I/O Instructions	
ldio.x	Load I/O
stio.x	Store I/O
ldint.x	Load interrupt vector
System Control Instructions	
flush	Cache flush
ld.c	Load from control register
st.c	Store to control register
lock	Begin interlocked sequence
unlock	End interlocked sequence
scyc.x	Special bus cycles
Assembler Pseudo-Operations	
Register to Register Move	
mov	Integer move
fmov.r	F-P reg-reg move
pfmov.r	Pipelined F-P reg-reg move
nop	Core no-operation
fnop	F-P no-operation
pfle.p	Pipelined F-P less-than or equal

(Courtesy of Intel Corporation)

integer (core) unit and which by the FPU. Programmers can specify a dual-instruction mode in one of the following ways:

1. By including in the mnemonic of a floating-point instruction a **d.** prefix.
2. By using the assembler directives *.dual* and *.enddual* arranged as follows:

   .dual
   code to be executed by the dual-instruction mode
   .enddual

Both of the above specifications cause the D bit of floating-point instructions to be set (see Fig. 10.3), permitting execution in the dual-instruction mode. Special dual-operation floating-point instructions (add and multiply, **pfam.p**, subtract and multiply, **pfsm.p**) use both the multiplier and adder units within the FPU in parallel to execute efficiently such common tasks as evaluating systems of linear equations, performing the fast Fourier transform (FFT), and graphics transformations.

The instructions **pfam.p**, **pfsm.p**, **pfmam.p**, and **pfmsm.p**, all operating on operands src1, src2, rdest, initiate both an adder operation and a multiplier operation. Six operands are required, but the instruction format specifies only three operands; therefore, there are special provisions for specifying the operands. These special provisions consist of:

1. Three special registers, KR, KI, and T, that can store values from one dual-operation instruction and supply them as inputs to subsequent dual-operation instructions.

    a. Registers KR and KI can store the value of src1 and subsequently supply that value to the multiplier pipeline in place of src1.

    b. Register T can store the last-stage result of the multiplier pipeline and subsequently supply that value to the adder pipeline in place of src1.

2. A four-bit datapath control field in the opcode that specifies the operands and loading of the special registers:

    a. Operand 1 of the multiplier can be KR, KI, or src1.

    b. Operand 2 of the multiplier can be src2 or the last-stage result of the adder pipeline.

    c. Operand 1 of the adder can be src1, T, or the last-stage result of the adder pipeline.

    d. Operand 2 of the adder can be src2, the last-stage result of the multiplier pipeline, or the last-stage result of the adder pipeline.

Unconditional branch instructions and the branch and test instruction are never delayed on the i860. Conditional branch instructions can be delayed (see chapter 2) by the user adding '.t' to the instruction mnemonic. The i860 uses a *scoreboarding* technique (see chapter 2) to guarantee proper operation of the code and prevent the use of incorrect data in a pipelined environment.

Memory organization
The i860 memory is byte-addressable with a paged virtual address memory of 4GB (2^{32} bytes). Data and instructions can be located anywhere in this address space. Normally, data are stored in memory in little-endian format. The i860 also offers the big-endian byte ordering as an option. Data consisting of n bytes are to be aligned on n-byte address boundaries. For instance, 64-bit (8-byte) data are to be aligned on 8-byte boundaries; that is, the three least-significant bits of the address must be zero.

For the 4KB page implementation, the i860 uses the page tables and the same format of virtual address as in the Intel x86 architecture [Tabk 94]. The *page directory* is pointed to by the **dirbase** register (see Fig. 10.1).

10.3 i860 Implementation
The current top implementation of the i860 architecture is the i860 XP. A block diagram of the i860 XP is shown in Fig. 10.4. It is a 2.55-million-transistors, three-layer metal, 0.8 micron CHMOS, 262-pin microprocessor. Its power

dissipation is 5W at 50MHz. It has an on-chip dual cache of 16KB code and 16KB data, for a total of 32KB [i860 91].

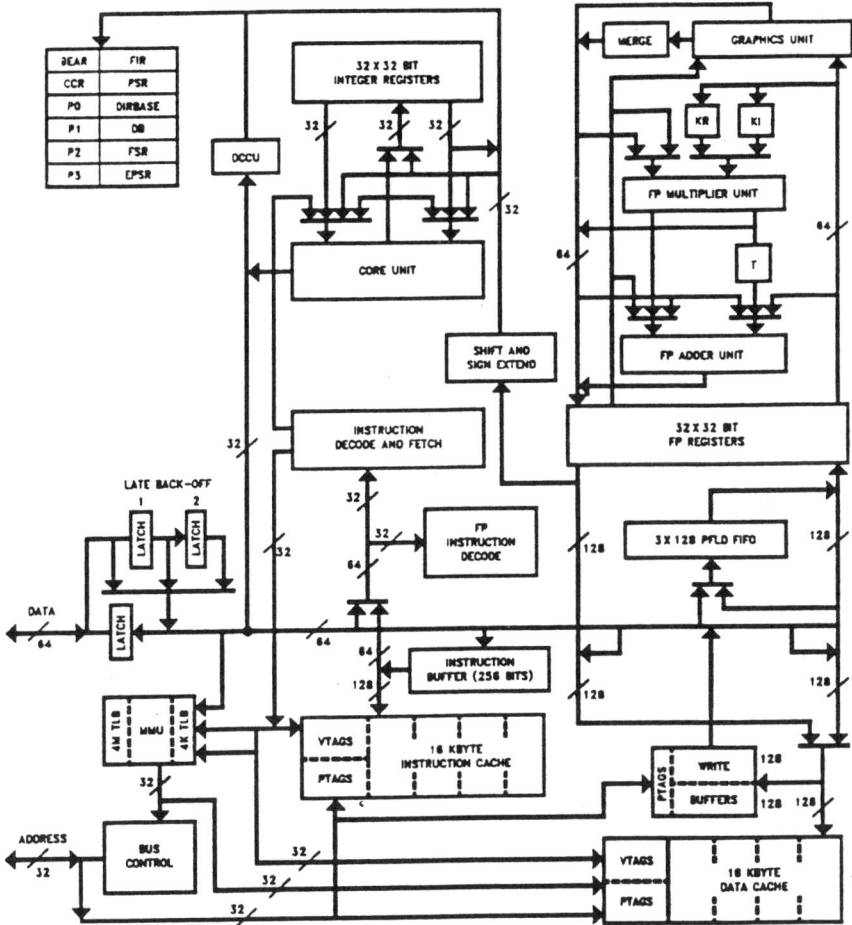

Fig. 10.4   The i860 XP *(Courtesy of Intel Corporation)*

The i860 integer instruction pipeline has four stages [Atki 91], as described in the example in chapter 1:

1. **F** — *fetch* instruction from instruction cache.
2. **D** — *decode* instruction and access register file.
3. **E**— *execute* operation.
4. **W** — *write* (store) result in the register file.

If the instruction is a branch, stage 3 becomes:

I — access *instruction cache* for target instruction and decode the instruction in the branch *delay* slot (next instruction to the branch). If it is a conditional branch, check condition code to determine if taken.

If the instruction is a subroutine call, then during stage 4 (W), write return address to the register file.

For floating-point instructions, the execute stage extends for three cycles: E1, E2, and E3. Thus, the floating-point pipeline is six stages deep.

The predecessor of the i860 XP is i860 XR. Their architecture is essentially identical. The i860 XR is a 1-million-transistors, 1 micron CHMOS, 168-pin chip. It has a dual cache of 4KB code and 8KB data, for a total of 12KB. Both caches use a random replacement policy [Smit 82]. Instructions that are new on the i860 XP: **pfld.q**, **scyc.x**, **ldio.x**, **stio.x**, **ldint.x** (Table 10.1).

Besides the **psr** and the **dirbase** system registers, defined earlier, there are the following 32-bit system registers on the i860 XP (Fig. 10.4, [i860 91]):

epsr — *extended psr*, contains additional state information for the current process beyond that stored in the **psr**.

db — *data breakpoint register*, used to generate a trap when the processor makes a data operand access to the address stored in this register.

fir — *fault instruction register*, contains the address of the trapping instruction, when a trap occurs.

fsr — *floating-point status register*, contains the floating-point trap and rounding mode status for the current process.

bear — *bus error address register*, receives the address of the cycle for bus or parity errors.

ccr — *concurrency control register*, controls the operation of the *concurrency control unit* (CCU).

P0, **P1**, **P2**, **P3** — *privileged registers* provided for the OS. May be used as interrupt stack pointer (SP), current user SP at the beginning of the trap handler, register values during trap handling, processor ID in a multiprocessor system.

System registers bear, ccr, and P0 to P3 are new on the i860 XP. Eight additional implemented bits were added in register epsr, and one in dirbase on the i860 XP.

The i860 XP features two page sizes: the regular 4KB and a large page size of 4MB, intended for lengthy software packages and graphics frame buffers. The TLB for 4KB pages has 64 entries encompassing $2^{12} * 2^6 = 2^{18}$ bytes $= 256$ KB of memory, and the 4MB page TLB has 16 entries, encompassing 64MB of memory. Both TLBs are four-way set-associative. A block diagram of the TLBs, and their address structure, are illustrated in Figs. 10.5(a) and (b). Both TLBs employ a random replacement algorithm because of its simplicity.

VIRTUAL ADDRESS

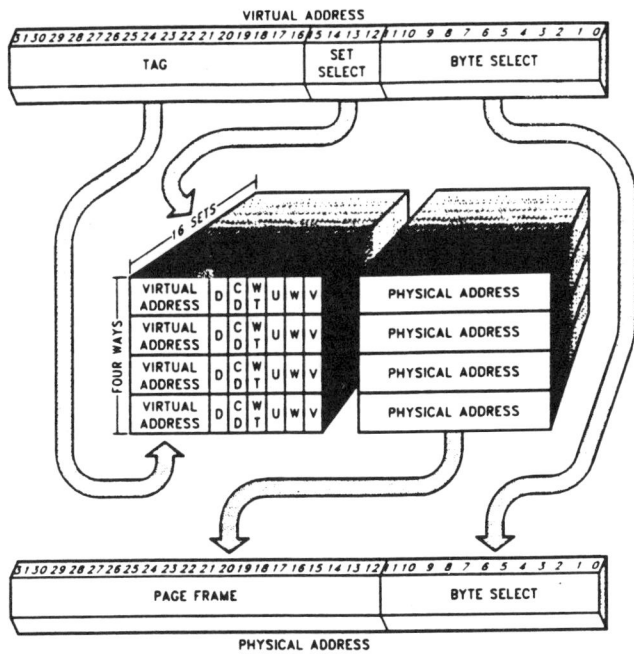

NOTES:
D Dirty
CD Cache Disable
WT Write-Through
U User Mode
W Writable
V Validity

PHYSICAL ADDRESS

Fig. 10.5(a) 4K TLB organization *(Courtesy of Intel Corporation)*

Because of the pipeline operation, a simultaneous access to both caches is required. However, the TLB can handle only one access at a time. In such a case, data access translation has a higher priority.

Each of the i860 XP caches is $16KB = 2^{14}$ bytes. Both are four-way set-associative (both i860 XR caches are two-way set-associative) with 32 bytes/line. Thus the number of lines in each cache is $2^{14}/2^5 = 2^9 = 512$ lines. The number of sets in each cache is therefore $2^9/2^2 = 2^7 = 128$ sets. The cache addressing scheme is shown in Fig. 10.6. For a 32-byte line we need a five-bit field to select a byte in a line, and for 128 sets we need a seven-bit field for set selection, a total of 12 bits, exactly the number of bits required for a 4KB = 2^{12} byte page offset. Thus, both the tag and the page number (non-zero part of the page base address) are 20-bit.

Each cache has two sets of tags: *virtual tags* used for internal access, and *physical tags* used for snooping (for cache coherency protocols in multiprocessors). The presence of both virtual and physical tags supports *aliasing*, a situation in which the TLBs associate in a single physical address with two or more virtual addresses. Cache line fills are generated only for read misses, not for write misses (a no-write-allocate policy; [HePa 90]).

Fig. 10.7 shows the organization of the i860 XP data cache. There are two state bits per physical tag (each line has a tag) and one validity bit per virtual tag.

254

VIRTUAL ADDRESS

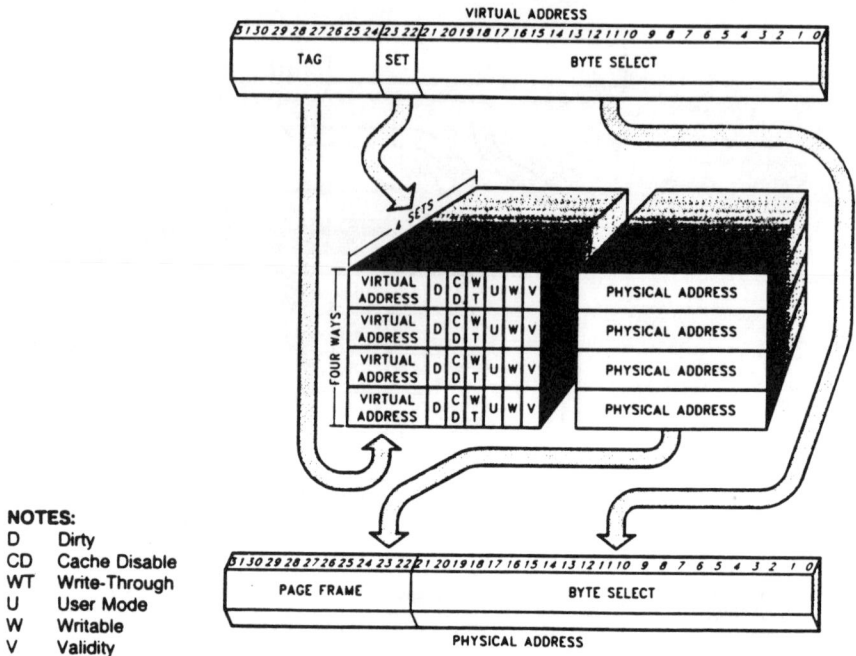

NOTES:
D   Dirty
CD   Cache Disable
WT   Write-Through
U   User Mode
W   Writable
V   Validity

Fig. 10.5(b)   4M TLB organization *(Courtesy of Intel Corporation)*

The *modified/exclusive/shared/invalid* (MESI) set of four states for the cache coherency protocol, listed in Table 10.2, is implemented. A *write-once* policy is implemented. A *write-through* is implemented for the first write into a line, while subsequent writes to the same line follow the *write-back* policy. The write-once policy helps to maintain cache coherency with a minimal amount of bus traffic. The first write (under write-through) broadcasts to other processors the fact that a line has been modified. The external system can dynamically change the update policy (write-back, write-through, write-once) of the i860 XP with each cache line.

Fig. 10.8 shows the organization of the instruction cache. Since instructions are not written into, no coherency problem exists, and no state bits are needed. There is only one validity bit per line (common to both virtual and physical tags). Aliasing support for instructions consists not simply of changing the virtual tag, but rather fetching a line whenever a virtual tag miss occurs. If the physical address already exists in the instruction cache, its line and its tags are overwritten. So, even though a physical line may be aliased, the processor never enters the line twice in the instruction cache.

Exceptions are called *traps* on the i860. When a trap occurs, execution of the current instruction is aborted. Except for bus error and parity error traps, the instruction is restartable. The information needed to restart the interrupted

INTERNALLY GENERATED ADDRESSES

31 30 29 28 27 26 25 24 23 22 21 20 19 18 17 16 15 14 13 12	11 10 9 8 7 6 5	4 3 2 1 0
CACHE TAG	SET SELECT	BYTE SELECT

128 SETS

FOUR WAYS

| VIRTUAL TAGS | 32-BYTE LINES | PHYSICAL TAGS |

31 30 29 28 27 26 25 24 23 22 21 20 19 18 17 16 15 14 13 12	11 10 9 8 7 6 5	4 3 2 1 0
CACHE TAG	SET SELECT	BYTE SELECT

EXTERNALLY GENERATED INQUIRY (SNOOP) ADDRESSES

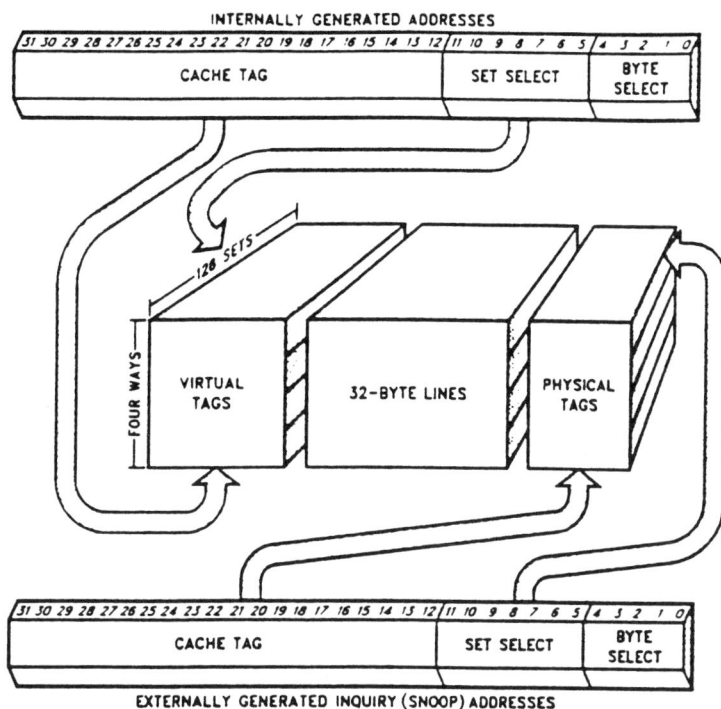

Fig. 10.6   Cache address usage *(Courtesy of Intel Corporation)*

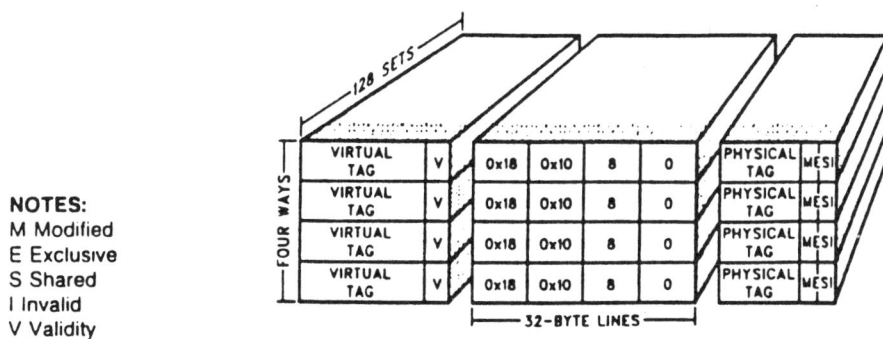

128 SETS

NOTES:
M Modified
E Exclusive
S Shared
I Invalid
V Validity

FOUR WAYS

VIRTUAL TAG	V	0x18	0x10	8	0	PHYSICAL TAG	MESI
VIRTUAL TAG	V	0x18	0x10	8	0	PHYSICAL TAG	MESI
VIRTUAL TAG	V	0x18	0x10	8	0	PHYSICAL TAG	MESI
VIRTUAL TAG	V	0x18	0x10	8	0	PHYSICAL TAG	MESI

32-BYTE LINES

Fig. 10.7   Data cache organization *(Courtesy of Intel Corporation)*

instruction is stored, and the processor executes an appropriate *trap handler* program in supervisor mode. Floating-point traps are triggered by the next floating-point instruction similar to the Alpha AXP's (see chapter 6) floating-point traps.

The i860 XP signals are shown in Fig. 10.9. There are 64 external data lines

Table 10.2 MESI Cache Line States

Cache Line State:	M Modified	E Exclusive	S Shared	I Invalid
This cache line is valid?	Yes	Yes	Yes	No
The memory copy is . . .	. . . out of date	. . . valid	. . . valid	—
Copies exist in other caches?	No	No	Maybe	Maybe
A write to this line . . .	. . . does not go to bus	. . . does not go to bus	. . . goes to bus and updates the cache	. . . goes directly to bus

(Courtesy of Intel Corporation)

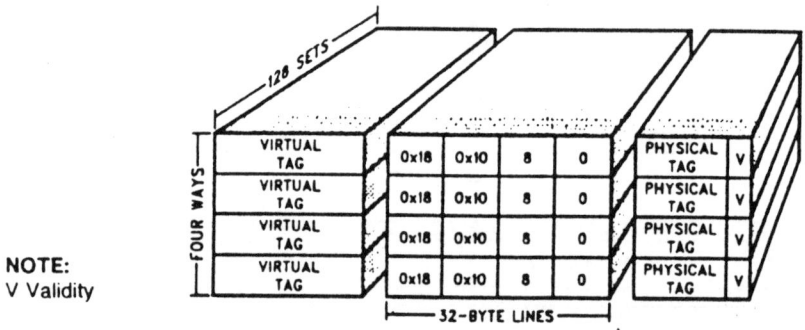

Fig. 10.8   Instruction cache organization *(Courtesy of Intel Corporation)*

D0 to D63. Of the 32 address lines, only lines A3 to A31 are external. However, there are eight byte enable lines BE0# to BE7# to identify each byte within a 64-bit doubleword. Tables 10.3, 10.4, and 10.5 list the operational interpretation of some combinations of i860 XP control and status signals.

10.4 Concluding Comments

The Intel i860 architecture and its microprocessor implementation have been discussed in the preceding sections. The i860 is extensively used both in Intel and in other manufacturers' applications, particularly in multiprocessors. The i860 XP has a relatively large total on-chip cache of 32KB. Its performance is competitive with other leading RISC and CISC microprocessors, operating at the same frequencies.

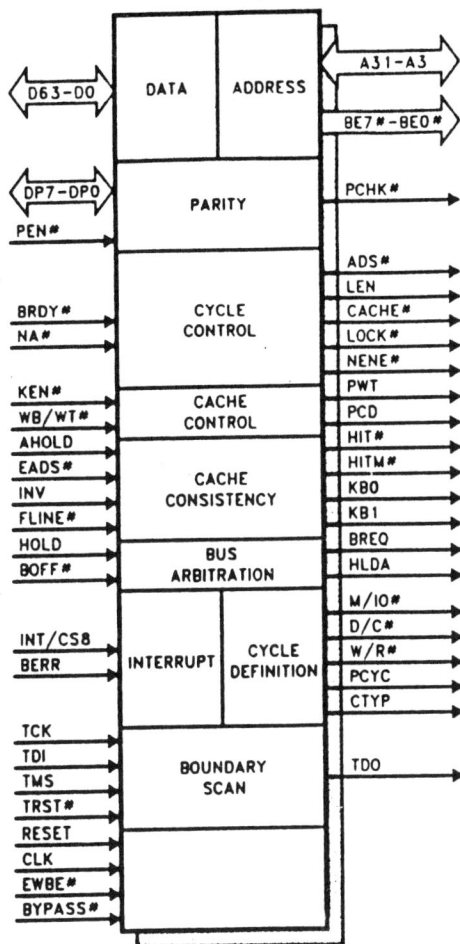

Fig. 10.9 Signal grouping *(Courtesy of Intel Corporation)*

Table 10.3 ADS# Initiated Bus Cycle Definitions

M/IO #	D/C #	W/R #	Bus Cycle Initiated
0	0	0	Interrupt Acknowledge
0	0	1	Special Cycle
0	1	0	I/O Read
0	1	1	I/O Write
1	0	0	Code Read
1	0	1	Reserved
1	1	0	Memory Read
1	1	1	Memory Write

(Courtesy of Intel Corporation)

Table 10.4 Memory Data Transfer Cycle Types

PCYC	CTYP	W/R #	Data Transfer Type
0	0	0	Normal read
0	1	0	Pipelined load (**pfld** instruction)
1	0	0	Page directory read
1	1	0	Page table read
0	0	1	Write-through (S-state hit)
0	1	1	Store miss or write-back
1	0	1	Page directory update
1	1	1	Page table update

NOTE:
PCYC and CTYP are defined only for memory data transfer
cycles (D/C # = 1, M/IO # = 1)

(Courtesy of Intel Corporation)

Table 10.5 Cycle Length Definition

W/R #	LEN	CACHE #	KEN #	Cycle Description	Burst Length
0	0	1	—	Noncacheable** 64-bit (or less) read	1
0	0	—	1	Noncacheable 64-bit (or less) read	1
1	0	1	—	64-bit (or less) write	1
—	0	1	—	I/O and Special Cycles	1
0	1	1	—	Noncacheable 128-bit read (p)fld.q	2
0	1	—	1	Noncacheable 128-bit read (p)fld.q	2
1	1	1	—	128-bit write **fst.q**	2
0	—	0	0	Cache line fill	4
1	—	0	—	Cache write-back	4

NOTE:
** Includes CS8-mode code fetches, which may be cached by the processor.
— Indicates 'don't care' values.

(Courtesy of Intel Corporation)

CHAPTER 11

The Motorola M88000 Family

11.1 Introductory Comments

Similarly to Intel, Motorola started its own RISC-type family of microprocessors, the M88000 family, after years of featuring a popular CISC-type family, the M68000 [Tabk 94]. The first members of the M88000 family are the MC88100 CPU and the MC88200 Cache MMU (CMMU) chips [Alsp 90, Mele 89, Tabk 94]. They were followed recently by the new-generation RISC MC88110, which is a two-issue superscalar [DiAl 92, M811 91]. The M88000 architecture will be presented in the next section, while the implemented microprocessors will be discussed in the subsequent sections.

11.2 M88000 Architecture

Register file

The M88000 register file (or: programming model) is shown in Fig. 11.1. It consists of the following parts:

1. *General register file* (GRF), consisting of 32 32-bit registers r0 to r31. Register r0 is permanently wired to a zero value, as it is in other RISC-type systems. Register r1 contains the *subroutine return pointer*. The content of register r1 is not protected; it can be overwritten by software.
2. *Extended register file* (XRF), consisting of 32 80-bit registers x0 to x31, intended for storing floating-point operands. The operands may be IEEE 754-1985 Standard 32-bit single-precision, 64-bit double-precision, or 80-bit extended precision. Register x0 is permanently wired to a positive zero value.
3. *Floating-point control register* (FPCR), 32-bit.
4. *Floating-point status register* (FPSR), 32-bit.
5. *Control registers*, cr0 to cr51, 32-bit. In supervisor programming model only.
6. *Floating-point exception cause register* (FPECR), fcr0, 32-bit. In supervisor programming model only.

Some of the control registers will be discussed later on in the next section dealing with M88000 microprocessor implementation.

GENERAL REGISTERS
r0 ZERO
r1 SUBROUTINE RETURN POINTER
r2
TEMPORARY STORAGE REGISTERS
r31

EXTENDED REGISTERS
x0 ZERO
x1
TEMPORARY STORAGE REGISTERS
x31

fcr62 FPSR FLOATING POINT STATUS REGISTER
fcr63 FPCR FLOATING POINT CONTROL REGISTER

USER PROGRAMMING MODEL

cr0	PID	PROCESSOR IDENTIFICATION
cr1	PSR	PROCESSOR STATUS REGISTER
cr2	EPSR	EXCEPTION PROCESSOR STATUS REGISTER
cr4	EXIP	EXCEPTION EXECUTING INSTRUCTION POINTER
cr5	ENIP	EXCEPTION NEXT INSTRUCTION POINTER
cr7	VBR	VECTOR BASE REGISTER
cr16	SR0	STORAGE REGISTER 0
cr17	SR1	STORAGE REGISTER 1
cr18	SR2	STORAGE REGISTER 2
cr19	SR3	STORAGE REGISTER 3
cr20	SR4	STORAGE REGISTER 4
cr25	ICMD	INSTRUCTION MMU/CACHE/TIC COMMAND
cr26	ICTL	INSTRUCTION MMU/CACHE CONTROL
cr27	ISAR	INSTRUCTION SYSTEM ADDRESS
cr28	ISAP	INSTRUCTION MMU SUPERVISOR AREA POINTER
cr29	IUAP	INSTRUCTION MMU USER AREA POINTER
cr30	IIR	INSTRUCTION MMU ATC INDEX REGISTER
cr31	IBP	INSTRUCTION MMU BATC R/W PORT
cr32	IPPU	INSTRUCTION MMU PATC R/W PORT (UPPER)
cr33	IPPL	INSTRUCTION MMU PATC R/W PORT (LOWER)
cr34	ISR	INSTRUCTION ACCESS STATUS REGISTER
cr35	ILAR	INSTRUCTION ACCESS LOGICAL ADDRESS
cr36	IPAR	INSTRUCTION ACCESS PHYSICAL ADDRESS
cr40	DCMD	DATA MMU/CACHE COMMAND
cr41	DCTL	DATA MMU/CACHE CONTROL
cr42	DSAR	DATA SYSTEM ADDRESS REGISTER
cr43	DSAP	DATA MMU SUPERVISOR AREA POINTER
cr44	DUAP	DATA MMU USER AREA POINTER
cr45	DIR	DATA MMU ATC INDEX REGISTER
cr46	DBP	DATA MMU BATC R/W PORT
cr47	DPPU	DATA MMU PATC R/W PORT (UPPER)
cr48	DPPL	DATA MMU PATC R/W PORT (LOWER)
cr49	DSR	DATA ACCESS STATUS REGISTER
cr50	DLAR	DATA ACCESS LOGICAL ADDRESS
cr51	DPAR	DATA ACCESS PHYSICAL ADDRESS
fcr0	FPECR	FLOATING-POINT EXCEPTION CAUSE REGISTER

SUPERVISOR PROGRAMMING MODEL

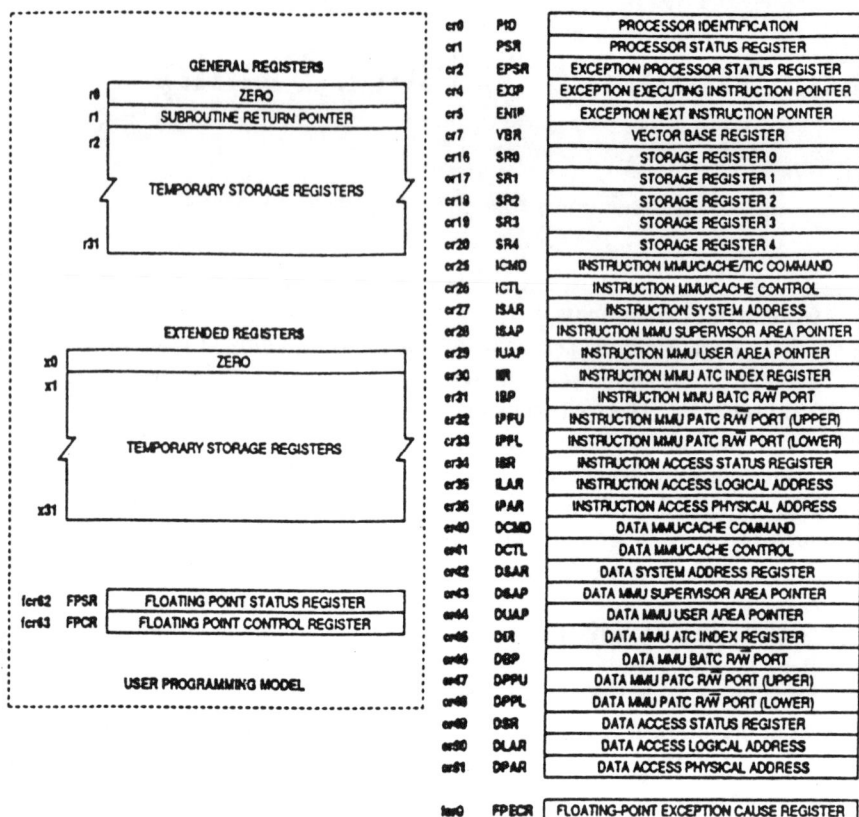

Fig. 11.1   M88000 programming model *(Courtesy of Motorola, Inc.)*

Data types

The following data types are recognized as operands by the M88000 architecture:

1. *Integer*.
   Byte   eight bits.
   Halfword   16 bits.
   Word   32 bits.
   Doubleword   64 bits.
2. *Bit-field*. One to 32 bits in a 32-bit register.
3. *Floating-point*.
   Single-precision   32 bits.
   Double-precision   64 bits.
   Double extended precision   80 bits.

4. *Graphics.*
32-bit packed nibbles (nibble = 4 bits), bytes, and halfwords.
64-bit packed nibbles, bytes, halfwords, and words.

The operand size for each instruction is either explicitly encoded in the instruction or implicitly defined by the instruction operation. Bit fields are defined by width and offset values given in the instruction or in a source register specified by the instruction. Data storage in general register and in the extended register files is illustrated in Figs. 11.2(a) and (b). Memory storage alignment of integer and floating-point operands is illustrated in Fig. 11.3. Attempting an incorrectly aligned data transfer will cause a misaligned reference exception, if this exception is not masked. The M88000 architecture supports both big-endian (by default) and little-endian byte ordering [M811 91].

Addressing modes
The M88000 addressing modes are classified into three categories as follows [M811 91]:

Computational
Register (general, extended, control).
Immediate (six-bit, 10-bit, 16-bit).
Load/Store/Exchange
Register indirect with immediate displacement.
Register indirect with index.
Register indirect with scaled index.
Flow control
Register indirect.
Register indirect with nine-bit vector table index.
PC-relative with 16-bit displacement.
PC-relative with 26-bit displacement.

Most of the above addressing modes are well known [Tabk 94]. The only addressing mode that requires further explanation is the *register indirect with nine-bit vector table index*. This mode is used by trap generation instructions (tb0, tb1, and tcnd). For this addressing mode there is a nine-bit VEC9 field (bits 8 to 0) in the instruction. This field is shifted three bits left, filling the three least significant bits with zeros, and concatenated with the upper 20 bits of the vector base address (which point to the exception vector table) to form a 32-bit address. The reason for the nine-bit VEC9 field is that there are $512 = 2^9$ exceptions featured by the M88000 architecture, and hence 512 vectors. Each vector takes up $8 = 2^3$ bytes, and therefore the shift left by three bits [M811 91].

Instruction formats
The M88000 instruction formats for three-operand register-to-register instructions,

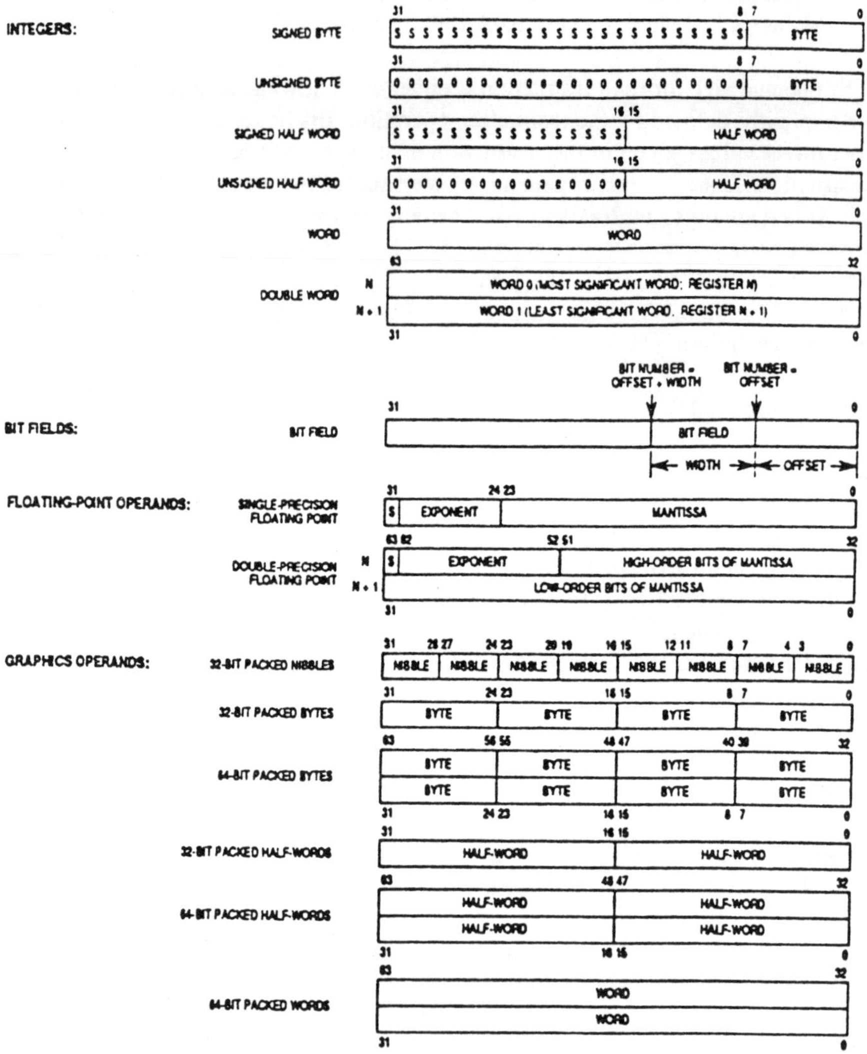

262

Fig. 11.2(a) Data organization in general registers *(Courtesy of Motorola, Inc.)*

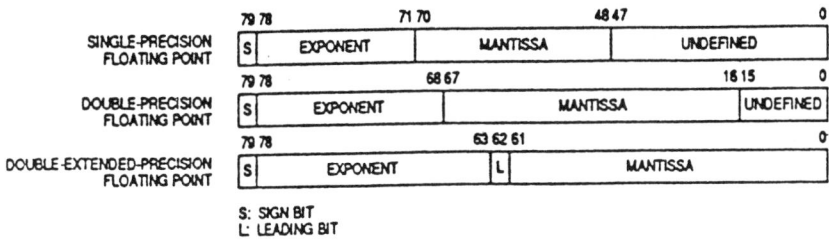

Fig. 11.2(b) Operands in extended register file *(Courtesy of Motorola, Inc.)*

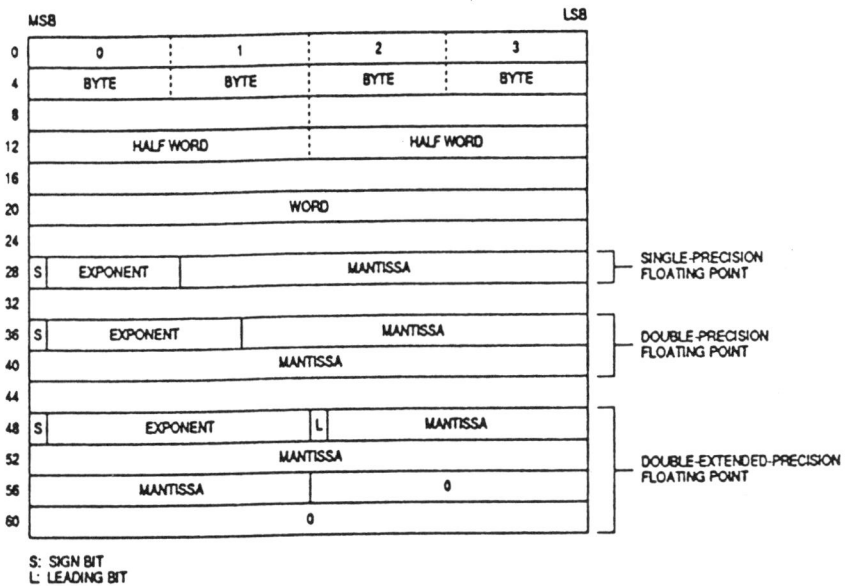

Fig. 11.3 Floating-point memory storage alignment *(Courtesy of Motorola, Inc.)*

for integer and floating-point operations, are illustrated in Fig. 11.4. In other formats the subopcode and S2 fields are superseded by fields for immediate operands. When the PC-relative with a 26-bit displacement mode is used (for br and bsr instructions), there is only a six-bit opcode field (bits 31 to 26) and then a 26-bit displacement field (bits 25 to 0).

Instruction set

The M88000 instruction set is listed in Table 11.1, subdivided into seven separate instruction groups. The total number of M88000 instructions is 66, a suitable

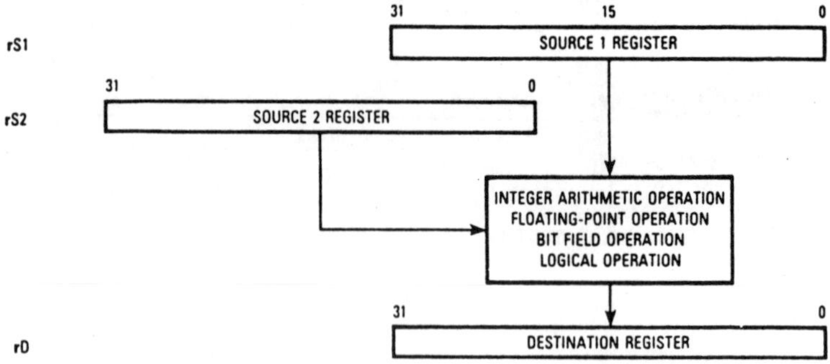

Instruction Format (Floating-Point)

31	26 25	21 20	16 15	5 4	0
1 0 0 0 0 1	D	S1	SUBOPCODE	S2	

D
: The D field specifies the destination register which receives the result of the operation.

S1
: The S1 field specifies the source 1 operand register. For the **int, nint, flt,** and **trnc** instructions, S1 must be zero.

SUBOPCODE
: This field identifies the floating-point instruction (**fadd, fcmp, fdiv, fmul, fsub, int, nint, flt,** and **trnc**).

S2
: The S2 field specifies the source 2 operand register.

Instruction Format (Non-Floating-Point)

31	26 25	21 20	16 15	5 4	0
1 1 1 1 0 1	D	S1	SUBOPCODE	S2	

D
: The D field specifies the destination register which receives the result of the operation. This field is ignored for instructions that do not generate results.

S1
: The S1 field specifies the source 1 operand register. For bit scan and the **rte** instructions, this field is ignored.

SUBOPCODE
: This field identifies the non-floating-point instruction (**add, addu, and, cmp, div, divu, ext, extu, ff0, ff1, mak, mul, or, rot, rte, set, sub, subu, trnc,** and **xor**).

S2
: The S2 field specifies the source 2 operand register. For the **rte** instruction this field is ignored.

Fig. 11.4   Instruction formats of the MC88100 *(Courtesy of Motorola, Inc.)*

number for a RISC-type system. All instructions are 32-bit long. The types of M88000 instructions and their number are listed next.

Table 11.1 MC88110 Instruction Set

Integer Arithmetic Instructions	
Mnemonic	Description
add	Signed Add
addu	Unsigned Add
cmp	Integer Compare
divs	Signed Divide
divu	Unsigned Divide
muls	Signed Multiply
mulu	Unsigned Multiply
sub	Signed Subtract
subu	Unsigned Subtract

Bit-Field Instructions	
Mnemonic	Description
clr	Clear Bit Field
ext	Extract Bit Field
extu	Unsigned Extract Bit Field
ff0	Find First Bit Clear
ff1	Find First Bit Set
mak	Make Bit Field
rot	Rotate Register
set	Set Bit Field

Logical Instructions	
Mnemonic	Description
and	And
mask	Logical Mask Immediate
or	Or
xor	Exclusive Or

Graphics Instructions	
Mnemonic	Description
padd	Pixel Add
padds	Pixel Add and Saturate
pcmp	Pixel Compare
pmul	Pixel Multiply
ppack	Pixel Truncate, Insert, and Pack
prot	Pixel Rotate Left
psub	Pixel Subtract
psubs	Pixel Subtract and Saturate
punpk	Pixel Unpack

Flow Control Instructions	
Mnemonic	Description
bb0	Branch on Bit Clear
bb1	Branch on Bit Set
bcnd	Conditional Branch
br	Unconditional Branch
bsr	Branch to Subroutine
illop	Illegal Operation
jmp	Unconditional Jump
jsr	Jump to Subroutine
rte	Return from Exception
tb0	Trap on Bit Clear
tb1	Trap on Bit Set
tbnd	Trap on Bounds Check
tcnd	Conditional Trap

Load/Store/Exchange Instructions	
Mnemonic	Description
ld	Load Register From Memory
lda	Load Address
ldcr	Load from Control Register
st	Store Register to Memory
stcr	Store to Control Register
xcr	Exchange Control Register
xmem	Exchange Register with Memory

Floating-Point Instructions	
Mnemonic	Description
fadd	Floating-Point Add
fcmp	Floating-Point Compare
fcmpu	Unordered Floating-Point Compare
fcvt	Convert Floating-Point Precision
fdiv	Floating-Point Divide
fldcr	Load from Floating-Point Control Register
flt	Convert Integer to Floating-Point
fmul	Floating-Point Multiply
fsqrt	Floating-Point Square Root
fstcr	Store to Floating-Point Control Register
fsub	Floating-Point Subtract
fxcr	Exchange Floating-Point Control Register
int	Round Floating-Point to Integer
mov	Register-to-Register Move
nint	Round Floating-Point to Nearest Integer
trnc	Truncate Floating-Point to Integer

(Courtesy of Motorola, Inc.)

Instruction Group	Number of Instructions
Integer arithmetic	9
Bit-field	8
Logical	4
Graphics	9
Flow control	13
Load/store/exchange	7
Floating-point	16

Examples:

add r5, r4, r1; r5 ← (r4) + (r1)

divs r11, r1, r2; r11 ← (r1)/(r2), signed divide, r11 receives the quotient

Floating-point operations permit the mixing of single-, double-, and extended-precision operands.

Examples:

fmul.dss   x1, x4, x8; x1 ← (x4) * (x8)

where s = single-precision, d = double-precision.
  The double-precision product of the single-precision contents of x4 and x8 is placed into x1.

fmul.xds   x2, x10, x12; x2 ← (x10) * (x12), where x = extended precision.

All combinations of s, d, or x are allowed as sources and destinations.

The M88000 offers the user an *optional delayed-branch* capability, attained by placing '.n' after the instruction mnemonic, such as in jmp.n or br.n (just writing 'jmp' or 'br' would be a regular, undelayed jump or branch; see chapter 2). It should be noted, however, that implementation of a delayed branch in superscalar systems introduces extra difficulties both in hardware and in software, and for this reason it is not recommended for use in such systems.

11.3 The MC88110
The MC88110 is a 1.3-million-transistors, triple-level metal, 0.8 micron CMOS, 299-pin microprocessor. It is a two-issue superscalar system with 10 on-chip operational units, also denoted as *execution units* [DiAl 92, M811 91]. A block diagram of the MC88110, and the execution units, are illustrated in Figs. 11.5(a) and (b). The architecture defines a major opcode subset denoted as a *special*

function unit (SFU); all floating-point instructions are encoded in SFU1, and all graphics instructions in SFU2 (see Fig. 11.5(b)). SFU3 to SFU7 are reserved for future extensions. The execution units are:

1., 2. *Integer.*
3. *Branch.*
4. *Bit-field.*
5. *Multiply* (integer and floating-point; Booth algorithm), pipelined.
6. *Floating add*, pipelined.
7. *Divide* (integer and floating-point), iterative, radix-8, three bits per clock.
8., 9. *Graphics.*
10. *Load/store.*

The abundance of execution units permits simultaneous execution of a large number of combinations of simultaneously fetched instructions. Even if both instructions are integer arithmetic, or both are graphics instructions, there are two identical execution units to execute them in parallel. This is indeed an important advantage in a superscalar system (see chapter 1).

The main part of the *superscalar instruction unit* (Fig. 11.5) is the *central instruction sequencer* (CIS), which dispatches instructions into the array of execution units [DiAl 92]. The CIS fetches instructions from the instruction cache, tracks resource availability and interinstruction dependencies, directs operand flow between the register files and execution units, and dispatches instructions to the individual execution units.

There is also a fully associative, 32-entry, logically addressed, *target instruction cache* (TIC). Each entry in the TIC contains the first two instructions of a branch target instruction stream, a 31-bit logical address tag, and a valid bit. The 31-bit tag holds a supervisor/user bit and the upper 30 bits of the address of the branch instruction. When a branch instruction occurs, the TIC is accessed in parallel with the decoding of the branch instruction. If there is a TIC hit, the two instructions corresponding to the branch instruction are sent from the TIC to the instruction unit. This eliminates much of the delay involved with changes in instruction flow [M811 91].

On each clock cycle, the CIS fetches two instructions from the instruction cache and two from the TIC. It decodes the appropriate instruction pair while fetching the necessary data operands from the register files (GRF or XRF). If all the required execution units and operands are available, the CIS simultaneously dispatches both instructions to their respective execution units. If the sequencer cannot dispatch both instructions, it tries to dispatch at least the first of the pair. In that case, the second instruction moves into the first issue slot, a new instruction is fetched to replace it, and the CIS tries to issue the new pair on the next clock cycle [DiAl 92].

Of particular interest is the MC88110 *load/store* execution unit [DiAl 92]. The unit provides a *stunt box* capability for holding memory references that are waiting

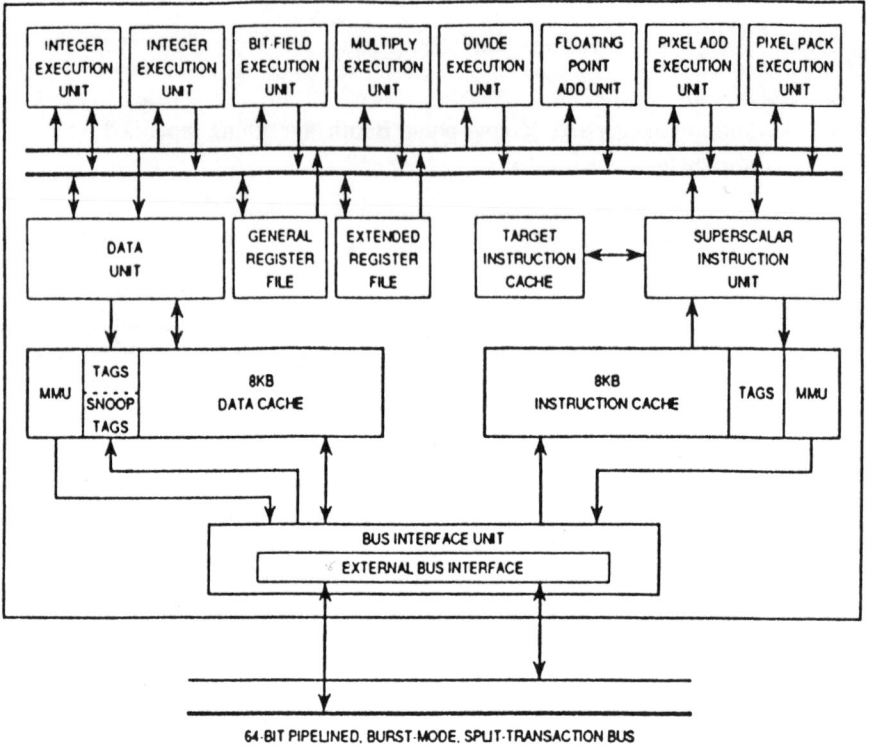

Fig. 11.5(a)   MC88110 block diagram *(Courtesy of Motorola, Inc.)*

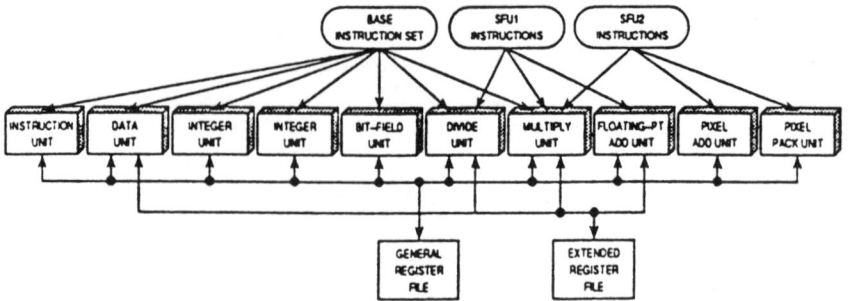

Fig. 11.5(b)   SFU hardware use *(Courtesy of Motorola, Inc.)*

for the memory system and allows *dynamic reordering* of load operations past stalled store operations. The term 'stunt box' refers to any device that allows reordering of memory references in the memory access system. The datapath from the load/store unit to the register files is 80 bits wide. On each clock cycle, the load/store unit can accept one new load or store instruction from the *instruction dispatch* unit. The dispatched instruction awaits access to the data cache in one of the two FIFO queues: the four-deep *load buffers* for load operations, and the three-deep *store reservation station* for store operations. Normal instruction dispatch and execution can continue while these instructions await service by the cache or memory system (provided that there is no data dependency on load instructions). Store instructions can be dispatched before the store data operand is available. Store instructions wait in the store queue until the instruction computing the required data completes execution. When the operand becomes available, the sequencer directs it into the store reservation station, and the associated store instruction becomes a candidate for access to the data cache. If a store instruction stalls in the reservation station waiting for its operand, subsequently issued load instructions can bypass the store and immediately access the cache. An *address comparator* detects address hazards and prevents loads from going ahead of stores to the same address, thus loading stale data. This load/store reordering feature allows runtime overlapping of tight loops by permitting loads at the top of a loop to proceed without having to wait for the completion of stores from the bottom of the previous iteration of the loop.

As with stores, the MC88110 provides a *reservation station* to avoid stalling on *conditional branches*. The sequencer *predicts* the branch direction, and instructions down the predicted path *execute conditionally*, or *speculatively*, until the branch operand is resolved. The static prediction of the branch direction is based on the opcode of the branch instruction. The *branch reservation station* provides a place to set aside the branch instruction so that instruction issue can continue while the branch condition can be resolved. If the prediction was incorrect, the system backs up to the branch, undoing all operations along the wrong path, and resumes execution along the correct path [DiAl 92].

The MC88110 has a dual cache, 8KB instruction, 8KB data, for a total of 16KB. Each cache is physically addressed, two-way set-associative, with 32 bytes/line. Each cache has $2^{13}/ 2^5 = 2^8 = 256$ lines, that is $256/2 = 128 = 2^7$ sets. Therefore, when addressing the cache we need five bits for the byte in line field, seven bits for the set field, and 20 bits for the tag. This fits exactly the virtual memory addressing for a 4KB $= 2^{12}$ bytes page, as practiced on the MC88100. Thus, the lowest 12 bits of the virtual address (bits 11 to 0) are the offset into a page, and at the same time the set (bits 11 to 5) and byte (bits 4 to 0) fields for cache access. The upper 20 bits are forwarded to the *address translation cache* (ATC) for translation into a 20-bit physical page number, to be compared with the 20-bit tags of the appropriate set in the cache. The data cache is write-back.

The MC88110 can also be connected to a secondary external cache, controlled by the MC88410 cache controller. The secondary cache can be configured out of

62110 SRAM chips, for a total size of 256KB to 1MB. The secondary cache is designed to be direct-mapped, write-back, with 32 or 64 bytes/line [DiAl 92].

The MC88110 features two types of ATC. One is the *page ATC* (PATC), which is fully associative and contains 32 entries embodying page number translations for 4KB pages. The PATC is automatically maintained by hardware or can be maintained by system software. The other ATC is the *block ATC* (BATC), which is fully associative, with eight entries, containing address translations for block sizes ranging from 512KB to 64MB. The term 'block' is just an M88000 term for optional larger page sizes [M811 91]. As in the latest implementations of the Motorola M68000 family [Tabk 94], the MC88110 features a dual MMU, illustrated in Fig. 11.6, the *instruction MMU* (IMMU) and the *data MMU* (DMMU). The IMMU and the instruction cache comprise the *instruction memory unit* (IMU), and the DMMU with the data cache comprise the *data memory unit* (DMU). As already argued in chapters 1 and 2, the memory unit duality permits the processor to deal with instruction and data accesses in parallel, thus supporting a more efficient handling of the pipeline. This is particularly important in superscalar systems.

The MC88110 page translation table structure is shown in Fig. 11.7, and the page table lookup is illustrated in Fig. 11.8. The extra S/U bit of the logical address differentiates between the supervisor and user modes, each of which has separate instruction and data areas in memory and separate address pointers (called *area descriptors*) into their segment tables. As can be seen in Fig. 11.8, the page table structure and the address partitioning of the MC88110 are identical to those of Intel [Tabk 94], except for some different terminology. The 'page table' term is the same on both. What is called 'page directory' in Intel, is called 'segment table' on the MC88110. All of the above have up to 1024 32-bit entries and may be up to 4KB in size (page size). What is called 'PTE' in Intel is called 'page descriptor' on the MC88110, and a 'PDE' in Intel is a 'segment descriptor' on the MC88110. Another difference is that there are four pointers on the MC88110 (and more than one segment table), while there is only one such pointer in Intel (CR3) and one table directory.

The MC88110 *processor status register* (PSR) is shown in Fig. 11.9. Only a part of its bits is currently implemented.

Bit 31, supervisor/user mode (MODE), MODE = 1 supervisor, MODE = 0 user.
Bit 30, byte ordering (BO), BO = 1 little-endian, BO = 0 big-endian.
Bit 29, serial mode (SER), SER = 1 serial instruction execution, SER = 0 concurrent execution.
Bit 28, carry (C), C = 1 carry generated by add or sub instructions, C = 0 carry not generated.
Bit 26, signed immediate mode (SGN), SGN = 1 immediate offsets and constants are signed, SGN = 0 immediate offsets and constants are unsigned.
Bit 25, serialize memory (SRM), SRM = 1 serialize memory instructions, SRM = 0 concurrent memory instruction execution.

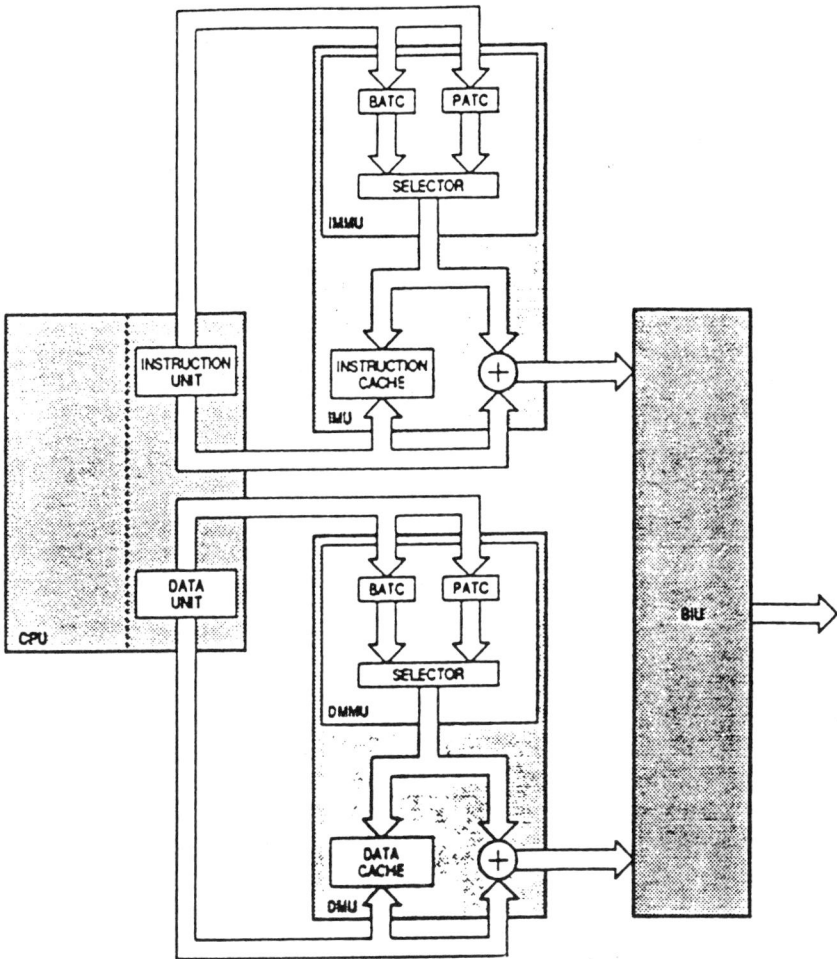

Fig. 11.6   MC88110 MMU block diagram *(Courtesy of Motorola, Inc.)*

Bits 9 to 3, SFU disable (SFUD), SFUD = 1 SFU disabled.
Bit 2, misaligned access exception mode mask (MXM), MXM = 1 exception disabled, MXM = 0 exception enabled.
Bit 1, interrupt disable (IND), IND = 1 external interrupts disabled, IND = 0 enabled.
Bit 0, exceptions freeze (EFRZ), EFRZ = 1 exceptions disabled, EFRZ = 0 enabled.

272

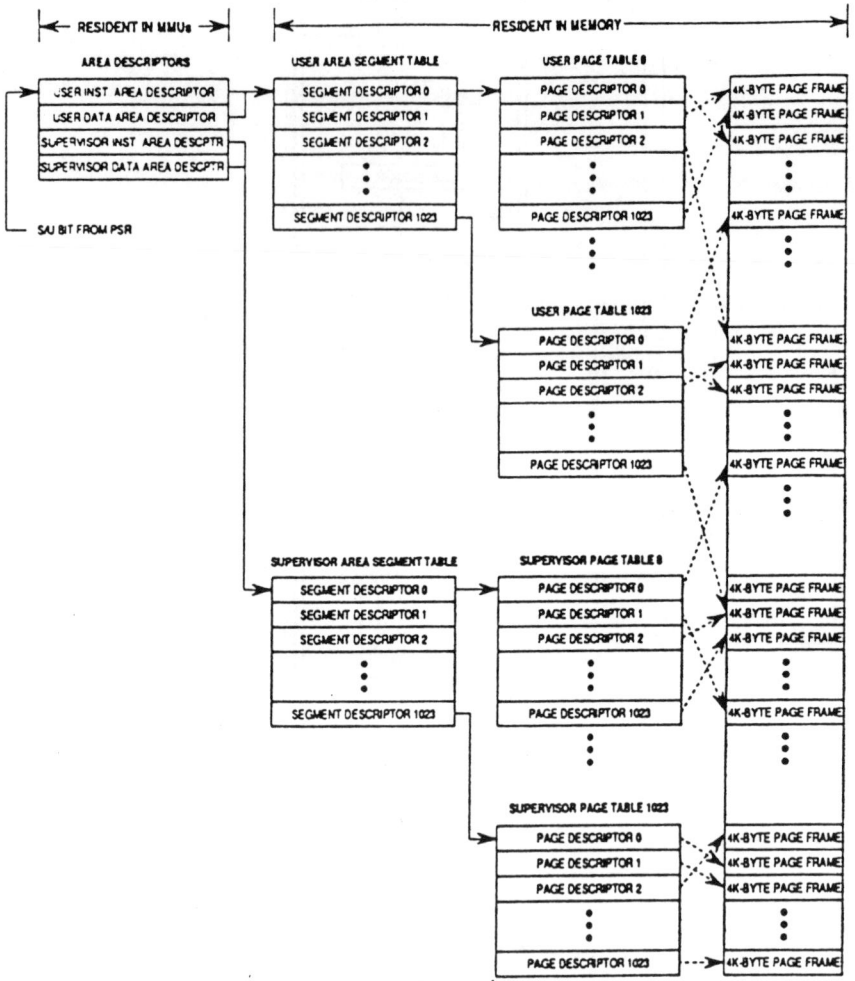

Fig. 11.7 Page translation table structure *(Courtesy of Motorola, Inc.)*

The M88000 architecture supports 512 exception vectors, stored in a *vector table*, pointed to by the *vector base register* (VBR), also known as control register 7 (cr7). The exception vector table implemented on the MC88110 is shown in Table 11.2. The lower 128 vectors (vectors 0 to 127) are reserved for hardware and supervisor use. They are not accessible from user trap instructions. The upper 384 vectors (numbers 128 to 511) are allocated for software traps. Each exception vector contains two instructions: typically, one instruction is a branch instruction to the exception handling routine, and the other is the first instruction of the corresponding

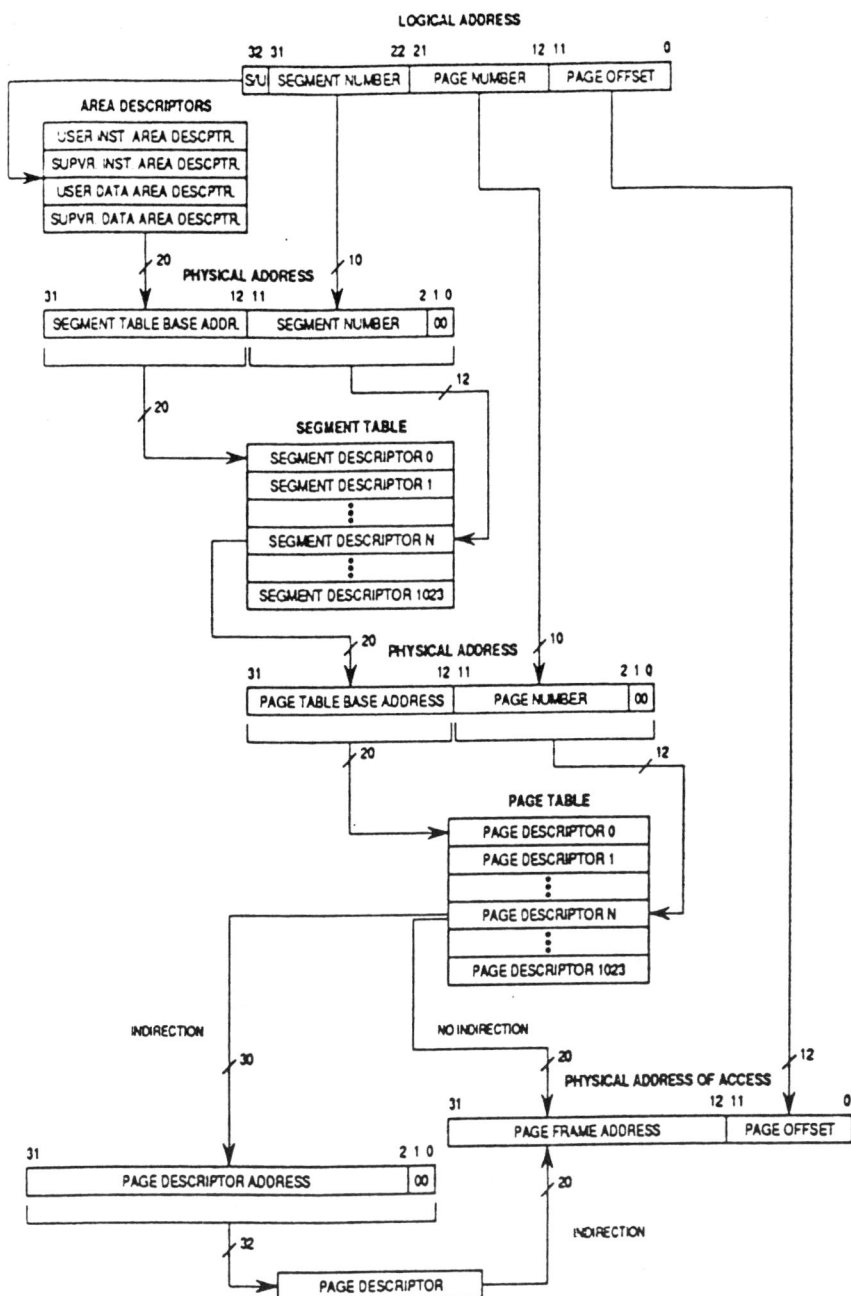

Fig. 11.8   Page table lookup *(Courtesy of Motorola, Inc.)*

31	30	29	28	27	26	25	24		10	9		3	2	1	0
MODE	BO	SER	C		SGN	SRM				SFU0			MXM	IND	EFRZ

☐ UNDEFINED-RESERVED FOR FUTURE USE

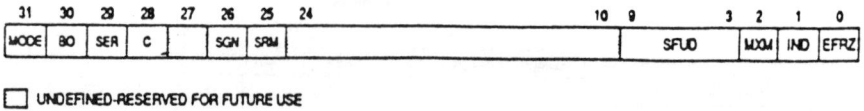

Fig. 11.9   Processor status register *(Courtesy of Motorola, Inc.)*

exception handling routine. The size of each exception vector is eight bytes (two instructions), and the size of the vector table is $512 * 8$ = 4KB. The exception-handling steps on the MC88110 are [M811 91]:

1. *Exception recognition* — the processor restores and forms the machine state associated with the faulting instruction.
2. *Exception processing* — the processor saves the execution context in exception-time registers, and changes program flow to the exception-handling routine.
3. *Exception handling* — the exception-handling software corrects the exception condition or performs the function initiated by the trap instruction.
4. *Return from exception* — the processor restores the execution context which was in effect before the exception occurred and resumes normal execution of program instructions.

The MC88110 has a *history buffer*, which records the relevant, user-visible machine state as instructions issue. The processor uses information stored in the history buffer to quickly restore the machine state back to the point of the exception. This is the same mechanism the MC88110 uses to recover from mispredicted branches [DiAl 92].

The pinout diagram of the MC88110 is shown in Fig. 11.10, and the signal summary is listed in Table 11.3. A great part of the MC88110 signals is implemented in PowerPC 601 (chapter 7).

11.4 The MC88100 and MC88200

The MC88100 is a 1.2 micron HCMOS, 180-pin CPU chip with an on-chip FPU. The MC88200 is a cache MMU (CMMU) chip with a 16KB cache, The MC88100 and the MC88200 interconnection is illustrated in Fig. 11.11. The minimum configuration is to connect two CMMU to one CPU chip (two separate buses); one CMMU acts as a data cache of 16KB, and the other as an instruction cache of 16KB, for a total of 32KB. However, up to four CMMUs can be connected on each side; 64KB data, 64KB instruction cache, for a total of 128KB of cache.

11.5 Concluding Comments

The M88000-family microprocessors have been implemented in numerous commercial systems. Of particular note is their implementation in multiprocessors

Table 11.2 Exception Vectors

Number	Vector Base Address Offset	Exception
0	$00	Reset
1	$08	Maskable Interrupt
2	$10	Instruction Access
3	$18	Data Access
4	$20	Misaligned Address
5	$28	Unimplemented Opcode
6	$30	Privilege Violation
7	$38	Bounds Check Violation
8	$40	Integer Divide-by-Zero
9	$48	Integer Overflow
10	$50	Unrecoverable Error
11	$58	Nonmaskable Interrupt
12	$60	Data MMU Read Miss
13	$68	Data MMU Write Miss
14	$70	Instruction MMU ATC Miss
15-113	—	Reserved
114	$390	SFU1—Floating-Point Exception
115	$398	Reserved
116	$3A0	SFU2—Graphics Exception
117	$3A8	Reserved
118	$3B0	SFU3—Unimplemented Opcode
119	$3B8	Reserved
120	$3C0	SFU4—Unimplemented Opcode
121	$3C8	Reserved
122	$3D0	SFU5—Unimplemented Opcode
123	$3D8	Reserved
124	$3E0	SFU6—Unimplemented Opcode
125	$3E8	Reserved
126	$3F0	SFU7—Unimplemented Opcode
127	$3F8	Reserved
128-511	—	Reserved--User Trap Vectors

(Courtesy of Motorola, Inc.)

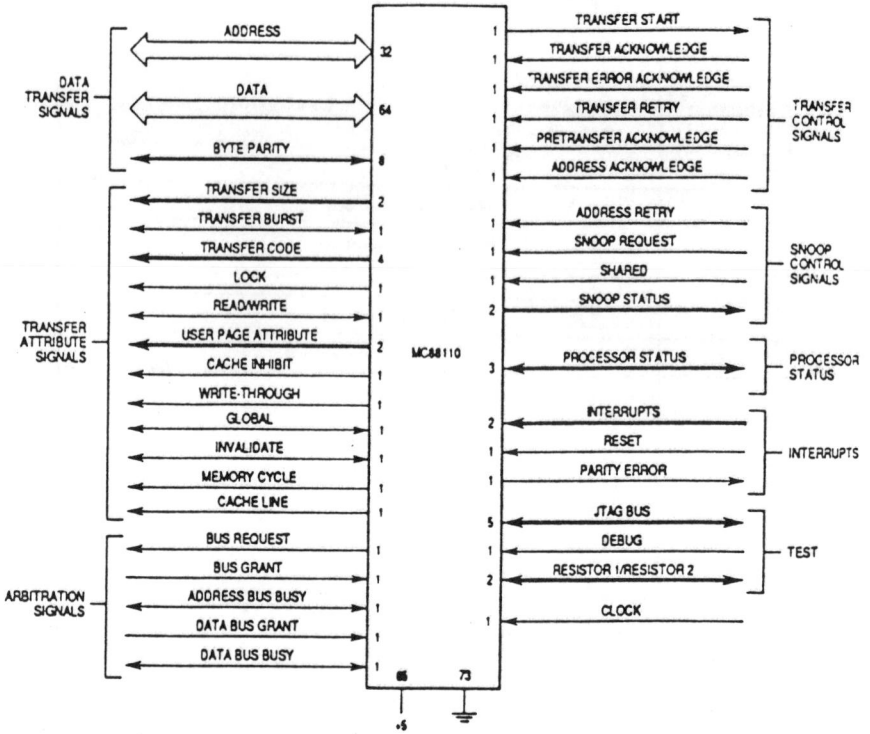

Fig. 11.10   MC88110 pinout *(Courtesy of Motorola, Inc.)*

such as the BBN Butterfly and the Encore [Tabk 90]. The MC88110 is an outstanding specimen of a two-issue superscalar system. It has 10 execution units, permitting very high flexibility in dispatching two instructions simultaneously for parallel execution. Barring data dependencies, such parallel execution should almost always be possible (almost, because two multiply instructions cannot be executed simultaneously, for instance). In any case, the MC88110 has fewer restrictions for parallel issue of two instructions than other systems. Should Motorola succeed in producing sample running above 100MHz, the MC88110 may outperform other RISC superscalar frontrunners.

Table 11.3 MC88110 Signal Summary

Function	Mnemonic	Count	Type	Active	Reset
Data Transfer					
Data Bus	D63–D0	64	I/O	High	Three-State
Address Bus	A31–A0	32	I/O	High	Three-State
Byte Parity	BP7–BP0	8	I/O	High	Three-State
Transfer Attributes					
Read/Write	R/W̄	1	I/O	High	Three-State
Lock	L̄K̄	1	Output	Low	Three-State
Cache Inhibit	C̄Ī	1	Output	Low	Three-State
Write-Through	W̄T̄	1	Output	Low	Three-State
User Page Attributes	ŪP̄Ā1̄–ŪP̄Ā0̄	2	Output	Low	Three-State
Transfer Burst	T̄B̄S̄T̄	1	I/O	Low	Three-State
Transfer Size	TSIZ1–TSIZ0	2	Output	High	Three-State
Transfer Code	TC3–TC0	4	Output	High	Three-State
Invalidate	ĪN̄V̄	1	I/O	Low	Three-State
Memory Cycle	M̄C̄	1	Output	Low	Three-State
Global	ḠB̄L̄	1	I/O	Low	Three-State
Cache Line	CLINE	1	Output	High	Three-State
Transfer Control					
Transfer Start	T̄S̄	1	Output	Low	Three-State
Transfer Acknowledge	T̄Ā	1	Input	Low	—
Pretransfer Ack	P̄T̄Ā	1	Input	Low	—
Transfer Error Ack	T̄Ē̄Ā	1	Input	Low	—
Transfer Retry	T̄R̄T̄R̄Ȳ	1	Input	Low	—
Address Acknowledge	ĀĀC̄K̄	1	Input	Low	—
Snoop Control					
Snoop Request	S̄R̄	2	Input	Low	—
Address Retry	ĀR̄T̄R̄Ȳ	1	Input	Low	—
Snoop Status	SSTAT1–SSTAT0	2	Output	Low	Three-State
Shared	S̄H̄D̄	1	Input	Low	—
Arbitration					
Bus Request	B̄R̄	1	Output	Low	Negated
Bus Grant	B̄Ḡ	1	Input	Low	—
Address Bus Busy	ĀB̄B̄	1	I/O	Low	Three-State
Data Bus Grant	D̄B̄Ḡ	1	Input	Low	—
Data Bus Busy	D̄B̄B̄	1	I/O	Low	Three-State

(Courtesy of Motorola, Inc.)

Table 11.3 MC88110 Signal Summary (continued)

Function	Mnemonic	Count	Type	Active	Reset
Processor Status					
Processor Status	PSTAT2– PSTAT0	3	Output	High	Input
Interrupt					
Nonmaskable Interrupt	N̄M̄Ī	1	Input	Low	Three-State
Interrupt	ĪN̄T̄	1	Input	Low	Three-State
Reset	R̄S̄T̄	1	Input	Low	Three-State
Byte Parity Error	B̄P̄Ē	1	Output	Low	Three-State
Clock					
Clock	CLK	1	Input	Rising Clock Edge	—
Test Pins					
Debug	D̄B̄Ū̄Ḡ	1	Input	Low	—
Resistor 1	RES1	1	Input	N/A	—
Resistor 2	RES2	1	Output	N/A	—
JTAG Test Reset	T̄R̄S̄T̄	1	Input	Low	—
JTAG Test Mode Select	TMS	1	Input	High	—
JTAG Test Clock	TCK	1	Input	Clock Edge	—
JTAG Test Data Input	TDI	1	Input	High	—
JTAG Test Data Output	TDO	1	Output	High	—

(Courtesy of Motorola, Inc.)

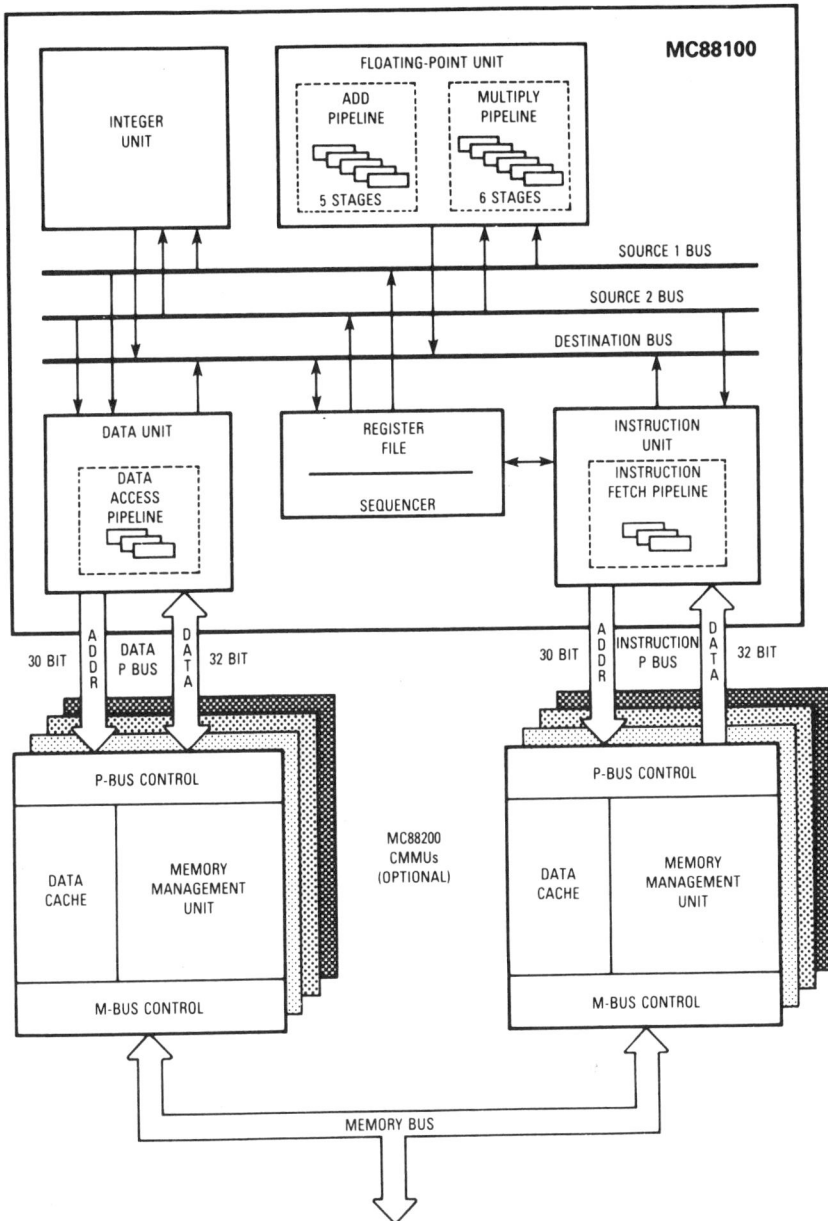

Fig. 11.11　MC88100/MC88200 block diagram *(Courtesy of Motorola, Inc.)*

CHAPTER 12

The Hewlett-Packard Precision Architecture (PA) Family

12.1 Introductory Comments

Hewlett-Packard (HP) was among the first industrial manufacturers to come out with a commercial RISC-type system in the mid-eighties [BiWo 86, Lee 89, Maho 86, PARI 90, Tabk 87, Tabk 94]. The architecture of this system was called *precision architecture* (PA) or *PA-RISC*. A number of microprocessors, implementing the PA, have been produced by HP in recent years. One of the latest implementations, the PA-7100 [Aspr 93, DWYF 92, Kneb 93], exceeded a number of notable RISC systems in its performance. The PA architecture will be presented in the next section, followed by a description of its microprocessor implementation.

12.2 The PA-RISC Architecture

When the HP team started to work on the PA-RISC, some of the design goals were to create a general-purpose architecture for use in commercial and technical applications [Lee 89]. The architecture was designed to be scalable across technologies, cost ranges and performance ranges, and provide price-performance advantages. The architecture was designed having in mind architectural longevity, allowing growth and extendibility, support of multiple operating environments, secure systems, and real-time environments. The PA-RISC is described in the next paragraphs of this section.

CPU registers

The PA-RISC features the following CPU registers [PARI 90]:

1. *General registers*, 32 32-bit, GR0 to GR31, shown in Fig. 12.1. Three of them have special functions:

GR0 is permanently wired to a zero value, as in most RISC systems.

GR1 is the target of the *add immediate left* (ADDIL) instruction.

GR31 is the instruction address offset link register for the base-relative interspace procedure call instruction *branch and link external* (BLE).

Registers GR1 and GR31 can also be used as general registers; however, software conventions may at times restrict their use. In the PA, bit count starts at the most significant bit (bit 0) and ends at the least significant bit (bit 31; big-endian bit ordering), as shown in Fig. 12.1 (same as in PowerPC and IBM architecture, see

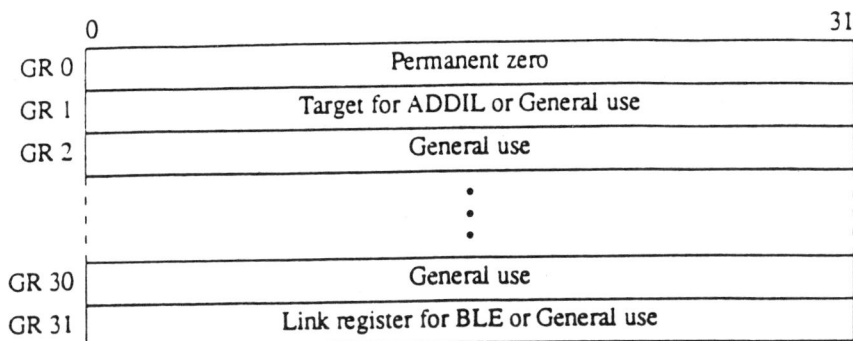

Fig. 12.1   General registers *(Courtesy of Hewlett-Packard, Inc.)*

chapter 7).

2. *Shadow registers*, seven 32-bit. Implementations may optionally choose to provide these registers into which the contents of GR1, GR8, GR9, GR16, GR17, GR24, and GR25 are copied upon interrupts (called in PA: '*interruptions*'). The content of these general registers is restored from their shadow registers upon a return from interrupt. Although shadow registers were initially declared to be optional by the PA-RISC architecture, every PA-RISC 1.1 processor implementation has provided them and they are now required by the architecture.

3. *Space registers*, eight registers SR0 to SR7, shown in Fig. 12.2, contain *space identifiers* for virtual addressing. Instructions specify SRs either directly in the instruction or indirectly through the most significant bits of the GR. Instruction addresses, computed by branch instructions, may use any of the SRs. SR0 is the instruction address space link register for the base-relative interspace procedure call instruction (BLE). Data operands can specify SR1 through SR3 explicitly, and SR4 through SR7 indirectly, via GRs. SR1 through SR7 have no special functions; however, their use will normally be constrained by software conventions. For instance, SR1 through SR3 provide general-use virtual pointers. SR4 tracks the instruction address (IA) space and provides access to literal data contained in the current code segment. SR5 points to a space containing process private data, SR6 to a space containing data shared by a group of processes, and SR7 to a space containing the OS public code, literals, and data. SR5 through SR7 can be modified only by code executing at the most privileged level. In different PA-RISC implementations, SRs may be nonexistent (level 0), 16 (level 1), 24 (level 1.5), or 32-bit wide (level 2). The software conventions shown in Fig. 12.2 are an example and do not necessarily correspond to any particular software implementation.

4. *Control registers*, 25 32-bit, CR0, CR8 through CR31, which contain system state information. Registers CR1 through CR7 are reserved for future use.

SR 0	Link code space ID
SR 1	General use
SR 2	General use
SR 3	General use
SR 4	Tracks IA space
SR 5	Process private data
SR 6	Shared data
SR 7	Operating system's public code, literals and data

Fig. 12.2   Space registers *(Courtesy of Hewlett-Packard, Inc.)*

5. *Floating-point registers,* 32 64-bit, which can also be used as 64 32-bit locations. Registers 0 through 3 contain the status (32-bit) and exception registers (seven 32-bit). Registers 4 through 31 are data registers. A 32-bit floating-point register is identified by appending a suffix in the instruction to the identifier of the 64-bit register within which it is contained. The suffix for the left-side 32-bit register is 'L'; the use of this suffix is optional. The suffix for the right-side 32-bit register is 'R'; its use is not optional.

Example: Left half of the 64-bit register 12 (bits 0 to 31) can be referred to as either 12 or 12L; the right half (bits 32 to 63) is referred to as 12R.

6. *Processor status word* (PSW), 32-bit, shown in Fig. 12.3.

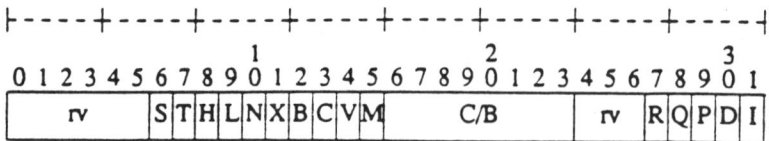

```
├ - - - - + - - - - + - - - - + - - - - + - - - - + - - - - + - - - - + - - - - ┤
                    1                   2                   3
  0 1 2 3 4 5 6 7 8 9 0 1 2 3 4 5 6 7 8 9 0 1 2 3 4 5 6 7 8 9 0 1
 ┌─────────┬─┬─┬─┬─┬─┬─┬─┬─┬─┬─────────────┬─────────┬─┬─┬─┬─┐
 │   rv    │S│T│H│L│N│X│B│C│V│M│    C/B    │   rv    │R│Q│P│D│I│
 └─────────┴─┴─┴─┴─┴─┴─┴─┴─┴─┴─────────────┴─────────┴─┴─┴─┴─┘
```

Fig. 12.3   Processor status word *(Courtesy of Hewlett-Packard, Inc.)*

The bit description of the PSW is as follows:

Bit 6 — secure interval timer (S). When S = 1, the interval timer is readable only by code executing at the most privileged level. When S = 0, it is readable at any privilege level.

Bit 7 — taken branch trap enable (T). When T = 1, any taken branch is terminated with a taken branch trap.

Bit 8 — higher-privilege transfer trap enable (H). When H = 1, a higher-privilege transfer trap occurs whenever the following instruction is of a higher privilege.

Bit 9 — lower-privilege transfer trap enable (L). When L = 1, a lower-privilege transfer trap occurs whenever the following instruction is of a lower privilege.

Bit 10 — nullify (N). When N = 1, the current instruction is nullified.

Bit 11 — data memory break disable (X). When X = 1, data memory break traps are disabled. X may be set by a return from interrupt instruction; it is set to 0 by other instructions.

Bit 12 — taken branch (B). B is set to 1 by any taken branch and set to 0 otherwise.

Bit 13 — code address translation enable (C). When C = 1, instruction addresses are translated and access rights checked.

Bit 14 — divide step correction (V). The integer division primitive instruction records immediate status in bit V to provide a non-restoring divide primitive.

Bit 15 — high-priority machine check mask (M). When M = 1, high-priority machine checks (HPMCs) are not allowed. Normally 0, M is set to 1 after an HPMC and cleared to 0 after all other interrupts.

Bits 16 to 23 — carry/borrow (C/B). Set on a carry by a set of arithmetic add instructions. Cleared on a borrow for subtract instructions.

Bit 27 — recovery counter enable (R). When R = 1, recovery counter traps occur if bit 0 of the recovery counter is a 1. This bit also enables decrementing of the recovery counter.

Bit 28 — interruption-state collection enable (Q). When Q = 1, interruption state is collected.

Bit 29 — protection identifier validation enable (P). When P = 1 and C = 1, instruction references check for valid protection identifiers (PIDs). When P = 1 and D = 1, data references check for valid PIDs. When P = 1, probe instructions check for valid PIDs.

Bit 30 — data address translation enable (D). When D = 1, data addresses are translated and access rights checked.

Bit 31 — external interrupt, power failure interrupt, and low-priority machine check interrupt unmask (I). When I = 1, these interrupts are unmasked and can cause an interruption. When I = 0, the interruptions are held pending.

Data types

Integer signed and unsigned:

Byte	8-bit
Halfword	16-bit
Word	32-bit

Integer unsigned:

Doubleword   64-bit

Floating-point:

IEEE 754-1985 Standard:
Single-precision   32-bit
Double-precision 64-bit
Quadruple-word (or: extended double) 128-bit (sign bit, 15-bit exponent, 112-bit mantissa). The IEEE Standard does not fully specify a quadruple precision format, but rather a range to which PA-RISC complies.

Packed decimal:

Consists of 7, 15, 23, or 31 BCD four-bit digits, aligned on a word boundary, and having a value of 0 to 9, followed by a four-bit sign. The standard sign for a positive number is X'C (X' denotes hexadecimal), but any value except X'D will be interpreted as positive. A minus sign is denoted by X'D. X'B is not supported as an alternative minus sign [PARI 90].

The alignment of the data operands in memory is illustrated in Fig. 12.4. As we can see, a big-endian byte ordering is used. In the latest version of PA-RISC architecture, both big- and little-endian byte ordering is supported. Bit 5 (E-bit) of PSW is cleared to 0 for big-endian, and set to 1 for little-endian, byte ordering.

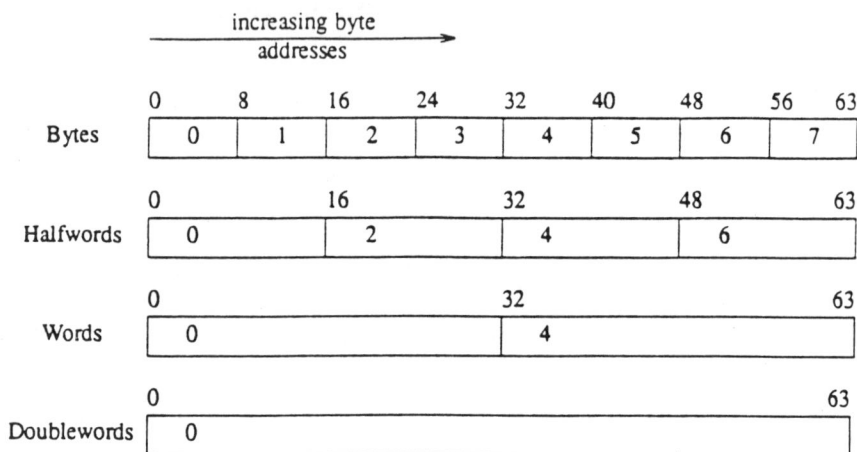

Fig. 12.4 Physical memory addressing and storage units *(Courtesy of Hewlett-Packard, Inc.)*

Addressing modes
The PA features the following addressing modes [PARI 90]:

Register.
Immediate.
Base with offset (displacement).
Base with scaled (shifted) index with offset.
Pre-decrement. If the displacement d is negative, its sign-extended value is added to the base register GRb and the result (the effective offset) is stored in GRb.
Post-increment. If d is positive, the effective offset is the original value in GRb. The sum of the content of GRb and the sign-extended value of d is stored in GRb.
PC-relative (IA-relative). In PA, what is usually called PC is called IA (instruction address).

Instruction formats

The PA-RISC instruction formats are shown in Fig. 12.5 [Lee 89], along with the abbreviations interpretation. One can easily recognize the three register fields for ALU instructions; with one register field interchangeable with an immediate operand field. In the load or store instruction formats, one register field serves for a destination (load) or a source (store), one register field for the base register, and one for a possible index register (interchangeable for use as an offset). For branch instructions, there are fields for a base register and for an offset.

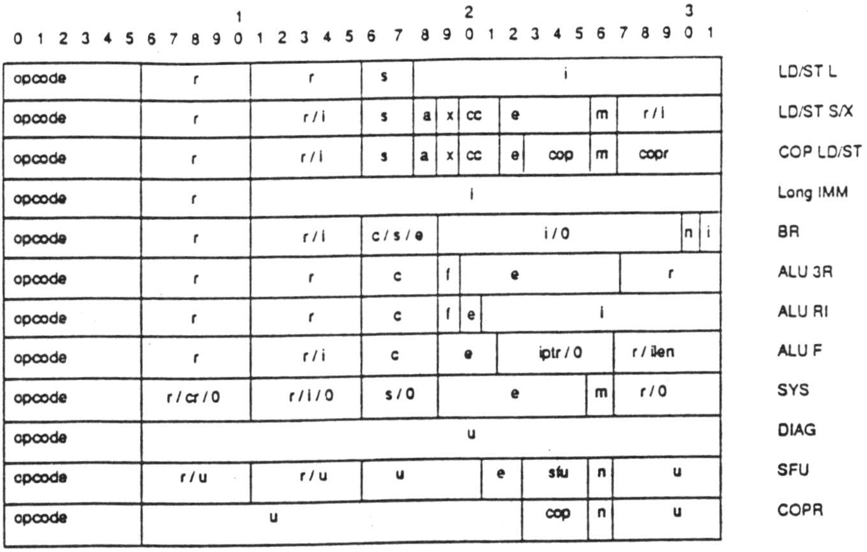

		1			2				3				
0 1 2 3 4 5 6 7 8 9	0 1 2 3 4 5 6 7	8 9	0 1 2 3 4 5 6 7 8 9	0 1									

opcode	r	r	s	i							LD/ST L
opcode	r	r / i	s	a	x	cc	e		m	r / i	LD/ST S/X
opcode	r	r / i	s	a	x	cc	e	cop	m	copr	COP LD/ST
opcode	r	i									Long IMM
opcode	r	r / i	c / s / e	i / 0					n	i	BR
opcode	r	r	c	f	e					r	ALU 3R
opcode	r	r	c	f	e	i					ALU RI
opcode	r	r / i	c	e	iptr / 0				r / ilen		ALU F
opcode	r / cr / 0	r / i / 0	s / 0	e				m	r / 0		SYS
opcode	u										DIAG
opcode	r / u	r / u	u		e	sfu	n	u			SFU
opcode	u				cop	n	u				COPR

Abbreviations for field names

r :   general register specifier

s :   space register specifier

i :   immediate (or displacement or offset)

a :   premodify versus postmodify, or index shifted by data size

x :   indexed (x = 0) versus short displacement (x = 1)

cc :   cache hints

e :   subop (opcode extension)

m :   modification specifier

n :   nullification specifier

c :   condition specifier

f :   falsify condition c

iptr: immediate pointer

ilen: immediate length

cr: control register

0 :   not used (set to zero)

u :   undefined (can be defined as instruction extension)

sfu :   special function unit identifier

cop :   coprocessor unit identifier

copr: coprocessor register

Fig. 12.5   Instruction formats *(Courtesy of Hewlett-Packard, Inc. and IEEE)*

Instruction set

A summary of the PA-RISC instruction set, subdivided into different categories, is listed in Table 12.1 [Lee 89]. The instructions are listed by their explicit names, without their mnemonics.

Table 12.1 Instruction Set

Memory Reference Instructions		Functional Instructions	
Load	{Word/Halfword/Byte} {Long/Indexed/Short} [Modified]	(a) Arithmetic	
Store	{Word/Halfword/Byte} {Long/Short} [Modified]	Add {Reg/Immed} [with carry] [and Trap on {overflow/cond/overflow or cond}]	
Load	Word Absolute {Indexed/Short}	Sub {Reg/Immed} [with borrow] [and Trap on {borrow/cond/borrow or cond}]	
Store	Word Absolute Short	Shift {One/Two/Three} And Add [and Trap on Overflow]	
Load	Offset	Divide Step	
Load	And Clear Word {Indexed/Short}	(b) Logical	
Store	Bytes Short	Or {Inclusive/Exclusive}	
		And {True/Complement}	
Branch Instructions		Compare {Reg/Immed} And Clear	
		Add Logical	
(a) Unconditional		Shift {One/Two/Three} And Add Logical	
		(c) Unit and Decimal	
Branch And Link {Displacement/Reg}		Unit Xor	
Branch Vectored		Unit Add Complement [and Trap on Condition]	
Branch External [and Link]		Decimal Correct	
Gateway		Intermediate Decimal Correct	
(b) Conditional		(d) Bit Manipulation	
Add {Reg/Immed} And Branch if {True/False}		Extract {Variable Pos/Constant Pos} {Signed/Unsigned}	
Compare {Reg/Immed} And Branch if {True/False}		Deposit {Variable Pos/Constant Pos} {Reg/Immed}	
Move {Reg/Immed} And Branch if {True/False}		Zero and Deposit {Variable Pos/Constant Pos} {Reg/Immed}	
Branch On Bit {Variable/Constant}		Shift Double {Variable Pos/Constant Pos}	
System Instructions		(e) Long Immediate	
		Add Immediate Left	
(a) System Control		Load Immediate Left	
System Mask {Set/Reset/Move to}		Assist Instructions	
Move {to/from} Control Register		(a) Special Function Unit Interface	
Move {to/from} Space Register		Spop {Zero/One/Two/Three}	
Load Space ID		(b) Coprocessor Interface	
Break			
Return From Interrupt		Copr Load {Word/Doubleword} {Indexed/Short}	
Diagnose		Copr Store {Word/Doubleword} {Indexed/Short}	
(b) Memory Management		Copr Operation	
Insert TLB {Instruction/Data} {Address/Protection}			
Purge TLB {Instruction/Data} [Entry]		**Key**	
Probe Access {Read/Write} {Reg/Immed}		Reg = register	
Load Physical Address		Immed = immediate	
Load Hash Address		Pos = position	
(c) Cache Management		cond = condition	
Flush {Instruction/Data} Cache [Entry]			
Purge Data Cache			
Sync			

*Curly brackets indicate that one alternative within the curly brackets is selected for a given instruction, while square brackets indicate an optional feature that can be specified in the instruction.

(Courtesy of Hewlett-Packard, Inc. and IEEE)

Addressing space

The PA-RISC architects felt that the longevity of an architecture lies in the range of its addressing capabilities rather than in the size of its words [Lee 89]. While processing 64-bit integers rather than 32-bit integers might increase accuracy, they did not consider the trade-off in the hardware required for 64-bit datapaths throughout the processor to be cost-effective for general-purpose computers. This was a sound decision conforming with the state of the art of the mid-eighties when PA was developed. As can be seen in earlier chapters, the designers of the early nineties Alpha AXP (chapter 6) and of the R4000 (chapter 9) did not think that way and have adopted a 64-bit integer datapath. The PA designers noted that computer usage has clearly tended towards the processing of larger programs and more data. For this reason they decided to provide up to a 64-bit virtual address range [Lee 89]. Eventually, PA-RISC will have a full 64-bit architecture extension. It should be noted that HP has been the first to ship full 64-bit virtual address space implementations.

The PA-RISC memory is byte-addressable. The PA-RISC distinguishes between an *absolute address* and a *virtual address*. When absolute addresses are used directly, no protection or access rights checks are performed. Virtual addresses are translated to absolute addresses and undergo protection and access rights checking. Memory accesses using absolute addresses are called *absolute accesses*, and those using virtual addresses are called *virtual accesses*. PA defines four levels of processor architecture in conjunction with memory access: levels 0, 1, 1.5, and 2. Level 0 systems support only absolute addressing and have no SRs. Level 1, 1.5, and 2 systems provide virtual addressing through the use of 16-, 24-, and 32-bit SRs, respectively [PARI 90].

Virtual memory is structured as a set of *virtual spaces*, each containing 4GB (2^{32} bytes). Level 1 processors have 2^{16}, level 1.5 processors have 2^{24}, and level 2 processors have 2^{32} address spaces.

During virtual address translation, a space is selected by a *space identifier* (space ID) contained in the 32-bit upper portion of the 64-bit virtual address. The byte *offset* within the space is specified by the lower 32 bits of the virtual address. The memory address space is also subdivided into 4KB pages, as it is in most other systems. Fig. 12.6 illustrates the structure of spaces, pages, and offsets. Support is provided for the emulation of larger page sizes (32KB). Eight contiguous pages, with the first of these pages beginning on a 32KB boundary, are referred to as a *page group* [PARI 90].

Registers SR0 through SR7 are used to compute instruction addresses for instruction cache flush, for TLB instructions, and for some branch target calculations. Addresses for instruction fetch and some branch target calculations are generated from the *instruction address* (IA) *queues*. When an instruction address is computed for an external branch target, the three-bit s-field in the instruction selects the SR to be used (see Fig. 12.5 for the BR instruction). Instruction addresses are aligned on word (four byte) boundaries and the least significant two bits of the offset are used to hold the *privilege level* (since these two bits are zero in the instruction address offset). The privilege level controls both instruction and data references.

288

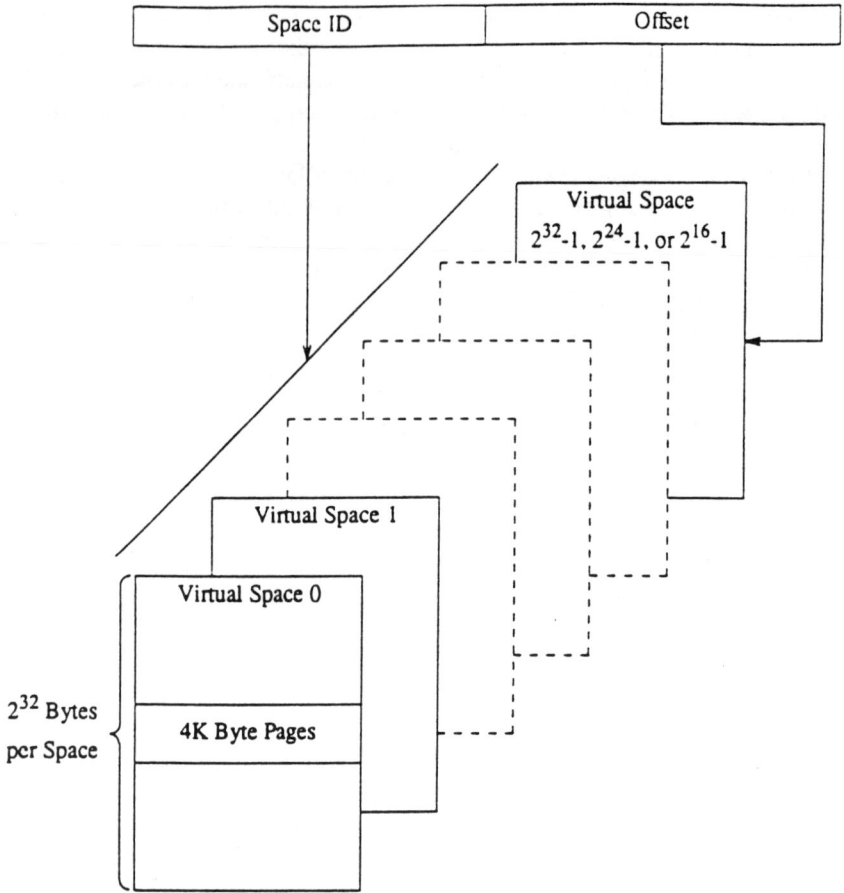

Fig. 12.6 Structure of spaces, pages and offsets *(Courtesy of Hewlett-Packard, Inc.)*

The current IA consists of a space ID and a 32-bit offset (Fig. 12.6). The current IA is maintained in the front elements of the IA space and offset queues. The 32-bit offset is computed by one of the addressing modes, which may use a base register, a scaled index register and a sign-extended displacement.

The space ID for data references is selected from SR1 through SR7 by the following procedure. The two-bit s-field of the instruction, when nonzero, selects corresponding SRs 1, 2, or 3. When the s-field is zero, the two most significant bits (bits 0 and 1) of the base register are used to select one of the SRs (SR4 through SR7). Adding four to these two bits generates the selected SR. Fig. 12.7 illustrates the space ID selection. Data references with the s-field zero permit addressing of four distinct spaces selected by program data. This is called *short pointer addressing* since a 32-bit value is an offset and selects an SR. Only a fourth of the space is directly addressable by the base register with short pointers, and the region corresponds to the quadrant selected by the upper two bits. For example, if a base register contains the value X'4000 1000 and the s-field is zero, SR5 is used (01 + 100; or 1 + 4) as the space ID and the second quadrant of the space is directly addressable.

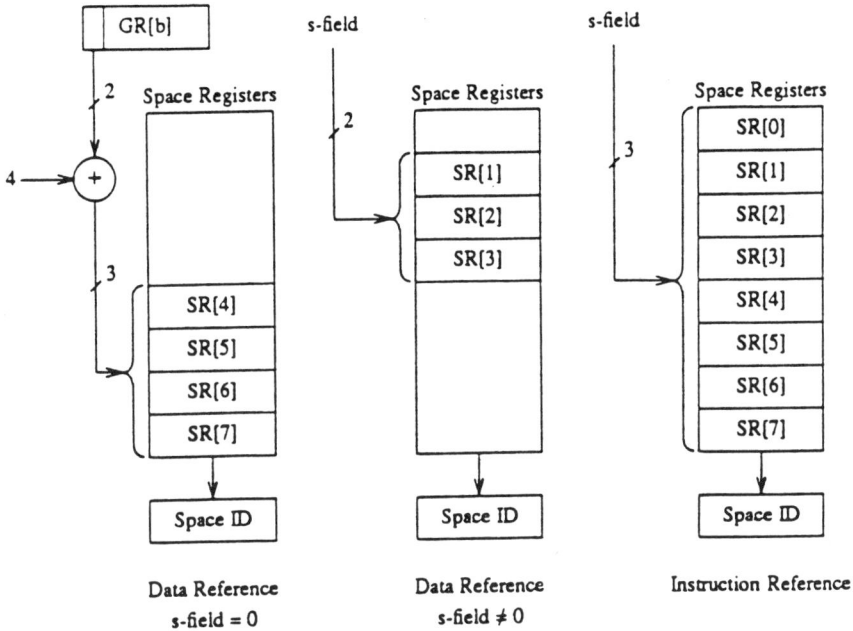

Fig. 12.7   Space identifier selection *(Courtesy of Hewlett-Packard, Inc.)*

12.3 PA-RISC Implementations
PA-7100

The first superscalar PA-RISC implementation is the PA-7100. It is a 0.8 micron CMOS, 850 000-transistors, 504-pin grid array (PGA) microprocessor. It can run at a frequency of up to 100MHz [Aspr 93, DWYF 92]. The PA-7100 is a two-issue superscalar; however, there is a restriction that only an integer and a floating-point instruction can be issued together for execution. It has a 64-bit data bus in and out of the chip. The PA-7100 has an on-chip FPU, but its cache is outside, unlike other recent RISC-type microprocessors, described earlier in chapters 6 through 11. One of the advantages of the PA-7100 outside cache is that it can be a very large one, of several megabytes, as opposed to current on-chip caches of a maximum total of 32 to 64KB. Certainly, a much higher hit ratio can be achieved with a larger cache.

   The PA-7100 has three bus outlets: one to the *system interface* (main memory, I/O, graphics), one to the *data cache* (D-cache), and one to the *instruction cache* (I-cache). The external D-cache can be configured from 4KB to 2MB. The I-cache can be configured from 4KB to 1MB. Both caches are *virtually addressed*, direct-mapped, with 32 bytes/line. Having no on-chip cache is certainly a disadvantage because of a possible longer access delay. This disadvantage is made up for by the fact that the size of the cache can reach a total of 3MB, tending to increase significantly the hit ratio. On the other hand, the cost of a 3MB primary cache may be quite high. The PA-7100 designers made a special effort to tune the processor operation to a relatively lower-cost SRAM cache [Aspr 93, DWYF 92]. The caches are wave-pipelined, and hence the ALU needs only to complete the 22 lower address bits before the cache SRAM has the full address. Cache SRAMs that can use a partial address for row address specification before column address specification improve the access time. Having a virtually addressed cache may pose another disadvantage because of address aliasing problems. On the other hand, such a cache does not need translation to a physical address, covering the tag field, which in turn speeds up the cache access.

The PA-7100 has a fully associative TLB with 120 fixed entries for 4KB pages. In addition, there are 16 variable size entries for spaces ranging from 512KB to 64MB. Thus, a large page option is implemented in effect, as in other systems.

The PA-7100 FPU fully complies with the IEEE 754-1985 Standard [IEEE 85]. It is composed of the following subunits [Aspr 93]:

1. *Floating-point register file*, as described in the previous section.
2. *Floating-point ALU*, which performs floating-point add, subtract, compare, complement, and convert instructions for both single- and double-precision operands.
3. *Floating-point multiplier*, performing multiplications of single- and double-precision floating-point operands. In addition, integer multiplications of 32-bit unsigned integers provide a 64-bit product. The *carry save* method [Hays 88] is used in the multiplication implementation.
4. *Floating-point divider*, performing division and square-root operations. The unit uses a modified radix-4 SRT (Sweeney-Robertson-Tocher) algorithm [Cava 84, Hwan 79, Robe 58].

PA-RISC has a five-operand floating-point instruction that performs:

$$C \leftarrow A * B$$

$$D \leftarrow D + E, \text{ in one cycle.}$$

This allows PA-RISC to execute the frequent multiply-add operation at a vector rate of one per clock cycle.

An alternate implementation is the PA-7100LC [Kneb 93]. The PA-7100LC is a 0.8 micron CMOS, 800 000-transistors, 432-pin ceramic PGA microprocessor. It can operate at frequencies of up to 75MHz. The PA-7100LC implements a 48-bit virtual address. One of the most significant improvements on the PA-7100LC is the addition of a second integer ALU, permitting simultaneous execution of two integer instructions, and thus improving the superscalar quality of operation of the PA-7100LC. In order to reduce the interfacing cost of the processor, an interface to a unified (as opposed to dual) external (off-chip) cache is provided. The external primary unified cache can be configured from 8KB to 2MB. As in the PA-7100, it is direct-mapped. The purpose of producing the PA-7100LC was to provide a lower-cost PA implementation processor without giving up on performance.

PA-7200

The PA-7200 is an enhanced version of the PA-7100 implementation [Kurp 94]. The PA-7200 is a 0.55 micron, three-level metal, 120MHz, 1.3 million-transistors, 540-pin ceramic PGA microprocessor. Its 64-bit bus is capable of supporting multiple processors and multiple outstanding read operations per processor. Some of the major enhancements realized on the PA-7200, compared to the PA-7100, are listed in the following paragraphs.

The technology was refined with a 0.55 micron CMOS, compared to 0.8 micron on the PA-7100. The operating frequency was raised from 100 to 120MHz. The number of transistors is 1.3 million on the PA-7200, as compared to 850 000 on the PA-7100. Both are two-issue superscalar. However, while the PA-7100 has only one integer ALU, a second integer ALU was added on the PA-7200. Whenever two integer arithmetic or logic instructions are issued together on the PA-7200, they can now be executed together, barring any data dependencies.

While the large primary dual cache is still external to the CPU chip as on the PA-7100, an additional on-chip *assist cache* was added on the PA-7200. The assist cache contains 64 fully associative 32-byte cache lines, for a total of 2KB. A content-addressable memory (CAM) is used to match a translated real line address with each entry's tag. For each cache access, 65 entries are checked for a valid match: 64 assist cache entries, and one off-chipcache entry. If there is a hit in either cache, the data are returned directly to the appropriate functional unit [Kurp 94]. In addition, the cache interface was enhanced to support single-cycle store operations.

A new processor-memory-I/O interconnect bus, called *Runway*, was introduced on the PA-7200. Runway is a synchronous 64-bit time-multiplexed address/data bus. The Runway protocol has been defined so that no logic needs to be performed in the same cycle as data transmission, which allows high-frequency implementations. The PA-7200 has been designed with a worst-case bus frequency of 120MHz in a four-way multiprocessor system, enabling sustained memory bandwidths of up to 768 MB/sec. Runway features include multiple outstanding split transactions from each bus module, predictive flow control, an efficient arbitration scheme, and a snoopy coherency protocol which allows flexible coherency check response time [Kurp 94].

PA-8000

The PA-8000 is the first 64-bit implementation of the HP PA-RISC architecture [Hunt 95]. It implements the new 64-bit PA2.0 architecture version of PA-RISC. It is a 3.8 million transistors, 0.5 micron, five layer, 180MHz microprocessor. The PA-8000 is a four-issue superscalar, and it contains five pairs (a total of ten) of the following execution units:

Integer ALU

Shift/Merge

Floating-point multiply/accumulate

Floating-point divide/square root

Load/Store

These functional units are arranged to allow up to four instructions per cycle to begin execution. To supply these functional units with enough operands to keep them busy, the PA-8000 incorporates a 56-entry *instruction reorder buffer* (IRB) and a dual-ported data cache. A block diagram of the PA-8000 is shown in Fig. 12.8 [Hunt 95].

The PA-8000 implements speculative execution (see chapter 1) in a number of ways. There is a branch prediction mechanism, predicting whether an unconditional branch will be taken or not taken. Subsequently, the outcome is corrected when the branch is resolved. Another way of PA-8000's speculative execution is executing new instructions before it is known whether an older instruction will signal an exception or trap. The result of the new instruction is eventually discarded if there is an exception or trap. Another case of speculative execution may be performing a new load before an older store instruction. If it happens to be at the same storage location, the situation is corrected and the premature incorrect load is eliminated. The PA-8000 has a 32-entry fully associated branch target address cache (BTAC), which associates the address by which a branch is fetched with the address of the target of the branch for branches which are predicted taken. On every instruction fetch, the address sent to the instruction cache is also sent to the BTAC. Whenever the BTAC signals a hit, the address supplied by the BTAC is used as the next fetch address. This means that correctly predicted taken branches which hit the BTAC suffer no penalty, since the quadword containing the branch target will arrive on chip the cycle after the branch itself arrives. A new entry is inserted into the BTAC each time a predicted-taken branch is fetched for which there is not already an entry in the BTAC. This insert does not cause any additional fetch penalty [Hunt 95].

The PA-8000 has a 256-entry branch history table (BHT; see chapter 1). The BHT is consulted to determine which way each branch should be predicted. Each entry in the BHT is a three-bit shift register which records the last three outcomes (taken or not taken) of a given branch. If a majority of the last three executions were actually taken, the fetch unit predicts that the branch will be taken again. The BHT is only updated as branch instructions are retired in order to prevent corrupting the history information with speculative executions of the branch [Hunt 95].

The PA-8000 has a fully dual-ported, 96-entry TLB. Each entry in the TLB may map any power-of-four-sized segment (page) of memory from 4KB to 16MB. The PA-8000 interfaces directly to the Runway bus, the same bus used by the PA-

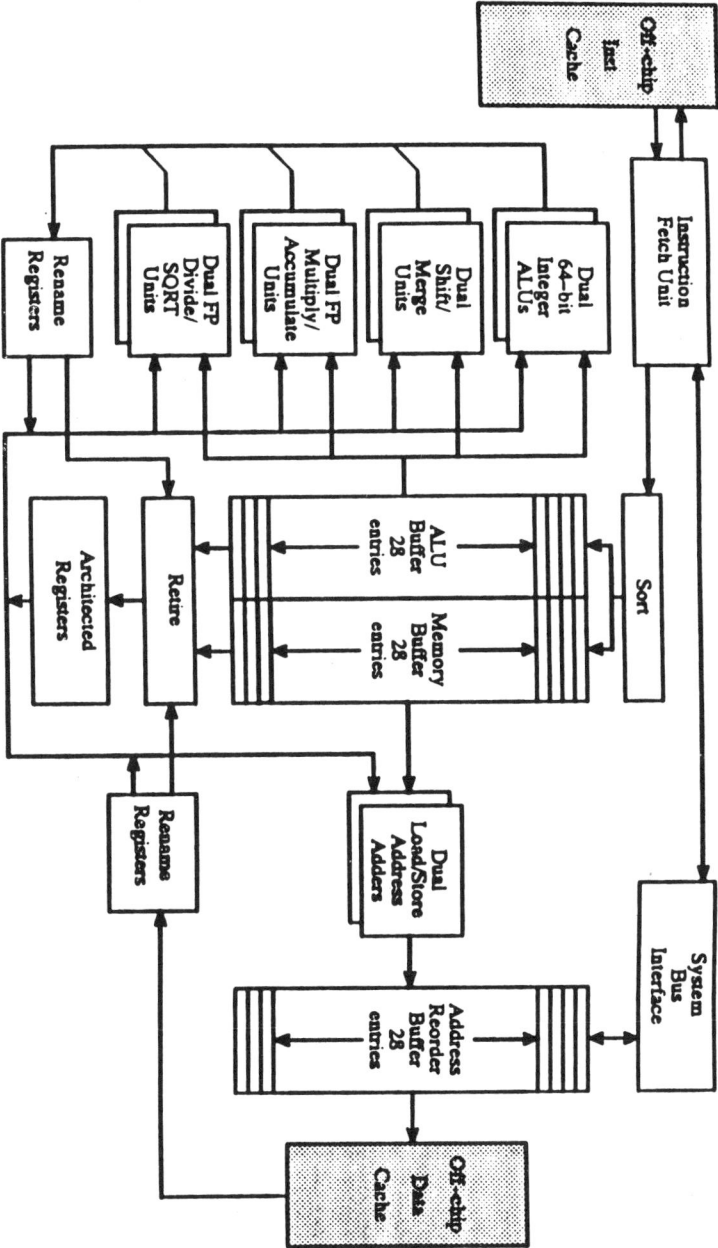

Fig. 12.8   PA-8000 block diagram (Courtesy of Hewlett-Packard, Inc. and IEEE)

7200 [Kurp 94]. The bus supports the full 40-bit physical address space of the PA-8000, allowing access to as much as 960GB of RAM. Arbitration takes place on separate wires; so it does not consume any bus cycles [Hunt 95].

12.4 Concluding Comments

A number implementation versions of PA microprocessors have been produced by HP. These microprocessors were and still are extensively used in many workstations and other computing systems. A Precision RISC organization (PRO) was established. The designers of HP are working on new and further improved versions of PA-RISC implementation microprocessors. Despite the fact that PA implementations do not yet have an on-chip cache, as many others do, their performance exceeds that of other notable RISC-type microprocessors. One of the PA implementation advantages that goes for it is their relatively high frequency of operation (over 100MHz for superscalar implementations). This advantage will be further extended in the forthcoming PA-RISC implementations.

CHAPTER 13

The INMOS Transputer

13.1 Introductory Comments

The transputer is produced by INMOS, a member of SGS-Thomson Microelectronics Group (US Headquarters in Phoenix, AZ). The first transputer microprocessor was launched in 1985 [Poun 91, Tabk 87], and a number of transputer implementations have been announced since then. The transputer is a RISC-type microprocessor, particularly suited for multiprocessor and multicomputer applications. This is mainly because of its on-chip four-way communication links. One of its particular and exclusive properties is that it includes part of the main memory on-chip. This makes it particularly suitable for compact embedded microcontroller applications. Another property that differentiates the transputer from other RISC-type systems is its very small CPU register file (six registers). It was designed from the beginning to be programmed by a special HLL called OCCAM [Occ2 88]. OCCAM belongs to the family of message-oriented HLLs [Tabk 90].

The architecture of the transputer will be described in the next section, and its implementations in the following one.

13.2 Transputer Architecture

Register file

The transputer architecture features a relatively small CPU register file of only six registers, illustrated in Fig 13.1 [T900 91]:

1. The *workspace pointer*, which points to an area of storage where local variables are kept.
2. The *instruction pointer*, which points to the next instruction to be executed (same as the PC in other systems).
3. The *operand register*, which is used in the formation of instruction operands.
4., 5., 6. The *Areg*, *Breg*, and *Creg* registers, which form an *evaluation stack*.

The transputer architecture is unique in the sense that it practices CPU stack operations [HePa 90]. Registers Areg, Breg, and Creg are sources and destinations for most arithmetic and logical operations. Loading a value into the evaluation stack pushes (Breg) into Creg, and (Areg) into Breg, before loading Areg. Storing a value from Areg into memory pops (Breg) into Areg and (Creg) into Breg. The

Registers	Locals	Program
Areg		
Breg		
Creg		
Workspace		
Next Instruction		
Operand		

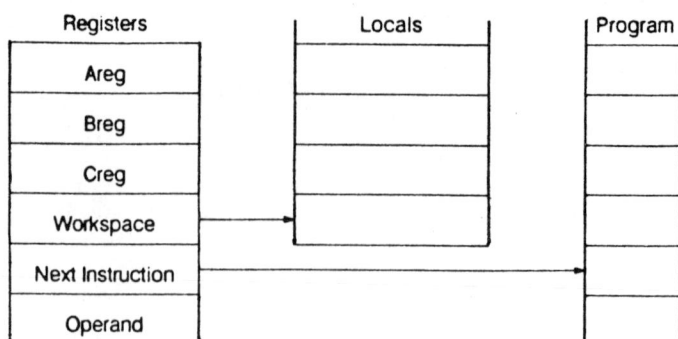

Fig. 13.1   Registers used in sequential integer processes *(Courtesy of INMOS)*

value left in Creg is undefined. The Areg serves as the top of the evaluation stack. Expressions are evaluated on the evaluation stack, and instructions refer to the stack implicitly. For example, the add instruction adds the top two values in the stack and places the result on the top of the stack. The main advantage of stack-oriented CPU architecture is that it saves space in the specification of instruction operands, since the stack operands are implicit [HePa 90]. The disadvantage is that there is much less flexibility of operand specification in stack-oriented architectures, compared to register-oriented architectures (such as in other systems described in chapters 6 to 12).

A separate floating-point evaluation stack is provided [T900 91], consisting of *FPAreg*, *FPBreg*, and *FPCreg*. The floating-point evaluation stack behaves in a similar way to the integer evaluation stack.

Any location in memory can be accessed relative to the workspace pointer, enabling the workspace to be of any size. The first 32 words (word = four bytes = 32 bits) relative to the workspace pointer may be placed in the on-chip *workspace cache*.

Instruction set

The transputer instruction set has been designed for simple and efficient compilation of HLLs [Tran 88]. All instructions have the same format, designed to give a compact representation of the operations occurring most frequently in programs. Each instruction consists of a single byte divided into two four-bit parts. The four most significant bits of the byte are a function code and the four least significant bits are a data value. The instruction format is illustrated in Fig. 13.2. This instruction format provides for sixteen functions, each with a data value ranging from 0 to 15 (0000 to 1111 binary). Thirteen of these values are used to encode the most important functions:

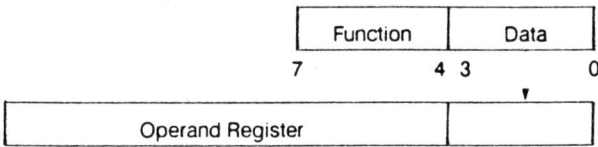

Function	Data
7   4 3   0

| Operand Register | |

Fig. 13.2   Instruction format *(Courtesy of INMOS)*

load constant
add constant
equals constant
load local
store local
load local pointer
load non-local
store non-local
load non-local pointer
jump
conditional jump
call
adjust workspace

Some of the most common operations in a program are the loading of small literal values and the loading and storing of a small number of variables. The load-constant instruction enables values between 0 and 15 to be loaded with a single byte instruction. The load-local and store-local instructions access locations in memory relative to the workspace pointer. The first 16 locations can be accessed using a single byte instruction. The load non-local and store non-local instructions behave similarly, except that they access locations in memory relative to the Areg register. Compact sequences of these instructions allow efficient access to data structures, and provide for simple implementations of HLLs such as OCCAM, Pascal or Ada.

Two more function codes, *prefix* and *negative prefix*, allow the operand of any instruction to be extended in length. All instructions are executed by loading the four data bits (see Fig. 13.2) into the least significant four bits of the operand register, which is then used as the instruction's operand. All instructions, except the prefix instructions, end by clearing the operand register to be ready for the next instruction. The prefix instruction loads its four data bits into the operand register and then shifts the operand register left four bits. The negative prefix instruction is similar, except that it complements the operand register before shifting it left. Consequently, operands can be extended to any length up to the length of the operand register by a sequence of prefix instructions. In particular, operands in the range of −256 to 255 can be represented using one prefix instruction.

The remaining function code, *operate*, causes its operand to be interpreted as an operation on the values stored in the evaluation stack. This allows up to 16 such operations to be encoded in a single byte instruction. However, the prefix instructions can be used to extend the operand of an operate instruction just like any other. The instruction representation therefore provides for an indefinite number of operations. Encoding of the indirect functions is chosen so that the most frequently occurring operations are represented without the use of a prefix instruction. These include arithmetic, logical, and comparison operations such as add, exclusive or, and greater than. Less frequently occurring operations have encodings that require a single prefix operation. Transputer implementation will be presented in the next section.

13.3 Transputer Implementation
The current top-level transputer implementation is the **IMS T9000**, or simply the T9000. The T9000 is a 32-bit, CMOS, 2 million-transistors microprocessor, running at 50MHz. Its block diagram is shown in Fig. 13.3 [T900 91].

The T9000 is a superscalar with a unified 16 Kbyte on-chip cache. The cache can also be configured as a 16 Kbyte main memory, or 8 Kbyte main memory and 8 Kbyte cache. The configuration with on-chip main memory permits the application of the T9000 as a compact embedded controller. For some applications, 16 Kbytes of memory may be enough and there is no need to use external memory chips. The T9000 has an on-chip FPU, incorporating hardware to perform divide and square-root operations. A separate workspace cache stores 32 words relative to the workspace pointer to provide zero delay access to local variables. The T9000 has four communication links for interprocessor interconnections.

Communication between processes takes place over channels, implemented in hardware. The same machine instructions are used for communication between processes on the same processor as for communication between processes on different T9000 processors. Communication between processes on different processors takes place over *virtual* channels. Virtual channels are multiplexed onto each physical link by the *virtual channel processor* (VCP). Communication between T9000 processors that are not directly connected is achieved by using a separate dynamic routing switch, the IMS C104.

The T9000 has four high-bandwidth serial communication links. To support virtual channels and dynamic message switching, and to provide a higher data bandwidth with high data integrity, each physical link consists of four wires (see Fig. 13.3), two in each direction, one carrying data and one carrying a strobe. The links are therefore referred to as data-strobe (DS) links. The four DS links support a total bidirectional bandwidth of 80 Mbytes/sec.

There is a highly integrated programmable memory interface (see Fig. 13.3), which supports a 4 Gbyte physical address space and provides a peak bandwidth of 50 Mwords/sec (200 Mbytes/sec). Four independent banks of external memory are supported, allowing the implementation of mixed memory systems, with support for DRAM, SRAM, EPROM, and VRAM. It has a 64-bit external data bus, and

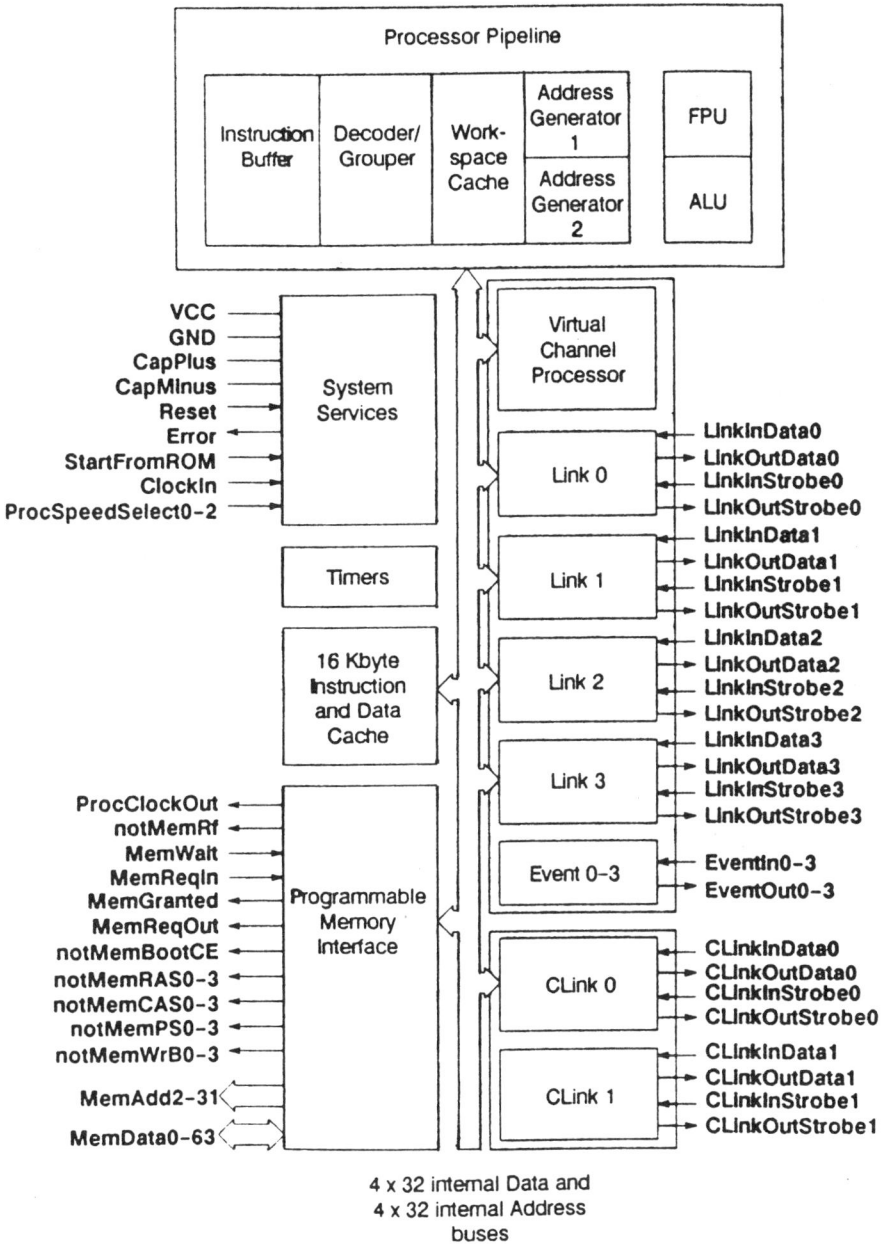

Fig. 13.3   IMS T9000 block diagram *(Courtesy of INMOS)*

each bank of memory can be configured to be eight, 16, 32, or 64 bits wide. The T9000 external pin designations are summarized in Table 13.1.

The T9000 features a five-stage instruction pipeline, illustrated in Fig. 13.4. The pipeline stages are [T900 91]:

[1] **Workspace cache**, which can fetch two local variables.

[2] **Non-local address**, which can perform two address calculations for accessing non-local or subscripted variables.

[3] **Main cache**, which can load two non-local variables.

[4] **ALU/FPU**, which can perform an integer or floating-point operation.

[5] **Write/Jump**, which can perform either a conditional jump or a write operation.

The T9000 features an *instruction grouping* unit (see Fig. 13.4) which permits the processor to act as a multiple-issue superscalar. The degree of issue depends on the sequence of instructions and their interdependence. The instruction grouping unit assembles groups of instructions from the instruction stream. These groups are chosen to make the best use of the available hardware, and one group can be sent through the pipeline every cycle. Instructions are put into groups in the order that they arrive in the CPU. Dependencies within the group are handled automatically by the pipeline.

The instruction grouping unit can be regarded as a hardware optimizer; it recognizes commonly occurring code sequences that the processor can execute effectively. The design of the grouping mechanism and the pipeline is based on analysis of the code typically generated by HLL compilers. The grouping of instructions takes advantage of the high degree of concurrency and multiple buses in the processor. For example, both caches are multiported and can each support two read operations by the CPU simultaneously. This allows two load local instructions to go into one group, and the group could also contain two sets of instructions to calculate addresses and fetch non-local variables. These could all be combined with an arithmetic operation such as add.

Example: Consider the assignment and expression evaluation of the following HLL statement:

$$a(i+1) = b(j+15) + c(k+7)$$

The transputer code produced is shown below along with the number of the pipeline stages in which it is executed (addr stands for address in the following table, page 302).

Table 13.1 T9000 Pin Designations

Pin	In/Out	Function
VCC, GND		Power supply and return
CapPlus, CapMinus		External capacitor for internal clock power supply
ClockIn	in	Input clock
ProcSpeedSelect0-2	in	Processor speed selectors
Reset	in	System reset
StartFromROM	in	Boot from external ROM or from link
Error	out	Error indicator

Pin	In/Out	Function
ProcClockOut	out	Processor clock
MemAdd2-31	out	Address bus
MemData0-63	in/out	Data bus
notMemRAS0-3	out	RAS strobes - one per bank
notMemCAS0-3	out	CAS strobes - one per bank
notMemPS0-3	out	Programmable strobes - one per bank
notMemWrB0-3 †	out	Byte-addressing write strobes
MemWait	in	Memory cycle extender
MemReqIn	in	Direct memory access request
MemGranted	out	Direct memory access granted
MemReqOut	out	Processor requires memory bus
notMemBootCE	out	Bootstrap ROM chip enable
notMemRf	out	Dynamic memory refresh indicator

† these pins have different functions depending on the external port sizes

Pin	In/Out	Function
EventIn0-3	in	Event inputs
EventOut0-3	out	Event outputs

Pin	In/Out	Function
LinkInData0-3	in	Link input data channels
LinkInStrobe0-3	in	Link input strobes
LinkOutData0-3	out	Link output data channels
LinkOutStrobe0-3	out	Link output strobes
CLinkInData0-1	in	Control link input data channels
CLinkInStrobe0-1	in	Control link input strobes
CLinkOutData0-1	out	Control link output data channels
CLinkOutStrobe0-1	out	Control link output strobes

(Courtesy of INMOS)

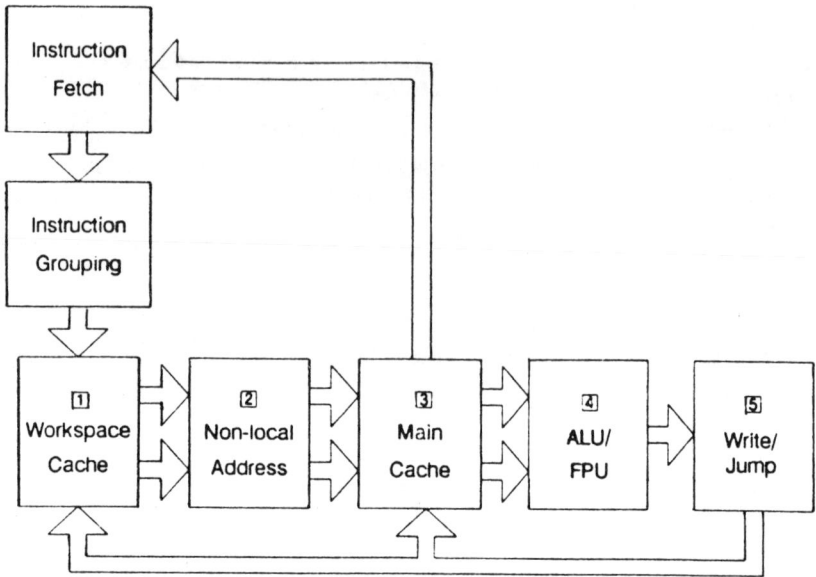

Fig. 13.4 Block diagram of grouper and pipeline *(Courtesy of INMOS)*

Instruction	Pipeline Stages	Operation
ldl j	[1]	load local variable j
ldl b	[1[	load base addr array b
wsub	[2]	calculate addr of b(j)
ldnl 15	[2] [3]	load value of b(j + 15)
ldl k	[1]	
ldl c	[1]	
wsub	[2]	
ldnl 7	[2] [3]	load value of c(k + 7)
add	[4]	add values on stack top
ldl i	[1]	
ldl a	[1]	
wsub	[2]	
stnl 1	[2] [5]	store into a (i + 1)

The above code sequence will be executed as three groups, in three CPU cycles as shown below. The exact content of each group will depend on the code that precedes and follows this. The first group might contain other instructions from earlier in the instruction stream.

First group: ldl, ldl, wsub, ldnl
Second group: ldl, ldl, wsub, ldnl, add
Third group: ldl, ldl, wsub, stnl

Since the processor can fetch one word, containing four bytes of instructions and data in each cycle, it is possible to achieve a continuous execution rate of four instructions per cycle. In other words, the T9000 can perform as a four-issue superscalar. However, if any of the instructions require more than one cycle to execute, then the instruction fetch mechanism can continue to fetch instructions so that larger groups can be built up. Up to eight instructions can be put into one group, and there may be five groups in the pipeline at any time [T900 91].

The T9000 memory hierarchy is illustrated in Fig. 13.5 [T900 91]. Besides the main on-chip cache of 16 Kbytes (unified for both code and data), there is also a workspace cache of 32 words (128 bytes) for local variables. The main cache consists of four independent banks, each containing 256 lines. Each line is four words (16 bytes) long. The four cache banks are accessed by a number of different functional units, as illustrated in Fig. 13.6. Some of these units have multiple ports into the cache, allowing simultaneous transfer of several data items. To allow four simultaneous read and write operations to take place in each cycle, there are four sets of address and data buses. An arbitrator controls access from the various functional units to the cache banks through a crossbar switch [Hwan 93, Tabk 90].

Each of the four cache banks is addressed by a quarter of the memory space. This division of the address space is done using bits 4 and 5 of the address. The lowest four bits (bits 3 to 0) are used to select a byte within a line. The same cache can also be configured to serve as 16 Kbytes of main memory, or 8 Kbytes main memory and 8 Kbytes unified cache. The cache is fully associative, using a write-back policy and a random replacement strategy [HePa 90, Smit 982]. The cache access is illustrated in Fig. 13.7. Bits 2 and 3 of the address identify the accessed word within a line. Bits 4 and 5 identify one of the four cache banks. The upper 26 bits of the address, usually called the 'tag', identify the particular line from memory residing in a particular line slot in the cache.

The T9000 has four data communication links (link 0, 1, 2, 3; see Fig. 13.3), each with a DMA controller and with the ability to synchronize with the scheduling of processes. The links and the DMA systems are controlled by a separate communications processor, the virtual channel processor (VCP), which works concurrently with the CPU. This supports practically a large number of virtual channels on each link. Each message sent across a link is divided into packets. Every packet requires a header to identify its destination process. Packets from different messages are interleaved on the link. Virtual channels are always created in pairs to form a virtual link. This means there is no need for a return address in packets: the acknowledgements are simply sent back along the other channel of the virtual link.

INMOS features a number of auxiliary chips in conjunction with its communication capabilities.

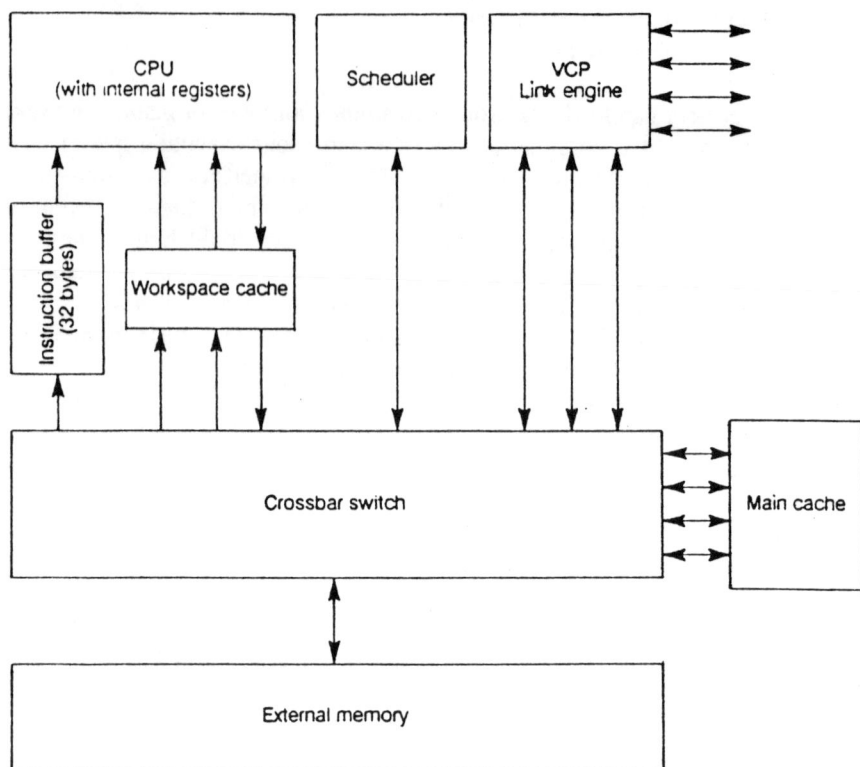

Fig. 13.5 IMS T9000 hierarchical memory system *(Courtesy of INMOS)*

The IMS C104 (or simply C104) packet routing switch connects 32 serial communication links to one another via a 32 by 32 non-blocking crossbar switch, enabling messages to be routed from any of its links to any other link. The links operate concurrently, and the transfer of a packet between one pair of links does not affect the data rate for another packet passing between a second pair of links. The C104 supports a rate of packet processing of up to 200 million packets per second. The C104 allows communication between T9000 transputers that are not directly connected. A single C104 can be used to connect up to 32 transputers. The C104 can also be connected to other C104s to make larger and more complex switching networks, linking any number of transputers and link adaptors, and any other devices that use the link protocol.

The IMS C100 (or simply C100) system protocol converter converts between protocols of different transputers, allowing the construction of mixed systems.

The T9000 belongs to the transputer family designated as T9. Earlier transputer implementations include:

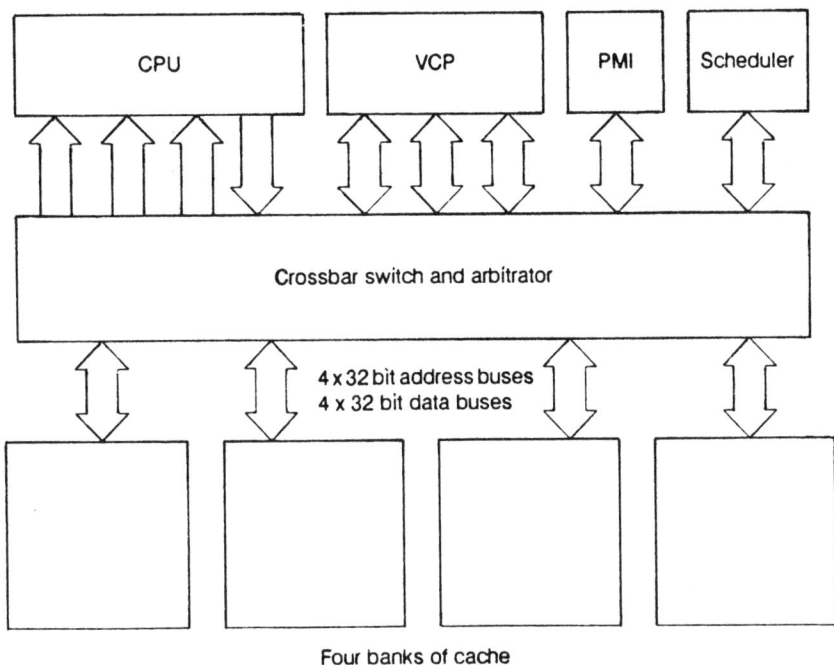

| CPU | VCP | PMI | Scheduler |

Crossbar switch and arbitrator

4 x 32 bit address buses
4 x 32 bit data buses

Four banks of cache

Fig. 13.6   Diagram of four banks of cache *(Courtesy of INMOS)*

T8 family (T800, T801, T805), 32-bit, with an on-chip FPU, 4 Kbyte on-chip memory, operating at frequencies of 20 to 30MHz.
T4 family (T400, T425), 32-bit, with 2 to 4 Kbyte on-chip memory, operating at a frequency of 20MHz.
T2 family (T222, T225), 16-bit, 4 Kbyte on-chip memory, 20MHz.

13.4 Concluding Comments
The transputer, and particularly the T9000, is capable of handling the generation, manipulation, and transmission of image data in applications such as multimedia, laser printers, graphic systems, image processing system, and industrial inspection systems. The transputer multiprocessor capability, scalable performance, and real-time responsiveness make it a suitable solution for applications including supercomputers, application accelerators, disk arrays, file servers, databases, and robotics. The particular combination of a high-performance processor and communication links with a packet-based protocol makes it highly applicable in communication areas, such as networking, LAN interfacing, internetworking, and packet-switching systems.

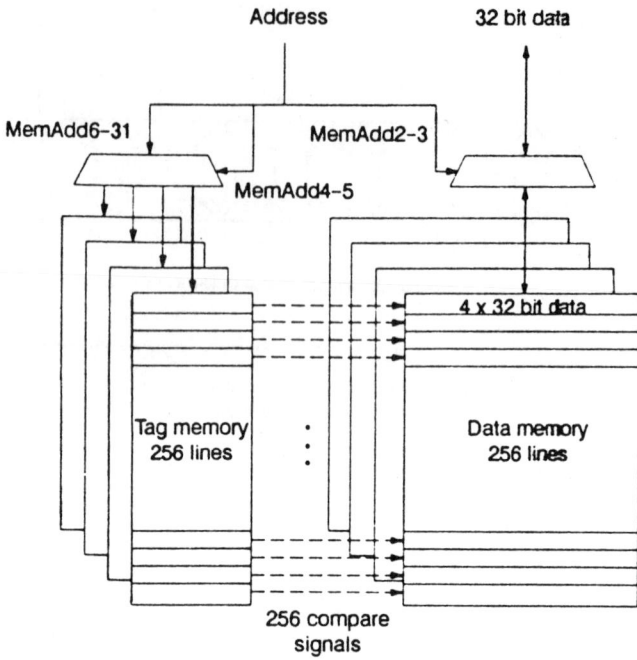

Fig. 13.7 Cache operation *(Courtesy of INMOS)*

PART 3

RISC EVALUATION AND APPLICATIONS

CHAPTER 14

Comparison and Performance of RISC Systems

14.1 Introductory Comments

A number of experimental and commercial RISC systems have been described in the preceding chapters. This chapter summarizes the properties of these systems, compares them and presents some experimental results on their performance.

A considerable amount of experimentation was conducted in conjunction with the first RISC system to be denoted by the name 'RISC' — the Berkeley RISC I and II (see chapter 3). Subsequently, the properties of the commercial RISC systems are compared and experimental results, conducted by some of the RISC manufacturers, are reported.

14.2 Performance Evaluation of the Berkeley RISC

Because of the inherent properties of the RISC architecture (small choice of instructions, formats and addressing modes), it is rather difficult and time-consuming to program in its assembly language. The Berkeley RISC developers adopted an efficient C language compiler for the RISC at an early state of the study [Kate 85, PaSe 82]. The main benchmark programs, used in the RISC performance evaluation, were written in (or translated into) the C language. The following computing systems were compared with the RISC:

Digital	VAX 11/780
Digital	PDP 11/70
Motorola	MC68000
Zilog	Z8002
BBN	C/70

The C compilers for all systems, except the PDP 11/70, were based on the UNIX portable C compiler [John 78]. The C compiler for the PDP 11/70 was based on the Ritchie C compiler [KeRi 78].

Eleven benchmark programs (in C language) were used [PaSe 82]:

E — Character String Search
F — Bit Set, Reset, Test
H — Linked List Insertion
K — Bit Matrix Transposition

I — Quicksort
Ackerman
Puzzle (Subscript)
Puzzle (Pointer)
Recursive Qsort
SED (UNIX-environment Batch Text Editor)
Towers of Hanoi (game program)

The first five benchmark programs are C versions of the so-called EDN benchmarks [GrHe 81].

The *Character String Search* (E) program examines a long character string for the first occurrence of a substring. If the search is successful, the procedure returns the substring's starting position. Otherwise, the procedure returns a 'not found' indicator. The starting addresses and the lengths of the string and substring are passed as parameters to the benchmark. This benchmark exercises an architecture's ability to move through character strings sequentially. The *Bit Set, Reset, Test* (F) benchmark tests sets or resets a bit within a tightly packed bit string beginning at a word boundary. This benchmark tests, sets, and then resets three bits. It checks an architecture's bit-manipulation capabilities. The *Linked List Insertion* (H) benchmark inserts five new entries into a doubly linked list. This benchmark tests pointer manipulation. The *Bit Matrix Transposition* (K) program takes a tightly packed, square bit matrix and transposes it. The matrix is of variable size and starts on a word boundary. This benchmark exercises an architecture's bit manipulation and looping capabilities. The *Quicksort* (I) performs a nonrecursive quick sorting algorithm on a large vector of fixed-length records. It contains no procedure calls. It thoroughly tests an architecture's addressing modes and character and stack manipulation capabilities. A recursive version of Quicksort, the *Recursive Qsort*, frequently used in UNIX, has also been used as one of the benchmark programs. It sorts 2600 fixed-length character strings. The *Puzzle* is a recursive bin-packing program that solves a three-dimensional puzzle. Two versions of this program have been used: the Puzzle-Subscript, denoted sometimes as Puzzle, and the Puzzle-Pointer, denoted as Ppuzzle. The *SED* (Stream-oriented text EDitor) is one of the UNIX software tools. It copies files to the standard output after they have been edited according to a script of commands. The *Ackerman* and the *Towers of Hanoi* are programs stressing recursive procedure calls; particularly the Ackerman, which requires more than 170 000 procedure calls [PaPi 82].

The average relative code size for the above 11 C benchmark programs is:

Machine	Code Size Relative to RISC
RISC I, II	1.0
VAX 11/780	0.8 ± 0.3
MC68000	0.9 ± 0.2
Z8002	1.2 ± 0.6
PDP 11/70	0.9 ± 0.4
BBN C/70	0.7 ± 0.2

Even in the worst case (C/70), the RISC code is no more than 50% larger on the average. In the Z8002, the RISC code is even 20% smaller. The results should have been expected. Since RISC uses the most frequently used instructions, the penalties of having a reduced instruction set are not excessive.

As far as execution speed is concerned, we have the following results [PaPi 82]:

Machine	Clock; MHz	Reg-to-Reg add; ns	b
RISC I	12	330	0.67
RISC II	8	500	1.00
VAX 11/780	5	400	1.7 ± 0.9
PDP 11/70	7.5	500	2.1 ± 1.2
MC68000	10	400	2.8 ± 1.4
BBN C/70	6.7	–	3.2 ± 2.2
Z8002	6	700	3.3 ± 1.3

where b = (Execution Time)/(8MHz RISC Execution Time) averaged over 11 C programs

As one can see, for the benchmarks chosen, the RISC is superior on the average. For the particular add instruction, the 12MHz RISC is also superior.

Data-Memory (M) traffic due to Call and Return instructions has also been monitored and expressed in units of words transferred and the percentage of all data-memory references:

Benchmarks		Puzzle	Quicksort
VAX 11/780:	words	440K	700K
	% of all data-M ref.	28%	50%
RISC:	words	8K	4K
	% of all data-M ref.	0.8%	1%

The extensive saving of Data-Memory traffic on the RISC contributes considerably to its overall enhancement of the throughput.

Another measurement, concerning the HLL performance of the RISC, was made in [PaPi 82]. The average of the following ratio was measured:

$$a = average \quad \frac{\text{Assembly Code Execution Time}}{\text{Compiler Code Execution Time}}$$

The results were:

Machine	a
RISC	0.90 ± 0.1
PDP 11/70	0.50 ± 0.2
Z8002	0.46 ± 0.3
VAX 11/780	0.45 ± 0.2
MC68000	0.34 ± 0.3

The lower this ratio, the more the programmer is tempted to program in assembly code. The above results indicate that the RISC programmer has a higher incentive to program in HLL [Kate 85].

The RISC does not have any floating-point supports in its architecture. Any floating-point calculations to be performed on a RISC are taken care of in two possible ways:

(a) Using a floating-point coprocessor
(b) By software subroutines

Both approaches have been experimented with by the Berkeley RISC researchers [Patt 84]. The Weitek floating-point two-chip set was used as a coprocessor. The Whetstone benchmark program [CuWi 75, WiCu 75], translated into C, has been implemented. The Whetstone benchmark, developed by the Central Computer Agency of the British Government, is a synthetic program that tests numerical computing by executing a substantial amount of floating-point arithmetic. The results were as follows:

Machine	Floating-point Implementation	Time (sec)
VAX 11/780	hardware (FPA)	2.2
VAX 11/750	hardware	3.4
RISC II (12MHz)	hardware (coprocessor)	4.5
VAX 11/780	microcode	5.5
RISC II (8MHz)	hardware (coprocessor)	6.4
VAX 11/750	microcode	8.4
68010 (10MHz)	software (assembly)	41.5
RISC II (12MHz)	software (C)	67.1
RISC II (8MHz)	software (C)	101.7

While the RISC performance with a coprocessor is quite competitive, its purely software performance for floating-point calculations is quite poor. The use of a coprocessor seems to be the most reasonable way of treating floating point on the Berkeley RISC.

The compile time for C benchmarks has also been evaluated running the VAX C compiler and the RISC C compiler *both* on the VAX 11/780 and on the RISC II at 8 and 12MHz. The total compile time for three benchmark programs in C (1d, sort, puzzle) is summarized below:

		Compile Time (sec)	$\dfrac{VAX}{RISC}$ Compile Time
VAX C Compiler			
on VAX		50.5	
on RISC II	8MHz	37.8	1.3
	12MHz	25.0	2.0
RISC C Compiler			
on VAX		62.5	
on RISC II	8MHz	40.4	1.5
	12MHz	26.7	2.3

We can see that the RISC C Compiler or the VAX Compiler, run on the RISC II at 12MHz, is twice as fast as the VAX C Compiler run on the VAX.

The Lisp and PSL (dialect of Lisp) performances were also tested for the RISC [Patt 84]. The programs tested were translated into the RISC machine code from the output of VAX Lisp compilers. The results were:

TAK Lisp Benchmark in Franz Lisp		TAK Lisp Benchmark in PSL	
Machine	Time (sec)	Machine	Time (sec)
MC68010 (10MHz)	13.7 no optimization	VAX 11/750	7.1 no optimization
VAX 11/780	8.3 no optimization	RISC II (8MHz)	2.6
RISC II (8MHz)	4.4	RISC II (12MHz)	1.7
VAX 11/750	3.6	VAX 11/750	1.4
RISC II (12MHz)	2.9		
MC68010 (10MHz)	2.5		
VAX 11/780	1.1		

The performance of RISC is quite competitive, at least compared to the VAX 11/750.

In the performance evaluation of RISC, one has to note two aspects not directly associated with the idea of a reduced instruction set:

(a) Use of an optimized C compiler;
(b) The presence of a large CPU register file and the 'register window' approach.

Both of the above contribute considerably to the enhancement of the RISC throughput, and both can be implemented in a CISC system as well. In other words, the above two aspects are not necessarily connected with the RISC general philosophy (see chapter 2). One has to add here though the following points:

1. From the VLSI viewpoint, it is precisely because of the RISC small control area (up to 10%) that it is possible to allocate a large CPU register file on the chip, as argued in chapter 2.
2. The presence of a large CPU register file is one of the RISC defining points, as stated in chapter 2.

Some researchers took up performance evaluation studies where the above aspects (a) and (b) of RISC were put to the test. Heath [Heat 84] has applied the optimized C compiler, running the same EDN benchmarks, to the MC68000 and the Z8002, with the following run time results (in msec):

Benchmark	RISC I	MC68000	Z8002
Character string (E)	460	1228 (2.8)	421 (0.9)
Bit set (F)	60	228 (4.8)	242 (4.0)
Linked list (H)	100	160 (1.6)	137 (1.4)
Quicksort (I)	50400	206640 (4.1)	149760 (3.0)
Bit matrix (K)	430	1720 (4.0)	1278 (3.0)
average		(3.5)	(2.5)

The numbers in parentheses indicate the number of times slower than the RISC I program.

Next, the programs were recoded in the RISC assembly code and run on a RISC I simulator and the other two machines. The RISC run assumed that the CPU had a total of 32 registers, eliminating the 'register window' concept. The running time (msec) results were:

Benchmark	RISC I	MC68000	Z8002
E	417	244 (0.59)	134 (0.32)
F	83	70 (0.84)	70 (0.85)
H	66	153 (2.32)	135 (2.05)
I	39449	33527 (0.85)	66000 (1.67)
K	772	368 (0.48)	369 (0.45
average		(1.01)	(1.07)

As should have been expected, the RISC performance dropped compared to the Berkeley results. Notwithstanding this drop of performance in the above experiments, they still indicate that even eliminating the large register file and 'register window' edge, the RISC is still comparable and competitive with some CISC microprocessors. One should also keep in mind that a large CPU register file is an integral part of the RISC attributes.

Similar studies were also reported in [HiSp 85]. One of the main conclusions of that project was that 'performance gains due to multiple register sets are independent of instruction set complexity'. As argued earlier in this section, this is a very logical statement, and it does not really require a lengthy simulation study to support it.

To summarize, most of the performance-evaluation studies point to the superiority (or at least non-inferiority) of the RISC with respect to other comparable computing systems. No study has demonstrated RISC inferiority, with or without the register window or the optimized C compiler.

14.3 Comparison of Commercial RISC Systems

The RISC-type microprocessors, described in chapters 6 through 13, will now be compared from several points of view involving their different features.

Technology features. RISC systems technology features are summarized in Table 14.1 They are all designed with 0.8 micron or less CMOS technology, more than one-layer metal, with over 150 pins. The DEC Alpha 21164 exceeds all others in its frequency of operation of 300MHz and in its transistor count of 9.3 million. The R10000 (see Table 14.9) is a significant runner-up at 200MHz.

Table 14.1 RISC Systems Technology

System	Technology	Transistors	Frequency	Pins
DEC 21164	0.5m,4L,CMOS	9 300 000	300 MHz	499 PGA
PowerPC 604	0.5m,4L,CMOS	3 600 000	100 MHz	304
SuperSPARC	0.8m,3L,BiCMOS	3 100 000	50 MHz	293 PGA
R4400	0.6m,2L,CMOS	2 200 000	75 MHz	179 PGA
i860 XP	0.8m,3L,CHMOS-V	2 550 000	50 MHz	262 PGA
MC88110	0.8m,3L,CMOS	1 300 000	50 MHz	299
PA7100	0.8m,3L,CMOS	850 000	100 MHz	504 PGA

PGA - pin grid array
m - micron
xL - x layer metal (x=2,3,4)
Note: Alpha and R4400 are 64-bit systems; all others are 32-bit

Architecture features. Some architectural features of the RISC systems (IU and FPU register files, virtual and physical addresses), are listed in Table 14.2. All systems feature separate IU and FPU register files. With the exception of the SuperSPARC with its large Berkeley RISC-style register file, all have 32 IU registers. The 32-register file is still quite large compared to CISC systems (actually double those of VAX and MC68000, and quadruple that of ix86), and at the same time conforming to some notable compilers, which explains their choice by most manufacturers. All systems have 32 FPU registers. The PA-7100 actually has 32 hardware FPU registers; however, the first four are assigned special tasks, so there are only 28 general-purpose FPU registers. The 21164 and R4400 are 64-bit systems, and this is why their IU registers are 64-bit wide. All systems have FPU registers that are at least 64-bit wide to accommodate IEEE 64-bit double-precision operands. The SuperSPARC and i860 XP registers can also be used as 16 64-bit registers (16×64). The FPU registers of the MC88110 are 80-bit wide to accommodate the 80-bit extended-precision operands. Most of the systems offer more than 32 bits of virtual address space: 64 bits by 21164, R4400, and PA-7100 (actually, the PA-7100 has 32-bit flat addressing with segment extension to 64 bits), and 52 bits by PowerPC 604. Two of the systems (SuperSPARC and R4400) offer a 36-bit physical address space, and the 21164 has a 40-bit physical address. The increase of address spaces beyond 32 bits is a trend that is expected to grow in future systems.

Table 14.2 RISC Systems Architecture

System	IU registers	FPU registers	VA bits	PA bits
DEC 21164	32x64	32x64	64	40
PowerPC 604	32x32	32x64	52^2	32
SuperSPARC	136x32	$32x32^1$	32	36
R4400	32x64	32x64	64	36
i860 XP	32x32	$32x32^1$	32	32
MC88110	32x32	32x80	32	32
PA7100	32x32	28x64	64^2	32

IU - integer unit   FPU - floating-point unit
VA - virtual address PA - physical address
1 - can also be used as 16x64 register file
2 - segmented; only 32-bit address calculations

Instruction level parallelism (ILP) features. The ILP features of the RISC systems are listed in Table 14.3. All practice ILP one way or another (as do the new CISCs Pentium and MC68060). Only the R4400 is superpipelined; all other are superscalar. Most processors listed in Table 14.3 are two-issue, the 21164 and the PowerPC 604 are four-issue, ànd the SuperSPARC is three-issue. The latest processors (see also Table 14.9), PowerPC 620 (chapter 7), UltraSPARC (chapter 8), and MIPS R8000 and R10000 (see chapter 9), are all four-issue superscalar. The processors differ in the number of functional units capable of simultaneous execution, and therefore there are differences in the amount of restrictions imposed on simultaneous issue of instructions. The one with the least restrictions is the MC88110 with its 10 functional units, which include two IUs and two graphics units. The most restricted is the i860 XP, where only an integer and a floating-point pair of instructions can be issued simultaneously under a special software arrangement.

RISC memory and cache organization comparison. The RISC systems cache and memory management features are presented in Table 14.4. All feature a dual primary cache. The largest total cache on chip is that of the 21164: 16KB primary (8KB code + 8KB data) and 96KB secondary. The only one without an on-chip cache is the PA-7100. Although its designers have tuned the external cache access

318

Table 14.3 RISC Systems ILP Features

System	ILP issue	IU units	FPU units	Graph. units
DEC 21164	4	2	2	0
PowerPC 604	4	5**	1	0
SuperSPARC	3	2	2	0
R4400	2*	1	3	0
i860 XP	2	1	2	1
MC88110	2	3	3	2
PA7100	2	1	3	0

* superpipelined; all others are superscalar. ** three IUs, the BPU, the LSU
ILP - instruction level parallelism.   IU - integer unit
FPU - floating-point unit. BPU - branch processing unit. LSU - load/store unit

for minimal delay, the access of an on-chip cache is still faster; PA-7100's high frequency of operation tends to 'cover up' for this obvious disadvantage, which may probably be corrected in future PA implementations. All mappings from direct to eight-way are used. All systems have on-chip logic to interface to an external secondary cache. The largest TLB is featured by the PowerPC 604: 256 entries. With the exception of the SuperSPARC, all systems feature additional page sizes (sometime called 'blocks', or 'spaces', but offering about the same options as larger pages). This follows some recent research results that point to an advantage of having optional larger page sizes.

Performance comparison
A number of benchmark performance experiments on an earlier generation of RISC-type systems, with the CISC i486 and MC68040, were reported in [Slat 91]. Some of these results are summarized in a different format in Table 14.5. The large disparity between the operating frequencies of the different processors being tested should be noted. Naturally, the PA-RISC (a PA microprocessor preceding the PA-7100), running at 66MHz, with the next runner-up at 40MHz, is ahead of any other processor in both integer and floating-point performance. It is felt that a more fair experimentation would be to test all processors at the same frequency. At this point, as a purely computational experiment, the results in Table 14.5 were scaled down to 25MHz, the lowest frequency reported in the table (for the MC68040). If the result in Table 14.5 was X, at a frequency Y, the scaled-down value $Z = 25X/Y$. The scaled-down results are shown in Table 14.6. Now the PA-RISC is left slightly behind the IBM RS/6000 in both integer and floating-point operation. It is also slightly outperformed by the MIPS R3000 in integer operation. Another interesting thing to observe is that while i486 (at 33MHz) outperforms MC68040 (at 25MHz) in the overall SPECmark figure in Table 14.5, the situation is reversed in Table 14.6, in which the i486 is assumed to be operating at 25MHz as well.

Table 14.4 RISC Systems Memory Organization

System	Icache,KB	Dcache,KB	Scache[2] ,KB	TLB entries	Page size
DEC 21164	8,direct	8,direct	96, 3-way	64 D+48 I	8 KB[3]
PowerPC 604	16, 4-way	16, 4-way	0	128+128	4 KB[4]
SuperSPARC	20, 5-way	16, 4-way	0	64	4 KB
R4400	16,direct	16,direct	0	96	4 KB[5]
i860 XP	16, 4-way	16, 4-way	0	64	4 KB, 4 MB
MC88110	8, 2-way	8, 2-way	0	40+40	4 KB[6]
PA7100	off-chip[1]	off-chip[1]	0	120 D+16 I	4 KB[7]

Icache - on-chip instruction cache; I - instruction
Dcache - on-chip data cache; D- data. Scache - on-chip secondary cache.
1 - off-chip 1 MB Icache, 2 MB Dcache
2 - all chips have on-chip logic for external cache interface
3 - pages can be grouped: blocks of 64 KB, 512 KB, 4 MB to use a single TLB entry
4 - PowerPC 604 has in addition blocks of 128 KB to 8 MB
5 - R4400 has a page size range of 4 KB to 16 MB, increasing by multiples of 4
6 - MC88110 has in addition blocks of 512 KB to 64 MB
7 - PA7100 has in addition spaces of 512 KB to 64 MB

Table 14.5 Geometric Means SPECmark Results

Processor	SPECmark	Integer-only	Fl.-pt.-only
PA-RISC, 66 MHZ	72.2	51.0	91.0
RS/6000, 30 MHz	34.7	24.0	44.3
SPARC, 40 MHz	21.2	20.8	21.6
R3000, 33 MHz	26.5	27.1	26.1
MC88100, 33 MHz	17.8	21.4	15.8
MC68040, 25 MHz	11.8	12.9	11.0
i486, 33 MHz	12.1	18.2	9.2
i860 XR, 40 MHz	24.7	19.3	29.2

Note: The above processors were within the following systems: PA-RISC: HP9000 model 730; IBM RS/6000 model 540; SPARC: Sun SPARCstation 2; R3000: MIPS RC3360; MC88100: Motorola Delta model 8612; i486: HP 425s; i860: Alacron AL860 [Slat 91]

The last-generation RISC systems are compared with the Pentium in Table 14.7, based on reports of experiments by Intel, also documented in [Stam 93]. There is again the disparity of frequencies for different processors. Even so, it is interesting to note that the CISC Pentium outperforms the RISC PowerPC 601 at the same frequency and the R4000 (100MHz inside, 50MHz outside) for integer operations. This should not come as a complete surprise. Intel has considerably improved the design of the Pentium, compared to the earlier members of the x86

Table 14.6 SPECmark Results at 25MHz

Processor	SPECmark	Integer-only	Fl.-pt.-only
PA-RISC	27.3	19.3	34.5
RS/6000	28.9	20.0	36.9
SPARC	13.3	13.0	13.5
R3000	20.0	20.5	27.3
MC88100	13.5	16.2	12.0
MC68040	11.8	12.9	11.0
i486	9.2	13.8	7.0
i860 XR	15.4	12.0	18.3

family. Although the Pentium is a CISC, it is a two-issue superscalar, with an on-chip dual cache (8KB code, 8KB data), and with a 64-bit bus in and out of the chip. This and other innovative features should explain why the CISC Pentium can successfully compete with the leading RISCs. In order to equalize the comparison, the results in columns SPECint92 and SPECfp92 were scaled to 66MHz for all systems, as was done in Table 14.6. While the R4400 outperformed all systems in integer operations, and the PA-7100 excelled in floating-point operations, the SuperSPARC comes out on top in both integer and floating-point operations in the equalized-frequency model. This should come as no surprise: the SuperSPARC is a three-issue superscalar with multiple execution units (both integer and floating-point), which alleviates restrictions on parallel execution of simultaneously issued instructions (see chapter 1). It should be borne in mind, however, that data attained at 'equalized' frequencies are rather artificial and should not be taken too seriously. Some processors compared in such a way may never achieve frequencies as high as some others. Therefore, there will always be a gap in their actual performance.

Independent experimental results were also reported by TI, the manufacturer of SuperSPARC and its co-designer with Sun. These results for SPECint92 are listed in Table 14.8. According to this report, the SuperSPARC at 50MHz outperforms all other systems. This becomes even clearer when the results are shown per MHz in the rightmost column of Table 14.8.

According to TI projections into the future, the next version of the SuperSPARC is expected to reach in 1994 a frequency of 90MHz, with a SPECint performance of up to 140, and a SPECfp performance of up to 210. This of course remains to be seen and compared with other systems in the future.

A comparison of the Pentium performance with that of the PowerPC 601, at the same frequency of 60MHz, was reported in [Half 93]. Using BYTE magazine benchmarks, the results indicated that the 601 outperformed the Pentium by a factor ranging from 1.44 to 4.7. The lower figures are for simple FPU operations, and the higher for bit-field operations. The Pentium actually outperformed the 601 on transcendental FPU operations.

Table 14.7 SPEC Performance Comparison

CPU (MHz)	SPECint92	int,66MHz	SPECfp92	fp,66MHz
i486DX (66)	32	32	16	16
Pentium (66)	65	65	57	57
21064 (150)	74	33	126	55
R4000 (100)	62	41	63	42
R4400 (150)	82	36	86	38
PA7100 (99)	80	53	151	101
MPC601 (66)	50	50	80	80
SSPARC (40)	53	87	63	104

MPC601 is the PowerPC 601 and SSPARC is the SuperSPARC

Table 14.8 Performance Comparison Reported by TI

System	Freq. MHz	SPECint92	SPECint/MHz
SuperSPARC	50	68	1.33
DEC 21064	133	65	0.54
Pentium	66	64	0.97
R4000	100	58	0.56
RS/6000	50	48	0.95
HP-PA 7100	50	37	0.81

TI - Texas Instruments

A comparison between DEC 21064- and PowerPC 601-based workstation performance was reported in [Amar 93]. The 21064-based workstation tested was the DEC 3000 Model 500X AXP, and the PowerPC 601-based was the HP 9000 Model 735. The 500X AXP has a 200MHz 21064 processor with a 512KB secondary off-chip cache. Although the 500X can support up to 256MB RAM, only a minimal configuration of 96MB was used. The HP 9000/735 had a 99MHz PA-7100 processor with an external primary cache of 256KB instruction and 256KB data (a total of 512KB) and 32MB RAM. The experimentation used the DN&R Labs' standard suite of UNIX workstation benchmarks. The performance was measured in units of Microvax II processing (MVUPs). Naturally, the 21064-based system, running at a double frequency with an on-chip cache, came out on top with an average 277.86 MVUPs, as opposed t the PA-7100-based systems which achieved 185.85 MVUPs.

Along with the new version of the Alpha AXP implementation, the 64-bit

21164 (see chapter 6), other high-performance 64-bit RISC processors have recently been announced: the PowerPC 620 (see chapter 7), the Sun Microsystems and TI UltraSPARC (see chapter 8), and the MIPS R10000 (see chapter 9). They all share the following properties:

1. All are 64-bit systems, keeping the 32-bit instruction formats for compatibility with previous 32-bit systems of the family.
2. All are 0.5 micron CMOS, four-layer metal.
3. All are four-issue superscalar.

Some of the different features of the above four processors are listed in Table 14.9. It should be noted that the SPEC data are estimated; at the time of this writing (end of 1994), none is available commercially. The Alpha AXP 21164 is most notable for its highest frequency of operation (300MHz) and the largest on-chip total cache of 112KB (8KB + 8KB L1; 96KB L2). It is the only processor with a significant on-chip secondary cache. Another detail worth noticing is the R10000 superior estimated floating-point performance. How it will turn out in actual experimentation remains to be seen. No doubt, R10000's 200MHz operation, a total of 64KB on-chip primary cache, and a total of 64 rename registers, will have a strong influence on its projected performance.

Pipelines of some notable RISC processors and their number of stages are listed in Table 14.10. Multiplicity of pipelines ranges from one to five and pipeline depth from two (for branch instructions) to 12 (for a memory reference in case of a miss in primary cache). Integer pipeline depth ranges from four to nine, and for the FPU from six to 10. It should be noted that, although a single instruction pipeline is counted on the PowerPC 604 and 620, it branches out into six separate execution units at the execute stage.

14.4 Concluding Comments

As impressive as some of the above benchmark results may be, it should be remembered that these results are for a restricted and limited quantity of programs. The results for many other programs may turn out to be quite different. Thus, the above results should be taken as indicative, but not conclusive. The same caution should be exercised with the numbers obtained by frequency scaling in Tables 14.6 and 14.7. After all, they do not represent the realistic state of affairs; if a microprocessor cannot run above a certain frequency, any numbers obtained assuming that it can, are only an indication of what *might* possibly be, but is not, or not yet. If microprocessor A attains a higher performance compared to B because A runs at a higher frequency, well, that is the reality. If the manufacturer of microprocessor A succeeded in creating a system capable of operating at a very high frequency, it should certainly enjoy the advantages coming out of such an achievement. One should also take into account that filling the chip with extra resources and increasing its density beyond certain limits may also limit the capability of the chip to operate at higher frequencies. The balance is somewhere in the middle: enough resources to run simultaneous operations in a superscalar environment, but not too many to inhibit high-frequency operation.

Table 14.9 High-performance 64-bit Superscalar RISC Systems

System:	21164	PowerPC 620	UltraSPARC	R10000
Frequency (MHz)	300	133	167	200
Transistorsx10^6	9.3	7.0	3.8	6.0
Pins	499	625	521	527
Functional units	4	6	9	5
On-chip L1 (KB)	8I/8D	32I/32D	16I/16D	32I/32D
On-chip L2 (KB)	96	-	-	-
Out-of-order execution	No	Yes	Yes	Yes
Speculative execution	No	Yes	Yes	Yes
Memory bus width, bits	128	128	128	64
Rename registers	-	8 IU/8 FPU	-	32 IU/32 FPU
SPECint92	330	225	275	300
SPECfp92	500	300	305	600

Where: I = Instruction   D = Data
    L1 = level 1 cache (primary)   L2 = level 2 cache (secondary)
    IU = integer unit   FPU = Floating-point unit
Note: SPEC data are estimated

Common properties for all four processors:

1.All are 64-bit systems, keeping the 32-bit instruction formats for compatibility with previous   32-bit systems of the family.
2.All are 0.5 micron CMOS, four-layer metal.
3.All are four-issue superscalar.

Table 14.10 Pipeline Comparison

System	No. of pipelines	IU stages	FPU stages	M ref. stages	Branch stages
DEC 21064	3	7	10	7	-
DEC 21164	3	7	9	12^1	-
PPC 601	4	4	6	5	2
PPC 603	5	4	6	5^2	3
PPC 604	1^3	6	-	-	-
PPC 620	1^3	5	-	-	-
UltraSPARC	2	9	9	-	-
SuperSPARC	1	8	-	-	-
MIPS R4000	1	8	-	-	-
MIPS R10000	5	5^4	7^4	6	-
HP PA-7100	1	5	-	-	-

IU = Integer Unit,   FPU = Floating-Point Unit,   M ref. = Memory reference
PPC = PowerPC,   HP = Hewlett-Packard,   PA = Precision Architecture

Comments:
1 - 7 stages only if there is an L1 hit.
2 - separate load and store pipelines.
3 - 6 execute units at execute stage.
4 - 2 pipelines

CHAPTER 15

RISC Applications in Parallel Computation

15.1 Introduction to Parallel Processing

Parallel computation has been one of the most active areas in computer development during the past years [Hwan 93]. From the very beginning of digital computer development, computer designers always tried to increase the speed of operations. There are a number of possible ways to achieve this. An obvious approach is to improve the technology implemented in the realization of the computer components. The current technology has gone a long way in this direction. The DEC Alpha AXP implementations run at a frequency of hundreds of MHz and we are promised even higher frequencies of operation, exceeding 500MHz by the end of the century. There is of course a natural limitation in technology development; no signal can propagate faster than the speed of light. Other obvious ways of improving the speed of operation of computers are in the refinement of the logic design of computer subsystems and in the development of more efficient computation algorithms.

There is, however, yet another way of increasing the speed of computation: by performing as many operations as possible simultaneously, concurrently, in parallel, instead of sequentially. This approach is called parallel processing [Hwan 93]. Pipelining, where the CPU treats several instructions, at their different stages, simultaneously, is one of the most widely used types of parallel processing (see chapter 1). Today, practically all modern computers implement pipelining. As argued in chapters 1 and 2, RISC processors are particularly efficient in handling pipelines, thus achieving higher performance and speed of operation. Instruction level parallelism (ILP), with the superscalar operation in particular, is one of the next logical steps in expanding concurrent operation and increasing speed (see chapter 1). Indeed, most recent processors, RISC (see part 2) or CISC (Pentium, MC68060 [Tabk 94]), are superscalar two- to four-issue. Naturally, RISC processors are better suited for handling high-issue superscalar and deep pipeline operations.

A natural expansion of the parallel processing concept is to develop systems with multiple execution units. As can be seen from the examples described in part 2, it is already practiced in most systems. One step further in the development of parallel processing is to design systems with multiple CPUs, or multiprocessors [Hwan 93, Tabk 90]. In a multiprocessing system, a number of processors can be busy on solving a part of a problem, or each processor can run a separate program

326

simultaneously. Either way of operation will increase the overall throughput of the system.

There exist many types of parallel processing systems. One of the most simple and widely accepted methods of parallel systems classification is the so-called Flynn classification [Flyn 72, Hwan 93, Tabk 90]. In this classification, we differentiate between instruction or control signal sequences (or streams) I, and data sequences (or streams) D. Thus, the four types of system according to the Flynn classification are:

1. *Single Instruction Single Data* (**SISD**) stream system. This is the regular single CPU system, also called a *uniprocessor*. However, even a uniprocessor of today may contain multiple ALUs, and implement pipelining and ILP.

2. *Single Instruction Multiple Data* (**SIMD**) stream system, illustrated in Fig. 15.1. The notation used in Fig. 15.1 is:

CU — control unit
Di — data stream i, i = 1, 2, ..., n
LMi — local memory i, i = 1, 2, ..., n
MM — main memory
Pri — processor (CPU) i, i = 1, 2, ..., n

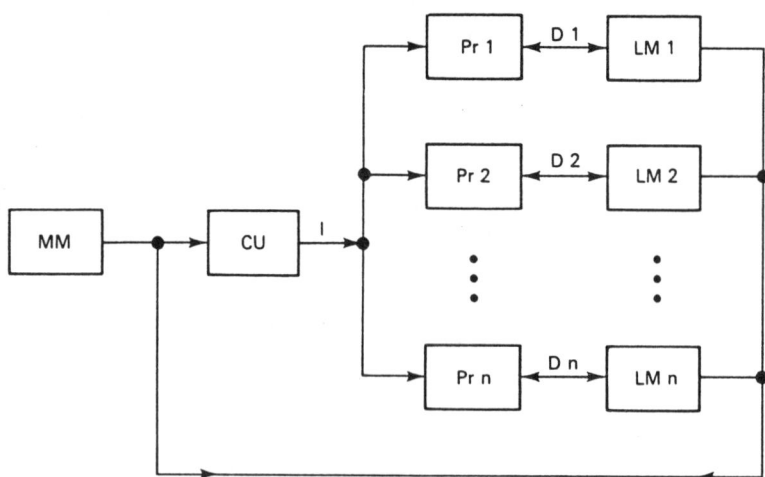

Fig. 15.1   SIMD

In this system, all n processors execute the same instruction concurrently on a different data stream. The single instruction stream I is supplied by the CU to all processors simultaneously.

3. *Multiple Instruction Single Data* (**MISD**) stream system. A sequence of data D is transmitted to a sequence of processors, each of which is controlled by a separate

CU and executes a different instruction sequence. The MISD structure has never been implemented in practice. It resembles a pipeline structure; however, the main difference is that a pipeline belongs to a single CPU and all of its stages are controlled by a single CU.

4. *Multiple Instruction Multiple Data* (**MIMD**) stream system, illustrated in Fig. 15.2. Each of the n processors executes a different instruction stream Ii on a different set of data. This is really the most general type of parallel processing. MIMD systems are also called *multiprocessors*.

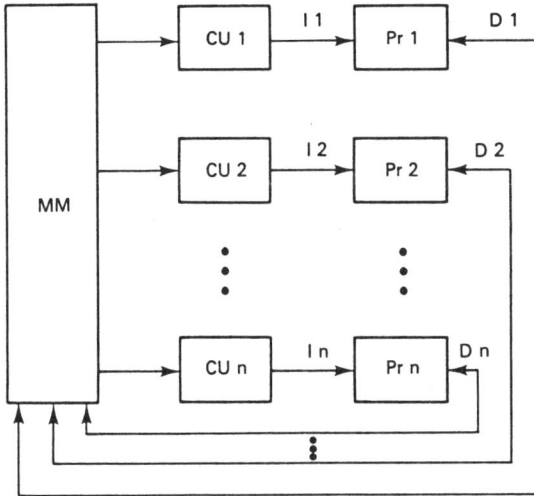

Fig. 15.2   MIMD

A widely accepted definition of multiprocessors is due to Enslow [Ensl 77]. According to Enslow, a multiprocessor must satisfy the following four properties:

1. It must contain two or more processors of approximately comparable capabilities.
2. All processors share access to a common memory. This does not preclude the existence of local memories for each or some of the processors.
3. All processors share access to a set of I/O resources. Some processors may own their own I/O devices.
4. The entire system is controlled by one operating system (OS).

A multiprocessor conforming to Enslow's definition, illustrated in Fig. 15.3, is sometimes called a *tightly coupled multiprocessor*. A *loosely coupled multiprocessor*, illustrated in Fig. 15.4, would tend to have much less shared and more local memories and I/O resources. Furthermore, a loosely coupled multiprocessor is more likely to have additional OS environments at each individual processor. A loosely coupled multiprocessor could sometimes be regarded as a computer network. If there is also a physical distribution of the processors, such a system can also be called a *distributed system*. In a distributed system, each processor may have its own autonomous OS. There exists, however, a high-level OS that unifies and integrates the control of the distributed processors. Since the overall system memory is distributed among multiple processors in loosely coupled systems, such systems may also be called *distributed memory systems*.

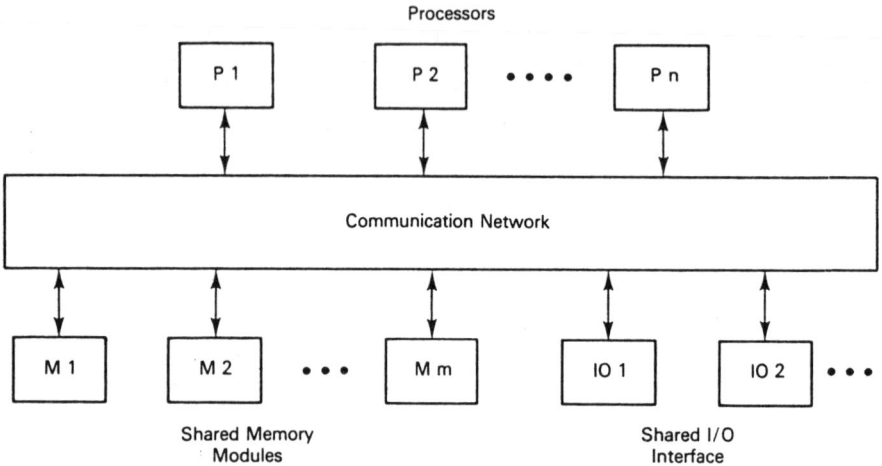

Fig. 15.3   Tightly coupled multiprocessor

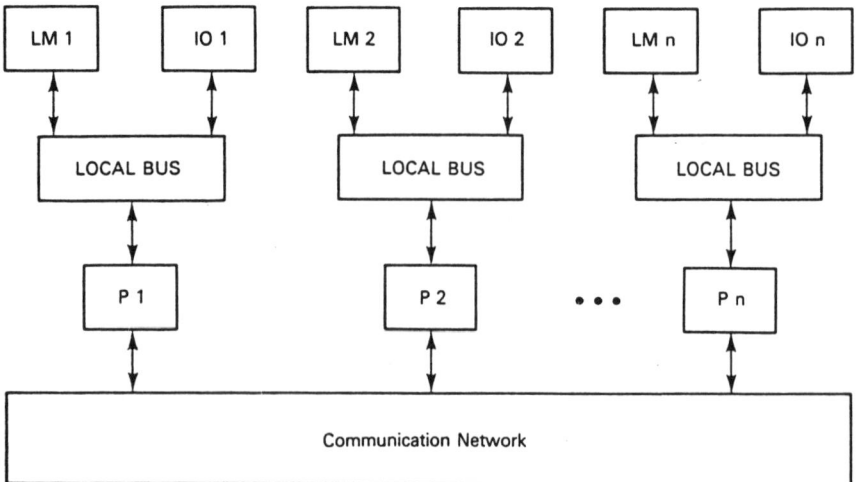

Fig. 15.4   Loosely coupled multiprocessor

As can be seen in Figs. 15.3 and 15.4, all processors and other resources of a multiprocessor are connected through a communication network. Its importance cannot be overemphasized. If parts of a large program are executed on different processors in a multiprocessor, there is always a need to communicate intermediate results between different parts of the program, allocated to different processors. There is also a need to coordinate between the operations in the different processors and synchronize them. Some operations on a certain processor may not begin until results attained at another processor arrive and become available. The transmission of intermediate results and synchronization signals is done via the communication network. The speed of transmission over this network, and possible delays incurred in it, are no less crucial than the speed of computation in the individual processors. If the communication network is inefficient with extensive delays, processors may be halted waiting for intermediate results. A case may be envisaged where a uniprocessor may perform better than a multiprocessor with an inefficient and slow communication network. For this reason, it is equally important to invest in the design of an efficient communication network in a multiprocessor, as it is to invest in the design of individual fast processors; both are equally important.

One of the most widely used communication networks in existing multiprocessors is the bus. All processors and other system resources are connected to the same bus over which all signals and data are transmitted. The reason for the bus popularity is its relative simplicity and low cost of realization. Subsystems may be easily added to or removed from the system. The problem with the bus is that only two devices at a time can establish communication over it (unless one device transmits information to several other devices simultaneously), thus creating a bottleneck. Therefore a bus-oriented system is a practical solution for multiprocessors with a relatively small number of processors (say up to 20 to 30). It is not an acceptable solution for massively parallel processors (MPP) with several hundred or more processors. A solution alleviating to some extent the bus bottleneck problem is the use of multiple buses in a system. In this case, if we have n buses, n pairs of devices at a time can communicate in principle. However, each device will have to be endowed with n ports of communication in order to sustain such an operation. Multiport systems are much more expensive. For this reason, a practical value for n would be about two to four in multibus systems.

An alternative communication network that became quite popular in the past decade is the *hypercube* [Hwan 93, Tabk 90]. The hypercube has $N = 2^n$ processor *nodes*, interconnected as n-dimensional binary cube. Each node contains a processor, local memory, I/O interface, and other auxiliary devices. Each node of an n-dimensional hypercube, or simply an *n-cube*, has a separate direct communication path to n other nodes. These paths correspond to the *edges*, or channels, of the hypercube. There are 2^n distinct n-bit binary addresses assigned to the nodes. Adjacent node addresses differ from each other in a single bit position. Hypercubes of the order zero to five (with $2^5 = 32$ nodes) are illustrated in Fig. 15.5. As can be seen, a zero-cube is just a single node, a one-cube is composed of two nodes connected by a single edge, a two-cube is a four-node square, and a three-cube is an eight-node cube with 12 edges.

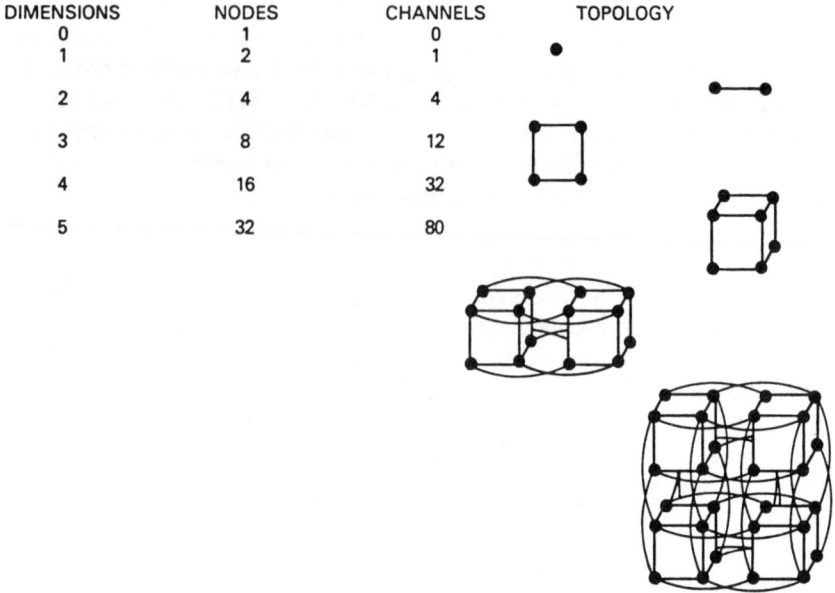

DIMENSIONS	NODES	CHANNELS	TOPOLOGY
0	1	0	
1	2	1	
2	4	4	
3	8	12	
4	16	32	
5	32	80	

Fig. 15.5   The hypercube topology *(Courtesy of Intel Corporation)*

The overall system memory is distributed among the nodes. Thus, the hypercube is an example of a distributed memory system. It also belongs to the loosely coupled category. Since many nodes can communicate between themselves simultaneously, there is much less of a bottleneck problem. On the other hand, the special hypercube structure may fit some classes of problem, but may at the same time be less efficient for others.

A multiprocessor communication network with the least possibility of developing bottleneck problems is the *crossbar*, illustrated in Fig. 15.6. If the total number of memory modules and I/O resources is no less than the number of processors, there is the possibility of concurrent communication between each processor and one of the memory modules or I/O resources. A bottleneck and a queue may arise only if several processors are attempting to access simultaneously the same memory module or the same I/O resource. The information in a crossbar network is routed through *crossbar switches* (CS) located at the intersection of each crossbar horizontal and vertical bus. A CS contains multiplexing and arbitration logic networks. If more than one processor attempts to access the same memory module, a priority queue can be established by the arbitration network. The main advantage of a crossbar network is its potential of high throughput by multiple concurrent communication paths. Its main disadvantage is an exceedingly high cost and hardware complexity. Assuming an n×n crossbar, we have n^2 CS units. Thus, the cost of an n-dimensional crossbar network is proportional to n^2.

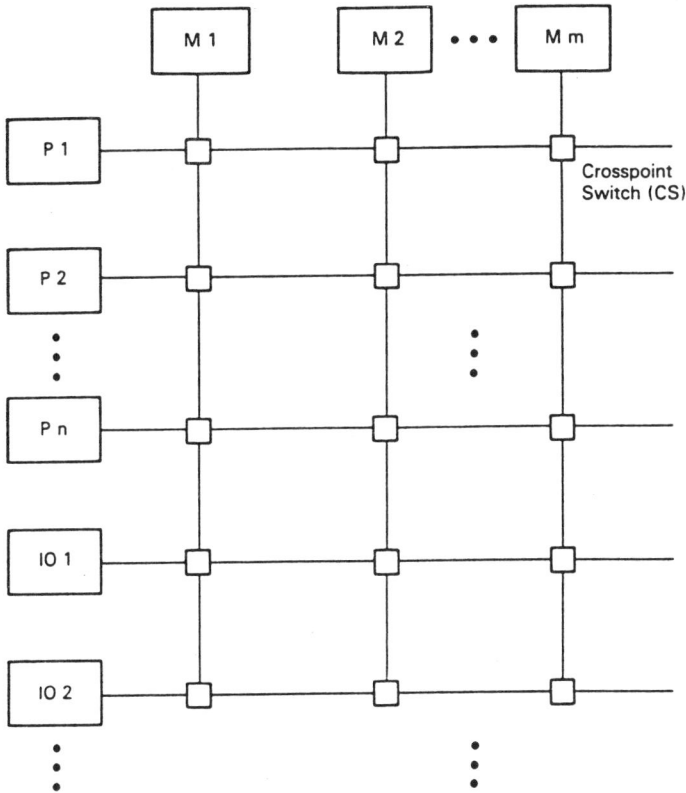

Fig. 15.6   Crossbar switch multiprocessor

A more general representation for multiprocessor communication networks is the *multistage network* or the *generalized cube network* [Sieg 90]. It is shown in [Sieg 90] that various types of multistage network, such as 'omega' or 'banyan', are equivalent to particular cases of the generalized cube network. A basic component of a multistage network is the two-input, two-output *interchange box*, illustrated in Fig. 15.7. The two inputs and outputs are labelled '0' and '1'. There are two control signals, associated with the interchange box, C0 and C1, which establish the interconnection between the input and output terminals as shown in Fig. 15.7.

A general multistage network has N inputs and N outputs. A generalized cube network is composed of m stages, where $N = 2^m$. Each stage has $N/2$ interchange boxes. An example of such a network for $N = 8$, $m = 3$, is shown in Fig. 15.8. The eight input and output links are labelled 0 to 7. Stage i (i = 0, 1, 2) of this network contains the cube i interconnection function for each pair of input labels of

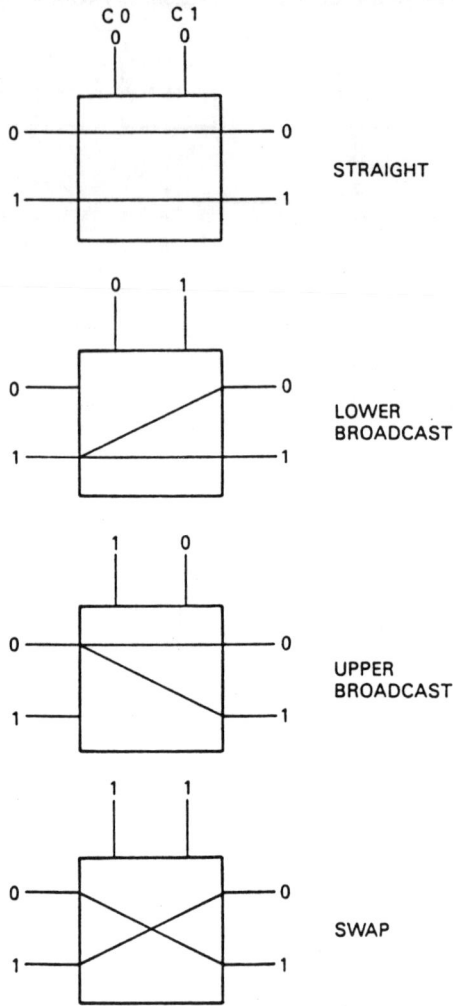

Fig. 15.7   Interchange box states

each interchange box. If the binary representation of any link label is:

$$L = b_{m-1} \ldots b_1 b_0$$

then the cube i interconnection function is defined:

$$\text{cube } i \, L = \text{cube } i(b_{m-1} \ldots b_1 b_0) = b_{m-1} \ldots b_{i+1} b_i' b_{i-1} \ldots b_1 b_0; \quad i = 0, 1, \ldots, m-1$$

where b_i' is the logic complement of b_i. In other words, the cube i interconnection function associates link L to link cube i(L), where cube i(L) is the link whose label differs from L in just the i-th bit position.

Example: In the system shown in Fig. 15.8, the following links are paired in stage $i = 2$:

0 000	1 001	2 010	3 011
4 100	5 101	6 110	7 111

in stage $i = 1$:

0 000	1 001	4 100	5 101
2 010	3 011	6 110	7 111

in stage $i = 0$:

0 000	2 010	4 100	6 110
1 001	3 011	5 101	7 111

The cube i definition corresponds to the earlier definition of a hypercube, where the labels of two adjacent nodes differ in just one bit.

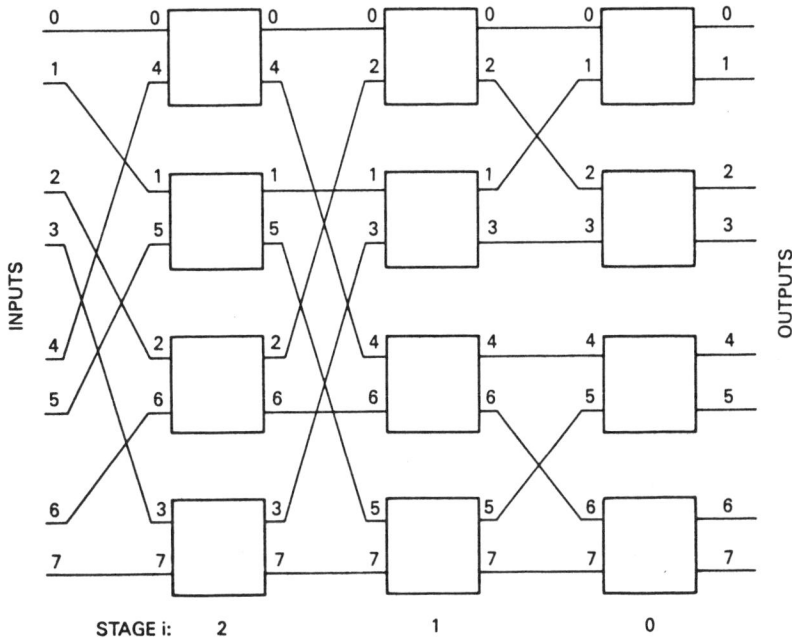

Fig. 15.8   Three-stage generalized cube network

In a multiprocessor system, the inputs and outputs of a multistage network can be connected to all of the processors (one input and one output to each processor), permitting direct intercommunication between them. When the number of processors N increases, the number of stages increases as $\log_2 N$, while the number of interchange boxes per stage is $N/2$. Thus, the total number of interchange boxes is $(N/2)\log_2 N$. Let us recall that, if the N processors are connected by a crossbar, the number of crosspoint switches is N^2. The multistage network is an economic alternative to the crossbar.

An interconnection network that recently became popular is the torus network, illustrated in Fig. 15.9. Its advantage is that it permits concurrent interconnection for data transmission between many pairs of nodes. It also has a high fault tolerance; if a node becomes faulty, it can easily be bypassed through other nodes. A natural extension of a two-dimensional torus, shown in Fig. 15.9, is a three-dimensional torus, used in the new CRAY T3D, described in the next section. The three-dimensional torus structure yields greater flexibility in signal routing in a multiprocessor system.

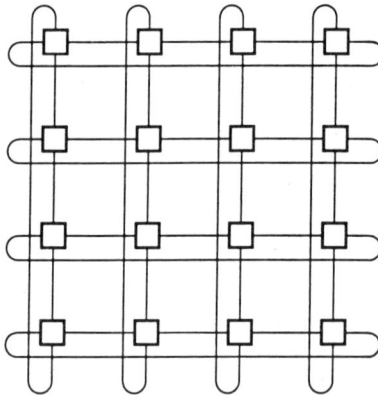

Fig. 15.9   Torus network

As stated earlier in this section, the quality of the interconnection networks in a multiprocessor is as important as the quality of its individual processors. RISC-type processors are particularly suited for implementation in multiprocessors because of their high performance and fast response in context switching. Indeed, many manufacturers of multiprocessors, who in the past used CISC or their own custom-made individual processors, are now switching to the use of off-the-shelf high-performance RISC-type processors. A notable example is the CRAY massively parallel processor T3D [Adms 94]. While CRAY used its own CPUs in its former multiprocessors, it will be using the RISC DEC Alpha AXP (see chapter 6) processors in its T3D. The CRAY T3D will serve as a major example of a RISC-based multiprocessor, and it will be described in detail in the next section.

Other RISC-based multiprocessor examples will be given in a subsequent section. Even though some of the manufacturers have gone out of business (such as Thinking Machines and Alliant), their products can still serve as interesting examples of multiprocessors.

15.2 The CRAY T3D Massively Parallel Processor

The CRAY T3D massively parallel processor is a large-scale distributed memory system, interconnected by a three-dimensional torus network [Adms 94]. Its primary components are processing element (PE) nodes, an interconnect network, and I/O gateways. A simplified diagram of the CRAY T3D system, illustrating its main components, is shown in Fig. 15.10. All applications programmed for the CRAY T3D system are compiled on a host system, which may by any Cray Research computer system that has an I/O subsystem model E (IOS-E), such as a CRAY C90 system.

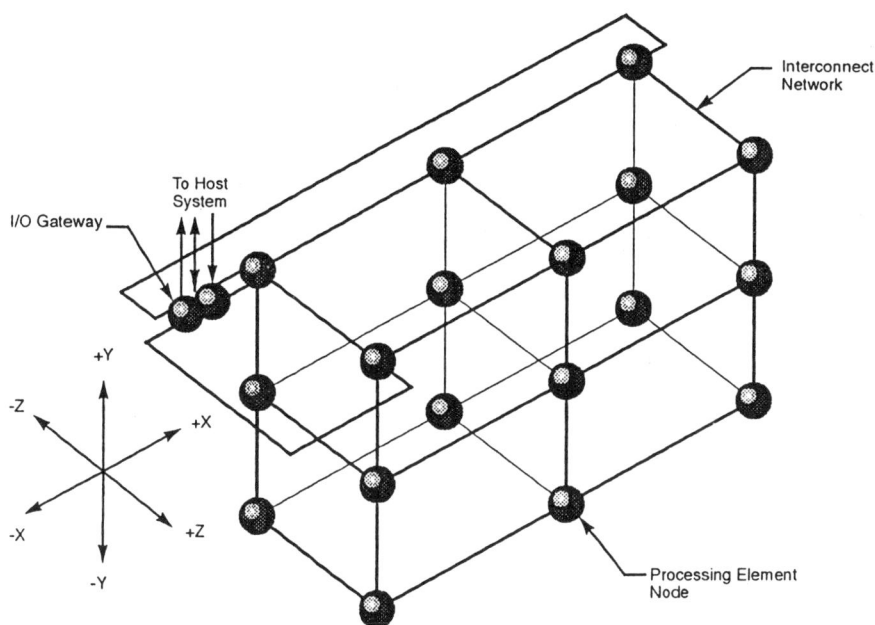

Fig. 15.10   CRAY T3D system components *(Courtesy of Cray Research, Inc.)*

Interconnect network

The CRAY T3D interconnect network provides communication paths among the PE nodes and the I/O gateways. It forms a three-dimensional matrix of paths that connect the nodes in the positive and negative X, Y, and Z directions (or dimensions), as shown in Fig. 15.10. The interconnect network is composed of communication links and network routers. Fig. 15.11 illustrates the interconnection of a PE node with the components of the interconnect network. A communication link transfers data and control information between two network routers. Each network router connects to a PE node or an I/O gateway node. Each communication link connects two nodes in one dimension.

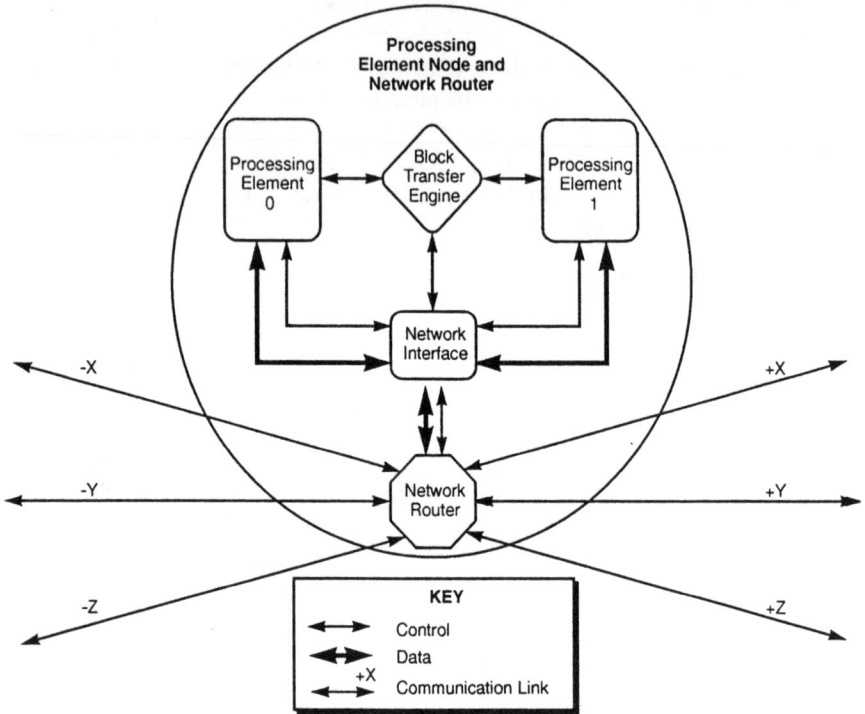

Fig. 15.11   Interconnect network components *(Courtesy of Cray Research, Inc.)*

A communication link consists of two unidirectional channels. Each channel contains data, control, and acknowledge signals, as shown in Fig. 15.12. There are 16 data lines in each channel. Data signals carry two types of information: *requests* or *responses*. Requests contain information that requests a node to perform an activity. For instance, a source node may send a request to a destination node to read data from local memory in the destination node. This request is sent over one channel in the communication link. Responses contain information that is the result of an activity. For instance, after receiving a request for read data, a destination node sends the response back to the source node over the other channel in the communication link. Requests and responses must be logically separated. This is done by providing separate buffers for requests and responses [Adms 94].

The *channel control* signals are controlled by the node sending information over the link. They are used to identify the transmitted information as a request or

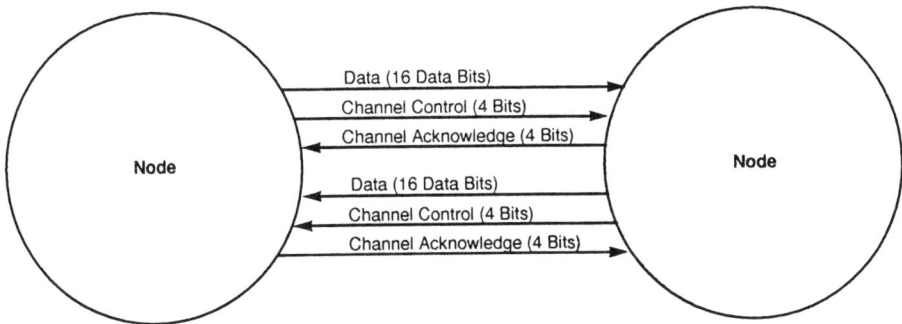

Fig. 15.12   Communication link channel signals *(Courtesy of Cray Research, Inc.)*

a response, and to identify which channel buffer in the receiving node will store the information. The *channel acknowledge* signals are controlled by the node receiving the information. The receiving node uses these signals to notify the sending node that the channel buffers in the receiving node are empty.

When a node sends information to another node, the information may travel through several communication links in the network. After information leaves a node, it travels through the network in the X dimension first, then through the Y dimension, and finally through the Z dimension, arriving at the destination node. This method of information travel is called *dimension order routing*.

Example: Node A in Fig. 15.13 sends request information to node B. The information first travels over one link in the +X direction. Because the information does not need to travel any farther in the X dimension, it switches direction to the Y dimension. After travelling over one link in the +Y direction, the information switches to the Z dimension and travels over one link in the +Z direction. Thus, the request information arrives at node B. If node B in Fig. 15.14 sends response information to node A, the information travels over one link in the −X direction and then changes direction into the Y dimension. It further travels over one link in the −Y direction, and one link in the −Z direction, bringing the response to node A [Adms 94].

Because information can travel in either the positive or negative direction of a dimension, faulty communication links can be bypassed and avoided. For instance, if node A in Fig. 15.15 sends information to node B, the information is supposed to travel over one link in the +X direction and one link in the +Y direction (see Fig. 15.13). Suppose the link in the +Y direction is faulty. The information may be routed over two links in the −Y direction, coming up around the torus, as shown in Fig. 15.15. It can then arrive at node B after travelling over a single link in the +Z direction.

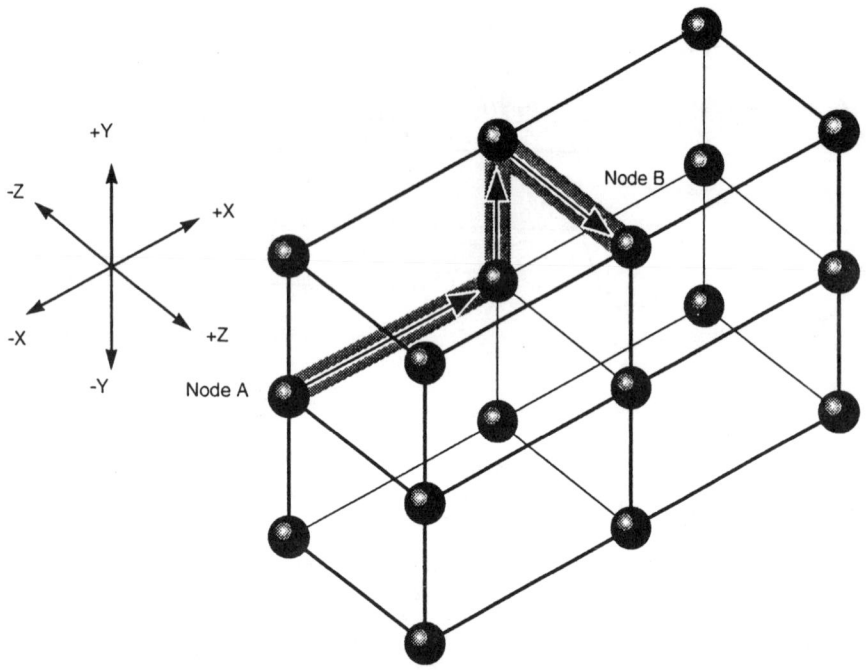

Fig. 15.13   +X, +Y, and +Z information travel *(Courtesy of Cray Research, Inc.)*

The CRAY T3D system uses virtual channels to prevent communication deadlock conditions. A *virtual channel* (VC) is created when request and response information travels over the same physical communication link but is stored in different buffers. The system contains four VC buffers:

VC	Task
0	Request buffer 0
1	Request buffer 1
2	Response buffer 0
3	Response buffer 1

Example: Fig. 15.16 shows four nodes in the X dimension. Each node is transferring request information to the node that is two links away in the +X direction. The dateline communication link is the communication link that connects nodes 1 and 2. The request information that is transferred from node 0 to node 2 and the request information that is transferred from node 1 to node 3 will at some time use the dateline communication link. Because of this characteristic, this

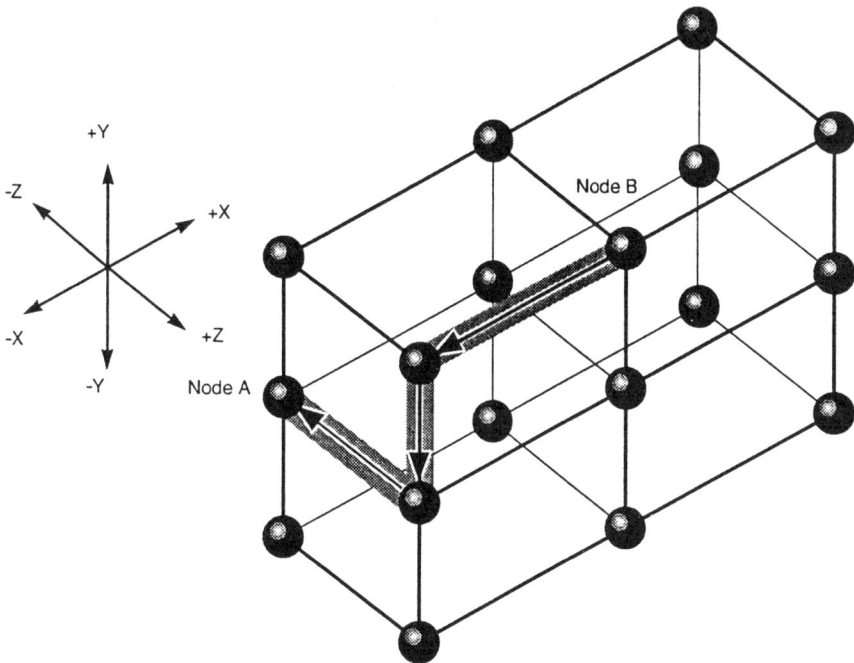

Fig. 15.14 –X, –Y, and –Z information travel *(Courtesy of Cray Research, Inc.)*

request information uses VC buffer 1 (request buffer 1). The request information that is transferred from node 2 to node 0 and the request information that is transferred from node 3 to node 1 will never use the dateline communication link. Because of this, this request information uses VC buffer 0 (request buffer 0).

Each VC buffer stores up to eight physical units (phits). Each phit contains 16 bits. A VC is reserved until all the phits of a packet have travelled through the VC buffer.

All information in the CRAY T3D system is transferred over communication links in the form of a *packet*. A packet contains two parts: a *header* and a *body*, as illustrated in Fig. 15.17 [Adms 94]. The header and body have variable lengths and are transferred over communication links one 16-bit phit at a time. Every packet contains a header. The header always contains routing information that steers the packet through the network, destination information that indicates which PE will receive the packet, and control information that instructs the destination PE to perform an operation. The header may also contain source information that indicates which PE created the packet and may contain memory address information.

When the network interface assembles a packet, it generates parity bits for the packet header information. Packet header information is checked for parity errors

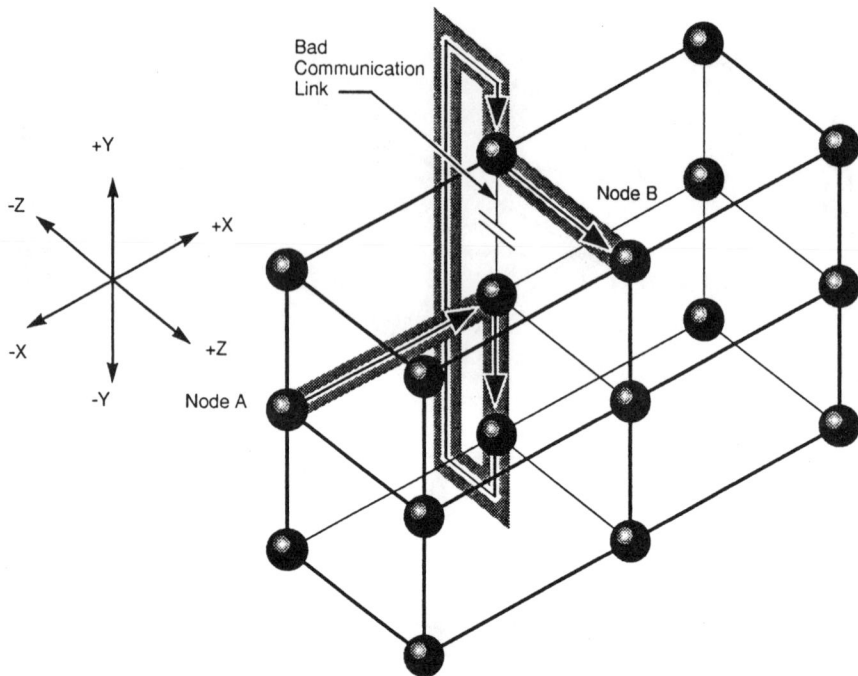

Fig. 15.15 Avoiding a faulty communication link *(Courtesy of Cray Research, Inc.)*

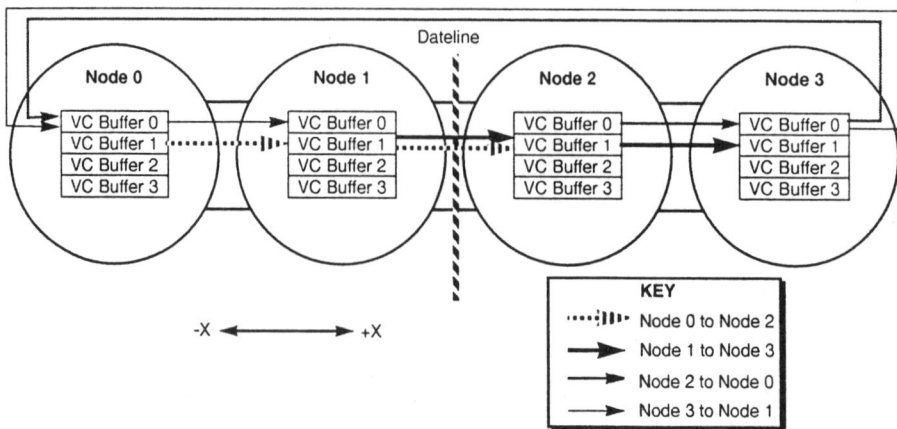

Fig. 15.16 Dateline communication link *(Courtesy of Cray Research, Inc.)*

each time the network interface receives a packet. A packet may or may not contain a body. The body of a packet contains one 64-bit word of data and 14 check bits of four 64-bit words of data and 56 check bits. Each processor uses the check bits to perform error detection and correction on the data that it receives.

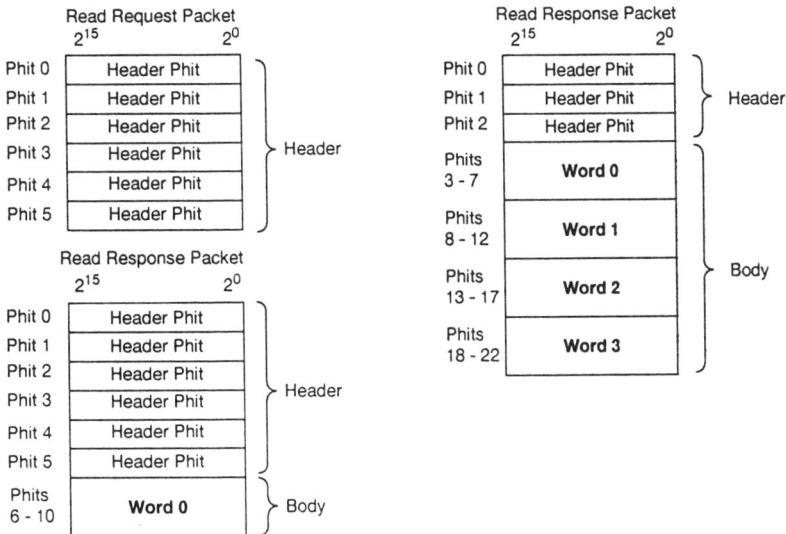

Fig. 15.17   Sample packet formats *(Courtesy of Cray Research, Inc.)*

The system *network routers* transfer packets of information through the communication links in the interconnect network. There are two types of network router:

1.   PE node network routers.
2.   I/O gateway network routers.

The PE node network routers contain three components: X, Y, and Z dimension switches. Fig. 15.18 illustrates the flow of packet information through a PE node network router. The X dimension switch controls the flow of packets through the X dimension communication links. Using the routing information in the packet and information received from the channel control signals, the X dimension switch steers packets from one X dimension communication link to the other, or from one X dimension communication link to the Y dimension switch. The Y and Z dimension switches function identically to the X dimension switch. The Y and Z dimension switches transfer packets over the Y and Z dimension communication links, respectively.

The I/O gateway network routers operate similarly to the PE node network routers; however, the I/O gateway network routers do not contain a Y dimension

342

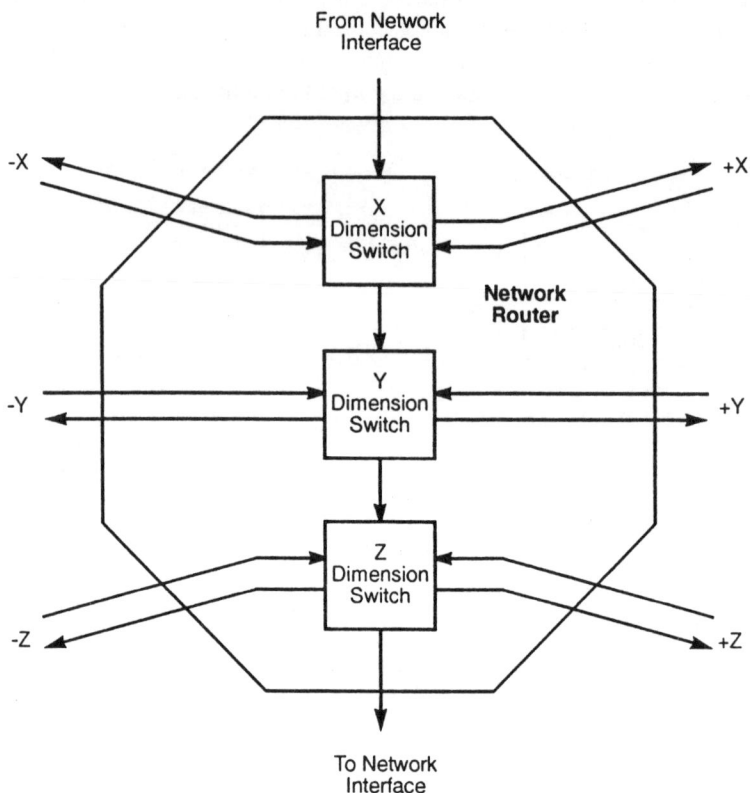

Fig. 15.18 PE node network routers *(Courtesy of Cray Research, Inc.)*

switch. Fig. 15.19 shows the components of the input node network router. The two network routers for an I/O gateway are connected to each other. The +X and +Z communication links from the input node network router connect to the output node network router. The –X and –Z communication links from the output node network router connect to the input node network router [Adms 94].

Processing element (PE) nodes
Processing element (PE) nodes perform all program instructions and store system data. Each PE node contains two PEs. More information on the structure of a PE is provided later in this section. Depending on the context, a PE is identified by one of three types of number:

1. Physical PE number.
2. Logical PE number.
3. Virtual PE number.

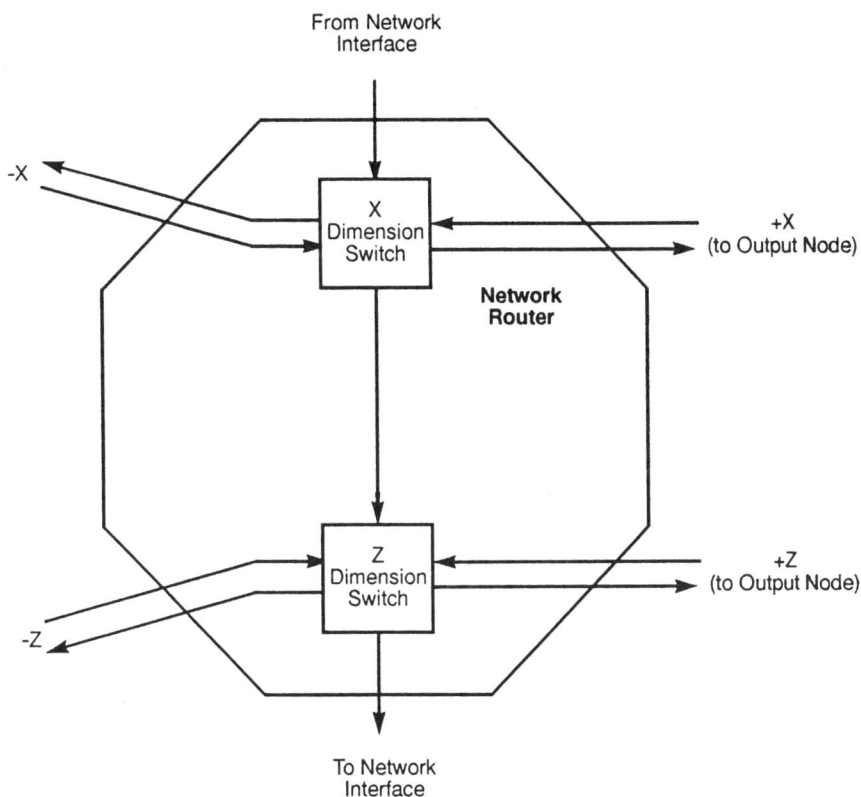

From Network
Interface

-X

X
Dimension
Switch

+X
(to Output Node)

**Network
Router**

Z
Dimension
Switch

+Z
(to Output Node)

-Z

To Network
Interface

Fig. 15.19   Input node network router *(Courtesy of Cray Research, Inc.)*

All three types of number consist of a PE bit, which identifies if the PE is PE 0 or PE 1 in a node (see Fig. 15.11), and a field containing the node number or node coordinates.

Every PE in the CRAY T3D system is assigned a unique number that indicates where the PE is physically located in a system. This number is the *physical PE number*. The support circuitry in each PE contains a register called the *physical PE register*. When a circuit board is placed in the system cabinet, hardware automatically sets the bits of the physical PE register to indicate where the PE is located in the cabinet [Adms 94].

Not all of the physical PEs in a CRAY T3D system are part of the logical system configuration. For instance, a 512-PE system contains 520 physical PEs (not including PEs in the I/O gateways). Of these 520 PEs, 512 PEs are used in the logical system and eight PEs (in four spare PE nodes) are used as spare PEs. Each physical PE used in a logical system is assigned a unique *logical PE number*. The logical PE number identifies where in the logical system of nodes a

PE is located. The logical nodes form a three-dimensional matrix of nodes.

Example: Fig. 15.20 shows the logical PE nodes for a 128-PE CRAY T3D system. Although the system actually contains 68 physical PE nodes, only 64 of the nodes, shown in Fig. 15.20, are used in the logical system. The remaining four spare physical nodes are physically connected to the interconnect network but are not given logical node numbers.

This type of configuration enables a spare node to logically replace a failing node. When this occurs, the spare node obtains a logical number and the failing node does not receive a new logical node number.

Example: If logical node $Z = 0$, $Y = 2$, $X = 3$ fails to operate properly, the physical node assigned to this number may be removed from the logical system. A spare node is then assigned the above logical node number, and the failing node does not receive a new number. Information is then rewritten into the routing tag look-up table of each node.

The *routing tag look-up table* contains information each node uses to create the routing tag in the header of a packet. Because the logical node number may correspond to any of the physical nodes, hardware in the nodes cannot use the logical node number to route data from one node to another. Each PE node uses a look-up table to obtain the routing tag. Circuitry in the node enters the logical node number into the routing tag look-up table. The routing tag look-up table then provides the routing tag for a packet, as illustrated in Fig. 15.21. The routing tag steers the packet from the physical source node to the physical destination node [Adms 94].

When an application is processed on a massively parallel processor (MPP), such as the CRAY T3D system, the support software running on the host system determines the resources needed for the application and creates a partition for the application to run in. A *partition* is a group of PEs and a portion of the barrier synchronization resources that are assigned to one application. The application uses *virtual PE numbers* to reference the PEs in the partition. There are two types of partition:

1. Operating system (OS) partition, when the application transfers data between PEs, involving the OS in the transfer. The OS converts the virtual PE numbers used by the application into logical PE numbers.
2. Hardware partition, when the application transfers data between PEs without involving the OS in the transfer. Hardware in each PE node converts the virtual PE numbers used by the application into logical PE numbers.

The virtual PE number contains two parts:

1. *Virtual node number*, which ranges from one to 10 bits and indicates which PE node in a hardware partition the PE resides in.

2. *PE bit*, which indicates if the PE is PE 0 or PE 1 in the node.

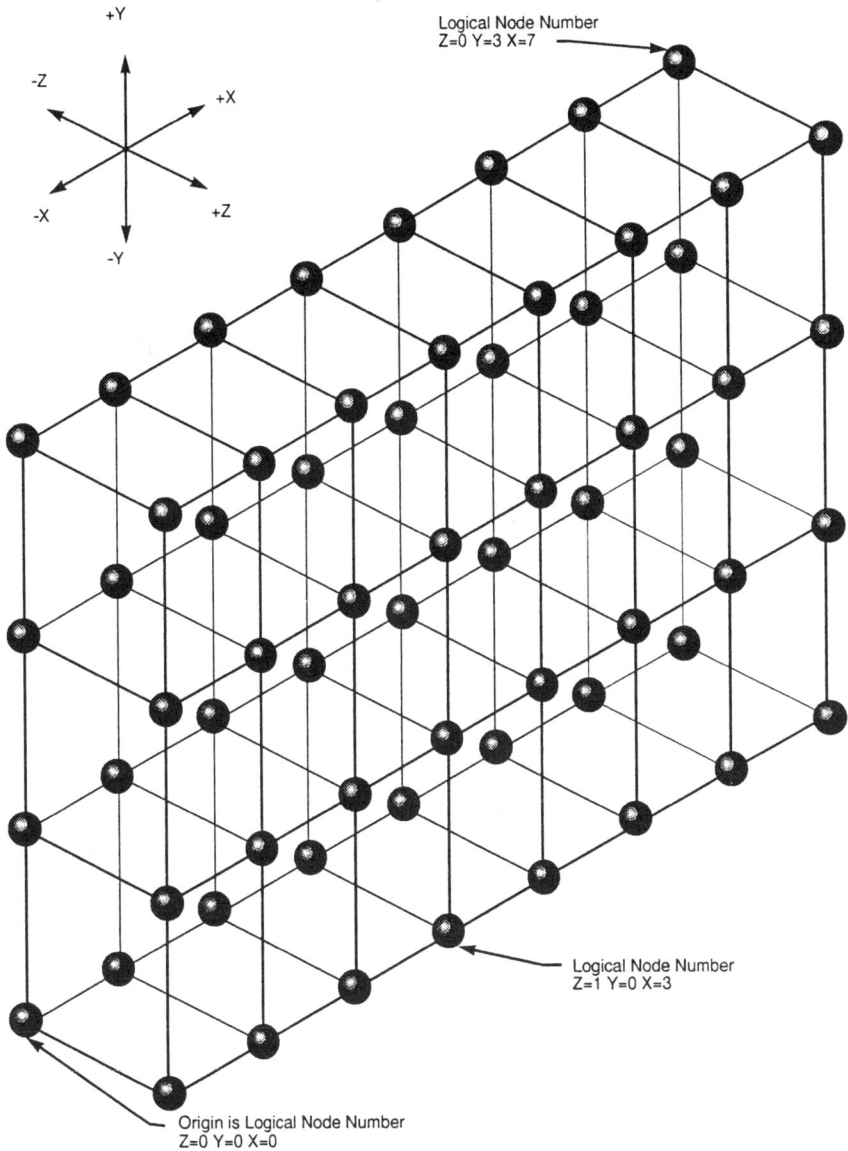

Fig. 15.20   Logical node numbers *(Courtesy of Cray Research, Inc.)*

The virtual node number has zero to three bits assigned to the X dimension, zero to four bits assigned to the Y dimension, and zero to three bits assigned to the Z dimension. By assigning bits of the virtual node number to the appropriate

Logical Node Number			Routing Tag		
X=0	Y=0	Z=0	ΔX=-1	ΔY=-1	ΔZ=-1
X=1	Y=1	Z=1	ΔX=0	ΔY=0	ΔZ=0
X=1	Y=2	Z=1	ΔX=0	ΔY=+1	ΔZ=0
X=1	Y=3	Z=1	ΔX=0	ΔY=+2	ΔZ=0
X=1	Y=4	Z=1	ΔX=0	ΔY=+3	ΔZ=0
X=1	Y=5	Z=1	ΔX=0	ΔY=+4	ΔZ=0

Destination Logical Node Number

X=1   Y=3   Z=1

Routing Tag

ΔX=0   ΔY=+2   ΔZ=0

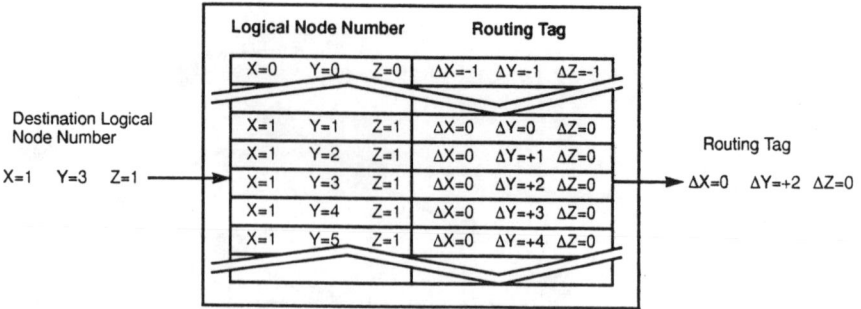

Fig. 15.21   Routing tag look-up table for logical node X = 1, Y = 1, Z = 1 *(Courtesy of Cray Research, Inc.)*

dimensions, software arranges the virtual nodes into one of several shapes.

Example: A three-bit virtual node number indicates that there are eight nodes in the hardware partition. These nodes may be arranged in one of 10 shapes. Table 15.1 lists the possible node shapes in this case. For each shape, the number of nodes in each dimension is limited to powers of two (1, 2, 4, 8, 16, and so on). Fig. 15.22 shows three of the eight-node partition shapes in a 128-PE CRAY T3D system. Continuing the example on virtual PE numbers, Fig. 15.23 shows a two-dimensional, eight-node partition. Each node in the partition is referred to by the three-bit virtual node numbers. This two-dimensional array of eight nodes may actually correspond to one of many eight-node two-dimensional arrays in the logical system. For instance, Fig. 15.24 shows two examples of how this two-dimensional array may be placed in the logical system of nodes in a 128-PE CRAY T3D system. A virtual node number does not always correspond to the same logical node number. For instance, Fig. 15.24 shows how virtual node $Y = 1$, $X = 2$ from Fig. 15.23 may correspond to either logical node number $Z = 1$, $Y = 2$, $X = 2$ or $Z = 1$, $Y = 3$, $X = 6$ [Adms 94].

Physically, each PE node resides on half of a circuit board in the system cabinet. Thus there are two PE nodes, or four processors (CPUs), per board. A functional block diagram of a PE node is shown in Fig. 15.25. Each PE node contains two PEs: PE 0 and PE 1. Each PE contains a processor (DEC Alpha AXP implementation; see chapter 6), local memory (DRAM), and support circuitry.

Memory

The CRAY T3D logically shared memory is physically distributed among the PE nodes of the system. It consists of the local memories of all PEs. Memory is logically shared because any processor can access information in the local memory of any PE without involving the processor in that PE. Fig. 15.26 illustrates the

Table 15.1 Eight-node Partition Shapes

Eight-node Array Shape in X, Y, Z	Description
8, 1, 1	One-dimensional array in the X dimension
1, 8, 1	One-dimensional array in the Y dimension
1, 1, 8	One-dimensional array in the Z dimension
1, 2, 4	Two-dimensional array in the Y-Z plane
1, 4, 2	Two-dimensional array in the Y-Z plane
2, 1, 4	Two-dimensional array in the X-Z plane
4, 1, 2	Two-dimensional array in the X-Z plane
2, 4, 1	Two-dimensional array in the X-Y plane
4, 2, 1	Two-dimensional array in the X-Y plane
2, 2, 2	Three-dimensional array

(Courtesy of Cray Research, Inc.)

physical distribution of memory in a 256-PE CRAY T3D system. Each local memory contains m 64-bit words. The size of the local memory depends on the type of the DRAM chips used in the system. The total size of shared memory is the product of m by the total number of PEs in the system. For instance, a system with m = 2 Mwords and 512 PEs has a total system shared (but distributed) memory of 1 Gword (or 8 Gbytes). The local memory size can be 2 Mwords for 4-Mbit DRAM chips, or 8 Mwords for 16-Mbit DRAM chips. Each processor uses memory addressing that references any word in shared memory. This address, the *virtual address*, is initially generated by the program compiler. The virtual address is converted into a logical node number, PE number, and address offset by the processor and other components in the PE node [Adms 94].

The PE support circuitry extends the control and addressing functions of the processor. These functions include the following tasks, to be discussed next:

Address interpretation.
Read and write operations.
Data prefetch.
Messaging.
Barrier synchronization.
Fetch and increment.
Status.

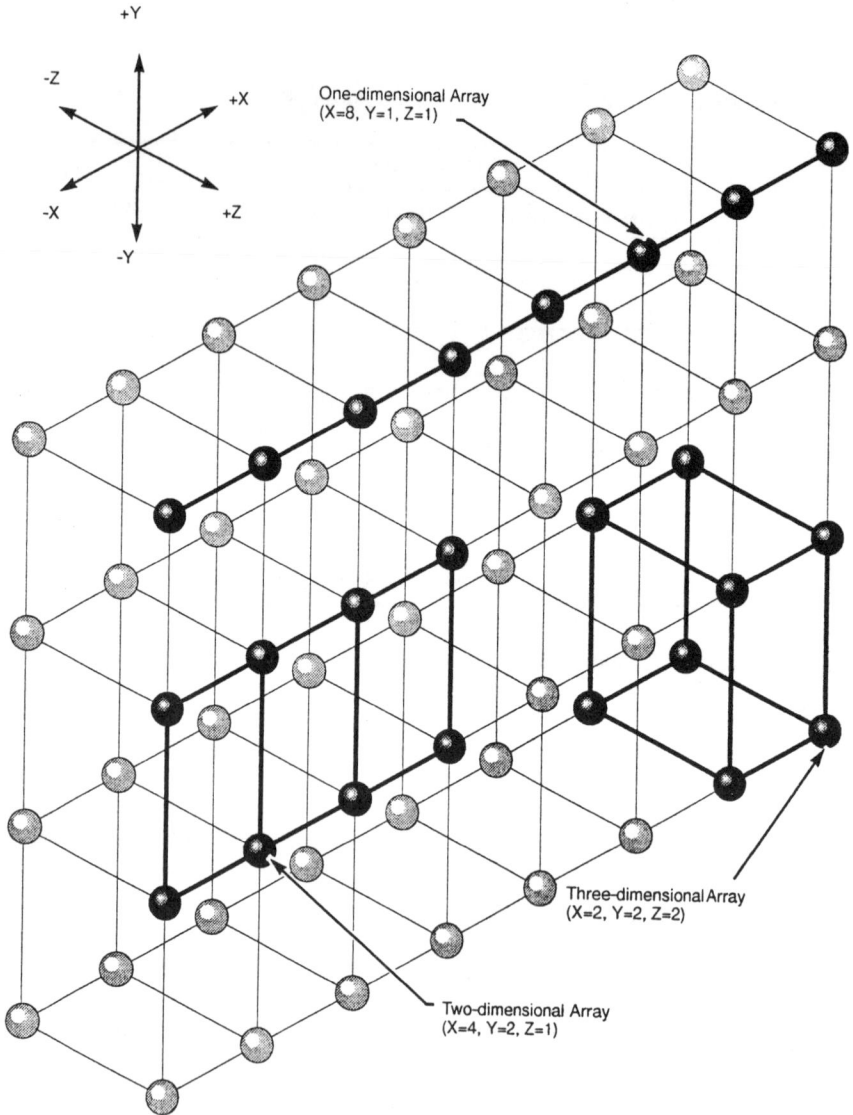

Fig. 15.22   Three eight-node partition shapes in a 128-PE CRAY T3D system *(Courtesy of Cray Research, Inc.)*

Address interpretation

The address output pins of the processor do not directly address physical memory. Instead, the support circuitry of the PE interprets the address and routes data

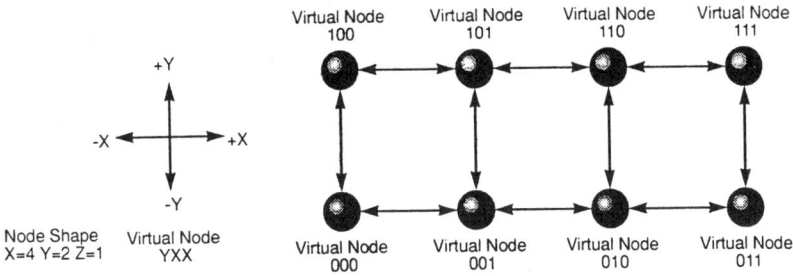

Fig. 15.23   Virtual node numbers of a two-dimensional array *(Courtesy of Cray Research, Inc.)*

between the processor and either local memory, memory-mapped registers, or memory in a remote PE. The support circuitry uses part of the address generated by the processor as an index into a 32-entry called the *data translation buffer (DTB) annex*. Each entry in the DTB annex contains a virtual or a logical PE number and a function code. The PE number is the number of the destination PE. The function code indicates what type of memory function (read, write, fetch-and-increment, message) the support circuitry will perform. The support circuitry compares the PE number received from the DTB annex with the number of the PE that contains the support circuitry. If they match, the processor is addressing local memory. If they do not match, the processor is addressing memory in another PE.

When the processor accesses local memory, the support circuitry uses the address from the processor as an address offset for data in local memory. The support circuitry then transfers data between the processor and local memory. When the processor accesses remote memory, the support circuitry sends the remote PE number along with the address offset and control information to the network interface for use in the header of a request packet. When the processor addresses a register in the support circuitry, the support circuitry routes the information to the appropriate register. In some cases, the support circuitry also performs a function related to the register [Adms 94].

Read and write operations
Read or load operations transfer data from memory into a CPU register. Information in the data cache may also be updated. After receiving address and cycle request information from the processor, the support circuitry retrieves a function code and PE number from an entry in the DTB annex. The value of the function code determines which read operation will be performed. There are two main types of read operation: noncacheable and cached. Cached read operations may be used to reduce delay of subsequent read operations from specified memory addresses. During noncacheable read operations, the support circuitry signals the processor not to update a line in the data cache. There are two types of noncacheable read operation:

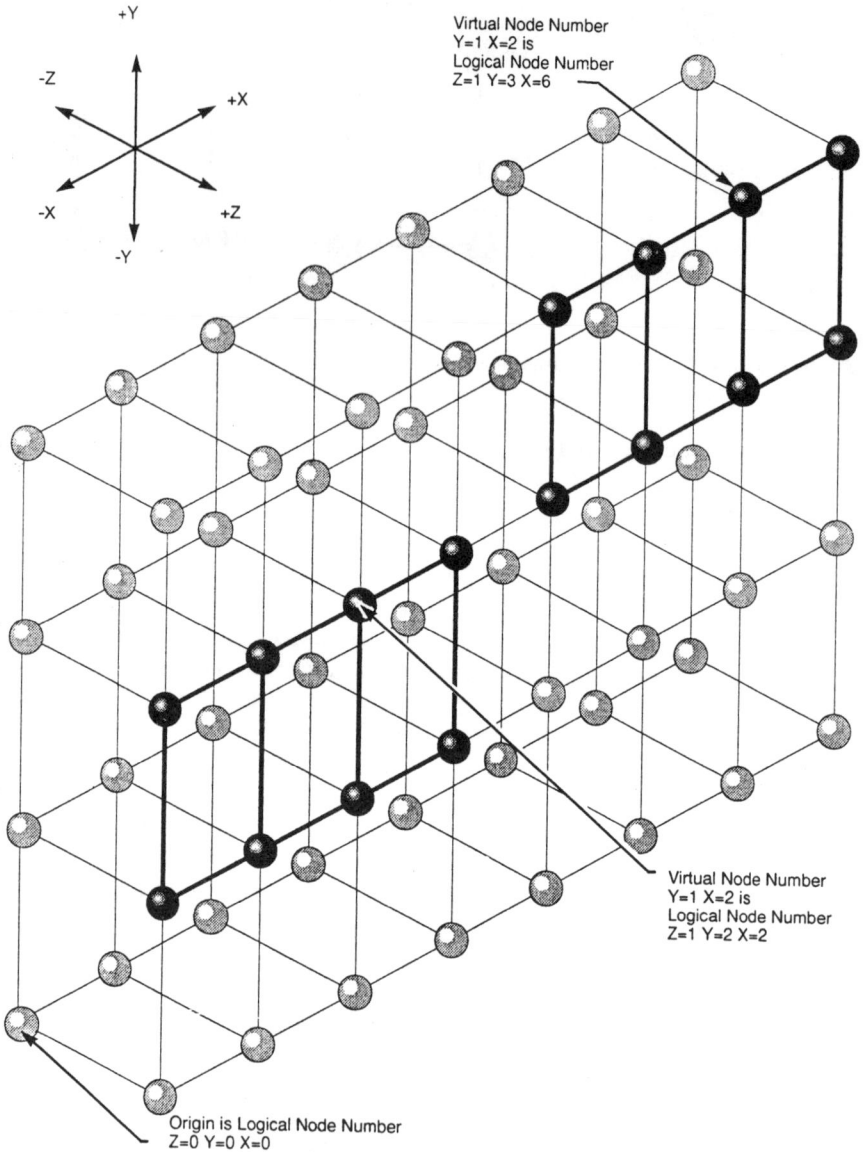

Fig. 15.24 Virtual and logical node numbers *(Courtesy of Cray Research, Inc.)*

1. Normal noncacheable read operations transfer data from memory to a CPU register without updating the data cache.

2. Noncacheable *atomic swap* read operations transfer a 64-bit word from memory to the CPU and then transfer another 64-bit word into the same memory location in an indivisible operation.

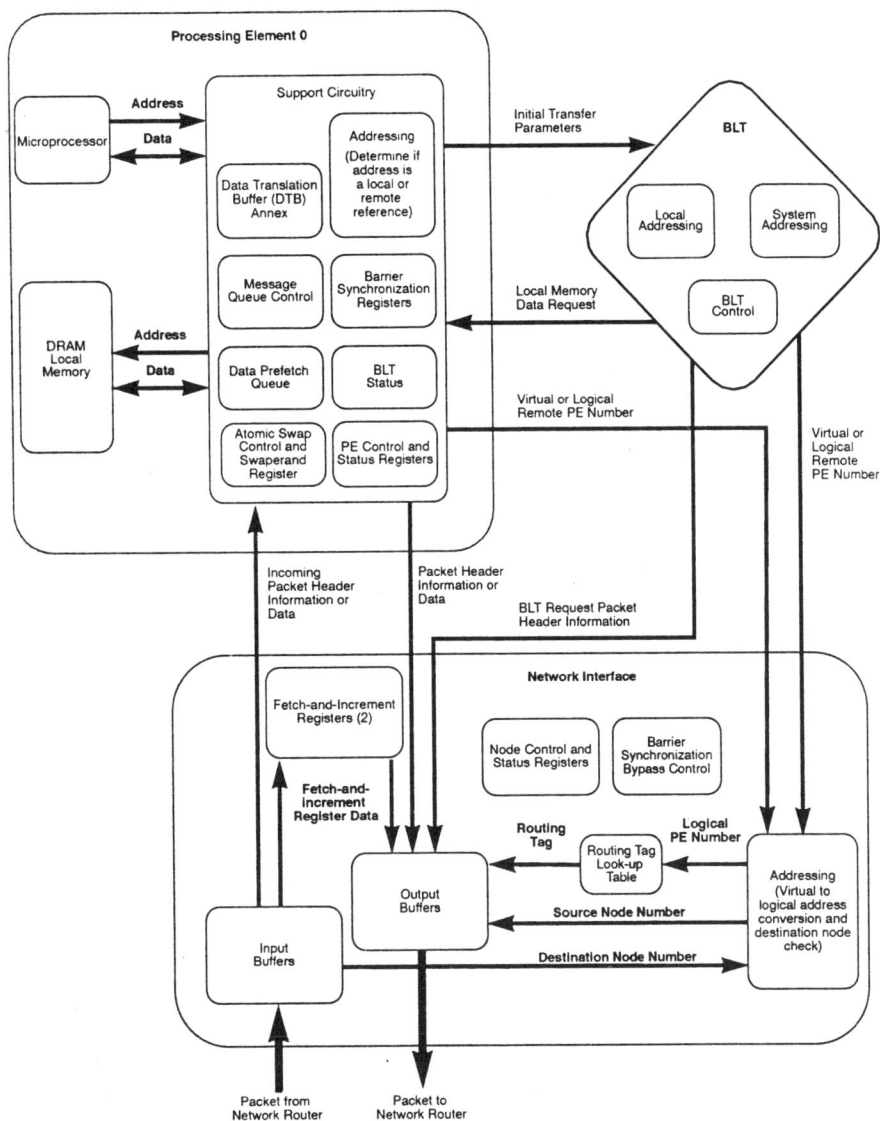

Fig. 15.25 PE node functional block diagram *(Courtesy of Cray Research, Inc.)*

Such operations are used in the handling of semaphores in multiprocessors [Hwan 93, Tabk 90]. Before initiating an atomic swap operation, the processor loads a 64-bit word into a register called the *swaperand register*, which is located in the

Local Memory in PE 0	Local Memory in PE 1	Local Memory in PE 2	Local Memory in PE 255
2^{63} — 2^0	2^{63} — 2^0	2^{63} — 2^0	2^{63} — 2^0
0 Data	0 Data	0 Data	0 Data
1 Data	1 Data	1 Data	1 Data
2 Data	2 Data	2 Data	2 Data
3 Data	3 Data	3 Data	3 Data
4 Data	4 Data	4 Data	4 Data
m-2 Data	m-2 Data	m-2 Data	m-2 Data
m-1 Data	m-1 Data	m-1 Data	m-1 Data

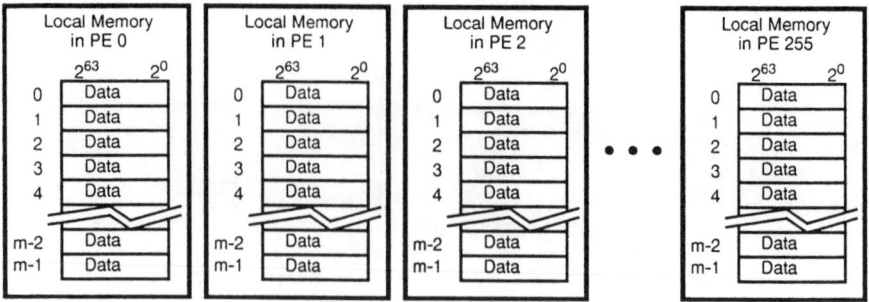

Fig. 15.26   Physical distribution of memory *(Courtesy of Cray Research, Inc.)*

support circuitry. During the atomic swap operation, the support circuitry transfers a word from memory to the CPU; then transfers the word from the swaperand register to the same memory location.

During cached read operations, the support circuitry signals the processor to update a line in the data cache. There are three types of cached read operation:

1. Normal cache read.
2. Cached atomic swap read.
3. Cached read ahead.

Normal cached read and cached atomic swap read operations operate the same as noncacheable normal read and noncacheable atomic swap read operations except that, when transferring data to the CPU, the support circuitry signals the processor to update a line in the data cache.

Cached read ahead operations are used to hide the delay of local memory read operations. The support circuitry contains a local memory read stage. After a cached read ahead operation has been performed, the local memory read stage buffers a four-word block of information (data or code) read from local memory. When the processor issues any type of cached or noncacheable read operation (except atomic swaps) with an address that matches the buffered block of data, data are transferred from the local memory read stage to the CPU. This action prevents the support circuitry from having to access memory to retrieve the block of data and decreases the delay for the read operation. Immediately after the support circuitry has sent the requested information to the CPU, it retrieves the next sequential block of information from local memory and places it in the local memory read stage. The buffered information remains stored until a memory-barrier instruction is issued or a read operation from a different local memory address occurs.

Write or store operations transfer data from the CPU to the memory. To initiate a write operation, the CPU provides the support circuitry with an address and with cycle request information. The processor may then continue issuing program instructions while the support circuitry completes the write operation. After receiving the address and cycle request information from the CPU, the support circuitry retrieves a function code and PE number from an entry in the DTB annex. The support circuitry then checks the value of the PE number read from the DTB annex. If the PE number is set to the local PE, the support circuitry writes up to four 64-bit words into local memory. If the PE number is set to a remote PE, the support circuitry creates a *write request packet* that contains up to four words of data and sends the request packet to the remote PE. After creating a write request packet, the support circuitry increments a counter (called the *outstanding write request counter*) that counts the number of write request packets created and sent to remote PEs. After receiving a write request packet, the support circuitry in the PE that requested the write operation decrements the outstanding write request counter. This action completes a write operation [Adms 94].

Data prefetch

When requested by the processor, the support circuitry performs a data prefetch operation. A data prefetch operation transfers one 64-bit word of data from memory in a remote PE to the *data prefetch queue* (see Fig. 15.25), which is located in the local PE support circuitry. The processor initiates a data prefetch operation when it encounters a *prefetch instruction* in a program. A programmer may place the prefetch instruction several instructions before the instruction that actually uses the prefetch data. This can be done by using the FETCH (prefetch data) or FETCH_M (prefetch data, modify intent) Alpha AXP architecture instructions, belonging to the miscellaneous type (see chapter 6, Table 6.10). When issuing the prefetch instruction, the processor signals the support circuitry that the next data transfer is a prefetch operation. After the processor has issued the prefetch instruction, the processor continues with other program instructions. For example, in order for software to issue a fetch-and-increment operation that will be stored in the prefetch queue, software issues a FETCH instruction with an address that points to the DTB annex entry with the function code set to indicate a fetch-and-increment function.

The support circuitry assembles information for a prefetch read request packet and sends the information to the remote PE over the interconnect network. After receiving the request packet, the support circuitry in the destination PE creates a prefetch read response packet that contains the word of data and indicates that the data are a prefetch response. The support circuitry in the remote PE then sends the response packet to the local PE over the interconnect network. The support circuitry of the local PE receives the prefetch response packet and stores the word of data in the data prefetch queue. When the processor issues the instruction that uses the data, the processor reads the data from the data prefetch queue instead of creating a read request packet and waiting for a response. The data prefetch queue stores a maximum of 16 words. The processor can issue up to 16 data prefetch instructions before reading the data out of the prefetch queue one word at a time [Adms 94].

Messaging

The messaging facility of the supporting circuitry transfers a special packet, called a message, from one PE to another. After receiving a message, the support circuitry interrupts the processor and places the message in a *message queue*, to be read by the processor. The message queue is located in a reserved portion of local memory. The message queue stores up to 4080 message packets and includes 16 reserved locations for a small amount of overflow (total of 256KB). The support circuitry places message packets in the message queue in the order that they are received.

To create a message, the processor fills one of its internal write buffer lines (by using an Alpha AXP store instruction; see chapter 6) with four words of data. The processor then transfers the data from the write buffer to the support circuitry. During the transfer, the processor also provides the support circuitry with an address and with cycle request information. The support circuitry then retrieves a function code and PE number from an entry in the DTB annex. The function code indicates that the support circuitry should perform a message write. The support circuitry then creates a message packet and sends it to the destination PE. For example, in order for software to issue a message send operation, a store instruction is issued with an address that points to the DTB annex entry with the function code set to indicate a message function.

After receiving the message packet, the support circuitry in the destination PE attempts to store the message in the message queue. If the message queue can accept the message, the support circuitry stores the message in the queue and sets the message hardware interrupt for the processor. A message acknowledge packet is then created and sent to the source PE. If the message queue at the destination is full and cannot accept the message, the support circuitry returns the message to the requesting PE by creating a no-acknowledge (NACK) packet. After receiving the NACK, the requesting PE can resend the message. Because of this feature, message delivery is guaranteed regardless of the amount of system message traffic.

In addition to message packets, the support circuitry may receive error messages and store them in the message queue. The network interface generates error messages if it receives a misrouted packet or if it receives a packet that contains parity errors. If a network error occurs, the network interface turns the packet it received into an error message and sends the error message to the appropriate PE in the node [Adms 94].

Barrier synchronization

There are two types of barrier synchronization operation on the CRAY T3D system: barriers and eurekas.

A *barrier* is a point in a program where a processor must wait until all other processors associated with the barrier have finished their part of the program instructions and communicated the results necessary for the processor to continue execution [Hwan 93, Tabk 90]. A programmer may use a barrier to ensure that all of the processors associated with a distributed, parallel loop in a program finish the instructions for the loop before continuing with other program instructions. The support circuitry in each PE contains two eight-bit registers called barrier register 0 and barrier register 1. Each bit in the barrier registers is connected to a separate barrier synchronization circuit handling the barrier synchronization operation.

Each of the barrier synchronization circuits may also be used for *eureka* synchronization. Eureka synchronization uses a point in program instructions where a processor is informed when the first processor associated with the eureka has finished its part in the program. Eureka synchronization has several uses, including database searches. Using eureka synchronization, a programmer can stop a database search as soon as any processor finds the data rather than waiting for all of the processors to exhaust the search [Adms 94].

Fetch and increment
The support circuitry also performs read or write operations to the fetch-and-increment registers. A fetch-and-increment register is a special register where, after reading information from a fetch-and-increment register, hardware in the PE node automatically increments the content of the register by one. Each PE node contains two 32-bit fetch-and-increment registers. The register size is large enough to contain a loop index value or an address offset value. These registers function independently of the PEs. Any PE may use any of the fetch-and-increment registers in a partition. These registers may be used to dynamically distribute independent iterations of a program loop to more than one processor.

Status
Each PE contains registers that indicate the status of PE operations. The status information includes error information and outstanding request information. The status information is used by the OS [Adms 94].

Block transfer engine (BLT)
The *block transfer engine* (BLT) is an asynchronous direct memory access (DMA) device that redistributes system data between globally addressable system memory and local memory in either of the PEs in a PE node (see Fig. 15.25). The BLT can create up to 65536 packets that contain one 64-bit word of data (or four 64-bit words) without interruption from the PE. The BLT performs four types of data transfer operation:

1. *Constant stride read* operation transfers data from fixed increment address locations in system memory to fixed increment address locations in local memory.
2. *Constant stride write* operation transfers the same type of data from local to system memory.
3. *Gather* operation transfers data from nonsequential memory locations in system memory to fixed increment address locations in local memory.
4. *Scatter* operation transfers data from fixed increment address locations in local memory to nonsequential address locations in system memory.

The BLT receives initial transfer parameters from one of the PEs in a PE node and then functions independently from the PEs. The BLT contains three main components (see Fig. 15.25):

1. System addressing portion of the BLT generates addresses that are used to reference a location in system memory (local or remote memory).
2. Local addressing portion of the BLT generates addresses that are used to reference location in the local PE. For instance, it may generate addresses that point to the location in local memory where data from a BLT read response packet will be stored.
3. Control portion of the BLT controls the BLT transfer. In addition, the control circuitry provides an interrupt to the PE when an error occurs, when the BLT is free to start a transfer, and when the BLT transfer is complete [Adms 94].

Network interface
The *network interface* (see Fig. 15.25) assembles outgoing request and response packets and steers incoming request and response packets to the correct PE in the node. The network interface also contains the fetch-and-increment registers and barrier synchronization bypass point control. When assembling an outgoing request or response packet, the network interface receives packet header information from PE 0, PE 1, or BLT. In addition, the network interface may receive data from a PE and receive a virtual or logical PE number from a PE or the BLT. If the PE number is a virtual PE number, the network interface converts it into a logical PE number. The network interface then converts the logical PE number into a routing tag that is used in the outgoing packet.

When receiving an incoming packet, the network interface checks the destination node number in the packet header. If the destination node number is the same as the number of the node that the network interface is in, the packet arrived in the correct node. The network interface then sends the packet to the destination PE. If the destination node number is incorrect, the network interface converts the packet into an error message and sends it to one of the PEs in the node [Adms 94].

I/O gateways
I/O gateways transfer system data and control information between the CRAY T3D system and the host system or the I/O cluster (IOC). The I/O gateways are connected to the interconnect network through network routers that have communication links in the X and Z dimensions only. The I/O gateways do not have connections in the Y dimension because the Y dimension connectors on an I/O gateway board were replaced with low-speed (LOSP) and high-speed (HISP) channel connectors. An I/O gateway can transfer information to any PE in the interconnect network. An I/O gateway contains an input node, an output node, and LOSP circuitry, as shown in Fig. 15.27.

The input node contains one PE, a network interface, a BLT, and HISP input

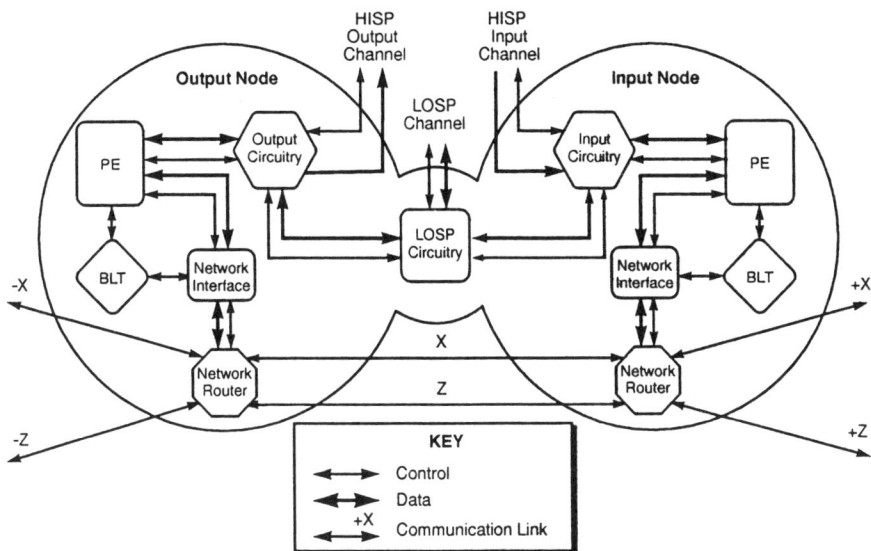

Fig. 15.27   I/O gateway *(Courtesy of Cray Research, Inc.)*

circuitry. The BLT and network interface in the input node are identical to the BLT and network interface used in the PE node. The PE in the input node is designed to interface with the HISP input circuitry. Thus, it does not contain the circuitry to perform all of the operations that a PE in a PE node performs. Instead, the circuitry is replaced with circuitry that interfaces with the HISP input circuitry. In addition, half of the local memory is replaced with HISP input circuitry that contains the HISP channel buffers. The HISP input circuitry receives incoming system data from the host system over the HISP channel. After receiving the data, the HISP input circuitry, PE, and BLT in the input node transfer the data to the destination PEs in the CRAY T3D system.

Except for HISP output circuitry replacing the HISP input circuitry, the output node is identical to the input node. The HISP output circuitry transmits outgoing system data to the host system over the HISP channel. After the PE and BLT in the output node have received data from source PEs in the CRAY T3D system, the HISP output circuitry transfers the data to the host system.

The LOSP circuitry transfers request and response information over the LOSP channel that connects the host and the CRAY T3D system. LOSP request and response information is used to control the transfer of system data over the HISP channel.

There are two types of I/O gateway: a master I/O gateway and a slave I/O gateway. The master gateway is the master component of a HISP channel and sends the address information to the host system during a HISP transfer. The slave gateway is the slave component of a HISP channel and receives the address information from the host system during a HISP transfer [Adms 94].

15.3 Other Examples of RISC-based Multiprocessors
Connection Machine CM-5

Connection Machine CM-5 is a scalable, distributed memory, RISC-based multiprocessor [CMT5 93, HiTu 93]. It is characterized by its creators as a coordinated homogeneous array of RISC multiprocessors, capable of supporting a wide range of applications and programming styles. Although the creator of CM-5, Thinking Machines, Inc., is out of business, the CM-5 can still serve as an interesting example of a RISC-based multiprocessor. The CM-5 coordination mechanisms are [HiTu 93]:

1. A low-delay, high-bandwidth communication mechanism that allows each processor to access data stored in memories of other processor nodes.
2. A fast global synchronization mechanism that allows the entire system, including the network, to be brought to a defined state at specific points in the course of a computation.

The CM-5 system, whose general diagram is shown in Fig. 15.28, consists of up to thousands of processing nodes (P), control processing nodes (CP), I/O control processing nodes (IOCP), I/O resources, interprocessor nodes data and control networks, and LAN and external I/O interfaces. The number of processors in systems currently installed ranges from 32 to 1024. Each processor accesses data stored in memories of remote nodes via the data network. One of the most important features of the CM-5 is its scalability. The current implementation, including networks, clocking, I/O system, and software, is designed to scale reliably up to 16384 processor nodes. The current CM-5 implementation uses a 32 to 40MHz SPARC (or SuperSPARC) microprocessor, with a 32MB memory per node. The CM-5 system software was designed to be largely processor-independent, so that the individual CPUs can be easily changed from implementation to implementation. A block diagram of a processor node, endowed with an additional four vector units (not all nodes have vector units), is shown in Fig. 15.29 [HiTu 93]. Besides the CPU, the processing node contains 32MB of memory, an interface to the control and data interconnection networks, and four independent vector units, each with a direct 64-bit path to an 8MB bank of memory.

A block diagram of a CM-5 control processor (CP) node is shown in Fig. 15.30. It consists of a SPARC CPU, memory, I/O (including local disks and Ethernet connections), and a CM-5 network interface, all connected to a standard 64-bit bus. Except for the network interface, this is a standard off-the-shelf workstation-class computer system. The network interface connects the CP to the rest of the system through the control and data networks. Each CP runs CMost, a UNIX-based OS with extensions for managing the parallel processing resources of

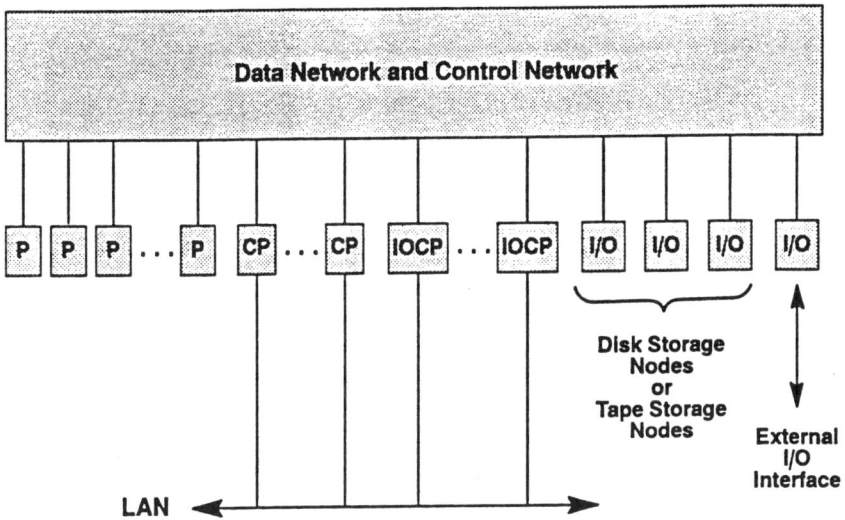

Fig. 15.28 CM-5 system components *(Courtesy of Thinking Machines, Inc.)*

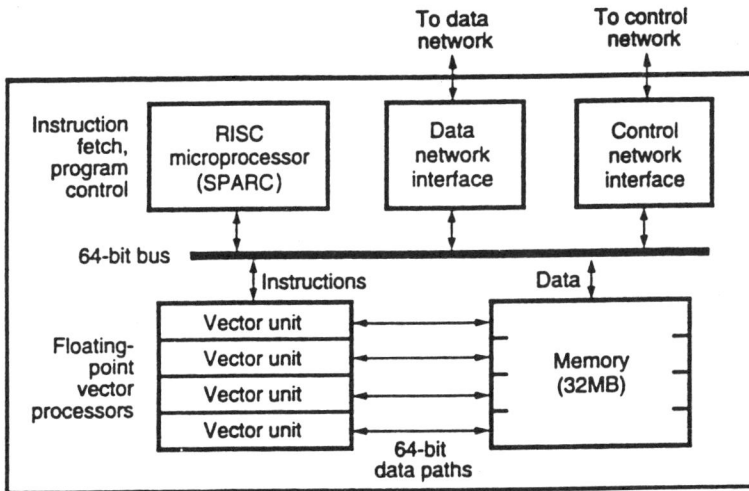

Fig. 15.29 CM-5 processor node *(Courtesy of Thinking Machines, Inc.)*

the CM-5. Some CPs are used to manage computational resources, and some are used to manage I/O resources [CMT5 93].

The CM-5 control network provides tightly-coupled communication services. It is optimized for fast response and low delay. Its functions include synchronizing the processing nodes, broadcasting a single value to every node, combining a value

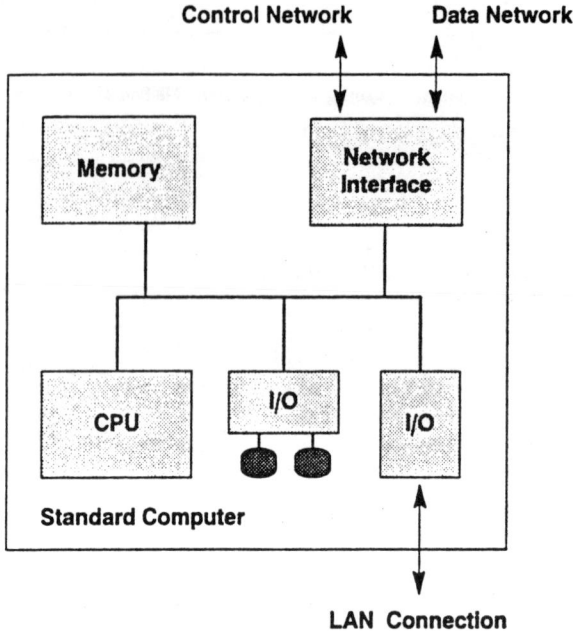

Fig. 15.30   Control processor *(Courtesy of Thinking Machines, Inc.)*

from every node to produce a single result, and computing certain parallel prefix operations. The data network provides loosely-coupled communication services. It is optimised for high bandwidth and good price/performance at any machine size. Its basic function is to provide point-to-point data delivery for tens of thousands of items simultaneously. Communication requests and data delivery need not be synchronized. Once the data network has accepted a message, it takes on all responsibility for its eventual delivery; the sending processor can then perform other computations while the message is in transit. Recipients may poll for messages or be notified by interrupt on arrival. The data network also transmits data between the processing nodes and I/O units [CMT5 93].

A CM-5 vector unit (VU), whose block diagram is shown in Fig. 15.31, is a memory controller and computational engine controller by a memory-mapped control register interface. VUs cannot fetch their own instructions; they merely react to instructions issued to them by the processor. The instruction format, instruction set, and maximum vector length have been chosen so that the processor can keep the vector units busy while having time of its own to fetch instructions (both its own and those for the VUs), calculate addresses, execute loop and branch instructions, and carry out other tasks. Each VU has 64 64-bit registers, which can also be addressed as 128 32-bit registers [CMT5 93].

The CM-5 data network is a fat tree, as illustrated in Fig. 15.32. The fat-tree structure has a number of advantages over the hypercube and two-dimensional mesh

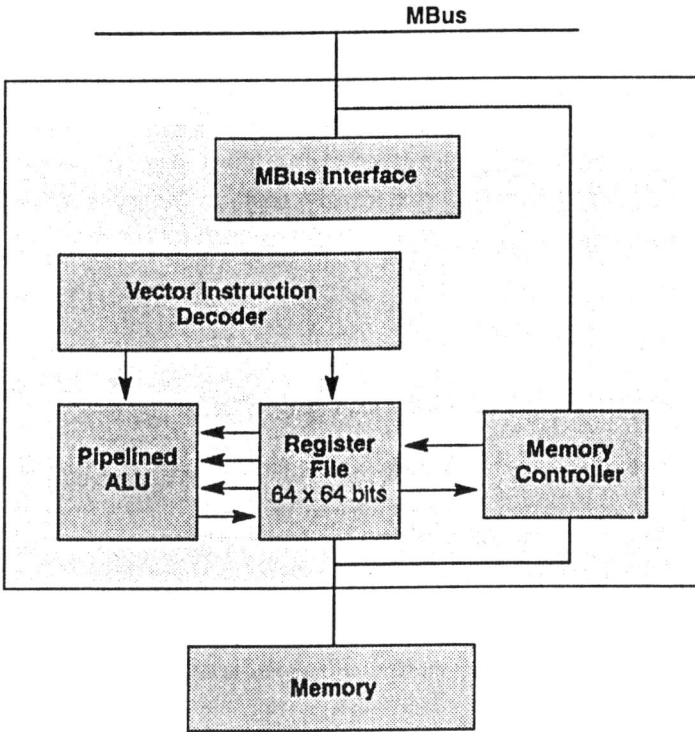

Fig. 15.31   Vector unit functional architecture *(Courtesy of Thinking Machines, Inc.)*

used in other systems. Like the mesh and hypercube, it can be divided into smaller pieces of the same topology. Traffic between two partitions in a fat tree does not interfere with traffic internal to a third partition, as may happen in a hypercube or a mesh [CMT5 93].

Intel Paragon XP/S

The Intel Paragon XP/S is an i860XP-based (see chapter 10) multiprocessor. It may contain over 2000 heterogeneous processor nodes, connected in a two-dimensional mesh, as illustrated in Fig. 15.33 [IntP 94]. The system is composed of general-purpose (GP) nodes which may serve three purposes: as a compute node executing the user applications, as an I/O node with an appropriate interface module plugged into the expansion port of the GP node, and as a service node executing user shell processes. The GP node, shown in Fig. 15.34, has one i860XP application processor dedicated to user processing, and a second i860XP processor dedicated to message passing operations. The node expansion port allows the GP

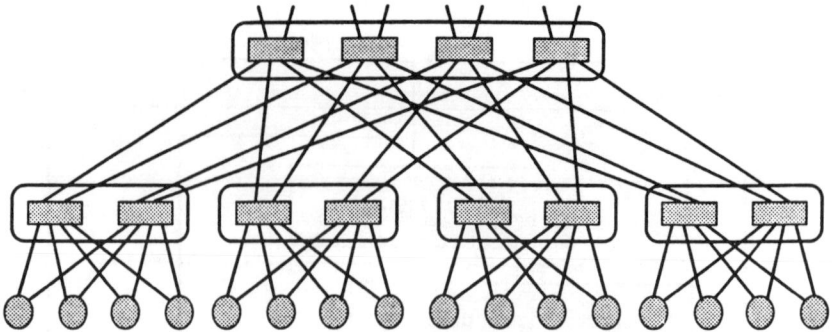

Fig. 15.32 CM-5 fat tree *(Courtesy of Thinking Machines, Inc.)*

nodes to serve for I/O or interactive use. GP nodes can be configured with 32, 96, or 160MB of high-speed DRAM.

When an application decides to send a message, the node's message processor handles message protocol processing and frees the application processor for numeric computing. Messaging software is executed from the message processor's internal cache (16KB code, 16KB data; see chapter 10), enabling overlapped communication and application processing to occur without incurring expensive context switching delays. The message processor is also used to implement efficient global operations such as synchronization and broadcasting [IntP 94].

All of the Paragon nodes utilize the same baseboard, referred to as the GP node board. When a GP node board is configured as an I/O node, an I/O interface is attached to the expansion port on the board and the appropriate software for the interface is downloaded when the system is booted. Supported I/O interfaces for the GP node include:

1. A multifunction I/O daughter card to support small computer system interface (SCSI) and Ethernet interfaces.
2. A high-performance parallel interface (HiPPI), for peak transfer rates of 80 to 100 MB/sec (full duplex) to stand-alone disk arrays, HiPPI switches, HiPPI graphics frame buffers, and other computer systems.

The Paragon OS is Intel's implementation of the open software foundation (OSF) OSF/1 Release 1.1 OS. It is an advanced microkernel architecture based on OSF/1 version 1.1, OSF/1 AD version 1.1, and Carnegie Mellon University Mach 3.0 kernel design, with components from Berkeley software distribution (BSD) release 4.3, and UNIX system laboratories (USL) System V release 3.2. Paragon OSF/1 R1.1 extends this base to provide a single system image across multiple nodes, effectively presenting one large system to the user.

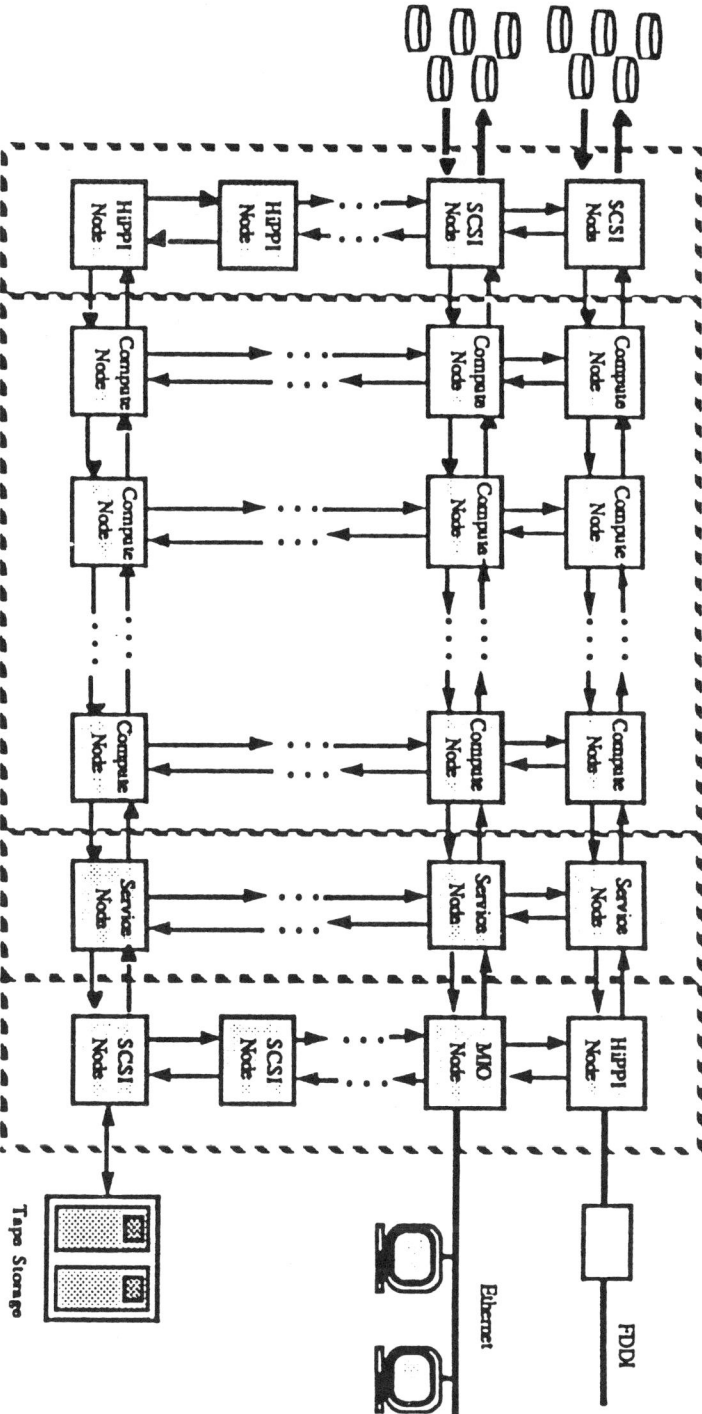

Fig. 15.33   The Paragon system (*Courtesy of Intel Corporation*)

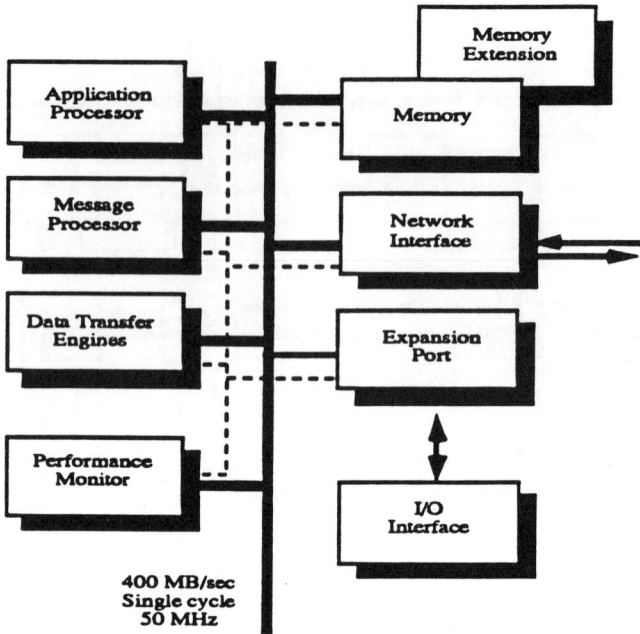

Fig. 15.34 Paragon GP node *(Courtesy of Intel Corporation)*

BBN TC2000

The TC2000 was developed by Bolt Beranek and Newman (BBN) Systems and Technologies (Cambridge, MA) [TC20 94]. It is a high-performance, fast-response, network interconnected multiprocessor [Hwan 93, Tabk 90]. The TC2000 is scalable both in computational and in I/O performance. It can be configured with up to 504 processors. Any TC2000 processor may be either PowerPC 604 (see chapter 7), or MC88100 (see chapter 11). The main memory of the TC2000 is distributed among its function cards, and it can be configured from 28MB to 64GB. The TC2000 features two types of function card:

1. **TC/F10** featuring two PowerPC 604 CPUs, 32 to 128MB memory, a VME 64 I/O interface, operating at 80MHz. A block diagram of the TC/F10 card is shown in Fig. 15.35.
2. **TC/FPV** featuring an MC88100 CPU and two MC88220 CMMUs (see chapter 11; the MC88220 is a more advanced, architecturally identical version of the MC88200), 4 to 16MB memory, a VME I/O interface, operating at 20MHz. A block diagram of the TC/FPV card is shown in Fig. 15.36.

Each TC2000 function card also contains a switch interface to the system's Butterfly network [Hwan 93, Tabk 90], and a test and control system slave processor,

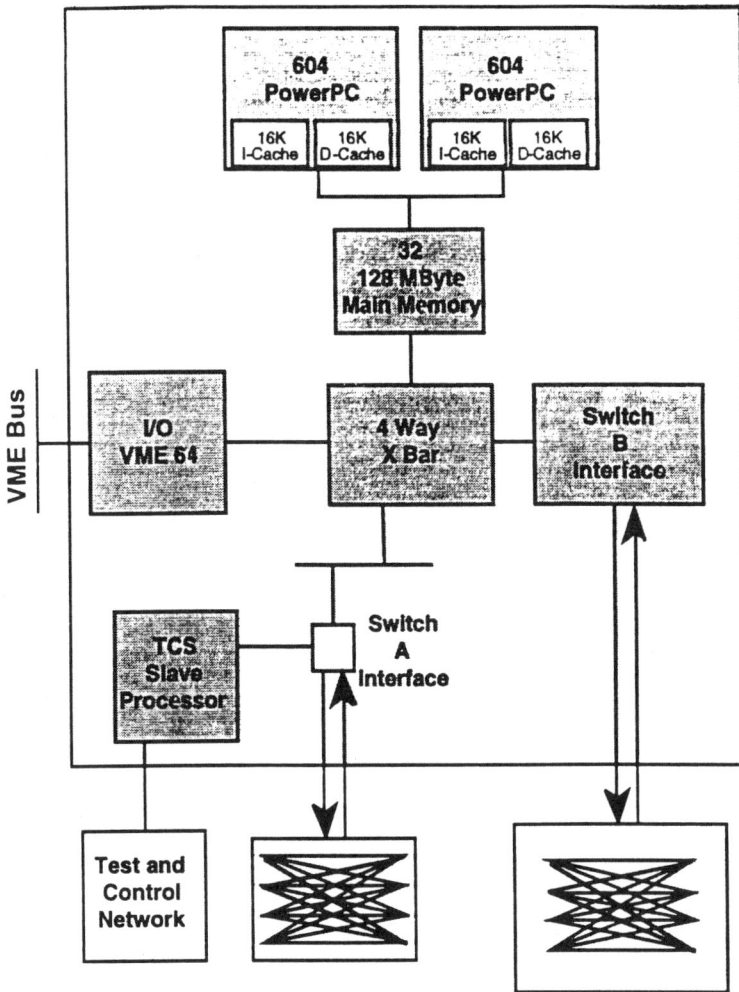

Fig. 15.35   TC2000 F10 card *(Courtesy of BBN)*

all connected to the on-board Tbus (on FPV), or on-board x bar switch (F10). Both types of card can be used in similar proportions in the same system. For applications requiring low computing and high I/O throughput, a preponderance of TC/FPVs (20MHz MC88100) may be used, while high-performance, computer-intensive applications would use a majority of TC/F10 (80MHz PowerPC 604) cards.

The system 64-port Butterfly switch is illustrated in Fig. 15.37. Each switch module is an 8×8 crossbar (see section 15.1) and can connect any input to any output. A two-stage Butterfly switch, like the one shown in Fig. 15.37, has up to

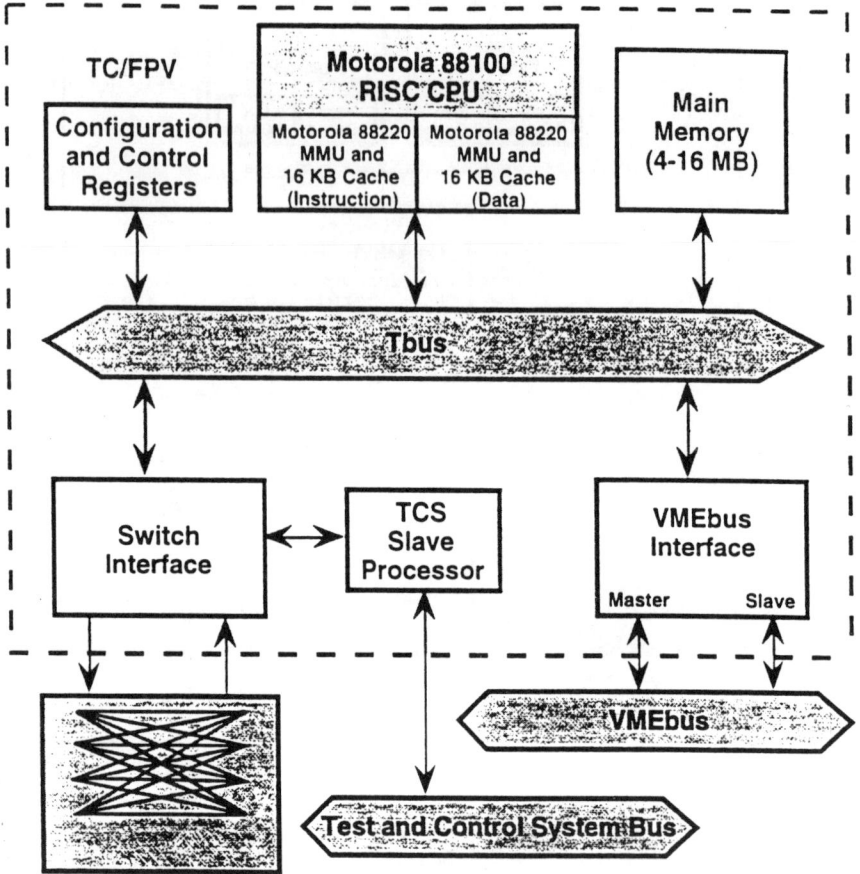

Fig. 15.36 TC2000 FPV card *(Courtesy of BBN)*

64 ports, while a three-stage switch can have up to 512 ports. The TC2000 offers two OS that can function concurrently on the same machine:

1. The nX OS, a general-purpose multiuser OS based on Berkeley UNIX 4.3 BSD.
2. The pSOS+m, a real-time OS from Integrated Systems, Inc.

15.4 Concluding Comments
A number of notable RISC-based multiprocessors have been surveyed in this chapter. Some of their properties are summarized in Table 15.2. It is quite obvious

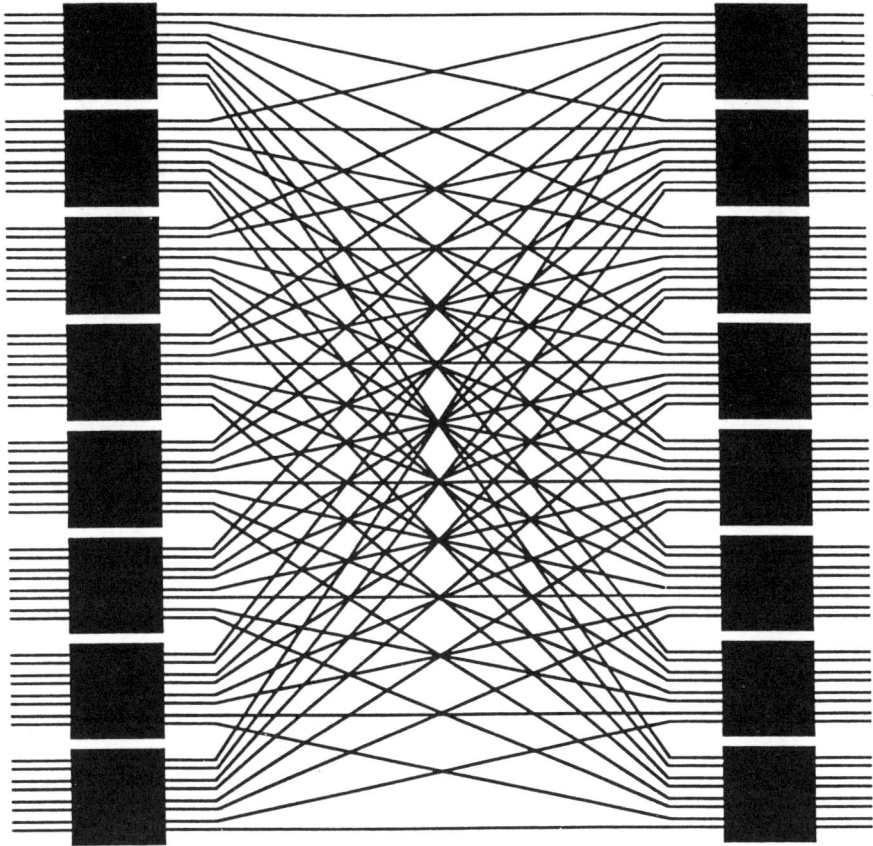

Fig. 15.37   A 64-port Butterfly network *(Courtesy of BBN)*

that the Alpha AXP 21064-based CRAY T3D, with a 2048 maximal configurable number of processors, operating at 150MHz, is the most powerful among the four. If the 21064 is eventually superseded by the 21164 (see chapter 6), its performance will certainly go up. Even with a configuration of a relatively small number of processors, say 32, the CRAY T3D can be a very powerful system. At the present time, new multiprocessors under development appear to be exclusively RISC-based because of the RISC high performance, low delays, and fast response. This trend is expected to continue.

Table 15.2 RISC-based Multiprocessors

System:	CRAY T3D	CM-5	Paragon	TC 2000
Processors	2048	1024	2048*	504
CPU (MHz)	21064 (150)	SPARC (40)	i860XP (50)	PowerPC604(80) MC88100 (20)
Network	3D Torus	Fat tree	Mesh	Butterfly + 8x8 crossbars
Max.MM (GB)	128	32	256	64
OS	UNIX-based	CMOST (UNIX)	OSF/1(Mach 3)	nX (UNIX) + pSOS + m

where: 3D = three-dimensional,   MM = main memory
    OS = operating system,   GB = gigabytes (2^{30} bytes)
    * Current maximal actual implementation. May be implemented with more processors in the future

CHAPTER 16

RISC Applications in Workstations

16.1 Introductory Comments

Workstations are powerful personal computers that may be connected in a network [HePa 90]. Current workstations may be as powerful (in speed, memory, and interface resource) as some mainframe computers. They may even be competitive with some systems termed as supercomputers. Workstations are just a particular case of a digital computer system small enough to be placed in an individual office, equipped with a keyboard, a screen, a mouse, a modem, and other resources. It may be connected through a network to other workstations, I/O devices (such as printers), and other computing systems.

Workstations which compete in their performance with other powerful computing systems must be endowed with powerful, high-performance processors. RISC-type processors have long ago proven themselves as very-high-performance processors. Today's leading processors of the Alpha AXP (chapter 6), PowerPC (chapter 7), and MIPS (chapter 9) families run within the interval of 150 to 300MHz (higher frequencies attained in laboratory environment), and they are high-issue superscalars. Indeed, RISC-type processors are pervasively used in recent most powerful workstations.

A number of existing RISC-based workstations will be surveyed in this chapter. One particular set of products, the Silicon Graphics CHALLENGE and Indy workstations, will be described in detail in the next section. As will be seen, some of these systems, such as the CHALLENGE, also fall into the category of multiprocessors. Introduction of multiprocessing is inevitable into high-performance workstations. A brief description of other workstations will follow in a subsequent section. Some properties of the workstations discussed in this chapter will be compared in the summarizing section.

16.2 The Silicon Graphics CHALLENGE and Indy Workstations
The CHALLENGE workstation

The CHALLENGE is a powerful, multiprocessing, workstation and network resource server [GaWi 94, Symm 93]. It is based on the POWERpath-2 system bus architecture. The CHALLENGE uses up to 36 MIPS R4400 (200MHz) processors (see chapter 9). CHALLENGE designers chose a *split transaction bus* for the POWERpath-2 to avoid stalling the entire bus for each memory reference, as happens in other systems. Since this is a coherent split transaction bus, the designers had to ensure that there were no conflicting transactions pending at the same time. For this reason, they implemented bus resource tags that track pending transactions. This is unlike other systems where the designers chose to enforce strict FIFO order on their split transaction buses, which is less complex but may degrade performance. The POWERpath-2 bus system, illustrated in Fig. 16.1, was designed with the following properties [GaWi 94]:

1. Sufficient headroom to support CPU, I/O, and networking technologies foreseeable during the life cycle of systems such as the CHALLENGE.
2. Protocol and bandwidth support for symmetric multiprocessing, providing high-bandwidth, low-delay, cache-coherent communication between processors, memory, and I/O.
3. Data rates (sustained 1.2 GB/sec transfer rate, sustained 9.5 million transactions per second) capable of supporting simultaneous memory access for as many as 36 high-performance microprocessors (such as the R4400).
4. I/O subsystems with data rates above 400 MB/sec.
5. Networking subsystems with data rate above 100 MB/sec.
6. Graphics subsystems with data rates above 150 MB/sec.
7. Multiple outstanding, variable duration split read transactions.
8. Independent 256 data, 40-bit address buses.
9. 47.6MHz synchronous signalling (21ns cycle).

The POWERpath-2 system has a 256-bit data bus dedicated to data transfer. It can sustain a transfer rate greater than 1.2 GB/sec. The POWERpath-2 system uses a 40-bit physical address space. It can support up to 16GB of contiguous memory.

As can be seen in Fig. 16.1, the POWERpath-2 system may be configured with up to nine CPU boards. Each CPU board, illustrated in Fig. 16.2, has four R4400 processors. Each R4400 CPU has its own secondary (L2) cache (in addition to its primary L1 on-chip cache of 16KB data and 16KB instruction; see chapter 9) and a cache controller (CC), realized on a separate CC chip. Each CPU is connected to the POWERpath-2 system bus through one address-path application specific integrated circuit (ASIC), the A chip, and four datapath chips, the D chips (see Fig. 16.2).

The CC chip implements a duplicate set of secondary cache tags that are used to handle cache coherency requests efficiently on the POWERpath-2 bus. Specifically, the CC chip has logic that allows read requests to complete with a higher priority than write requests; it buffers cache line write-backs until an outstanding read request completes. CHALLENGE designers decided to implement memory write-backs during cache intervention transactions, which causes more work for the memory subsystem but is helpful in cleaning cache lines during transfer, avoiding future write-backs if they are not necessary. In addition, the CC chip implements buffers and queues that improve overall system performance by scheduling read and write operations intelligently. It contains 102000 gates in a 383-pin PPGA (plastic PGA).

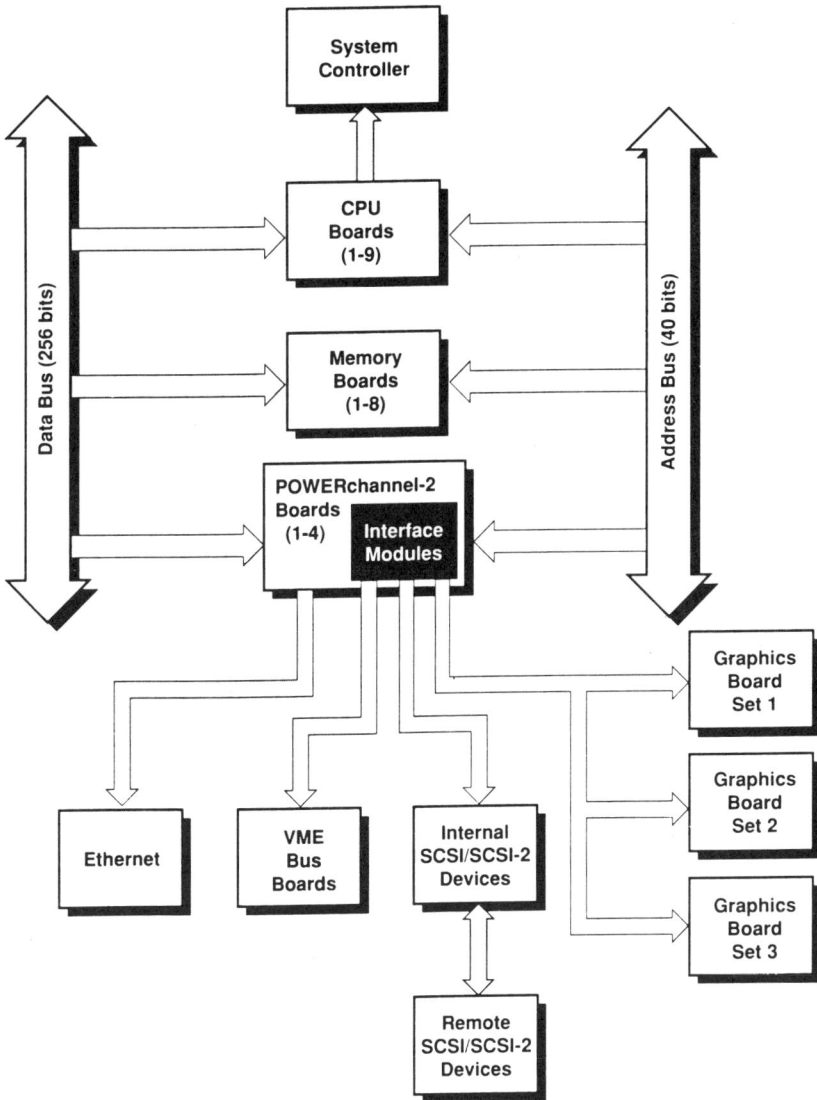

Fig. 16.1 POWERpath-2 system bus block diagram *(Courtesy of Silicon Graphics, Inc.)*

The POWERpath-2 cache coherency protocol is almost identical to the Illinois protocol [PaPa 84], except that the cache to cache transfers are used only for dirty data [GaWi 94]. Each cache has four states: invalid, exclusive, dirty exclusive, and shared. Transition between cache states is caused by actions initiated by the

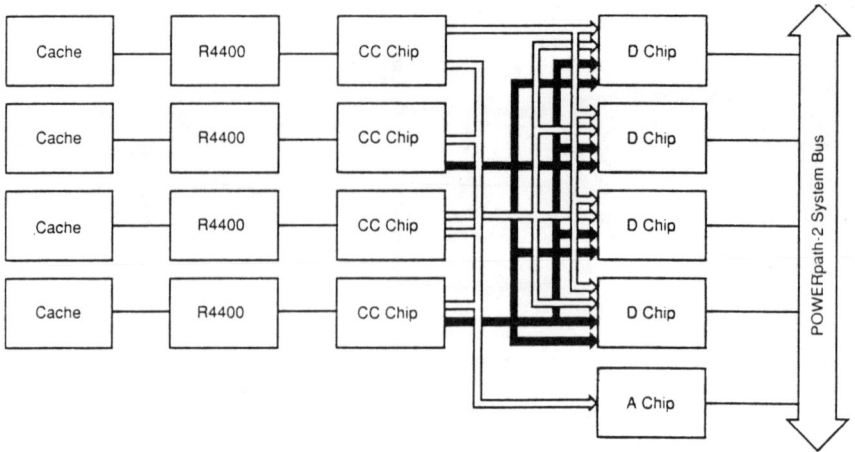

Fig. 16.2   Functional block diagram of the CHALLENGE CPU board *(Courtesy of Silicon Graphics, Inc.)*

processor or by a coherency transaction signal appearing on the bus. In order to eliminate unnecessary cache contention between the processor and the snoopy bus mechanism, a duplicate set of cache tags [ArBa 86] is maintained by the processor interface ASIC. A processor cache will only be accessed for coherency reasons if the data in question actually reside in that cache; bus traffic targeting lines not cached by the local processor will not affect the processor or its cache [GaWi 94].

The A chip services the address requests of all four processors on the CPU board. Like the CC chip, the A chip has a prioritized read request path to minimize read delay. The A chip handles bus arbitration, and prioritizes read requests over write requests on the bus itself. It also supports 'piggyback' read requests. This performance optimization for tightly coupled multiprocessing programs allows several processors to share read request and response cycles on the bus. Even though the A chip services four processors, each processor has its own dedicated path to the bus. This allows processors located on different boards the same performance advantages normally associated with processors that share the same board. The A chip contains 91000 gates in a 299-pin PPGA (plastic PGA).

The D chip is a bit-sliced datapath that narrows the 256 bits of POWERpath-2 system bus data to a 64-bit bus that matches the size of the MIPS R4400 system interface bus (see chapter 9). Each processor has its own 64-bit path dedicated for transfers to the system bus; so, again, there is no contention between processors sharing the same CPU board. The datapath between the CC chip and D chips is bidirectional. To minimize read delay, the default direction for this bus is towards the processor. The D chip contains 45000 gates in a 299-pin PPGA.

The CHALLENGE memory board supports two-way interleaving at the cache block level. A single memory board can be expanded to 2GB. Two memory boards support up to four-way memory interleaving; four memory boards support up to eight-way interleaving. Each memory board, illustrated in Fig. 16.3, consists of two DRAM array leaves. Each leaf contains four banks. Other board key components are one address control ASIC (the MA chip) and four data control ASICs (the MD chips). The MA ASIC is a gate array that provides the interface between the memory array and the system address lines. Its 94000 gates are packaged in a 299-pin PPGA. The MA ASIC includes bus arbitration and acknowledge logic, decode logic, and two interleaved DRAM controllers. Each DRAM controller generates multiplexed memory address lines plus control lines sufficient to control two banks of DRAM. In addition, the MA chip generates and receives signals that allow it to control the MD chips.

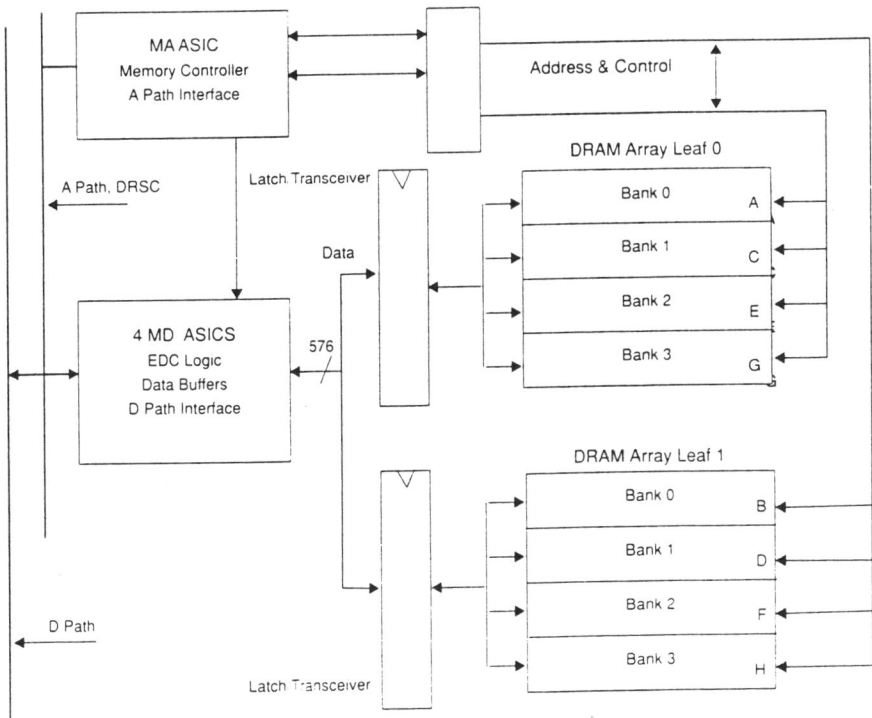

Fig. 16.3   POWERpath-2 interleaved memory board block diagram *(Courtesy of Silicon Graphics, Inc.)*

The four MD ASICs provide error detection and correction and data buffering for the transfer of data between the 576-bit-wide memory array and the 264-bit-wide D path (see Fig. 16.3), including error correction code (ECC) bits. The four chips are identical; each drives one quarter of the bus. Each MD chip contains approximately 55000 gates in a 383 PPGA package. Controlled by the MA ASIC, the MD chips perform no action on their own except for notifying the MA chip when they detect an error.

The memory array consists of eight banks of 144 four-bit-wide DRAMs of either 16 Mbit or 64 Mbit. Normally, at least two memory banks are populated. For maximum performance, the two banks must be located on different memory leaves; all memory banks must have the same number of populated leaves. In cases where half the system bus's rated performance is sufficient, however, a system can be configured with a single memory bank.

The POWERpath-2 system bus uses a *distributed arbitration* scheme to minimize the delay of transmission of information, while the I/O bus uses a *centralized* scheme. CHALLENGE designers chose a centralized scheme for the I/O bus because, rather than being a peer bus, the I/O bus to system bus interface is a centralized location for decision making. Also, system delay is less of a problem in I/O as long as throughput can be maintained. Arbitration requests and grants are pipelined to allow full bus utilization; so the centralized scheme will not impact throughput [GaWi 94].

The CHALLENGE I/O subsystem consists of one or more POWERchannel-2 boards, which plug directly into the POWERpath-2 system bus, and HIO (high-performance I/O) modules (see Fig. 16.4). The F and S HIO modules are daughter boards that plug into POWERchannel-2 boards to allow expansion and customization. Controllers for I/O devices connect to the 64-bit-wide HIO bus. The HIO bus connects to the POWERpath-2 bus through the IA and ID chips (see Fig. 16.4). These chips form an asynchronous boundary to modulate between the 1.2 GB/sec bandwidth on the system bus and the 320 MB/sec bandwidth on the HIO bus. The bandwidth of the HIO bus is adequate to support a graphics subsystem, a VME64 bus, and as many as eight SCSI-2 channels operating simultaneously. Up to two HIO modules plug into the HIO bus on each POWERchannel-2 board.

The IA and ID chips act as bus adapters that connect the HIO bus to the much faster POWERpath-2 system bus. In addition to making the necessary conversions back and forth between the two buses, the IA and ID chips perform virtual address mapping for scatter/gather DMA operations and maintain cache coherency between the system bus and the I/O subsystem. A fully associative four-line cache allows non-block write operations performed by I/O controllers to be combined efficiently. POWERchannel-2 contains two flat cable interfaces (FCI). FCIs are synchronous, point-to-point interfaces that allow communication between devices connected by a cable. The FCIs operate at up to 160 MB/sec. The two FCIs on the first POWERchannel-2 in a system are connected to the VME channel adapter module (VCAM) board, which contains a VME adapter and a connection to a graphics subsystem. When additional FCIs are required for multiple graphics subsystems or multiple VME buses, F HIO modules can be used to connect them.

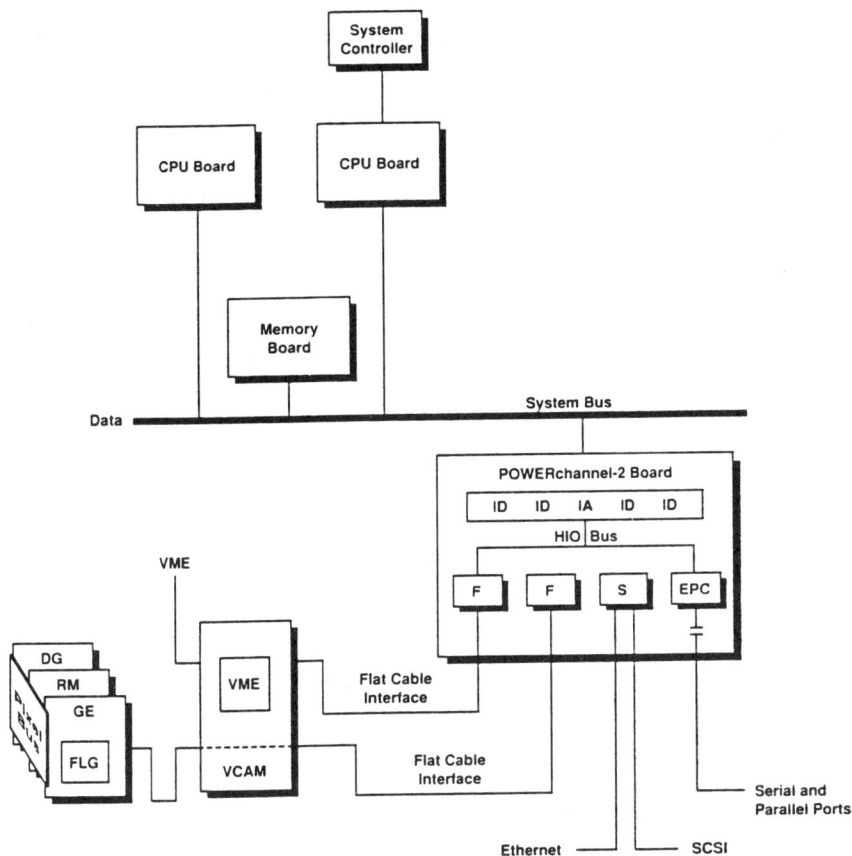

Fig. 16.4 Block diagram of the POWERchannel-2 board in context *(Courtesy of Silicon Graphics, Inc.)*

The Indy workstation

The Indy is a R4000-based workstation [Indy 93]. It can be configured either with a R4000PC or a R4000SC (see chapter 9) module. The R4000SC module also includes a unified off-chip 1 MB secondary cache. Either module runs at 50MHz externally and 100MHz internally. The Indy workstation, shown in Fig. 16.5, contains six major subsystems: CPU module, memory, graphics, I/O, video, and graphics I/O (GIO) expansion subsystems. The electronics are partitioned into the system board, the graphics board, and the CPU module daughter card as illustrated in Fig. 16.5. The CPU module contains the R4000 processor, EEPROM, oscillator, and cache RAM. It is connected to the memory subsystem by a 64-bit (plus eight bits parity) multiplexed address and data CPU bus (see Fig. 16.5). The CPU bus transfers data at a rate of 267 MB/sec to and from the memory subsystem.

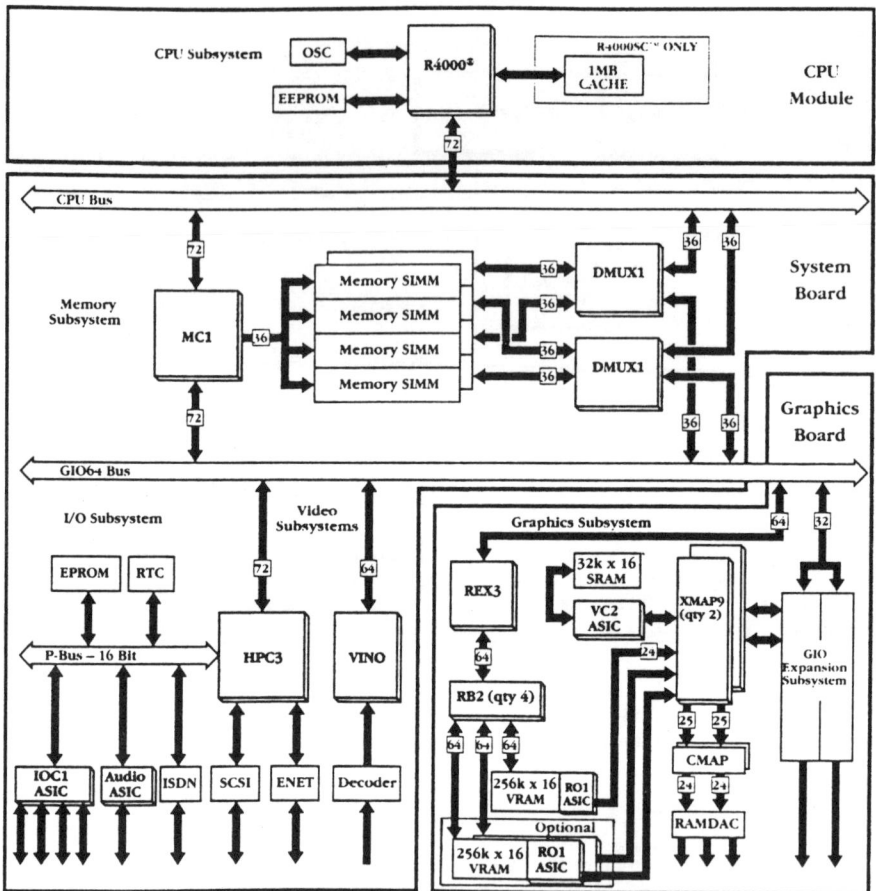

Fig. 16.5 Indy system electronics partitioned into subsystems and boards. Shaded components represent custom ASICs from Silicon Graphics *(Courtesy of Silicon Graphics, Inc.)*

The memory subsystem contains memory control, data bus routing, and eight SIMM (single in-line memory module) sockets for main memory. A 64-bit (plus parity) multiplexed address and data GIO64 bus connects the memory subsystem to I/O, graphics, video, and the GIO expansion subsystems.

The I/O subsystem contains a central I/O controller to collect data from relatively slow peripherals and transfer them into main memory at high speeds. This controller includes support for boot PROMs, processor interrupts, a real-time clock, serial ports, a parallel port, ISDN, and audio. These peripherals are interfaced to the I/O controller by a 16-bit peripheral bus called the P-bus. The controller also supports a SCSI controller and an Ethernet (ENET) controller which are connected directly for increased bandwidth (see Fig. 16.5).

The video subsystem contains a video decoder chip set to convert analog video into digital pixels. The output of the decoder is connected to a video controller ASIC which formats and sizes the pixels and transfers them into system memory. The graphics subsystem consists of the raster engine, the frame buffer, video timing controller, and the digital-to-analog converters (DACs). It is connected to the GIO64 bus. The GIO expansion subsystem is connected to 32 bits of the GIO64 bus. It also has a direct connection to the video backend section of the graphics subsystem.

Silicon Graphics developed several custom ASICs to aid communication between the system and the buses.

MC1 serves as the GIO64 bus arbiter, which provides an interface between the CPU and the GIO64 bus. It is also the memory controller, allowing DMA by devices other than the CPU.

DMUX1 are datapath chips, controlled by the MC1 chip, that isolate the CPU bus from the GIO64 bus. They also perform the memory interleaving functions.

HPC3 provides an interface to peripheral I/O, the audio system, and other devices on the P-bus, connecting them to the GIO64 bus.

IOC1 provides interrupt control, two general-purpose serial ports, a parallel port, and a keyboard/mouse controller.

REX3 (on the graphics board) connects the graphics subsystem to the GIO64 bus and renders pixels into the frame buffer.

HAL2 (audio) provides the datapath and control logic to interface the HPC3 P-bus and audio.

VINO processes digital video pixels and transfers them by a DMA operation into system memory.

A block diagram of the MC1 (memory controller) ASIC is shown in Fig. 16.6. It performs the following functions:

1. It controls the flow of data between main memory and the CPU.
2. It serves as a DMA controller for all memory requests from the graphics system or any other devices on the GIO64 bus.
3. It acts as a system arbiter for the GIO64 bus.
4. It provides single-word accesses for the CPU to GIO64 bus devices and to the graphics system.
5. It passes on interrupts from the IOC1 ASIC to the CPU.
6. It initiates the CPU on power-up, executes CPU requests, refreshes memory, and checks data parity in memory.

The DMUX1 ASICs are a two-chip slice of a data crossbar between the CPU, main memory, and the GIO64 bus. They form a datapath with control signals

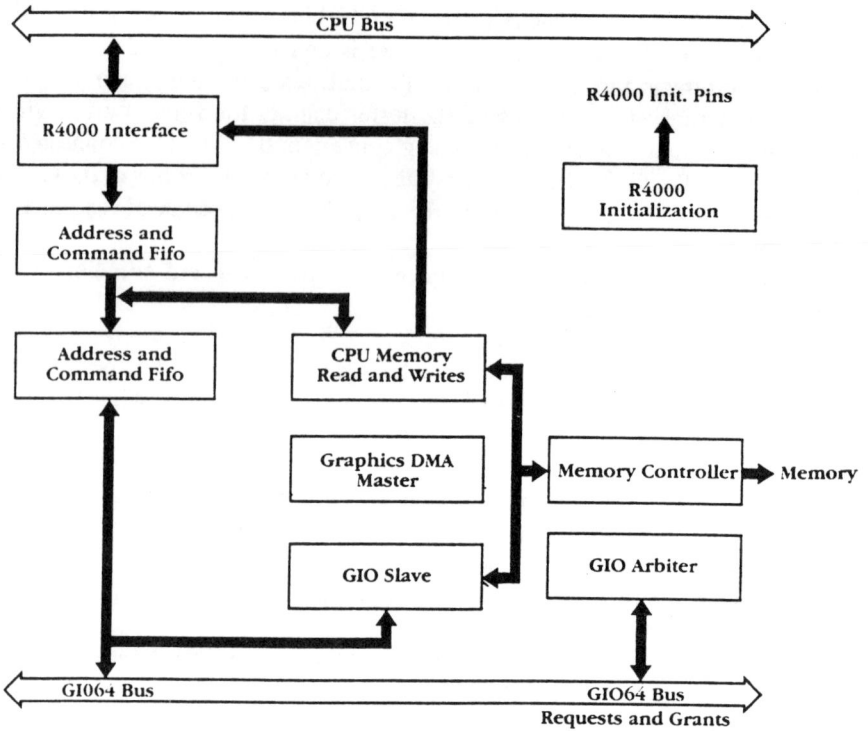

Fig. 16.6 A block diagram of the MC1 ASIC *(Courtesy of Silicon Graphics, Inc.)*

generated by the MC1. They isolate the CPU bus from the memory system and the GIO64 bus. They also contain synchronization FIFOs to perform flow control between the various subsystems, and they interleave main memory to increase peak memory bandwidth. Main memory, which is controlled by the MC1 and DMUX1 ASICs, provides system access to large amounts of DRAM. The DMUX1 chips facilitate the creation of a 72-bit-wide two-way interleaved memory system, as illustrated in Fig. 16.7. Main memory can be configured from 16MB to 256MB.

Indy supports a single ISDN (integrated services digital network) basic rate interface, integrated onto the system board, accessed by the S access point, as shown in Fig. 16.8. The ISDN supports the point-to-point protocol (PPP), enabling networking across ISDN B-channels, providing the full 64 Kbit/sec bandwidth of each B-channel. The application software interface (ASI) developed by the National ISDN User's Forum is expected to become a standard in the USA. ISDN features include:

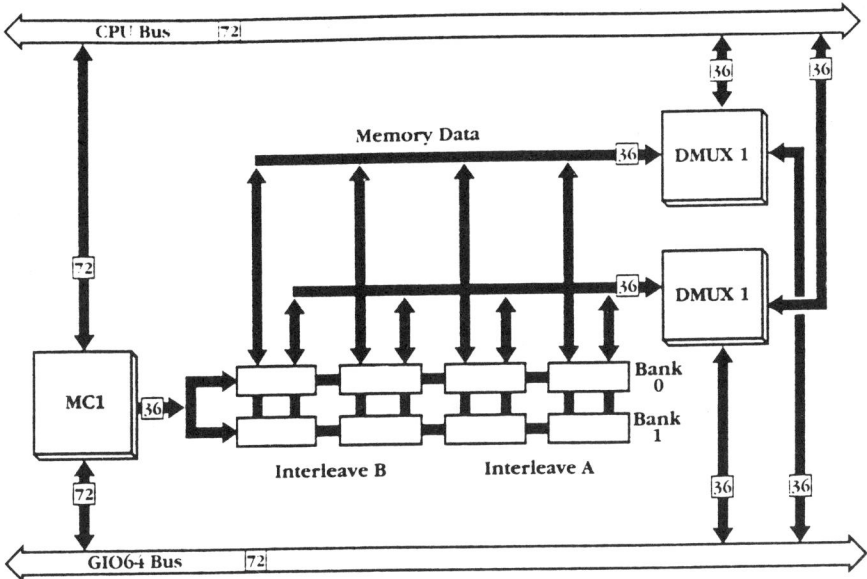

Fig. 16.7 Indy memory interleaving *(Courtesy of Silicon Graphics, Inc.)*

1. Single S RJ45 connector.
2. Hardware HDLC framing on both B-channels for data communication and networking applications.
3. Three DMA channels: one to transmit and one each for the receive direction on each B-channel.
4. Separate 64-byte transmit and receive FIFOs on each B-channel and on the D-channel.

The interface is based on the S interface chip and the HDLC controller chip. The S interface chip provides the interface to the four-wire S interface, HDLC formatting on the B-channel, two FIFOs for the D-channel transmit and receive data, and host access to the D-channel data. The HDLC controller chip provides the DMA interface to the B-channels, HDLC formatting on the B-channels, and four FIFOs for the B-channel transmit and receive data. The isolation transformers provide the coupling and high-voltage isolation between the S interface and the Indy system. The S interface chip and the HDLC controller chip are both connected to the P-bus. Both chips contain registers that may be accessed by the host CPU. The HDLC controller chip is connected to three DMA channels that are contained in the HPC3 ASIC.

The Indy system board provides the ability to record, process, synthetize, and play professional quality audio. Fig. 16.9 illustrates the Indy audio architecture. The Indy audio support system provides a built-in speaker, front volume controls,

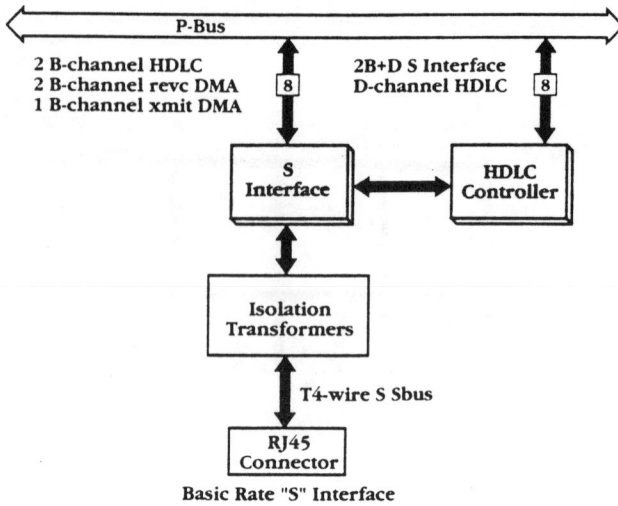

Fig. 16.8   ISDN interface architecture *(Courtesy of Silicon Graphics, Inc.)*

stereo line level analog audio I/O, stereo headphone output, digital audio I/O, sampling rates of 48, 44.1, 32, 16, 8kHz, microphone input with DC power, simultaneous input and output, independent input and output rates, output rate that can be synchronized to the digital input rate, analog signal processing, Silicon Graphics audio library (AL), microphone input that supports stereo microphones, and other features.

The Indy audio system is built around a central controller chip, the HAL2 ASIC, two stereo audio Codec chips, an AES transmitter chip, an AES receiver chip, a microphone input circuit, a headphone/speaker amplifier circuit, and a four-channel-mode output switch. The HAL2 contains the datapath and control logic to interface the HPC3 P-bus and the audio devices on the module. Indy audio uses a pair of stereo audio Codecs. These chips are highly integrated monolithic CMOS mixed-signal devices that make use of the latest signal conversion technology. In the normal mode of operation, the Codec A digital-to-analog converter (DAC) is used for analog output and the Codec B analog-to-digital converter (ADC) is used for analog input. The analog input to Codec B is selectable from either the line or microphone inputs under software control. The analog output signal from Codec A is routed both to line-out and to the stereo headphone/internal loudspeaker circuit.

The Indy video subsystem provides a low-cost way to capture and use video and video mail as a computer data type in presentations, in user-to-user communication, and in documentation and training. The subsystem displays video live in a window with simultaneous software compression of the video as it is saved on the system disk. Indy comes standard with the IndyCam, a digital color video camera. There are three video input ports, shown in Fig. 16.10, to support

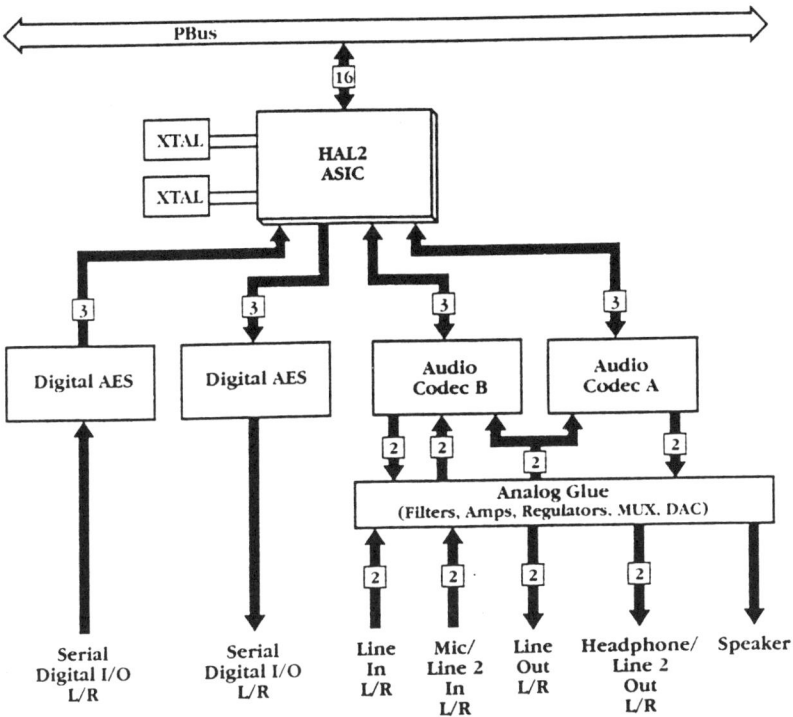

Fig. 16.9   Indy audio architecture *(Courtesy of Silicon Graphics, Inc.)*

different video formats:

1. NTSC/PAL composite analog video.
2. NTSC/PAL S-video analog video.
3. SGI (Silicon Graphics, Inc.) digital video.

The video subsystem inputs video, digitizes the analog video, processes the digital pixels as requested, and then puts the pixels on the GIO64 bus. The subsystem provides pixel formatting and DMA hardware to assist software implemented real-time video compression and decompression.

The video subsystem is built around the VINO ASIC shown in Fig. 16.11. There are two DMA channels A and B within the VINO. Either channel can be assigned to the digital video input or the analog input bus. Both channels can be used simultaneously; however, only one analog format can be used at any one time. For instance, the following channel combinations are possible:

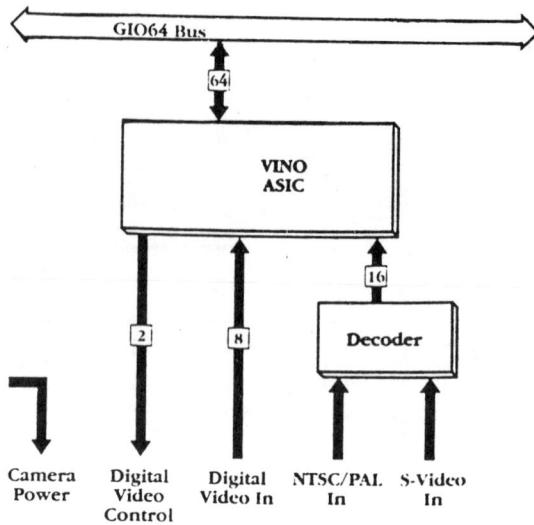

Fig. 16.10   Video subsystem architecture *(Courtesy of Silicon Graphics, Inc.)*

Both channels can be connected to the digital video port.
One channel can be connected to the digital video input and one to either analog video input.
Both channels can be connected to the analog composite video input.
Both channels can be connected to the S-video input.

Digital video from the digital video port is sent directly to the VINO. Analog video from either the composite or S-video port is first transferred to a digital decoder chip set for conversion to digital pixels which are then sent to the VINO. The VINO can then resize the digital pixels and color space convert them before it transfers them directly (by DMA) into system memory. The clipping, decimation/filtering, color space conversion, and dithering processes are optional, allowing NTSC/PAL video with full spatial, temporal, and color information.

The Indy graphics board system, shown in Fig. 16.12, comes standard on the Indy. It contains the following subsystems:

1.   The raster engine REX3 ASIC, which converts geometric data processed by the CPU into pixel and line data that it then writes into the framebuffer.
2.   The framebuffer VRAM, which contains the pixel color and overlay data for the 1280×1024 display, and the CID planes for arbitrary window clipping operations.
3.   The VC2 video controller ASIC, XMAP9 ASICs, and CMAP which, together with a 24-bit DAC, generate video signals sent to the monitor.

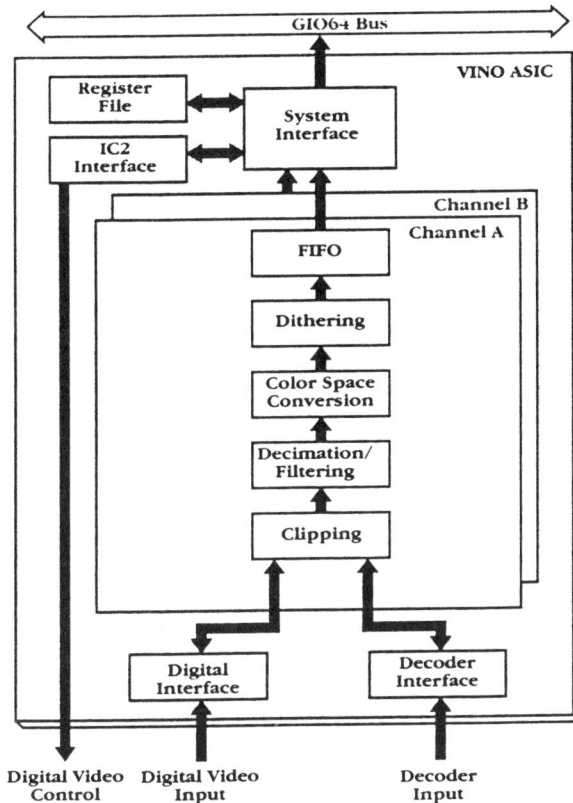

Fig. 16.11 VINO ASIC block diagram *(Courtesy of Silicon Graphics, Inc.)*

The GIO32-bus expansion subsystem is also integrated onto the Indy graphics board. The main bus on the Indy graphics board provides a communication path between the elements of the graphics subsystem. The Indy graphics board is connected to the GIO64 bus via the REX3 ASIC, which can access data from the CPU at a burst rate of 267 MB/sec.

16.3 Examples of Other RISC-based Workstations
Alpha AXP-based workstations
AlphaStation 800 5/300

The AlphaStation 800 5/300, also known as *Alcor*, uses DECchip 21164 (266 to 300MHz) as its processor. Its primary components include [ZuML 95]:

1. Main memory, configurable from 32MB to 4GB, using industry standard SIMMs. There is a 256-bit high-bandwidth datapath to memory.

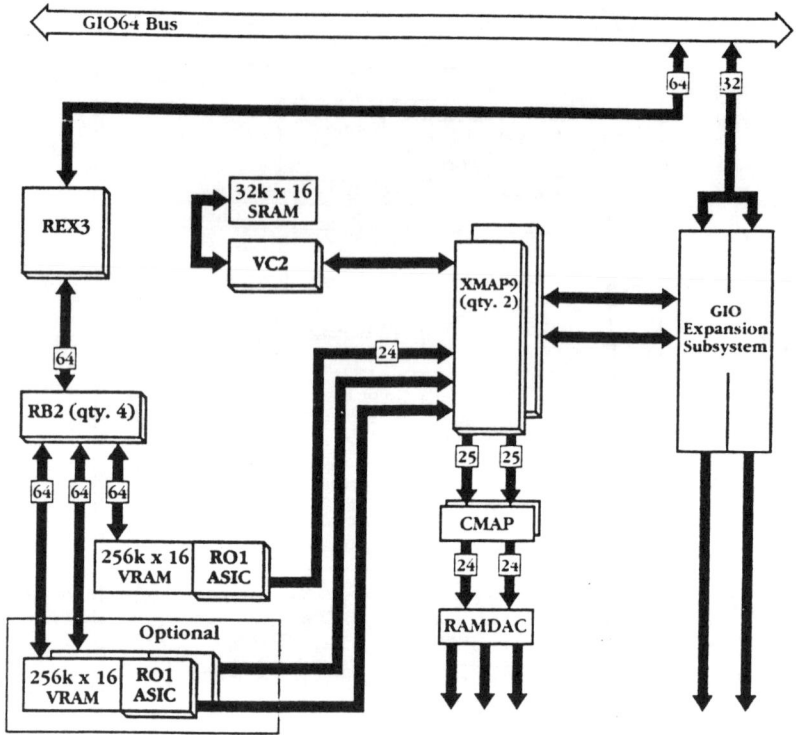

Fig. 16.12 The Indy graphics board *(Courtesy of Silicon Graphics, Inc.)*

2.   Plug-in, optional external write-back cache, configurable from 2 to 16MB, with a 64-byte line size. Since the 21164 contains a 16KB primary cache (L1: 8KB I-cache, 8KB D-cache) and a 96KB on-chip secondary cache (L2), the external cache is a third-level cache (L3). Access time to L3 is a multiple of processor cycle time and depends on SRAM parts used (typically 25ns for first 128-bit data, 22ns for remaining data with 12ns SRAM).

3.   There are eight interface option slots:

Four peripheral component interconnect (PCI) slots.

Three extended industry standard architecture (EISA) slots.

One PCI/EISA shared slot.

4.   Synchronous timing design: memory, cache, and PCI timing are multiples of processor cycle time. Thus, the PCI clock, the memory block, and the cache loop are all synchronous to one another. The designers avoided an asynchronous design, because it suffers from longer delays due to the synchronizers, and is more difficult to verify with regard to timing. The design uses a single-phase clock, apart from the memory controller, which uses a double-frequency clock to provide a finer

15ns resolution for the memory timing pulses. Phase lock loop (PLL) devices control the clock skew on the system board and in the ASICs. The PLL in the ASICs also generates the double-frequency clock [ZuML 95].
5. An X-bus for the real-time clock, keyboard controller, configuration RAM, and the operator control panel logic.

The system's 64-bit PCI bus provides bandwidth in excess of 260 MB/sec, which is achievable for large DMA read operations. The system can transfer data from memory to I/O space at 152 MB/sec. These transfers are particularly useful in graphics and multimedia applications.

The Alcor system design minimized logic on the mother board in favor of more expansion slots. This approach allows the user the flexibility to configure to the user's requirements, without providing unnecessary and costly functionality on the mother board. Moreover, the system design allows for easier future upgrades. The Alcor system uses option cards for SCSI, Ethernet, graphics, and audio [ZuML 95].

DECpc AXP 150
The DECpc AXP 150 is the first Alpha AXP-based (see chapter 6) personal computer (PC), developed by DEC [CKFa 94]. Its block diagram is shown in Fig. 16.13. The AXP 150 CPU is a 150MHz 21064 microprocessor. It generates a 25MHz clock that runs most of the logic. Sections of the I/O system run at 8.33MHz, generated by the EISA (extended industry standard architecture) chip set. The PC has a 512KB backup cache (L2). Its main memory can be configured from 16 to 256MB. The memory — CPU data bus is 128-bits wide. The memory was designed to use 36-bit-wide SIMMs (single in-line memory modules) to handle both 1 M- and 4 M-deep SIMMs, and to handle both the single- and double-banked versions of the SIMMs.

DEC AlphaServer 2100
The DEC AlphaServer 2100 is a symmetric multiprocessor (SMP) superserver [Hays 94], configurable with one to four, 190MHz, 21064 processors. Each processor board includes a 1MB secondary cache. The main memory can be configured from 32MB to 2GB (the initially marketed product has 64MB). The system includes a 2GB disk, CD-ROM, floppy-disk drive, and eight EISA (extended industry standard architecture) and three PCI (peripheral component interconnect) slots. The OS featured includes Open VMS, DEC ODF/1, and SMP version of OSF/1.

DEC 3000 workstations
The DEC 3000 model 700 system features a 225MHz 21064A CPU, and model 900 implements a 275MHz 21064A CPU. Model 700 is a desktop workstation. It comes with 64MB of main memory, and a 1.05GB hard disk drive. Model 900 is a deskside workstation which includes 64MB of main memory, and a 2GB hard

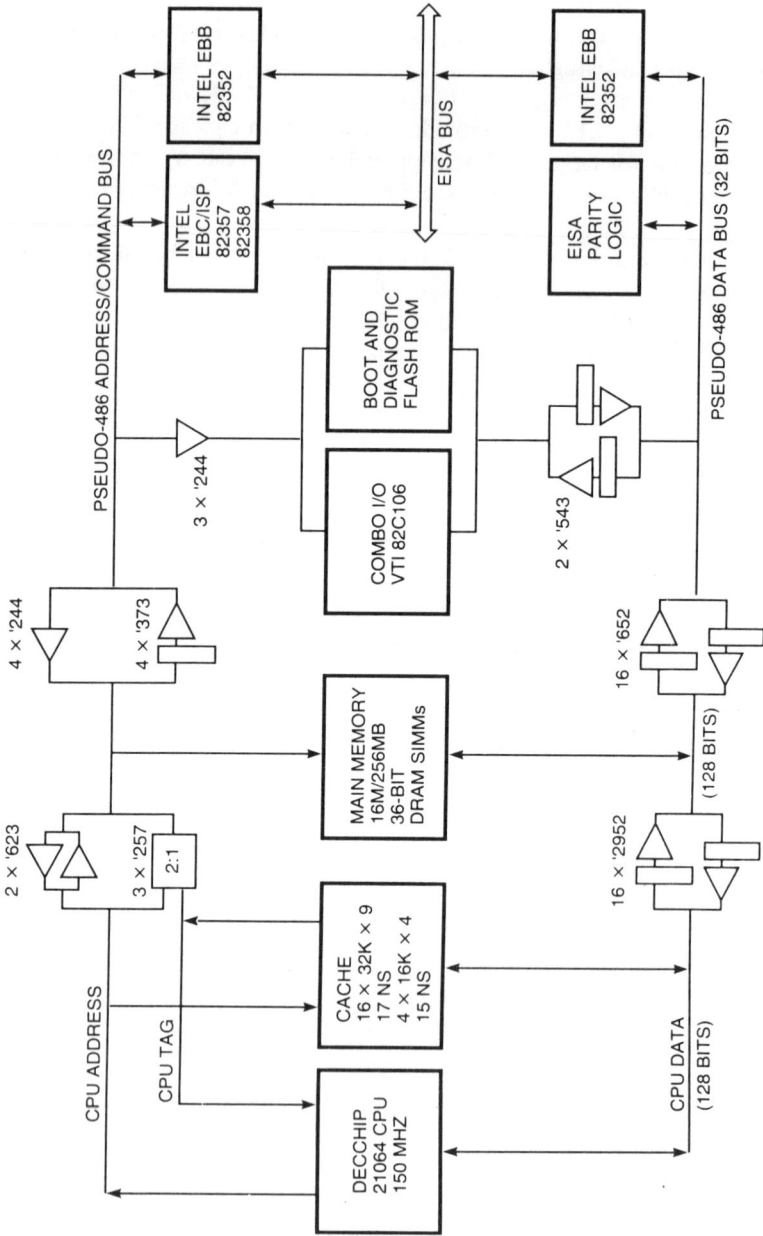

Fig. 16.13 Block diagram of the DECpc AXP 150 product *(Courtesy of DEC)*

disk drive. Both models include a 600MB CD-ROM drive, two SCSI-2 controllers (maximum I/O throughput of 10 MB/sec each), and 2MB of I/O cache. Both models' standard packages include the new ZLX-E1 accelerated 2-D eight-bit plane graphics controller and a 21-inch color monitor. The controller can display 256 colors at up to 1024-line by 1280-pixel resolution. The models can work with either DEC OSF/1 or Open VMS OS.

ALPINE Alpha-based workstations
Aspen Systems, Inc. (Wheat Ridge, CO) produces a set of Alpha AXP-based workstations called ALPINE. The systems currently featured are:

System	CPU	Frequency (MHz)	RAM (MB)	L2 (MB)
ALPINE 166RS	21064	166	16	0.5
ALPINE 200RS	21064	200	16	0.5
ALPINE 200XS	21064	200	16	2.0
ALPINE 233XS	21064A	233	32	2.0
ALPINE 275XS	21064A	275	64	2.0

All systems feature an SCSI-2 DMA controller (10 MB/sec), three PCI connectors (max. 132 MB/sec, 33MHz), three ISA-compliant connectors, 1GB hard disk drive, two floppy-disk drives, two high-speed RS-232 serial connectors, one high-speed bidirectional parallel port, one PS/2-compliant mouse connector, and high-speed video graphics.

Cobra AXP 275 PC
The Cobra 275 PC was developed by Carrera Computers, Inc. (Laguna Hills, CA). It implements a 275MHz 21064 CPU. It features a 128-bit memory bus, a 128-bit processor bus, 64MB RAM, 2GB disk, CD-ROM drive, 3.5in. floppy-disk drive, PCI video adapter, two 32-bit PCI, three 16-bit ISA expansion slots, PCI SCSI-2 controller, PCI-based Ethernet controller, and two asynchronous serial ports. Its performance is advertised to be 170 SPECint92 and 290 SPECfp92.

Alta AT/V64 Alpha-based board
The Alta AT/V64 board, manufactured by Alta Technology (Sandy, Utah) is intended to serve either as an individual microcomputer or as a processor board in a scalable parallel processing system. It can be configured either with a 200MHz 21064 or a 275MHz 21064A. Each node has four serial links (TLINKS) for attachment of additional processors. AT/nodes interface with a variety of host architectures using Alta's host system interface (HSI) products. The HSI provides a gateway between a specific host architecture (such as SBus or EISA) and the TLINKS and control signals required for a network of processors. The 21064 CPU on an AT/node is attached to a transputer (see chapter 13), which acts as a control

and communication processor. It is the transputer that supplied the serial TLINK connections. Alpha programs are compiled and configured on a host workstation and then downloaded from the host (using HSI), booted by the control processor, after which the 21064 becomes the 'master' and the control processor becomes the 'slave'. The 21064 makes requests of the control processor for services such as communication and process management, and the control processor provides the services through 32KB of dual port memory and control signals. The CPU is connected to the system memory through a 128-bit data bus. The node can be configured with 16 to 128MB of RAM. A parallel processing system can be configured with up to 16 processor nodes for a total memory of 2GB.

PowerPC-based systems
Power Macintosh 8100/80
The Power Macintosh 8100/80 system of Apple Computer, Inc. (Cupertino, CA) implements an 80MHz PowerPC 601 microprocessor (see chapter 7) as its CPU. The system features a 256KB secondary cache (L2) and an 8MB or 16MB main memory RAM, expandable to 264MB. There is a second version of the 8100/80, the 8100/80AV, which adds S-video and composite video input and output for use with televisions, video cameras and video recorders. Both systems feature DRAM display support. The 8100/80 features 2MB of VRAM for second display support, expandable to 4MB. The 8100/80AV features 2MB of VRAM for second display including NTSC or PAL monitors. The 8100/80 has nine, and the 8100/80AV has 11, built-in ports to support a wide range of peripherals. Both systems feature three NuBus slots for expansion cards, optional internal CD-ROM drive, on-board Ethernet, and double-speed SCSI. Both systems run Macintosh, MS-DOS, and Windows applications. Both systems read Macintosh, Windows, MS-DOS, and ProDOS floppy-disk formats.

Motorola PowerPC-based Ultra and Atlas
Motorola (Tempe, AZ) features a new family of PowerPC-based OEM single-board computer products Ultra and Atlas. The systems implement either a 66MHz PowerPC 603 or a 100MHz PowerPC 604 (see chapter 7) microprocessor as a CPU. The systems feature up to 128MB DRAM, a PCI local bus for I/O peripherals, PCI and ISA expansion slots, an eight-bit SCSI-2 bus interface with 32-bit PCI local bus burst DMA, an Ethernet transceiver interface with 32-PCI local bus DMA, 10base-2 and 10base-T interfaces, a floppy port, an IDE port, and a mouse and keyboard ports. The boards also provide two serial communication ports in addition to an IEEE 1284 Centronics compatible bidirectional parallel port. The Ultra also accommodates a 16-bit stereo audio capability, a range of Super VGA (SVGA) graphics with resolutions up to 1024 bits × 768 lines and 64K colors non-interlaced, and 1280 bits × 1024 lines and 64K colors interlaced. The Ultra and Atlas are designed to support Microsoft's Windows NT OS and provide a platform for Windows NT development.

SuperSPARC-based workstations
SPARCstation
Sun Microsystems (Mountain View, CA) has been producing SPARCstation workstations for a long time. Its latest SuperSPARC-based (see chapter 8) workstations are SPARCstation 10 and SPARCstation 20. The main models of SPARCstation 10 are models 40 and 51. Their primary differences are:

Feature	Frequency (MHz)	Secondary Cache (MB)
Model 40	40	none
Model 51	50	1

Both models can be configured with up to 512MB main memory and a 1.05 to 41GB disk. The main models of SPARCstation 20 are 50, 51, 61. Their main features are:

Feature	Frequency (MHz)	Secondary Cache (MB)
Model 50	50	none
Model 51	50	1
Model 61	60	1

All three models can be configured with up to 512MB main memory and a disk from 1.05GB to 69GB SCSI (or 138GB with array). The top model 61 of the above features a bandwidth of 144 bits, SIMM size of 16MB or 64MB, SCSI bandwidth of 10 MB/sec, four SBus slots, two MBus slots, two serial ports, one parallel port, 16-bit (CD quality) audio, an internal speaker, and two Ethernet ports. In addition to the above, there are also three multiprocessor versions of SPARCstation 20: models 502MP, 612MP, and 514MP. Models 502MP and 612MP feature two processors, and model 514MP has four processors. Models 502MP and 514MP implement a 50MHz SuperSPARC, while model 612MP implements a 60MHz SuperSPARC. Models 612MP and 514MP feature a 1MB secondary cache per processor, while model 502MP does not.

SPARCserver
Sun Microsystems also features multiprocessing SuperSPARC-based (version 8) servers: SPARCserver 10 and SPARCserver 1000. SPARCserver 10 can be configured with one (models 30 and 41), two (model 52), or four (model 54) CPUs. Models 41, 52, and 54 have a 1MB secondary cache per CPU. All models have a main memory of up to 512MB, two 64-bit MBus slots for multiprocessing, two Ethernet ports, SCSI-2 synchronous interface, two serial ports, one Centronics-compatible parallel port, CD-quality 16-bit audio (8 to 48kHz; optional speaker

box and microphone), ISDN interface, four SBus 32-bit expansion slots, and up to 1GB internal disk.

SPARCserver 1000 is a multiprocessing server than can be configured with one to eight SuperSPARC (version 8) CPUs with 1MB L2 cache each. Main memory can be expanded up to 2GB per system using 32MB SIMMs. The system includes up to four boards per system, two serial ports per system board, three SBus 32-bit expansion slots per system board, a keyboard and mouse port, an Ethernet port per system board, SCSI-2 synchronous port per system board, a maximum of three 2.1GB internal disk cards, and a 644MB CD-ROM.

SPARC CPU-10/9U

FORCE Computers, Inc. (San Jose, CA) produces a VMEbus-based, SPARCstation 10 compatible workstation SPARC CPU-10/9U (there is also a CPU-10 model). The CPU is a SuperSPARC running at 40, 50, or 60MHz, with an optional 1MB L2 cache. On-board DRAM is offered for 32, 128, or 640MB. Overall DRAM capacity is 32 to 1024MB. The system includes four SBus expansion slots, VMEbus interface, VMEbus interrupt handler (1 through 7, selectable), an Ethernet port, asynchronous/synchronous serial ports, SCSI controller, ISDN and audio controller, a floppy-disk controller, a keyboard, a mouse, a clock/calendar, a 512KB boot EPROM, and a 2MB (1.5MB user accessible) flash EEPROM.

The CPU-10/9U runs current versions of SunOS/Solaris. It implements the IEEE 1014-compatible VMEbus interface. It is intended for use in UNIX and real-time applications. It is binary compatible with SPARCstation 10.

16.4 Concluding Comments

A number of prominent RISC-based workstations, servers, and PCs have been surveyed in this chapter. The uniprocessor systems are summarized in Table 16.1. From the viewpoint of pure potential processing speed, it is obvious that the 275MHz Alpha AXP 21064-based ALPINE 275XS with its 2MB secondary cache (L2) has a very strong edge over the other systems. Undoubtedly, some of the Alpha AXP-based systems will feature the 300MHz 21164 (see chapter 6), further increasing the performance gap. This gap will be decreased, however, when the MIPS-based systems feature the R10000 (see chapter 9), and the SuperSPARC will be replaced by the UltraSPARC (see chapter 8) in the SPARCstations. It is also expected that the PowerPC-based systems (Macintosh and Ultra) will feature the PowerPC 620 (see chapter 7), considerably increasing their potential performance. It should be noted that the SuperSPARC-based systems are stronger with regard to the maximal configurable main memory.

The multiprocessor RISC-based workstations and servers are summarized in Table 16.2. It is obvious that the 36-processor (200MHz R4400) CHALLENGE with its up to 4MB secondary cache per CPU, and a total system configurable main memory of up to 16GB, is the most powerful.

With the appearance of the recent Alpha AXP 21164, PowerPC 620,

UltraSPARC, and MIPS R10000, we are going to see supercomputer-caliber desktop performance in the near future.

Table 16.1 RISC-based Workstations

System	CPU (MHz)	L2 (MB)	MM (MB)
Indy	R4000 (100)	1.0	256
DECpc AXP 150	21064 (150)	0.5	256
ALPINE 275XS	21064A (275)	2.0	64
Cobra AXP 275PC	21064A (275)	-	64
Macintosh 8100/80	PowerPC 601 (80)	0.25	264
Motorola Ultra	PowerPC 604 (100)	-	128
SPARCstation 20/61	SuperSPARC (60)	1.0	512
Force CPU-10/9U	SuperSPARC (60)	1.0	1024

where L2 = secondary off-chip cache, MM = maximal configurable main memory

Table 16.2 RISC-based Multiprocessor Workstations

System (N)	CPU (MHz)	L2 (MB)	MM (GB)
CHALLENGE (36)	R4400 (200)	4.0	16
DEC 2100 A500MP (4)	21064 (190)	1.0	2
SPARCserver 1000 (8)	SuperSPARC (60)	1.0	2

where N = maximal number of CPUs, L2 = maximal configurable secondary cache per CPU
MM = maximal configurable main memory for the whole system

MB = megabytes = 2^{20} bytes, GB = gigabytes = 2^{30} bytes

CHAPTER 17

RISC Applications in Real-time Systems

17.1 Introductory Comments: Real-time Concepts and RISC

Because of the RISC microprocessors' relative simplicity, high performance, and fast response, they are particularly suitable for real-time applications. *Real-time computing systems* can be defined as computing systems required to yield results at specific deadlines during actual implementation [HaSt 91, Savi 85, Stan 88]. Real-time systems can be interactive, where an operator at a terminal expects an immediate response before taking the next step in the operation. Real-time systems are utilized in many cases such as process control systems, where a computer is directing or monitoring an ongoing physical process.

Real-time systems are applied in a variety of areas. Industrial real-time applications may involve control of chemical processes, machine control, and data acquisition for medical equipment, for power systems, and for avionics. Real-time industry applications may include field command control communication (C-cube) systems, instrument panels and monitoring systems. Real-time computing systems are also used in the management and handling of satellite communication. In the office business market, real-time systems are used for airline reservation operations, data acquisition for financial transactions, control of laser copiers and printers, and many other applications.

No matter what the nature of the application, *timing* (or rather obtaining the result on time) is one of the most critical issues in real-time systems. The real-time computing system receives, periodically, a certain amount of input signals in the form of operator requests from a terminal or from sensor measurements. The input signals undergo processing by the computing system, according to established algorithms, appropriate for the application, yielding a set of output results. The output results may appear as messages on a terminal screen or as signals directed to various locations of the system. These output signals must be made available by a prescribed deadline. Any tardiness or delay may result in a faulty operation of the system. The output results should be held available for a sufficient time for the rest of the system to act upon them. Once the results have been used and acted upon, space for new results of the next cycle should be provided.

Based on the above considerations, we can define the following timing measures that can be applied to real-time systems:

Response time — time the real-time system takes to recognize and respond to an external event. To be more precise, the time interval between the appearance of an input signal and the appearance of an output result.

Survival time — time during which output data will remain available to be noticed and acted upon.

Throughput — total number of events that the system can handle in a given time period. When measured in bits/sec, it is called *bandwidth*.

Recovery time (cleanup time) — the time it takes to provide space for the output results of the next cycle after having acquired and acted upon the previous results.

Of the above timing measures, the response time is the most crucial for real-time applications. Its value, compared to the required information update period, will establish whether a given computing system is fit for a specific real-time implementation.

Let us now look more closely at the specific tasks that a real-time computing system is usually required to perform. It should also be noted that the organization, implementing the real-time system, may have additional computational tasks, not necessarily connected with the real-time operation. We can, therefore, classify the tasks in the following manner:

1.   Direct real-time tasks repeated at specified time periods (sometimes called *sampling periods*):

(a) Acquisition of input variables through sensors, keyboard, or other devices. In many cases, the input signals must undergo an additional transformation, in order to be treatable by the computing system (such as A/D conversion, sampling and hold).

(b) Application of computational algorithms by the processing subsystem. The algorithms depend on the nature of the real-time operation. The worst-case computing time of the algorithms should be below the operational sampling period.

(c) Transmission of output results to the terminals and/or control signal application points. This may require in many cases transformation operations such as processing for video display and D/A conversion.

2.   Indirect tasks associated with the real-time operation, such as diagnostics, memory check, and non-real-time update of process status. The results of these tasks are not expected at specific deadlines; however, they are still to be performed to assure reliable operation and maintenance of the system.

3.   Non-real-time tasks or computational tasks required by the organization implementing the real-time system, but unrelated to the real-time operation.

As we can see, the computing system managing the real-time operation is called upon to perform a great variety of tasks, many of which are to be performed periodically (tasks 1(a), (b), (c)), within prescribed periods of time. The more tasks required of the system and the shorter the sampling period, the more powerful, faster, and more *predictable* will the computing system have to be. RISC-type systems have been repeatedly shown to be faster than CISC-type systems. Because of the RISC hardware simplicity and its high performance, it is easier to predict its time of computation for different tasks. Naturally, some RISC-type processors were chosen as CPUs for real-time applications by a number of manufacturers. Because of the possible multiplicity of tasks imposed on a real-time system, it sometimes makes sense to configure it as a multiprocessor [Tabk 90], a feature practiced by a number of real-time systems manufacturers.

17.2 The PowerPC-based MVME 1600

The MVME 1600 is a VMEbus, PowerPC-based (see chapter 7), microprocessor module, featured by Motorola (Phoenix, AZ). It features two types of module:

1. MVME 1600/PM 603, with a PowerPC 603 processor, operating at 66MHz.
2. MVME 1600/PM 604, with a PowerPC 604 processor, operating at 100MHz.

The MP 603 offers workstation-level performance packed into a low-power, low-cost design, particularly suited for embedded real-time control and monitoring applications. The MP 604 constitutes a high-velocity system for sophisticated control and mid-range servers. A block diagram of the MVME 1600 is shown in Fig. 17.1.

A key feature of the MVME 1600 is the use of the *peripheral component interconnect* (PCI) for the on-board local bus peripherals. PCI is also used to support an industry standard mezzanine interface (IEEE P1386.1 Standard) *PCI mezzanine card* (PMC). PMC modules provide a wide variety of I/O expansion for FDDI, graphics, or additional Ethernet or SCSI ports. One single PMC module can be installed on the MVME 1600 and still occupy only one VME slot. The MVME 1600 features:

1. User expandable shared DRAM of 8 to 128MB.
2. Single 32-bit PMC expansion slot.
3. Non-volatile RAM (NVRAM) of $8K \times 8$ and time-of-day clock with removable battery backup.
4. Four serial communication ports, two asynchronous and two asynchronous/synchronous.
5. Four 16-bit times and watchdog timer.
6. 16-bit SCSI-2 bus interface with 32-bit PCI local bus burst DMA.
7. Ethernet transceiver interface with 32-bit PCI local bus DMA.
8. Super VGA graphics port.
9. Eight-bit bidirectional parallel port, IEEE 1284 Centronics compatible.
10. VMEexec real-time development environment support. VMEexec includes a real-time executive and a suite of development tools for designing embedded applications in a UNIX environment.
11. On-board debugger and diagnostic firmware.

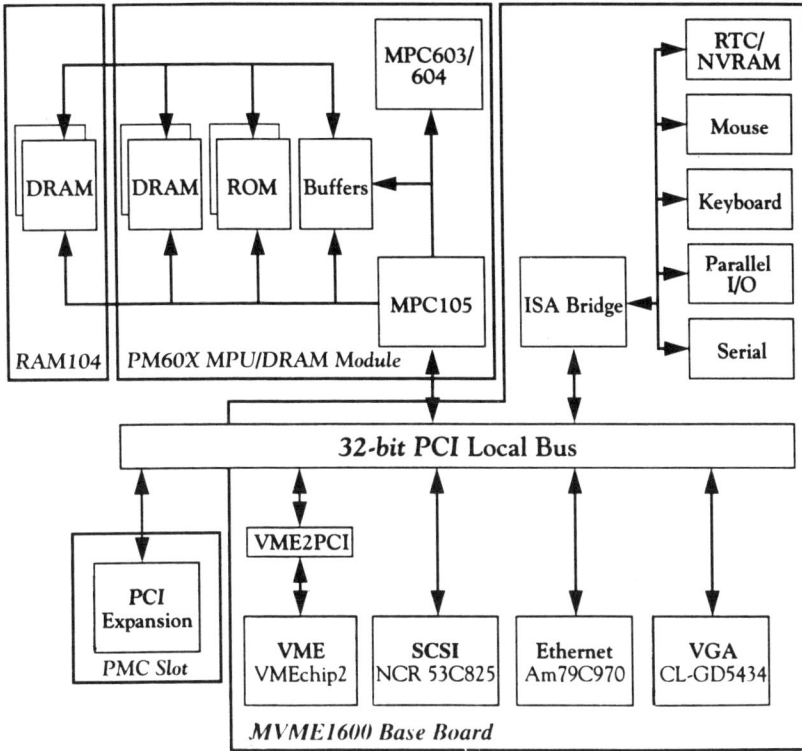

Fig. 17.1   MVME 1600 block diagram *(Courtesy of Motorola, Inc.)*

Development software for the MVME 1600 includes the on-board debugger/ monitor firmware and the VMEexec development environment, which provides the application developer with a complete set of tools. Operating in a point-and-click environment, the developer moves from source code editor, to compiler, to loader, to debugger, to performance analyzer, to source code browser, to archiver in any sequence using a graphical user interface. The C and C++ compilers provide flexibility and range in writing real-time applications. A set of flexible utilities for target environment build and load are provided under the same user interface. The VMEexec development environment is packaged in start-up kits which provide the real-time programmer with the necessary tools to build, test, and deploy a complete run-time environment for the MVME 1600 boards. The start-up kits include all utilities and libraries, a pSOS+ kernel, the pROBE+ target debugger, a UNIX system V application programming interface library, a STREAMS interface to Ethernet, FDDI, X.25, and OSI networks, and board support packages for Motorola's family of VMEbus processor modules.

17.3 Examples of Other RISC-based Real-time Systems
Heurikon Daytona system

The Heurikon (Madison, WI) Daytona system is a fully integrated real-time graphics workstation consisting of a Silicon Graphics Indy workstation (see chapter 16) embedded in a VMEbus system enclosure. Fig. 17.2 illustrates the structure of the Daytona system. The Daytona is configurable with up to nine of Heurikon's real-time target CPU boards. These boards can be based either on the RISC-type MIPS R3500 or on the CISC MC68040 [Tabk 94]. The RISC-based board, denoted as HKMIPS/V3500, features the MIPS R3500 processor, produced by IDT (Integrated Device Technology, Inc., Santa Clara, CA). The R3500 combines both the R3000 CPU and the R3010 floating-point coprocessor (see chapter 9) on the same chip. It operates at 40MHz. The architecture of the R3500 is identical to that of the R3000. It has a 64-entry TLB and a five-stage instruction pipeline, identical to that of the R3000.

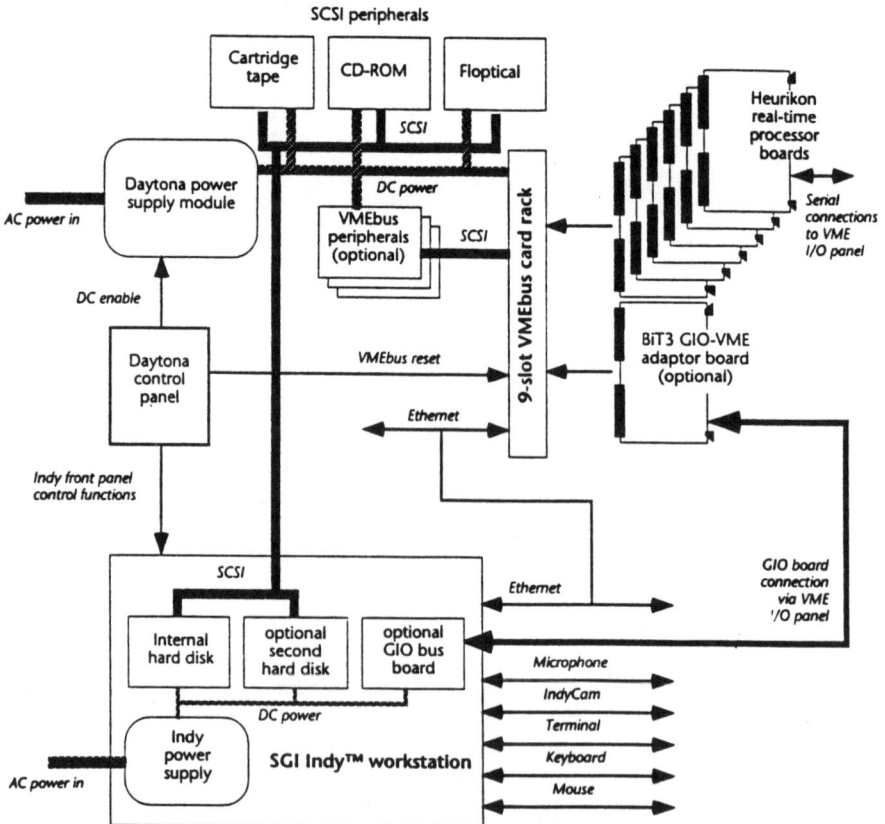

Fig. 17.2   Daytona block diagram *(Courtesy of Heurikon Corporation)*

The HKMIPS/V3500 has an off-chip primary 64KB instruction cache and a 64KB data cache. The caches are direct-mapped and interleaved on a common set of data and address lines from the CPU. The board main memory can be configured as 8, 16, or 32MB DRAM. There is also a memory capability of up to 1MB non-volatile boot PROM for storage of system software and 32KB of non-volatile RAM (NVRAM) for user definable functions. The system features a VMEbus architecture with 32-bit datapath, 32-bit addressing, and seven bus interrupts. There are four serial ports: two asynchronous serial ports provided via two Western Digital 8250 UARTs and two additional serial ports provided via a Z85C30 chip. There are also two programmable AMD 82C54-based timers, and three independent 16-bit counters. The Intel 82596CA 32-bit local area network (LAN) chip is used for interface with Ethernet. It conforms to IEEE 802.3 Standard, supports up to 10 Mbit/sec transfers, and has on-chip DMA and memory management. The HKMIPS/V3500 includes an NCR 53C710 SCSI I/O processor.

The Daytona combines IRIX, Silicon Graphics' UNIX system V.4 OS, with Wind River's VxWorks real-time development environment. The IRIX OS provides development tools, media capabilities, networking facilities, and a programmer-friendly interface to offer an application development platform. IRIX's extensions also enable implementation of soft real-time tasks, such as those with non-critical time constraints. IRIX's extensions also enable implementation of soft real-time tasks, such as those with non-critical time constraints. IRIX serves as the high-level platform to develop real-time code that will run and be debugged under VxWorks. The VxWorks compact ROMable kernel resides on each real-time target and handles the debugging, testing, and running of real-time applications. The kernel, designed for hard real-time, provides context switch times of less than 1.5 microseconds and interrupt delay of less than 8 microseconds.

Encore Infinity R/T Model 300
The Encore Infinity R/T Model 300 is an Alpha AXP-based real-time system manufactured by Encore Computer Corporation (Fort Lauderdale, FL). Its CPU is a 150MHz DEC 21064 microprocessor. In addition it has an Intel i960 I/O coprocessor. It can be configured with a 512KB secondary cache (L2) and up to 128MB of on-board main memory. It features six independent 32-bit counter/timers, Ethernet interface, two serial ports, and two SCSI-2 controllers. The Ethernet access is implemented using the Intel 82590CA Ethernet controller. The SCSI-2 controller functions are provided by the NCR53C710 system. The system conforms to the VMEbus protocol specification. Its OS is the UNIX-based OSF/1.

Force CPU-3CE
A SPARC-based real-time board CPU-3CE, suitable for embedded applications, is produced by Force Computers, Inc. (San Jose, CA). Its CPU is a 40 or 60MHz MicroSPARC (see chapter 8). The CPU-3CE features:

1. Main memory of 8, 16, 32, or 64MB DRAM.
2. Boot firmware on a 512KB flash EEPROM.
3. User flash EEPROM of 1MB.
4. Ethernet interface integrated in the NCR 89C100, compatible with the industry-standard AM7990 Ethernet controller. The 89C100 includes a DMA controller.
5. SCSI-2 interface, 10 MB/sec.
6. Centronics-compatible parallel port.
7. Two serial I/O channels.
8. Keyboard and mouse ports.
9. Floppy-disk controller.
10. An MK48T08 real-time clock non-volatile RAM (RTC/NVRAM), 6KB.
11. A watchdog timer.
12. Sbus interface (two slots).
13. VMEbus interface based on the Sun S4-VME chip.

The main CPU-3CE OS is the Solaris. It is UNIX-based, and it comprises the SunOS, a networking environment, the OpenWindows environment based on the X-Window standard, and a graphical user interface. Both Solaris 1.1, based on SunOS 4.1.3 (a BSD UNIX derivative), and Solaris 2.x, based on UNIX SVR4, are ported on the CPU-3CE. For applications that require fast and deterministic real-time response, a board support package for the VxWorks real-time OS is available. VxWorks enables the CPU-3CE to run as a standalone real-time system in an Ethernet and/or VMEbus network of UNIX boards or systems.

SKYbolt
The SKYbolt system is manufactured by Sky Computers, Inc. (Chelmsford, MA). It features two CPUs, and it uses a host system. The main CPU is an Intel i860XR (see chapter 10), operating at a frequency of 40MHz. The second CPU is an Intel i960KA [HiTa 92], which is an I/O processor (IOP) handling the SKYbolt's three gateways: the VME bus, the VSB bus, and the auxiliary port. The i960KA also executes a kernel which binds the SKYbolt to the host server process. The host system, operating under the host OS, provides the operator interface routines and peripheral device management. The host system CPU may be an MC680x0 on a Sun-3, or a SPARC on a SPARCstation or Sun-4. The OS is SunOS 4.0x. The system can be configured with 256KB secondary cache (L2) and with up to 64MB DRAM main memory. There is also an option of attaching to the system a SKYbolt Shamrock daughter card that contains four i860XR processors and 16 or 64MB DRAM.

17.4 Concluding Comments
Some examples of RISC-based real-time boards have been presented in the preceding two sections. Some of these systems' properties are summarized in Table 17.1. Obviously, the Alpha AXP-based Infinity R/T, running at 150MHz,

with 512KB of secondary cache, and up to 128MB of main memory, appears to be the frontrunner. The reason for this is its top frequency of operation, top secondary cache, and top total main memory (matched by MVME 1600 only).

Table 17.1 RISC-based Real-time Systems

System:	1600	Daytona	Infinity	CPU-3CE	SKYbolt
CPU (MHz)	PPC 604 (100)	R3500 (40)	21064 (150)	MicroSPARC (60)	i860XR (40)
L1 cache(KB)	16I+16D on-chip	64I+64D off-chip	8I+8D on-chip	4I+2D on-chip	4I+8D on-chip
L2 cache(KB)	-	-	512	-	256
MM (MB)	128	32	128	64	64
OS	VMEexec	IRIX+ VxWorks	OSF/1	Solaris+ VxWorks	SunOS 4.0x

where: L1 = primary cache, L2 = secondary cache, MM = main memory (maximal)
        I = instruction,   D = data,   OS = operating system

The 40MHz SKYbolt has an off-chip secondary cache L2 of 256KB (no L2 on MVME 1600), which might compensate somewhat for its relatively low frequency of operation. Moreover, the SKYbolt can be configured with six CPUs (using the Shamrock daughter card and the i960 IOP) running in parallel. The 40MHz Daytona has a rather large off-chip primary cache of a total of 128KB (64KB I-cache, 64KB D-cache). The 60MHz CPU-3CE comes close in its frequency of operation to that of the PowerPC 603 (66MHz). All in all, the above systems have some very useful components for real-time operation. More RISC-based real-time boards are expected to be developed in the near future.

CHAPTER 18

RISC Systems: Past, Present, Future

In the concluding chapter (15) of "RISC Systems" (1990), some predictions were made concerning the future development of RISC-type processors. It was predicted that 'over the next few years, some new RISC systems, unknown today, will be announced'. Indeed, quite a few new RISC systems appeared within the following four years. These new systems include the DEC Alpha AXP architecture 21064 and 21164 processors (see chapter 6), the IBM, Motorola, Apple PowerPC architecture 601, 603, 604, and 620 processors (see chapter 7), the Sun Microsystems and TI SuperSPARC and UltraSPARC (see chapter 8), the MIPS R4000, R8000, and R10000 (see chapter 9), the Intel i860XP (see chapter 10), the Motorola MC88110 (see chapter 11), and the Hewlett-Packard PA-RISC 7100 (see chapter 12).

It was predicted that 'more and more resources will be put on the processor chip'. Indeed, it has been done on a large scale. While at that time the top transistor count was 1.2 million (i860), the transistor count of today pushes the ten million with 9.3 million transistors on the DEC 21164 (see chapter 6). It seems that the promise of 50 to 100 million on-chip transistors by the end of the century becomes more of a reality as time goes on. The 21164 has a total of 112KB cache on-chip: 16KB primary (8KB instruction, 8KB data) and 96KB secondary cache. It is the largest on-chip cache to date, and the 21164 is so far the only processor with an on-chip secondary cache. Undoubtedly, these values will increase in the future. Moreover, in some systems, we may see some significant on-chip main memory. While at the writing of "RISC Systems" not all processors had an on-chip FPU, almost every major, high-performance current RISC (or CISC for that matter) processor now has an on-chip FPU. Other special operational subsystems will be added in the future. In 1989, the i860 (see chapter 10) was the only chip with an on-chip graphics unit. Today, the MC88110 (see chapter 11) has two graphics units. This trend is expected to continue in other systems, possibly implementing additional types of special computational unit.

It was predicted that 'we should also expect an expansion in the standard word length ... some new RISC systems will indeed be full-scale 64-bit machines'. Indeed, the new top-level systems such as the DEC Alpha AXP 21064, 21164, the PowerPC 620, the Sun and TI UltraSPARC, and the MIPS R4000 and R10000 are full-scale 64-bit processors.

While the RISC systems of the late eighties implemented a scalar pipeline, issuing a single instruction per cycle, practically all current major processors,

RISC or CISC (Pentium, MC68060 [Tabk 94]), implement instruction level parallelism (ILP), most being superscalar, issuing more than one instruction per cycle (see chapter 1). For instance, the major current RISC systems mentioned above, such as the 21164, PowerPC 620, UltraSPARC, and R10000, are all four-issue superscalar.

While the RISC CMOS-based processors, described in "RISC Systems", ran at below 50MHz, most current major CMOS-based systems run at between 100 and 200MHz. The Alpha-based systems run at over 200MHz, with the 21164 at 300MHz. The frequency of operation is expected to increase in the coming years. Even now, laboratory experiments conducted at up to 500MHz are reported [Gepp 95].

Another trend in the development of computing systems is multiprocessing (see chapter 15). Practically all modern multiprocessors, with just a few exceptions, implement RISC-type processors as individual CPUs within the system. This occurs not only in massively parallel processors (MPPs) but also in smaller-scale systems. There are a number of workstations which implement a number of RISC-type processors (see chapter 16). While at the moment most of the personal computers (PCs) and workstations implement CISC-type processors, such as the Intel x86 (taking up a major part of the market) or Motorola M68000 families [Tabk 94], the trend is to increase the percentage of RISC-type systems in the individual computing systems area. Even some of the most recent CISC-type systems contain certain attributes practiced earlier by RISC systems only. For instance, the Pentium of the Intel x86 family and the MC68060 of the Motorola M68000 family are both two-issue superscalars with two parallel integer computation pipelines, and both implement an on-chip dual cache (Motorola has been implementing an on-chip dual cache in its earlier MC68030 and MC68040 as well [Tabk 94]). Undoubtedly, some of the future processors will be hybrid systems implementing RISC properties (see chapter 2) and conforming to earlier, possibly CISC-type, architectures. The PowerPC (see chapter 7), for instance, is a fully fledged RISC system carrying certain elements of the earlier IBM 360 and 370 architecture.

A distinct new development in recent years is the cooperation of several outstanding computer companies leading to the creation of new systems. Some recent examples of such fruitful cooperation are IBM/Motorola/Apple creating the PowerPC (see chapter 7), Sun Microsystems and Texas Instruments (TI) creating the SuperSPARC and the UltraSPARC (see chapter 8), and MIPS (Silicon Graphics) and Toshiba creating the R8000 (see chapter 9). Intel (the creator of the x86, i860, and i960 families) and Hewlett-Packard (HP; creator of the PA-RISC family, see chapter 12) are currently working on the development of a new system. Such a trend of mutual collaboration between leading computer companies is expected to continue. More new and exciting developments are just around the corner.

References

[Adms 86] G.D. Adams, Functional Specification and Simulation of a Floating Point Coprocessor for SPUR, Report No. UCB/CSD 87/311, Computer Science Division, University of California, Berkeley, CA, August 1986

[Adms 94] Don Adams, *CRAY T3D System Architecture Overview*, Publication No. HR-04033, Cray Research, Inc., Chippewa Falls, WI, 25 February 1994

[AhHU 75] A.V. Aho, J. Hopcroft, J. Ullman, *The Design and Analysis of Computer Algorithms*, Addison-Wesley, Reading, MA, 1975

[AlBe 93] M.S. Allen, M.C. Becker, Multiprocessing Aspects of the PowerPC 601, Proc. COMPCON 93, pp. 117-126, San Francisco, CA, 22-26 February 1993

[Alex 93] N. Alexandridis, *Design of Microprocessor-Based Systems*, Prentice-Hall, Englewood Cliffs, NJ, 1993

[Amar 93] C. Amaru, DEC, HP Seek High-End Workstation Supremacy, Digital News & Review, 23 August 1993

[ArBa 86] J. Archibald, J.L. Baer, Cache Coherence Protocols: Evaluation using Multiprocessor Simulation Model, ACM Trans. on Computer Systems, Vol. 4, No. 4, pp. 273-298, November 1986

[Aspr 93] T. Asprey et al., Performance Features of the PA7100 Microprocessor, IEEE MICRO, Vol. 13, No. 3, pp. 22-35, June 1993

[Atki 91] M. Atkins, Performance and the i860 Microprocessor, IEEE MICRO, Vol. 11, No. 5, pp. 24-27, 72-78, October 1991

[Azar 84] H. Azaria, Preliminary Analysis of RISC Architecture Performance, Microprocessing and Microprogramming, Vol. 14, No. 3, 4, pp. 133-137, October/November 1984

[AzTa 80] H. Azaria, D. Tabak, Bit-Sliced Realization of a CMOVE Architecture Microcomputer, EUROMICRO Journal, Vol. 6, No. 6, pp. 373-380, November 1980

[AzTa 81] H. Azaria, D. Tabak, A CMOVE Distributed Processing System, in L. Richter, P. Le Beaux, G. Chroust (eds.), *Implementing Functions: Microprocessors and Firmware*, North Holland, Amsterdam, 1981

[AzTa 83a] H. Azaria, D. Tabak, Design Considerations of a Single-Instruction Microcomputer — A Case Study, Microprocessing and Microprogramming, Vol. 11, No. 3, 4, pp. 187-194, March/April 1983

[AzTa 83b] H. Azaria, D. Tabak, The MODHEL Microcomputer for RISCS Study, Microprocessing and Microprogramming, Vol. 12, No. 3, 4, pp. 199-206, October/November 1984

[BaKe 95] P. Bannon, J. Keller, Internal Architecture of Alpha 21164 Microprocessor, Proc. COMPCON 95, pp. 79-87, San Francisco, CA, 6-8 March 1995

[BAMo 93] M.C. Becker, M.S. Allen, C.R. Moore, J.S. Muhich, D.P. Tuttle, The PowerPC 601 Microprocessor, IEEE MICRO, Vol. 13, No. 5, pp. 54-68, October 1993

[BaWh 90] H.B. Bakoglu, T. Whiteside, RISC System/6000 Hardware Overview, IBM RISC System/6000 Technology, pp. 8-15, SA 23-2619, IBM Corporation, 1990

[BiSh 88] L. Bic, A.C. Shaw, The Logical Design of OS, Prentice-Hall, Englewood Cliffs, NJ, 1988

[BiWo 86] J.S. Birnbaum, W.S. Worley, Beyond RISC: High Precision Architecture, HP Journal, Vol. 36, No. 8, pp. 4-10, August 1985 (also in Proc. COMPCON 86, pp. 40-47, San Francisco, CA, March 1986)

[BlKr 92] G. Blanck, S. Kreuger, The SuperSPARC Microprocessor, Proc. COMPCON 92, San Francisco, CA, February 1992

[BuPa 93] M. Butler, Y. Patt, A Comparative Performance Evaluation of Various State Maintenance Mechanisms, Proc. 26th Annual Symposium on Microarchitecture, MICRO-26, pp. 70-79, Austin, TX, 1-3 December 1993

[Burg 94] B. Burgess et al., The PowerPC 603 Microprocessor, Communications of the ACM, Vol. 37, No. 6, pp. 34-42, June 1994

[Cava 84] J.J.F. Cavanagh, Digital Computer Arithmetic, McGraw-Hill, NY, 1984

[ChBJ 92] J.B. Chen, A. Borg, N.P. Jouppi, A Simulation Based Study of TLB Performance, Proc. 19th Annual Int. Symp. on Computer Architecture (ISCA 92), pp. 114-123, Gold Coast, Queensland, Australia, 19-21 May 1992

[CKFa 94] D.G. Conroy, T.E. Kopec, J.R. Falcone, The Evolution of the Alpha AXP PC, Digital Technical Journal, Vol. 6, No. 1, pp. 54-65, Winter 1994

[ClSt 80] D.W. Clark, W.D. Strecker, Comments on "The Case for the RISC", Computer Architecture News, Vol. 8, No. 6, pp. 34-38, 15 October 1980

[CMT5 93] Connection Machine CM-5 Technical Summary, Thinking Machines Corporation, Cambridge, MA, November 1993

[Colw 85] R.P. Colwell et al., Computers, Complexity and Controversy, IEEE Computer, Vol. 18, No. 9, pp. 8-19, September 1985

[Colw 88] R.P. Colwell et al., A VLIW Architecture for a Trace Scheduling Compiler, IEEE Trans. on Computers, Vol. 37, No. 8, pp. 967-979, August 1988

[CuWi 75] H.J. Curnow, B.A. Wichmann, A Synthetic Benchmark, Computer Journal, Vol. 19, No. 1, 1975

404

[DaPT 88] J.M. Davila, A.J. Phillips, D. Tabak, Floating Point Arithmetic on a RISC, Microprocessing and Microprogramming, Vol. 23, No. 1-5, pp. 179-184, 1988

[DECM 92] DECchip 21064-AA Microprocessor Hardware Reference Manual, DEC, Order No. EC-N0079-72, Maynard, MA, October 1992

[Denn 72] P.J. Denning, On Modeling Program Behavior, Proc. Spring Joint Computer Conference, Vol. 40, pp. 937-944, AFIPS Press, Arlington, VA, 1972

[Deut 83] L.P. Deutsch, *The Dorado Smalltalk-80 Implementation: Hardware Architecture's Impact on Software Architecture*, Addison-Wesley, Reading, MA, 1983

[DiAl 92] K. Diefendorff, M. Allen, Organization of the Motorola 88110 Superscalar RISC Microprocessor, IEEE MICRO, Vol. 12, No. 2, pp. 40-63, April 1992

[Dief 94] K. Diefendorff, History of the PowerPC Architecture, Communications of the ACM, Vol. 37, No. 6, pp. 28-33, June 1994

[DiOH 94] K. Diefendorff, R. Oehler, R. Hochsprung, Evolution of the PowerPC Architecture, IEEE MICRO, Vol. 14, No. 2, pp. 34-49, April 1994

[Dobb 92] D.W. Dobberpuhl et al., A 200 Mhz 64-bit Dual-issue CMOS Microprocessor, Digital Technical Journal, Vol. 4, No. 4, pp. 35-50, Special Issue 1992

[Dong 85] J.J. Dongarra, Performance of Various Computers using Standard Linear Equations Software in a Fortran Environment, Comp. Arch. News, Vol. 13, No. 1, pp. 3-11, March 1985

[DuBo 88] D.K. DuBose, Extended RISC, M.S. Thesis, George Mason University, Fairfax, VA, 1988

[DuFT 86] D.K. DuBose, D.K. Fotakis, D. Tabak, A Microcoded RISC, Proc. 19th Annual Workshop on Microprogramming, MICRO 19, pp. 124-128, New York, 15-17 October 1986

[DWYF 92] E. DeLano, W. Walker, J. Yetter, M. Forsyth, A High Speed Superscalar PA-RISC Processor, Proc. COMPCON 92, pp. 116-121, San Francisco, CA, 24-28 February 1992

[EdRu 94] J. Edmondson, P. Rubinfeld, An Overview of the Alpha AXP 21164 Microarchitecture, Proc. Hot Chips VI Symposium, pp. 1-8, Stanford University, Palo Alto, CA, August 1994

[Ensl 77] P.H. Enslow, Multiprocessor Organization, ACM Computing Surveys, Vol. 9, No. 1, pp. 103-129, March 1977

[Fair 82] D.A. Fairclough, A Unique Microprocessor Instruction Set, IEEE MICRO, Vol. 2, No. 2, pp. 8-18, May 1982

[FlMM 87] M.J. Flynn, C.L. Mitchell, J.M. Mulder, And Now a Case for More Complex Instruction Sets, IEEE Computer, Vol. 20, No. 9, pp. 71-83, September 1987

[Flyn 72] M.J. Flynn, Some Computer Organizations and their Effectiveness, IEEE Trans. on Computers, Vol. C-21, No. 9, pp. 948-960, September 1972

[Gabr 85] R.P. Gabriel, *Performance and Evaluation of LISP Systems*, MIT Press, Cambridge, MA, 1985

[Garn 88] R.B. Garner, SPARC — Scalable RISC Architecture, Sun Technology, No.. 1, No. 3, pp. 42-55, Summer 1988

[GaWi 94] M. Galles, E. Williams, Performance Optimizations, Implementation, and Verification of the SGI Challenge Multiprocessor, Proc. 27th Annual Hawaii Int. Conf. on System Science, HICSS 27, Vol. 1, pp. 134-143, January 1994

[Gepp 95] L. Geppeert, Solid State, IEEE Spectrum, Vol. 32, No. 1, pp. 35-39, January 1995

[GoRo 83] A.J. Goldberg, D. Robson, *Smalltalk-80: The Language and its Implementation*, Addison-Wesley, Reading, MA, 1983

[Gree 95] D. Greeley et al., UltraSPARC: The Next Generation Superscalar 64-bit SPARC, Proc. COMPCON 95, pp. 442-451, San Francisco, CA, 6-8 March 1995

[GrHe 81] R.G. Grappel, J.E. Hemmengway, A Tale of Four Microprocessors: Benchmarks Quantify Performance, Electronic Design News, Vol. 26, No. 7, pp. 179-265, 1 April 1981

[GrOe 90] R.D. Groves, R. Oehler, IBM's RISC System/6000 Processor Architecture, Microprocessors and Microsystems, Vol. 14, No. 6, pp. 357-366, July/August 1990

[Half 93] T.R. Halfhill, PowerOpen Gives Users Freedom of Choice, BYTE, August 1993

[HaSt 91] W.A. Halang, A.D. Stoyenko, *Constructing Predictable Real Time Systems*, Kluwer, Norwell, MA, 1991

[HaVZ 90] V.C. Hamacher, Z.G. Vranesic, S.G. Zaky, *Computer Organization*, 3rd ed., McGraw-Hill, NY, 1990

[Hays 88] J.P. Hayes, *Computer Architecture and Organization*, 2nd ed., McGraw-Hill, NY, 1988

[Hays 94] F.M. Hayes, Design of the AlphaServer Multiprocessor Server System, Digital Technical Journal, Vol. 6, No. 3, pp. 8-19, Summer 1994

[Heat 84] J.L. Heath, Reevaluation of the RISC I, Computer Architecture News, Vol. 12, No. 1, pp. 3-10, March 1984

[Hein 93] J. Heinrich, *MIPS R4000 Microprocessor User's Manual*, PTR Prentice-Hall, Englewood Cliffs, NJ, 1993

[Hein 94] J. Heinrich, *MIPS R10000 Microprocessor User's Manual*, MIPS Technologies, Inc., Mountain View, CA, 1994

[Henn 82] J.L. Hennessy et al., The MIPS Machine, Proc. COMPCON 82, pp. 2-7, San Francisco, CA, February 1982

[Henn 84] J.L. Hennessy, VLSI Processor Architecture, IEEE Trans. on Computers, Vol. C-33, No. 12, pp. 1221-1246, December 1984

[HePa 90] J.L. Hennessy, D.A. Patterson, *Computer Architecture: A Quantitative Approach*, Morgan Kaufmann, San Mateo, CA, 1990

[HePa 94]   J.L. Hennessy, D.A. Patterson, *Computer Organization and Design, The Hardware/Software Approach*, Morgan Kaufmann, San Mateo, CA, 1994

[Hill 88]   M.D. Hill, A Case for Direct-Mapped Caches, IEEE Computer, Vol. 21, No. 12, pp. 25-40, December 1988

[HiSm 89]   M.D. Hill, A.J. Smith, Evaluating Associativity in CPU Caches, IEEE Trans. on Computers, Vol. 38, No. 12, pp. 1612-1630, December 1989

[HiSp 85]   C.Y. Hitchcock, H.M.B. Sprunt, Analyzing Multiple Register Sets, Proc. 12th Annual Int. Symp. on Computer Architecture (ISCA 85), pp. 55-63, Boston, MA, 17-19 June 1985

[HiTa 92]   K.J. Hintz, D. Tabak, *Microcontrollers: Architecture, Implementation, and Programming*, McGraw-Hill, NY, 1992

[HiTu 93]   W.D. Hillis, L.W. Tucker, The CM-5 Connection Machine: A Scalable Supercomputer, Communications of the ACM, Vol. 36, No. 11, pp. 31-40, November 1993

[Hunt 95]   D. Hunt, Advanced Performance Features of the 64-bit PA-8000, Proc. COMPCON 95, pp. 123-128, San Francisco, CA, 6-8 March 1995

[Hwan 79]   K. Hwang, *Computer Arithmetic*, Wiley, NY, 1979

[Hwan 93]   K. Hwang, *Advanced Computer Architecture*, McGraw-Hill, NY, 1993

[HwPa 87]   W.W. Hwu, Y.N. Patt, Checkpoint Repair of Out-of-Order Execution Machines, Proc. 14th Annual Int. Symp. on Computer Architecture (ISCA 87), pp. 18-26, Pittsburgh, PA, June 1987

[i860 91]   *i860 XP Microprocessor Data Book*, Intel Corporation Order No. 240874-002, November 1991

[IEEE 85]   *IEEE Standard 754-1985 for Binary Floating-Point Arithmetic*, IEEE Computer Society Press, Los Alamos, CA, 1985

[Indy 93]   *Indy*, Technical Report No. INDY-TR(06/93), Silicon Graphics Computer Systems, Mountain View, CA, 1993

[IntP 94]   *Intel Paragon XP/S Technical Summary*, Intel Supercomputer Systems Division, Document No. SSD9401R13N, Beaverton, OR, January 1994

[John 78]   S.C. Johnson, A Portable Compiler: Theory and Practice, Proc. Fifth Annual ACM Symp. on Programming Languages, pp. 97-104, January 1978

[Joup 89]   N.P. Jouppi, The Nonuniform Distribution of Instruction-Level and Machine Parallelism and its Effect on Performance, IEEE Trans. on Computers, Vol. 38, No. 12, pp. 1645-1658, December 1989

[JoWa 89]   N.P. Jouppi, D. Wall, Available Instruction Level Parallelism for Superscalar and Superpipelined Machines, Proc. Third Int. Conf. on Architectural Support for Programming Languages and OS (ASPLOS), pp. 272-282, Boston, MA, April 1989

[KaHe 92]   G. Kane, J. Heinrich, *MIPS RISC Architecture*, Prentice-Hall, Englewood Cliffs, NJ, 1992

[KaPa 86]   R.H. Katz, D.A. Patterson, A VLSI RISC Multiprocessor Workstation, Proc. ICCD 86, pp. 94-96, New York, October 1986

[Kate 85]   M.G.H. Katevenis, *Reduced Instruction Set Computer Architectures for VLSI*, MIT Press, Cambridge, MA, 1985

[KeRi 78]   B.W. Kernighan, D.M. Ritchie, *The C Programming Language*, Prentice-Hall, Englewood Cliffs, NJ, 1978

[KlWi 88]   S.R. Kleinman, D. Williams, Sun OS on SPARC, Sun Technology, Vol. 1, No. 3, pp. 56-63, Summer 1988

[Kneb 93]   P. Knebel et al., HP's PA7100LC: A Low-Cost Superscalar PA-RISC Processor, Proc. COMPCON 93, pp. 441-447, San Francisco, CA, 22-26 February 1993

[Kohn 95]   L. Kohn et al., The Visual Instruction Set (VIS) in UltraSPARC, Proc. COMPCON 95, pp. 462-469, San Francisco, CA, 6-8 March 1995

[KoMa 89]   L. Kohn, N. Margulis, Introducing the Intel i860 64-bit Microprocessor, IEEE MICRO, Vol. 9, No. 4, pp. 15-30, August 1989

[Kurp 94]   G. Kurpanek et al., PA7200: A PA-RISC Processor with Integrated High Performance MP Bus Interface, Proc. COMPCON 94, pp. 375-382, San Francisco, CA, February 1994

[Latt 81]   W.W. Lattin et al., A Methodology for VLSI Chip Design, Lambda, pp. 34-44, Second Quarter 1981

[Lee 89]   R.B. Lee, Precision Architecture, IEEE Computer, Vol. 22, No. 1, pp. 78-91, August 1989

[LeEc 84]   H.M. Levy, R.H. Eckhouse, Jr., *Computer Programming and Architecture: The VAX-11*, Digital Press, Bedford, MA, 1984

[Leeu 90]   G. Leeuwrik, D.R. Miller, D.J. Quammen, R. Senko, D. Tabak, Hardware Design of the Multris Microprocessor, Microprocessing and Microprogramming, Vol. 28, No. 1-5, pp. 117-122, March 1990

[Leon 87]   T.E. Leonard, ed., *VAX Architecture Reference Manual*, Digital Press, Bedford, MA, 1987

[LiGi 86]   Y.C. Liu, G.A. Gibson, *Microcomputer Systems: The 8086/8088 Family*, 2nd ed., Prentice-Hall, Englewood Cliffs, NJ, 1986

[Lipo 76]   G.J. Lipovski, The Architecture of a Simple, Effective, Control Processor, in M. Sami, J. Wilmink, R. Zaks (eds.), *Microprocessing and Microprogramming*, EUROMICRO 76, pp. 7-18, North Holland, Amsterdam, 1976

Lipo 78]   G.J. Lipovski, On Conditional Moves in Control Processors, Proc. 2nd Rocky Mountain Symp. on Microprocessors, pp. 63-94, Pingree Park, CO, 1978

[M811 91]   *MC88110 User's Manual*, Motorola, UM88110/AD, 1991

[Maho 86]   M.J. Mahon et al., HP PA: The Processor, HP Journal, Vol. 37, No. 8, pp. 4-21, August 1986

[MaTA 91]   S. Makhdoom, D. Tabak, R. Auletta, Register File/Cache Microarchitecture Study using VHDL, Proc. 24th Annual Int. Symp. on Microarchitecture, MICRO-24, pp. 217-222, Albuquerque, NM, 18-20 November 1991

408

[McKi 94]   D.L. McKinney et al., Digital's DEC Chip 21066: The First Cost-Focused Alpha AXP Chip, Digital Technical Journal, Vol. 6, No. 1, pp. 66-77, Winter 1994

[McLe 93]   E. McLellan, The Alpha AXP Architecture and 21064 Processor, IEEE MICRO, Vol. 13, No. 3, pp. 36-47, June 1993

[Mele 89]   C. Melear, The Design of the 88000 RISC Family, IEEE MICRO, Vol. 9, No. 2, pp. 26-38, April 1989

[Milu 86]   V.M. Milutinovic, ed., Special Issue of IEEE Computer, Vol. 19, No. 10, October 1986

[MiWV 92]   S. Mirapuri, M. Woodacre, N. Vasseghi, The MIPS R4000 Processor, IEEE MICRO, Vol. 12, No. 2, pp. 10-22, April 1992

[Moor 93]   C.R. Moore, The PowerPC 601 Microprocessor, Proc. COMPCON 93, pp. 109-116, San Francisco, CA, 22-26 February 1993

[MoSt 94]   C.R. Moore, R.C. Stanphill, The PowerPC Alliance, Communications of the ACM, Vol. 37, No. 6, pp. 25-27, June 1994

[MPVa 93]   M. Moudgill, K. Pingali, S. Vassiliadis, Register Renaming and Dynamic Speculation: An Alternative Approach, Proc. 26th Annual Symp. on Microarchitecture, MICRO-26, pp. 202-218, Austin, TX, 1-3 December 1993

[MR40 91]   *MIPS R4000 Microprocessor User's Manual*, MIPS Computer Systems, Inc., 1991

[Myrs 82]   G.J. Myers, *Advances in Computer Architecture*, 2nd ed., Wiley, NY, 1982

[Occ2 88]   *OCCAM 2 Reference Manual*, Prentice-Hall, Englewood Cliffs, NJ, 1988

[OeBl 91]   R.E. Oehler, M.W. Blasgen, IBM RS/6000: Architecture and Performance, IEEE MICRO, Vol. 11, No. 3, pp. 14-17, 56-62, June 1991

[P604 94]   *PowerPC 604 RISC Microprocessor Technical Summary*, Motorola, Inc., Order No. MPC604/D, Rev. 1, Austin, TX, May 1994

[PaDi 80]   D.A. Patterson, D.R. Ditzel, The Case for the RISC, Computer Architecture News, Vol. 8, No. 6, pp. 25-33, 15 October 1980

[PaPa 84]   M. Paramarcos, J. Patel, A Low Overhead Coherent Solution for Multiprocessors with Private Cache Memories, Proc. 11th Int. Symp. on Computer Architecture (ISCA), pp. 348-354, Ann Arbor, MI, June 1984

[Papd 91]   G.M. Papadopoulos, *Implementation of a General-Purpose Dataflow Multiprocessor*, MIT Press, Cambridge, MA, 1991

[PaPi 82]   D.A. Patterson, R.S. Piepho, Assessing RISC in HLL Support, IEEE MICRO, Vol. 2, No. 4, pp. 9-19, November 1982

[PARI 90]   *PA-RISC 1.1 Architecture and Instruction Set Reference Manual*, HP No. 09740-90039, November 1990

[PaSe 82]   D.A. Patterson, C.H. Sequin, A VLSI RISC, IEEE Computer, Vol. 15, No. 9, pp. 8-21, September 1982

[PaSi 93]   G. Papp,. E. Silha, PowerPC: A Performance Architecture, Proc. COMPCON 93, pp. 104-108, San Francisco, CA, 22-26 February 1993

[Patt 82] D.A. Patterson, A RISCy Approach to Computer Design, Proc. COMPCON 1982, pp. 8-14, San Francisco, CA, 1982

[Patt 84] D.A. Patterson, RISC Watch, Computer Architecture News, Vol. 12, No. 1, pp. 11-19, March 1984

[Patt 85] D.A. Patterson, Reduced Instruction Set Computers, Communications of the ACM, Vol. 28, No. 1, pp. 8-21, January 1985

[Paul 94] R.P. Paul, *SPARC Architecture, Assembly Language Programming, and C*, Prentice-Hall, Englewood Cliffs, NJ, 1994

[PeSW 91] C. Peterson, J. Sutton, P. Wiley, iWarp: A 100-MOPS LIW Microprocessor for Multicomputers, IEEE MICRO, Vol. 11, No. 3, pp. 26-29, 81-87, June 1991

[PoPC 93] *PowerPC 601 User's Manual*, Motorola, Inc., MPC601UM/AD, Rev. 1, June 1993

[Poun 91] D. Pountain, The Transputer Strikes Back, BYTE, pp. 265-275, August 1991

[Prot 88] D.A. Protopapas, *Microcomputer Hardware Design*, Prentice-Hall, Englewood Cliffs, NJ, 1988

[Przy 84] S.A. Przybylski et al., Organization and VLSI Implementation of MIPS, J. VLSI and Computer Systems, Vol. 1, No. 2, pp. 170-208, Spring 1984

[Przy 90] S.A. Przybylski, *Cache and Memory Hierarchy Design*, Morgan Kaufmann, San Mateo, CA, 1990

[QDuT 88] D.J. Quammen, D.K. DuBose, D. Tabak, A RISC Architecture for Multitasking, Proc. 21st Annual Hawaii Int. Conf. on System Sciences, HICSS 21, Vol. 1, pp. 230-237, January 1988

[QuMT 89] D.J. Quammen, D.R. Miller, D. Tabak, Register Window Management for a Real-Time Multitasking RISC, Proc. 22nd Annual Hawaii Int. Conf. on System Sciences, HICSS 22, Vol. 1, pp. 135-142, 3-6 January 1989

[Radi 83] G. Radin, The 801 Minicomputer, IBM J. R. & D., Vol. 27, No. 3, pp. 237-246, May 1983

[Rafi 84] M. Rafiquzzaman, *Microprocessors and Microcomputer Development Systems*, Harper & Row, NY, 1984

[RauF 93] B.R. Rau, J.A. Fisher, Instruction Level Parallel Processing: History, Overview, and Perspective, J. Supercomputing, Vol. 7, No. 1/2, pp. 9-50, May 1993

[Rhod 94] S. Rhodes, *MIPS R8000 Microprocessor Chip Set User's Manual*, MIPS Technologies, Inc., Mountain View, CA, 1994

[Robe 58] J.E. Robertson, A New Class of Digital Division Methods, IEEE Trans. on Computers, Vol. C-7, No. 3, pp. 218-222, September 1958

[Savi 85] S. Savitzky, *Real-Time Microprocessor Systems*, Van Nostrand Reingold, NY, 1985

[SBNe 82] D.P. Siewiorek, C.G. Bell, A. Newell, *Computer Structures: Principles and Examples*, McGraw-Hill, NY, 1982

[ShAz 85]   I. Shallom, H. Azaria, Architectural Concepts of an Optimal Instruction Set Selection Procedure Machine, Microprocessing and Microprogramming, Vol. 16, No. 2, 3, pp. 113-119, September/October 1985

[ShPh 94]   J. Shipnes, M. Phillip, A Modular Approach to Motorola PowerPC Compilers, Communications of the ACM, Vol. 37, No. 6, pp. 56-63, June 1994

[Sieg 90]   H.J. Siegel, *Interconnection Networks for Large-Scale Parallel Processing*, 2nd ed., McGraw-Hill, NY, 1990

[Sits 92a]   R.L. Sites, Alpha AXP Architecture, Digital Technical Journal, Vol. 4, No. 4, pp. 19-34, Special Issue, 1992

[Sits 92b]   R.L. Sites, ed., *Alpha Architecture Reference Manual*, Digital Press, Burlington, MA, 1992

[Sits 93]   R.L. Sites, Alpha AXP Architecture, Communications of the ACM, Vol. 36, No. 2, pp. 33-44, February 1993

[Slat 91]   M. Slater, PA Workstations Set Price/Performance Records, Microprocessor Report, Vol.5, No. 6, 3 April 1991

[Smit 78]   A.J. Smith, A Comparative Study of Set Associative Memory Mapping Algorithms and their Use for Cache and Main Memory, IEEE Trans. on Software Eng., Vol. SE-4, No. 2, pp. 121-130, March 1978

[Smit 82]   A.J. Smith, Cache Memories, Computing Surveys, Vol. 14, No. 3, pp. 473-530, September 1982

[Smit 85]   A.J. Smith, Cache Evaluation and the Impact of Workload Choice, Proc. 12th Annual Int. Symp. on Computer Architecture (ISCA 85), pp. 64-73, Boston, MA, 17-19 June 1985

[Smit 87]   A.J. Smith, Line (Block) Size Choice for CPU Cache Memories, IEEE Trans. on Computers, Vol. C-36, No. 9, pp. 1063-1075, September 1987

[SmPl 85]   J.E. Smith, A.R. Pleszkun, Implementation of Precise Interrupts in Pipelined Processors, Proc. 12th Annual Int. Symp. on Computer Architecture (ISCA 85), pp. 36-44, Boston, MA, 17-19 June 1985

[SmWe 94]   J.E. Smith, S. Weiss, PowerPC 601 and Alpha 21064: A Tale of Two RISCs, IEEE Computer, Vol. 27, No. 6, pp. 46-58, June 1994

[Sprc 90]   *SPARC RISC User's Guide*, Ross Technology, Inc., Austin, TX, 2nd ed., February 1990

[SSII 95]   STP1021 SuperSPARC II Addendum, Revision 1.3, Sun Microsystems, Mountain View, CA, January 1995

[SSPC 92]   *SuperSPARC User's Guide*, TI Document 2647726-9721, October 1992

[Stal 93]   W. Stallings, *Computer Organisation and Architecture*, Macmillan, NY, 1993

[Stan 88]   J.A. Stankovic, Misconceptions About Real-Time Computing, IEEE Computer, Vol. 21, No. 10, pp. 10-19, October 1988

[Symm 93] *Symmetric M ultiprocessing Systems*, T echnical Report No. EVER-IND-TR(01/93), Silicon Graphics Computer Systems, Mountain View, CA, 1993

[T900 91] *The T9000 Transputer Products Overview Manual*, INMOS (SGS-Thomson Microelectronics Group), Phoenix, AZ, 1991

[Tabk 87] D. Tabak, *RISC Architecture*, Research Studies Press, UK, and Wiley, NY, 1987

[Tabk 90] D. Tabak, *Multiprocessors*, Prentice-Hall, Englewood Cliffs, NJ, 1990

[Tabk 94] D. Tabak, *Advanced Microprocessors*, 2nd ed., McGraw-Hill, NY, 1994

[TaLi 80] D. Tabak, G.J. Lipovski, MOVE Architecture in Digital Controllers, IEEE Trans. on Computers, Vol. C-29, No. 2, pp. 180-190, February 1980

[Tall 92] M. Talluri, S. Kong, M.D. Hill, D.A. Patterson, Tradeoffs in Supporting Two Page Sizes, Proc. 19th Annual Int. Symp. on Computer Architecture (ISCA 92), pp. 415-424, Gold Coast, Queensland, Australia, 19-21 May 1992

[TaSe 83] Y. Tamir, C.H. Sequin, Strategies for Managing the Register File in RISC, IEEE Trans. on Computers, Vol. C-32, No. 11, pp. 977-989, November 1983

[TC20 94] *TC2000 Product Summary*, BBN Systems and Technologies, Cambridge, MA, October 1994

[ThRy 94] T. Thompson, B. Ryan, PowerPC 620 Soars, BYTE, pp. 113-120, November 1994

[Tran 88] *The Transputer Instruction Set — A Compiler Writer's Guide*, Prentice-Hall, Englewood Cliffs, NJ, 1988

[Uffe 91] J. Uffenbeck, *Microcomputers and Microprocessors*, 2nd ed., Prentice-Hall, Englewood Cliffs, NJ, 1991

[Ungr 87] D.M. Ungar, *The Design and Evaluation of a High Performance Smalltalk System*, MIT Press, Cambridge, MA, 1987

[UnPa 87] D.M. Ungar, D.A. Patterson, What Price Smalltalk?, IEEE Computer, Vol. 20, No. 1, pp. 67-74, January 1987

[Wall 88] D.W. Wall, Register Windows vs. Register Allocation, Proc. Conf. on Programming Language Design and Implementation (SIGPLAN '88), pp. 67-78, Atlanta, GA, 22-24 June 1988

[WeGe 94] D. Weaver, T. Germond, *The SPARC Architecture Manual, Version 9*, SPARC International, Inc., and Prentice-Hall, Englewood Cliffs, NJ, 1994

[Weic 84] R.P. Weicker, Dhrystone: A Synthetic Systems Programming Benchmark, Communications of the ACM, Vol. 27, No. 10, pp. 1013-1030, October 1984

[WeSm 94] S. Weiss, J.M. Smith, *POWER and PowerPC*, Morgan Kaufmann, Inc., San Francisco, CA, 1994

[WiCu 75]   B.A. Wichmann, H.J. Curnow, The Design of Synthetic Programs, **in** *Benchmarking: Computer Evaluation and Measurement*, pp. 89-114, Wiley, London, 1975

[ZuML 95]   J. Zurawski, J. Murray, P. Lemmon, The Design of the AlphaStation 800 5/300 Workstation, Proc. COMPCON 95, pp. 88-94, San Francisco, CA, 6-8 March 1995

Glossary of Abbreviations

ABI	Application Binary Interface
ADC	Analog to Digital Converter
AIX	Advanced Interactive Executive
ALU	Arithmetic Logic Unit
AMD	Advanced Micro Devices
AMU	Arithmetic Move Unit
ANDES	Architecture with Non-sequential Dynamic Execution Scheduling
ANSI	American National Standards Institute
AP	Argument Pointer
ARI	Address Register Indirect
ARM	Acorn RISC Machine
ASCII	American Standard Code for Information Interchange
ASI	1. Address Space Identifier
	2. Application Software Interface
ASIC	Application Specific Integrated Circuit
ATC	Address Translation Cache
AU	Address Unit
B	Byte
BAT	Block Address Translation
BATC	Block ATC
BBN	Bolt, Beranek and Newman
BCD	Binary Coded Decimal
BE	Byte Enable
BEAR	Bus Error Address Register
BGU	Ben Gurion University
BHT	Branch History Table
BiCMOS	Bipolar CMOS
BIST	Built-In Self Test
BIT	Bipolar Integrated Technology
BIU	Bus Interface Unit
BLT	Block Transfer Engine
BMIC	Bus Master Interface Controller
BPC	Breakpoint Program Counter

BPU	Branch Processing Unit
BSD	Berkeley Software Distribution
BTAC	Branch Target Address Cache
BTC	Branch Target Cache
BTLB	Block TLB
BU	Bus Unit

C	Carry
CA	1. Core Architecture
	2. Channel Attention
CACP	Centralized Arbitration Control Point
CACR	Cache Control Register
CAD	Computer-Aided Design
CAMMU	Cache and MMU
CAR	Compare Address Register
CC	Cache Controller
CCR	1. Condition Code Register
	2. Concurrency Control Register
CD	Cache Disable
CDC	Control Data Corporation
CF	Carry Flag
CFG	Configuration
CFP	Current Frame Pointer
CIO	Channel Input/Output
CIS	Central Instruction Sequencer
CISC	Complex Instruction Set Computer
CLA	Carry Look Ahead
CMMU	Cache/MMU
CMOS	Complementary MOS
CMOVE	Conditional Move
CP	1. Control Parity
	2. Control Processing node
CPGA	Ceramic PGA
CPU	Central Processing Unit
CR	1. Control Register
	2. Condition Register
CRB	Cache Reload Buffer
CROM	Control ROM
CS	Crossbar Switch
CSA	Carry Save Adder
CSQ	Completed Store Queue
CTR	Count Register
CU	Control Unit
CWP	Current Window Pointer

DAC	Digital-to-Analog Converter
DAE	Data Access and Alignment Exception
DAR	Data Address Register
DARPA	Defense Advanced Research Project Agency
DB	Data Breakpoint register
DBAT	Data Block Address Translation
DCL	DEC's Command Language
DCU	Data Cache Unit
DE	Data Execution
DEC	Digital Equipment Corporation
DEN	Data Enable
DEQ	Decode Queue
DES	Data Execution Section
DFC	Destination Function Code
DI	Disable Interrupt
DIP	Dual In-Line Packages
DIR	Data Input Register
DM	Data Memory
DMA	1. Data Memory Access
	2. Data Memory Address
DMAC	DMA Controller
DMD	Data Memory Data
DMMU	Data MMU
DMT	Data Memory Transaction
DMU	Data Memory Unit
DOR	Data Output Register
DOS	Disk OS
DP	Data Parity
DRAM	Dynamic RAM
DSISR	1. Data Storage Interrupt Status Register
	2. DAE Source Instruction Service Register
DSL	Description Language
DST	Destination
DTB	Data Translation Buffer
DTT	Data Transparent Translation
EA	Effective Address
EAR	External Address Register
ECC	Error Correction Code
ECL	Emitter Current Logic
ECM	Emulator Control Module
EFS	Extended File System
EISA	Extended Industry Standard Architecture
EM	Emulate Coprocessor

EMI	Electromagnetic Interference
EPROM	Erasable PROM
EPSR	1. Exception-time PSR
	2. Extended PSR
ERAT	Effective-to-Real Address Translation
ES	Error Summary
EU	Execution Unit
EVT	Exception Vector Table
FCC	Federal Communications Commission
FCI	Flat Cable Interface
FCOP	Floating-point Coprocessor
FCR	Floating-point Control Register
FCU	Floating-point Conversion Unit
FDC	Floppy-Disk Controller
FDDI	Fiber Distributed Data Interface
FEU	Floating-point Execution Unit
FFT	Fast Fourier Transform
FGR	Floating-point General-purpose Register
FGU	Floating-point/Graphics Unit
FIFO	First In, First Out
FIP	Fetch Instruction Pointer
FIR	1. Fetch Instruction Register
	2. Fault Instruction Register
FNU	Floating-point Normalization Unit
FP	Frame Pointer
FPA	Floating-Point Accelerator
FPC	Floating-Point Controller
FPCR	Floating-Point Control Register
FPECR	Floating-Point Exception Cause Register
FPIAR	Floating-Point Instruction Address Register
FPP	Floating-Point Processor
FPR	Floating-Point Register
FPSCR	Floating-Point Status and Control Register
FPSR	Floating-Point Status Register
FPU	Floating-Point Unit
FQ	Floating-Point Queue
FRF	Floating-point Register File
FSQ	Finished Store Queue
FSR	Floating-point Status Register
FW	Free Window
FWB	Floating-point Write-Back
FXU	Fixed-point Unit

G	Giga (times 10^9)
GaAs	Gallium Arsenide
GIO	Graphics I/O
GMU	George Mason University
GP	General Purpose
GPR	General-Purpose Register
GR	General Register
GRF	General Register File
HID	Hardware Implementation Dependent
HIO	High-performance I/O
HiPPI	High-Performance Parallel Interface
HISP	High Speed
HLL	High-Level Language
HP	Hewlett Packard
HPC	High-Performance Computing
HPMC	High-Priority Machine Check
HSI	Host System Interface
Hz	Hertz
IA	Instruction Address
IAR	Instruction Address Register
IBAT	Instruction Block Address Translation
IBM	International Business Machines
IC	Integrated Circuit
ICD	In-Circuit Debugger
ICR	Interrupt Control Register
ICU	1. Interrupt Control Unit
	2. Instruction Cache Unit
ID	Instruction Decode
IDT	Integrated Device Technology
IEEE	Institute of Electrical and Electronics Engineers
IEU	Integer Execution Unit
IF	1. Instruction Fetch
	2. Instruction Format
IFU	Instruction Fetch Unit
ILP	Instruction Level Parallelism
IMMU	Instruction MMU
IMU	Instruction Memory Unit
I/O	Input/Output
IOC	1. I/O Controller
	2. I/O Cluster
IOCC	I/O Channel Controller
IOCP	I/O Control Processing Node

IOP	I/O Processor
IP	1. Instruction Pointer
	2. Integer Processor
IPL	Initial Program Load
IPR	Internal Processor Register
IR	Instruction Register
IRB	Instruction Reorder Buffer
IRF	Integer Register File
IRQ	Interrupt Request
ISA	Instruction Set Architecture
ISDN	Integrated Services Digital Network
ISO	International Standards Organization
ISP	1. Integrated System Peripheral
	2. Interrupt Stack Pointer
ISR	Interrupt Service Routine
ITB	Instruction Translation Buffer
ITLB	Instruction TLB
ITT	Instruction Transparent Translation
IU	1. Integer Unit
	2. Instruction Unit
JAL	Jump And Link (also JMPL)
K	Kilo (times 10^3)
KART	Keyboard Asynchronous Receiver-Transmitter
KHz	Kilohertz (10^3 Hertz)
L	Longword (32 bits)
LA	Logic Analyzer
LAN	Local Area Network
LBA	Local Block Address
LBP	Laser Beam Print
LDC	Lock Data Cache
LIC	Lock Instruction Cache
LIFO	Last In, First Out
LIO	Local I/O
LOSP	Low Speed
LPA	Logical Page Address
LR	1. Logical Register
	2. Link Register
LRU	Least Recently Used
LSB	Least Significant Bit
LSI	Large Scale Integration
LSU	Load/Store Unit

LSW	Logical Status Word
M	1. Memory (also MEM)
	2. Mega (times 10^6)
MAG	Memory Address Generator
MAR	Memory Address Register
MBUS	Memory Bus
MC	Motorola Company
McD	McDonnell-Douglas
MCIU	Multiple-Cycle IU
MCR	Memory Management Control
MEM	Memory (also M)
MEMC	Memory Controller
MESI	Modified, Exclusive, Shared, Invalid
MFLOPS	Millions of Floating-point Operations Per Second
MHz	Megahertz (10^6 Hertz)
MIMD	Multiple Instruction, Multiple Data
MIPS	1. Microprocessor without Interlocked Pipeline Stages
	2. Millions of Instructions Per Second
MIRIS	Microcoded RISC
MM	Main Memory
MMU	Memory Management Unit
MODEM	Modulator/Demodulator
MOPS	Millions of Operations Per Second
MOS	Metal Oxide Semiconductor
MP	Monitor Coprocessor
MPE	Multiprogramming Executive
MPP	Massively Parallel Processor
MQ	Multiplier and Quotient
MSB	Most Significant Bit
MSI	Medium-Scale Integration
MSR	1. Memory management Status Register
	2. Machine Status Register
MSW	Machine Status Word
MULTRIS	Multitasking RISC
MVUP	MicroVAX II Units of Processing
MW	Map Window
MWI	Map Window Index
N	1. Negative
	2. Nonsequential
NA	Numerics Architecture
NACK	No-Acknowledge
NaN	Not a Number

NE	Numerics Exception
NEC	Nippon Electric Company
NFS	Network File System
NIP	Next Instruction Pointer
NMI	Nonmaskable Interrupt
NMOS	N-channel MOS
NOP	No Operation
NS	National Semiconductor
ns	nanosecond (10^{-9} second)
NT	Nested Task
NVRAM	Non-Volatile RAM
NWINDOWS	Number of Windows
NYU	New York University
OB	Overflow Bit
OD	Operand Decode
OEA	Operating Environment Architecture
OF	Operand Fetch
OPR	Overflow Pointer Register
OS	1. Operating System
	2. Operand Store
OSF	Open Software Foundation
OT	Overflow Type
OW	Object Window
P	Processing Node
PA	1. Precision Architecture
	2. Protected Architecture
PAL	Privileged Architecture Library
PARIS	Parallel RISC
PATC	Page ATC
PBA	Physical Block Address
PBUS	Processor Bus
PC	1. Program Counter
	2. Personal Computer
PCB	Process-Control Block
PCC	Process Cycle Counter
PCI	Peripheral Component Interconnect
PCS	Program Control Section
PCU	Program Control Unit
PDE	Page Directory Entry
PDH	Processor Dependent Hardware
PE	1. Protection Enable
	2. Processing Element

PF	Parity Flag
PFA	Page Frame Address
PFP	Previous Frame Pointer
PFT	Page Frame Table
PG	Paging Enable
PGA	Pin Grid Array
PIC	Programmable Interrupt Controller
PID	Protection Identifier
PL	Privilege Level
PLL	Phase-Lock Loop
PM	Program Memory
PMC	PCI Mezzanine Card
PMMU	Paged MMU
PMOS	P-channel MOS
POWER	Performance Optimized With Enhanced RISC
PPGA	Plastic PGA
PPP	Point-to-Point Protocol
PPU	Peripheral Processing Unit
PR	Parameter Register
PROM	Programmable ROM
PSCU	Program Status Control Unit
PSR	Processor Status Register
PSW	Processor Status Word
PT	Program Time
PTE	Page Table Entry
PVR	Processor Version Register
PWT	Page Write Through
QNaN	Quiet NaN
R	Referenced
RA	Real Address
RAM	Random-Access Memory
RB	Reorder Buffer
RCA	Radio Corporation of America
RD	Read
RE	Result Even
RET	Return Instruction
RF	Register File
RIP	Return Instruction Pointer
RISC	Reduced-Instruction-Set Computer
RISCS	RISC Space
RMO	Relaxed Memory Order
RMW	Read-Modify-Write

RO	Result Odd
ROB	Reorder Buffer
ROM	Read-Only Memory
ROMP	Research Office product division MicroProcessor
ROS	Read-Only Storage
RPN	Real Page Number
RS	1. RISC System
	2. Reservation Station
RTN	Register Transfer Notation
RWM	Read Write Memory
S	1. Sign
	2. Sequential
SAPR	Supervisor Area Pointer Register
SAST	Stand Alone Self-Test
SB	1. Scoreboard
	2. Static Base
SCIU	Single-Cycle IU
SCSI	Small Computer Systems Interface
SCU	Storage Control Unit
SDR	Search Description Register
SE	Sign-Extended
SF	1. Sign Flag
	2. Stack Flag
SFC	Source Function Code
SFIP	Shadow FIP
SFU	Special Function Unit
SGI	Silicon Graphics Incorporated
SIC	Single-Instruction Computer
SIMD	Single Instruction, Multiple Data
SIMM	Single In-line Memory Module
SIO	System I/O
SLA	Serial Link Adapter
SLB	Segment Lookaside Buffer
SMD	Storage Module Device
SMP	Symmetric Multiprocessor
SNaN	Signalling NaN
SNIP	Shadow NIP
SOAR	Smalltalk On A RISC
SP	Stack Pointer
SPARC	Scalable Processor Architecture
SPR	Special-Purpose Register
SPUR	Symbolic Processing Using RISC
SQW	Stack/Queue Window

SQWI	SQW Index
SR	1. Status Register
	2. Segment Register
	3. Shadow Register
SRAM	Static RAM
SRP	Supervisor Root Pointer
SRU	System Register Unit
STDIO	Standard I/O
SSW	System Status Word
SVGA	Super VGA
SWP	Saved Window Pointer
SX	Storage and Execution
SXIP	Shadow XIP
T	Temporary
TB	1. Translation Buffer
	2. Time Base
TBR	Trap Base Register
TC	Translation Control Register
TCW	Tag and translation Control Word
TEAR	Translation Exception Address Register
TEX	Translation Exception
TF	Trap Enable Flag
TGI	Target Interface Adapter
TI	1. Table Index
	2. Texas Instruments
TIC	Target Instruction Cache
TID	Transaction Identifier
TLB	Translation Lookaside Buffer
TR	Temporary Register
TS	1. Task Switched
	2. Translate Supervisor
TTL	Transistor-Transistor Logic
TU	Translate User
UARP	User Area Pointer Register
UART	Universal Asynchronous Receiver Transmitter
UCLA	University of California at Los Angeles
UISA	User Instruction Set Architecture
URP	User Root Pointer
USL	UNIX System Laboratories
USP	User Stack Pointer
UTLB	Unified TLB
UWS	Ultrix Worksystem Software

V	1. oVerflow
	2. Valid
VA	Virtual Address
VADS	Verdix Ada Development System
VBR	Vector Base Register
VC	1. Virtual Channel
	2. Video Controller
VCAM	VME Channel Adapter Module
VCP	Virtual Channel Processor
VEA	Virtual Environment Architecture
VGA	Video Graphics Array
VHDL	VHSIC Hardware Description Language
VHSIC	Very-High-Speed Integrated Circuits
VIDC	Video Controller
VIS	Visual Instruction Set
VLIW	Very-Large Instruction Word
VLSI	Very-Large-Scale Integration
VM	1. Virtual Memory
	2. Virtual Mode
VRAM	Video RAM
VU	Vector Unit

W	Word
WB	Write-Back
WIM	Window Invalid Mask
WP	Write Protect
WR	Write
WT	1. Windows Transferred
	2. Writes Transparent

X	Extend Flag
XA	Extended Architecture
XER	Exception Register
XIP	Execution Instruction Pointer
XRF	Extended Register File

Z	1. Zero
	2. Zilog
ZF	Zero Flag

Index